An Engineer's Guide
to MATLAB®

An Engineer's Guide
to MATLAB®

Edward B. Magrab

University of Maryland
Mechanical Engineering Department

Contributing Authors:

**Shapour Azarm, Balakumar Balachandran,
James H. Duncan, Keith E. Herold, Gregory C. Walsh**

University of Maryland
Mechanical Engineering Department

Prentice
Hall

Prentice Hall
Upper Saddle River, NJ 07458

Library of Congress Cataloging-in-Publication Data

Magrab, Edward B..
  An engineer's guide to MATLAB / by Edward B. Magrab.
   p. cm.
   ISBN 0-13-011335-2 (pbk.)
   1. MATLAB (Computer program language) I. Title

QA76.73.P22 S43 2000
005.13 ' 3--dc21   00-051528
                    CIP

Acquisitions editor: *Laura Curless*
Editorial assistant: *Laurie Friedman*
Editorial/production supervision: *Rose Kernan*
Vice-president of editorial development, ECS: *Marcia Horton*
Executive managing editor: *Vince O'Brien*
Managing editor: *David A. George*
Vice-president of production and manufacturing: *David W. Riccardi*
Cover design: *Bruce Kenselaar*
Creative director: *Jayne Conte*
Manufacturing manager: *Trudy Pisciotti*
Manufacturing buyer: *Pat Brown*
Marketing manager: *Danny Hoyt*

© 2000 by Prentice Hall
Prentice-Hall, Inc.
Upper Saddle River, New Jersey 07458

The author and publisher of this book have used their best efforts in preparing this book. These efforts include the development, research, and testing of the theories and programs to determine their effectiveness. The author and publisher make no warranty of any kind, expressed or implied, with regard to these programs or the documentation contained in this book. The author and publisher shall not be liable in any event for incidental or consequential damages in connection with, or arising out of, the furnishing, performance, or use of these programs.

Printed in the United States of America
10 9 8 7 6 5 4 3 2

ISBN 0-13-011335-2

Prentice-Hall International (UK) Limited, *London*
Prentice-Hall of Australia Pty. Limited, *Sydney*
Prentice-Hall Canada Inc., *Toronto*
Prentice-Hall Hispanoamericana, S.A., *Mexico*
Prentice-Hall of India Private Limited, *New Delhi*
Prentice-Hall of Japan, Inc., *Tokyo*
Pearson Education Asia Pte Ltd
Editora Prentice-Hall do Brasil, Ltda., *Rio de Janeiro*

For June Coleman Magrab, my muse

CONTENTS

9   Dynamics and Vibrations   *Balakumar Balachandran* **321**

10 Control Systems   *Gregory C. Walsh* **391**

PREFACE

The primary goal of this book is to guide the reader in developing a strong working knowledge of MATLAB to solve engineering problems. Typically, solving these problems involves writing relatively short, one-time-use programs. Therefore, in this book we attempt to teach how to effectively develop such programs in MATLAB, ones that are compact, yet readable, are easy to debug, and execute fast.

The first seven chapters of the book are intended for use in a sophomore/junior level class that introduces programming and the use of computer languages in engineering. In the remaining seven chapters we present applications of MATLAB to a wide range of engineering topics. The emphasis of the book is on using MATLAB to obtain solutions to several classes of engineering problems, not the technical subject matter *per se*. Therefore, the technical material is presented in summary form only and no attempt has been made to present the basic material in each of these topic areas. The book also can be used in the following ways: (1) as a companion book to junior, senior and graduate level textbooks in engineering; (2) as a reference book for obtaining numerical solutions to a wide range of engineering problems, and; (3) as a source of applications of a wide variety of MATLAB solution techniques.

Engineering programming applications are typically used to do the following: (1) analyze a predictive model, such as an algebraic equation, an ordinary or partial differential equation or an approximation to these; (2) obtain statistical inferences from data; (3) visualize a model or data to enhance one's understanding; (4) either verify or obtain an empirical model from experimental results; and (5) monitor/control/analyze external events. In this book all but the last application are addressed.

The presentation of the material in this book is made with the assumption that the reader can employ the engineering approach to problem solving; that is, one that uses approximate mathematical models to predict the response of elements, devices, and systems. This approach also requires that one have a good comprehension of the physical problem so that he or she can tell when the model's results are correct, or at least reasonable. These qualities are an important prerequisite to creating programs that function correctly. The book also assumes that the reader is moderately fluent in calculus and engineering mathematics.

The first seven chapters are devoted to the introduction of MATLAB, where vector and matrix notation and definitions are introduced immediately and their fundamental importance to using MATLAB effectively is demonstrated. Numerous examples and detailed explanations are used to proceed through the material. The scripts and functions used to solve the example problems emphasize the employment of a relatively small number of readable MATLAB expressions to generate primarily graphical presentations of the results. This approach reinforces the importance of the vector/matrix formulations and the advantages of the resulting compactness of the code. Many of the example problems have been selected to illustrate the graphical presentation of data.

The approach used in the first seven chapters is then applied in the remaining seven chapters, each of which presents the application of MATLAB solution methods and toolboxes to classes of problems in the following areas: design of machine elements, dynamics and vibrations, controls, fluid mechanics, heat transfer, optimization, and engineering statistics. The material in these chapters is illustrated by numerous MATLAB solutions to classes of problems, and includes brief discussions of the program listings and their results. Each chapter provides exercises for which many of the solutions require annotated two or three-dimensional figures.

The MATLAB scripts and functions developed throughout the book use the most appropriate MATLAB function to obtain the numerical results and they have been verified to work correctly through version 5.3 (Release 11). We assume that the reader has access to all functions demonstrated. Furthermore, we have tried to keep to a minimum much of the detailed information that is readily available from the on-line help files. However, for a number of frequently used functions and for many functions in the toolboxes we have included a sufficient amount of information so that the reader can clearly determine what equations the functions solve and how the numerical method represented by the function can be used. In addition, several of the chapters use MATLABís controls, statistics, optimization and partial differential equation toolboxes, thereby extending the traditional range of the types of problems usually examined. Furthermore, we present solution techniques that take advantage of MATLABís numerical procedures where practical, as opposed to first obtaining algebraic solutions and then programming them.

Several preliminary versions of the book have been used over the last five semesters in the Mechanical Engineering department at the University of Maryland, both in an introductory MATLAB course and as companion material in junior and senior level courses in vibrations, controls, heat transfer, fluid mechanics, optimization, solid mechanics, and engineering statistics. The authors have found that with a good working knowledge of MATLAB they could expand the type of realistic engineering problems that could be examined in these classes, and they have frequently marveled at the relative ease with which these solutions could be obtained. We hope that the reader will also reap the rewards of applying MATLAB to determine the solutions to his or her engineering problems.

E. B. Magrab
S. Azarm
B. Balachandran
J. H. Duncan
K. E. Herold
G. C. Walsh

College Park, MD
March 2000

C H A P T E R   1

INTRODUCTION

Edward B. Magrab

The fundamental characteristics of the MATLAB environment and its basic syntax are introduced.

1.1 INTRODUCTION

MATLAB, which derives its name from *Mat*rix *Lab*oratory, is a computing language devoted to processing data in the form of matrices of numbers. MATLAB integrates computation and visualization into a flexible computer environment, and provides a diverse family of built-in functions that can be used in a straightforward manner to obtain numerical solutions to a wide range of engineering problems.

1.2 WAYS TO USE MATLAB

When the MATLAB program is launched, the user is placed in a window where a blinking[1] cursor appears immediately after the prompt ">>". This window, commonly called the

---

[1] The MATLAB window's look, management, and file management descriptions relate to a Windows™ environment. Equivalent procedures are used with other operating systems.

MATLAB command window, is a workspace that is equivalent to a blank sheet of paper. The space appearing immediately after the ">>" is called the command line. One enters numerical values for a matrix by simply typing a matrix of numbers on the command line in the prescribed format discussed in Section 2.4. To identify these numbers with a variable name, the variable name followed by an equal sign should precede them. If no variable name is used, then MATLAB assigns it the generic name *ans*. In either case the matrix can be recalled for either display to the command window or for use in another MATLAB expression by simply typing either the user-specified variable name or *ans*. However, if the same variable name is used to identify another matrix of numbers, or another set of numbers is typed at the command line without specifying a variable name, then the previously entered numbers for either the variable name or *ans*, as the case may be, will be overwritten. In addition, typing `clear` clears the workspace. This command is discussed in more detail below.

MATLAB permits one to perform arithmetic, trigonometric, and exponential operations (e.g., addition, division, cosine, and logarithm) on the variables in the same manner as with a calculator. These operations are performed by what MATLAB calls functions. In addition to these basic calculator-type functions, MATLAB has a large collection of functions that perform very sophisticated mathematical operations. MATLAB also provides the means whereby users can create their own functions, as described in Chapter 5. Another use of these functions is to allow a structured approach to managing the programming task. They differ from expressions entered at the command line in that MATLAB allots them their own private workspace and they have formally defined input-output relationships with the MATLAB environment.

When the user is required to enter many expressions or to repeatedly retype a series of expressions at the command window, the task can become tedious. To alleviate this potential problem, MATLAB has introduced script files—files that contain a list of commands, each of which will be operated on by MATLAB as if they were typed at the command line in the command window. A script file is created in either a word processor, a text editor, or the MATLAB-supplied text editor and debugger,[2] and saved as a <u>text</u> file with the suffix ".m". If a word processor or text editor is used, then the file is executed by typing the file name without the suffix ".m" in the MATLAB command window. If the MATLAB editor is used, then clicking on *Tools* and selecting *Run* executes the script. However, before doing this the file must first be saved.

Script files are usually employed in those cases where:

1. The program will contain more than a few lines of code.

2. The program will be used again.

3. A permanent record is desired.

4. It is expected that occasional upgrading will be required.

5. Substantial debugging is required.

6. One wants to transfer the listing to another person or organization.

---

[2] Clicking either the leftmost icon in the MATLAB command window (the white rectangle) or selecting from the *File* pull-down menu *New* or *M-File* accesses the MATLAB Editor/Debugger.

In addition, a script or a function typically has the following attributes:

1. *Documentation*, which, at a minimum, indicates the:

> Purpose and operations performed
> Programmer's Name
> Date originated
> Date(s) revised
> Description of the input(s): number, meaning, and type
> Description of the output(s): number, meaning, and type

2. *Input*, which includes numerous checks to ensure that all input values have the qualities required for the script/function to work properly.

3. *Initialization*, where the appropriate variables are assigned their numerical values.

4. *Computation*, where the major numerical evaluations are performed.

5. *Output*, where the results are presented as graphical and/or annotated numerical quantities.

1.3 CREATING VARIABLE NAMES

MATLAB permits the user to create variable names with a length of up to 31 alphanumeric characters, with the characters after the thirty-first being ignored. Each variable name must start with either an uppercase or lowercase letter, which can then be followed by any combination of uppercase and lowercase letters, numbers, and the underscore character (_). No blank spaces may appear between these characters. Variable names are case sensitive, so that a variable named *junk* is different from *junK*. There are two commonly used conventions: one that uses the underscore and one that uses capital letters. For example, if the exit pressure is a quantity that is being evaluated, then it could be defined in a MATLAB command line, script, or function as either *exit_pressure* or *ExitPressure*.

The most commonly used characters and symbols that have been set aside by MATLAB, along with their meanings, are shown in Table A.1 in the Appendix at the end of this chapter.

1.4 MANAGEMENT OF VARIABLES

During any MATLAB session—that is, during any time until the program is exited—MATLAB retains in its memory the most recently obtained values of all variables defined by each expression that has been either typed or evaluated from a script file, unless the `clear` function is invoked. The `clear` function deletes all the variables from memory. As mentioned previously, the numerical values assigned most recently to these variables are accessible anytime during the session (provided that `clear` hasn't been used) by simply typing the variable's name or using it in an expression. These variables are referred to as global variables.

Typing done in the MATLAB command window remains in the window and can be accessed by scrolling back until the scrolling memory has been exceeded, at which point the earliest entered information is lost. However, the expressions evaluated from a script file are not available, although the variable names and their numerical values are available as indicated in the preceding paragraph. This record of previously typed expressions can be removed by going to the *Edit* pull-down menu at the top of the MATLAB command window and selecting *Clear Session*, which clears the MATLAB command window, but does not delete the variables, which have to be removed by using `clear`. Also, the copy and paste icons can be used either to reproduce previously typed expressions in the current (active) line in the MATLAB command window or to paste MATLAB expressions either from the MATLAB command window into a word processor's window or vice versa.

For a listing of what variables have been created since the use of the last application of `clear`, one either types `whos` in the MATLAB command window or goes to the pull-down *File* menu and selects *Show Workspace*, which creates a window with this information. Either method reveals the names of the variables, their size, the number of bytes of storage that each variable uses, and their type: numerical, string (Section 3.1), symbolic, or an `inline` object (Section 5.3). The advantage of the latter method is that if one keeps the window active, this information is readily available, because MATLAB continually updates it.

1.5 ACCESSING SCRIPTS AND FUNCTION FILES

Script files and functions are run by typing their file name (without the ".m") in the MATLAB command window. However, MATLAB must be provided with the path to the directory in which the file resides. The path information is entered by going to the *File* pull-down menu and selecting *Set Path*. This opens the *Path Browser*. Click on *Browse* and choose the directory. Then go to *Path* and select *Add to Path* and either *Add to Front* or *Add to Back*. More than one directory may be added while in *Path Browser*. Before leaving the *Path Browser* it is suggested that you select *File* and then *Save Path*, which saves these paths for the next time MATLAB is used.

1.6 COMMAND WINDOW MANAGEMENT

To make the letters and numbers that appear in the command window more readable, MATLAB offers several options with the `format` function. Two that are particularly useful are the phrases

        format compact

and

        format long e

The former removes most empty (blank) lines and the latter provides a toggle from the default format of 5 digits to a format with 16 digits plus a 3-digit exponent. The `format long e` option is useful when debugging scripts that produce numbers that either change by very small amounts or vary over a wide range. To toggle back to the default settings type the phrase

```
format short
```

To change either the font, size, or style of type that appears in the MATLAB command window, go to the *File* pull-down menu and select *Preferences*. In this window select *Command Window Font* and make your selections.

Two keyboard entries that are very useful are ^c (Ctrl and c simultaneously) and ^p (Ctrl and p simultaneously). Application of ^p places in the MATLAB command window the last entry typed from the keyboard, which can then be implemented by pressing *Enter*. Also, prior to pressing *Enter* one can modify the expression. If *Enter* is not pressed and instead ^p is entered again, then the next most recently typed entry replaces the most recent entry, and so on. This same result can be obtained using the up-arrow ($\uparrow$) and down-arrow ($\downarrow$) keys.

The application of ^c is used either to abort a running script or function or to exit a paused script or function.

1.7 SCRIPT AND FUNCTION OUTPUT TO THE COMMAND WINDOW

If either a script or a function requires the user to enter a numerical value (or a series of numerical values if the quantity is either a vector or a matrix—see Sections 2.3 and 2.4) from the MATLAB command window, then the script (or function) contains the statement

VariableName = input('Any message')

where input is a MATLAB function and *Any message* is displayed in the MATLAB command window. After this expression is executed, the response typed, and *Enter* pressed, the value (or series of values) entered is assigned to *VariableName*. Other methods of data entry are given in Section 3.3, and further clarifications of the usage of input are given in Section 3.2.

On the other hand, there are two ways to get program results to the command window. The first is simply to omit the semicolon (;) at the end of an expression. This is illustrated in Section 1.8. (See also Table A.1 in the Appendix at the end of the chapter.) In this case, MATLAB displays in the MATLAB command window the variable's name followed by an equal sign, and then skips to the next line and displays the value(s) of the variable. This method is useful during debugging. When output values are to be annotated for clarity, then one uses either

```
disp
```

or

```
fprintf
```

which are discussed in Section 3.1.

1.7.1 Online Help

MATLAB has a complete online help capability, which can be accessed several ways. One way is to click on the question mark (?) icon on the toolbar. This opens the *Help* window, which should be minimized after each use so as to be readily available from both the MATLAB command window and from the word processor/text editor window. Another way is to type in the MATLAB command window

        help FunctionName

where *FunctionName* is the name of the function about which information is sought.

A third way is to select *Help Desk (HTML)* from the *Help* pull-down menu, which opens the computer system's web browser to display a more complete description of the command(s) in question. This form of information can also be accessed by clicking on the *Go to Help Desk* icon in the MATLAB help window that is accessed with the question mark (?) icon in the MATLAB command window.

1.8 BASIC MATLAB SYNTAX

MATLAB requires that all variable names (except those used by the Symbolic Toolbox) be assigned numerical values prior to being used in an expression. Typing the variable name, an equal sign, the numerical value(s), and then *Enter* performs the assignment. Thus, if we let $p = 7.1$, $x = 4.92$ and $k = -1.7$, then the following interaction in the MATLAB command window is obtained.

```
» p = 7.1          ←——— User types
p =
    7.1000      ⌐ ←——— System responds
» x = 4.92         ←——— User types
x =
    4.9200      ⌐ ←——— System responds
» k = -1.7         ←——— User types
k =
   -1.7000      ⌐ ←——— System responds
```

If one wants to suppress the system's response, then a semicolon (;) is placed as the last character of the expression. Thus,

```
»  p = 7.1;
»  x = 4.92;
»  k = -1.7;
»
```

MATLAB also lets one place several expressions on one line, a line being terminated by *Enter*. In this case, each expression is separated by either a comma (,) or a semicolon (;). When a comma is used, the system echoes the input. Thus, if the following is typed,

» p = 7.1, x = 4.92, k = −1.7

then the system responds with

```
p =
   7.1000
x =
   4.9200
k =
  −1.7000
»
```

The use of semicolons instead of the commas would have suppressed this output.

The five arithmetic operators to perform scalar addition, subtraction, multiplication, division and exponentiation are +, −, *, /, and ^, respectively. For example, the mathematical expression

$$t = \left(\frac{1}{1+px}\right)^k$$

is written in MATLAB as

t = (1/(1+p*x))^k

The quantities p, x, and k must be assigned numerical values by the user prior to the execution of this statement. If this has not been done, then an error message to that effect will appear. Assuming that the quantities p, x and k are those entered previously, the system returns[3]

440.8779

The parentheses in the MATLAB expression for t have to be used so that the mathematical operations are performed on the proper collections of quantities in their proper order within each set of parentheses. There is a hierarchy that MATLAB uses to compute arithmetic statements so that the number of parentheses can be minimized. However, parentheses that are unnecessary from MATLAB's point of view can still be used to remove visual ambiguity and make the expression easier to understand. The highest level is exponentiation, followed by multiplication and division, and then addition and subtraction. Within each set of parentheses and with all expressions in general, MATLAB performs its operations from left to right. Consider the examples shown in Table 1.1 involving the scalar quantities c, d, g, and x. The MATLAB function

---

[3] From this point forward we shall not always reproduce the command window literally, and instead just indicate the output (answers) in a format appropriate to its context.

TABLE 1.1
Examples of MATLAB Syntax

Mathematical expression	MATLAB expression
$1 - dc^{x+2}$	1-d*c^(x+2)
$dc^x + 2$	d*c^x+2 or 2+d*c^x
$(2/d)c^{x+2}$	(2/d)*c^(x+2) or 2/d*c^(x+2) or 2*c^(x+2)/d
$(dc^x + 2)/g^{2.7}$	(d*c^x+2)/g^2.7
$\sqrt{dc^x + 2}$	(d*c^x+2)^0.5 or sqrt(d*c^x+2)

> sqrt

takes the square root of its argument.

MATLAB also includes a large set of elementary, and not so elementary, functions. Some of the elementary ones are listed in Tables 1.2 and 1.3. The arguments to these functions can be scalars, vectors, or matrices. The definitions of vectors and matrices and their creation in MATLAB are given in Sections 2.3 and 2.3.

An example of the use of MATLAB's built-in functions is illustrated by considering the following expression:

$$y = \sqrt{\left| \pi - \sin(x)/\cosh(a) - \ln_e(x+a) \right|}$$

In MATLAB this expression is written as

> y = sqrt(abs(pi-sin(x)/cosh(a)-log(x+a)))

where the built-in function $pi = \pi$. It is assumed that x and a have been assigned numerical values prior to the execution of this statement.

1.9 SOME SUGGESTIONS ON HOW TO USE MATLAB

Listed below are some suggestions on how to use the MATLAB environment to efficiently create MATLAB scripts and functions.

- *Use the Help files extensively.* This will minimize errors caused by incorrect syntax and by incorrect or inappropriate application of a MATLAB function.

- *Write scripts and functions in a text editor and save them as m files.* This will save time, save the code, and greatly facilitate the debugging process, especially if the MATLAB editor/debugger is used.

- *Attempt to minimize the number of expressions comprising scripts and functions.* This usually leads to a tradeoff between readability and compactness, but it can encourage the search for MATLAB functions and procedures that can perform some of the steps faster and more directly.

TABLE 1.2
Some Elementary MATLAB Functions

Mathematical function	MATLAB expression
e^x	exp(x)
$\sqrt{x}$	sqrt(x)
$\ln(x)$ or $\log_e(x)$	log(x)
$\log_{10}(x)$	log10(x)
$|x|$	abs(x)
signum	sign(x)

TABLE 1.3
MATLAB's Trigonometric and Hyperbolic Functions

	Trigonometric		Hyperbolic	
Function	Function	Inverse function	Function	Inverse function
sine	sin(x)	asin(x)	sinh(x)	asinh(x)
cosine	cos(x)	acos(x)	cosh(x)	acosh(x)
tangent	tan(x)	atan(x) ⊠	tanh(x)	atanh(x)
secant	sec(x)	asec(x)	sech(x)	asech(x)
cosecant	csc(x)	acsc(x)	csch(x)	acsch(x)
cotangent	cot(x)	acot(x)	coth(x)	acoth(x)

⊠ atan2(y,x) is the four quadrant version.

- *When practical use graphical output as the script or function is being developed. This usually shortens the code development process by identifying potential coding errors and can facilitate the understanding of the physical process being modeled or analyzed.*

- *Most important, verify by independent means that the outputs from the scripts and functions are correct.*

EXERCISES

1.1 The following expressions[4] describe the principal contact stresses in the x-, y-, and z-directions, respectively, when two spheres are pressed together with a force F.

---

[4] J. E. Shigley and C. R. Mischke, *Mechanical Engineering Design*, 5th ed., McGraw-Hill, New York, 1989.

$$\sigma_x = \sigma_y = -p_{max}\left[\left(1-\frac{z}{a}\tan^{-1}\left(\frac{a}{z}\right)\right)(1-\upsilon_1)-0.5\left(1+\frac{z^2}{a^2}\right)^{-1}\right]$$

$$\sigma_z = \frac{-p_{max}}{1+z^2/a^2}$$

where

$$a = \sqrt[3]{\frac{3F}{8}\frac{(1-v_1^2)/E_1+(1-v_2^2)/E_2}{1/d_1+1/d_2}}$$

$$p_{max} = \frac{3F}{2\pi a^2}$$

and v_j, E_j and d_j, $j = 1,2$, are the Poisson's ratio, Young's modulus, and diameter, respectively, of the two spheres.

Write these equations in MATLAB notation. Check your expressions with the following values: $v_1 = v_2 = 0.3$, $E_1 = E_2 = 3 \times 10^7$, $d_1 = 1.5$, $d_2 = 2.75$, $F = 100$ lb., and $z = 0.01$ in. Save these expressions for plotting in Exercise 6.4. [Answer: $a = 0.0130$ in, $p_{max} = 281,580$ psi, $\sigma_x = -108,580$ psi, and $\sigma_z = -177,120$ psi.]

1.2 The following expressions[5] describe the principal contact stresses in the x-, y- and z-directions, respectively, when two cylinders, whose axes are parallel, are pressed together with a force F.

$$\sigma_x = -2v_2 p_{max}\left(\sqrt{1+\frac{z^2}{b^2}}-\frac{z}{b}\right)$$

$$\sigma_y = -p_{max}\left(\left(2-\left(1+\frac{z^2}{b^2}\right)^{-1}\right)\sqrt{1+\frac{z^2}{b^2}}-2\frac{z}{b}\right)$$

$$\sigma_z = \frac{-p_{max}}{\sqrt{1+z^2/b^2}}$$

$$\tau_{yz} = 0.5(\sigma_y - \sigma_z)$$

where

$$p_{max} = \frac{2F}{\pi b L}$$

$$b = \sqrt{\frac{2F}{\pi L}\frac{(1-v_1^2)/E_1+(1-v_2^2)/E_2}{1/d_1+1/d_2}}$$

and v_j, E_j, and d_j, $j = 1,2$, are the Poisson's ratio, Young's modulus, and diameter, respectively, of the two cylinders.

---

[5] J. E. Shigley and C. R. Mischke, *ibid*

Write these equations in MATLAB notation. Check your expressions with the following values: $v_1 = v_2 = 0.3$, $E_1 = E_2 = 3\times10^7$, $d_1 = 1.5$, $d_2 = 2.75$, $F = 100$ lb., $L = 2$, and $z = 0.001$ in. Save these expressions for plotting in Exercise 6.5. [Answer: $b = 0.0014$ in, $p_{max} = 23{,}251$ psi, $\sigma_x = -7{,}085.7$ psi, $\sigma_y = -4{,}843.8$ psi and $\sigma_z = -18{,}775$ psi.]

1.3 The load number of a hydrodynamic bearing is given by[6]

$$N_L = \frac{\pi\varepsilon\sqrt{\pi^2\left(1-\varepsilon^2\right)+16\varepsilon^2}}{\left(1-\varepsilon^2\right)^2}$$

where ε is the eccentricity ratio.

Write this equation in MATLAB notation. Check your expression with the following value: $\varepsilon = 0.8$. [Answer: $N_L = 72.022$.]

1.4 Consider a threaded bolt of height h and whose material has a Young's modulus E. The stiffness k of the bolt when it is passed through a hole of diameter d_0 can be estimated from[7]

$$k = \frac{\pi E d_o \tan 30°}{\ln\dfrac{\left(d_2 - d_0\right)\left(d_1 + d_0\right)}{\left(d_2 + d_0\right)\left(d_1 - d_0\right)}}$$

where d_1 is the diameter of the washer under the bolt, and

$$d_2 = d_1 + h\tan 30°$$

Write these equations in MATLAB notation. Remember that the arguments of trigonometric functions must be in radians. Check your expression with the following values: $h = 1.25$, $d_0 = 0.25$, $d_1 = 0.625$, and $E = 3\times10^7$. [Answer: $d_2 = 1.3467$ in and $k = 2.8842\times10^7$ lb/in.]

1.5 The radial and tangential stresses in long tubes due to a temperature T_a at its inner surface of radius a and temperature T_b at its outer surface of radius b are, respectively,[8]

$$\sigma_r = \frac{\alpha E\left(T_a - T_b\right)}{2(1-v)\ln(b/a)}\left[\frac{a^2}{b^2-a^2}\left(\frac{b^2}{r^2}-1\right)\ln\left(\frac{b}{a}\right)-\ln\left(\frac{b}{r}\right)\right]$$

$$\sigma_t = \frac{\alpha E\left(T_a - T_b\right)}{2(1-v)\ln(b/a)}\left[1-\frac{a^2}{b^2-a^2}\left(\frac{b^2}{r^2}+1\right)\ln\left(\frac{b}{a}\right)-\ln\left(\frac{b}{r}\right)\right]$$

where r is the radial coordinate of the tube, E is the Young's modulus of the tube material, and α is the coefficient of thermal expansion.

The temperature distribution through the wall of the tube in the radial direction is

$$T = T_b + \frac{\left(T_a - T_b\right)\ln(b/r)}{\ln(b/a)}$$

---

[6] R. L. Norton, *Machine Design, An Integrated Approach*, Prentice-Hall, Upper Saddle River, NJ, 1996.
[7] A. H. Burr and J. B. Cheatham, *Mechanical Analysis and Design*, 2nd ed., Prentice Hall, Upper Saddle River, NJ, 1995, p. 423.
[8] A. H. Burr and J. B. Cheatham, *ibid.*, p. 496.

Write these equations in MATLAB notation. Check your expressions with the following values: α = 1.2×10^{-5}, $E = 3\times10^{7}$, $v = 0.3$, $T_a = 500$, $T_b = 300$, $a = 0.25$, $b = 0.5$, $r = 0.375$. [Answer: σ_r = $-8,011.5$, $\sigma_t = 5,231.9$ and $T = 383.0075$.]

1.6 The time it takes to increase the value of an amount of money P, called the principal, to an amount $r_p P$ when the money appreciates i % n times per year (ni is the yearly percentage appreciation) is

$$T = \frac{\ln r_p}{n\ln(1+0.01i)} \quad \text{years}$$

Write this equation in MATLAB notation. Check your expression with the following values: r_p = 2, $i = 0.5$, and $n = 12$. [Answer: $T = 11.5813$ years.]

1.7 The mass flow rate of a gas escaping from a tank at pressure p_0 and under reversible adiabatic conditions is proportional to[9]

$$\psi = \sqrt{\frac{k}{k-1}}\sqrt{\left(\frac{p_e}{p_0}\right)^{2/k} - \left(\frac{p_e}{p_0}\right)^{(k+1)/k}}$$

where p_e is the pressure exterior to the tank's exit and k is the adiabatic reversible gas constant.

Write this equation in MATLAB notation. Check your expression with the following values: k = 1.4 and $p_e/p_0 = 0.3$. [Answer: $\psi = 0.4271$.]

1.8 The discharge factor for flow through an open channel of parabolic cross section is[10]

$$K = \frac{1.2}{x}\left[\sqrt{16x^2+1} + \frac{1}{4x}\ln\left(\sqrt{16x^2+1}+4x\right)\right]^{-2/3}$$

where x is the ratio of the maximum water depth to the breadth of the channel at the top of the water.

Write this equation in MATLAB notation. Check your expression with the following value: x = 0.45. [Answer: $K = 1.3394$.]

1.9 Show that with the following astonishing formula[11] one can approximate π to within less than 10^{-7} with one term ($n = 0$) and to within less than 10^{-15} with two terms ($n = 0, 1$). In fact, for each term used the approximation of π improves by almost a factor of 10^{-8}. Thus, summing the first four terms ($n = 0$, 1, 2, 3) one would obtain the first 31 digits of π, a fact that can be verified only with MATLAB's Symbolic toolbox.

$$\frac{1}{\pi} = \frac{\sqrt{8}}{9801}\sum_{n=0}^{\infty}\frac{(4n)!(1103+26390n)}{(n!)^4 396^{4n}}$$

Note: The factorial is evaluated using gamma as follows: gamma(n+1) = n!; gamma($4n$+1) = ($4n$)! n = 0, 1, ...

---

[9] W. Beitz and K. H. Kuttner, Eds., *Handbook of Mechanical Engineering*, Springer-Verlag, New York, 1994, p. C15.
[10] H. W. King, *Handbook of Hydraulics*, 4th ed., McGraw-Hill, NY, 1954, p. 7–24.
[11] S. Ramanujan, "Modular equations and approximations to π," *Quart. J. Math*, **45**, pp. 350–372.

Write these equations in MATLAB notation. Check your expressions with the following values: $v_1 = v_2 = 0.3$, $E_1 = E_2 = 3\times10^7$, $d_1 = 1.5$, $d_2 = 2.75$, $F = 100$ lb., $L = 2$, and $z = 0.001$ in. Save these expressions for plotting in Exercise 6.5. [Answer: $b = 0.0014$ in, $p_{max} = 23{,}251$ psi, $\sigma_x = -7{,}085.7$ psi, $\sigma_y = -4{,}843.8$ psi and $\sigma_z = -18{,}775$ psi.]

1.3 The load number of a hydrodynamic bearing is given by[6]

$$N_L = \frac{\pi\varepsilon\sqrt{\pi^2\left(1-\varepsilon^2\right)+16\varepsilon^2}}{\left(1-\varepsilon^2\right)^2}$$

where ε is the eccentricity ratio.

Write this equation in MATLAB notation. Check your expression with the following value: $\varepsilon = 0.8$. [Answer: $N_L = 72.022$.]

1.4 Consider a threaded bolt of height h and whose material has a Young's modulus E. The stiffness k of the bolt when it is passed through a hole of diameter d_0 can be estimated from[7]

$$k = \frac{\pi E d_o \tan 30^\circ}{\ln\dfrac{(d_2-d_0)(d_1+d_0)}{(d_2+d_0)(d_1-d_0)}}$$

where d_1 is the diameter of the washer under the bolt, and

$$d_2 = d_1 + h\tan 30^\circ$$

Write these equations in MATLAB notation. Remember that the arguments of trigonometric functions must be in radians. Check your expression with the following values: $h = 1.25$, $d_0 = 0.25$, $d_1 = 0.625$, and $E = 3\times10^7$. [Answer: $d_2 = 1.3467$ in and $k = 2.8842\times10^7$ lb/in.]

1.5 The radial and tangential stresses in long tubes due to a temperature T_a at its inner surface of radius a and temperature T_b at its outer surface of radius b are, respectively,[8]

$$\sigma_r = \frac{\alpha E(T_a - T_b)}{2(1-\upsilon)\ln(b/a)}\left[\frac{a^2}{b^2-a^2}\left(\frac{b^2}{r^2}-1\right)\ln\left(\frac{b}{a}\right)-\ln\left(\frac{b}{r}\right)\right]$$

$$\sigma_t = \frac{\alpha E(T_a - T_b)}{2(1-\upsilon)\ln(b/a)}\left[1-\frac{a^2}{b^2-a^2}\left(\frac{b^2}{r^2}+1\right)\ln\left(\frac{b}{a}\right)-\ln\left(\frac{b}{r}\right)\right]$$

where r is the radial coordinate of the tube, E is the Young's modulus of the tube material, and α is the coefficient of thermal expansion.

The temperature distribution through the wall of the tube in the radial direction is

$$T = T_b + \frac{(T_a - T_b)\ln(b/r)}{\ln(b/a)}$$

[6] R. L. Norton, *Machine Design, An Integrated Approach*, Prentice-Hall, Upper Saddle River, NJ, 1996.
[7] A. H. Burr and J. B. Cheatham, *Mechanical Analysis and Design*, 2nd ed., Prentice Hall, Upper Saddle River, NJ, 1995, p. 423.
[8] A. H. Burr and J. B. Cheatham, *ibid.*, p. 496.

Write these equations in MATLAB notation. Check your expressions with the following values: α = 1.2×10^{-5}, $E = 3 \times 10^7$, $v = 0.3$, $T_a = 500$, $T_b = 300$, $a = 0.25$, $b = 0.5$, $r = 0.375$. [Answer: σ_r = $-8,011.5$, $\sigma_t = 5,231.9$ and $T = 383.0075$.]

1.6 The time it takes to increase the value of an amount of money P, called the principal, to an amount $r_p P$ when the money appreciates i % n times per year (ni is the yearly percentage appreciation) is

$$T = \frac{\ln r_p}{n \ln(1 + 0.01i)} \quad \text{years}$$

Write this equation in MATLAB notation. Check your expression with the following values: r_p = 2, $i = 0.5$, and $n = 12$. [Answer: $T = 11.5813$ years.]

1.7 The mass flow rate of a gas escaping from a tank at pressure p_0 and under reversible adiabatic conditions is proportional to[9]

$$\psi = \sqrt{\frac{k}{k-1}} \sqrt{\left(\frac{p_e}{p_0}\right)^{2/k} - \left(\frac{p_e}{p_0}\right)^{(k+1)/k}}$$

where p_e is the pressure exterior to the tank's exit and k is the adiabatic reversible gas constant.
Write this equation in MATLAB notation. Check your expression with the following values: k = 1.4 and $p_e/p_0 = 0.3$. [Answer: $\psi = 0.4271$.]

1.8 The discharge factor for flow through an open channel of parabolic cross section is[10]

$$K = \frac{1.2}{x}\left[\sqrt{16x^2 + 1} + \frac{1}{4x}\ln\left(\sqrt{16x^2 + 1} + 4x\right)\right]^{-2/3}$$

where x is the ratio of the maximum water depth to the breadth of the channel at the top of the water.
Write this equation in MATLAB notation. Check your expression with the following value: x = 0.45. [Answer: $K = 1.3394$.]

1.9 Show that with the following astonishing formula[11] one can approximate π to within less than 10^{-7} with one term ($n = 0$) and to within less than 10^{-15} with two terms ($n = 0, 1$). In fact, for each term used the approximation of π improves by almost a factor of 10^{-8}. Thus, summing the first four terms ($n = 0$, $1, 2, 3$) one would obtain the first 31 digits of π, a fact that can be verified only with MATLAB's Symbolic toolbox.

$$\frac{1}{\pi} = \frac{\sqrt{8}}{9801}\sum_{n=0}^{\infty}\frac{(4n)!(1103 + 26390n)}{(n!)^4 396^{4n}}$$

Note: The factorial is evaluated using gamma as follows: gamma(n+1) = n!; gamma($4n$+1) = ($4n$)! n = $0, 1, \ldots$.

---

[9] W. Beitz and K. H. Kuttner, Eds., *Handbook of Mechanical Engineering*, Springer-Verlag, New York, 1994, p. C15.
[10] H. W. King, *Handbook of Hydraulics*, 4th ed., McGraw-Hill, NY, 1954, p. 7–24.
[11] S. Ramanujan, "Modular equations and approximations to π," *Quart. J. Math*, **45**, pp. 350–372.

APPENDIX A

Summary of MATLAB Special Characters

TABLE A.1
MATLAB's Special Characters and a Summary of Their Usage

Character	Name	Usage
.	Period	(a) Decimal point.
		(b) Part of arithmetic operators to indicate a special type of vector or matrix operation, called the dot operation, such as $c = a.*b$.
,	Comma	(a) Separator within parentheses of matrix elements such as $b(2,7)$ and functions such as `besselj(1, x)` or brackets creating vectors such as v = [1,x] or the output of function arguments such as [x,s] = max(a).
		(b) Placed at the end of an expression when several expressions appear on one line.
;	Semicolon	(a) Suppresses display of the results when placed at end of an expression, or series of expressions, appearing on one line.
		(b) Indicates the end of a row in matrix creation statement such as $m = [x\,y\,z;\,a\;b\;c]$.
:	Colon	(a) Separator in the vector creation expression x = a:b:c.
		(b) For a matrix z it indicates "all rows" when written as $z(:,k)$ or "all columns" when written as $z(k,:)$.
( )	Parentheses	(a) Denote subscript of an element of matrix z, where $z(j, k)$ is the element in row j and column k.
		(b) Delimiters in mathematical expressions such as $a^\wedge(b+c)$.
		(c) Delimiters for the arguments of functions, such as $\sin(x)$.
[ ]	Brackets	Creates an array of numbers, either a vector or a matrix, or strings (literals).
{ }	Braces	Creates a cell matrix or structure.
%	Percentage	Comment delimiter; used to indicate the beginning of a comment wherein the MATLAB compiler ignores everything to its right. The exception is when it is used inside a pair of quotes to define a string such as a = 'p1 = 14 % of the total'.
'	Quote or Apostrophe	(a) '*Expression*' indicates that *Expression* is a string (literal)
		(b) Indicates the transpose of a vector or matrix.
...	Ellipsis	Continuation of a MATLAB expression to the next line. Used to create more readable code.
	Blank	Context dependent: either ignored, indicates a delimiter in a data creation statement such as c = [a b] or is a character in a string statement.

C H A P T E R   2

MATRICES AND MATLAB

Edward B. Magrab

The fundamental MATLAB syntax is introduced in the context of vectors and matrices and their manipulation.

2.1 INTRODUCTION

MATLAB is a language whose operating instructions and syntax are based on a set of fundamental matrix operations and their extensions. Therefore, in order to fully utilize the advantages and compactness of the MATLAB language, we summarize some basic matrix definitions, and symbolism and present several examples of their usage. The material presented in this section is used extensively in the code developed throughout this and subsequent chapters.

2.2 MATRICES AND VECTORS

An array a of m rows and n columns is called a matrix of order $(m \times n)$, which consists of a total of mn elements arranged in the following rectangular array:

$$a = \begin{bmatrix} a_{11} & a_{12} & \cdots & a_{1n} \\ a_{21} & a_{22} & & \\ \vdots & & \ddots & \\ a_{m1} & & & a_{mn} \end{bmatrix} \rightarrow (m \times n)$$

The elements of the matrix are denoted a_{ij}, where i indicates the row number and j the column number. The order of a matrix a is determined from

```
size(a)
```

or

```
[m,n] = size(a)
```

In the first form, `size` displays two values: the first is the number of rows (m), and the second is the number of columns (n). In the second notation, $[m,n]$ means that m is assigned the value for the number of rows and n the number of columns. This is more fully explained in Section 5.2.

Several special cases of this general matrix are as follows.

2.2.1 Square Matrix

When $m = n$ we have a square matrix.

2.2.2 Diagonal Matrix

When $a_{ij} = 0$, $i \neq j$, and $m = n$ we have the diagonal matrix

$$a = \begin{bmatrix} a_{11} & 0 & \cdots & 0 \\ 0 & a_{22} & & \\ \vdots & & \ddots & \\ 0 & & & a_{nn} \end{bmatrix} \rightarrow (n \times n)$$

Thus, if $a = [1\ 3\ 8]$ (see Section 2.3 for the creation of vectors), then

```
a = [1 3 8];
z = diag(a)
```

gives

```
z =
    1   0   0
    0   3   0
    0   0   8
```

which is MATLAB's display of the (3×3) matrix

$$\begin{bmatrix} 1 & 0 & 0 \\ 0 & 3 & 0 \\ 0 & 0 & 8 \end{bmatrix}$$

On the other hand, if b is a square matrix, then

    diag(b)

returns the diagonal elements of b.

When $a_{ii} = 1$ and $m = n$ we have the unit matrix I, that is,

$$I = \begin{bmatrix} 1 & 0 & \cdots & 0 \\ 0 & 1 & & \\ \vdots & & \ddots & \\ 0 & & & 1 \end{bmatrix}$$

The MATLAB expression for a unit matrix is

    eye(n)

where n is the order of the square matrix. Thus, the MATLAB expression

    c = eye(3)

gives

```
c =
    1   0   0
    0   1   0
    0   0   1
```

2.2.3 Column and Row Matrices (Vectors)

When $a_{ij} = a_{i1}$ (i.e., there is only one column), then a is called a column matrix or, more commonly, a vector—that is,

$$a = \begin{bmatrix} a_{11} \\ a_{21} \\ \vdots \\ a_{m1} \end{bmatrix} = \begin{bmatrix} a_1 \\ a_2 \\ \vdots \\ a_m \end{bmatrix} \rightarrow (m \times 1)$$

However, when $a_{ij} = a_{1j}$, that is, we have only one row, then a is called a row matrix or a vector—that is,

$$a = \begin{bmatrix} a_{11} & a_{12} & \cdots & a_{1n} \end{bmatrix} = \begin{bmatrix} a_1 & a_2 & \cdots & a_n \end{bmatrix} \rightarrow (1 \times n)$$

This is the default definition of a vector in MATLAB.

2.2.4 Transpose of a Matrix and a Vector

The transpose of a matrix is denoted by an apostrophe ('), and is defined as follows. When a is the $(m \times n)$ matrix

$$a = \begin{bmatrix} a_{11} & a_{12} & \cdots & a_{1n} \\ a_{21} & a_{22} & & \\ \vdots & & \ddots & \\ a_{m1} & & & a_{mn} \end{bmatrix} \rightarrow (m \times n)$$

then its transpose $w = a'$ is the following $(n \times m)$ matrix

$$w = a' = \begin{bmatrix} w_{11} = a_{11} & w_{12} = a_{21} & \cdots & w_{1m} = a_{m1} \\ w_{21} = a_{12} & w_{22} = a_{22} & & \\ \vdots & & \ddots & \\ w_{n1} = a_{1n} & & & w_{nm} = a_{mn} \end{bmatrix} \rightarrow (n \times m)$$

For column and row vectors, we have the following. If

$$a = \begin{bmatrix} a_1 \\ a_2 \\ \vdots \\ a_m \end{bmatrix} \rightarrow (m \times 1) \qquad \text{then} \qquad a' = \begin{bmatrix} a_1 a_2 \cdots a_m \end{bmatrix} \rightarrow (1 \times m)$$

and, if

$$a = \begin{bmatrix} a_1 a_2 \cdots a_m \end{bmatrix} \rightarrow (1 \times m) \qquad \text{then} \qquad a' = \begin{bmatrix} a_1 \\ a_2 \\ \vdots \\ a_m \end{bmatrix} \rightarrow (m \times 1)$$

The length of a vector a, that is, its number of elements, can be determined by using either

    L = length(a)

or

    L = size(a)

whereas the order of a matrix is determined only from size. The advantage of using size is that it is not necessary to know *a priori* whether a is a vector or a matrix. However, for vectors length is more convenient to use.

2.3 CREATION OF VECTORS

Vectors are expressed as either

$$f = [a \, x \, b \, ...] \quad \text{or} \quad f = [a, x, b, ...]$$

where a, x, b, ... are either variable names, numbers, expressions, or strings (see Section 3.2). If they are either variable names or expressions, then all variable names and the variable names comprising the expressions must be defined such that a numerical value has been obtained for each of these variable names prior to the execution of this statement. Expressions and numbers can appear in any combination and in any order. In the form

$$f = [a \, x \, b \, ...]$$

the space (blank) between symbols is required, whereas in the form

$$f = [a, x, b, ...]$$

it is optional.

It is important to note, however, that if a, say, is an expression that is explicitly written in the location where a is, then there may be no spaces between any of the alphanumeric characters and the mathematical operator symbols. For example, if $a = h + d^g$, then f is written as either

$$f = [h+d^\wedge g \, x \, b \, ...]$$

or

$$f = [h+d^\wedge g, x, b, ...]$$

MATLAB gives several other ways to assign numerical values to the elements of a vector and a matrix. The techniques for the creation of matrices are given in Section 2.4. The first means, described below, uses the colon notation to specify the range of the values and the increment between adjacent values. The second method specifies the range of the values and the number of values desired. In the former method, the increment is either important or has been specified, whereas in the latter method the number of values is important. Using the colon notation to create a vector we have x = s:d:f

where

> s = start or initial value
>
> d = increment or decrement
>
> f = end or final value

Thus, the following row vector x is created

$$x = [s \; s+d \; s+2d \; ... \; s+nd]$$

where $s+nd \leq f$. Note that the number of values n created for x is not specified directly. The quantities s, d, and f can be any combination of numerical values, variable names, and expressions. The number of terms that this expression has created is determined from

n = length(x)

When d is omitted MATLAB assumes that $d = 1$. Then

x = s:f

creates the vector

$$x = [s, s+1, s+2, ... , s+n]$$

where $s+n \leq f$. Again s and f can be any combination of numerical values, variable names, and expressions.

On the other hand, one can specify n equally spaced values starting at s and ending at f as follows:

x = linspace(s, f, n)

where the increment (decrement) is computed by MATLAB from

$$d = \frac{f-s}{n-1}$$

The values of s and f can be either positive or negative and either $s > f$ or $s < f$. When n is not specified it is assigned a value of 100. Thus, linspace creates the vector

$$x = [s \; s+d \; s+2d \; ... \; f = s+(n-1)d]$$

If equal spacing on a logarithmic scale is desired then

x = logspace(s, f, n)

where the initial value is 10^s, the final value is 10^f and d is defined above. Thus,

$$x = [10^s \ 10^{s+d} \ 10^{s+2d} \ \dots \ 10^f]$$

When n is not specified MATLAB assigns it a value of 50.

To further examine MATLAB's treatment of vectors let

$$b = [b_1 \ b_2 \ b_3 \ \dots \ b_n]$$

This means that we have created a vector b that has one row and n columns. If we use MATLAB's subscript notation to locate b_3, then we write $b(3)$; that is, MATLAB will indicate that $b(3)$ has the numerical value assigned to b_3, the third element of the vector. However, MATLAB's interpreter is smart enough to know that the matrix b is a $(1 \times n)$ matrix, and in some sense it ignores the double subscript requirement. That is, writing $b(3)$ in the case where b is a vector defined above is the same as writing it as $b(1,3)$. If one were to either directly or implicitly require $b(3,1)$, then an error message would appear because this row (the third row) hasn't been defined (created).

Conversely, if we let

$$b = [b_1 \ b_2 \ b_3 \ \dots \ b_n]'$$

we have created a column vector—that is, a $(n \times 1)$ matrix. If we want to locate the third element of this vector, then we again write $b(3)$ and MATLAB returns the numerical value corresponding to b_3. This is the same as having written $b(3,1)$. If one were to either directly or implicitly require $b(1,3)$, then an error message would appear because this column (the third column) hasn't been defined (created).

Suppose that we now want to create a vector x that is to have the seven values [−2, 1, 3, 5, 7, 9, 10]. This can be created with either the statement

    x = [−2 1:2:9 10]

or

    x = [−2, 1, 3, 5, 7, 9, 10]

which means that the elements of this vector are: $x_1 = -2$, $x_2 = 1$, $x_3 = 3$, $x_4 = 5$, $x_5 = 7$, $x_6 = 9$ and $x_7 = 10$, and $length(x) = 7$. We access the elements of x with the MATLAB expression $x(j), j = 1, 2, \dots, 7$. For example, the expression $x(5)$ returns the value 7.

When we add or subtract a scalar from a vector, the scalar is added or subtracted from each element of the vector. Thus,

    z = x−1

results in $z = [-3 \ 0 \ 2 \ 4 \ 6 \ 8 \ 9]$. However, the rules for multiplication, division, and exponentiation have some restrictions. See Section 2.6.

On the other hand, we may want to modify only some of the elements of a vector. For example, let $z = [-2 \ 1 \ 3 \ 5 \ 7 \ 9 \ 10]$. Then to divide the second element by 2 we have

    z = [−2 1 3 5 7 9 10];

z(2) = z(2)/2;

which results in z = [−2 0.5 3 5 7 9 10]. If, further, we multiply the third and fourth elements by 3 and subtract 1 we have

z = [−2 1 3 5 7 9 10];
z(2) = z(2)/2;
z(3:4) = z(3:4)*3−1;

which results in z = [−2 0.5 8 14 7 9 10]. Notice that the rest of the elements remain unaltered.

There are several other ways in which one can access the elements of a vector. Consider the eight-element vector

y = [−1 6 15 −7 31 2 −4 −5];

If one wanted to create a new vector x composed of the third through fifth elements of y, then

x = y(3:5)

creates the three-element vector x = [15 −7 31].

Suppose, instead, we wanted to create a vector x composed of the first two and the last two elements of y. This can be done either by

x = [y(1) y(2) y(7) y(8)]

or by

x = y([1 2 7 8])

or by first defining the vector and employing it as follows

index = [1 2 7 8];
x = y(index)

The last two representations have many useful applications. Let us assume that corresponding to the vector y is the following vector z, which is also a vector with eight elements. Thus,

y = [−1 6 15 −7 31 2 −4 −5];
z = [10 20 30 40 50 60 70 80];

Suppose that we would like to sort the vector y in ascending order (most negative to most positive) using the sort function, and then rearrange the order of the elements of z to correspond to the new order of the elements of *y*. Thus, from the *Help* file we find that one form of the `sort` function is

> [ynew,indx] = sort(y)

where *ynew* is the vector with the rearranged (sorted) elements of *y* and *indx* is a vector containing the *original* locations of the elements in *y*. Thus, the script

> y = [−1 6 15 −7 31 2 −4 −5];
> z = [10 20 30 40 50 60 70 80];
> [ynew,indx] = sort(y)
> znew = z(indx)

when executed, gives

> ynew→[-7 -5 -4 -1 2 6 15 31]
> indx→[4 8 7 1 6 2 3 5]
> znew→[40 80 70 10 60 20 30 50]

Therefore, we see that *indx*(1) = 4 means that *ynew*(1) used to be *y*(4). Thus, to obtain the corresponding *z* we simply define *znew* as the vector *z* whose indices (order) are now given by *indx*.

We can extend this capability further by introducing `find`, which determines the locations (not the values) of all the elements in a vector (or matrix) that satisfy a user-specified condition or expression. We illustrate its usage by creating a new vector *s* that contains only those elements of *y* that are either negative or zero. The MATLAB relational operator `<=` stands for ≤ (see Table 4.1). Then

> y = [−1 6 15 −7 31 2 −4 −5];
> indxx = find(y<=0)

gives

> indxx→[1 4 7 8]

Therefore,

> y = [−1 6 15 −7 31 2 −4 −5];
> indxx = find(y<=0);
> s = y(indxx)

results in

> s→[-1 -7 -4 -5]

These expressions could have been written compactly as

$$y = [-1\ 6\ 15\ -7\ 31\ 2\ -4\ -5];$$
$$s = y(\texttt{find}(y<=0))$$

See Section 6.3.8 for another application of $\texttt{find}$.

One of the great advantages of MATLAB's implicit vector and matrix notation is that it provides the user with a compact way of performing a series of operations on an array of values. For example, suppose that we would like to determine $\sin(x)$ when x varies by $\pi/5$ from $-\pi \le x \le \pi$. Then the MATLAB statements

```
x = -pi:pi/5:pi;
y = sin(x)
```

yield the following vector of $n = \texttt{length}(y) = 11$ elements:

$y \rightarrow$[0.0000 -0.5878 -0.9511 -0.9511 -0.5878 0.0000 0.5878 0.9511 0.9511
        0.5878 0.0000]

2.4 CREATION OF MATRICES

The (4×3) matrix a

$$a = \begin{bmatrix} a_{11} & a_{12} & a_{13} \\ a_{21} & a_{22} & a_{23} \\ a_{31} & a_{32} & a_{33} \\ a_{41} & a_{42} & a_{43} \end{bmatrix} \rightarrow (4\times3)$$

is created in any of the following ways. Consider the three quantities a_{11}, a_{12}, and a_{13}. These can be combined to create a vector v_1 by

$$v_1 = [\ a_{11}\ a_{12}\ a_{13}]$$

In a similar manner, we can create three more vectors v_2, v_3, and v_4:

$$v_2 = [\ a_{21}\ a_{22}\ a_{23}]$$
$$v_3 = [\ a_{31}\ a_{32}\ a_{33}]$$
$$v_4 = [\ a_{41}\ a_{42}\ a_{43}]$$

We now use these four vectors to create a matrix a as follows:

$$a = [\ v_1;\ v_2;\ v_3;\ v_4]$$

where the semicolons are used to indicate the end of a row. Each row must have the *same* number of columns. This expression could have also been created directly with

$$a = [\ a_{11}\ a_{12}\ a_{13};\ a_{21}\ a_{22}\ a_{23};\ a_{31}\ a_{32}\ a_{33};\ a_{41}\ a_{42}\ a_{43}]$$

or, if a more readable presentation is desired,

$$a = [a_{11}\ a_{12}\ a_{13};\ldots$$
$$a_{21}\ a_{22}\ a_{23};\ldots$$
$$a_{31}\ a_{32}\ a_{33};\ldots$$
$$a_{41}\ a_{42}\ a_{43}]$$

where the ellipses (...) are required. See Table A.1 in the Appendix at the end of Chapter 1. Lastly, the matrix can also created by simply using *Enter* to indicate the end of a row as follows:

```
a = [a11 a12 a13
     a21 a22 a23
     a31 a32 a33
     a41 a42 a43];
```

In all the forms above, the a_{ij} are numbers, variable names, expressions, or strings. If they are either variable names or expressions, then the variable names or the variable names comprising the expressions must have been assigned numerical values, either by the user or from previously executed expressions, prior to the execution of this statement. Expressions and numbers can appear in any combination. If they are strings, then the number of characters in each row must be the same. See Section 3.1.

Two other useful functions that can be used to generate data for the elements of a matrix are:

```
one = ones(r,c)
```

which creates an ($r \times c$) matrix in which each element has the value 1, and

```
zero = zeros(r,c)
```

which creates an ($r \times c$) matrix in which each element has the value 0. These functions are convenient replacements for the equivalent expressions: $one(1:r,1:c) = 1$ and $zero(1:r,1:c) = 0$.

Thus,

```
on = ones(2,5)
```

creates the (2×5) matrix

```
1   1   1   1   1
1   1   1   1   1
```

and

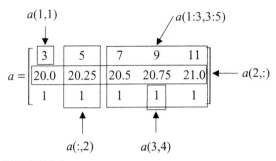

FIGURE 2.1
Accessing elements of a matrix.

    zer = zeros(3,2)

creates the (3×2) matrix of zeros

    0   0
    0   0
    0   0

Now consider the construction of the (3×5) matrix

$$a = \begin{bmatrix} 3 & 5 & 7 & 9 & 11 \\ 20.0 & 20.25 & 20.5 & 20.75 & 21.0 \\ 1 & 1 & 1 & 1 & 1 \end{bmatrix} \rightarrow (3 \times 5)$$

This is created with the statement

    a = [3:2:11; linspace(20,21,5); ones(1,5)]

which yields

    3.0000   5.0000   7.0000   9.0000   11.0000
    20.0000   20.2500   20.5000   20.7500   21.0000
    1.0000   1.0000   1.0000   1.0000   1.0000

We access the elements of this matrix as shown in Figure 2.1. Thus,

    $a(1, 1) \rightarrow 3$
    $a(3, 4) \rightarrow 1$
    $a(:,2) \rightarrow [5\ 20.25\ 1]'$
    $a(2,:) \rightarrow [20\ 20.25\ 20.5\ 20.75\ 21]$

and

$$a(1:3,3:5) \rightarrow [7\ 9\ 11;\ 20.5\ 20.75\ 21;\ 1\ 1\ 1]$$

which is a (3×3) matrix. The notation

$$a(:,2)$$

means "all the rows of column 2," and

$$a(2,:)$$

means "all the columns of row 2." Also, we see that in writing the indices of a, one can employ the colon notation, where the increment in this case is equal to +1. Thus,

$$a(1:3,3:5)$$

means that the rows of a start at 1 and end at 3, and the columns of a start at 3 and end at 5. Thus, if

$$b = a(1:3,3:5) = \begin{bmatrix} 7 & 9 & 11 \\ 20.5 & 20.75 & 21 \\ 1 & 1 & 1 \end{bmatrix} \rightarrow (3 \times 3)$$

then we have defined a new (3×3) matrix b.

Let us now create a matrix that is the same size as a but with all of its elements equal to 4. This is done with the expressions

```
a = [3:2:11; linspace(20,21,5); ones(1,5)];
z = 4*ones(size(a))
```

which creates

```
4   4   4   4   4
4   4   4   4   4
4   4   4   4   4
```

One can alter elements of a matrix in a manner similar to that used for vectors. Let

```
z = magic(4)
```

which displays

```
16  2   3  13
 5 11  10   8
```

```
9   7   6 12
4  14  15  1
```

The `magic` function creates a matrix in which the sum of elements in all columns and rows and the two diagonals are equal. For a (4×4) matrix the value is 34. Let us divide all the elements in row 2 by 2 and then add all the elements in column 2 to those in column 4 and place the result in column 4. The script is

```
z = magic(4);
z(2,:) = z(2,:)/2;
z(:,4) = z(:,4)+z(:,2);
```

which results in elements of the matrix z having the following values.

```
16    2    3  15
 2.5  5.5  5   9.5
 9    7    6  19
 4   14   15  15
```

To set all the diagonal elements of the original matrix to zero we use

```
z = magic(4);
z = z–diag(diag(z))
```

which results in

```
0  2   3   13
5  0  10   8
9  7   0  12
4 14  15   0
```

To replace all the diagonal elements with the value 5 we have

```
z = magic(4);
z = z–diag(diag(z))+5*eye(4)
```

which results in

```
5  2   3  13
5  5  10   8
9  7   5  12
4 14  15   5
```

To place the values 11, 23, 54, and 61 in the diagonal elements of z we have

```
z=magic(4);
z=z–diag(diag(z))+diag([11 23 54 61])
```

which results in

```
11   2    3   13
5    23  10   8
9    7   54   12
4    14  15   61
```

MATLAB provides two functions that can be used to create matrices by replicating a scalar, column or row vector, or matrix a specified number of times. These two functions are:

```
repmat
```

and

```
meshgrid
```

which uses `repmat`. The general form of `repmat` is

```
repmat(x, r, c)
```

where x is either a scalar, vector, or matrix, r is the number times that the rows of x will be replicated, and c is the number of times that the columns of x will be replicated. For example, the function `repmat` can be used to create either a column or row vector of arbitrary length in which each element of the vector has the same numerical value. Thus, if we wish to create a row vector w composed of six values of the number 45.72, then

w = `repmat`(45.72,1,6)

This expression is equivalent to

w = [45.72, 45.72, 45.72, 45.72, 45.72, 45.72]

This vector could have also been created with

w(1,1:6) = 45.72

If, instead, we want to create a (3×3) matrix of these values, then we have

w = `repmat`(45.72,3,3)

which could also have been created using

w(1:3,1:3) = 45.72

Either of these expressions will produce in the MATLAB command window

```
45.7200  45.7200  45.7200
45.7200  45.7200  45.7200
45.7200  45.7200  45.7200
```

Now consider the vector

$$s = [a_1 \; a_2 \; a_3 \; a_4]$$

The expression

v = repmat(s, 3, 1)

creates the numerical equivalent[1] of the matrix

$$v = \begin{bmatrix} a_1 & a_2 & a_3 & a_4 \\ a_1 & a_2 & a_3 & a_4 \\ a_1 & a_2 & a_3 & a_4 \end{bmatrix}$$

That is, it creates three rows of the vector v, with each row in this case having four columns. The expression

repmat(s, 3, 2)

creates the numerical equivalent of the matrix

$$v = \begin{bmatrix} a_1 & a_2 & a_3 & a_4 & a_1 & a_2 & a_3 & a_4 \\ a_1 & a_2 & a_3 & a_4 & a_1 & a_2 & a_3 & a_4 \\ a_1 & a_2 & a_3 & a_4 & a_1 & a_2 & a_3 & a_4 \end{bmatrix}$$

On the other hand, the command

v = repmat(s', 1, 3)

yields a matrix of three columns of the numerical equivalent of the column vector s', with each column in this case having four rows:

---

[1] By numerical equivalent we mean that in MATLAB the v_{ij} have had numerical values assigned to them. The notation here is used to better illustrate what repmat does by symbolically showing the arrangement of the elements of the resulting array.

$$v = \begin{bmatrix} a_1 & a_1 & a_1 \\ a_2 & a_2 & a_2 \\ a_3 & a_3 & a_3 \\ a_4 & a_4 & a_4 \end{bmatrix}$$

The expression

    repmat(s', 2, 3)

gives the numerical equivalent of the matrix

$$v = \begin{bmatrix} a_1 & a_1 & a_1 \\ a_2 & a_2 & a_2 \\ a_3 & a_3 & a_3 \\ a_4 & a_4 & a_4 \\ a_1 & a_1 & a_1 \\ a_2 & a_2 & a_2 \\ a_3 & a_3 & a_3 \\ a_4 & a_4 & a_4 \end{bmatrix}$$

If we have two row vectors s and t, then the MATLAB expression

    [u,v] = meshgrid(s,t)

gives the same result as that produced by the two commands:

    u = repmat(s,length(t),1)
    v = repmat(t',1,length(s))

In either case, u and v are each matrices of order (length(t)×length(s)). Thus, if

$$s = [s_1 \ s_2 \ s_3 \ s_4]$$
$$t = [t_1 \ t_2 \ t_3]$$

then

    [u,v] = meshgrid (s,t)

produces the numerical equivalent of the two (3×4) matrices

$$u = \begin{bmatrix} s_1 & s_2 & s_3 & s_4 \\ s_1 & s_2 & s_3 & s_4 \\ s_1 & s_2 & s_3 & s_4 \end{bmatrix} \tag{2.1a}$$

$$v = \begin{bmatrix} t_1 & t_1 & t_1 & t_1 \\ t_2 & t_2 & t_2 & t_2 \\ t_3 & t_3 & t_3 & t_3 \end{bmatrix} \qquad (2.1b)$$

The meshgrid function can also be used to return only one matrix as follows

w = meshgrid(s,t)

which creates $w = u$, where u is given by Eq. (2.1a). This form is illustrated in Example 2.2.

There are two matrix manipulation functions that are useful in certain applications: fliplr(a) and flipud(a), which flip the rows and columns, respectively. Consider the (2×5) matrix

$$a = \begin{bmatrix} a_{11} & a_{12} & a_{13} & a_{14} & a_{15} \\ a_{21} & a_{22} & a_{23} & a_{24} & a_{25} \end{bmatrix} \rightarrow (2 \times 5)$$

which is created with the statement

$$a = [a_{11}\, a_{12}\, a_{13}\, a_{14}\, a_{15};\, a_{21}\, a_{22}\, a_{23}\, a_{24}\, a_{25}]$$

Then,

$$\text{fliplr}(a) = \begin{bmatrix} a_{15} & a_{14} & a_{13} & a_{12} & a_{11} \\ a_{25} & a_{24} & a_{23} & a_{22} & a_{21} \end{bmatrix} \rightarrow (2 \times 5)$$

$$\text{flipud}(a) = \begin{bmatrix} a_{21} & a_{22} & a_{23} & a_{24} & a_{25} \\ a_{11} & a_{12} & a_{13} & a_{14} & a_{15} \end{bmatrix} \rightarrow (2 \times 5)$$

and

$$\text{flipud(fliplr}(a)) = \begin{bmatrix} a_{25} & a_{24} & a_{23} & a_{22} & a_{21} \\ a_{15} & a_{14} & a_{13} & a_{12} & a_{11} \end{bmatrix} \rightarrow (2 \times 5)$$

The results of the fliplr(a) and flipud(a) functions can also be obtained with the colon notation in the matrix's subscripts: For example,

c = fliplr(a)

produces the same results as

c = a(:,length(a):–1:1)

Now consider the vector

$$c = [a \ \text{fliplr}(a)]' = \begin{bmatrix} a_{11} & a_{21} \\ a_{12} & a_{22} \\ a_{13} & a_{21} \\ a_{14} & a_{24} \\ a_{15} & a_{25} \\ a_{15} & a_{25} \\ a_{14} & a_{24} \\ a_{13} & a_{23} \\ a_{12} & a_{22} \\ a_{11} & a_{21} \end{bmatrix} \rightarrow (10 \times 2)$$

which has created two identical rows: 5 and 6. Suppose that we wish to remove one of these repeating rows. This is done by setting one of the rows to a null value using the expression [], where there is no space (blank) between the brackets. Then, either the expression

   c(length(a),:) = []

or

   c(length(a)+1,:) = []

creates

$$c = \begin{bmatrix} a_{11} & a_{21} \\ a_{12} & a_{22} \\ a_{13} & a_{23} \\ a_{14} & a_{24} \\ a_{15} & a_{25} \\ a_{14} & a_{24} \\ a_{13} & a_{23} \\ a_{12} & a_{22} \\ a_{11} & a_{21} \end{bmatrix} \rightarrow (9 \times 2)$$

where the order of c is now (9×2). The expression c(length(a),:) = [] means that all the columns of row number length(a) in c are to be assigned the value [] (removed, in this case). Although we know that the length of a is 5, it is good practice to let MATLAB do the counting; hence, the use of the function length(a).

   We further clarify the above notations by presenting the results of three different MATLAB operations. First we create the following two (2×5) matrices a and b

$$a = \begin{bmatrix} a_{11} & a_{12} & a_{13} & a_{14} & a_{15} \\ a_{21} & a_{22} & a_{23} & a_{24} & a_{25} \end{bmatrix} \qquad b = \begin{bmatrix} b_{11} & b_{12} & b_{13} & b_{14} & b_{15} \\ b_{21} & b_{22} & b_{23} & b_{24} & b_{25} \end{bmatrix}$$

Now consider their use in the following three MATLAB operations:

Addition: $c = a + b$

$$c = \begin{bmatrix} a_{11}+b_{11} & a_{12}+b_{12} & a_{13}+b_{13} & a_{14}+b_{14} & a_{15}+b_{15} \\ a_{21}+b_{21} & a_{22}+b_{22} & a_{23}+b_{23} & a_{24}+b_{24} & a_{25}+b_{25} \end{bmatrix} \rightarrow (2 \times 5)$$

Thus, c is a (2×5) matrix.

Column augmentation: $c = [a\ b]$

$$c = \begin{bmatrix} a_{11} & a_{12} & a_{13} & a_{14} & a_{15} & b_{11} & b_{12} & b_{13} & b_{14} & b_{15} \\ a_{21} & a_{22} & a_{23} & a_{24} & a_{25} & b_{21} & b_{22} & b_{23} & b_{24} & b_{25} \end{bmatrix} \rightarrow (2 \times 10)$$

Thus, c is (2×10) matrix.

Row augmentation: $c = [a;\ b]$

$$c = \begin{bmatrix} a_{11} & a_{12} & a_{13} & a_{14} & a_{15} \\ a_{21} & a_{22} & a_{23} & a_{24} & a_{25} \\ b_{11} & b_{12} & b_{13} & b_{14} & b_{15} \\ b_{21} & b_{22} & b_{23} & b_{24} & b_{25} \end{bmatrix} \rightarrow (4 \times 5)$$

Thus, c is (4×5) matrix.

Furthermore, if

$$x = [x_1\ x_2\ x_3]$$
$$y = [y_1\ y_2\ y_3]$$

then either

$$z = [x'\ y']$$

or

$$z = [x;y]'$$

produces

$$z = \begin{bmatrix} x_1 & y_1 \\ x_2 & y_2 \\ x_3 & y_3 \end{bmatrix} \rightarrow (2 \times 3)$$

whereas

$$z = [x';y']$$

yields

$$z = \begin{bmatrix} x_1 \\ x_2 \\ x_3 \\ y_1 \\ y_2 \\ y_3 \end{bmatrix} \rightarrow (6 \times 1)$$

These relationships are very useful when placing data in a specified or required order.

2.5 DOT OPERATIONS

We now introduce MATLAB's dot (.) notation, which is MATLAB's syntax for performing, on matrices of the *same* order, arithmetic operations on an element by element basis. Consider the following (3×4) matrices:

$$x = \begin{bmatrix} x_{11} & x_{12} & x_{13} & x_{14} \\ x_{21} & x_{22} & x_{23} & x_{24} \\ x_{31} & x_{32} & x_{33} & x_{34} \end{bmatrix}$$

and

$$m = \begin{bmatrix} m_{11} & m_{12} & m_{13} & m_{14} \\ m_{21} & m_{22} & m_{23} & m_{24} \\ m_{31} & m_{32} & m_{33} & m_{34} \end{bmatrix}$$

We now write out explicitly the following MATLAB dot (.) operations:

$$z_m = x.*m = \begin{bmatrix} x_{11}*m_{11} & x_{12}*m_{12} & x_{13}*m_{13} & x_{14}*m_{14} \\ x_{21}*m_{21} & x_{22}*m_{22} & x_{23}*m_{23} & x_{24}*m_{24} \\ x_{31}*m_{31} & x_{32}*m_{32} & x_{33}*m_{33} & x_{34}*m_{34} \end{bmatrix} \quad (2.2a)$$

$$z_d = x./m = \begin{bmatrix} x_{11}/m_{11} & x_{12}/m_{12} & x_{13}/m_{13} & x_{14}/m_{14} \\ x_{21}/m_{21} & x_{22}/m_{22} & x_{23}/m_{23} & x_{24}/m_{24} \\ x_{31}/m_{31} & x_{32}/m_{32} & x_{33}/m_{33} & x_{34}/m_{34} \end{bmatrix} \quad (2.2b)$$

$$z_e = x.^{\wedge} m = \begin{bmatrix} x_{11}^{\wedge} m_{11} & x_{12}^{\wedge} m_{12} & x_{13}^{\wedge} m_{13} & x_{14}^{\wedge} m_{14} \\ x_{21}^{\wedge} m_{21} & x_{22}^{\wedge} m_{22} & x_{23}^{\wedge} m_{23} & x_{24}^{\wedge} m_{24} \\ x_{31}^{\wedge} m_{31} & x_{32}^{\wedge} m_{32} & x_{33}^{\wedge} m_{33} & x_{34}^{\wedge} m_{34} \end{bmatrix} \tag{2.2c}$$

In other words

$$z_{mij} = x_{ij} m_{ij} \qquad \{\text{or } zm(i,j) = x(i,j)*m(i,j)\}$$

$$z_{dij} = x_{ij}/m_{ij} \qquad \{\text{or } zd(i,j) = x(i,j)/m(i,j)\}$$

$$z_{eij} = x_{ij}^{m_{ij}} \qquad \{\text{or } ze(i,j) = x(i,j)^{\wedge}m(i,j)\}$$

for $i = 1,2,3$ and $j = 1,2,3,4$. Note that the dot (.) must be placed before the symbol for multiplication, division, and exponentiation. The dot operation for either addition or subtraction is not required, since the matrix notation causes the same operation; that is—an element by element addition or subtraction. See Eq. (2.6).

We now examine several special cases of these three operations. For dot multiplication, we see that if $x = x_0$, a scalar constant, then the dot operation is not needed since

$$x_0.* m = \begin{bmatrix} x_0 * m_{11} & x_0 * m_{12} & x_0 * m_{13} & x_0 * m_{14} \\ x_0 * m_{21} & x_0 * m_{22} & x_0 * m_{23} & x_0 * m_{24} \\ x_0 * m_{31} & x_0 * m_{32} & x_0 * m_{33} & x_0 * m_{34} \end{bmatrix} = x_0 \begin{bmatrix} m_{11} & m_{12} & m_{13} & m_{14} \\ m_{21} & m_{22} & m_{23} & m_{24} \\ m_{31} & m_{32} & m_{33} & m_{34} \end{bmatrix} = x_0 * m$$

Similarly when $m = m_0 = $ scalar constant we find that

$$x.*m = x*m_0$$

For dot division when $m = m_0$, a scalar constant, we have

$$x./m_0 = \begin{bmatrix} x_{11}/m_0 & x_{12}/m_0 & x_{13}/m_0 & x_{14}/m_0 \\ x_{21}/m_0 & x_{22}/m_0 & x_{23}/m_0 & x_{24}/m_0 \\ x_{31}/m_0 & x_{32}/m_0 & x_{33}/m_0 & x_{34}/m_0 \end{bmatrix}$$

$$= \frac{1}{m_0} \begin{bmatrix} x_{11} & x_{12} & x_{13} & x_{14} \\ x_{21} & x_{22} & x_{23} & x_{24} \\ x_{31} & x_{32} & x_{33} & x_{34} \end{bmatrix} = x/m_0$$

and, thus, the dot operation is not required. However, when $x = x_0$, a scalar constant, we find that

$$x_0./m = \begin{bmatrix} x_0/m_{11} & x_0/m_{12} & x_0/m_{13} & x_0/m_{14} \\ x_0/m_{21} & x_0/m_{22} & x_0/m_{23} & x_0/m_{24} \\ x_0/m_{31} & x_0/m_{32} & x_0/m_{33} & x_0/m_{34} \end{bmatrix}$$

$$= x_0 \begin{bmatrix} 1/m_{11} & 1/m_{12} & 1/m_{13} & 1/m_{14} \\ 1/m_{21} & 1/m_{22} & 1/m_{23} & 1/m_{24} \\ 1/m_{31} & 1/m_{32} & 1/m_{33} & 1/m_{34} \end{bmatrix} = x_0./m$$

and the dot operation is required.

From the examination of this last case it should be apparent that whether $m = m_0$, a scalar constant or $x = x_0$, a scalar constant, we are required always to use the dot operation for exponentiation. Thus, if $z = x.^m$, then

$$z = x_0.^m$$

and

$$z = x.^{m_0}$$

To illustrate the dot operation for exponentiation consider the computation of 2^j for $j = 1, 2, ..., 8$. The script is:

```
x = 1:8;
y = 2.^x
```

which yields

2 4 8 16 32 64 128 256

Thus, the placement of a decimal point before the exponentiation operator ($^$) signifies to MATLAB that it is to take the scalar 2 and compute its power at each of the values of x and then place the results in the corresponding elements of a vector y of the same length. The previous script can be written more compactly as:

```
y = 2.^(1:8)    % or y = 2.^[1:8]
```

If the problem were reversed and we had wanted to determine x^2, then the script is

```
y = (1:8).^2   % or y = [1:8].^2
```

which yields

1 4 9 16 25 36 49 64

If we let $f(y)$ stand for the operation of any function, such as `sin`, `cosh`, `besselj`, etc., on the matrix y, then if y, for example, is a (3×4) matrix:

$$z = f(y) = \begin{bmatrix} f(y_{11}) & f(y_{12}) & f(y_{13}) & f(y_{14}) \\ f(y_{21}) & f(y_{22}) & f(y_{23}) & f(y_{24}) \\ f(y_{31}) & f(y_{32}) & f(y_{33}) & f(y_{34}) \end{bmatrix}$$

It should be realized that we could combine the dot operations provided that the order of each quantity is the same. For example, if a, b, c, d, and f are each a (3×2) matrix, then the expression

$$z = \left[\tan a - f\left(\frac{b}{c}\right)^d\right]^2$$

is written as

    z = (tan(a)–f.*(b./c).^d).^2;

which results in the elements of z having the numerical values computed from the following expressions:

$$z = \begin{bmatrix} (\tan(a_{11}) - f_{11} * (b_{11}/c_{11})^\wedge d_{11})^\wedge 2 & (\tan(a_{12}) - f_{12} * (b_{12}/c_{12})^\wedge d_{12})^\wedge 2 \\ (\tan(a_{21}) - f_{21} * (b_{21}/c_{21})^\wedge d_{21})^\wedge 2 & (\tan(a_{22}) - f_{22} * (b_{22}/c_{22})^\wedge d_{22})^\wedge 2 \\ (\tan(a_{31}) - f_{31} * (b_{31}/c_{31})^\wedge d_{31})^\wedge 2 & (\tan(a_{32}) - f_{32} * (b_{32}/c_{32})^\wedge d_{32})^\wedge 2 \end{bmatrix}$$

To show another application of the dot operations, let us return to the meshgrid example wherein the two vectors $s = [s_1\ s_2\ s_3\ s_4]$ and $t = [t_1\ t_2\ t_3]$ were used in the statement

    [u,v] = meshgrid(s,t)

to produce the two (3×4) matrices

$$u = \begin{bmatrix} s_1 & s_2 & s_3 & s_4 \\ s_1 & s_2 & s_3 & s_4 \\ s_1 & s_2 & s_3 & s_4 \end{bmatrix} \quad \text{and} \quad v = \begin{bmatrix} t_1 & t_1 & t_1 & t_1 \\ t_2 & t_2 & t_2 & t_2 \\ t_3 & t_3 & t_3 & t_3 \end{bmatrix} \qquad (2.3)$$

Suppose that we wish to multiply the corresponding elements of u and v. Then the dot multiplication

    z = u.*v

results in (recall Eq. (2.2a))

$$z = \begin{bmatrix} s_1 * t_1 & s_2 * t_1 & s_3 * t_1 & s_4 * t_1 \\ s_1 * t_2 & s_2 * t_2 & s_3 * t_2 & s_4 * t_2 \\ s_1 * t_3 & s_2 * t_3 & s_3 * t_3 & s_4 * t_3 \end{bmatrix} \qquad (2.4)$$

The elements of z can be interpreted as corresponding to the product of all combinations of the elements of vectors s and t. A similar interpretation is obtained when addition, subtraction, division, and exponentiation are performed, since the multiplication symbol (*) can be replaced by the respective operator.

We now examine the

sum

and

cumsum

functions, which are often used in conjunction with these dot operations. Let us examine sum first. When the argument of sum is a vector, the sum function sums over the length of the vector and returns a scalar value. When the argument is a matrix, the function sums the columns of the matrix, and returns a row vector whose length is equal to the number of columns of the original matrix. Thus, if z is a (3×4) matrix with elements z_{ij}, then

$$\text{sum}(z) = \left[\sum_{n=1}^{3} z_{n1} \quad \sum_{n=1}^{3} z_{n2} \quad \sum_{n=1}^{3} z_{n3} \quad \sum_{n=1}^{3} z_{n4} \right] \rightarrow (1 \times 4) \tag{2.5a}$$

is a four-element vector, whereas

$$\text{sum}(z') = \left[\sum_{n=1}^{4} z_{1n} \quad \sum_{n=1}^{4} z_{2n} \quad \sum_{n=1}^{4} z_{3n} \right] \rightarrow (1 \times 3) \tag{2.5b}$$

is a three-element vector. It should be realized that z can be the result of any of the above dot operations and their combinations.

The cumsum function for a vector v composed of n elements v_j is another vector of length n whose elements are

$$y = \text{cumsum}(v) = \left[\sum_{k=1}^{1} v_k \quad \sum_{k=1}^{2} v_k \quad \cdots \quad \sum_{k=1}^{n} v_k \right] \rightarrow (1 \times n)$$

On the other hand if w is (m×n) matrix composed of elements w_{jk}, then cumsum(w) is the following matrix

$$y = \text{cumsum}(w) = \begin{bmatrix} \sum_{k=1}^{1} w_{k1} & \sum_{k=1}^{1} w_{k2} & \cdots & \sum_{k=1}^{1} w_{kn} \\ \sum_{k=1}^{2} w_{k1} & \sum_{k=1}^{2} w_{k2} & & \\ \vdots & & \ddots & \\ \sum_{k=1}^{m} w_{k1} & & & \sum_{k=1}^{m} w_{kn} \end{bmatrix} \rightarrow (m \times n)$$

To illustrate the use of sum consider the following equation:

$$z = \sum_{m=1}^{4} m^m$$

The script to evaluate this expression is

```
m = 1:4;
z = sum(m.^m)
```

which, when executed, gives $z = 288$. This can be written more compactly as

```
z = sum((1:4).^(1:4))
```

We now summarize the results of this section by evaluating the following expression[2] for $N = 305$ and five equally spaced values of x from $0 \le x \le 2$.

$$\operatorname{sech} x = 4\pi \sum_{n=1,3,5}^{N \to \infty} \frac{n(-1)^{(n-1)/2}}{(n\pi)^2 + 4x^2}$$

We shall also compare the summed values to its exact values. The script is

```
nn = 1:2:305;                                          % (1×153)
xx = linspace(0,2,5);                                  % (1×5)
[x,n] = meshgrid(xx,nn);                               % (153×5)
s = 4*pi*sum(n.*(-1).^((n-1)/2)./((pi*n).^2+4*x.^2));  % (1×5)
se = sech(xx);                                         % (1×5)
compare = [s' se']                                     % (5×2)
```

which, upon execution, displays in the MATLAB command window

```
1.0021   1.0000
0.8889   0.8868
0.6501   0.6481
0.4272   0.4251
0.2679   0.2658
```

We have selected the order of the arguments of meshgrid to produce matrices of order (153×5) since sum performs the summation on all the elements of the rows on a column-by-column basis. This script can be written more compactly as

```
[x,n] = meshgrid(linspace(0,2,5),1:2:305);
s = 4*pi*sum(n.*(-1).^((n-1)/2)./((pi*n).^2+4*x.^2));
```

---

[2] L. B. W. Jolley, *Summation of Series*, 2nd ed., Dover Publications, New York, 1961.

compare = [s' sech(linspace(0,2,5)')]

2.6 MATHEMATICAL OPERATIONS WITH MATRICES

We now define several fundamental matrix operations: addition, subtraction, multiplication, inversion, determinants, and solutions of equations and roots (eigenvalues). These results are then used to obtain numerical solutions to classes of engineering problems.

2.6.1 Addition and Subtraction

If we have two matrices a and b, each of the order $(m \times n)$, then

$$a \pm b = \begin{bmatrix} a_{11} \pm b_{11} & a_{12} \pm b_{12} & \cdots & a_{1n} \pm b_{1n} \\ a_{21} \pm b_{21} & a_{22} \pm b_{22} & & \\ \vdots & & \ddots & \\ a_{m1} \pm b_{m1} & & & a_{mn} \pm b_{mn} \end{bmatrix} \rightarrow (m \times n) \qquad (2.6)$$

2.6.2 Multiplication

If we have an $(m \times k)$ matrix a and a $(k \times n)$ matrix b, then

$$c = ab = \begin{bmatrix} \sum_{j=1}^{k} a_{1j} b_{j1} & \sum_{j=1}^{k} a_{1j} b_{j2} & \cdots & \sum_{j=1}^{k} a_{1j} b_{jn} \\ \sum_{j=1}^{k} a_{2j} b_{j1} & \sum_{j=1}^{k} a_{2j} b_{j2} & & \vdots \\ \vdots & & \ddots & \\ \sum_{j=1}^{k} a_{mj} b_{j1} & \cdots & & \sum_{j=1}^{k} a_{mj} b_{jn} \end{bmatrix} \rightarrow (m \times n) \qquad (2.7)$$

where c is of order $(m \times n)$. Notice that the product of two matrices is defined only when the adjacent integers of their respective orders are equal, k in this case. In other words, $(m \times k)(k \times n) = (m \times n)$, where the notation indicates that we have summed the k terms as indicated in Eq. (2.7). The MATLAB expression for matrix multiplication is

c = a*b

The extension of Eq. (2.7) to the matrix multiplication $f = cd = abd$ is given in Example 2.5, Eq. (2.15).

When $m = n$ it should be noted that, in general, $ab \neq ba$. It can be shown that if $c = ab$, then

$$c' = (ab)' = b'a'$$

Also, if a is a unit matrix ($a = I$) and $m = n$, then

$$Ib = bI = b$$

Let us examine the results of the matrix multiplication further and give one interpretation of the result. Consider the following series:[3]

$$w(x, y) = \sum_{j=1}^{k} d_j e_j(x) g_j(y) = \sum_{j=1}^{k} f_j(x) g_j(y)$$

Suppose that we are interested in the value of $w(x, y)$ over a range of values for x and y: $x = x_1, x_2, \ldots, x_m$ and $y = y_1, y_2, \ldots, y_n$. Then one can consider

$$w(x_i, y_j) = \sum_{l=1}^{k} f_l(x_i) g_l(y_j) \quad i = 1,2,\ldots,m \quad j = 1,2,\ldots,n$$

as one element of a matrix w of order ($m \times n$) as follows. Let f be a matrix of order ($m \times k$)

$$f = \begin{bmatrix} f_1(x_1) & f_2(x_1) & \cdots & f_k(x_1) \\ f_1(x_2) & f_2(x_2) & & \\ \vdots & & \ddots & \\ f_1(x_m) & \cdots & & f_k(x_m) \end{bmatrix} \rightarrow (m \times k)$$

and g be a matrix of order ($k \times n$)

$$f = \begin{bmatrix} g_1(y_1) & g_1(y_2) & \cdots & g_1(y_n) \\ g_2(y_1) & g_2(y_2) & & \\ \vdots & & \ddots & \\ g_k(y_1) & \cdots & & g_k(y_n) \end{bmatrix} \rightarrow (k \times n)$$

Then, from Eq. (2.7),

$$w = fg = \begin{bmatrix} \sum_{j=1}^{k} f_j(x_1)g_j(y_1) & \sum_{j=1}^{k} f_j(x_1)g_j(y_2) & \cdots & \sum_{j=1}^{k} f_j(x_1)g_j(y_n) \\ \sum_{j=1}^{k} f_j(x_2)g_j(y_1) & \sum_{k=1}^{k} f_j(x_2)g_j(y_2) & & \vdots \\ \vdots & & \ddots & \\ \sum_{j=1}^{k} f_j(x_m)g_j(y_1) & \cdots & & \sum_{j=1}^{k} f_j(x_m)g_j(y_n) \end{bmatrix} \rightarrow (m \times n) \quad (2.8)$$

---

[3] This form of a series results from a family of solutions to differential equations with certain boundary conditions.

In other words, this matrix multiplication performs the summation of the series at each combination of values for x and y. As we shall see subsequently, this observation provides a very compact means of summing a series at each point in a grid that is defined by all combinations of the elements of the vectors x and y.

We now consider three special cases of this general matrix multiplication:

1. The product of a row and a column vector.

2. The product of a column and a row vector.

3. The product of a row vector and a matrix.

These three cases will provide one means by which we can take advantage of MATLAB's compact notation and matrix solution methods for a class of engineering problems.

Case 1—Product of a row and column vector. Let a be the row vector

$$a = [a_1 \ a_2 \ ... \ a_k] \to (1 \times k)$$

which is of order $(1 \times k)$ and b be the column vector

$$b = [b_1 \ b_2 \ ... \ b_k]' \to (k \times 1)$$

which is of order $(k \times 1)$. Then the product $d = ab$ is the scalar

$$d = ab = \begin{bmatrix} a_1 & a_2 & \cdots & a_k \end{bmatrix} \begin{bmatrix} b_1 \\ b_1 \\ \vdots \\ b_k \end{bmatrix} = \left[\sum_{j=1}^{k} a_j b_j \right] = \sum_{j=1}^{k} a_j b_j \to (1 \times 1) \tag{2.9}$$

since the product of the orders gives $(1 \times k)(k \times 1) = (1 \times 1)$. This is called the dot product of two vectors. The MATLAB expression for matrix multiplication of the two vectors as defined above is either

    d = a*b

or

    d = dot(a,b)

If c is an $(n \times n)$ matrix and x is an $(n \times 1)$ column vector, then

$$f = x'cx = \sum_{i=1}^{n} \sum_{j=1}^{n} x_i c_{ij} x_j \tag{2.10}$$

which is also a scalar since the product of their orders gives $(1 \times n)(n \times n)(n \times 1) = (1 \times 1)$. The MATLAB expression for Eq. (2.10) is

    f = x'*c*x

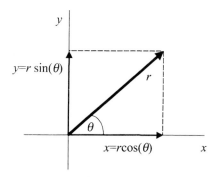

FIGURE 2.2
Transformation from polar to Cartesian coordinates.

This combination of operations is useful in solving eigenvalue problems. (See Chapter 9.)

Case 2—Product of a column and row vector. Let b be an $(m{\times}1)$ column vector and a a $(1{\times}n)$ row vector. Then the product $h = ba$ is

$$h = ba = \begin{bmatrix} b_1 \\ b_2 \\ \vdots \\ b_m \end{bmatrix} \begin{bmatrix} a_1 & a_2 & \cdots & a_n \end{bmatrix} = \begin{bmatrix} b_1 a_1 & b_1 a_2 & \cdots & b_1 a_n \\ b_2 a_1 & b_2 a_2 & & \\ \vdots & & \ddots & \\ b_m a_1 & & \cdots & b_m a_n \end{bmatrix} \rightarrow (m \times n) \qquad (2.11)$$

which is a matrix of order $(m{\times}n)$, since the product of their orders gives $(m{\times}1)(1{\times}n) = (m{\times}n)$. Thus, the elements of h (which are $h_{ij} = b_i a_j$) are the individual products of all the combinations of the elements of b and a.

As an example of the utility of this relationship we examine the transformation from polar coordinates to Cartesian coordinates shown in Figure 2.2—that is,

$$x = r\cos(\theta)$$
$$y = r\sin(\theta)$$

If we have a vector of radial values $r = [r_1 \ r_2 \ ... \ r_m]$ and a vector of angular values $\theta = [\theta_1 \ \theta_2 \ ... \ \theta_n]$, then the corresponding Cartesian coordinates are[4]

$$x = r' * \cos(\theta) = \begin{bmatrix} r_1 \\ r_2 \\ \vdots \\ r_m \end{bmatrix} \begin{bmatrix} \cos\theta_1 & \cos\theta_2 & \cdots & \cos\theta_n \end{bmatrix}$$

---

[4] This conversion can also be performed with `pol2cart`; however, this function is restricted to the case when $m = n$.

$$= \begin{bmatrix} r_1 \cos\theta_1 & r_1 \cos\theta_2 & \cdots & r_1 \cos\theta_n \\ r_2 \cos\theta_1 & r_2 \cos\theta_2 & & \\ \vdots & & \ddots & \\ r_m \cos\theta_1 & & \cdots & r_m \cos\theta_n \end{bmatrix} \qquad (2.12a)$$

and

$$y = r' * \sin(\theta) = \begin{bmatrix} r_1 \\ r_2 \\ \vdots \\ r_m \end{bmatrix} \begin{bmatrix} \sin\theta_1 & \sin\theta_2 & \cdots & \sin\theta_n \end{bmatrix}$$

$$= \begin{bmatrix} r_1 \sin\theta_1 & r_1 \sin\theta_2 & \cdots & r_1 \sin\theta_n \\ r_2 \sin\theta_1 & r_2 \sin\theta_2 & & \\ \vdots & & \ddots & \\ r_m \sin\theta_1 & & \cdots & r_m \sin\theta_n \end{bmatrix} \qquad (2.12b)$$

Thus we have mapped the polar coordinates into their Cartesian counterparts. This procedure is very useful in the plotting of results, as illustrated in the following example.

Example 2.1 Mode shape of a circular membrane

Consider the following mode shape for a solid circular membrane clamped along its outer boundary $r = 1$:

$$z(r,\phi) = J_1(3.8316r)\cos(\phi)$$

where $J_1(x)$ is the Bessel function[5] of the first kind of order 1 and (r,ϕ) are the polar coordinates of any point on the membrane. The Bessel function is determined by

```
besselj(n,x)
```

where n is the order and x its argument. The origin of the coordinate system is at the center of the membrane. The value 3.8316 is one of the natural frequency coefficients for this membrane. This mode shape can be plotted using the surface plotting function

```
mesh(x,y,z)
```

where (x,y) are the planar coordinates of a point on the surface $z(x,y)$. The mesh function is discussed in detail in Section 7.2. Thus, if we plot the surface every $\Delta r = 0.05$ and every $\theta = \pi/20$, then the script is

---

[5] See, for example, F. B. Hildebrand, *Advanced Calculus for Applications*, Prentice-Hall, Saddle River, NJ, 1976.

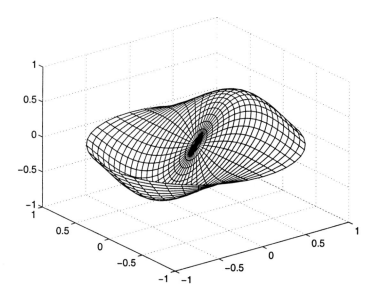

FIGURE 2.3
A mode shape of a clamped solid circular membrane.

```
r = [0:0.05:1]';                        % (21×1)
phi = 0:pi/20:2*pi;                     % (1×41)
x = r*cos(phi);                        % (21×41)
y = r*sin(phi);                        % (21×41)
z = besselj(1,3.8316*r)*cos(phi);      % (21×41)
mesh(x,y,z)
```

In this case *phi* is a (1×41) matrix and *r* is a (21×1) matrix. Then, from Eq. (2.12) *x*, *y* and *z* are each a (21×41) matrix. The coordinate transformations are required because the surface has to be plotted in the Cartesian coordinate system. It should also be realized that this technique works because the functions cos, sin, and besselj accept vectors for their arguments and return vectors of the same order. The execution of this script results in Figure 2.3.

Example 2.2 A solution to the Laplace equation

The solution of the Laplace equation subject to the boundary conditions $u(0,\eta) = u(1,\eta) = u(\xi,1) = 0$ and $u(\xi,0) = \xi(1-\xi)$ is

$$u(\xi,\eta) = 4 \sum_{n=1}^{N \to \infty} \frac{1 - \cos n\pi}{(n\pi)^3} e^{-n\pi\xi} \sin n\pi\eta$$

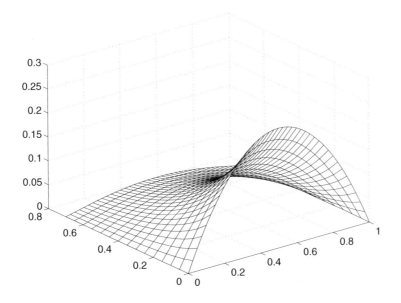

FIGURE 2.4
Display of a solution to the Laplace equation.

where $0 \le \eta \le 1$ and $\xi \ge 0$. We shall plot the surface $u(\xi,\eta)$ using $\mathrm{mesh}(\eta,\xi,u(\xi,\eta))$ for $N = 25$ and for increments $\Delta\eta = 0.025$ and $\Delta\xi = 0.05$ up to $\xi_{\max} = 0.7$. The script is

```
n = (1:25)*pi;                          % (1×25)
eta = 0:0.025:1;                        % (1×41)
xi = 0:0.05:0.7;                        % (1×15)
tempc = meshgrid((1−cos(n))./n.^3,xi);  % (15×25)
tempe = exp(−n'*xi)';                   % (15×25)
tempec = tempc.*tempe;                  % (15×25)
temps = sin(n'*eta);                    % (25×41)
z = 4*tempec*temps;                     % (15×41)
mesh(eta,xi,z)
```

The result is shown in Figure 2.4. The matrix multiplication *tempec*temps* produces the summation of the series over all *n* at all combinations of *eta* and *xi* as indicated in Eq. (2.8). In the mesh command MATLAB allows one to have the first two arguments, *eta* and *xi*, be vectors whose lengths agree with the respective values comprising the order of *z*. See the help file for mesh. This script can be written more compactly as

```
n = (1:25)*pi;
eta = 0:0.025:1;
```

```
xi = 0:0.05:0.7;
z = 4*meshgrid((1−cos(n))./n.^3,xi).*exp(−n'*xi)'*sin(n'*eta);
mesh(eta,xi,z)
```

since MATLAB evaluates expressions from left to right.

Case 3—Product of a row vector and a matrix. Let b be an $(m \times n)$ matrix and a a $(1 \times m)$ row vector. Then the product $g = ab$ is

$$g = ab = \begin{bmatrix} a_1 & a_2 & \cdots & a_m \end{bmatrix} \begin{bmatrix} b_{11} & b_{12} & \cdots & b_{1n} \\ b_{21} & b_{22} & & \\ \vdots & & \ddots & \\ b_{m1} & & \cdots & b_{mn} \end{bmatrix} \tag{2.13}$$

$$= \begin{bmatrix} \displaystyle\sum_{k=1}^{m} a_k b_{k1} & \displaystyle\sum_{k=1}^{m} a_k b_{k2} & \cdots & \displaystyle\sum_{k=1}^{m} a_k b_{kn} \end{bmatrix} \rightarrow (1 \times n)$$

which is a row vector of order $(1 \times n)$, since the product of their orders gives $(1 \times m)(m \times n) = (1 \times n)$.

This result can be interpreted as follows. Consider the series[6]

$$r(x) = \sum_{j=1}^{m} p_j h_j(x) \tag{2.14}$$

Suppose that we are interested in the value of $r(x)$ over a range of values $x_1, x_2, \ldots, x_n$. Then one can consider

$$r(x_i) = \sum_{j=1}^{m} p_j h_j(x_i) \qquad i = 1, 2, \ldots, n$$

one element of a vector r of order $(1 \times n)$ as follows. Let p be a vector of order $(1 \times m)$ with elements p_j and v the $(m \times n)$ matrix

$$v = \begin{bmatrix} h_1(x_1) & h_1(x_2) & \cdots & h_1(x_n) \\ h_2(x_1) & h_2(x_2) & & \\ \vdots & & \ddots & \\ h_m(x_1) & & & h_m(x_n) \end{bmatrix} \rightarrow (m \times n)$$

Then $r = pv$ gives

---

[6] Series of this form result from the solution of differential equations with certain boundary conditions and from Fourier series expansions of periodic functions.

$$r = pv = \left[\sum_{j=1}^{m} p_j h_j(x_1) \quad \sum_{j=1}^{m} p_j h_j(x_2) \quad \cdots \quad \sum_{j=1}^{m} p_j h_j(x_n) \right] \rightarrow (1 \times n)$$

Several illustrations of the uses of these results are given in the following examples.

Example 2.3 Summation of a Fourier series

The Fourier series representation of a rectangular pulse of duration d and period T is given by[7]

$$f(\tau) = \frac{d}{T} \left[1 + 2 \sum_{n=1}^{\infty} \frac{\sin(n\pi d / T)}{n\pi} \frac{1}{d/T} \cos(2\pi n\tau) \right]$$

where $\tau = t/T$. We see that this equation is of the form given by Eq. (2.14).

Let us sum 150 terms of $f(\tau)$ and plot it from $-1/2 < \tau < 1/2$ when $d/T = 0.25$. To do this we use plot(x,y) where $x = \tau$ and $y = f(\tau)$. (See Section 6.2 for a discussion of plot.) The script is

```
n = 1:150;                    % (1×150)
tau = linspace(-.5,.5,100);   % (1×100)
sn = sin(pi*n/4)./(pi*n/4);   % (1×150)
cntau = cos(2*pi*n'*tau);     % (150×100)
f = 0.25*(1+2*sn*cntau);      % (1×100)
plot(tau,f)
```

We see that the determination of f uses vector multiplication and dot division. The result of the dot division to produce sn is a vector of order (1×150), and the vector multiplication to produce $cntau$ creates a (150×100) matrix as shown in Eq. (2.11). According to Eq. (2.13), $sn*cntau$ is a row vector whose elements are the sum of the series at each value of τ. The execution of this script results in Figure 2.5.

Example 2.4 Normal cumulative distribution function

An approximation to the normal (gaussian) cumulative probability distribution function, which estimates the probability P that $0 \le X \le x$ is given as[8]

$$P(x) = P(X \le x) \cong 1 - \frac{1}{\sqrt{2\pi}} e^{-x^2/2} \sum_{m=1}^{5} b_m \left(1 + 0.2316419x \right)^{-m} \quad 0 \le x \le \infty$$

where $0.5 \le P(x) \le 1$, and

---

[7] See, for example, H. P. Hsu, *Applied Fourier Analysis*, Harcourt Brace Jovanovich, San Diego, CA, 1984.
[8] M. Abramowitz and I. A. Stegun, *Handbook Of Mathematical Functions*, National Bureau of Standards, Applied Mathematics Series 55, U.S. Government Printing Office, Washingtom D.C., 1964, p. 932.

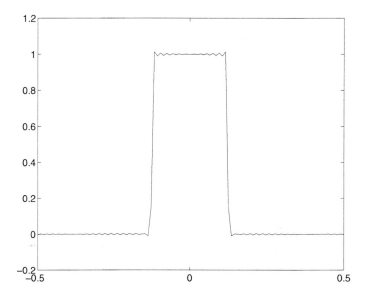

FIGURE 2.5
Fourier series summation of a periodic pulse.

$$b_1 = 0.319381530$$
$$b_2 = -0.356563782$$
$$b_3 = 1.781477937$$
$$b_4 = -1.821255978$$
$$b_5 = 1.330274429$$

The region for $-\infty \le x \le 0$ is obtained from $1 - P(|x|)$, where $0 \le 1 - P(|x|) \le 0.5$.

The objective is to compute and plot the cumulative distribution for $-3 \le x \le 3$ every $\Delta x = 0.2$. The script is

```
b = [0.319381530 -0.356563782 1.781477937 -1.821255978 1.330274429];  % (1×5)
m = 1:length(b);                    % (1×5)
x = 0:0.2:3;                        % (1×16)
mm = meshgrid(m,x);                 % (16×5)
bb = meshgrid(b,x);                 % (16×5)
temp = (1./(1+0.231641*x ))';       % (16×1)
zxx = meshgrid(temp,m)';            % (16×5)
bzm = sum((bb.*(zxx.^mm))');        % sum[(16×5)']→sum[(5×16)]→(1×16)
px = 1-bzm.*exp(-0.5*x.^2)/sqrt(pi*2); % (1×16)
plot(x,px,'k',-fliplr(x),fliplr(1-px),'k')
```

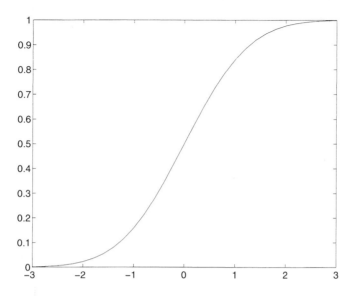

FIGURE 2.6
Normal cumulative probability distribution.

The length of x is 16 and that of m is 5. Thus, the order of the three matrices *mm*, *bb*, and *zxx* created by the `meshgrid` function are each of order (16×5). The quantity (bb.*(zxx.^mm))' is a (5×16) matrix and, as shown in Eq. (2.5), `sum`((bb.*(zxx.^mm))') is a (1×16) vector. Furthermore, `exp`(−0.5*x.^2) is a (1×16) vector. Consequently, bzm.*exp(−0.5*x.^2) is a (1×16) vector. When each element of this vector is subtracted from 1 each result represents $P(x)$ at each of the 16 values of x. The `plot` function, which is discussed in detail in Section 6.2, uses two sets of triplets for its arguments. The third term of each triplet tells the plotting routine to use the same color for each portion of the line, in this case black. The first pair of each triplet gives the x and y values to be displayed. The expression −`fliplr`(x) is the same as creating a new vector $z = -3{:}0.2{:}0$. The expression `fliplr`(1−px) reverses the order of the elements of the vector $1-px$, and creates a vector whose elements correspond to the negative x-values given by −`fliplr`(x). The execution of this script results in Figure 2.6.

Example 2.5 Evaluation of series with double summations

Consider the following double summation of the form:

$$w(x_i, y_j, t) = \sum_{n}^{N} \sum_{m}^{M} f_n(x_i) g_m(y_j) h_{nm}(t) \qquad i = 1,2,...s \quad j = 1,2,...p$$

where $x = [x_1 \; x_2 \; \ldots \; x_s]$ and $y = [y_1 \; y_2 \; \ldots \; y_p]$. If we assume that $N = M = k$ and let $t = t_0$, an assigned (numerical) value, then we can evaluate this series in the following manner. First we note that if we take the $(m \times n)$ matrix given by Eq. (2.7) and multiply it with a matrix d of order $(n \times p)$ and elements d_{ij}, then the result is the following $(m \times p)$ matrix:

$$
w = cd = abd = \begin{bmatrix}
\sum_{l=1}^{n}\sum_{j=1}^{k} a_{1j}b_{jl}d_{l1} & \sum_{l=1}^{n}\sum_{j=1}^{k} a_{1j}b_{jl}d_{l2} & \cdots & \sum_{l=1}^{n}\sum_{j=1}^{k} a_{1j}b_{jl}d_{lp} \\
\sum_{l=1}^{n}\sum_{j=1}^{k} a_{2j}b_{jl}d_{l1} & \sum_{l=1}^{n}\sum_{j=1}^{k} a_{2j}b_{jl}d_{l2} & & \vdots \\
\vdots & & \ddots & \\
\sum_{l=1}^{n}\sum_{j=1}^{k} a_{mj}b_{jl}d_{l1} & \cdots & & \sum_{l=1}^{n}\sum_{j=1}^{k} a_{mj}b_{jl}d_{lp}
\end{bmatrix} \to (m \times p)
$$

$$(2.15)$$

We now form $f_n(x)$ into the following matrix of order $(k \times s)$

$$
f = \begin{bmatrix}
f_1(x_1) & f_2(x_1) & \cdots & f_s(x_1) \\
f_1(x_2) & f_2(x_2) & & \vdots \\
\vdots & & \ddots & \\
f_1(x_k) & \cdots & & f_s(x_k)
\end{bmatrix} \to (k \times s)
$$

$g_m(y)$ into the following matrix of order $(k \times p)$

$$
g = \begin{bmatrix}
g_1(y_1) & g_1(y_2) & \cdots & g_1(y_p) \\
g_2(y_1) & g_2(y_2) & & \\
\vdots & & \ddots & \\
g_k(y_1) & \cdots & & g_k(y_p)
\end{bmatrix} \to (k \times p)
$$

and $h_{nm}(t_0)$ into the following matrix of order $(k \times k)$

$$
h = \begin{bmatrix}
h_{11}(t_0) & h_{12}(t_0) & \cdots & h_{1k}(t_0) \\
h_{21}(t_0) & h_{22}(t_0) & & \vdots \\
\vdots & & \ddots & \\
h_{k1}(t_0) & \cdots & & h_{kk}(t_0)
\end{bmatrix} \to (k \times k)
$$

Then, since $n = k$ in Eq. (2.15), the product $f'hg$ is the following matrix w of order $(s \times p)$

$$
w = \begin{bmatrix}
w(x_1, y_1, t_0) & w(x_1, y_2, t_0) & \cdots & w(x_1, y_p, t_0) \\
w(x_2, y_1, t_0) & w(x_2, y_2, t_0) & & \vdots \\
\vdots & & \ddots & \\
w(x_s, y_1, t_0) & \cdots & & w(x_s, y_p, t_0)
\end{bmatrix} \to (s \times p)
$$

where

$$w(x_i, y_j, t_0) = \sum_{n=1}^{k} \sum_{m=1}^{k} f_n(x_i) h_{nm}(t_0) g_m(y_j)$$

To illustrate this procedure consider the following series,[9] which represents the non-dimensional, normalized displacement response of a square membrane subjected to an initial displacement $w(\eta, \xi, 0) = \eta \xi (\eta - 1)(\xi - 1)$:

$$w(\eta, \xi, \tau) = \sum_{n=0}^{k} \sum_{m=0}^{k} \frac{\sin((2n+1)\pi\eta)\sin((2m+1)\pi\xi)}{(2n+1)^3 + (2m+1)^3} \cos\left(\pi\tau \sqrt{(2n+1)^2 + (2m+1)^2} \right)$$

where $\eta = x/b$, $\xi = y/b$, b is the length of a side of the membrane, $\tau = ct_0/b$, c is the wave speed in the membrane, and t is time.

The script to evaluate this series at $\tau = 0$ and $k = 10$ is

```
tau = 0; n = 0:10; m = n; xi = 0:0.1:1; eta = xi;
nden = meshgrid((2*n+1).^3,xi);
mden = meshgrid((2*m+1).^3,eta);
snx = sin(pi*(2*n+1)'*xi);
sme = sin(pi*(2*m+1)'*eta);
xterm = snx./nden';
yterm = sme./mden';
[n2,m2] = meshgrid(2*n+1,2*m+1,1);
w = xterm'*cos(pi*tau*sqrt(n2.^2+m2.^2))*yterm;
mesh(xi,eta,w)
```

The vectors n, m, xi, and eta are each (1×11) vectors. The first two $\texttt{meshgrid}$ functions create two (11×11) matrices for $ndem$ and $mden$. The vector multiplications that give snx and sme permit the dot divisions that produce $xterm$ and $yterm$. The third $\texttt{meshgrid}$ function produces two (11×11) matrices for $n2$ and $m2$. Thus, w is a (11×11) matrix. The $\texttt{mesh}$ function is similar to the $\texttt{surf}$ function, the primary distinction being that in the resulting figure the color of the patches is white. See Section 7.2. When executed, the script produces the surface shown in Figure 2.7.

2.6.3 Matrix Inverse

The inverse of a square matrix a is an operation such that

$$a^{-1}a = aa^{-1} = I$$

provided that a is not singular, that is, its determinant (see Section 2.6.4) is not equal to zero ($|a| \neq 0$). The superscript "−1" denotes the inverse. The expression for obtaining the inverse of matrix a is either

---

[9] H. P. Hsu, *ibid.*, p. 202.

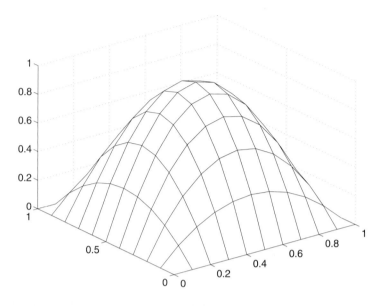

FIGURE 2.7
Shape of a square membrane at $\tau = 0$.

    inv(a)

or

    a^−1

It is important to note that $1/a \neq a^\wedge(-1)$; $1/a$ will cause an error. The inverse can also be obtained using the backslash operator as shown in Section 2.6.5.

2.6.4 Determinants

A determinant of order n is defined as

$$|a| = \begin{vmatrix} a_{11} & a_{12} & \cdots & a_{1n} \\ a_{21} & a_{22} & & \vdots \\ \vdots & & \cdots & \\ a_{n1} & \cdots & & a_{nn} \end{vmatrix}$$

For $n = 2$:

$$|a| = a_{11}a_{22} - a_{12}a_{21}$$

For $n = 3$:

$$|a| = a_{11}a_{22}a_{33} + a_{12}a_{23}a_{31} + a_{13}a_{21}a_{32} - a_{13}a_{22}a_{31}$$
$$- a_{11}a_{23}a_{32} - a_{12}a_{21}a_{33}$$

The MATLAB expression for the determinant is

```
det(a)
```

For example, if a is defined as

$$a = \begin{bmatrix} 1 & 3 \\ 4 & 2 \end{bmatrix}$$

then

```
a = [ 1 3; 4 2];
d = det(a)
```

gives, upon execution, $d = -10$.

A class of problems that occurs in several engineering applications results in a determinant of the form

$$|a - \lambda b| = 0$$

where a and b are ($n{\times}n$) matrices and λ_j, j = 1, 2, , ..., n are the roots (sometimes called eigenvalues) of this equation. The solution of this polynomial equation is obtained from

```
lambda = eig(a,b)
```

Example 2.6 Transformation of a polynomial

A polynomial of the form

$$ax^2 + by^2 + cz^2 + 2dxy + 2exz + 2gyz$$

where a, b, c, d, e, and g are real numbers, can be transformed into the real diagonal form

$$r_1 x'^2 + r_2 y'^2 + r_3 z'^2$$

where x', y', and z' is another coordinate system whose origin is also at $(0,0,0)$, $r_1 \geq r_2 \geq r_3$ are the roots of

$$|A - rI| = 0$$

and A is the real symmetric matrix

$$A = \begin{bmatrix} a & d & e \\ d & b & g \\ e & g & c \end{bmatrix}$$

Consider the polynomial

$$4x^2 + 3y^2 - z^2 - 12xy + 4exz - 8gyz$$

Thus

$$A = \begin{bmatrix} 4 & -6 & 2 \\ -6 & 3 & -4 \\ 2 & -4 & -1 \end{bmatrix}$$

To determine the roots r_j we have

r = eig([4 −6 2;−6 3 −4;2 −4 −1])

which, upon execution, gives the column vector $r = [-4.0000\ -1.0000\ 11.0000]'$. Notice that the roots are not in any particular order. To place them in the desired order we use `sort`. However, `sort` arranges the values in ascending order (most negative to most positive), only. Therefore, we can use either of the following expressions, which work for any combination of positive and negative real values, to obtain the values in descending order.

Form #1

r = −sort(−r)

which gives $r = [11.0000\ -1.0000\ -4.0000]'$.

Form #2

r = flipud(sort(r))

which also gives $r = [11.0000\ -1.0000\ -4.0000]'$. If r were a row vector, then we would replace `flipud` with `fliplr`.

The real diagonal form is, therefore,

$$11x'^2 - y'^2 - 4z'^2$$

We could also have written these statements more compactly as

r = −sort(−eig([4 −6 2;−6 3 −4;2 −4 −1]))

2.6.5 Solution of a System of Equations

Consider the following system of n equations and n unknowns x_k, $k = 1, 2, \ldots, n$:

$$a_{11}x_1 + a_{12}x_2 + \cdots + a_{1n}x_n = b_1$$
$$a_{21}x_1 + a_{22}x_2 + \cdots + a_{2n}x_n = b_2$$
$$\vdots$$
$$a_{n1}x_1 + a_{n2}x_2 + \cdots + a_{nn}x_n = b_n$$

We can rewrite this system of equations in matrix notation as follows:

$$ax = b$$

where a is the $(n \times n)$ matrix

$$a = \begin{bmatrix} a_{11} & a_{12} & \cdots & a_{1n} \\ a_{21} & a_{22} & & \vdots \\ \vdots & & \ddots & \\ a_{n1} & \cdots & & a_{nn} \end{bmatrix} \rightarrow (n \times n)$$

and x and b are, respectively, the $(n \times 1)$ column vectors

$$x = \begin{bmatrix} x_1 \\ x_2 \\ \vdots \\ x_n \end{bmatrix} \rightarrow (n \times 1) \qquad b = \begin{bmatrix} b_1 \\ b_2 \\ \vdots \\ b_n \end{bmatrix} \rightarrow (n \times 1)$$

The symbolic solution is obtained by pre-multiplying both sides of the matrix equation by a^{-1}. Thus,

$$a^{-1}ax = a^{-1}b$$
$$x = a^{-1}b$$

since $a^{-1}a = I$ and $Ix = x$. The preferred expression for solving this system of equations is[10]

    x = a\b

where the backslash operator indicates matrix division and is referred to by MATLAB as left matrix divide. Left division uses a procedure that is more numerically stable when compared to the methods used for either of the following alternative notations:

    x = a^-1*b

---

[10] The notation $a \backslash b$ can be applied even when a is not a square matrix, whereas $\mathtt{inv}(a)$ is only applicable when a is square. That is, if a is an $(m \times n)$ matrix, x an $(n \times 1)$ vector and b an $(m \times 1)$ vector, then if $ax = b$, left division $a \backslash b$ finds $x = cb$, where $c = (a'a)^{-1}a'$ is the pseudo-inverse of a.

or

```
x = inv(a)*b
```

As an example consider the following system of equations:

$$8x_1 + x_2 + 6x_3 = 7.5$$
$$3x_1 + 5x_2 + 7x_3 = 4$$
$$4x_1 + 9x_2 + 2x_3 = 12$$

which, in matrix notation, is

$$\begin{bmatrix} 8 & 1 & 6 \\ 3 & 5 & 7 \\ 4 & 9 & 2 \end{bmatrix} \begin{bmatrix} x_1 \\ x_2 \\ x_3 \end{bmatrix} = \begin{bmatrix} 7.5 \\ 4 \\ 12 \end{bmatrix}$$

The solution is obtained with the following script:

```
a = [8 1 6; 3 5 7; 4 9 2];
b = [7.5 4 12]';
x = a\b
```

which gives $x = [1.2931 \ 0.8972 \ -0.6236]'$. This script could also have been written compactly as

```
x = [8 1 6; 3 5 7; 4 9 2]\[7.5 4 12]'
```

As a check we set

```
z = a*x
```

and find numerically that $z = b$.

Example 2.7 Solution of a system of coupled equations

In the determination of the solution to the static deflection of a square plate clamped on all four of its edges and subjected to a uniform loading over its surface, one must first obtain the constants E_m from the truncation of the following infinite set of equations:[11]

$$a_i E_i + \sum_{m=1,3,\dots} b_{im} E_m = c_i \qquad i = 1,3,5,\dots$$

where

---

[11] S. Timoshenko and S. Woinowsky-Krieger, *Theory of Plates and Shells*, McGraw-Hill, New York, 1959, pp. 197-202.

$$a_i = \frac{1}{i}\left(\tanh\alpha_i + \frac{\alpha_i}{\cosh^2\alpha_i}\right)$$

$$b_{im} = 8i\left(\pi m^3\left(1 + \frac{i^2}{m^2}\right)^2\right)^{-1}$$

$$c_i = \frac{4}{\pi^3 i^4}\left(\frac{\alpha_i}{\cosh^2\alpha_i} - \tanh\alpha_i\right)$$

and $\alpha_i = i\pi/2$. If we take only the first four terms of this system, then we have

$$\begin{bmatrix} a_1 + b_{11} & b_{13} & b_{15} & b_{17} \\ b_{31} & a_3 + b_{33} & b_{35} & b_{37} \\ b_{51} & b_{53} & a_5 + b_{55} & b_{57} \\ b_{71} & b_{73} & b_{75} & a_7 + b_{77} \end{bmatrix} \begin{bmatrix} E_1 \\ E_3 \\ E_5 \\ E_7 \end{bmatrix} = \begin{bmatrix} c_1 \\ c_3 \\ c_5 \\ c_7 \end{bmatrix}$$

The solution of these four equations is obtained with the following script:

```
m = 1:2:7; i = m; alp = m*pi/2;
ai = (tanh(alp)+alp./(cosh(alp).^2))./i;             % (1×4)
ci = 4.*(alp./(cosh(alp).^2)-tanh(alp))./((pi^3)*i.^4);   % (1×4)
[ii,mm] = meshgrid(i,m);                              % (4×4)
bim = (8/pi)*ii./(((1+(ii.^2)./(mm.^2)).^2).*mm.^3);  % (4×4)
format long e
ee = (diag(ai)+bim)\ci'
format short
```

The `meshgrid` function produces two (4×4) matrices in the manner shown in Eq. (2.3), which are then used to determine *bim*; see Eq. (2.4). Even though the subscripts are odd numbers, the length of each vector is 4. The execution of the script yields the column vector, whose following numerical values have been truncated for clarity:

ee→[-0.048000 0.004903 0.002296 0.001111]′

Thus: E_1 = ee(1,1) = −0.048000; E_3 = ee(2,1) = 0.004903; E_5 = ee(3,1) = 0.002296; and E_7 = ee(4,1) = 0.001111.

EXERCISES

Section 2.3

2.1 Create two vectors, one whose elements are $2n-1$ and the other whose elements are $2n+1$, $n = 0, 1, ..., 7$. Call the former *a* and the latter *b*.

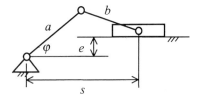

FIGURE 2.8
Slider crank mechanism.

a) What is the sum of a and b?

b) What is the difference of a and b?

c) What is the product $a'b$ and the value of its determinant?

d) What is the product ab'?

2.2 Given the vector $x = [17\ -3\ -47\ 5\ 29\ -37\ 51\ -7\ 19]$. Create a script that rearranges them into the following vector: $y = [-3\ -7\ -37\ -47\ 51\ 29\ 19\ 17\ 5]$. The script should be written to work on a vector of arbitrary length. Place the value 0 (for the general vector) with the negative quantities; that is, when a 0 is an element of the vector it will be the first element of y.

Section 2.4

2.3 Let $z = \texttt{magic(5)}$.

(a) Perform the following operations to z in the order given:

(i) Divide column 2 by $\sqrt{3}$;

(ii) Add the elements of the third row to those in the fifth row (the third row remains unchanged);

(iii) Multiply the first column by the fourth column and place the result in the first column;

(iv) Set the diagonal elements to 2.

(b) If the final result obtained in (a) is denoted q, then display the diagonal of qq'.
[Answer: [486 104189 7300 44522 111024]'.]

(c) Display the square of each element of q.

Section 2.5

2.4 The displacement of the slider of the slider crank mechanism shown in Figure 2.8 is given by

$$s = a\cos(\varphi) + \sqrt{b^2 - (a\sin(\varphi) - e)^2}$$

Plot the displacement s as a function of the angle φ (in degrees) when $a = 1$, $b = 1.5$, $e = 0.3$, and $0 \le \varphi \le 360°$—that is, use $\texttt{plot}(\varphi,s)$.

2.5 The percentage of the total power P in a periodic series of rectangular-shaped pulses as a function of the number of terms N_H in its series expansion is

$$P = 100P_o/P_T\%$$

where P_T is the total nondimensional power in the signal,

$$P_o = 1 + 2 \sum_{n=1}^{N_H} \frac{\sin^2(n\pi\tau_o/T)}{(n\pi\tau_o/T)^2}$$

and τ_o/T is the ratio of the pulse duration to its period. If we let $\tau_o/T = 1/\sqrt{19}$, then $P_T \cong 4.3589$. For this case plot the percentage total power as a function of N_H for $2 \le N_H \le 25$.

2.6 Consider the following product[12]

$$S_N = \prod_{n=1}^{N} \left(1 - \frac{x^2}{n^2 - a^2} \right)$$

where, when $N \to \infty$,

$$S_\infty = \frac{a}{\sin \pi a \sqrt{a^2 + x^2}} \sin\left(\pi \sqrt{a^2 + x^2} \right)$$

A percentage error is defined as

$$e_N = 100 \frac{S_N - S_\infty}{S_\infty} \%$$

If x varies from 1 to 5 by 0.5 and $a = \sqrt{2.8}$, then what is the percentage error at these nine values of x when $N = 100$. Use the function prod. [Answer: e_{100} = [1.0001 2.2643 4.0610 6.4176 9.3707 12.9670 17.2642 22.3330 28.2588].]

2.7 One means of obtaining an estimate of a parameter δ appearing in the Weibull probability density function (see Section 14.2.2 and Exercise 5.2(l)) is obtained from

$$\delta = \left[\frac{1}{n} \sum_{i=1}^{n} x_i^\beta \right]^{1/\beta}$$

where x_i are a random sample of size n and β is another (known) parameter. If x = [72 82 97 103 113 117 126 127 127 139 154 159 199 207] and $\beta = 3.644$, then determine the value of δ. [Answer: δ = 144.2741.]

2.8 The transformation from spherical to Cartesian coordinates is given by

$$x = b \sin\phi \cos\theta$$
$$y = b \sin\phi \sin\theta$$
$$z = b \cos\phi$$

Take 10 equally spaced values of ϕ in the range $0 \le \phi \le 90°$ and 24 equally spaced values of θ in the range $0 \le \theta \le 360°$ and plot the hemisphere using mesh(x, y, z) when $b = 2$.

2.9 Evaluate the following series for $N = 25$ and 5 equally spaced values of x from $0.1 \le x \le 1$.

---

[12] L. B. W. Jolley, *ibid.*

$$\sum_{N\to-\infty}^{N\to\infty} \frac{1}{n^4+x^4} = \frac{2\pi^4}{y^3}\frac{\sinh y + \sin y}{\cosh y - \cos y} \qquad y = \pi x\sqrt{2}$$

Compare these values with exact values.

2.10 The series representation for the Bessel function of the first kind of order n is given by

$$J_n(x) = \sum_{k=0}^{K\to\infty} \frac{(-1)^k (x/2)^{2k+n}}{k!\,\Gamma(k+1+n)}$$

For $K = 25$ determine a vector of values of $J_n(x)$ for $n = 2$ and 6 equally spaced values in the range $1 \le x \le 6$. Both the gamma function Γ and the factorial are obtained with gamma. Compare your answers with those obtained from MATLAB's built-in function besselj(n,x).

Section 2.6.2

2.11 A matrix is said to be an orthogonal matrix if

$$X'X = I$$

and, therefore, $(X'X)^{-1} = I$. Show that each of the following matrices is orthogonal. See also Section 4.3.1.

$$w = \frac{1}{2}\begin{bmatrix} -1 & -1 \\ 1 & -1 \\ -1 & 1 \\ 1 & 1 \end{bmatrix} \qquad q = \frac{1}{2}\begin{bmatrix} 1 & -1 & -1 & 1 \\ 1 & 1 & -1 & -1 \\ 1 & -1 & 1 & -1 \\ 1 & 1 & 1 & 1 \end{bmatrix}$$

2.12 Consider the planar three degree-of-freedom linkages shown in Figure 2.9. The location and orientation of point O_3 with respect to the fixed coordinate system O_0 is

$$T_3 = A_1 A_2 A_3$$

where

$$A_j = \begin{bmatrix} \cos\theta_j & -\sin\theta_j & 0 & a_j\cos\theta_j \\ \sin\theta_j & \cos\theta_j & 0 & a_j\sin\theta_j \\ 0 & 0 & 1 & 0 \\ 0 & 0 & 0 & 1 \end{bmatrix} \qquad j = 1,2,3$$

and

$$T_3 = \begin{bmatrix} u_x & v_x & 0 & q_x \\ u_y & v_y & 0 & q_y \\ 0 & 0 & 1 & 0 \\ 0 & 0 & 0 & 1 \end{bmatrix}$$

The components q_x and q_y are the (x,y)-coordinates of the point O_3 with respect to the coordinate system centered at O_0. If $\theta_j = 30°$, $j = 1, 2, 3$, and $a_1 = 1$, $a_2 = 2$ and $a_3 = 3$, then what is the location of

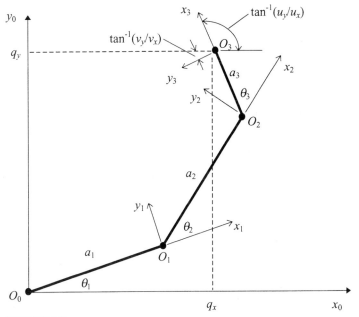

FIGURE 2.9
Planar three degree-of-freedom linkage.

point O_3 with respect to the coordinate system centered at O_0 and the orientation of the (x_3, y_3) axes system. [Answer: $q_x = 1.8660$, $q_y = 5.2321$, x_3 is parallel to y_0 and y_3 is parallel to x_0, but in the opposite direction.]

2.13 In multiple linear regression analysis the following matrix quantity has some utility (see Exercise 14.13)

$$H = X(X'X)^{-1}X'$$

If

$$X = \begin{bmatrix} 17 & 31 & 5 \\ 6 & 5 & 4 \\ 19 & 28 & 9 \\ 12 & 11 & 10 \end{bmatrix}$$

determine the diagonal of H. [Answer: diagonal $H = [0.7294\ 0.9041\ 0.4477\ 0.9188]'$.]

2.14 Plot the series[13] given below over the indicated ranges of τ. Unless otherwise stated, use 200 terms to sum each series. Obtain the solutions without using sum.

---

[13] H. P. Hsu, *ibid.*

a) Square wave

$$f(\tau) = \frac{4}{\pi} \sum_{n=1,3,5...} \frac{1}{n} \sin(2n\pi\tau) \qquad -\frac{1}{2} \le \tau \le \frac{1}{2}$$

b) Sawtooth

$$f(\tau) = \frac{1}{2} + \frac{1}{\pi} \sum_{n=1} \frac{1}{n} \sin(2n\pi\tau) \qquad -1 \le \tau \le 1$$

c) Sawtooth

$$f(\tau) = \frac{1}{2} - \frac{1}{\pi} \sum_{n=1} \frac{1}{n} \sin(2n\pi\tau) \qquad -1 \le \tau \le 1$$

d) Triangular wave

$$f(\tau) = \frac{\pi}{2} - \frac{4}{\pi} \sum_{n=1} \frac{1}{(2n-1)^2} \cos\big((2n-1)\pi\tau\big) \qquad -1 \le \tau \le 1$$

e) Rectified sine wave

$$f(\tau) = \frac{2}{\pi} + \frac{4}{\pi} \sum_{n=1} \frac{1}{1-4n^2} \cos(2n\pi\tau) \qquad -1 \le \tau \le 1$$

f) Half sine wave

$$f(\tau) = \frac{1}{\pi} + \frac{1}{2} \sin \pi\tau - \frac{2}{\pi} \sum_{n=2,4,6,...}^{106} \frac{\cos n\pi\tau}{n^2 - 1} \qquad -2 \le \tau \le 2$$

g) Exponential

$$f(\tau) = \frac{e^{2\pi} - 1}{\pi} \left[\frac{1}{2} + \sum_{n=1}^{250} \frac{1}{1+n^2} (\cos n\tau - n \sin n\tau) \right] \qquad 0 \le \tau \le 4\pi$$

Use 350 values of τ to display the results.

h) Trapezoidal

$$f(\tau) = \frac{4}{\alpha^2} \sum_{n=1,3,5,...}^{105} \frac{\sin n\pi\alpha}{(\pi n)^2} \sin n\pi\tau \qquad -2 \le \tau \le 2$$

Let $\alpha = 0.25$.

2.15 Consider the following two series:[14]

---

[14] L. B. W. Jolley, *ibid.*

$$S_{1N} = \sum_{n=1}^{N} \frac{\cos(n\theta)}{n^2 + a^2} \qquad 0 < \theta < \pi$$

$$S_{2N} = \sum_{n=1}^{N} \frac{n\sin(n\theta)}{n^2 + a^2} \qquad 0 < \theta < 2\pi$$

where, when $N \to \infty$,

$$S_{1\infty} = \frac{\pi \cosh[a(\pi - \theta)]}{2a \sinh \pi a} - \frac{1}{2a^2} \qquad 0 < \theta < \pi$$

$$S_{2\infty} = \frac{\pi \sinh[a(\pi - \theta)]}{2 \sinh \pi a} \qquad 0 < \theta < 2\pi$$

A percentage error is defined as

$$e_{jN} = 100 \frac{S_{jN} - S_{j\infty}}{S_{j\infty}} \% \qquad j = 1,2$$

If θ varies from $10°$ to $80°$ every $10°$ and $a = \sqrt{3}$, then what is the percentage error for these two series at these eight values of θ when $N = 25$. Obtain the results without using sum. [Answer: $e_1 = [-1.2435$ 0.8565 0.8728 -1.9417 -0.9579 -8.1206 0.7239 1.1661] and $e_2 = [8.0538$ 10.4192 -8.9135 -5.4994 12.9734 -0.5090 -17.2259 11.2961].]

2.16 The nondimensional steady-state temperature distribution in a rectangular plate that is subjected to a constant temperature along the edge $\eta = 1$ is given by[15]

$$T(x,y) = \frac{4}{\pi} \sum_{n=1,3,5}^{\infty} \frac{\sinh(n\pi\alpha\eta)}{n\sinh(n\pi\alpha)} \sin(n\pi\xi)$$

where $\eta = x/d$, $\xi = y/b$, d and b are the lengths of the plate in the x and y directions, respectively, $\alpha = d/b$, $0 \le \eta \le 1$, and $0 \le \xi \le 1$. Display the temperature distribution throughout the plate when $\alpha = 2$ using mesh. Let $\Delta\eta = \Delta\xi = 1/14$. Obtain the results without using sum.

2.17 The displacement of a wave propagating in a string subject to an initial velocity of zero and an initial displacement of

$$u(\eta,0) = \frac{\eta}{a} \qquad 0 \le \eta \le a$$

$$u(\eta,0) = \frac{1-\eta}{1-a} \qquad a \le \eta \le 1$$

is given by

$$u(\eta,\tau) = \frac{2}{a\pi(1-a)} \sum_{n=1}^{N \to \infty} \frac{\sin n\pi a}{n^2} \sin(n\pi\eta)\cos(n\pi\tau)$$

---

[15] H. P. Hsu, *ibid.*

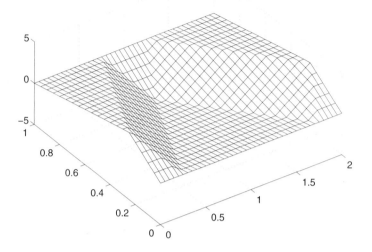

FIGURE 2.10
Propagation of an initial displacement in a string.

Display $u(\eta, \tau)$ when $N = 50$, $a = 0.25$, $\Delta\eta = 0.05$, and $\Delta\tau = 0.05$, where $0 \le \tau \le 2$. Obtain the solution without using sum. The result is shown in the Figure 2.10, which was obtained after using the rotate icon in the figure window.

Section 2.6.5

2.18 Given the following system of equations.

$$16s + 32u + 33p + 13w = 91$$
$$5s + 11u + 10p + 8w = 16$$
$$9s + 7u + 6p + 12w = 5$$
$$34s + 14u + 15p + w = 43$$

Determine the values of s, u, p, and w. What is the value of the determinant of the coefficients? [Answer: $s = -0.1258$, $u = -8.7133$, $p = 11.2875$ and $w = -0.0500$. Determinant = 7,680.]

2.19 Consider two long cylinders of two different materials where one cylinder just fits inside the other cylinder. The inner radius of the inner cylinder is a, and its outer radius is b. The inner radius of the outer cylinder is also b, and its outer radius is c. The Young's modulus and Poisson ratio of the inner cylinder are E_1 and v_1, respectively, and those of the outer cylinder E_2 and v_2, respectively. The radial stress σ_{rr}, hoop stress $\sigma_{\theta\theta}$, and radial displacement u_r are given by, respectively,

$$\sigma_{rri}(r) = \frac{A_i}{r^2} + B_i$$

$$\sigma_{\theta\theta i}(r) = \frac{-A_i}{r^2} + B_i \tag{a}$$

$$u_{ri}(r) = \frac{-(1+\upsilon_i)}{rE_i} A_i + \frac{(1-\upsilon_i)}{E_i} rB_i$$

where $i = 1$ refers to the inner cylinder and $i = 2$ the outer.

If the outer surface of the outer cylinder is subjected to a compressive radial displacement U_o and the inner surface of the inner cylinder has no radial stress, then the following four boundary conditions can be used to determine A_i and B_i, $i = 1,2$:

$$\sigma_{rr1}(a) = 0$$
$$\sigma_{rr1}(b) = \sigma_{rr2}(b) \tag{b}$$
$$u_{r1}(b) = u_{r2}(b)$$
$$u_{r2}(c) = -U_o$$

Substituting Eqs. (a) into (b) results in the following systems of equations.

$$\begin{bmatrix} 1 & a^2 & 0 & 0 \\ 1 & b^2 & -1 & -b^2 \\ -(1+v_1) & (1-v_1)b^2 & (1+v_2)E_1/E_2 & -(1-v_2)b^2 E_1/E_2 \\ 0 & 0 & -(1+v_2) & (1-v_2)c^2 \end{bmatrix} \begin{bmatrix} A_1 \\ B_1 \\ A_2 \\ B_2 \end{bmatrix} = \begin{Bmatrix} 0 \\ 0 \\ 0 \\ -U_o E_2 c \end{Bmatrix}$$

What is the hoop stress in the inner and outer cylinders at $r = b$ when $v_1 = v_2 = 0.4$, $E_1 = 3 \times 10^5$ psi, $E_2 = 3.5 \times 10^4$ psi, $U_o = 0.01$ inch, $a = 0.192$ inch, $b = 0.25$ inch and $c = 0.312$ inch? [Answer: $\sigma_{\theta\theta1}(b) = -9571.8$ psi and $\sigma_{\theta\theta2}(b) = -1989.3$ psi.]

C H A P T E R   3

DATA INPUT/OUTPUT

Edward B. Magrab

The means of displaying annotated numerical results in the MATLAB command window and storing and retrieving data from files are presented.

3.1 STRINGS (LITERALS) AND ANNOTATED OUTPUT

MATLAB allows the creation, storage, and manipulation of matrices of any combination of letters, numbers, and special characters as quantities called strings. Strings are defined in a manner similar to that for vectors and matrices, except that a pair of single quotes encloses the collection of alphanumeric characters (' ... '). However, each character in the string occupies one element in a vector or a matrix.

Consider the following examples. Let s be the string 'testing123'. The MATLAB expression to define this string is the vector

    s = 'testing123'

or

    s = ['testing123']

where each character within the pair of single quotes is a location in the vector s. Thus,

$s(7) \rightarrow$ g
$s(3:6) \rightarrow$ stin
fliplr(s) $\rightarrow$ 321gnitset

and length(s) = 10. The concatenation of strings is analogous to that for numerical values. Thus,

sc = [s fliplr(s)]

produces the string

testing123321gnitset

whereas

scs = [s; fliplr(s)]

is a matrix with

scs(1,:) $\rightarrow$ testing123
scs(2,:) $\rightarrow$ 321gnitset

Notice that both rows of *scs* have the same number of characters (columns).

If we place a string in each row of a matrix, we have a convenient way in which to access string expressions. The requirement is that each row must contain the same number of characters. This requirement can be met by employing blanks to pad the rest of the string when the individual string expressions are of unequal length. Thus, if

lab = ['first ';'last ';'middle']

then

lab(1,:) $\rightarrow$ first*b*
lab(2,:) $\rightarrow$ last*bb*
lab(3,:) $\rightarrow$ middle

and *b* is a blank space. Fortunately, MATLAB provides a way to do this padding for us using

str2mat

Thus, the above expression can be replaced by the easier-to-use expression

lab = str2mat('first','last','middle')

where each string expression is a row in the matrix *lab*, which is a (3×6) array. The trailing blanks can be removed with

```
deblank
```

To convert a numerical value to a string we use

```
num2str
```

Let *num* be either a number, a matrix of numbers, or an expression resulting in a number or a matrix of numbers. Then, to convert this to a string we have

```
z = num2str(num)
```

where *z* is a string variable.

The function num2str is most often used to place annotated numerical output in the MATLAB command window or on a figure. A typical construct would be to concatenate the converted numerical value with some identifying text. Thus, if *num* is, say, the weight in kilograms, and it is to be identified as such, then to display it to the MATLAB command window we use the disp function as follows:

```
num = 12.567;
z = num2str(num);
disp(['Product weight = ' z ' kg'])
```

or, more compactly,

```
num = 12.567;
disp(['Product weight = ' num2str(num) ' kg'])
```

When executed this results in

Product weight = 12.567 kg

being displayed in the MATLAB command window. Internally, this string is a vector of length 26. Notice that blank spaces are acceptable string characters and are preserved as such.

If *num* is the vector of weights, then

```
num = [12.567 3.458 9.111];
disp(['Product weight = ' num2str(num) ' kg'])
```

displays

Product weight = 12.567   3.458   9.111 kg

However, to create annotation that accompanies each value of *num* we use the following
script

```
num = [12.567 3.458 9.111];
n = length(num);
disp([repmat('Product weight = ',n,1) num2str(num') repmat(' kg',n,1)])
```

which, upon execution, displays

```
Product weight = 12.567 kg
Product weight =  3.458 kg
Product weight =  9.111 kg
```

If one were to display *num* without annotation, then

```
num = [12.567 3.458 9.111];
disp(num)
```

displays in the MATLAB command window

```
12.5670    3.4580    9.1110
```

whereas

```
num = [12.567 3.458 9.111];
disp(num')
```

displays

```
12.5670
3.4580
9.1110
```

MATLAB also permits one to specify the number of digits of the number to be
converted to a string as follows:

```
num2str(a,N)
```

where a is the number being converted to a string and N is the number of digits. If the
number of digits specified is less than the number of digits to the left of the decimal place,
then MATLAB converts the number to its exponential representation with number of
significant digits equal to N.

Consider the following examples in which $a = 1000\pi = 3141.592653589$. Then

```
num2str(a,1) → 3e+003
```

num2str(a,3) → 3.14e+003
num2str(a,4) → 3142
num2str(a,5) → 3141.5
num2str(a,8) → 3141.5927

Notice that the decimal point (.) does not count as a digit.

An alternative function that can be used to display formatted data to the MATLAB command window is fprintf, which has a slight advantage over disp in that it can better control the format of the numerical values. The syntax of the fprintf function to print to the MATLAB command window is

fprintf(1,'%....', variables)

where the first argument, the '1', indicates that the output is to be to the MATLAB command window, and everything inside the quotes is the format specification pertaining to *variables*. When *variables* is a vector or a matrix, the format specification is cycled through the format specification on a column-by-column basis. The order of the format specifications corresponds to the order of the variables. The % symbol precedes each specific format specification. A commonly used format specification is of the form

*x.y*f

The *f* is one of several format types. See the MATLAB Help file for fprintf for other formats. The *x* is an integer that specifies the total number of digits of the number and *y* the number of these digits that will appear to the right of the decimal. We illustrate the use of fprintf by displaying the vector

num = [12 −14 3.458 0.11167];

several different ways.

To display this vector on one line using fprintf we have

num = [12 −14 3.458 0.11167];
fprintf(1,'%5.3f ', num)

which results in

12.000 -14.000 3.458 0.112 »

Notice that *num*(1) and *num*(2) had three zeros added to its representation, whereas *num*(4) was rounded to 3 digits after the decimal. Also, the >> indicates that on the same line that the data were printed we now can execute another MATLAB expression. To get to the next line, one presses *Enter*. If we want to display these values as a column of four numbers, we use the delimiter \n as follows:

```
num = [12 −14 3.458 0.11167];
fprintf(1,'%5.3f\n', num)
```

which results in

```
12.000
-14.000
3.458
0.112
```

To reproduce the four numbers with the same digital precision as given we have

```
num = [12 −14 3.458 0.11167];
fprintf(1,'%2.0f %2.0f %5.3f %5.5f ', num)
```

where we placed two blanks (spaces) between each *f* and % so that the numbers are separated by two spaces. The execution of this expression gives

```
12  -14  3.458  0.11167 »
```

To annotate each number, we use the following:

```
num = [12 −14 3.458 0.11167];
fprintf(1,'weight = %2.0f kg  pressure = %2.0f Pa  time = %5.3f s  length = %5.5f
          m\n', num)
```

which results in

```
weight = 12  kg pressure = -14 Pa  time = 3.458 s  length = 0.11167 m
```

To display the values in a column, the script is

```
num = [12 −14 3.458 0.11167];
fprintf(1,'weight = %2.0f kg\npressure = %2.0f Pa\ntime = %5.3f s\nlength =
          %5.5f m\n', num)
```

which results in

```
weight = 12  kg
pressure = -14 Pa
time = 3.458 s
length = 0.11167 m
```

If we are willing to have each number appear with the same format, then we can simplify the format specification and still generate annotated output, albeit in a somewhat less informative manner, as follows:

```
num = [12 −14 3.458 0.11167];
nn = 1:length(num);
fprintf(1,'x(%1.0f) = %7.5f\n',[nn; num])
```

which results in

```
x(1) = 12.00000
x(2) = -14.00000
x(3) = 3.45800
x(4) = 0.11167
```

3.2 ENTERING DATA WITH INPUT

Arrays of data can be solicited by a script or function and then entered by the user using input. In addition, input can display to the MATLAB command window a message instructing the user what is to be entered. However, the actual form of the data depends on whether the data is a scalar, vector, or matrix and whether these quantities are numbers or strings. We now illustrate these various cases. Other methods of data entry are discussed in Sections 3.3 and 5.2.

3.2.1 Entering a Scalar

To input a single numerical quantity we use

```
InputData = input('Enter the temperature in degrees C: ');
```

which displays in the MATLAB command window

```
Enter the temperature in degrees C: 121.7
```

where the number 121.7 was entered by the user. The semicolon at the end of the expression suppresses the echoing of the value entered.

One can also perform modification to user-entered values in the same expression. For example,

```
InputData = input('Enter the starting angle in degrees: ')*pi/180;
```

which displays

```
Enter the starting angle in degrees: 45
```

where the value 45 was entered by the user. However, the value of *InputData* is 0.7854 (= $45\pi/180$).

As another example, consider the conversion of temperature from °C to °F.

InputData = 1.8*input('Enter the temperature in degrees C: ')+32;

which displays

Enter the temperature in degrees C: 100

where the value 100 was entered by the user. However, the value of *InputData* is 212.

The message may be printed on several lines by including within the message's quotation delimiters a \n at the appropriate places. Thus,

InputData = input('Enter the starting angle\n in degrees: ')*pi/180;

displays

Enter the starting angle
in degrees:

3.2.2 Entering a String

To input a single string quantity we use

InputData = input('Enter file name, including its extension: ','s');

which displays in the MATLAB command window

Enter file name, including its extension: DataSet3.txt

where the string *DataSet3.txt* was entered by the user. Notice that no single quotation marks are required. This is made possible by the 's' in the second argument of input.

3.2.3 Entering a Vector

To input a vector of numerical values we use

InputData = input('Enter the temperatures in degrees C: ');

which displays in the MATLAB command window

Enter the temperatures in degrees C: [120 141 169 201]

where the vector of numbers [120 141 169 201] was entered by the user. The square brackets are required. If a column vector was to be entered, then the user's response would be [120 141 169 201]'.

3.2.4 Entering a Matrix

To input a matrix of numerical values we use

> InputData = `input`('Enter the three temperatures in degrees C\nat levels 1 and 2: ');

which displays in the MATLAB command window

> Enter the three temperatures in degrees C
> at levels 1 and 2: [67 35 91;44 51 103]

where the array [67 35 91;44 51 103] was entered by the user. The variable *InputData* is now a (2×3) array.

3.3 INPUT/OUTPUT DATA FILES

As shown in the previous section, one method of entering data for execution by a script is to use `input`. The second means is to define data within a script using the methods discussed in Sections 2.3 and 2.4. These data creation statements can also appear in a function, which is discussed in Chapter 5. In fact, one can define a function such that it only contains data. See Section 5.2 for an example.

There is still another way to enter data, and that is to place data in an ASCII text file and use

> `load`

The `load` function reads data on a row-by-row basis, with each row separated by a carriage return and with each data value separated by either a blank or a comma. The number of columns of data in each row must be the same, and the number of rows in each column must be equal. These requirements are analogous to those that must be followed when creating matrices. Here the carriage return is used instead of the semicolon. When creating a row vector, one enters the data without using the carriage return. When creating a column vector, each data value is followed by a carriage return.

Let us illustrate two ways to use `load`. For specificity we shall assume that the data reside in the file *DataSection33.txt* in the form

> 11 12 13
> 21 22 23
> 31 32 33
> 41 42 43

The useful part about the `load` function is that the file name without the extension (the suffix ".txt") becomes the name of the variable whose vector or matrix elements are the data as they appear in the file. Thus, in the script the variable named *DataSection33* is a (4×3) matrix of numbers, and it is used in the script as if a variable named *DataSection33* had been placed on the left side of an equal sign.

The expression is either

    `load` DataSection33.txt

or

    `load` 'DataSection33.txt'

or

    `load`('DataSection33.txt')

It is assumed that the path to this file has been specified. If not, use either `cd` or go to *Set Path* in the *File* pull-down menu. These three forms are used when the filename is known at the time of the creation of a script and will not change. Thus, if we wanted to square each element of the matrix, then

    `load` 'DataSection33.txt'
    y = DataSection33.^2

results in

121	144	169
441	484	529
961	1024	1089
1681	1764	1849

On the other hand, if one wanted to operate on data in different files, each having a different file name, then we have to employ a different technique. Here the user will enter the file name when requested to do so by the script or function and, as before, the script will square all the data residing in the file whose name is specified when the script is executed. The script is

    FileName1 = `input`('Enter file name containing data (including suffix): ','s');
    `load`(FileName1);
    m = `findstr`(FileName1,'.');
    data1 = `eval`(FileName1(1:m-1));
    y = data1.^2

The `findstr` function locates the position of the first occurrence in the string of characters within the apostrophes (' '), in this case the period (.), and brings back its value. We have used it here to limit the string of characters comprising *FileName1* to those up to, but not including, the period; hence the *m*−1. Thus, we have stripped the suffix from the file's name. Since the stripped version of *FileName1* is still unknown to the remaining expressions in the script, it must be converted to a numerical quantity. This is done by the `eval` function, which evaluates the string quantity appearing in its argument.

If one wants to save numerical values resulting from a script to a file, then we use

```
save
```

Suppose that we would like to save the square of each value in *DataSection33.txt* as ASCII text. Then the script is

```
load 'DataSection33.txt'
y = DataSection33.^2
save SavedDataSection33.txt' y -ascii
```

which results in a text file whose contents are

```
1.2100000e+002  1.4400000e+002  1.6900000e+002
4.4100000e+002  4.8400000e+002  5.2900000e+002
9.6100000e+002  1.0240000e+003  1.0890000e+003
1.6810000e+003  1.7640000e+003  1.8490000e+003
```

When just the file name is given, MATLAB places the file in the default directory. In order to place the file in a specific directory, the entire path name must be given. For example,

```
load 'DataSection33.txt'
y = DataSection33.^2;
save 'c:\Matlab mfiles\Matlab results\SavedDataSection33.txt' y -ascii
```

Notice that we have selected the form that uses the quotes around the entire path name and file name. This is necessary because of the appearance of the colon and the blank spaces in the path name. Also, if we want to save additional quantities in this file, we would append their respective variable names to the `save` statement as follows. Suppose that the above script also computed the square root of the values in *DataSection33.txt*. Then,

```
load 'DataSection33.txt'
y = DataSection33.^2;
z = sqrt(DataSection33);
save 'c:\Matlab mfiles\Matlab results\SavedDataSection33.txt ' y z -ascii
```

The data in the file would now contain a matrix of eight rows each with three columns. The data in the first four rows would correspond to y and those in the last four rows to z.

The procedure to save figures is given in Section 6.1.

EXERCISES

3.1 The Fibonacci numbers can be generated from the relation

$$F_n = \frac{1}{\sqrt{5}}\left[\left(\frac{1+\sqrt{5}}{2}\right)^n - \left(\frac{1-\sqrt{5}}{2}\right)^n\right] \qquad n = 0,1,2,...$$

Generate the first sixteen numbers using both `fprintf` and `disp` and present them to the MATLAB command window as follows:

```
F 0 =  0
F 1 =  1
F 2 =  1
F 3 =  2
  ⋮
F15 = 610
```

C H A P T E R 4

PROGRAM FLOW CONTROL

Edward B. Magrab

The various means of controlling the order in which a program's expressions get evaluated are presented, along with a representative set of relational and logical operators that are used to accomplish this control.

4.1 INTRODUCTION

The control of the order in which a program's expressions get evaluated are performed by four program flow control structures: `while`, `if`, `for`, and `switch`. Each time one of these statements appears, it must be followed at a later place within the program by an `end` statement. All expressions that appear between the control structure statement and the `end` statement are executed until all requirements of the structure are satisfied. Each of these control structure statements can appear as often as necessary within each other or within themselves. When this occurs, they are called nested structures.

Control structures frequently rely on relational and logical operators to determine whether or not a condition has been met. When a condition has been met, the structure

TABLE 4.1
Several Relational and Logical Operators

Conditional	Mathematical symbol	MATLAB symbol
Relational operators		
equal	=	==
not equal	≠	~=
less than	<	<
greater than	>	>
less than or equal	≤	<=
greater than or equal	≥	>=
Logical operators		
and	AND	&
or	OR	|
not	NOT	~

directs the program to a specific part of the program to execute one or more expressions. Several of MATLAB's relational and logical operators are given in Table 4.1.

When using control structures, it is recommended that the statements following each control structure definition up to, but not including, the end statement be indented. This greatly improves the readability of the script or function. When the structures are nested, the entire nested structure is indented, with the nested structure's indentation preserved. When using MATLAB's editor/debugger, this is done automatically.

One can use the logical operators appearing in Table 4.1 to create a logical function whose output is 1 if the logical operation is true and 0 if it is false. Suppose that we want to create a function $g(x)$ such that

$$g(x) = f(x) \qquad a \le x < b$$
$$= 0 \qquad \text{otherwise}$$

The logical operator is formed by

y = (a<=x & x<b);

where a and b have been assigned numerical values prior to this statement and

(a<=x & x<b)

is the logical operator that has a value of 1 (true) when $x \ge a$ and $x < b$. Its value is 0 (false) for all other values of x. Thus, if we let $a = -1$, $b = 2$, $f(x) = e^{x/2}$, and $x = [-4 \ -1 \ 1 \ 4]$, then a script using this logical operator is

```
a = -1; b = 2;
x = [-4 -1 1 4];
gofx = exp(x/2).*(a<=x & x<b)
```

which, upon execution, yields *gofx* = [0 0.6065 1.6487 0].

4.2 CONTROL OF PROGRAM FLOW

4.2.1 While Loop

The while loop repeats one or more statements an indefinite number of times, leaving the loop only when a specified condition has been satisfied. Its general form is

```
while condition
  statements
end
```

where the expression defining *condition* can be composed of one or more of the variables evaluated by *statements*.

We now present two examples of while loops. The first can be used to ensure that user-entered data are within specified limits. The second can be used when certain convergence criteria have to be satisfied.

Example 4.1 Correctly entering data

The following excerpt from a program asks the user to enter a number from 1 to 8, and continues to ask the user until the entry is in the requested range. The input function prints the message appearing in quotes to the MATLAB window and waits until the user enters a value, at which point the program sets that value to *nfnum*. The symbol "|" is the logical OR.

```
nfnum = 0;
while (nfnum<1)|(nfnum>8)
  nfnum = input('Enter a number from 1 to 8: ');
end
```

The quantity *nfnum* is initially set equal to a value (in this case zero) that causes the while test (*nfnum*<1)|(*nfnum*>8) to enter the while structure. After reaching the last expression prior to the end statement, the program returns to the while test expression to determine whether or not it is satisfied. If it is not satisfied, it executes the next line in the structure, otherwise it proceeds to the next statement after the end statement. Notice that we have employed the preferred practice of placing the structure's initializing value—*nfnum* in this case—just prior to its entry into the structure.

Example 4.2 Convergence of a series

Let us determine and display the number of terms that it takes for the series

$$S_N = \sum_{n=1}^{N} \frac{1}{n^2}$$

to converge to within 0.01% of its exact value, which is $S_\infty = \pi^2/6$. The script is

```
series = 1; k = 2; exact = pi^2/6;
while abs((series- exact)/exact) >= 1e- 4
  series = series+1/k^2;
  k = k+1;
end
disp(['# terms = 'num2str(k- 1)])
```

The quantity *series* is initially set equal to a value (1 in this case) that causes the `while` test abs((*series-exact*)/*exact*) to enter the `while` structure. After reaching the last expression prior to the `end` statement, the program returns to the `while` test expression to determine whether or not it is satisfied. If it is not satisfied, it executes the next line in the structure; otherwise, it proceeds to the next statement after the `end` statement, which in this case displays the result to the MATLAB command window.

We have used the absolute value of the test condition (*series-exact*)/*exact*) in order to avoid any instance when the difference *series-exact* is negative, which would be less than 10^{-4} (since it is a negative number), but whose magnitude may not be < 10^{-4}. This avoids having to know *a priori* whether or not the quantity *series* approaches the limit from above or below. One must also be very careful when establishing the test criterion for the termination of the `while` loop, for, if improperly or poorly stated, one may stay in the loop indefinitely—that is, until control and c are pressed simultaneously.

4.2.2 `If` Statements

The general form of the `if` statement is

```
if condition #1
  expressions #1
elseif condition #2
  expressions #2
else
  expressions #3
end
```

When condition #1 is satisfied, expressions #1 are executed, followed by the next statement after the outermost `end` statement. When condition #1 is not satisfied, then condition #2 is examined. If it is satisfied, then expressions #2 are executed, and followed by the next statement after the outermost `end` statement. If neither condition #1 nor condition #2 is satisfied, then expressions #3 are executed, and then followed by the next statement after the outermost `end` statement. The statements `elseif` and `else` are optional. Also, there can be more than one `elseif` statement.

The following script illustrates the use of the `if` statement. The quantities j, x, and *nnum* have numerical values that were either assigned or determined from a computational procedure earlier in the program.

```
if j == 1
    z = sin(x) ;          ←——— Executed only when j = 1.
    if nnum<=4            ←——— This if statement encountered only when j = 1.
        nr = 1 ;
        nc = 1;          ←——— These statements executed only when j = 1 and nnum ≤ 4.
    else
        nr = 1 ;
        nc = 2;          ←——— These statements executed only when j = 1 and nnum > 4.
    end
else
    nr = 2;              ←——— These statements executed only when j ≠ 1.
    nc = 1;
end
```

Notice that we have a nested `if` statement and, therefore, we require a second `end` statement. Also note how the indenting of the expressions inside the various nested structures makes the code more readable.

Example 4.3 Fatigue strength factors

Consider the relationships that govern the correction factors used to estimate the fatigue strength of metals.

Factor	Range	Correction
Load	Bending	$C_{load} = 1$
	Axial	$C_{load} = 0.70$
Size	$d \leq 8$ mm	$C_{size} = 1$
	$8 \leq d \leq 250$ mm	$C_{size} = 1.189 d^{-0.097}$
Temperature	$T < 450\ °C$	$C_{temp} = 1$
	$450 \leq T\ °C$	$C_{temp} = 1 - 0.0032(T - 840)$

A portion of a script that can be used to determine these factors is given below. The values of *lode*, d and *temp* have had numerical values either assigned or computed previously in the program. The quantity *lode* is a string.

```
if lode == 'bending'
    cload = 1;
else
```

```
   cload = 0.7;
end
if d<=8
  csize = 1;
else
  csize = 1.189*d^(-0.097);
end
if temp<=450
  ctemp = 1;
else
  ctemp = 1-0.0032*(T-840);
end
```

We also could have written this script as

```
if lode == 'bending', cload = 1; else, cload = 0.7; end
if d<=8, csize = 1; else, csize = 1.189*d^(-0.097); end
if temp<=450, ctemp = 1; else, ctemp = 1- 0.0032*(T-840); end
```

As discussed in Section 1.8, the separator for each expression on one line is either a comma (,) or a semicolon (;).

4.2.3 For Loop

A for loop repeats a series of statements a specific number of times. Its general form is

```
for variable = expression
    statements
end
```

where one or more of the *statements* can be a function of *variable*.

Example 4.4 Total interest of a loan

We shall compute the total interest on a loan when the amount of the loan is L, its duration m months, and its annual percentage interest I_a. The monthly payment p_{mon} is

$$p_{mon} = \frac{iL}{1-(1+i)^{-m}}$$

where

$$i = I_a/1200$$

is the monthly interest rate expressed as a decimal number. Each month, as the loan is being paid off, a portion of the payment is used to pay the interest, and the remainder is applied to the unpaid loan amount. The unpaid loan amount after each payment is called the balance. Mathematically we express these relations as follows. If $b_0 = L$, then

$$i_n = ib_{n-1}$$
$$P_n = p_{mon} - i_n \qquad n = 1,2,3,...,m$$
$$b_n = b_{n-1} - P_n$$

where i_n is the portion of p_{mon} that goes towards the payment of the interest and P_n is the portion of the payment that goes towards the reduction of the balance b_n—that is, the amount required to pay off the loan. The total interest paid at the end of the loan's duration is

$$i_T = \sum_{j=1}^{m} i_j$$

The script to compute i_T is

```
loan = input('Enter loan amount: ');                    ⎤
durat = input('Enter term of loan in months: ');        ⎥  ← Input
int = input('Enter annual interest rate: ')/1200;       ⎦
ints = zeros(durat,1);                                  ⎤
prins = ints;                                           ⎥
bals = ints;                                            ⎥  ← Initialization
pmon = (loan*int)/(1- (1+int)^(- durat));               ⎥
bals(1) = loan;                                         ⎦
for m = 2:durat+1                                       ⎤
    ints(m) = int*bals(m- 1);                           ⎥
    prins(m) = pmon- ints(m);                           ⎥  ← Computation
    bals(m) = bals(m- 1)- prins(m);                     ⎦
end
fprintf(1,'Total interest = $%8.2f\n',sum(ints))        ← Output
```

As noted in Section 1.2, this script follows a program's usual structure: input, initialization, computations, and output, which in this case is the display of the results to the MATLAB command window. Execution of the script gives

```
Enter loan amount: 100000
Enter term of loan in months: 360
Enter annual interest rate: 8
Total interest = $164155.25
```

The first three lines are the user's response to the script's sequentially displayed queries, wherein the user entered the three numerical quantities shown after each query, and the last line is the answer.

It is recommended by MATLAB that prior to entering a for loop, or nested for loops, in which vectors or arrays are created by specifying their subscripts, one should size the array with the zeros function prior to entering the for loops. This greatly decreases the execution time of this portion of the script, because otherwise, MATLAB would be dynamically allocating memory during the execution of the `for` loop, thereby incurring substantial overhead.

Example 4.5 Equivalent implementation of `find`

We shall assume that we are given a vector g of positive and negative numbers and of arbitrary length. The objective is to create a script that performs the same function as the expression

   indx = find(g>a)

where a is specified by the user. We shall check the script with $a = 4$ and with the vector $g = [4\ 4\ 7\ 10 - 6\ 42\ 1\ 0]$. The script is

```
g = [4 4 7 10 – 6 42 1 0]; a = 4;
k = 0;
indx = [];
for n = 1:length(g)
 if g(n)>a
  k = k+1;
  indx(k) = n;
 end
end
disp(['Element locations for g(n)>' num2str(a) ': ' num2str(indx)])
```

which, upon execution, displays to the MATLAB command window

   Element locations for g(n)>4: 3 4 6

An alternative way to obtain *indx* is

```
g = [4 4 7 10 – 6 42 1 0]; a = 4;
k = 0;
indx = [];
for n = 1:length(g)
 if g(n)>a
  indx = [indx n];
 end
end
disp(['Element locations for g(n)>' num2str(a) ': ' num2str(indx)])
```

Example 4.6 Equivalent implementation of `cumsum`

For a given vector c of arbitrary length, we shall create a script that provides the same results as

    Csum = cumsum(c)

We shall check the script with the vector $c = [4\ 4\ 7\ 10\ -6\ 42\ 1\ 0]$. The script is

```
c = [4 4 7 10 - 6 42 1 0];
Csum(1) = c(1);
for k = 2:length(c)
  Csum(k) = Csum(k- 1)+c(k);
end
disp(['Cumsum of c = ' num2str (Csum)])
```

which, upon execution, displays to the MATLAB command window

    Cumsum of c = 4   8 15 19 61 62 62

An alternative way to obtain *Csum* is

```
c = [4 4 7 10 - 6 42 1 0];
Csum(1) = c(1);
for k = 2:length(c)
  Csum = [Csum Csum(k- 1)+c(k)];
end
disp(['Cumsum of c = ' num2str(Csum)])
```

Example 4.7 Equivalent implementation of `diag`

For an $(n \times n)$ matrix b we shall create a two part script that provides the same result as

    v = diag(b)

in the first part and the same result as

    d = diag(v)

in the second part, where v was obtained in the first part. We shall check the results using b = magic(4) and assume that we can not use colon notation and `zeros`. The script is

```
b = magic(4); [r c] = size(b);
for k = 1:r
```

```
  v(k) = b(k,k);
end
disp(['Diagonal elements of b = '])
disp(num2str(v))
for n = 1:r
 for m = 1:r
  if n == m
    d(n,m) = v(n);
  else
    d(n,m) = 0.0;
   end
  end
end
disp(['Diagonal matrix d ='])
disp(num2str(d))
```

which, upon execution, displays to the MATLAB command window

```
Diagonal elements of b =
16 11  6  1
Diagonal matrix d =
16  0   0  0
0   11  0  0
0    0. 6  0
0    0   0  1
```

If we allow ourselves to use the colon notation, then the script simplifies to

```
b = magic(4); [r c] = size(b);
for k = 1:r
 v(k) = b(k,k);
end
disp(['Diagonal elements of b = '])
disp(num2str(v))
d(1:r,1:c) = 0.0;
for n = 1:r
 d(n,n) = v(n);
end
disp(['Diagonal matrix d ='])
disp(num2str(d))
```

4.2.4 Early Termination of Either a `for` or `while` Loop

The `break` function is used to terminate either a `for` or `while` loop. If the `break` function is within nested `for` or `while` loops, then it returns to the next higher level `for` or `while` loop. Consider the following portion of a script:

```
for j = 1:14
    ⋮
    b = 1
    while b<25
        ⋮
        if n<0
          break
        end
        ⋮
    end
    ⋮
end
```

When $n < 0$ the `while` loop is exited and the script continues from the next statement *after* this end statement

To terminate the script (or function; see Chapter 5) because a specified condition had not been satisfied, one would use `error`. The `error` function is usually used to ensure that the program is using numerical values that lead to meaningful results. When the program encounters the `error` function it will display the message contained within it to the MATLAB command window. After displaying the message the execution of the script or function is terminated and control is returned to the command line in the MATLAB command window. The `error` function can be used anywhere within a script or function and is not limited to `for` and `while` structures.

4.2.5 `Switch` Statement

The general form of the `switch` statement is

```
switch switch_expression
    case case_expression #1
        statements #1
    case case_expression #2
        statements #2
            ⋮
    case case_expression #n
        statements #n
    otherwise
        statements #n+1
end
```

The first *case_expression #j*, *j* = 1, 2, ... , *n*, that is encountered in which *case_expression #j* = *switch_expression* will cause *statements #j* to be executed. Only one case is executed. Following the execution of *statements #j*, the next statement to be executed is that following the end statement. If none of the *case_expression #j* is satisfied, then *statements #n*+1 are executed. However, the otherwise statement is optional. If the otherwise statement has been omitted and *case_expression #j* does not equal *switch_expression* for any *j*, then the next statement after the end statement is executed.

The switch structure is, essentially, an alternative to using a series of if-elseif-else-end structures. The following switch structure acts as indicated. The quantity *k* has been assigned a value or had its value computed prior to encountering this structure.

```
a = 3;
switch k
 case 1
  disp('Case 1' )          ← This statement executed only when k = 1.
 case {2,3}
  disp('Case 2 or 3' )     ← This statement executed only when k = 2, 3.
 case a^2
  disp('Case 9' )          ← This statement executed only when k = 9.
 otherwise
  disp('Otherwise')        ← This statement executed only when k ≠ 1, 2, 3 or 9.
end
```

Example 4.8 Plotting four views of a surface

Consider the situation where one plots four views of a surface $z(x,y)$ in four separate quadrants of one figure window. The script is given below. The subplot function divides the window into a grid, in this case a 2×2 grid. The indicator *k* specifies where the figure is located in the grid: *k* = 1 upper left; *k* = 2 upper right; *k* = 3 lower left; *k* = 4 lower right. (See Chapters 6 and 7 for more details about this and the other plotting functions.) The surf function plots a 3-D perspective of the array of values for *z* as a function of *x* and *y*. The view function sets the viewing angles. The quantities *x*, *y*, and *z* either have been previously assigned values or had their values previously computed.

```
for  k = 1:4
 subplot(2,2,k)
 surf(x,y,z)
 switch k
  case 1
    view(−37.5,30)
  case 2
    view(−70,30)
  case 3
    view(−37.5,50)
```

```
  case 4
    view(-70,50)
 end
end
```

4.3 TWO APPLICATIONS OF PROGRAM CONTROL STRUCTURES

We shall now present two examples of scripts that use combinations of these program control structures.

4.3.1 Generation of a 2^k Factorial Table

Experiments performed on systems influenced by several factors are usually designed so that the procedure requires that all combinations of all the levels (settings) of each factor are used for each complete run of the experiment. Such an experimental design is called a factorial experiment. If the experiment contains k factors, and each factor is considered at only two levels, then the experiment is called a 2^k factorial design. The convention is to denote the value of the high level of a factor with a "+", and the value of the low level with a "−". The factors are denoted A and B for $k = 2$; A, B, and C for $k = 3$; and A, B, C, and D for $k = 4$.

Consider the tabulations in Table 4.2. The + and − signs in each column represent +1 and −1, respectively. The columns labeled A, B, C, and D are the primary factors. The remaining columns represent all the interaction terms, which are obtained by multiplying the corresponding signs in the columns of the primary factors or previously determined interactions as indicated. Thus, the signs in the columns designating the interaction ABC are obtained by multiplying the signs in the columns labeled either A, B, and C or AB and C or A and BC. For example, in row seven ($m = 7$) $A = -1$, $B = +1$, and $C = +1$; therefore, the sign in the seventh row of the column labeled ABC is −1 [= (−1)(+1)(+1)]. Furthermore, for the 2^2 experiment the first three columns and the rows $m = 1, 2, \ldots, 4$ are used; for the 2^3 experiment the first seven columns and the rows $m = 1, 2, \ldots, 8$ are used; and for the 2^4 experiment all fifteen columns and the rows $m = 1, 2, \ldots, 16$ are used. Also note that the first $2^{(k-1)}$ rows ($k > 2$) are repeated to form the rows below the horizontal lines in Table 4.2 as the number of factors increases.

The results presented in Table 4.2 are fundamental to the analysis of data obtained from a 2^k factorial design. (See Section 14.6.2.) Therefore, we will write a script to generate the values ±1 appearing in this table for $k = 2$, 3 or 4. The script is

```
k = input('Enter number of factors (= 2, 3, or 4)');
s = ones(2^k,2^k- 1);
for r = 1:2:2^k
  s(r,1) = -1;
end
for c = 2:k
  e = 2^(c- 1);
  for r = 1:e
    s(r,e) = - 1;
  end
```

TABLE 4.2
2^k Factorial Signs

Factors and their interactions															
1	2	3	4	5	6	7	8	9	10	11	12	13	14	15	
$k=2$			$k=3$				$k=4$								
A	B	AB	C	AC	BC	ABC	D	AD	BD	ABD	CD	ACD	BCD	ABCD	m
−	−	+	−	+	+	−	−	+	+	−	+	−	−	+	1
+	−	−	−	−	+	+	−	−	+	+	+	+	−	−	2
−	+	−	−	+	−	+	−	+	−	+	+	−	+	−	3
+	+	+	−	−	−	−	−	−	−	−	+	+	+	+	$4=2^2$
−	−	+	+	−	−	+	−	+	+	−	−	+	+	−	5
+	−	−	+	+	−	−	−	−	+	+	−	−	+	+	6
−	+	−	+	−	+	−	−	+	−	+	−	+	−	+	7
+	+	+	+	+	+	+	−	−	−	−	−	−	−	−	$8=2^3$
−	−	+	−	+	+	−	+	+	−	+	−	+	+	−	9
+	−	−	−	−	+	+	+	−	−	−	−	−	+	+	10
−	+	−	−	+	−	+	+	+	+	−	−	+	−	+	11
+	+	+	−	−	−	−	+	−	+	+	−	−	−	−	12
−	−	+	+	−	−	+	+	+	−	+	+	−	−	+	13
+	−	−	+	+	−	−	+	−	−	−	+	+	−	−	14
−	+	−	+	−	+	−	+	+	+	−	+	−	+	−	15
+	+	+	+	+	+	+	+	−	+	+	+	+	+	+	$16=2^4$

```
for r = e+1:2^(k)
  s(r,2^(c− 2)) = s(r− e,2^(c− 2));
  end
end
for m = 2:k
  e = 2^(m− 1);
  for j = 1:e− 1
    s(:,e+j) = s(:,j).*s(:,e);
  end
end
disp(s)
```

When this script is executed the following is displayed.

    Enter number of factors (= 2, 3, or 4) 3

```
-1  -1   1  -1   1   1  -1
 1  -1  -1  -1  -1   1   1
-1   1  -1  -1   1  -1   1
 1   1   1  -1  -1  -1  -1
-1  -1   1   1  -1  -1   1
 1  -1  -1   1   1  -1  -1
-1   1  -1   1  -1   1  -1
 1   1   1   1   1   1   1
```

The last digit of the first line, the 3, is the user's response.

It is noted that if $z = s/2^{k/2}$, then the matrix z is an orthogonal matrix, which has the property (recall Exercise 2.11)

$$I = z'z$$

where I, in this case, is a (7×7) unit matrix.

4.3.2 Multiple Root Finding Using Interval Halving[1]

MATLAB has a function fzero that is used to determine the value of x that makes $f(x)$ very closely equal to zero, provided that fzero is given a good estimate of the location of the root. (See Section 5.5.1.) However, it only finds one zero at a time; to find additional zeros one must call fzero again with another estimate of where the next zero can be found.

Let us assume that we would like to find automatically a series of positive values of x (x_1, x_2, ...) that make $f(x) = 0$. This assumes, of course, that $f(x)$ has multiple zeros and, therefore, the sign of $f(x)$ alternates as x increases.

One technique to find the zeros of a function is called interval halving.[2] Referring to Figure 4.1, this technique works as follows. The independent variable x is given a starting value $x = x_{start}$ and the sign of $f(x_{start})$ is determined. The variable x is then incremented by an amount Δ and the sign of $f(x_{start}+\Delta)$ is determined. The signs of these two values are compared. If the signs are the same (as they are in Figure 4.1), then x is again incremented by Δ and the sign of $f(x+2\Delta)$ is evaluated and compared to that of $f(x_{start})$. If the signs are different, then the current value of x is decremented by half the interval size—that is, by $\Delta/2$. From Figure 4.1 we see that the sign change occurs at $x = x_{start} + 3\Delta$, so that after the sign change has been detected the next value for x is $x = x_{start} + 5\Delta/2$. The sign of $f(x_{start}+5\Delta/2)$ is then compared to $f(x_{start})$. If it is the same, then half the current interval is added to the current value of x, otherwise it is subtracted from the current value of x. In this example the sign of $f(x_{start})$ is the same as $f(x_{start}+5\Delta/2)$ so that the next point that $f(x)$ is evaluated at is $x_{start} + 11\Delta/4$. This process is repeated until the incremental change in x divided by the current value of x is less than some tolerance; that is, $\Delta_{current}/x_{current} < t_o$, the tolerance. When this tolerance criteria has been satisfied, then the root $x_1 = x_{current}$. The process is continued

---

[1] See, for example, S. C. Chapra and R. P. Canale, *Numerical Methods for Engineers*, 2nd ed., McGraw-Hill, New York, 1988, p. 128ff.

[2] Although this method will find the roots, it is not the best way to do it, for the techniques that are used in fzero require 2 to 3 times fewer interations to find a root to within a specified precision.

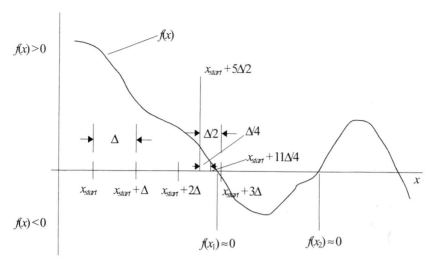

FIGURE 4.1
Interval halving scheme.

until the desired number of x_j has been determined. After each x_j has been obtained we set $x_{start} = 1.05x_j$, reset Δ is to its original value, and repeat the process.

The objective is to write a script using the interval halving technique to determine the first 5 values of x that set the function

$$f(x) = \cos(ax) \cong 0$$

where a is a constant. These x_j are said to satisfy this equation when the incremental change in x divided by x is less than $t_o = 10^{-6}$. Also $x_j \geq x_{start} \geq 0$ for $j = 1, 2, ..., n$. Thus, in general, the inputs to the root-finding portion of the program are n, x_{start}, t_o, and Δ, and for this particular $f(x)$ the quantity a.

In Chapter 5, we shall convert this script into a function so that we can determine the roots for an arbitrary $f(x)$. See Figure 5.1. Thus, $n = 5$, $t_o = 10^{-6}$ and we shall let $x_{start} = 0.2$, $\Delta = 0.3$, and $a = \pi$. The script is

```
n = 5; a = pi; increment = 0.3; tolerance = 1e– 6; xstart = 0.2;
x = xstart;
dx = increment;
for m = 1:n
  s1 = sign(cos(a*x));
  while dx/x >tolerance
    if s1 ~= sign(cos(a*(x+dx)))
      dx = dx/2;
    else
      x = x+dx;
    end
```

```
    end
  · route(m) = x;
    dx = increment;
    x = 1.05*x;
    end
    disp(route)
```

which, when executed, displays

$$0.5000 \quad 1.5000 \quad 2.5000 \quad 3.5000 \quad 4.5000$$

EXERCISES

4.1 Create a script that performs the equivalent function of the logical operator introduced in Section 4.1 for any vector of values h, such that the output vector v of the logical operator indicates which of its elements satisfy $h > a$ and $h < b$. Test your script with $h = [1\ 3\ 6\ -7\ -45\ 12\ 17\ 9]$, $a = 3$ and $b = 13$. [Answer: $v = [0\ 0\ 1\ 0\ 0\ 1\ 0\ 1]$.]

4.2 The estimate of the variance of n samples x_i is determined from

$$s_n^2 = \frac{1}{n-1}\left[\sum_{j=1}^{n} x_j^2 - n\bar{x}_n^2\right] \qquad n > 1$$

where

$$\bar{x}_n = \frac{1}{n}\sum_{j=1}^{n} x_j$$

is an estimate of the mean. The variance is determined from `var`.

   Write a script that determines s_n^2 as a function of n for $n > 1$ for the following data: $x = [45\ 38\ 47\ 41\ 35\ 43]$. [Answer: $[24.5000\ 22.3333\ 16.2500\ 24.2000\ 19.9000]$.]

4.3 For a given $a > 0$ the following relationship will determine the positive value of the $\sqrt{a}$ to within a tolerance t_0 for any starting value (guess) $x_0 > 0$

$$x_{n+1} = \frac{1}{2}\left(x_n + \frac{a}{x_n}\right) \qquad n = 0,1,2,\dots$$

where $x_{n+1} \cong \sqrt{a}$. (When $x_0 < 0$ the negative square root is found.) Write a script that determines $\sqrt{a}$ to within $|x_n - x_{n+1}| < 10^{-6}$ for $a = 7$. How many iterations does it take if (a) $x_0 = 3$; and (b) $x_0 = 100$. The first iteration is the determination of x_1. [Hint: Notice that the above relationship is not an explicit function of n. Here the subscript n is simply an indicator that the next (new) value x_{n+1} is a function of the previous (old) value x_n. Thus, each time through the loop the old and new values keep changing. Therefore, has to keep track of n in order to record the number of times this relationship is used until the convergence criterion is met.] [Answer: (a) $n_{\text{iterations}} = 4$; and (b) $n_{\text{iterations}} = 10$.]

4.4 Consider the following relation

$$x_{n+1} = x_n^2 + 0.25 \quad n = 0,1,2,...,N$$

For $x_0 = 0$, write two scripts that plot the values of x_n for $n = 0, 5, 10, ..., 200$. In the first script use a for loop and the second script a while loop. To what value does x_N appear to converge? For the third argument of the plot function use plot(..., ..., 'ks'), which will plot the values of x_n as squares. The x-axis values are the values of n and the y-axis values are the x_n. Note that all x_n, $n = 0,1,2,...,200$ must be computed, but only every fifth x_n is plotted. Also, this exercise differs from Exercise 4.3 in that the values of x_n must be saved as elements of a vector so that the appropriate elements can be subsequently displayed.

4.5 The chi-square statistic is used to perform goodness-of-fit tests. (See Exercise 14.6.) It is defined as

$$\chi^2 = \sum_{i=1}^{k} \frac{(x_i - e_i)^2}{e_i}$$

where e_i and x_i are independent vectors of length k.

If $e_i < 5$, then the e_i and x_i must be combined with their respective e_{i+1} and x_{i+1} values. If the sum of $e_i + e_{i+1}$ is still < 5, then e_{i+2} is added to the sum of $e_i + e_{i+1}$. This process is repeated until the sum is ≥ 5. When $e_i \geq 5$ and the sum of the remaining e_{i+1}, e_{i+2}, ..., e_k, is less than 5, then these remaining values are added to e_i.

Write a script that computes χ^2 under the conditions described above. Check your results with the following vectors, which represent three different cases:

(i) $x = [1\ 7\ 8\ 6\ 5\ 7\ 3\ 5\ 4]$ and $e = [2\ 6\ 10\ 4\ 3\ 6\ 1\ 2\ 3]$;

(ii) $x = [7\ 11\ 13\ 6]$ and $e = [6\ 10\ 15\ 7]$;

(iii) $x = [3\ 14\ 20\ 25\ 14\ 6\ 2\ 0\ 1\ 0]$ and $e = [4\ 12\ 19\ 19\ 14\ 8\ 4\ 2\ 1\ 1]$.

Save this script for use in Exercise 14.6(b). Hint: The most compact script will be obtained by performing tests on the elements of cumsum(e), where the length of e changes as the evaluation procedure progresses. [Answers:

(i) $e_{modified} = [8\ 10\ 7\ 6\ 6]$, $x_{modified} = [8\ 8\ 11\ 7\ 12]$, $\chi^2 = 8.8524$;

(ii) $e_{modified} = [6\ 10\ 15\ 7]$, $x_{modified} = [7\ 11\ 13\ 6]$, $\chi^2 = 0.6762$;

(iii) $e_{modified} = [16\ 19\ 19\ 14\ 8\ 8]$, $x_{modified} = [17\ 20\ 25\ 14\ 6\ 3]$, $\chi^2 = 5.6349$.]

4.6 Given two polynomials:

$$y(x) = p_1 x^n + p_2 x^{n-1} + ... + p_n x + p_{n+1}$$
$$z(x) = s_1 x^m + s_2 x^{m-1} + ... + s_m x + s_{m+1}$$

write a script to add them; that is, $h(x) = y(x) + z(x)$, when $m = n$, $m < n$, and $m > n$. Polynomials are added by adding the coefficients of the terms with the same exponent. Assume that the input to the script are the vectors $p = [p_1\ p_2\ ...\ p_n\ p_{n+1}]$ and $s = [s_1\ s_2\ ...\ s_m\ s_{m+1}]$.

Check your script with the following data sets:

(i) $p = [1\ 2\ 3\ 4]$ and $s = [10\ 20\ 30\ 40]$;

(ii) $p = [11\ 12\ 13\ 14]$ and $s = [101\ 102]$;

(iii) $p = [43\ 54\ 55]$ and $s = [77\ 66\ 88\ 44\ 33]$.

[Answers: (i) h = [11 22 33 44]; (ii) h = [11 12 114 116]; (iii) h = [77 66. 131 98 88].]

4.7 Write a script that computes the day of week for the years 1999 and 2000, when its input is of the form: month/day/year - xx/xx/xxxx. Have the script output the results in the following manner:

The date 5/31/2000 is the 152 day of the year and falls on a Wednesday.

The functions str2num, deblank, and findstr should prove helpful.

C H A P T E R 5

FUNCTIONS

Edward B. Magrab

The creation of functions and their various uses within MATLAB are described, and several built-in functions that are frequently used to obtain numerical solutions to engineering problems are illustrated.

5.1 INTRODUCTION

One form of an m file is the script file. A second type of m file is the function file. Function files are script files that create their own local and independent workspace within MATLAB. All variable names defined within a function are local to that function and neither affect nor are affected by these same variable names being used in any script or other function file. All of MATLAB's built-in functions are of this type. The first non-comment line of a function file must follow a prescribed format, which is given in Section 5.2. Typically, user-created MATLAB programs consist of a script file and employ any number of user-created functions and MATLAB's built-in functions.

5.1.1 Why Use Functions

There are several reasons to create functions, besides the fact that several MATLAB built-in functions require them. (See Section 5.5.) They include:

1. Avoiding duplicate code
2. Limiting the effect of changes to specific sections of the code
3. Promoting code reuse
4. Reducing the complexity of the overall code by making it more readable and manageable
5. Isolating complex operations
6. Improving portability
7. Making debugging and error isolation easier
8. Improving performance because each routine can be "optimized"

The compartmentalization brought about by the use of functions also tends to minimize the unintended use of data by portions of the program, because data to each function is provided only on a need-to-know basis.

5.1.2 Naming Functions

The names of functions should be chosen so that they are meaningful and indicate what the routine does. Typical lengths of function names are between 9 and 20 characters and should employ standard or consistent conventions. For example, all script file names could begin with *scr* and all function names without this prefix. The proper choice of function names can also minimize the use of comments within the function itself. Recall, also, the naming conventions suggested in Section 1.3.

5.1.3 Length of Functions

The length of a function can vary from two lines to more than hundreds of lines of code. However, the length of a function should be governed, in part, by its functional cohesion – that is, the degree to which it does one thing and not anything else. For example, sin(x) is 100% cohesive, whereas a function *sincostan*(x), which computes the sin, cos, and tangent, would be less cohesive because it does three separate things, each of which is unrelated to the other. A function can be created with numerous highly cohesive functions to create another cohesive function. An additional advantage of the creation of highly cohesive functions is their reliability—that is, lower error rate. Also, when functions have a low degree of cohesion, there is often difficulty in isolating errors.

5.1.4 Debugging Functions

During the creation of functions (and scripts), the code should be independently verified to ensure that it is working correctly after every few lines of code are written. MATLAB is particularly well-suited to this type of procedure, which simply involves omitting the semicolon at the end of each expression. Furthermore, one incurs very little time penalty when omitting the semicolon, except in those programs using large vectors and matrices or iterative solution techniques. The verification should be performed with some type of independent calculation or estimation. During the verification/debugging stage, the lines of code that may be inserted to provide intermediate output should be commented out, not deleted, until the entire function has been verified to be working correctly. Only after a function is working correctly should it be improved to decrease its execution time, if necessary. Creating correctly performing programs is always the primary goal.

5.2 THE FUNCTION FILE

A function has at least two lines of program code, the first line of which has a format required by MATLAB. There is no terminating character or expression for the function program such as the `end` statement, which is required for the `for`, `while`, `if`, and `switch` structures. Furthermore, the name of the m file should be the same as the name of the function, except that the file name has the extension ".m".

The number of variables and their type (scalar, vector, matrix) that are brought in and out of the function are controlled by the function interface, which is the first non-comment line of the function program. This "interface" has the general form shown in the following generic example of a function.

```
function OutputVariable = FunctionName(InputVariables)
% comments
expression(s)
```

Comments immediately following the function interface statement are used by MATLAB to create this function's Help information—that is, when one types at the MATLAB command line

```
help FunctionName
```

all the initial contiguous comments will appear in the MATLAB command window. Any comments appearing prior to the `function` statement will not be part of the Help information.

The expressions are written in the same manner as for a script, except that each variable name used within the function must be defined either in the names used for the input variables or by one of the expressions in the function. The output variables may be a scalar, vector, or matrix and may be composed of either numerical values or strings. There may be any number of input variables, with each input variable separated by a comma. The input variables may be scalars, vectors, or matrices and may be composed of either numerical values or strings. Thus, if there are three input variables a, b, and c, then the interface line of the function program is

```
function OutputVariable = FunctionName(a,b,c)
```

There are several concepts that must be understood to correctly create functions. The first is that the variable names used in the function definition do not have to match the corresponding names used when the function is called from the MATLAB command window, a script, or another function. Instead, it is the locations of the input variables within the argument list inside the parentheses that govern the transfer of information—that is, the first argument in the calling statement transfers its value(s) to the first argument in the function interface definition, and so on. The names assigned should be thought of as placeholders.

Second, the names selected for each argument are local to the function program and have meaning only within the context of the function program. The same names can be used in an entirely different context in the script file that calls this function or in another function used by this function. However, the names appearing for each input variable of the function statement must be the same type, either scalar, vector, matrix, or string, in the calling statement as in the function program in order for the function's expressions to work as intended. For example, the multiplication of two row vectors may result in an error message if the variables do not have the correct order. Furthermore, the names used for the input variables of the function statement are equivalent to their appearing on the left side of an equal sign. Thus, in the example above, the input variables (a, b, c) are equivalent to the expressions: $a = ...$; $b = ...$; and $c = ...$. Finally, there are several forms that *OutputVariable* can take, each of which has an impact on how the results returned by the function statement can be used. These are discussed below.

The function file may be stored in any directory to which a path has been or will be defined and has the file name *FunctionName.m*. To illustrate the creation of a function, we will examine one example and three of the forms that it can have.

5.2.1 Form #1: Input Arguments Individually Identified and One Output Variable

Consider the following equations that are to be computed in a function:

$$x = \cos(at) + b$$

$$y = |x| + c$$

The values of x and y are to be returned by the function. We now create a function that we call *ComputeXY*, which is saved as a file named *ComputeXY.m*, to compute these quantities:[1]

```
function zanswer = ComputeXY(t,a,b,c)
% Computation of -
%   x = cos(at)+b
%   y = |x|+c
% Scalars: a,b,c
% Vector: t
% Matrix: zanswer
x = cos(a*t)+b;
zanswer = [x; abs(x)+c];
```

When one types in the MATLAB command window

```
help ComputeXY
```

the following is displayed

```
Computation of -
   x = cos(at)+b
   y = |x|+c
Scalars: a,b,c
Vector: t
Matrix: zanswer
```

MATLAB identifies functions by their file names, not by the characteristics of their input and output variables. Therefore, one must ensure that the number and the type of the input and output variables are correct with respect to how they are to be used by the function. These restrictions should be denoted in the function's comments intended for the response to the `help` request. In this case, we shall assume that t is either a scalar or a vector, and that a, b, and c are scalars. Thus, when t is a vector of length n_t the function returns a $(2 \times n_t)$ matrix *zanswer* such that *zanswer*$(1,:) = x(:)$ and *zanswer*$(2,:) = y(:)$.

We now shift our attention to the portion of a script file that calls this function. One possible scenario is

```
vick = ComputeXY(0:pi/4:pi, 1.4, 2, 0.75);
```

---

[1] The comments are included in this example to show its usage. In the large majority of scripts and functions presented in this book, the comment lines have been omitted in order to make the listings themselves more readable. However, in most cases the important features of the programs are discussed within the text accompanying each script or function, or they are obvious from its context.

By virtue of the location within the parentheses, this means that with reference to the function, $t = 0$, $\pi/4$, $\pi/2$, $3\pi/4$, and π, $a = 1.4$, $b = 2$, and $c = 0.75$. Upon executing this statement we obtain:

$vick(1,:) \rightarrow$ [3.0000   2.4540   1.4122   1.0123   1.6910]
$vick(2,:) \rightarrow$ [3.7500   3.2040   2.1622   1.7623   2.4410]

where $x = vick(1,:)$ and $y = vick(2,:)$. It should be noted that if the function *zanswer* had been instead written as

zanswer = [x abs(x)+c];

then the execution of *ComputeXY* would return the $(1 \times 2n_t)$ vector

$vick \rightarrow$ [3.0000 2.4540 1.4122 1.0123 1.6910 3.7500 3.2040 2.1622
              1.7623 2.4410]

In this case, $x = vick(1:5)$ and $y = vick(6:10)$.

5.2.2 Form #2: Input Arguments Represented as a Vector and One Output Variable

Function program   Corresponding script

```
function zanswer = ComputeXY(t,w)     vick = ComputeXY(0:pi/4:pi,[1.4 2
x = cos(w(1)*t)+w(2);                                          0.75]);
zanswer = [x; abs(x)+w(3)];
```

It is seen that by virtue of their placement in the vector w: $w(1) = a = 1.4$; $w(2) = b = 2$; and $w(3) = c = 0.75$, where a, b, and c refer to the three quantities defined in Form #1.

5.2.3 Form #3: Input Arguments Represented as a Vector and Each Output Variable Individually Identified

Function program   Corresponding script

```
function [x,y] = ComputeXY(t,w)     [u,v] = ComputeXY(0:pi/4:pi, [1.4 2
x = cos(w(1)*t)+w(2);                                        0.75]);
y = abs(x)+w(3);
```

In the statement `function [x,y]` ... the comma is required, but in $[u,v] = ...$ the commas can be replaced by a blank space. In the script file, if the call to *ComputeXY* were written as $q = ComputeXY(...)$, then only the first value would be assigned to q; that is, q would correspond to the vector x. Thus, when

$$[u,v] = \text{ComputeXY}(0:pi/4:pi, [1.4\ 2\ .75]);$$

is executed, we obtain

$$u \rightarrow [3.0000\ \ 2.4540\ \ 1.4122\ \ 1.0123\ \ 1.6910]$$
$$v \rightarrow [3.7500\ \ 3.2040\ \ 2.1622\ \ 1.7623\ \ 2.4410]$$

whereas when

$$q = \text{ComputeXY}(0:pi/4:pi, [1.4\ 2\ .75]);$$

is executed, we have

$$q \rightarrow [3.0000\ \ 2.4540\ \ 1.4122\ \ 1.0123\ \ 1.6910]$$

and the quantity corresponding to *y* is not available to the script.

Consequently, the form of the left-hand side of the function call most often matches that of the function definition itself. However, many of the MATLAB built-in functions take advantage of this property and make its usage context dependent. See, for one example, the *Help* file for `polyval`.

Since the arguments in the function definition are just placeholders for the numerical values that will reside in their respective places when the function is executed, one can, when appropriate, insert any correctly constructed expression in the calling statement. To illustrate this, consider the following script file for the function in Form #3:

```
n = 4;
c = linspace(1,1.4,n);
for k = 1:n
  [u,v] = ComputeXY(0:pi/4:pi, [c(k) sqrt(1.8/(1+k)^3) 1/.85]);
    ⋮
```

As a final remark, we illustrate the case where the results of a function are returned as a vector and are redefined in the script file as one row of a matrix. For simplification, we will assume that we are interested only in the values of *x* and that these values are returned inside a `for` loop. Thus, a segment of a program could be

```
n = 4;
c = linspace(1,1.4,n);
p = zeros(4,n);
for k = 1:4
  p(k,:) = ComputeXY(0:pi/4:pi, [c(k) sqrt(1.8/(1+k)^3) 1/.85]);
    ⋮
```

It is seen that p $(= u = \cos(at) + b)$ in this case will be a $(4{\times}5)$ matrix, since $k = 1, 2, 3, 4$ and the length of the vector t is 5. Recall that the notation $p(k,:)$ means that the kth row of matrix p is to have its column elements assigned the corresponding values of the columns of the row vector returned by *ComputeXY*.

5.2.4 Two Special Cases

Functions can also be created either to plot only to the MATLAB command window or to write only data to files. In these cases, no values are transferred back to the calling program. Then, the interface line of the function simplifies to

```
function FunctionName(InputVariables)
```

When a function is used only to store data in a prescribed manner, the function does not require any arguments. In this case, the interface line of the function has the form

```
function OutputVariables = FunctionName
```

or

```
function [a,b, ...] = FunctionName
```

Functions normally return when the last statement of the function is reached. To force an earlier return one uses

```
return
```

Consider the following example representing a portion of a function:

```
function c = FunctionName(x,a,b)
  if length(x) == 1|nargin ~= 3
   c = x
   return
  end
  ⋮
```

where `nargin` gives the number of input variables that are actually used to call the function.

5.3 INLINE

One can create a local function, either in the MATLAB command window, a script, or function, using `inline`, which has the advantage that it doesn't have to be saved in a separate file. However, it does have several limitations. It cannot call another `inline` function, it can be composed of only one MATLAB expression, and it can bring back only one variable—that is, Form #3 is not allowed. Thus, any function requiring logic or multiple operations to arrive at the final result cannot employ `inline`.

The general form of `inline` is

FunctionName = `inline`('expression', 'p1','p2',...)

where *expression* itself is any valid MATLAB expression and *p1, p2, ...* are the names of all the variables appearing in *expression*. We illustrate `inline` with the following example. Let us create a function *FofX* that evaluates

$$f(x) = x^2 \cos(ax) - b$$

where *a* and *b* are scalars. Then

FofX = `inline`('x.^2.*cos(a*x)–b','x','a','b')

displays in the MATLAB command window

```
FofX =
    Inline function:
    FofX(x,a,b) = x.^2.*cos(a*x)-b
```

If we had ended the expression with a semicolon, then this display would have been suppressed.

Thus, when we enter the following expression in the MATLAB command window,

g = FofX([`pi/3 pi/3.5`],4,1)

the system responds with $g = [-1.5483 \ -1.7259]$.

The `inline` form for functions has utility in many MATLAB commands that require one to first create a function that the command will subsequently evaluate. Several examples of its usage are given in Section 5.5.

5.4 CREATING FUNCTIONS THAT USE `feval` (FUNCTION OF FUNCTIONS)

There are many MATLAB built-in functions that require the user to create user-defined functions in a form specified by that built-in function. Several such functions are discussed in Section 5.5. In addition, there are situations when the user would also like to have this capability. MATLAB provides the means to do this with

`feval`

We will explain how this procedure works with an example based on the results of Section 4.3.2, where a root-finding program to determine the *m* lowest roots of a specific function $f(x) = 0$ was presented. We will now redefine this script as a function whose name is *ManyZeros*, which resides in the file *ManyZeros.m*. The function $f(x)$ and its name will now be arbitrary. In addition, it will be assumed that $f(x)$ has, in general, to be passed several parameters, which are part of its definition. Furthermore, we recall that the root-finding program requires four inputs: m, the number of the lowest roots desired; x_s, the starting value for search; t, the computational tolerance that determines the degree of closeness to zero of $f(x_{root})$; and Δ, the initial search increment.

For this example we shall let

$$f(x) = \cos(\beta x) - a \qquad a \le 1$$

Thus, we have to transfer to the user-defined function program two quantities: β and a. This user-defined function will be called *CosBeta*, and it resides in the file *CosBeta.m*. To implement these functions we also need a script file. The functions and the script are shown in Figure 5.1. According to the MATLAB help file, the first argument of `feval` is the name of the function and the additional arguments are the parameters to be transferred to the function. The function *ManyZeros* requires the following input variables: (1) the name of the function defining $f(x)$, which is the string variable *zname* (= 'CosBeta'); and (2) six parameters, the first four of which correspond to m, x_s, t, and Δ, and the remaining two, β and a, which are to be transferred to the function *CosBeta*. Depending on the value of m, the result c is either a scalar ($m = 1$) or a vector of length m.

To access the function *CosBeta* and bring back its numerical value, we use the MATLAB function `feval`. The MATLAB function `sign` then evaluates the sign of the numerical value brought back by `feval`. Also notice that the variable names defined in the function's input variables in the script file and the two function files are mostly different. This has been done to emphasize that only the locations and the subsequent usage of the arguments are important and not their alphanumeric descriptors, since the variable names are local to their respective functions.

5.5 MATLAB FUNCTIONS THAT USE `FEVAL`

MATLAB provides several functions that evaluate user-defined functions. The ones that we shall illustrate are:

> `fzero`—finds one root of $f(x) = 0$
>
> `roots`—finds the roots of a polynomial
>
> `quad8`—numerically integrates $f(x)$ in a specified interval
>
> `trapz`—numerically integrates $f(x)$ in a specified interval
>
> `polyarea`—determines the area within closed curves
>
> `fminbnd`—finds a local minimum of $f(x)$ in a specified interval
>
> `ode45`—numerically integrates a system of ordinary differential equations
>
> `fsolve`—numerically solves a system of nonlinear equations

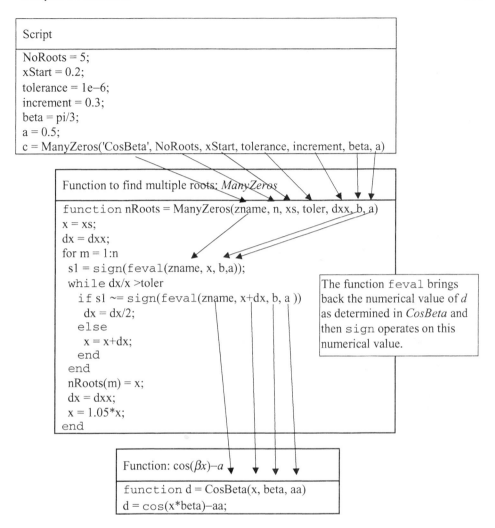

Script

```
NoRoots = 5;
xStart = 0.2;
tolerance = 1e–6;
increment = 0.3;
beta = pi/3;
a = 0.5;
c = ManyZeros('CosBeta', NoRoots, xStart, tolerance, increment, beta, a)
```

Function to find multiple roots: *ManyZeros*

```
function nRoots = ManyZeros(zname, n, xs, toler, dxx, b, a)
x = xs;
dx = dxx;
for m = 1:n
  s1 = sign(feval(zname, x, b,a));
  while dx/x >toler
    if s1 ~= sign(feval(zname, x+dx, b, a ))
      dx = dx/2;
    else
      x = x+dx;
    end
  end
  nRoots(m) = x;
  dx = dxx;
  x = 1.05*x;
end
```

The function `feval` brings back the numerical value of *d* as determined in *CosBeta* and then `sign` operates on this numerical value.

Function: $\cos(\beta x) - a$

```
function d = CosBeta(x, beta, aa)
d = cos(x*beta)–aa;
```

FIGURE 5.1
Graphical representation of the use of `feval` with user-defined functions.

When using these built-in functions the arguments of the user defined functions and/or their output have to conform to specific requirements. These different requirements are illustrated in the following sections and are also clearly specified in the *Help* file for that function.

5.5.1 Zeros of Functions—`fzero` and `roots/poly`

The built-in function `fzero` finds one solution to $f(x) = 0$ within a tolerance t_o in either the neighborhood of x_o or within the range $[x_1 \; x_2]$. It can also transfer p_j parameters to the function defining $f(x)$. The general expression is

```
fzero(FunctionName,x0,options,p1,p2,...)
```

where *FunctionName* is either the name of the function file in *single quotes*, but without the suffix ".m" or the variable name of the function *without any quotes* when created by `inline`, x0 = x_o or x0 = [x_1 x_2], p1, p2, etc., are the parameters p_j, and *options* is set using

```
optimset
```

The built-in function `optimset` is a general parameter adjusting function that is used by several MATLAB functions, primarily from the optimization toolbox. As a minimum it is recommended that `optimset` be used to turn the display off. Thus,

```
options = optimset('display','off');
```

would precede each use of `fzero`. See the *Help* file for `optimset` for the types of attributes that can altered, which vary depending on the function.

The interface for the function has the form

```
function z = FunctionName(x,p1,p2,...)
```

where *x* is the independent variable that `fzero` is changing in order to find a value such that $f(x = z) \cong 0$. The independent variable must always appear in this location. This requirement is true for most user-defined functions that are created for evaluation by MATLAB functions and is true for all functions illustrated in this chapter. We shall now illustrate the use of `fzero`.

The function $f(x)$ can be either a MATLAB function or a user-created one. Let us assume that we want to determine a root of cos(*x*) near *x* = 6. Then the statements

```
options = optimset('display','off');
w = fzero('cos',2*pi, options)/pi
```

yield *w* = 1.5000; that is, cos(1.5π) = 0. However,

```
options = optimset('display','off');
w = fzero('cos',2.04*pi,options)/pi
```

yields *w* = 2.5000, but

```
options = optimset('display','off');
w = fzero('cos',2.03*pi,options)/pi
```

yields *w* = 1.5000.

Thus, for multiple-valued functions one should use the form x0 = [x_1 x_2] and specify the region explicitly. However, an error results if the sign of $f(x_1)$ does not differ from the sign of $f(x_2)$. Thus,

> options = optimset('display','off');
> w = fzero('cos',[0 2*pi],options)/pi

causes an error, whereas

> options = optimset('display','off');
> w = fzero('cos',[0.6*pi 2*pi],options)/pi

yields, as before, $w = 1.5000$. Hence, for multivalued functions whose properties are not known *a priori*, one should plot the function first to determine approximately where its roots are.

On the other hand, if the root of $J_1(x) = 0$ (the Bessel[2] function of the first kind of order 1) near 3 was of interest, then the statement

> options = optimset('display','off');
> w = fzero('besselj',3,options)

would *not* work as intended because the arguments to besselj are besselj(n,x), where n is the order (= 1 in this case) and x is the independent variable. Therefore, n is the first argument and not x. Hence, we have to create a new function

> function v = besseljx(x,n)
> v = besselj(n,x);

and then call fzero as follows

> options = optimset('display','off');
> a = fzero('besseljx',3,options,1)

which brings back the correct result of $a = 3.8317$. Notice that in order to transfer the parameter $p_1 = 1$ to the function *besseljx*, we had to place a value of 1 in the fourth location of fzero.

For another example consider the equation from which the natural frequency coefficients for a beam clamped at both ends can be determined:

$$f(x) = \cos(x)\cosh(x) - 1$$

We first create a function called *ccbeam*

> function s = ccbeam(x)

---

[2] See, for example, F. B. Hildebrand, *Advanced Calculus for Applications*, Prentice-Hall, Saddle River, NJ, 1976.

```
s = cos(x)*cosh(x)–1;
```

Then

```
options = optimset('display','off');
q = fzero('ccbeam',4,options)
```

returns $q = 4.7300$. The function $f(x)$ is graphed in Figures 6.8 and 6.9.

We could have also determined this root using `inline` in either of the following two ways.

Form #1

```
qcc = inline('cos(x)*cosh(x)–1','x');
options = optimset('display','off');
q = fzero(qcc,4,options)
```

Form #2

```
options = optimset('display','off');
q = fzero(inline('cos(x)*cosh(x)–1','x'),4,options)
```

As mentioned previously, when *qcc* is defined by the `inline` function it does not have single quotes around it. This is true for all of MATLAB's built-in functions that require a user-defined function. When the function is to be used more than one time in a script, Form #1 has to be used, since with Form #2 the function has not been defined in a way that makes it available to any other expressions in the script. Form #1 is usually preferable.

We now determine the lowest 5 roots (not including $x = 0$) of

$$f(\mathrm{x}) = \cos(x)\cosh(x) - 1$$

The procedure is to first graph the function over a range of x to observe the approximate locations of x at which $f(x) = 0$. This information is then used to obtain five ranges over which `fzero` is to search for a root. The script is

```
qcc = inline('cos(x).*cosh(x)–1','x');
options = optimset('display','off');
% x = linspace(0,20);
% plot(x,qcc(x))
% axis([0 20 –10 10])
xo = [3 5];
for n = 1:5
  q(n) = fzero(qcc,xo,options);
  xo = [1.05*q(n) q(n)+4];
end
```

```
disp(['Lowest five roots are: ' num2str(q)])
```

which, upon execution, displays to the MATLAB command window

Lowest five roots are: 4.73004 7.8532 10.9956 14.1372 17.2788

In order to easily plot the function *qcc*, we used dot operations in its definition. These dot operations are not required by `fzero`. Secondly, because the magnitude of *qcc* varies over a very large positive and negative range, we employed `axis` to limit the values displayed, thereby greatly increasing the graph's resolution. In this case, we limited the *y*-axis to ± 10. See Section 6.2. From the graph we determined that the search region for *x* could be from a value that was 5% greater than the previous root location to the previous root location plus 4, which always placed the upper limit of the search region slightly beyond the next zero location. In the actual development of the script the last six expressions were not written until the first five expressions were executed and the results analyzed. Therefore, once this information had been determined it was no longer needed and the expressions were commented out.

If $f(x)$ were such that a constant value, 4 in the case, didn't exist and instead several different values C_j, $j = 1, 2, 3, 4$ were required, then the above script would become

```
qcc = inline('cos(x).*cosh(x)–1','x');
options = optimset('display','off');
C = [4 5 6 5 0];
xo = [3 5];
for n = 1:5
  q(n) = fzero(qcc,xo,options);
  xo = [1.05*q(n) q(n)+C(n)];
end
disp(['Lowest five roots are: ' num2str(q)])
```

The vector *C* has had added to it a fifth element 0 that is not used by the `fzero`, but is required because of the value of subscript of *C*.

For a last example let us determine the value of *a* that satisfies

$$\sum_{j=1}^{1000} \frac{1}{j^2 - a} = 0$$

and display its annotated value to the MATLAB command window with eight digits. We first create a function called *suma*

```
function z = suma(a)
z = sum(1./([1:1000].^2–a));
```

Then, with an initial guess of $\pi/2$ we have

```
options = optimset('display','off');
fofa = fzero('suma',pi/2,options);
disp(['The value of a is ' num2str(fofa,8) '. '])
```

which, upon execution, gives

The value of a is 2.0465776.

If we use `inline` we obtain the value of a with

```
options = optimset('display','off');
fofa = fzero(inline('sum(1./([1:1000].^2–a))','a'),pi/2,options);
disp(['The value of a is ' num2str(fofa,8) '. '])
```

When $f(x)$ is a polynomial of the form

$$f(x) = c_1 x^n + c_2 x^{n-1} + \ldots + c_n x + c_{n+1}$$

its roots can more easily be found using

```
roots(c)
```

where $c = [c_1\ c_2\ \ldots\ c_{n+1}]$. For example, if

$$f(x) = x^4 - 10x^3 + 35x^2 - 50x + 24$$

then

```
r = roots([1 –10 35 –50 24])
```

gives $r = [4\ 3\ 2\ 1]'$. The inverse of `roots` is

```
c = poly(rts)
```

which returns c, the polynomial's coefficients, and *rts* is a vector of roots. In the general case, *rts* is a vector of real and/or complex numbers.

Polynomials can also be multiplied using

```
conv(a,b)
```

where a and b are vectors containing the coefficients of the respective polynomials. For example, suppose we had another polynomial

$$g(x) = x^2 - 4$$

Then the product $h(x) = g(x)f(x)$ is obtained from

$$h = \text{conv}([1\ 0\ -4],[1\ -10\ 35\ -50\ 24])$$

which results in

$$h \rightarrow [1\ -10\ 31\ -10\ -116\ 200\ -96]$$

Thus, the polynomial is

$$h(x) = x^6 - 10x^5 + 31x^4 - 10x^3 - 116x^2 + 200x - 96$$

The roots of this polynomial should be the roots of $f(x)$ and the roots of $g(x)$, which are ±2.0. Thus,

$$rh = \text{roots}([1\ -10\ 31\ -10\ -116\ 200\ -96])$$

results in

$$rh \rightarrow [4.0000\ -2.0000\ 3.0000\ 2.0000\ 2.0000\ 1.0000]'$$

Notice that the results of roots are in an arbitrary order.

5.5.2 Numerical Integration—quad8, trapz, and polyarea

The built-in function quad8 numerically integrates $f(x)$ from a lower limit a to an upper limit b to within a tolerance t_o. It can also transfer p_j parameters to the function defining $f(x)$. The general expression for quad8 is[3]

quad8(FunctionName,a,b,t0,tc,p1,p2,...)

where *FunctionName* is either the name of the function file in *single quotes*, but without the suffix ".m" or the variable name of the function *without any quotes* when created by inline, a = a, b = b, t0 = t_o (when omitted the default value is used), p1, etc., are the parameters p_j, and, when tc ≠ [], quad8 provides intermediate output.

The interface for this function has the form

function z = FunctionName(x,p1,p2,...)

where x is the independent variable that quad8 is integrating over. The independent variable must always appear in this location. We shall now illustrate the use of quad8.

Two quantities that are frequently of interest in mechanics are the area of a two-dimensional shape and the location of its centroid. Let us assume that we have two curves $y_j = f_j(x)$, $j = 1, 2$, and that the two curves intersect at x_1 and x_2. Then the area between the two intersection points of the curves is:

---

[3] The double integration of a function $g(x,y)$ is obtained from dblquad; however, one cannot pass any parameters to it.

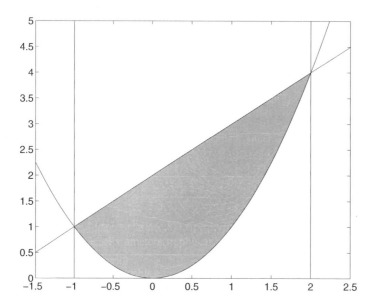

FIGURE 5.2
Determination of the centroid of the filled area.

$$A = \int dA = \int_{x_1}^{x_2} (y_2 - y_1)dx$$

and the location of the area's centroid about the origin is

$$x_c = \frac{1}{A}\int xdA = \frac{1}{A}\int_{x_1}^{x_2} x(y_2 - y_1)dx$$

$$y_c = \frac{1}{A}\int ydA = \frac{1}{A}\int_{x_1}^{x_2}\frac{1}{2}(y_2 + y_1)dA = \frac{1}{2A}\int_{x_1}^{x_2}(y_2^2 - y_1^2)dx$$

Suppose that $y_2 = x + 2$ and $y_1 = x^2$, which are shown in Figure 5.2. Then it is straightforward to show that the intersections occur at $x_1 = -1$ and $x_2 = 2$. The integrations yield $A = 4.5$, $x_c = 0.5$ and $y_c = 1.6$. We now repeat these calculations numerically.

Since the expressions for these curves are relatively simple, we use `inline` and `quad8` to obtain the following script.

```
area = quad8(inline('x+2','x'),−1,2)−quad8(inline('x.^2', 'x'),−1,2)
xc = quad8(inline('x.*((x+2)−x.^2)', 'x'),−1,2)/area
yc = quad8(inline('((x+2).^2−x.^4)/2', 'x'),−1,2)/area
```

The execution of the script gives: *area* = 4.5000, *xc* = 0.5000 and *yc* = 1.6000.
    Another way to obtain an approximation to a single integral is with

```
trapz(x,y)
```

In this case one specifies the values of *x* and the corresponding values of *y* as arrays. The function then performs the summation of the product of the average of adjacent *y* values and the corresponding *x* interval separating them. Even though it may, at times, be less accurate it has the convenience of not having to create a function as required by quad8. Furthermore, it must be used when the argument of the integral is available only as arrays of numbers. To solve the previous example with trapz we have

```
x = linspace(-1,2,150);
y = x+2-x.^2;
area = trapz(x,y)
xc = trapz(x,x.*y)/area
yc = trapz(x,(x+2).^2-x.^4)/2/area
```

When the script is executed, the results to five significant digits are *area* = 4.4998, *xc* = 0.5000, and *yc* = 1.6000.
    The area of closed curves can also be approximated by

```
polyarea(x,y)
```

where (*x,y*) are the coordinates of the connected straight lines forming an approximation to these curves. In our particular example, one of the curves is a straight line, with endpoints (−1,1) and (2,4). The script to compute the area with polyarea is

```
x = linspace(-1,2);
y = x.^2;
x = [-1 2 x];
y = [1 4 y];
area = polyarea(x,y)
```

which, when executed, results in *area* = 4.4995.
    Consider the following integral from which the length of a line in space can be determined:

$$L = \int_a^b \sqrt{\left(\frac{dx}{dt}\right)^2 + \left(\frac{dy}{dt}\right)^2 + \left(\frac{dz}{dt}\right)^2}\, dt \approx \sum_{i=1}^{N} \sqrt{(\Delta_i x)^2 + (\Delta_i y)^2 + (\Delta_i z)^2}$$

where

$$\Delta_i x = x(t_{i+1}) - x(t_i)$$
$$\Delta_i y = y(t_{i+1}) - y(t_i)$$
$$\Delta_i z = z(t_{i+1}) - z(t_i)$$

and $t_1 = a$ and $t_{N+1} = b$. The quantities $\Delta_i x$, $\Delta_i y$, and $\Delta_i z$, can be evaluated with

```
diff
```

which computes from a vector $x = [x_1 \; x_2 \; \ldots \; x_n]$ a vector q with $n - 1$ elements of the form

$$q = [x_2-x_1, \, x_3-x_2, \, \ldots, \, x_n-x_{n-1}]$$

For a vector x, `diff` is simply

```
q = x(2:end)-x(1:end-1);
```

where end = length(x) is a MATLAB function.

To illustrate the determination of the approximation to L we let

$$x = 2t$$
$$y = t^2$$
$$z = \ln t$$

for $1 \le t \le 2$ and $n = 25$. The script is

```
t = linspace(1,2,25);
L = sum(sqrt(diff(2*t).^2+diff(t.^2).^2+diff(log(t)).^2))
```

which, upon execution, yields $L = 3.6931$.

5.5.3 Local Minimum of a Function—`fminbnd`

The function `fminbnd`, from the Optimization Toolbox, finds a local minimum of $f(x)$ in the interval $a \le x \le b$ within a tolerance t_o. It can also transfer p_j parameters to the function defining $f(x)$. The general expression for `fminbnd` is

```
fminbnd(FunctionName,a,b,options,p1,p2,...)
```

where *FunctionName* is either the name of the function file in *single quotes*, but without the suffix ".m" or the variable name of the function *without any quotes* when created by `inline`, a = a, b = b, *options* is an optional vector whose parameters are set with `optimset` (see the *Help* file for `optimset`), and p1, etc., are the parameters p_j.

The interface for this function has the form

```
function z = FunctionName(x,p1,p2,...)
```

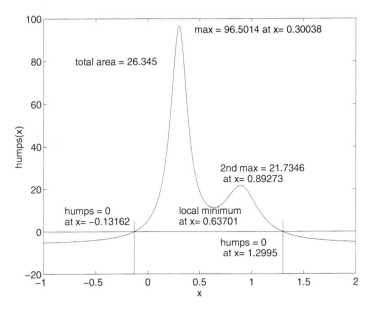

FIGURE 5.3
Properties of MATLAB's demonstration function humps.

where x is the independent variable that fminbnd is varying in order to minimize $f(x)$. The independent variable must always appear in this location. We shall now illustrate the use of fminbnd.

Consider the MATLAB demonstration function humps, which is shown in Figure 5.3. The minimum value of the function between $0 \le x \le 1$ is determined from the statements

```
options = optimset('display','off');
xmin = fminbnd('humps ',0,1,options)
```

which gives $xmin = x_{min} = 0.6370$. On the other hand, if we want to find the maximum value of humps in this interval, then we have to recognize that fminbnd must operate on the negative or the reciprocal of humps. Thus, using the negative of humps we create the script

```
options = optimset('display','off');
w = fminbnd(inline('–humps(x)', 'x '),0,1,options)
```

which gives $w = 0.300376$. The magnitude of humps at this maximum is determined from

```
wmax = humps(0.300376)
```

which yields $w_{max} = 96.5014$.

The other quantities appearing in Figure 5.3 can be verified using the techniques discussed in Sections 5.5.1 and 5.5.2.

5.5.4 Numerical Solutions of Ordinary Differential Equations—ode45

The function ode45 returns the numerical solution to a system of n first-order ordinary differential equations

$$\frac{dy_j}{dt} = f_j(t, y_1, y_2, ..., y_n) \qquad j = 1, 2, ..., n$$

over the interval $t_o \le t \le t_f$ subject to the initial conditions $y_j(t_o) = a_j$, $j = 1, 2, ..., n$, where a_j are constants. The arguments of ode45 are as follows:

$[t, y]$ = ode45(FunctionName, $[\,t_o\ t_f]$, $[a_1\ a_2\ ...\ a_n]'$,options,$p_1, p_2, ...$)

where the output t is a column vector of the times $t_o \le t \le t_f$ that are determined by ode45, the output y is the matrix of solutions such that the rows correspond to the times t and the columns correspond to the solutions:

$$y(:,1) = y_1(t)$$
$$y(:,2) = y_2(t)$$
$$...$$
$$y(:,n) = y_n(t)$$

The first argument of ode45 is *FunctionName*, which is either the name of the function file in *single quotes*, but without the suffix ".m" or the variable name of the function *without any quotes* when created by inline. Its form must be as follows:

function yprime = FunctionName(t,y,flag,p1,p2,...)

where t is the independent variable, y is a vector whose elements correspond to y_j, *flag* is a string of lower case letters that is not employed in this book but must be present (see the odefile *Help* file), $p1$, $p2$, ... are parameters passed to *FunctionName*, and *yprime* is a column vector of length n (rows) whose elements are $f_j(t, y_1, y_2, ..., y_n)$, $j = 1, 2, ..., n$; that is,

$$yprime = [f_1; f_2; ...; f_n]$$

The variable names *yprime, FunctionName*, etc. are assigned by the programmer.

The second argument of ode45 is a two-element vector giving the starting and ending times over which the numerical solution will be obtained. This quantity can, instead, be a vector of the times $[t_o\ t_1\ t_2\ ...\ t_f]$ at which the solutions will be obtained. The third argument is a vector of initial conditions $y_j(t_o) = a_j$. The fourth argument, *options*, is usually set to null (see the ode45 *Help* file), and the remaining arguments are those that are passed to *FunctionName*.

There are four other ordinary differential equation solvers in MATLAB, each of which has its advantages depending on the particular properties of the differential equation. They are ode23, ode113, ode15s, and ode23s. Their use is the same as described for ode45. See the MATLAB users guide and their respective *Help* files for details.

We now illustrate the usage of this function by considering the nondimensional second-order ordinary differential equation

$$\frac{d^2y}{dt^2} + 2\xi\frac{dy}{dt} + y = h(t) \tag{5.1}$$

This can be rewritten as a system of two first-order equations with the substitution

$$y_1 = y$$
$$y_2 = \frac{dy}{dt}$$

Then

$$\frac{dy_1}{dt} = y_2$$
$$\frac{dy_2}{dt} = -2\xi y_2 - y_1 + h$$

Let us consider three cases, each of which uses $\xi = 0.15$, $t_o = 0$, and $t_f = 35$:

Case (1)

$$y_1(0) = 0$$
$$y_2(0) = 0$$
$$h(t) = u(t)$$

where $u(t)$ is the unit step function.

Case (2)

$$y_1(0) = 1$$
$$y_2(0) = 0$$
$$h(t) = 0$$

Case (3)

$$y_1(0) = 0$$
$$y_2(0) = 0$$
$$h(t) = \sin(\pi t/5) \quad t \le 5$$
$$= 0 \quad t > 5$$

We first create a function that will handle these three cases and present its output in the form required by ode45:

```
function s = ForcingFunction(t,w,flag,x,c)
```

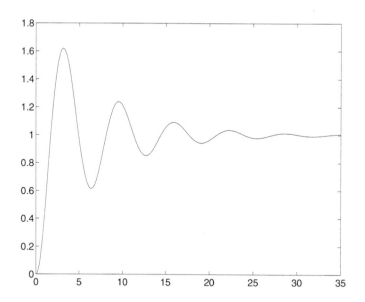

FIGURE 5.4
Response of Eq. (5.1) to a unit step function.

```
switch c
  case 1
   s = [w(2); –2*x*w(2)–w(1)+1];
  case 2
   s = [w(2); –2*x*w(2)–w(1)];
  case 3
   h = sin(pi*t/5).*(t<=5);
   s = [w(2); –2*x*w(2)–w(1)+h];
end
```

where $w(1) = y_1(t)$, $w(2) = y_2(t)$, and $x = \xi$.

Case 1: $y_1(0) = 0$, $y_2(0) = 0$, and $h(t) = u(t)$. The script is:

```
[tt,yy] = ode45('ForcingFunction',[0 35], [0 0]',[],0.15,1);
plot(tt,yy(:,1))
```

which results in Figure 5.4. Thus

$$yy(:,1) = y_1(t) = y(t)$$
$$yy(:,2) = y_2(t) = dy/dt$$

Another way to get the step response of an ordinary differential equation is to use

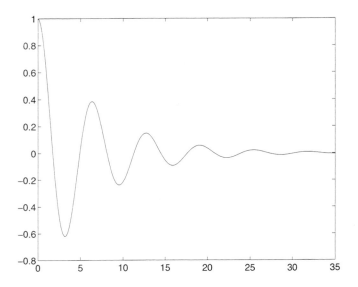

FIGURE 5.5
Response of Eq. (5.1) to an initial condition.

```
step
```

from the Controls toolbox. See Chapters 9 and 10.

Case 2: $y_1(0) = 1$, $y_2(0) = 0$, and $h(t) = 0$. The script is:

```
[tt,yy] = ode45('ForcingFunction',[0 35], [1 0]',[],0.15,2);
plot(tt,yy(:,1))
```

which results in Figure 5.5.

Case 3: $y_1(0) = 0$, $y_2(0) = 0$, and $h(t) = \sin(\pi t/5)$, $t \le 5$, and $h(t) = 0$, $t > 5$. In this case we specify the values of t, which is done by replacing the second argument with a vector of the times. The script is:

```
[tt,yy] = ode45('ForcingFunction',linspace(0,35,200), [0 0]',[],0.15,3);
plot(tt,yy(:,1))
```

which when executed, results in Figure 5.6.

We now consider several additional examples that extend the basic usage of ode45.

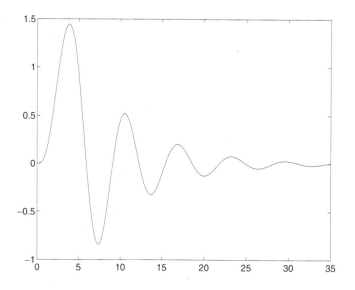

FIGURE 5.6
Response of Eq. (5.1) to a half sine wave.

Example 5.1 Natural convection along a heated vertical plate

The equations describing the natural convection along a heated vertical plate in contact with a cooler fluid is given by (see Section 12.3.2)

$$\frac{d^3 f}{d\eta^3} + 3f\frac{d^2 f}{d\eta^2} - 2\left(\frac{df}{d\eta}\right)^2 + T^* = 0$$

$$\frac{d^2 T^*}{d\eta^2} + 3\Pr f\frac{dT^*}{d\eta} = 0$$

When Pr = 0.7 the boundary conditions at $\eta = 0$ are

$$f = 0 \qquad \frac{df}{d\eta} = 0 \qquad \frac{d^2 f}{d\eta^2} = 0.68$$

$$T^* = 1 \qquad \frac{dT^*}{d\eta} = -0.50$$

This system can be decomposed into a system of five first-order equations by introducing the following set of dependent variables:

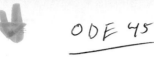

$$O D E \ 45$$

$$y_1 = f \qquad y_4 = T^*$$

$$y_2 = \frac{df}{d\eta} \qquad y_5 = \frac{dT^*}{d\eta}$$

$$y_3 = \frac{d^2 f}{d\eta^2}$$

where y_1 is the stream function, y_2 is the velocity, y_3 is the shear, y_4 is the temperature, and y_5 is the heat flux. Then the differential equations in terms of these new variables are

$$\frac{dy_1}{d\eta} = y_2 \qquad\qquad \frac{dy_4}{d\eta} = y_5$$

$$\frac{dy_2}{d\eta} = y_3 \qquad\qquad \frac{dy_5}{d\eta} = -3 \Pr y_1 y_5$$

$$\frac{dy_3}{d\eta} = 2 y_2^2 - 3 y_1 y_3 - y_4$$

The corresponding boundary conditions at $\eta = 0$ are

$$y_1(0) = 0 \qquad y_4(0) = 1$$

$$y_2(0) = 0 \qquad y_5(0) = -0.50$$

$$y_3(0) = 0.68$$

To solve this system of equations we first must create the following function to specify the column vector representing the right-hand side of the five first order differential equations, the f_j.

```
function ff = NaturalConv(x,y,flag,Pr)
ff = [y(2); y(3); -3*y(1)*y(3)+2*y(2)^2-y(4); y(5); -3*Pr*y(1)*y(5)];
```

The script is

```
y0 = [0 0 0.68 1 -0.50];
Pr = 0.7;
[eta ff] = ode45('NaturalConv',[0 20],y0,[],Pr);
```

The results are shown in Figure 12.14.

Example 5.2 Inverted pendulum

Consider the inverted pendulum attached to a disk as shown in Figure 10.35. Its linearized equations of motion are

$$ml^2 \frac{d^2\theta}{dt^2} + mrl\frac{d^2\psi}{dt^2} = mgl\theta + b_1\frac{d\theta}{dt}$$

$$mrl\frac{d^2\theta}{dt^2} + \left(J + mr^2\right)\frac{d^2\psi}{dt^2} = b_2\frac{d\psi}{dt} + \tau_m$$

where m is the mass of the bob, l the length of the pendulum, r is the radius of the disk which is also the radius of the bob attachment, d is the thickness of the disk, $J = \rho\pi dr^4/4$ is the inertia of the disk, b_1 is the friction coefficient of the revolute joint of the pendulum, b_2 is the friction in the revolute joint of the disk, and τ_m is the torque applied by the motor attached to the base of the disk.

If we define the following set of dependent variables

$$x_1(t) = \theta(t) \qquad x_3(t) = \frac{d\theta}{dt}$$

$$x_2(t) = \psi(t) \qquad x_4(t) = \frac{d\psi}{dt}$$

then the governing equations become, in matrix form,

$$M\dot{x} = Qx + W$$

where

$$M = \begin{bmatrix} 1 & 0 & 0 & 0 \\ 0 & 1 & 0 & 0 \\ 0 & 0 & ml^2 & mlr \\ 0 & 0 & mlr & J+mr^2 \end{bmatrix} \qquad Q = \begin{bmatrix} 0 & 0 & 1 & 0 \\ 0 & 0 & 0 & 1 \\ mgl & 0 & b_1 & 0 \\ 0 & 0 & 0 & b_2 \end{bmatrix}$$

$$W = \begin{bmatrix} 0 \\ 0 \\ 0 \\ \tau_m \end{bmatrix} \qquad x = \begin{bmatrix} x_1 \\ x_2 \\ x_3 \\ x_4 \end{bmatrix} \qquad \dot{x} = \begin{bmatrix} dx_1/dt \\ dx_2/dt \\ dx_3/dt \\ dx_4/dt \end{bmatrix}$$

In order to obtain the four first-order ordinary differential equations required by ode45, we must solve this system of equations for dx_i/dt. Thus,

$$\dot{x} = M^{-1}Qx + M^{-1}W$$

provided that the determinant of $M \neq 0$. In this case, $\det(M) = ml^2J \neq 0$.

First we create the following function to specify the right-hand sides of the four first-order ordinary differential equations.

```
function p = InvPend(t,x,flag,taum,m,r,L,d,g,rho,b1,b2)
J = 0.25*pi*rho*d*r^4;
M = [1 0 0 0; 0 1 0 0; 0 0 m*L^2 m*r*L; 0 0 m*r*L J+m*r^2];
```

Q = [0 0 1 0; 0 0 0 1; m*g*L 0 b1 0; 0 0 0 b2];
W = [0;0;0;taum];
p = inv(M)*Q*x+inv(M)*W;

where *p* is column vector. Ordinarily, at this point one would use *InvPend* to find either the response of the system to a suddenly applied torque or to a set of initial conditions. Unfortunately, this system is unstable and a formal solution doesn't yield any useful information. In addition, the solution quickly leaves the region in which the linearization used to obtain these equations is valid. However, the system can be stabilized using a suitable control system as discussed in detail in Section 10.5.3.

Example 5.3 Boundary conditions specified at each end of the domain

Consider the ordinary differential equation

$$\frac{d^2y}{dx^2} + ky = x \qquad 0 \le x \le 1$$

subject to the boundary conditions

$$y(0) = 0 \qquad y(1) = 0$$

Since ode45 requires that we specify the boundary (initial) conditions at $x = 0$ only, we must use a procedure that determines the value of $dy(0)/dx$ such that $y(1) \to 0$. This procedure requires an interative process whereby the value of $dy(0)/dx$ is varied until it eventually produces a value for $y(1)$ that is very close to zero.[4] Since we have only one unknown, $dy(0)/dx$, we can use fzero to find this value. For higher order differential equations we use fsolve instead of fzero. See Sections 8.2.1 and 12.3.1.

First we transform the equation into a pair of first order differential equations as shown earlier in this section to obtain

$$\frac{dy_1}{dx} = y_2$$

$$\frac{dy_2}{dx} = x - ky_1$$

The function representing these equations in the form required by ode45 is

```
function f = ExampleODE(x,y,flag,k)
f = [y(2);x–k*y(1)];
```

Next we create a function that can be used by fzero to determine the value of $dy(0)/dx$.

---

[4] This technique, which converts the boundary-value problem to an initial value problem, is known as the shooting method.

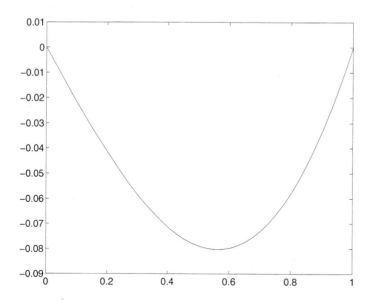

FIGURE 5.7
y(*x*) for Example 5.3.

```
function z = Slope(s,k)
[x,y] = ode45('ExampleODE',[0 1],[0 s]',[],k);
z = y(end,1);
```

where $y(\text{end},1) = y(1)$ and $s = dy(0)/dx$. Notice that `fzero` will be varying *s* in order to make $z \to 0$.

The script to determine *y*(*x*) when *k* = 2 is

```
options = optimset('display','off');
k = 2; guess = -0.1;
bc = fzero('Slope',guess,options,k);
[x,y] = ode45('ExampleODE',[0 1],[0 bc]',[],k);
disp(['Slope at x = 0 is ' num2str(bc)])
plot(x,y(:,1))
```

which, upon execution, displays

Slope at x = 0 is -0.21586

to the MATLAB command window and creates the results shown in Figure 5.7. It should be realized that in the script $bc = y(1,2)$. For another application of this technique see Section 11.3.2.

5.5.5 Numerical Solutions of Nonlinear Equations—`fsolve`

The built-in function `fsolve` in the Optimization Toolbox finds the numerical solution to a system of n nonlinear equations $f_n(x_1, x_2,..., x_n) = 0$ in the x_n unknowns using a starting guess $x_s = [x_{s1}\ x_{s2}\ ...\ x_{sn}]$. It can also transfer p_j parameters to the function defining $f_n(x)$. The general expression for `fsolve` is

> `fsolve(FunctionName,xs,options,p1,p2,...)`

where *FunctionName* is either the name of the function file in *single quotes*, but without the suffix ".m" or the variable name of the function *without any quotes* when created by `inline`, $xs = x_s$, *options* is an optional vector whose parameters are set with `optimset` (see `optimset` in the *Help* file), and p1, etc., are the parameters p_j.

The interface for this function has the form

> `function z = FunctionName(x,p1,p2,...)`
> `z = [f1;f2;...;fn];`

where x is a vector of the n quantities to be determined, x_n, and z is a column vector composed of n MATLAB expressions for the n nonlinear equations $f_n(x_1, x_2,..., x_n)$ in terms of the elements of x.

Consider the following system of equations, which results from an intermediate step in the inverse kinematics solution for the three degree-of-freedom linkages shown in Figure 2.7:

$$r_1 - a_1 \cos(\theta_1) - a_2 \cos(\theta_1 + \theta_2) = 0$$
$$r_2 - a_1 \sin(\theta_1) - a_2 \sin(\theta_1 + \theta_2) = 0$$

To solve this system of equations we first create a function *kinematics*, which puts these equations in the form required by `fsolve`. Thus,

> `function w = kinematics(theta,a1,a2,r1,r2)`
> `w = [a1*cos(theta(1))+a2*cos(theta(1)+theta(2))–r1;...`
> `       a1*sin(theta(1))+a2*sin(theta(1)+theta(2))–r2];`

where *theta*(1) = θ_1 and *theta*(2) = θ_2.

Let $r_1 = 1.8$, $r_2 = 2.1$, $a_1 = 1.0$ and $a_2 = 2$, and let our initial guesses for θ_1 and θ_2 be $\pi/6$. Then the script is

> `options = optimset('display','off');`
> `z = fsolve('kinematics',[pi/6 pi/6],options,1,2,1.8,2.1)*180/pi`

which upon execution gives $\theta_1 = z(1) = 16.6026°$ and $\theta_2 = z(2) = 48.5095°$. Another set of angles will be found when the initial guess is $\theta_1 = \theta_2 = \pi$. Thus, fsolve must be used with caution, especially if more than one solution exists.

As another example of multiple solutions consider the interaction of an ellipse

$$g(x, y) = x^2/4 + y^2 - 1$$

with the parabola

$$f(x, y) = y - 4x^2 + 3$$

A graph of these two functions reveals that they intersect at four points. Thus, the value returned by fsolve will be sensitive to the initial guess. We illustrate this by first creating the function

```
function w = fgsolve(xy)
w = [0.25*xy(1).^2+xy(2).^2−1; xy(2)−4*xy(1).^2+3];
```

where $xy(1) = x$ and $xy(2) = y$. The script to determine the solution with initial guesses of $x = 0.5$ and $y = -0.5$ is

```
options = optimset('display','off');
xy = fsolve('fgsolve',[0.5,−0.5],options)
```

Upon execution, we find that $x = xy(1) = 0.7188$ and $y = xy(2) = -0.9332$. If, instead, we had chosen for our initial guess $x = -0.5$ and $y = 0.5$, we would have obtained $x = xy(1) = -0.9837$ and $y = xy(2) = 0.8707$.

5.6 EXAMPLES OF SEVERAL OTHER MATLAB FUNCTIONS

There are many other general-purpose functions in MATLAB that have a wide range of use in obtaining numerical solutions to engineering problems. We shall present a few of them in this section employing specific applications.

5.6.1 Fitting Data With Polynomials—polyfit/polyval

A notch sensitivity factor q for metals can be defined in terms of a Neuber's constant $\sqrt{a}$ and the notch radius r as follows:

$$q = \left(1 + \frac{\sqrt{a}}{\sqrt{r}}\right)^{-1}$$

The value of $\sqrt{a}$ is different for different metals, and is a function of the ultimate strength S_u of the material. It can be estimated by fitting a polynomial to experimentally obtained data

TABLE 5.1
Neuber's Constant for Steel

S_u (ksi)	$\sqrt{a}$ ($\sqrt{\text{in}}$)	S_u (ksi)	$\sqrt{a}$ ($\sqrt{\text{in}}$)
50	0.130	170	0.028
70	0.092	190	0.020
90	0.072	210	0.015
110	0.057	230	0.010
130	0.046	250	0.007
150	0.037		

of $\sqrt{a}$ as a function of S_u for a given metal. Once we have this polynomial we can determine the value of q for a given value of r and S_u.

Let us consider the data given in the Table 5.1 for steel. Using these data we first determine the coefficients of a fourth-order polynomial that expresses $\sqrt{a}$ as a function of S_u, and then use this polynomial to obtain q for a given r and S_u.

In order to fit a polynomial to a set of data we use

```
polyfit
```

to obtain the coefficients of the polynomial, and we use

```
polyval
```

to evaluate it. If the general form of the polynomial is

$$y(x) = p_1 x^n + p_2 x^{n-1} + \ldots + p_n x + p_{n+1} \tag{5.2}$$

then the statement to obtain its coefficients is

```
p = polyfit(x,y,n)
```

where n is the order of the polynomial, $p = [p_1\ p_2\ \ldots\ p_n\ p_{n+1}]$ is a vector of length $n+1$ representing the coefficients of the polynomial in Eq. (5.2), and x and y are each vectors of length $m \geq n + 1$; they are the data to which the polynomial is fitted, with x the input and y the output.

To evaluate Eq. (5.2) once we have p we use

```
y = polyval(p,x)
```

where p is a vector of length $n+1$ that has been determined from `polyfit` and x is either a scalar or a vector of points at which the polynomial will be evaluated. In general, the values of p in `polyval` can be arbitrarily selected. In the present case we are interested in the specific set that has been determined by `polyfit`.

To fit the data appearing in Table 5.1 and to obtain the value of $\sqrt{a}$ for any value $50 \le S_u \le 250$ and $0 < r < 0.2$ we use the following script. For simplicity, we assume that we enter one set of S_u and r at a time. Furthermore, we place the data appearing in Table 5.1 in a function called *NeuberData*. The generation of a set of graphs that display the values of q for a range of data is given in Figure 6.19b.

The function for the data is

```
function nd = NeuberData
nd = [50, .13; 70, .092; 90, .072; 110, .057; 130, .046; 150, .037; ...
      170, .028; 190, .020; 210, .015; 230, .010; 250, .007];
```

where $nd(:,1) = S_u$ and $nd(:,2) = r$. The script is

```
ncs = NeuberData
p = polyfit(ncs(:,1),ncs(:,2),4);
r = input('Enter notch radius (0 < r < 0.2) ');
Su = input('Enter ultimate strength of material (50 < Su < 250) ');
q = 1/(1+polyval(p,Su)/sqrt(r));
disp(['Notch sensitivity = ' num2str(q)])
```

Executing this script yields

```
Enter notch radius (0 < r < 0.2) .1
Enter ultimate strength of material (50 < Su < 250) 135
Notch sensitivity = 0.87999
```

where the script displayed the first two lines sequentially and the user entered the numbers .1 and 135, respectively, after each line was displayed. The system then computed the value of q and displayed the third line.

5.6.2 Interpolation of Data—`interp1`

Let us return to the numerical solution of Eq. (5.1) to a step function, which is shown in Figure 5.4. We are interested in determining the value of the percentage overshoot of the system's output $p_{overshoot}$ and its rise time t_r. The rise time is defined as the time it takes for the system's output to go from 10% to 90% of its steady state (long-time) response, denoted y_{ss}, when $\xi > 0$ and when subjected to a unit step function at its input. Thus,

$$t_r = t_h - t_l$$

where t_h and t_l are determined, respectively, from

$$y(t_h) = 0.9 \, y_{ss}$$
$$y(t_l) = 0.1 \, y_{ss}$$

The percentage overshoot is defined as follows. If the maximum value of the output response is y_{max} and the steady state value is y_{ss}, then the percentage overshoot is

$$p_{overshoot} = 100(y_{max} - y_{ss})/y_{ss}$$

Since $y(t)$ has been obtained numerically, neither `fzero` nor `fminbnd` can be used. A means of overcoming this limitation is given in Section 5.6.3. Therefore, to find these quantities we use

```
interp1
```

to determine t_h and t_l and

```
max
```

to determine the location of y_{max}. The general expression for `interp1` is

```
V = interp1(u,v,U)
```

where v is $v(u)$, u and v are vectors of the same length, and U is a scalar or vector of values of u for which V desired. V has the same length as U. Thus, the script is

```
[t,y] = ode45('ForcingFunction',[0 35], [0 0]',[],0.15,1);
[ymax,tmax] = max(y(:,1));
tr = interp1(y(1:tmax),t(1:tmax),[.1 .9]);
povershoot = 100*(ymax−y(end,1))/y(end,1);
disp(['Percentage overshoot = ' num2str(povershoot,4) ' %'])
disp(['Rise time = ' num2str(tr(2)−tr(1),4) ' seconds'])
```

which, upon execution, displays to the MATLAB command window

Percentage overshoot = 61.23 %
Rise time = 1.153 seconds

The first line of the script has already been discussed in Section 5.5.4. Recall that y is a two-column vector, the first column corresponding to $y(t)$ and the second to dy/dt. The second line is another form of output for the `max` function, which corresponds to Form #3 of Section 5.2. (See the *Help* file for `max`.) The second output *tmax* is the *index* of the array $y(:,1)$ at which the maximum value of $y(:,1)$ occurs. In this case it is the 39th element of the array (*tmax* = 39); thus, $y(39,1) = ymax = 1.6207$. The `interp1` function requires that its first argument be monotonic. Therefore, we must terminate the array $y(:,1)$ at its maximum value (index = *tmax*), because after this point $y(:,1)$ starts to decrease.

5.6.3 Fitting Data with `spline`

We shall generate some exponentially decaying oscillatory data and then fit these data with a series of splines using

`spline`

Then we shall determine the period of one of its oscillations and compute its damping from the logarithmic decrement.

The general expression for `spline` is

Y = spline(x,y,X)

where y is $y(x)$, x and y are vectors of the same length that are used to create the functional relationship $y(x)$, and X is a scalar or vector for which the values of $Y = y(X)$ are desired.

The data will be generated by sampling the following function[5] over a range of nondimensional times τ for a given damping coefficient $\xi < 1.0$.

$$f(\tau,\xi) = \frac{e^{-\xi\tau}}{\cos\alpha}\cos\left(\tau\sqrt{1-\xi^2} + \alpha\right) \qquad (5.2)$$

where

$$\alpha = \tan^{-1}\frac{-\xi}{\sqrt{1-\xi^2}}$$

We shall evaluate this equation in a function called *DampedSineWave*, which is given by

```
function f = DampedSineWave(tau,xi)
alpha = atan(-xi/sqrt(1-xi^2));
f = exp(-xi*tau).*cos(tau*sqrt(1-xi^2)+alpha)/cos(alpha);
```

Let us sample 10 equally-spaced points of $f(\tau,\xi)$ over the range $0 \le \tau \le 20$ and plot the resulting piece-wise polynomial with the original wave form for $\xi = 0.1$. The script is

```
n = 10; xi = 0.1;
tau = linspace(0,20,n);
data = DampedSineWave(tau,xi);
newdata = linspace(0,20,200);
plot(newdata,spline(tau,data,newdata),'k--',newdata, ...
        DampedSineWave(newdata,xi),'k-')
```

---

[5] See, for example, S. S. Rao, *Mechanical Vibrations*, Addison-Wesley, Reading, MA, 1986, pp. 80–82.

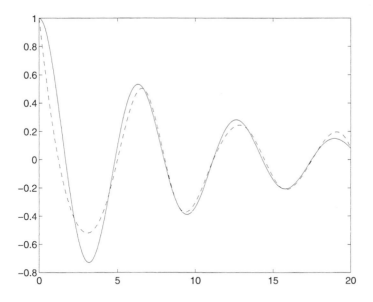

FIGURE 5.8
Comparison of a damped sine wave (solid line) with an approximation (dashed line) obtained with a spline using 10 equally spaced points in the range $0 \leq \tau \leq 20$.

which, when executed, produces Figure 5.8. It is seen that the results are fairly good. The curves become visually indistinguishable from each other when the number of equally spaced sampled points increases to 15. However, in the next phase of examining these fitted data we will have to use a value of $n = 40$ in order to get excellent numerical agreement between our estimated values and the exact values. A detailed discussion of `plot` is given in Section 6.2.

The logarithmic decrement represents the rate at which the amplitude of a free damped vibration decreases, and is defined as[6]

$$\Delta = \ln \frac{x_1}{x_2} = \frac{2\pi\xi}{\sqrt{1-\xi^2}}$$

where

$$x_1 = f(\tau_1, \xi)$$
$$x_2 = f(\tau_1 + T, \xi)$$

are given by Eq. (5.2) and T is the period of damped oscillation.

---

[6] S. S. Rao, *ibid*.

To determine ξ from a determination of x_1 and x_2 we use the following procedure. We will fit 40 equally spaced sampled points with `spline` over the range $0 \le \tau \le 20$. Then we will create a vector of 200 time data points and use them to compute, from our fitted function, the values of the damped sine wave. From the resulting vector we find the index of the value at which the approximate minimum value of $f(\tau, \xi)$ occurs. We then use twice this minimum value as the upper range of the guess in `fminbnd`, which will determine more precisely the time at which this minimum value occurs. Twice this minimum time is the period T. Then we compute the logarithm of the ratio of the amplitudes at $0.05T$ and $1.05T$, which is the value Δ, and use `fzero` to solve for ξ in the above equation. The script that performs these operations is

```
n = 40; xi = 0.1;
tau = linspace(0,20,n);
data = DampedSineWave(tau,xi);
tx = linspace(0,20,200);
datafit = inline('spline(tau,data,tx)','tx','tau','data');
[datamin imin] = min(datafit(tx,tau,data));
options = optimset('display','off');
periodT = 2*fminbnd(datafit,0,2*tx(imin),options,tau,data);
delta = log(datafit(.05*periodT,tau,data)/datafit(1.05*periodT,tau,data));
logdec = inline('s/sqrt(1-s^2)-d/2/pi','s','d');
xiEst = fzero(logdec,[0.01 .999],options,delta);
dif = 100*(xiEst-xi)/xi;
disp(['Estimated xi = 'num2str(xiEst)'  Exact xi = ' num2str(xi) ...
           ' Difference = ' num2str(dif) '%'])
```

Execution of this script, for $\xi = 0.1$, displays to the MATLAB command window

Estimated xi = 0.10006   Exact xi = 0.1   Difference = 0.063776%

and, for $\xi = 0.95$,

Estimated xi = 0.94383   Exact xi = 0.95   Difference = -0.64952%

Setting $n = 100$ reduces the error in the latter case to -0.26%.

5.6.4 Digital Signal Processing—`fft` and `ifft`

Discrete Fourier Transform. The Fourier transform of a real function $g(t)$ that is sampled every Δt over an interval $0 \le t \le T$ can be approximated by its discrete Fourier transform

$$G_n = G(n\Delta f) = \Delta t \sum_{k=0}^{N-1} g_k e^{-j2\pi nk/N} \qquad n = 0,1,...,N-1$$

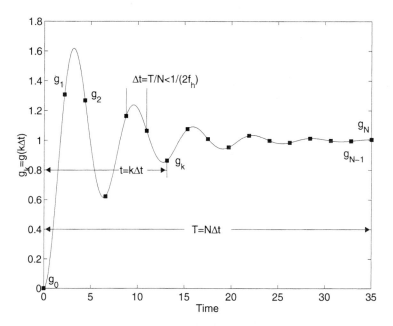

FIGURE 5.9
Sampled waveform.

where $g_k = g(k\Delta t)$, $\Delta f = 1/T$, $T = N\Delta t$ and N is the number of samples. Refer to Figure 5.9. In general, G_n is a complex quantity. The restriction on Δt is that

$$\alpha\Delta t < \frac{1}{f_h}$$

where f_h is the highest frequency in $g(t)$ and $\alpha \geq 2$. The quantity G_n is called the amplitude density of $g(t)$ and has the units amplitude-second or, equivalently, amplitude/Hz.

The inverse transform is approximated by

$$g_k = \Delta f \sum_{n=0}^{N-1} G_n e^{j2\pi nk/N} \qquad k = 0,1,...,N-1$$

In order to estimate the magnitude of the amplitude A_n corresponding to each G_n at its corresponding frequency $n\Delta f$ one multiplies G_n by Δf; thus,

$$A_n = \Delta f G_n$$

and, therefore,

$$A_n = \frac{1}{N} \sum_{k=0}^{N-1} g_k e^{-j2\pi nk/N} \qquad n = 0,1,\dots,N-1$$

since $\Delta f \Delta t = 1/N$. The average power in the signal is

$$P_{avg} = \sum_{n=0}^{N-1} |A_n|^2$$

One often plots $|A_n|$ as a function of $n\Delta f$ to obtain an amplitude spectral plot. In this case we have that[7]

$$|A_n|_s = 2|A_n| \qquad n = 0,1,\dots,N/2-1$$

These expressions are best evaluated using the fast Fourier transform, which is a very efficient algorithm for numerically evaluating the discrete Fourier transform. It's most effective when the number of sampled data points is a power of 2—that is; $N = 2^m$, where m is a positive integer. MATLAB implements this algorithm with

    fft(g,N)

and its inverse with

    ifft(G,N)

where

        fft returns $G_n/\Delta t$

and

        ifft returns $g_k/\Delta f$

Weighting Functions. There are many situations when it is desirable to weight $g(t)$ by a suitable function to provide better resolution or other properties in the transformed domain. The procedure is to modify the original signal prior to performing the discrete Fourier transform in such a way that the effects of the changes caused by the windowing function to the signal's mean value and the signal's average power are removed. Thus, if the sampled values of the weighting function are $w_n = w(n\Delta t)$, then the corrected signal g_{cn} is given by[8]

$$g_{cn} = k_2 w_n (g_n - k_1) \qquad n = 0,1,\dots,N-1$$

---

[7] See, for example, J. S. Bendat and A. G. Piersol, *Engineering Applications of Correlation and Spectral Analysis*, John Wiley & Sons, New York, 1980.

[8] E. C. Ifeachor and B. W. Jervis, *Digital Signal Processing: A Practical Approach*, Addison-Wesley, Harlow, England, 1993, p. 593.

where

$$k_1 = \sum_{n=0}^{N-1} w_n g_n \Bigg/ \sum_{n=0}^{N-1} w_n$$

corrects for the mean of the windowing function and

$$k_2 = \left[N \Bigg/ \sum_{n=0}^{N-1} w_n^2 \right]^{1/2}$$

corrects for the average power of the windowing function. One then takes the discrete Fourier transform of g_{cn}.

MATLAB's Digital Signal Processing Toolbox contains eight commonly used weighting functions.

Cross Correlation. The cross correlation of two finite-duration deterministic signals $x(t)$ and $y(t)$ is given by

$$R_{xy}(\tau) = \int_{-\infty}^{\infty} x(t)y(t+\tau)dt \qquad -\infty < \tau < \infty$$

It is current practice to evaluate this quantity from the inverse Fourier transform of the cross-spectral density function $S_{xy}(\omega)$:

$$R_{xy}(\tau) = F^{-1}\big[S_{xy}(\omega)\big]$$

where $F^{-1}(...)$ indicates the inverse Fourier transform and

$$S_{xy}(\omega) = X(\omega)Y^*(\omega)$$

The quantities $X(\omega)$ and $Y(\omega)$ are the Fourier transforms of $x(t)$ and $y(t)$, respectively, and the asterisk denotes the complex conjugate. To convert $R_{xy}(\tau)$ to its proper units requires that we multiply $S_{xy}(\omega)$ by $\Delta t = T/N$.

We shall illustrate these relationships with two examples.

Example 5.4 Fourier transform of a sine wave

Let

$$g(t) = A_o \sin(2\pi f_o t) \qquad 0 \le t \le T = 2^K / f_o \quad K = 0,1,2,...$$

Thus,

$$\Delta t < 1/(2f_o) \quad \text{or} \quad m - K > 1$$

since

$$f_h = f_o = 2^K / T$$

and

$$\Delta t = 2^{-m}T$$

We assume that $g(t)$ is weighted by the Hamming function, which is given by

$$w(t) = 0.54 - 0.46\cos(2\pi t/T) \qquad 0 \le t \le T$$
$$= 0 \qquad \text{otherwise}$$

The script to compute and plot the corrected weighted signal $g_c(t)$ and the amplitude spectrum A_n and display the average power in the signal, which is $P_{avg} = A_o^2/2$, is as follows. We assume that $A_o = 2.5$, $f_o = 10$ Hz, $K = 5$, and $m = 10$ ($N = 1024$).

```
k = 5; m = 10; fo = 10; Ao = 2.5;
N = 2^m; T = 2^k/fo;
ts = (0:N-1)*T/N;
df = (0:N/2-1)/T;
whamm = 0.54-0.46*cos(2*pi*ts/T);
SampledSignal = Ao*sin(2*pi*fo*ts);
k1 = sum(whamm.*SampledSignal)/sum(whamm);
k2 = sqrt(N/sum(whamm.^2));
CorrectedSignal = whamm.*(SampledSignal-k1)*k2;
figure(1)
plot(ts,CorrectedSignal)
figure(2)
An = abs(fft(CorrectedSignal,N))/N;
plot(df,2*An(1:N/2))
disp(['Average power = ' num2str(sum(An.^2))])
```

Execution of the script results in Figures 5.10 and 5.11 and the following message being displayed to the MATLAB command window.

Average power = 3.125

The MATLAB function `figure` is used to provide two separate figure windows. See Section 6.1. Notice that the amplitude of the sine wave does not equal 2.5. This value will be obtained, however, when the weighting function is removed.

Example 5.5 Cross correlation of two pulses

We now determine the cross-correlation function for the two pulses shown in Figure 5.12, which are expressed as

$$x(t) = A_x\left[u(t) - u(t - T_o)\right] \qquad t \ge 0$$
$$y(t) = A_y\left[u(t - T_1) - u(t - T_1 - T_2)\right] \qquad t \ge 0$$

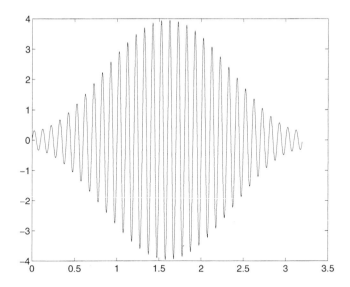

FIGURE 5.10
Sine wave modified by the Hamming weighting function.

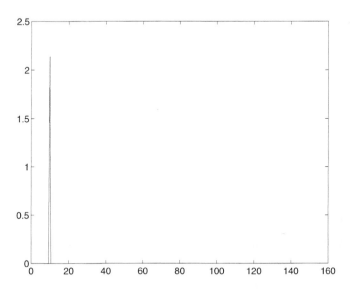

FIGURE 5.11
Amplitude spectrum of a sine wave using a Hamming weighting function.

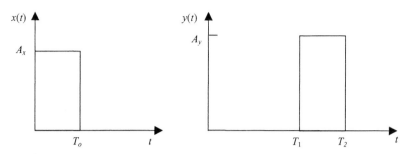

FIGURE 5.12
Two pulses.

where $u(t)$ is the unit step function. We assume that $A_x = A_y = 1$, $T_o = 0.01$ s, $T_1 = 2T_o$, $T_2 = T_1 + T_o$, $T = T_2 + T_o$ and $N = 2^{10}$. The script is

```
To = 0.01; T1 = 2*To; T2 = T1+To; Tend = T2+To;
N = 2^10; deltaT = Tend/N; ampl = 1;
t = linspace(0,Tend,N);
PulseCrossCorr = inline('ampl*((t-Ts>=0)-(t-Te>0))','t','Ts','Te','ampl');
x = PulseCrossCorr(t,0,To,ampl);
y = PulseCrossCorr(t,T1,T2,ampl);
X = fft(x,N);
Y = conj(fft(y,N));
Rxy = ifft(X.*Y*deltaT,N);
plot(t,real(Rxy))
```

Execution of the script results in Figure 5.13. The function `real` removes residual imaginary parts due to numerical round-off errors.

EXERCISES

Section 5.5.1

5.1 The principal stresses can be determined from the roots of the polynomial[9]

$$\sigma^3 - C_2\sigma^2 - C_1\sigma - C_0 = 0$$

where

$$C_2 = \sigma_x + \sigma_y + \sigma_z$$
$$C_1 = \tau_{xy}^2 + \tau_{yz}^2 + \tau_{zx}^2 - \sigma_x\sigma_y - \sigma_y\sigma_z - \sigma_z\sigma_x$$

---

[9] See, for example, J. E. Shigley and C. R. Mischke, *Mechanical Engineering Design*, 5th ed., McGraw-Hill, New York, 1989.

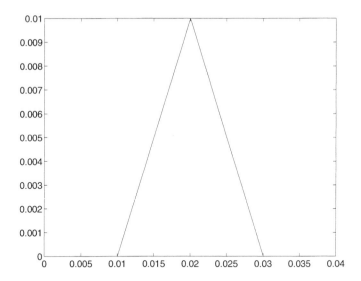

FIGURE 5.13
Cross-correlation function of two pulses of equal duration.

$$C_0 = \sigma_x \sigma_y \sigma_z + 2\tau_{xy}\tau_{yz}\tau_{zx} - \sigma_x \tau_{yz}^2 - \sigma_y \tau_{zx}^2 - \sigma_z \tau_{xy}^2$$

and σ_x, σ_y, σ_z, are the applied normal stresses and τ_{xy}, τ_{yz}, τ_{zx}, are the applied shear stresses. If the roots of the equation are σ_1, σ_2, and σ_3 (the three principal stresses), where $\sigma_1 > \sigma_2 > \sigma_3$, then the principal shear stresses are

$$\tau_{12} = (\sigma_1 - \sigma_2)/2 \qquad \tau_{23} = (\sigma_2 - \sigma_3)/2 \qquad \tau_{13} = (\sigma_1 - \sigma_3)/2$$

where $\tau_{max} = \tau_{13}$.

Determine the principal stresses and corresponding principal shear stresses when

$\sigma_x = 100$	$\tau_{xy} = -40$
$\sigma_y = -60$	$\tau_{yz} = 50$
$\sigma_z = 80$	$\tau_{zx} = 70$

The root finding function does not order the roots. To accomplish this use `sort` in the manner discussed at the end of Example 2.2 in Section 2.5.4. [Answer: $\sigma_1 = 160.7444$, $\sigma_2 = 54.8980$, $\sigma_3 = -95.6424$, $\tau_{12} = 52.9232$, $\tau_{23} = 75.2702$, and $\tau_{13} = 128.1934$.]

5.2 Unless indicated otherwise, find the lowest five positive roots of the following equations using `fzero`. Use the form of `fzero` that requires the function to explore only a specified region [x_0 x_1]. Plot each function prior to determining the roots. Use `axis` to increase the graph's resolution.

a) The following equation arises in the vibration of strings:[10]

---

[10] E. B. Magrab, *Vibration of Elastic Structural Members*, Sijthoff & Noordhoff, The Netherlands, 1979, p. 58.

$$\tan x = x$$

b) The following equation arises in the heat flow in slabs.[11] Obtain the roots for the two separate cases: $p = 0.1$ and 1.

$$2\cot x = \frac{x}{p} - \frac{p}{x}$$

c) The following equation[12] arises in the vibrations of annular membranes. Assume that $b = 2$.

$$J_0(x)Y_0(xb) - J_0(xb)Y_0(x) = 0$$

Use `besselj` and `bessely`, respectively, for $J_0(x)$ and $Y_0(x)$, which are the Bessel functions of the first and second kind, respectively, of order 0.

d) The following equation[13] arises in the vibrations of a cantilever beam carrying a concentrated mass M_0 at its free end. Obtain the roots for the three separate cases: $M_0/m_0 = 0$, 0.2, and 1.

$$(M_0/m_0)\Omega[\cos(\Omega)\sinh(\Omega) - \sin(\Omega)\cosh(\Omega)] + \cos(\Omega)\cosh(\Omega) + 1 = 0$$

e) The following equation[14] arises in the vibrations of a beam clamped at one end and simply supported at its other end.

$$\tanh(\Omega) - \tan(\Omega) = 0$$

f) The following equation[15] arises in the vibrations of a solid circular plate clamped on its outer boundary.

$$J_m(\Omega)I_{m+1}(\Omega) + I_m(\Omega)J_{m+1}(\Omega) = 0$$

where $J_m(x)$ is the Bessel function of the first kind of order m and $I_m(x)$ is the modified Bessel function of the first kind of order m. Use `besselj` and `besseli`, respectively, for $J_m(x)$ and $I_m(x)$. Find the lowest three roots for $m = 0$, 1, and 2. Save the script for Exercise 7.4.

g) The following equation[16] arises in the determination of the in-plane symmetric modes of a suspended cable. Find the lowest root when $\lambda^2 = 2\pi^2$, $4\pi^2$, and $8\pi^2$. This solution must be obtained interactively by graphing the equation first. Use the `axis` function to limit the vertical axis from -10 to 20. See Section 6.2.

$$\tan \Omega = \Omega - \frac{4\Omega^3}{\lambda^2}$$

h) In the analysis of nonuniform flow in an open channel of trapezoidal cross section, the ratio of the depth of the fluid to the height of the energy gradient x is determined from[17]

$$(1 + c_0 x)^2 (x^2 - x^3) = c_1$$

---

[11] M. N. Ozisik, *Heat Conduction*, 2nd ed., John Wiley & Sons, New York, 1993, p. 47.
[12] E. B. Magrab, *ibid.*, p. 83.
[13] E. B. Magrab, *ibid.*, p. 130.
[14] E. B. Magrab, *ibid.*, p. 130.
[15] E. B. Magrab, *ibid.*, p. 252.
[16] M. Irvine, *Cable Structures*, Dover Publications, Inc., New York, 1981, p. 95.
[17] H. W. King, *Handbook of Hydraulics*, 4th ed., McGraw-Hill, New York, 1954, p. 8-1.

where $0 \le c_0 \le 11$ and $0.005 \le c_1 \le 12.3$ are functions of the geometry of the channel and the flow rate. However, not all combinations of c_0 and c_1 are appropriate. Find the pairs of real values of x between 0 and 1 that satisfy this equation for: (1) $c_0 = 0.4$ and $c_1 = 0.2$; and (2) $c_0 = 7.0$ and $c_1 = 4.0$. Use two methods: fzero and roots. To use roots the equation is rewritten as

$$-c_0^2 x^5 + \left(c_0^2 - 2c_0\right)x^4 + \left(2c_0 - 1\right)x^3 + x^2 - c_1 = 0$$

i) The wave angle β $(0 < \beta \le \pi/2)$ of a disturbance wave on top of a fluid in an open channel in which the velocity of the fluid is greater than the wave speed in the fluid is determined from[18]

$$2N_F^2 \sin^2(\beta)\tan^2(\beta - \theta) = \tan(\beta)\tan(\beta - \theta) + \tan^2(\beta) \qquad \beta > \theta$$

where θ is the wall deflection angle and $1 \le N_F \le 12$ is the Froude number. Determine the values of β, in degrees, in the range $\theta < \beta \le 90°$ when $\theta = 35°$ and $N_F = 5$. Plot the function first.

j) The internal rate of return i_{rr} is an accounting metric that represents the percentage interest earned on the unrecovered balance of an investment. It is determined from[19]

$$\sum_{k=0}^{n} F_k \left(1 + i_{rr}\right)^{-k} = 0$$

where n is the number of periods, i_{rr} is the internal rate expressed as a decimal number and F_k is the cash flow in each period: positive cash flow means money is received and negative flow means money is disbursed. Determine i_{rr} when $F_0 = -\$1000$, $F_1 = -\$800$, $F_2 = \$500$, $F_3 = \$500$, $F_4 = \$500$ and $F_5 = \$1,200$.

k) If one invests an amount P and receives an amount A each period from this investment, then the number of periods n required for pay back of P at an interest rate i per period (expressed as a decimal number) is determined from[20]

$$\frac{A}{P} = \frac{i(1+i)^n}{(1+i)^n - 1}$$

If $i = 12\%$ per year and $A/P = 0.16$, then determine n, the number of years for pay back.

l) An estimate of a parameter β appearing in the Weibull probability density function (see Section 14.2.2) requires the solution of the following equation:[21]

$$\beta = \left[\frac{\displaystyle\sum_{i=1}^{n} x_i^\beta \ln(x_i)}{\displaystyle\sum_{i=1}^{n} x_i^\beta} - \frac{1}{n}\sum_{i=1}^{n} \ln(x_i)\right]^{-1}$$

---

[18] N. H. C. Hwang and C. E. Hita, *Fundamentals of Hydraulic Engineering Systems*, 2nd ed., Prentice Hall, Englewood Cliffs, NJ, 1987, p. 222.
[19] G. J. Theusen and W. J. Fabrycky, *Engineering Economy*, 8th ed., Prentice-Hall, Englewood Cliffs, NJ, 1993, p. 176,.
[20] G. J. Theusen and W. J. Fabrycky, *ibid.*, p. 188.
[21] D. C. Montgomery and G. C. Runger, *Applied Statistics and Probability for Engineers*, John Wiley & Sons, New York, 1994, p. 299.

where x_i are a random sample of size n. If

$$x = [72\ 82\ 97\ 103\ 113\ 117\ 126\ 127\ 127\ 139\ 154\ 159\ 199\ 207]$$

then determine the value of β.

m) In determining the surface contact shear stress between a sphere and a plane, which is a model of the effects of a bearing against a surface, the value of a ratio x is obtained from[22]

$$x \ln\left(\sqrt{x^2 - 1} + x\right) - \sqrt{x^2 - 1} - Cx = 0$$

where $x > 1$ and $C < 1$. For $C = 0.5$ determine x.

5.3 Find the three real roots of[23]

$$x^4 = 2^x$$

[Hint: First plot the function over the following two different regions: $-1 \le x \le 2$ and $2 \le x \le 17$.]

5.4 The computational formula for the generalized equation for the compressibility factor Z of a gas is given by[24]

$$Z(r,\tau) = 1 + r \sum_{i=1}^{6} A_i \tau^{i-1} + r^2 \sum_{i=7}^{10} A_i \tau^{i-7} + r^3 \sum_{i=11}^{13} A_i \tau^{i-11} + r^4 A_{14}\tau + r^5\left(A_{15}\tau^2 + A_{16}\tau^3\right) + r^6 A_{17}\tau^2$$

$$+ r^7\left(A_{18}\tau + A_{19}\tau^3\right) + r^8 A_{20}\tau^3 + r^2 e^{-0.0588r^2}\left[A_{21}\tau^3 + A_{22}\tau^4 + r^2\left(A_{23}\tau^3 + A_{24}\tau^5\right)\right.$$

$$+ r^4\left(A_{25}\tau^3 + A_{26}\tau^4\right) + r^6\left(A_{27}\tau^3 + A_{28}\tau^5\right) + r^8\left(A_{29}\tau^3 + A_{30}\tau^4\right)$$

$$\left. + r^{10}\left(A_{31}\tau^3 + A_{32}\tau^4 + A_{33}\tau^5\right)\right]$$

where $\tau = T_c/T$ $(0.4 \le \tau \le 1)$, $r = RT_c/P_cv$, R is the gas constant in (MPa-m^3)/(kg-K), T is the temperature in K, P is the pressure in MPa, v is the volume in m^3/kg, T_c and P_c are the critical temperature and pressure, respectively, and the values of the 33 constants are given in Table 5.2.

(a) Create a function to determine $Z(r,\tau)$. Check your function, using `format long e`, with the following test values:

(i) $Z(1,1) = 0.70242396927$

(ii) $Z(1/0.3,1) = 0.29999999980$

(iii) $Z(2.5,0.5) = 0.99221853928$

Save this function and those created to satisfy (b) and (c) below for use in Exercise 6.12.

(b) The above quantity is used in the formula

$$Z(r,\tau) = \frac{p\tau}{r} = \frac{Pv}{RT} \tag{a}$$

---

[22] W. Changsen, *Analysis of Rolling Element Bearings*, Mechanical Engineering Publishers, London, 1991, p. 80.
[23] Problem suggested by Prof. Jeffery M. Cooper, Department of Mathematics, University of Maryland, College Park, MD.
[24] W. C. Reynolds, "Thermodynamic Properties in SI," Department of Mechanical Engineering, Stanford University, Stanford, CA, 1979.

TABLE 5.2
Constants in Generalized Formula for Z

j	A_j	j	A_j	j	A_j
1	0.062432384	12	−0.000727155024313	23	−0.0845194493813
2	0.12721477	13	−0.00452454652610	24	−0.00340931311928
3	−0.93633233	14	0.00130468724100	25	−0.00195127049901
4	0.70184411	15	−0.000222165128409	26	$4.93899910978 \times 10^{-5}$
5	−0.35160896	16	−0.00198140535656	27	$-4.93264612930 \times 10^{-5}$
6	0.056450032	17	$5.97573972921 \times 10^{-5}$	28	$8.85666572382 \times 10^{-7}$
7	0.0299561469907	18	$-3.64135349702 \times 10^{-6}$	29	$5.34788029553 \times 10^{-8}$
8	−0.0318174367647	19	$8.41364845386 \times 10^{-6}$	30	$-5.93420559192 \times 10^{-8}$
9	−0.0168211055517	20	$-9.82868858822 \times 10^{-9}$	31	$-9.06813326929 \times 10^{-9}$
10	1.60204060081	21	−1.57683056810	32	$1.61822407265 \times 10^{-9}$
11	−0.00109996740746	22	0.0400728988908	33	$-3.32044793915 \times 10^{-10}$

where $p = P/P_c$ ($1 \leq p \leq 6$). Determine the value of r and $Z(r,\tau)$ using Eq. (a) for: (i) $p = 0.6$ and $\tau = 1/1.05$; and (ii) $p = 2.18$ and $\tau = 1/1.2$. [Answer: (i) $Z = 0.8013$ at $r = 0.7131$; (ii) $Z = 0.5412$ at $r = 3.3567$.]

(c) Use Eq. (a) to determine the value τ and $Z(r,\tau)$ when: (i) $p = 0.6$ and $r = 1/1.4$; and (ii) $p = 2.18$ and $r = 1/0.6$. [Answer: (i) $Z = 0.8007$ at $\tau = 0.9532$; (ii) $Z = 0.8508$ at $\tau = 0.6505$.]

5.5 The pressure drop of a fluid flowing in a pipe is a function of the pipe's coefficient of friction λ, which can be estimated from the Colebrook formula[25]

$$\lambda = \left[-2\log_{10}\left(\frac{2.51}{R_e \sqrt{\lambda}} + \frac{0.27}{d/k} \right) \right]^{-2} \qquad R_e \geq 4000$$

where R_e is the Reynolds number, d is the diameter of the pipe, and k is the surface roughness. For smooth pipes ($k \cong 0$ or $d/k > 100,000$)

$$\lambda = \left[-2\log_{10}\left(\frac{R_e \sqrt{\lambda}}{2.51} \right) \right]^{-2} \qquad R_e \geq 4000$$

For fully developed turbulent flow, the coefficient of friction is given by

$$\lambda = \left[2\log_{10}\left(3.7 \frac{d}{k} \right) \right]^{-2}$$

---

[25] N. H. C. Hwang and C. E. Hita, *ibid.*, p. 68.

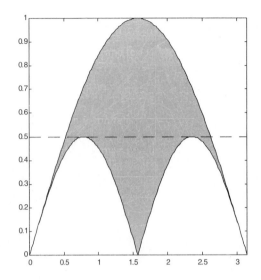

FIGURE 5.14
Figure for Exercise 5.6.

which is independent of R_e. It is a special case of the general Colebrook formula, and has utility in that it can be used to obtain a starting guess in iterative-type problems such as that described in Section 11.2.3.

If the values of λ range from 0.008 to 0.08, then find the value of λ when $R_e = 10^5$ and (1) $d/k = 200$ and (2) $k = 0$. Save the function and script for use in Exercise 6.11. [Answer: (1) $\lambda = 0.0313$ and (2) $\lambda = 0.0180$.]

Section 5.5.2

5.6 Find the area between the two sine curves shown in Figure 5.14 using `quad8` and `trapz`.

5.7 In determining the load distribution in axial thrust bearings under an eccentric load the following integral must be evaluated[26]

$$I_m(\varepsilon) = \frac{1}{2\pi} \int_{-a}^{a} \left[1 - (1 - \cos(x))/2\varepsilon\right]^c \cos(mx) dx$$

where $\varepsilon > 0$, $m = 0$ or 1,

$$a = \cos^{-1}(1 - 2\varepsilon)$$

and $c = 1.5$ for ball bearings and $c = 1.1$ for roller bearings. Determine the value of $I_1(0.6)$ for a ball bearing. [Answer: $I_1(0.6) = 0.2416$.]

---

[26] W. Changsen, *ibid.*, p. 92.

5.8 Given

$$\int_0^\infty E_{\lambda,b}(\lambda,T)d\lambda = \sigma T^4$$

where

$$E_{\lambda,b}(\lambda,T) = \frac{C_1}{\lambda^5\left[\exp\left(C_2/\lambda T\right)-1\right]}$$

and λ is the wavelength in μm, T is the temperature in Kelvin, $C_1 = 3.742\times10^8$ W·μm^4/m^2, $C_2 = 1.439\times10^4$ μm·K, and $\sigma = 5.667\times10^{-8}$ W/m^2·K^4 is the Stephan-Boltzmann constant. Perform this integration numerically for $T = 300$, 400, and 500 K and determine the percentage error of the approximate results compared to the exact value. A note of caution: Both integration limits give considerable difficulty numerically. Therefore, approximate the integral using a lower limit of 1 μm and an upper limit of 150 μm. These limits were determined from the graph of $E_{\lambda,b}$ at the three temperatures and from the values of the integration limits that could be used without causing warning messages from quad8. [Answer: error$_{300}$ = -0.145%, error$_{400}$ = -0.061%, error$_{500}$ = -0.030%.] (See also Exercise 12.6.)

Section 5.5.3

5.9 The relationship between the lead angle of a worm gear λ, the ratio $\beta = N_1/N_2$, where N_1 is the number of teeth on the worm gear and N_2 is the number of teeth on the driven gear, the center distance C between shafts, and the normal diametral pitch P_{dn} is[27]

$$K = \frac{2P_{dn}C}{N_2} = \frac{\beta}{\sin\lambda} + \frac{1}{\cos\lambda}$$

Over the range of practical interest $1 \le K \le 2$, $1° \le \lambda \le 40°$, and $0.02 \le \beta \le 0.30$. For certain combinations of values λ can have one value, two values, or no value.

a) Find the value of λ that makes K a minimum when $\beta = 0.02, 0.05, 0.08, 0.11, 0.15, 0.18, 0.23$, and 0.30. Save the script for use in Exercise 6.8.

b) For $K = 1.5$ and $\beta = 0.16$ find the value(s) of λ.

5.10 Consider Eq. (5.1) and its numerical solution to a step input. Determine the value of ξ that makes the following quantity a minimum:

$$f(\xi) = \sum_{n=1}^{N}\left(y(t_n)-1\right)^2$$

Let ξ range from 0.05 to 1.5 in increments of 0.05. It should be realized that fminbnd cannot be used because $f(\xi)$ is an array of numerical values; use min to bring back the index of ξ and the value of ξ at that index.

5.11 In Exercise 1.7 the mass flow rate of a gas escaping from a tank at pressure p_0 and under reversible adiabatic conditions was proportional to

---

[27] M. F. Spotts and T. E. Shoup, *Design of Machine Elements*, Prentice Hall, Upper Saddle River, NJ, 1998, p. 613.

$$\psi = \sqrt{\frac{k}{k-1}} \sqrt{\left(\frac{p_e}{p_0}\right)^{2/k} - \left(\frac{p_e}{p_0}\right)^{(k+1)/k}}$$

where p_e is the pressure exterior to the tank's exit and k is the adiabatic reversible gas constant. The maximum value occurs at

$$\frac{p_e}{p_0} = \left(\frac{2}{k+1}\right)^{\frac{k}{k-1}}$$

Verify this maximum value numerically for $k = 1.4$ using `fminbnd` and using `min` with 200 equally spaced values for $0 \le p_e/p_0 \le 1$.

Section 5.5.4

5.12 Consider the motion of a projectile that leaves a point $(0,0)$ with an initial velocity v_0 and at an angle with the horizontal of α. If the projectile lands at a location (x_e, y_e) and is subjected to a drag during flight that is proportional to the square of its velocity, then the four first-order equations governing its flight are[28]

$$\frac{dv_x}{dx} = -c_d v \qquad \frac{dv_y}{dx} = \frac{-(g + c_d v v_y)}{v_x} \qquad \frac{dy}{dx} = \frac{v_y}{v_x} \qquad \frac{dt}{dx} = \frac{1}{v_x}$$

where y is the vertical height of the projectile, x is the horizontal distance of travel; t is time; v_x and v_y are the horizontal and vertical components of the velocity v, respectively; c_d is the drag coefficient; g is the gravity constant; and

$$v = \sqrt{v_x^2 + v_y^2}$$

These equations are valid only when v_0 is large enough so that v_x is greater than zero when it reaches x_e. The test for this condition can be stated as, say, $|v_x| > v_0 \times 10^{-6}$. If this condition is not satisfied, then the program's execution must be terminated. Use `error` to cause the termination. This check is placed in the beginning of the function that is called by `ode45`. The initial conditions are

$$v_{0x} = v_0 \cos(\alpha) \qquad v_{0y} = v_0 \sin(\alpha) \qquad y = 0 \qquad t = 0$$

From the order in which the equations are written let $y_1(x) = v_x$, $y_2(x) = v_y$, $y_3(x) = y$, and $y_4(x) = t$.

(a) Plot the projectile path for $v_0 = 600$ fps, $c_d = 0.002$, and $\alpha = 45°$ until the projectile reaches $y_e = 0$— that is, plot only those points for which $y_e > 0$. Let $x_{final} = 1000$ ft in `ode45`.

(b) What is the value of the maximum elevation of the projectile and at what distance does this occur. Use `fminbnd` and `spline` to obtain these values. [Answer: $y_{max} = 474.8285$ ft at $x = 648.1205$ ft.]

(c) What is the value of x_e when $y_e = 0$ and the time of travel to reach this point. Use `interp1` to determine these values. [Answer: $x_e = 975.3240$ and the time of travel is 10.6246 s.]

5.13 A bungee jumper is preparing to make a high altitude jump from a hot-air balloon using a length L of bungee line. In order to do so safely the peak acceleration, velocity, and total drop distance must be

---

[28] H. B. Wilson and L. H. Turcotte, *Advanced Mathematics and Mechanics Applications Using MATLAB*, 2nd ed., CRC Press, Boca Raton, FL, 1997, p. 294.

predicted so that the arresting force is not to great and the balloon will be high enough so that the jumper doesn't hit the ground. Taking into account the aerodynamic drag forces the governing equation is[29]

$$\frac{d^2x}{dt^2} + c_o \text{signum}(dx/dt)\left(\frac{dx}{dt}\right)^2 + \frac{k}{m_J}(x-L)u(x-L) = g$$

where $g = 9.8$ m/s^2 is the acceleration of gravity, c_d is proportional to the drag coefficient and has the units of m^{-1}, k is the spring constant of the bungee cord in N/m, m_J is the mass of the jumper, and $u(z)$ is the unit step function—that is, $u(z) = 0$ when $z \leq 0$ and $u(z) = 1$ when $z > 0$. The programming is greatly simplified if the logical operator described in Section 4.1 is used to describe $u(t)$.

If $L = 150$ m, $m_J = 70$ kg, $k = 10$ N/m, $c_o = 0.00324$ m^{-1}, and the initial conditions are zero, then show that:

(1) The maximum value of x is -308.47 m, which occurs at 11.47 s

(2) The jumper will reach 150 m in 5.988 s traveling at a velocity of -43.48 m/s

(3) The maximum acceleration will be -12.82 m/s^2 (-1.308 g) at 11.18 s

Also plot the displacement, velocity, and acceleration. The acceleration can be obtained by approximating the derivative of the velocity using `diff`. The numerical results stated above were obtained using `spline` on the output from `ode45`.

5.14 Consider an inverted pendulum that is composed of a weightless rigid rod of length L to which a mass m and a linear spring of spring constant k are attached at its free end. The pendulum is initially vertical. The unstretched length of the spring is L. The rotation of the pendulum's pivot has a damping c, and the pendulum is driven by a moment $M(t)$. The governing equation describing the angular motion is[30]

$$\frac{d^2\theta}{d\tau^2} + \alpha\frac{d\theta}{d\tau} - \sin\theta + \beta\left(1 - \frac{1}{\sqrt{5-4\cos\theta}}\right)\sin\theta = P(t)$$

where

$$\beta = \frac{2kL}{mg} \qquad P = \frac{M}{mgL} \qquad \tau = t\sqrt{\frac{g}{L}} \qquad \alpha = (c/m)\sqrt{L/g}$$

and t is time.

If $M = 0$, $\beta = 10$, $\alpha = 0.1$, $\theta(0) = \pi/4$, and $d\theta(0)/d\tau = 0$, then plot the rotation θ as a function of τ for 1,000 equally spaced values of τ from $0 \leq \tau \leq 50$, and, in a separate figure, plot $\theta(\tau)$ versus $d\theta(\tau)/d\tau$.

5.15 Consider a uniform inextensible cable of length L_o and weight per unit length w that hangs between two fixed points $x = 0$ and $x = L$ such that $L < L_o$. If the cable has no flexural rigidity and can only support tensile forces T, then the governing equation of the non dimensional deflection $z(\eta)$ of the cable is[31]

---

[29] See, for example, D. M. Etter, *Engineering Problem Solving with MATLAB*, Prentice Hall, Upper Saddle River, NJ, 1997, pp. 220–221.
[30] H. B. Wilson and L. H. Turcotte, *ibid.*, p. 279.
[31] M. Irvine, *ibid.*, p. 4.

$$\frac{d^2z}{d\eta^2} = \beta\sqrt{1+\left(\frac{dz}{d\eta}\right)^2}$$

where $\eta = x/L$, $\beta = wL/H$, H is the horizontal component of T and a negative z indicates a downward deflection. The corresponding length L_o of the cable is equal to

$$L_o = L\int_0^1\sqrt{1+\left(\frac{dz}{d\eta}\right)^2}\,d\eta$$

from which one can determine β and, hence, H when w, L and L_o are given. The boundary conditions are

$$z(0) = 0 \qquad z(1) = 0$$

Determine the value of β and the slope $dz(0)/d\eta$ when $L_o/L = 1.2$. The solution technique requires nested iteration loops: the innermost loop determines the value of the slope $dz(0)/d\eta$ for which $z(1) = 0$, and the outermost one determines the value of β that satisfies the integral. The nesting is required because the determination of the slope $dz(0)/d\eta$ requires the value of β. The integration must be performed with `trapz`. [Answer: $\beta = 2.1284$, $dz(0)/d\eta = -1.2768$.]

5.16 The oscillations of the height Z of the separation between the fluid levels in two rectangular prismatic reservoirs connected by a long pipeline can be determined from[32]

$$\frac{d^2Z}{dt^2} + \text{signum}(dZ/dt)p\left(\frac{dZ}{dt}\right)^2 + qZ = 0$$

If $p = 0.375$ m^{-1}, $q = 7.4\times10^{-4}$ s^{-2} and the initial conditions are $Z(0) = Z_n$ m and $dZ(0)/dt = 0$ m/s, then determine the value of the *first* occurrence of t_n, $n = 1$, 2, for which $Z(t_n) = 0$ when $Z_1 = 10$ m and $Z_2 = 50$ m. Use `interp1` to determine t_n. The quantity signum is determined with `sign`. Suggestion: Plot the results for one value of Z_n and then from the characteristics of the curve use an appropriate combination of `min` and `find` to select the middle index of the small range of values over which `interp1` should perform the interpolation. [Answers: $t_1 = 114.2692$ s and $t_2 = 276.1428$ s.]

Section 5.5.5

5.17 (a) Use `fsolve` to find the values of θ in degrees and k that satisfy the following equations when $a = 1$ and $b = 3$.

$$b = k(1-\cos\theta)$$
$$a = k(\theta - \sin\theta)$$

(b) The two equations in (a) can be combined into the following one equation:

$$b(\theta - \sin\theta) - a(1-\cos\theta) = 0$$

Use `fzero` to determine the value of θ when $a = 1$ and $b = 3$, and then use one of the equations in (a) to determine k. [Answers: k = 6.9189 and $\theta = 55.4999°$.]

---

[32] D. N. Roy, *Applied Fluid Mechanics*, Ellis Horwood Limited, Chichester, England, 1988, pp. 290–293.

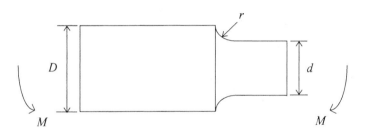

FIGURE 5.15
Geometry and loading for a stress concentration factor.

5.18 (a) Use `fsolve` to determine from the following equations the values of Q, T_A, and T_B when $\sigma = 5.667 \times 10^{-8}$, $T_1 = 373$ K, and $T_2 = 293$ K.

$$T_1^4 - T_A^4 = Q/\sigma$$
$$T_A^4 - T_B^4 = Q/\sigma$$
$$T_B^4 - T_2^4 = Q/\sigma$$

(b) The equations in (a) can also be written as

$$\begin{bmatrix} 1 & 0 & 1/\sigma \\ 1 & -1 & -1/\sigma \\ 0 & 1 & -1/\sigma \end{bmatrix} \begin{Bmatrix} x \\ y \\ Q \end{Bmatrix} = \begin{Bmatrix} T_1^4 \\ 0 \\ T_2^4 \end{Bmatrix}$$

where $x = T_A^4$ and $y = T_B^4$. Determine the values of Q, T_A, and T_B from this system of equations using left division. [Answer: $T_A = 352.052$, $T_B = 326.5116$ and $Q = 226.4312$.]

Section 5.6.1

5.19 The stress concentration factor for a stepped circular shaft shown in Figure 5.15 is approximated by[33]

$$K_t = c \left(\frac{D-d}{2d} \right)^{-a}$$

where c and a are given in Table 5.3. Obtain two expressions, one for c and the other for a, as a function of D/d two ways: (1) with a fifth-order polynomial and (2) with a spline. For both methods, compare the values of K_t obtained with the two sets of fitted values to those obtained with the original values given in Table 5.3. Which is the better method to use in this case.

Section 5.6.4

5.20 Consider the following signal

---

[33] R. L. Norton, *Machine Design, An Integrated Approach*, Prentice Hall, Upper Saddle River, NJ, 1996, p. 1,005ff.

TABLE 5.3
Stress Concentration Factor Constants

D/d	c	a
6.00	0.88	0.33
3.00	0.89	0.31
2.00	0.91	0.29
1.50	0.94	0.26
1.20	0.97	0.22
1.10	0.95	0.24
1.07	0.98	0.21
1.05	0.98	0.20
1.03	0.98	0.18
1.01	0.92	0.17

TABLE 5.4
Constants Defining the Signal in Exercise 5.20

n	$\omega_n/2\pi$	ζ_n	H_n
1	5	0.1	1
2	9	0.04	1.3
3	9.4	0.04	1.3
4	20	0.03	1.8

$$f(t) = \sum_{n=1}^{4} H_n e^{-\zeta_n \omega_n t} \sin\left(\sqrt{1-\zeta_n^2}\,\omega_n t\right) \quad 0 \le t \le T$$

where the values of the constants are given in Table 5.4. For $N = 2^{10}$ and $\Delta t = 2\pi/(4\omega_4)$:

(a) Plot the amplitude spectrum for this signal with and without Hamming. The results should look like those shown in Figure 5.16.

(b) Determine the frequencies at which the peaks occur. [Hint: Use several applications of find and diff.] [Answers: No Hamming: [4.84375 9.14063 20.0781] Hz; with Hamming: [4.92188 9.0625 9.45313 20.0781] Hz.]

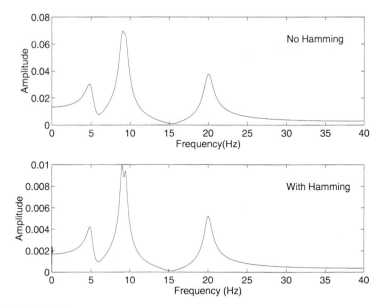

FIGURE 5.16
Results from the solution to Exercise 5.20(a).

C H A P T E R   6

2D GRAPHICS

Edward B. Magrab

The implementation of a wide selection of two-dimensional plotting capabilities is presented.

6.1 INTRODUCTION

MATLAB provides a wide selection of very flexible and easy-to-implement two- and three-dimensional plotting capabilities. The plotting functions can be grouped into three categories: graphics management, curve and surface generation, and annotation and graph characteristics. Although there are quite a few plotting functions, for the most part their syntax is similar and they can be annotated with the same set of functions. The functions whose usage we shall illustrate in this and the next chapter are:

Management	Generation	Annotation and Characteristics
`figure`	**2-D**	`xlabel`
`subplot`	`plot`	`ylabel`
`zoom`	`polar`	`zlabel` (3D only)
`hold`	`fill`	`text`
`view` (3D only)	`plotyy`	`text3` (3D only)
`rotate3d` (3D only)	**3-D**	`title`
	`plot3`	`legend` (2D only)
	`surf, surfc`	`box`
	`mesh, meshz`	`set`
	`contour, contour3,`	`grid`
	`    contourf`	`axis, axis equal,`
	`waterfall`	`    axis off`
	`cylinder`	`colorbar` (3D only)
		`clabel`
		`colormap` (3D only)

Other specialized plotting functions, such as `bar` and `hist`, are employed in later chapters.

When generating graphed entities one should expend the effort so that each figure (1) meets the solution's objective by illustrating what is important and (2) exhibits clarity and specificity by being fully annotated with the axes labeled, the figure titled, curves identified (if more than one), and important numerical values displayed. However, any devices that are used to enhance the figure, such as color, line type, symbols, and text should do so without being distracting.

A typical set of graph-creating expressions consists of management functions, followed by one or more graph-generation functions, and followed in turn by annotation functions, which may be followed by additional management functions. However, except for the management functions, the order of these functions is, in most applications, arbitrary. Also, the employment of the annotation and graph characteristic functions is optional. MATLAB scales the axes and labels the axes' magnitudes, even if more than one set of data is plotted. Thus, one can always obtain a partially annotated graph, provided that the function's syntax has been used correctly.

A graph is created in a figure window, which is a window created by MATLAB at execution time, when any one of its graph management, generation, or annotation and characteristics functions is invoked. When a program, either a script or function, uses more than one graph-generation function MATLAB creates a new figure window. However, any previously created window is removed prior to creating the new figure window. To retain each new graph in its own figure window, one must use

`figure(n)`

where *n* is an integer. If the argument of `window` is omitted, then MATLAB gives it the next integer value.

One can also place several independently created graphs in one figure window with

```
subplot(i,j,k)
```

The first two arguments divide the window into sectors (rows and columns), and the third indicates in which sector a graph is to be placed. A value of 1 for this argument indicates the upper left corner, and the sum of the number of rows and columns indicates the lower right corner. As the numbers increase, they indicate the sectors from left to right, starting at the top row. Any annotation and management functions that appear in the program after a `figure`/`subplot` expression apply only to that sector indicated by the third argument of `subplot`. Within each sector, any compatible set of the 2D or 3D graph generation functions can be used. Refer to Figure 6.1 to see several examples of how `figure` and `subplot` are used. It is noted that if only one figure window is needed, `figure` can be omitted, even if `subplot` is used.

Since each graph-generation function creates a new figure window,[1] in order to draw more than one curve, surface, or line (or combination of these) on a given graph, one must use

```
hold on
```

which holds the current window (or `subplot` sector) active. However, one must use a compatible set of graph-generation functions, such as `surf` and `plot3` or `plot` and `fill`. All figures that have been created can be copied to the Windows clipboard by selecting *Copy Figure* from the *Edit* pull-down menu within each figure's window. This figure can then be transferred (pasted) to a page in a word processor program and will be in the Windows metafile format.

MATLAB provides the means to convert a figure to a format compatible with many common print devices. For example, if one wants to save the graphics appearing in the active figure window as a level-2 encapsulated postscript file for black-and-white printers with the name *FileName*, then one uses the following expression:

```
print -deps2 'c:\path\FileName.eps'
```

where *path* describes the directory and subdirectory names where the file will reside. For other options, see the Help file for `print`. On the other hand, if one wants to insert a level-2 encapsulated postscript file into an MS Word document such that a "tiff" preview image of the figure is displayed, then one uses the following expression[2]

```
print -deps2 -tiff 'c:\path\FileName.eps'
```

---

[1] The MATLAB window look, management, and file management descriptions relate to a Windows environment. Equivalent procedures are used with other operating systems.
[2] In order to use this file in MS Word, the appropriate encapsulated postscript filters must be installed. These are part of MS Word, but are not always installed when MS Word is installed. In this case run MS Word setup and install the desired filters.

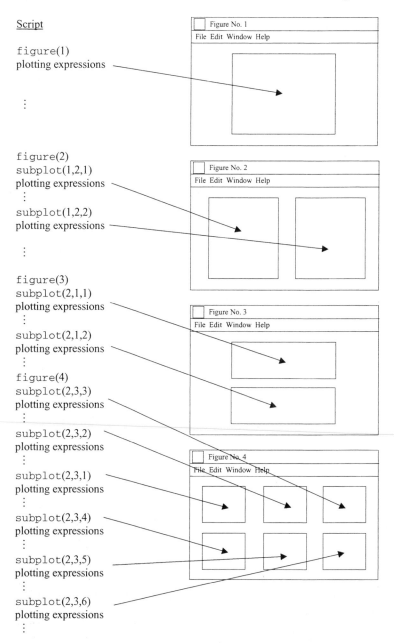

FIGURE 6.1
Examples of the use of various combinations of figure and subplot.

6.2 BASIC 2D PLOTTING COMMANDS

The basic 2D plotting command is

```
plot(u1,v1,c1,u2,v2,c2, ...)
```

where u_j and v_j are the x and y coordinates, respectively, of a point or a series of points. They are either a pair of numbers, vectors of the same length, matrices of the same order, or expressions that, when evaluated, result in one of these three quantities. The quantity c_j is string of characters: one character specifies the line/point color, one character specifies the point type if points are to be plotted, and up to two characters are used to specify the line characteristics. When a series of points are to be plotted, one of the characters of c_j can be, for example, an 's' to plot a square or an asterisk '*' to plot an asterisk. When the points, whether or not they are to be displayed, are to be connected with (straight) lines, the characters of c_j can be, for example, a '-' for a solid line and a '--' for a dashed line. When both the lines and points are to be plotted with the same color, the c_j contains both descriptors. For example, if we were to plot blue dashed lines connecting blue diamonds, c_j would be 'b--d'. The order of the three sets of characters within the single quotes is not important. When both lines and points are to be plotted but the number of points defining the line is different from the number of points that are to be plotted, c_1 contains the symbol for the line type and c_2 contains the symbol for the point type, or *vice versa*. See the Help file for `plot` for a list of the colors and line and point types provided. If c_j is omitted, then the system's default values are used. If more than one curve is drawn, then the line colors change according to the default sequence.

We now describe the statements used to draw points, lines, circles, expressions, families of curves, and curves described by multiple functions.

6.2.1 Points

To place a red asterisk at the location (2,4), the plotting instruction is

```
plot(2,4,'r*')
```

6.2.2 Lines

To draw a straight line that goes from (0,0) to (1,2) using the default line type (solid) and the default color (blue), the plotting instruction is

```
plot([0 1],[0 2])
```

Notice that the first two-element vector [0 1] represents the values of the x coordinates, and the second two-element vector [0 2] represents the values of the y coordinates. Thus, the first element of each vector defines the (x,y) coordinates of one endpoint of the line, and the second elements of these vectors are the coordinates of the other endpoint.

Suppose that we want to draw a set of n unconnected lines whose end points are (x_{1n}, y_{1n}) and (x_{2n}, y_{2n}). To accomplish this we create four vectors:

$$x_j = [x_{j1} \; x_{j2} \; ... \; x_{jn}]$$
$$y_j = [y_{j1} \; y_{j2} \; ... \; y_{jn}] \quad j = 1, 2$$

Then the `plot` instruction is[3]

```
plot([x1;x2],[y1;y2])
```

where [x1;x2] and [y1;y2] are each (2×n) matrices.

To illustrate this expression, let us draw four vertical lines from $y = 0$ to $y = \cos(\pi x/20)$ when $x = 2, 4, 6,$ and 8. The script is

```
x = 2:2:8;
plot([x; x],[zeros(1,length(x));cos(pi*x/20)],'k')
```

since $x_1 = x_2$. The color is specified so that the lines all have the same color, black in this case. The function `zeros` is used to create a vector of 0's of the same length as x. The result is shown in Figure 6.2a. Unfortunately, because of MATLAB's automatic scaling of the axes, the first and last lines are coincident with the box around the figure. Therefore, one has to adjust the axes so that these lines are visible. This adjustment is done with

```
axis([xmin xmax ymin ymax])
```

where x_{min}, x_{max}, y_{min}, and y_{max} are the minimum and maximum values of the x and y axes, respectively. Thus, the revised script is

```
x = 2:2:8;
plot([x; x],[zeros(1,length(x));cos(pi*x/20)],'k')
axis([1 9 0 1])
```

The revised graph is shown in Figure 6.2b.

Obtaining the values of the axis limits and then redefining one or more of them as needed can provide additional flexibility. The limits are obtained from

```
v = axis;
```

in which v is a four-element vector:

$$v(1) = x_{min} \quad v(3) = y_{min}$$
$$v(2) = x_{max} \quad v(4) = y_{max}$$

Thus, to obtain the revised figure, Figure 6.2b, the script could be further revised as follows:

```
x = 2:2:8;
plot([x; x],[zeros(1,length(x));cos(pi*x/20)],'k')
```

---

[3] This `plot` expression is, in some respects, a generalization of the `stem` function, which assumes that $x_1 = x_2$ and that $y_1 = 0$.

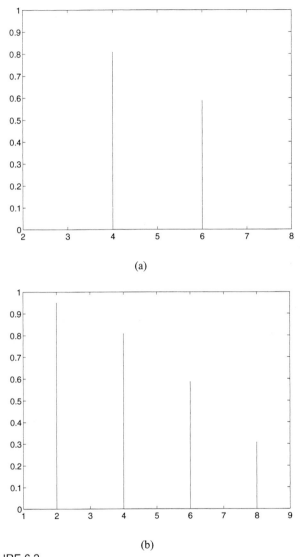

FIGURE 6.2
(a) Situation where the figure box hides lines; (b) use of `axis` to broaden the axis limits so that all lines can be seen.

```
v = axis;
v(1) = 1;
v(2) = 9;
axis(v)
```

6.2.3 Circles

To draw a circle of radius r whose center is located at (a, b) in a Cartesian coordinate system, one has to first transform them to Cartesian coordinates (recall Figure 2.2)

$$x = a + r\cos(\theta)$$
$$y = b + r\sin(\theta)$$

where $0 \le \theta \le \theta_1 \le 2\pi$. When $\theta_1 < 2\pi$, we draw an arc of a circle. If we assume that $\theta_1 = 2\pi$, $a = 1$, $b = 2$, and $r = 0.5$, then the script to draw the circle is

```
theta = linspace(0,2*pi);
plot(1+0.5*cos(theta),2+0.5*sin(theta))
axis equal
```

The `axis equal` function proportions the graph so that the circles appear as circles, rather than as ellipses.

The script to draw a family of six concentric circles, whose initial radius of 0.5 increases in increments of 0.25 and whose centers are indicated by a plus sign, is

```
theta = linspace(0,2*pi,50);        % (1×50)
rad = 0.5:0.25:1.75;                 % (1×6)
x = 1+cos(theta)'*rad;               % (50×6)
y = 2+sin(theta)'*rad;               % (50×6)
plot(x,y,'k',1,2,'k+')
axis equal
```

The values in the matrices are plotted column by column. Since we wanted all 50 values of *theta* to be drawn at each value of *rad*, we formed them as (50×6) matrices. If the string 'k' were omitted, then each circle would have been drawn in a different color. The execution of this script yields Figure 6.3.

6.2.4 Function *vs.* Function

A Lissajous figure is obtained when $\sin(n\theta)$ is plotted against $\sin(m\theta + \theta_1)$, where m and n are positive numbers, $0 \le \theta \le 2\pi$, and $0 \le \theta_1 < 2\pi$. Let us consider the case where $n = 1$, $m = 2$, and $\theta_1 = \pi/4$ (45°). If we take 101 equally spaced θ, then the script is

```
theta = linspace(0,2*pi,101);
plot(sin(theta),sin(2*theta+pi/4))
```

Execution of this script results in Figure 6.4a. We could also draw the Lissajous without reference to an axis system by adding

```
axis off
```

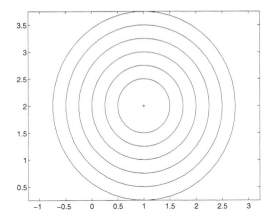

FIGURE 6.3.
Concentric circles.

to the script, which results in Figure 6.4b.

6.2.5 Family of Curves

One way to draw a family of curves was presented in the previous drawing of six concentric circles. In general, MATLAB allows one to have one axis represented by a vector and the other by a matrix. It will draw the curves by drawing the vector versus either the columns or the rows of the matrix, depending on which one matches the length of the vector.

Consider the case of drawing a family of parabolas

$$y = a^2 - x^2$$

for $-5 \leq x \leq 5$ and $a = 1, 2, ..., 5$. The script is

```
x = -5:0.2:5;
a = 1:5;
[xx,aa] = meshgrid(x.^2,a.^2);
plot(x,aa-xx,'k')
```

which results in Figure 6.5.

Now consider the visualization of the convergence of the series

$$S_N = \sum_{j=1}^{N} \frac{1}{(a+j)^2}$$

for $N = 1, 2, ..., 10$ and $a = 1, 2,$ and 3. In this case, we use cumsum (recall Section 2.5) to obtain the following script:

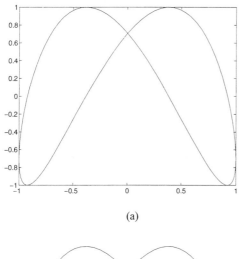

(a)

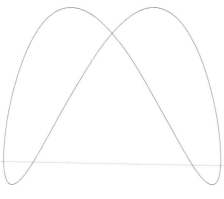

(b)

FIGURE 6.4.
(a) Lissajous figure; (b) Lissajous figure using `axis off`.

```
aa = 1:3;                  % (1×3)
N = 1:10;                  % (1×10)
[a,k] = meshgrid(aa,N);    % (10×3)
S = cumsum(1./(a+k).^2);   % (10×3)
plot(N,S,'k')
```

which, when executed, results in Figure 6.6.

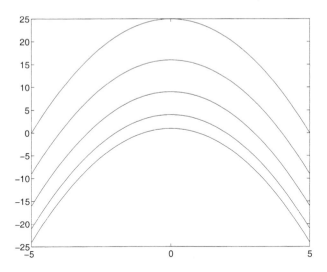

FIGURE 6.5
Family of parabolas.

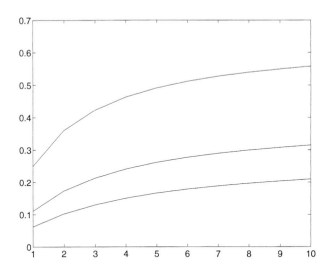

FIGURE 6.6
Visualization of the convergence of a series.

6.2.6 Multiple Functions on One Figure[4]

Consider the three functions

$$g_1(x) = 0.1x^2$$
$$g_2(y) = \cos^2 y$$
$$g_3(z) = e^{-0.3z}$$

where $0 \le x = y = z \le 3.5$. We can draw these three functions on one figure in either of three ways:

```
x = linspace(0,3.5);
plot(x,[0.1*x.^2; cos(x).^2;exp(–0.3*x)],'k')
```

or

```
x = linspace(0,3.5);
plot(x,0.1*x.^2,'k',x,cos(x).^2,'k',x,exp(–0.3*x),'k')
```

or

```
x = linspace(0,3.5);
plot(x,0.1*x.^2,'k')
hold on
plot(x,cos(x).^2,'k')
plot(x,exp(–0.3*x),'k')
```

Execution of any of these three scripts will produce Figure 6.7a, wherein all the curves have the same color: black.

On the other hand, if the range of the independent variable for each of these functions is different, then only the second and third scripts can be used. For example, if $0 \le x \le 3$, $1 \le y \le 4$, and $2 \le z \le 5$, then the form of the second script above is used as follows:

```
x = linspace(0,3,45);
y = linspace(1,4,55);
z = linspace(2,5,65);
plot(x,0.1*x.^2,'k-',y,cos(y).^2,'k--',z,exp(–0.3*z),'k-.')
```

which, upon execution, results in Figure 6.7b. Notice that we have plotted each function with a different line type and that each curve was plotted with a different number of points.

---

[4] To plot two different types of graphs with two different ordinates use `plotyy`. This is presented in Section 6.3.6. Also see the script that created Figure 14.1.

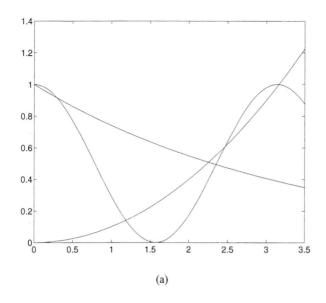

(a)

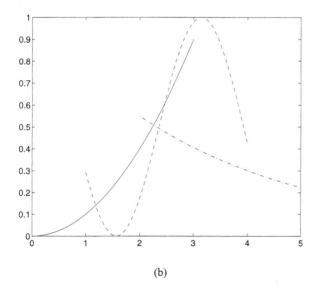

(b)

FIGURE 6.7
(a) Three different functions over the same range; (b) three different functions over three different ranges.

6.3 GRAPH ANNOTATION AND VISUAL ENHANCEMENT

6.3.1 Axes and Curve Labels, Figure Titles, Legends, Text, and Other Attributes

We shall now illustrate, through an example, how to enhance a graph:

- With axis labels, figure titles, labeled curves, legends, filled areas, and placement of text
- By altering the attributes of the axes, curve lines, and the text
- By using Greek letters, mathematical symbols, and subscripts and superscripts

Let us draw, label, title and annotate the relationship of two intersecting curves, $\cos(x)$ and $1/\cosh(x)$, over the range $0 \le x \le 6$. In this range, these two curves intersect at $x = 4.73$. Recall the example in Section 5.5.1. We shall also draw a vertical line through the intersecting point and denote the value of x near this intersection. The script to perform this is

```
x = 0:.05:6;
plot(x,cos(x),'k',x,1./cosh(x),'k',[4.73 4.73],[-1 1],'k')
xlabel('x')
ylabel('Value of functions')
title('Visualization of two intersecting curves')
text(4.8,-.1,'x = 4.73')
text(2.1,.3,'1/cosh(x)')
text(1.2,-.4,'cos(x)')
```

Execution of the script results in Figure 6.8. The coordinate values for the location of the various texts are chosen after only the `plot` function is executed—that is, after only the first two lines of the script have been written and the resulting figure examined. Then the `text` functions are added.

We can modify these results so that the area between the two curves in the range $0 \le x \le 4.73$ is filled with the color cyan. To fill the area contained within these two curves we use

```
fill
```

which requires that these two curves be turned into a connected polygon. In doing this, we must also create a new range for x: $0 \le x \le 4.73$. To accomplish this, the following expressions are appended to the above script:

```
xn = linspace(0,4.73,50);
hold on
fill([xn fliplr(xn)], [1./cosh(xn) fliplr(cos(xn))],'c');
```

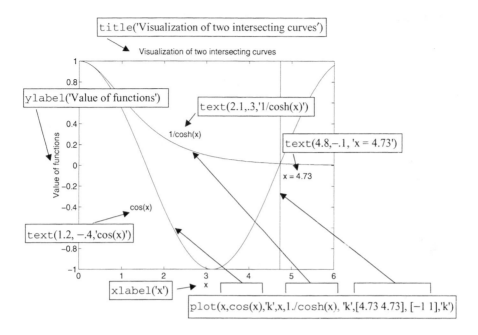

FIGURE 6.8.
Expressions that create and annotate the figure shown.

The result of appending this script to the previous one gives Figure 6.9. The connected polygon is created by forming the vector [1./cosh(xn) fliplr(cos(xn))], which is the concatenation of the top curve 1/cosh(x) and the reversal of the vector of cos(x), the bottom curve. Corresponding to this new vector is the new x-coordinate vector [xn fliplr(xn)], which is formed by the concatenation of the new values of x and its reversed values.

If, instead of using fill, the area between these two curves is delineated by a series of 20 equally spaced vertical lines, then the script is

```
x = 0:.05:6;
plot(x,cos(x),'k',x,1./cosh(x),'k',[4.73 4.73],[−1 1],'k')
hold on
xx = linspace(0,4.73,20);
plot([xx;xx],[cos(xx);1./cosh(xx)],'k-')
```

When executed, this script produces the results shown in Figure 6.10a.

To create 20 equally spaced horizontal lines, we have to work with the inverse functions $\cos^{-1}(x)$ and $\cosh^{-1}(x)$. For this case the script is

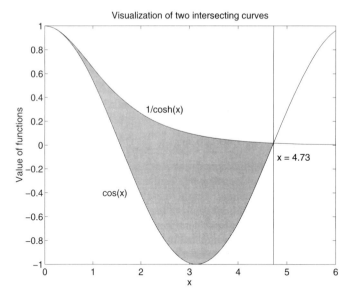

FIGURE 6.9.
Modification of Figure 6.8 with the area between the curves filled in.

```
x = 0:.05:6;
plot(x,cos(x),'k',x,1./cosh(x), 'k',[4.73 4.73], [−1 1],'k')
hold on
y1 = linspace(1,0.01,10);
plot([acos(y1);acosh(1./y1)],[y1;y1],'k-')
y2 = linspace(0.01,−1,10);
plot([acos(y2);pi+fliplr(acos(y1))],[y2;y2],'k-')
```

which, upon execution, results in Figure 6.10b. Both of these scripts can be combined to produce a hatched effect shown in Figure 6.11.

There is another way that we can identify the curves in Figure 6.9, and that is with

```
legend
```

The legend function differs from text in that text can be used as many times as practical, whereas legend can only be used once. The number of arguments of the legend function equals the number of different lines being drawn by one or more plot functions. There is also an additional (last) argument, which is optional. Each argument (except the last one) is a string that carries the alphanumeric identifier for each line. The value of the optional argument (1, 2, 3, or 4) places the legend in one of the four corners of the figure, to the right of the figure (−1), or in the 'best' location (0)—that is, one that interferes least with the data. When this last argument is omitted, the legend is placed in its default location, which is the upper right-hand corner. However, one can omit this argument

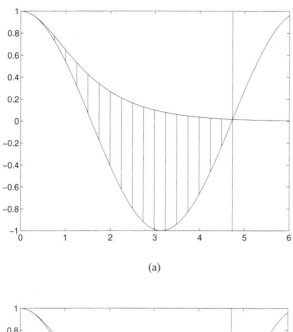

(a)

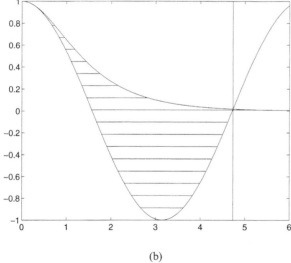

(b)

FIGURE 6.10
Area between two intersecting curves filled with equally spaced (a) vertical lines; (b) horizontal lines.

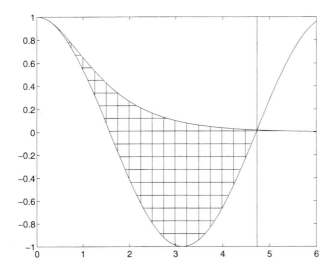

FIGURE 6.11
Area between two intersecting curves filled with hatched effect.

and use the mouse to place the legend. Simply click on the legend and, with the mouse button depressed, move the legend to its desired location. However, this placement is temporary in that when this figure is closed and then created at another time, the legend will again appear at its default location and again must be relocated in this manner.

We shall illustrate the use of the `legend` function by reexamining a variation of the plotting of the quantities appearing in the script to produce Figure 6.8. Consider the statements

```
x = 0:.05:6;
plot(x,cos(x),'k-',x,1./cosh(x), 'k--')
legend('cos(x) ', '1/cosh(x) ',3)
```

The above script produces Figure 6.12. The third argument of each triplet in the `plot` function specifies that the lines are to be drawn in black, with cos(*x*) appearing as a solid line and 1/cosh(*x*) as a dashed line. The `legend`'s arguments are order dependent. The first argument relates to the first curve drawn, the second to the second line drawn, and so on. If there are several `plot` functions used, then the order continues with the first argument of the second `plot` function following the last string identifying the last curve plotted in the previous `plot` statement. Only one `legend` function can be used per `figure` or `subplot`. The number 3 in the `legend` function places the legend in the lower left-hand corner of the figure.

Figure 6.12 could have also been obtained from the script

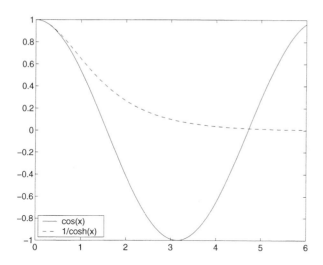

FIGURE 6.12
Use of the legend function.

```
x = 0:.05:6;
plot(x,cos(x),'k-')
hold on
plot(x,1./cosh(x),'k--')
legend('cos(x) ', '1/cosh(x) ',3)
```

When the line types and colors are not specified in the plot function, the legend function uses the default line type (solid) and the default color sequence—that is, the lines in the legend are solid lines of different colors.

MATLAB provides the capability to make changes to virtually all characteristics of the elements that comprise a graph. Several that we shall illustrate are the font type and size of the text characters and axes numbers, along with the line widths of the axes and the curves. A complete discussion of all the properties can be found in the HTML version of the help files. The default value of the line width is 0.5. The default value for the axis labels and text font size is 10, and the default font name for both is Helvetica.

Let us return to the script that generated Figure 6.8, which was, in part,

```
x = 0:.05:6;
plot(x,cos(x),'k',x,1./cosh(x),'k',[4.73 4.73],[–1 1],'k')
text(4.8,–.1,'x = 4.73')
text(2.1,.3,'1/cosh(x)')
text(1.2,–.4,'cos(x)')
```

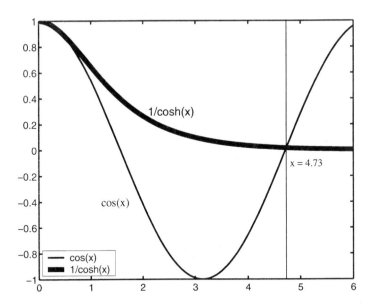

FIGURE 6.13
Change of font sizes, font type, and line widths.

We shall now modify this script to make the axis lines a little thicker, draw the curves with lines of different thickness, place a legend in the lower left-hand corner, and print the text in three different size fonts and two different types. The revised script is

```
x = 0:.05:6;
h = plot(x,cos(x),'k',x,1./cosh(x),'k',[4.73 4.73],[-1 1],'k');
text(4.8,-.1,'x = 4.73','fontname','times','fontsize',14)
text(2.1,.3,'1/cosh(x)','fontsize',16)
text(1.2,-.4,'cos(x)', 'fontsize',16,'fontname','times')
set(gca,'fontsize',14,'LineWidth',2)
PropertyName = {'LineWidth','LineWidth','LineWidth'};
PropertyValue = {2.5, 2.5, 2.5; 7, 7, 7; 1, 1, 1};
set(h,PropertyName,PropertyValue)
[legendhandle objecthandle] = legend('cos(x) ', '1/cosh(x) ',3);
set(objecthandle(1),'fontsize',14,'color','r')
```

which, when executed, results in Figure 6.13. The construct $h = $ plot$(\ldots)$ places in column vector h three values, called handles, which provide MATLAB the identity of the specific entity (curve) that is to be accessed. There are three values for h in this case because in this plot function we are drawing three different curves: $\cos(x)$, $1/\cosh(x)$, and a vertical line at $x = 4.73$. Knowing the identifying number for each curve, which is assigned in the order in which they appear, we use the last `set` function to change each line width to the value indicated. The first `set` function uses the MATLAB function `gca` (= **g**et handle to **c**urrent **a**xis), which brings back the handle for the axis. In this case, we changed two attributes of the axes: line width and font size. The form of legend brings back the various handles to the attributes of the lines (*legendhandle*) and the text (*objecthandle*). The attributes of the text in the legend is accessed with *objecthandle*(1), where we have chosen to change the font size of the letters in the legend and their color to red.

The changes to the attributes of the text, curves, and axes can also be made directly in the figure window using the appropriate icons at its top and/or by selecting the appropriate operation from its *Tools* menu. After the changes have been made the figure can be saved. However, when the script or function that generated this figure is run again these alterations and additions will not be there, and they must be made again.

Another attribute that can be used with `text` is `rotation`, which will rotate the text an angle θ degrees with respect to the horizontal axis. This attribute is illustrated in Figure 6.20 of Section 6.3.6.

There is also the capability to annotate the graph with upper- and lower-case Greek letters, subscripts and superscripts, and a range of mathematical symbols. These annotations can be done with `xlabel`, `ylabel`, `zlabel`, `text`, `legend` and `title`. The formatting instructions follow the LaTeX language,[5] and are in addition to the text modification commands discussed previously.

Subscripts are created with the underscore (_) and superscripts with the exponentiation operator (^). The creation of the Greek letters is obtained by the spelling of the letter and preceding the spelling by a backslash (\), as shown in Table 6.1. Upper-case Greek letters are obtained by capitalizing the first letter of the spelling. However, since many of the upper-case Greek letters are the same as upper-case English letters, only those that are different are given in Table 6.1. The remaining upper case Greek letters are obtained by simply using the appropriate upper case English letters.

The creation of the mathematical symbols is obtained by their special spellings preceded by a backslash (\). Some of the more commonly used symbols are also given in Table 6.1. The general syntax is to place a set of concatenated instructions between a pair of apostrophes. When certain groups of symbols are to be kept together, such as an expression that is to appear in an exponent, they are placed between a pair of braces ({}). We shall now illustrate these procedures with an example.

Let us compute and plot the following function for $\beta = 3$ and $1 \le \Omega_1 \le 2$, and label the figure accordingly:

$$g_2 = 1 + e^{-\Omega_1^\beta}$$

The script is

```
Omega1 = linspace(1,2); beta = 3;
plot(Omega1,1+exp(–Omega1.^beta),'k')
title('Plot of g_2 versus \Omega_1 for \beta = 3')
ylabel('g_2')
```

---

[5] See, for example, L. Lamport, *LaTeX: A Document Preparation System*, Addison-Wesley, Reading, MA, 1987.

TABLE 6.1
Upper and Lower Case Greek Letters and Some Mathematical Symbols

Lower case				Upper case		Mathematical			
Symbol	Syntax	Symbol	Syntax	Symbol	Syntax	Symbol	Syntax	Symbol	Syntax
α	\alpha	ν	\nu	Γ	\Gamma	$\leq$	\leq	$\circ$	\circ
β	\beta	ξ	\xi	Δ	\Delta	$\geq$	\geq	$\ll$	\ll
γ	\gamma	o	o	Θ	\Theta	$\neq$	\neq	$\gg$	\gg
δ	\delta	π	\pi	Λ	\Lambda	$\pm$	\pm	'	\prime
ε	\epsilon	ρ	\rho	Ξ	\Xi	$\times$	\times	$\Leftarrow$	\Leftarrow
ζ	\zeta	σ	\sigma	Π	\Pi	∞	\infty	$\angle$	\angle
η	\eta	τ	\tau	Σ	\Sigma	$\sum$	\sum	$\sqrt{}$	\surd
θ	\theta	υ	\upsilon	Υ	\Upsilon	$\int$	\int	#	\#
ι	\iota	ϕ	\phi	Φ	\Phi	$\div$	\div	\$	\\$
κ	\kappa	χ	\chi	Ψ	\Psi	$\sim$	\sim	%	\%
λ	\lambda	ψ	\psi	Ω	\Omega	$\leftarrow$	\leftarrow	&	\&
μ	\mu	ω	\omega			$\uparrow$	\uparrow	{	\\{

```
xlabel('\Omega_1')
text(1.2,1.2,'g_2=1+e^{-\Omega_1^\beta}','fontsize',16)
```

The execution of this script results in Figure 6.14.

6.3.2 Repeating Curves: Display of cot(x) From $0 \leq x \leq m\pi$

We shall display the cot(x) from $0 < x < m\pi$, where m is either 2, 3, ..., or 6, and is selected by the user. The choice $m = 2$ is shown in Figure 6.15. The y-axis limits are set to ± 8, and the x-axis limits vary from 0 to $m\pi$. Since $\cot(0) = \infty$ and $\cot(\pi) = -\infty$, we start and end x so as not to include these values. Also, the cotangent repeats itself every $m\pi$ and, therefore, needs only to be computed once for $0 < x < \pi$ and then plotted using these values in the region $(m - 1)\pi < x < m\pi$, $m > 1$ by simply incrementing the x-axis values by $x + (m-1)\pi$. The script is

```
m = input('Enter number of repetitions of cot function (integer from 2 to 6) = ');
the = linspace(0.12,pi-0.12,50);
ct = cot(the);
hold on
for n = 1:m
  plot([(2*n-1)*pi/2 (2*n-1)*pi/2],[-8/40 8/40],'k-')
  if n == 1
```

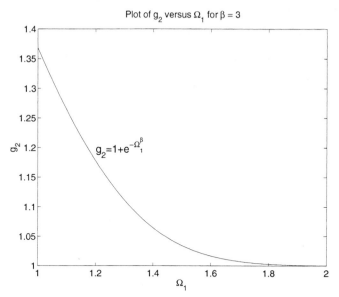

FIGURE 6.14
Annotation with superscripts, subscripts, and Greek letters.

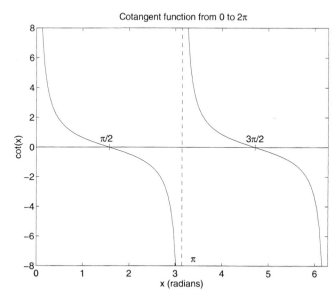

FIGURE 6.15
Cotangent function from 0 to 2π.

```
   text((2*n–1)*pi/2–pi/(8*m), .6, '\pi/2')
     text(n*pi+pi/(8*m), –7.5, '\pi')
   else
     text((2*n–1)*pi/2–pi/(8*m),0.6, [num2str((2*n–1),2) '\pi/2'])
     if n<m
       text(n*pi+pi/(8*m), –7.5,[num2str(n,1) '\pi'])
     end
   end
   if n == m
     plot(the+(n–1)*pi,ct,'k-')
   else
     plot(the+(n–1)*pi,ct,'k-',[n*pi n*pi],[–8 8],'k--')
   end
 end
 plot([0 m*pi],[0 0],'k-')
 axis([0 m*pi –8 8])
 xlabel('x (radians)')
 ylabel('cot(x)')
 title(['Cotangent function from 0 to ' num2str(m,1),'\pi'])
 box on
```

It is seen that almost all of the script is devoted to annotating the figure. Only two statements are used to compute $\cot(x)$.

6.3.3 Polar Plot: Far Field Radiation Pattern of a Sound Source

The normalized sound pressure at a large distance from the center of a circular piston in an infinite baffle that is vibrating at a frequency f is given by

$$p(r,\theta) = \left| \frac{J_1(ka\theta)}{ka\theta} \right| \qquad ka^2 \ll r \quad \text{and} \quad a \ll r$$

where r is the radial distance from the center of the piston, θ is the angle of r with respect to the plane of the baffle, k is the wave number, a is the radius of the piston, and $J_1(x)$ is the Bessel function of the first kind of order 1. The wave number is the reciprocal of the wavelength of the sound at frequency f; thus, ka is dimensionless. This model is a fair approximation to the angular dispersion of sound from a loudspeaker.

We wish to create a polar plot of the normalized radiation pattern for $ka = 6\pi$ when θ ranges from $-\pi/2 < \theta < \pi/2$. We have chosen this solution also to illustrate the use of the zoom function, since, as we shall see, this radiation pattern exhibits side lobes that are not distinguishable in the M<small>ATLAB</small>-scaled figure. The script is

```
theta = linspace(–pi/2,pi/2,300);
rad = abs(besselj(1,6*pi*theta)./(6*pi*theta));
polar(theta, rad/max(rad))
zoom on
```

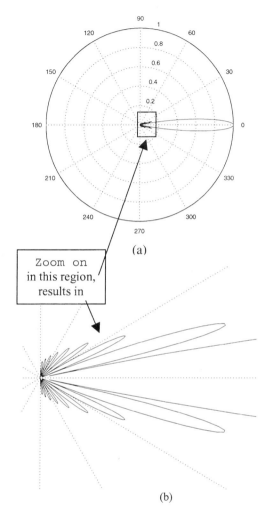

FIGURE 6.16
(a) Polar representation of a radiation pattern; (b) magnified region.

    The foregoing script gives the curve shown in Figure 6.16a. Notice that the values of θ are such that $ka\theta \neq 0$. The max function finds the maximum value in the vector *rad* so that the ratio *rad*/max(*rad*) is the normalized radiation pattern whose maximum value is 1. The function zoom on lets us use the left mouse button to define a rectangular region that will, upon release of the mouse button, fill the plotting area. This region is indicated by the rectangle in Figure 6.16a and becomes, upon release of the button, that shown in Figure 6.16b. To return the figure to its original size the right mouse button is pressed one or more

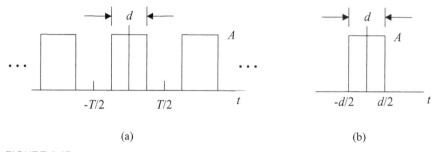

(a)   (b)

FIGURE 6.17
(a) Periodic rectangular pulse train; (b) single rectangular pulse.

times when the cursor is in the figure's window. One turns the zoom feature off by typing either `zoom off` or `zoom`. This procedure can also be performed using the pan and zoom icons in the figure window instead of typing `zoom on`.

6.3.4 Multiple Figures: Spectral Plot for a Periodic Pulse Train and a Single Pulse

Consider a periodic series of rectangular pulses, shown in Figure 6.17a, whose pulse duration is d and whose period is T. This signal can be represented as (recall Example 2.3):

$$g(t) = \frac{f(t)T}{Ad} = c_0 + 2 \sum_{n=1}^{\infty} c_n \cos(n\omega_0 t)$$

where $\omega_0 = 2\pi / T$ and

$$c_0 = 1$$
$$c_n = \frac{\sin(n\pi d / T)}{(n\pi d / T)} \qquad n = 1, 2, \ldots$$

The c_n are the normalized amplitudes of each harmonic comprising the signal. When one plots $|c_n|$ as a function of n, the resulting plot is called the amplitude spectrum for the signal. The spectral plot has frequency content only at the harmonics of ω_0—that is, at $n\omega_0$—and is zero everywhere else. It is seen that $c_n = 0$ whenever

$$\frac{n\pi d}{T} = m\pi \qquad \text{or} \qquad n = \frac{m}{(d / T)}$$

On the other hand, if we have a single pulse, as shown in Figure 6.17b, its frequency spectrum is

$$F(0) = 1$$
$$F(\omega) = \frac{G(\omega)}{Ad} = \frac{\sin(\omega d / 2)}{(\omega d / 2)} \qquad \omega > 0$$

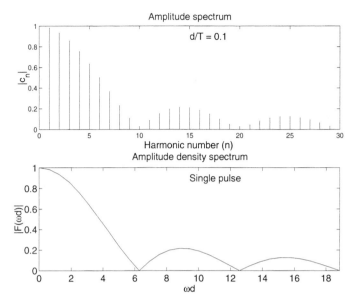

FIGURE 6.18
Frequency spectra of (a) periodic pulse shown in Figure 6.17a and (b) single pulse shown in Figure 6.17b.

The absolute value of $G(\omega)$ is called the amplitude density spectrum.

Let us generate two figures, one of $|c_n|$ vs. n for $n = 1, 2,..., 30$ when $d/T = 0.1$, and the second of $|F(\omega d)|$ vs. ωd, where $0 \le \omega d \le 6\pi$. To create the first figure, we use the technique described in Section 6.2.2 to draw a series of unconnected straight lines. These two figures will be plotted one above the other. Note that special care has to be taken to avoid dividing by zero. The results of the following script are shown in Figure 6.18.

```
n = 1:30;
cn = [1 abs(sin(0.1*pi*n)./(0.1*pi*n))];
n = [0 n];
subplot(2,1,1)
plot([n;n],[zeros(1,length(cn));cn], 'k')
xlabel('Harmonic number (n) ')
ylabel('|c_n|')
text(15,.9,'d/T = 0.1')
title('Amplitude spectrum')
w = pi/5:pi/5:6*pi;
subplot(2,1,2)
plot([0 w],[1 abs(sin(w/2)./(w/2))], 'k')
axis([0 6*pi 0 1])
xlabel('\omegad')
```

```
ylabel('|F(\omegad)|')
text(3*pi,.9,'Single pulse')
title('Amplitude density spectrum')
```

To avoid dividing by zero, we used the following technique. The harmonic number vector is initially defined as $n = 1{:}30$ so that we can easily compute $|c_n|$ over this range using dot division. Then we create the two vectors that include $n = 0$ and $c_0 = 1$, respectively, as indicated in the second and third lines. The same technique is used to evaluate $|F(\omega)|$. Notice that this technique eliminates the need for any programming logic.

6.3.5 Multiple Curves: Notch Sensitivity for Steel

We now return to the example given in Section 5.6.1 and plot the notch sensitivity constant q over a range of values for $50 \le S_u \le 250$ and $0 < r < 0.2$. To make the script a little more readable we create a function for the data that are to be fitted. Thus,

```
function ns = DataNeuber
ns = [50, .13; 70, .092; 90, .072; 110, .057; 130, .046; 150, .037; ...
      170, .028; 190, .020; 210, .015; 230, .010; 250, .007];
```

The following script consists of two parts. The first part obtains the values of the coefficients of the fourth-order polynomial used to fit these data, and then displays the data points and the polynomial that fits these points. The second part uses the polynomial to generate a family of curves of notch sensitivity q versus the notch radius for several values of the ultimate strength of steel, S_u. The execution of the script results in Figures 6.19a and 6.19b.

```
st = 50:10:250; skip = 1:2:11; loc = 0.25:0.08:0.65;
ncs = DataNeuber;
p = polyfit(ncs(:,1),ncs(:,2),4);
figure(1)
plot(st, polyval(p,st),'k', ncs(:,1),ncs(:,2),'ks')
title('Neuber constant: 4th order fit for steel')
xlabel('Ultimate strength of steel (ksi)')
ylabel('\surda')
figure(2)
[s,r] = meshgrid(ncs(skip,1),0.0025:0.0025:0.2);
notch = inline('1./(1+polyval(p,s)./sqrt(r))','p','s','r');
plot(r,notch(p,s,r),'k')
hold on
plot([repmat(0.125,1,6); repmat(0.1,1,6)],[loc;notch(p,ncs(skip,1)',0.1)],'k')
text(repmat(00.13,1,6),loc, num2str(ncs(skip,1)))
text(0.145,0.65,'ultimate strength')
text(0.145,0.62,'(\times1000)')
xlabel('r')
```

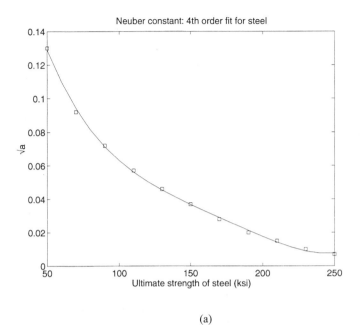

(a)

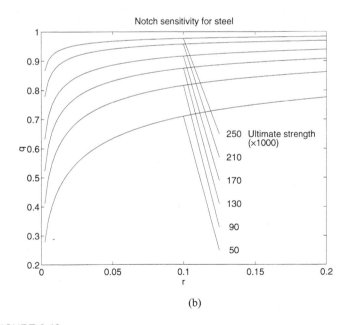

(b)

FIGURE 6.19
(a) Neuber's constant for steel; (b) notch sensitivity for steel as a function of notch radius r.

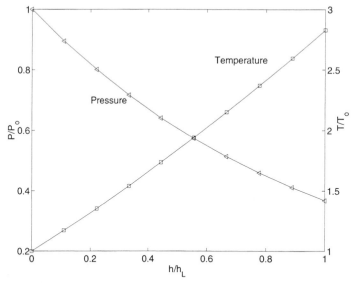

FIGURE 6.20
Two different quantities plotted with `plotyy`.

```
ylabel('q')
title('Notch sensitivity for steel')
```

The `meshgrid` function creates two (80×6) arrays, where the rows are the values of r and the columns the values of S_u. Since the expressions in the `inline` function *notch* were written using the dot notation we can enter these arrays for their appropriate arguments. The placing of the curve's identifying lines is done with the last `plot` function. We use the same techniques introduced previously to draw a series of unconnected straight lines. Note, however, that we had to transpose $ncs(:,1)$ from a column vector to a row vector. To place text adjacent to the ends of these lines we created a vector for the x and y coordinates, with the corresponding text given by converting the first column of $ncs(:,1)$ to a string using `num2str`. We selected every other element of *ncs* by incrementing its first subscript by 2.

6.3.6 Multiple Curves with Different *y*-Axes: `plotyy`

Consider two nondimensional quantities, a pressure ratio and a temperature ratio, each of which is a function of a height ratio h/h_L. Assume that these ratios are given by

$$\frac{T}{T_o} = \left(1 + \frac{h}{h_L}\right)^{1.5} \quad \text{and} \quad \frac{P}{P_0} = e^{-h/h_L}$$

The following script shows how to plot these two ratios over the range $0 \le h/h_L \le 1$ on one annotated graph with `plotyy`. When this script is executed we obtain Figure 6.20.

```
hoverhL = linspace(0,1,10);
ToverTo = (1+hoverhL).^1.5;
PoverPo = exp(-hoverhL);
[ax,h1,h2] = plotyy(hoverhL,PoverPo,hoverhL,ToverTo);
xlabel('h/h_L')
ylabel('P/P_o')
v = axis;
text(v(2)*1.06,v(3)+(v(4)-v(3))/2,'T/T_o','rotation',90)
text(v(1)+(v(2)-v(1))/5,v(3)+(v(4)-v(3))/1.6,'Pressure')
text(v(2)/1.6,v(4)/1.2,'Temperature')
set(h2,'Marker','s')
set(h1,'Marker','<')
```

The function `plotyy` plots each of the curves and gives the proper scale values for each of them. It does this by assigning the left-hand vertical axis to the first pair of variables in the `plotyy` arguments and assigning the axis values to the right-hand vertical axis according to the second pair of variables. However, one can label the left-hand vertical axis only with `ylabel`. Also, `plotyy` does not permit one to specify the line types for each of the curves. Therefore, in order to label the right-hand vertical axis and to give each curve its own line identifier, we use the form of `plotyy` shown in the script. The quantity $ax(1)$ and $ax(2)$ are the handles to the left- and right-hand axes, respectively. The quantity $h1$ and $h2$ are the handles to the first and second curves, respectively, as indicated by the order in which they appear in `plotyy`. The `set` function is used to set the property `Marker` of the handle identifier appearing in the first argument of the `set` function. In the first `set` function it sets each of the points plotted to a square, and in the second `set` function, it sets them to a triangle pointing left. The attribute `rotation` in the first `text` expression rotates the text 90° as shown.

6.3.7 Reading Numerical Values from Graphs: `ginput`

MATLAB provides the ability to record the (x,y) coordinates directly from a graph with `ginput`. This function can either be typed directly in the MATLAB command window or be part of a script. We illustrate its usage with a script based on the *DampSineWave* function created in Section 5.6.3. Our objective is to determine its damped period from the graph using the average of several readings from a succession of local amplitude maxima, and from the average of several readings of at the function's zero crossings. These average values are then compared to the following analytically obtained value of the period T

$$T = \frac{2\pi}{\sqrt{1-\xi^2}}$$

where ξ is the dimensionless damping coefficient.
    The function is typically used as

[x,y] = ginput

where *x* and *y* are each a vector of values corresponding to the coordinates of the cursor (center of the cross hairs) on the figure at the location at which the left mouse button was pressed. The cursor can be positioned as many times as appropriate. After the last point has been recorded, one hits *Enter*. To have the best resolution when using this method, one should maximize the graphics window prior to starting this process.

If we let $\xi = 0.1$ and τ range from $0 \le \tau \le 30$, then the script is

```
tau = linspace(0,30,200); xi = 0.10;
plot(tau,DampedSineWave(tau,xi),'k')
grid on
[tim,amp] = ginput;
disp(' tau      ampl')
disp(num2str([tim amp]))
disp(['Analytically determined period = ' num2str(2*pi/sqrt(1-xi^2))])
disp(['Average period graphically obtained = ' num2str(mean(diff(tim)))])
disp(['Standard deviation = ' num2str(std(diff(tim)))])
```

When the script has been executed and five data points have been collected from the zero crossings, we obtain

```
   tau       ampl
1.68539  -0.00137931
7.99358  -0.00137931
14.3018  -0.00137931
20.61    -0.00137931
26.9181  -0.00137931
Analytically determined period = 6.3148
Average period graphically obtained = 6.3082
Standard deviation = 2.2933e-015
```

When five data points have been collected from the local maxima we obtain

```
   tau      ampl
   0      0.995862
6.30819   0.528276
12.5682   0.28
18.9246   0.147586
25.2327   0.0772414
Analytically determined period = 6.3148
Average period graphically obtained = 6.3082
Standard deviation = 0.039318
```

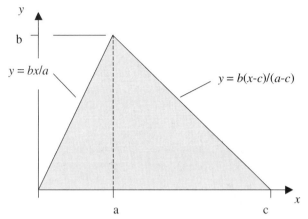

FIGURE 6.21
Triangle whose area will be approximated using random numbers.

6.3.8 Area Fill Using Random Numbers

We shall determine the approximate area of a triangle using randomly generated coordinates, and fill the area occupied by the triangle by displaying only those points that lie within its domain. The random numbers are created by

$$r = \text{unifrnd}(a1,a2,m,n)$$

which generates an ($n \times m$) array of numbers having a uniform (equal) probability of assuming any value within the specified interval (a_1, a_2).

Consider the triangle shown in Figure 6.21. Its area is $A_e = 0.5bc$. Its approximate area is the fraction of randomly generated points that fall within its borders multiplied by the total possible area, bc. If we let $b = 1$, $c = 2$, and $a = c/4$, and we examine 3,000 pairs of points, then the script to perform these operations is

```
b = 1;c = 2;a = 0.25*c;
exactarea = 0.5*b*c;
N = 3000;
x = unifrnd(0,c,1,N);
y = unifrnd(0,b,1,N);
indL = find(x<=a);
nxL = x(indL);
nyL = y(indL);
indyL = find(nyL<=b*nxL/a);
indR = find(x>a&x<=c);
nxR = x(indR);
nyR = y(indR);
```

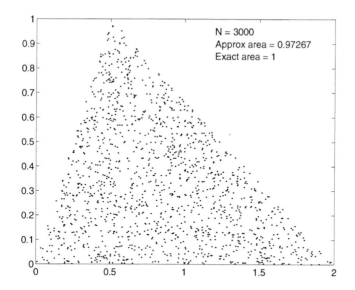

FIGURE 6.22
Triangle filled with randomly generated points.

```
indyR = find(nyR<=b/(a–c)*(nxR–c));
approxA = b*c*(length(indyL)+length(indyR))/N;
plot(nxL(indyL),nyL(indyL),'k.',nxR(indyR),nyR(indyR),'k.')
text(0.6*c, 0.95,['N = ' num2str(N)])
text(0.6*c,0.90,['Approx area = ' num2str(approxA)])
text(0.6*c,0.85,['Exact area = ' num2str(exactarea)])
```

Execution of this script results in Figure 6.22.

EXERCISES

Note: The actual plotting in all the exercises can be done using vector and dot operations and meshgrid. Use the for structure only to increment through a range of parameters as appropriate.

6.1 The force on a Belleville spring (see Figure 5.33) is proportional to C_1, where

$$C_1 = 0.5d_t^3 - 1.5h_t d_t^2 + \left(1 + h_t^2\right)d_t$$

and $h_t = h/t$, $d_t = \delta/t$, and δ is the deflection of the spring. Plot C_1 as a function of d_t when h_t varies from 1 to 3 in increments of 0.25 and d_t varies from 0 to 5. Label the curves and limit the y-axis to 8. The results should look like those shown in Figure 6.23.

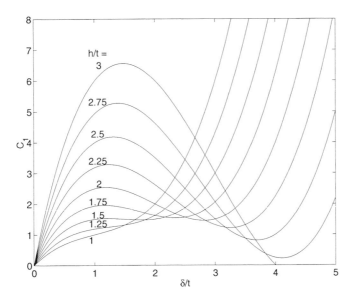

FIGURE 6.23
Belleville spring constant C_1.

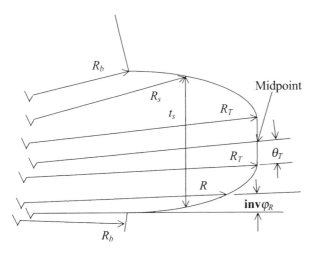

FIGURE 6.24
Nomenclature of a gear tooth.

6.2 Consider the gear tooth shown in Figure 6.24. If the gear has n teeth, then each tooth appears every $2\pi/n$ radians. Let R_b be the radius of the base circle, R_T the radius of the tooth tip circle, and R

TABLE 6.2
Definitions of the Various Sectors of the Gear Tooth Shown in Figure 6.24

R	ψ	Definitions
$R_b \le R \le R_T$	$\mathbf{inv}(\varphi(R))$	$\varphi(R) = \cos^{-1}(R_b/R)$
		$\mathbf{inv}(x) = \tan(x) - x$
R_T	$\mathbf{inv}(\varphi(R_T)) \le \psi \le \mathbf{inv}(\varphi(R_T)) + 2\theta_T$	$\theta_T = 0.5t_s/R_s + \mathbf{inv}(\varphi_s) - \mathbf{inv}(\varphi(R_T))$
$R_b \le R \le R_T$	$2[\theta_T + \mathbf{inv}(\varphi(R_T))] - \mathbf{inv}(\varphi(R))$	
R_b	$2[\theta_T + \mathbf{inv}(\varphi(R_T))] \le \psi \le 2\pi/n$	

$(R_b \le R \le R_T)$ the radius of a point on the profile of the tooth. Then the polar coordinates of the profile of one gear tooth (R, ψ), including the space between an adjacent tooth, are given in Table 6.2. In Table 6.2 φ_s is the gear pressure angle, either 14.5°, 20°, or 25°, $R_s = nm/2$ is the standard pitch radius, m is the gear module, and t_s is the tooth thickness at R_s.

If a gear has 24 teeth, a pressure angle of 20°, a module of 10 mm, a tooth thickness of 14.022 mm, a base radius of 90.21 mm and a tip radius of 106 mm, then draw the gear two ways: using `polar` and using `plot`.

6.3 The efficiency, in percent, of a power screw, when the friction of the collar is ignored, is (see Exercise 8.8)

$$e = 100 \frac{\cos(\alpha) - \mu \tan(\lambda)}{\cos(\alpha) + \mu \cot(\lambda)} \%$$

where μ is the coefficient of friction, λ is the lead angle of the screw and α is the thread angle. Plot the efficiency as a function of λ for $0 < \lambda < 90°$, $\mu = 0.02$, 0.05, 0.10,.0.15, 0.20, and 0.25, and for two thread angles: $\alpha = 7°$ and 14.5°. Label the figure and the individual curves and use the `axis` function to limit the efficiency to 0 to 100%. The results should look like those shown in Figure 6.25.

6.4 Using the results of Exercise 1.1, plot σ_x/p_{max}, σ_z/p_{max} and $\tau_{xz}/p_{max} = \tau_{yz}/p_{max} = 0.5(\sigma_x/p_{max} - \sigma_z/p_{max})$ as a function of z/a for $v_1 = 0.3$. Label the figure and identify the curves.

6.5 Using the results of Exercise 1.2, plot σ_x/p_{max}, σ_y/p_{max}, σ_z/p_{max} and τ_{yz}/p_{max} as a function of z/b for $v = 0.3$. Label the figure and identify the curves.

6.6 Plot the following curves.[6] All require the `axis equal` function.

Cycloid $(-\pi \le \varphi \le 3\pi;\ r_a = 0.5, 1, 1.5)$

$$x = r_a \varphi - \sin\varphi$$
$$y = r_a - \cos\varphi$$

Lemniscate $(-\pi/4 \le \varphi \le \pi/4)$

$$x = \cos\varphi\sqrt{2\cos(2\varphi)}$$
$$y = \sin\varphi\sqrt{2\cos(2\varphi)}$$

---

[6] D. von Seggern, *CRC Standard Curves and Surfaces*, CRC Press, Inc., Boca Raton, FL, 1993.

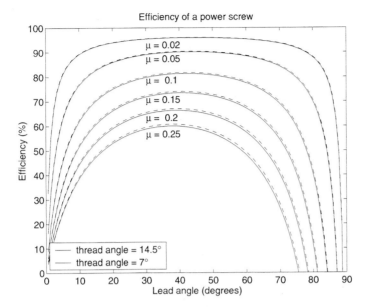

FIGURE 6.25
Efficiency of a power screw.

Spiral $(0 \le \varphi \le 6\pi)$

    Archimedean

$$x = \varphi \cos\varphi$$
$$y = \varphi \sin\varphi$$

    Logarithmic $(k = 0.1)$

$$x = e^{k\varphi} \cos\varphi$$
$$y = e^{k\varphi} \sin\varphi$$

Cardioid $(0 \le \varphi \le 2\pi)$

$$y = 2\cos\varphi - \cos 2\varphi$$
$$y = 2\sin\varphi - \sin 2\varphi$$

Astroid $(0 \le \varphi \le 2\pi)$

$$x = 4\cos^3\varphi$$
$$y = 4\sin^3\varphi$$

Epicycloid $(R_r = 3, a_r = 0.5, 1$ or 2, and $0 \le \varphi \le 2\pi$; $R_r = 2.5, a_r = 2$ and $0 \le \varphi \le 6\pi)$

$$x = (R_r + 1)\cos\varphi - a_r \cos(\varphi(R_r + 1))$$
$$y = (R_r + 1)\sin\varphi - a_r \sin(\varphi(R_r + 1))$$

TABLE 6.3
Constants Used to Determine μ

SAE Number	j	A_j	B_j
10	1	9.1209	3.5605
20	2	9.1067	3.5385
30	3	8.9939	3.4777
40	4	8.9133	3.4292
50	5	8.5194	3.2621
60	6	8.3666	3.1884

Hypocycloid ($R_r = 3$, $a_r = 0.5$, 1 or 2, and $0 \le \varphi \le 2\pi$)

$$x = (R_r - 1)\cos\varphi + a_r \cos(\varphi(R_r - 1))$$
$$y = (R_r - 1)\sin\varphi - a_r \sin(\varphi(R_r - 1))$$

6.7 The absolute viscosity of the oil in μreyn (lb-s/in^2) can be estimated within $\pm 10\%$ from the relationship

$$\mu = 10^{C-1}$$

where

$$C = 10^{A_j - B_j \log_{10} T_o}$$

and $T_o = 255.2 + 5/9T$ °K, where T is the temperature of the oil in °F, and A_j and B_j are given in Table 6.2 as a function of the oil's SAE number. Plot, on two side-by-side figures, the $\log_{10}\log_{10}(10\mu)$ as a function of the $\log_{10}(T_o)$ and μ as a function of the T_o for the six oils given in Table 6.3. (See, also, Section 8.6.)

6.8 The relationship between the lead angle of a worm gear λ, the ratio $\beta = N_1/N_2$, where N_1 is the number of teeth on the worm gear and N_2 is the number of teeth on the driven gear, the center distance between shafts C, and the normal diametral pitch P_{dn} is

$$K = \frac{2P_{dn}C}{N_2} = \frac{\beta}{\sin\lambda} + \frac{1}{\cos\lambda}$$

Plot K vs. λ for $1° \le \lambda \le 40°$ and $\beta = 0.02, 0.05, 0.08, 0.11, 0.15, 0.18, 0.23, 0.30$. Label the figure and the curves. Limit the range of the y-axis from 1 to 2. On the same figure plot the results of Exercise 5.9(a) by drawing a line that connects the minimum values of each curve. Do this by incorporating the appropriate function(s) and portions of the script from Exercise 5.9(a) into the script written for this exercise. The results should look like those shown in Figure 6.26.

6.9 Write a script that produces three or more circles around a central circle of radius $r_b = 1.5$ as shown for $n = 5$ circles in Figure 6.27. The radius r_s of the outer circles is

$$r_s = \frac{r_b \sin(\pi/n)}{1 - \sin(\pi/n)}$$

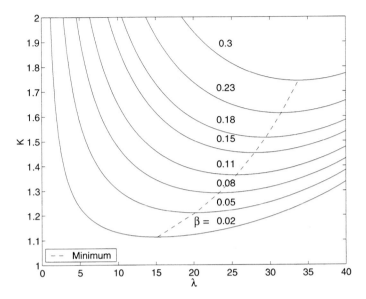

FIGURE 6.26
Lead angle of a worm gear.

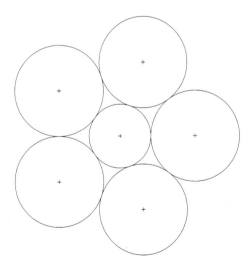

FIGURE 6.27
Five circles on a circle.

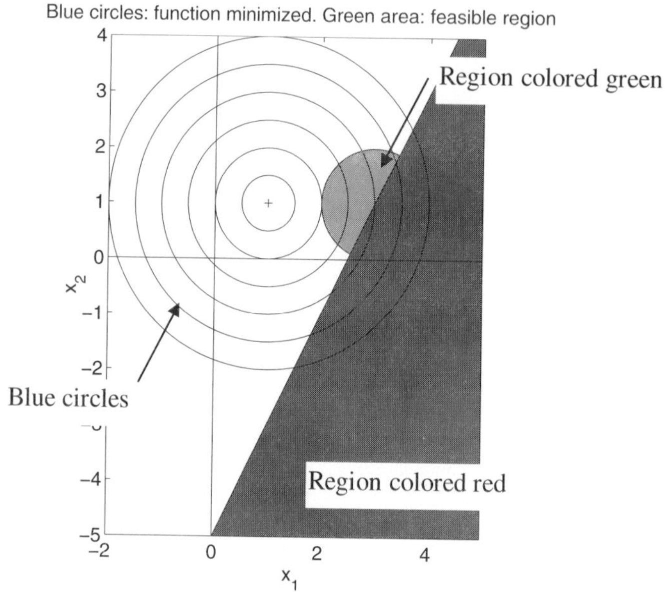

Blue circles: function minimized. Green area: feasible region

FIGURE 6.28
Solution to Exercise 6.10.

Have the script ask the user for the number of circles. The script can be written without using the `for` loop.

6.10 In optimization analysis it is often beneficial to plot the function being optimized (called the objective function) and its constraints (regions in which the solution is required to reside). Consider the requirement to minimize

$$f(x_1, x_2) = (x_1 - 1)^2 + (x_2 - 1)^2$$

subject to the constraints

$$g_1 = (x_1 - 3)^2 + (x_2 - 1)^2 - 1 \le 0$$
$$g_2 = 2x_1 - x_2 - 5 \le 0$$

Thus, the solution x_{m1} and x_{m2} must be on the circle $f(x_1, x_2)$ and within the region specified by g_1 and g_2.

Plot the above objective function (circles) and the region in which the solution must lie. The results should be made to look like those shown in Figure 6.28. To obtain this result, the function `fill` will have to be used and applied in the proper order.

6.11 In Exercise 5.5 we gave the following Colebrook formula from which the pipe's coefficient of friction λ could be estimated:

$$\lambda = \left[-2\log_{10}\left(\frac{2.51}{R_e\sqrt{\lambda}} + \frac{0.27}{d/k} \right) \right]^{-2} \qquad R_e \ge 4000$$

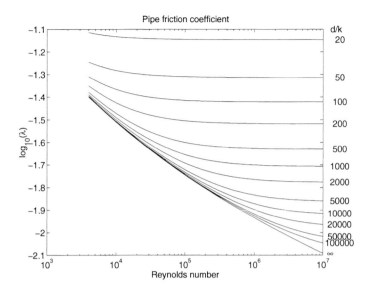

FIGURE 6.29
Moody diagram.

where R_e is the Reynolds number, d is the diameter of the pipe, and k is the surface roughness. For smooth pipes ($k \cong 0$; $d/k > 100{,}000$)

$$\lambda = \left[2\log_{10}\left(\frac{R_e \sqrt{\lambda}}{2.51} \right) \right]^{-2} \qquad R_e \geq 4000$$

Plot $\log_{10}(\lambda)$ as a function of $\log_{10}(R_e)$, $4\times10^3 \leq R_e \leq 10^7$, for $d/k = 20$, 50, 100, 200, 500, 1,000, 2,000, 5,000, 10,000, 20,000, 50,000, 100,000, and ∞ ($k = 0$). Use `semilogx` instead of `plot`. Label the figure and the curves. Place the identifiers for the curves to the right of $R_e = 10^7$—that is, outside the figure's right-hand vertical axis. The resulting figure is known as the Moody diagram of friction factors for pipe flow. The results should look like those in Figure 6.29.

6.12 Recall Exercise 5.4 wherein we used the following compressibility equation for gases:

$$Z(r,\tau) = \frac{p\tau}{r} = \frac{Pv}{RT}$$

where $Z(r, \tau)$ is defined in Exercise 5.4. Use the techniques of Exercises 5.4(b) and 5.4(c) to generate Figures 6.30(a) and 6.30(b). In Figure 6.30a, when τ is held constant let $.05 \leq r \leq 3.4$ in `fzero`, and when r is held constant let $0.4 \leq \tau \leq 2.5$ in `fzero`. To create the dashed curves use the `find` function to simplify things. In Figure 6.30b, when τ is held constant and is less than $1/1.3$ use a guess of $r = 4$ in `fzero`. When $\tau \geq 1/1.3$ and $p < 3$ use a guess of 2, otherwise use a guess of 3.3 in `fzero`. When r is held constant use a guess of $\tau = 0.6$.

6.13 Consider the following polynomial from $-12 \leq x \leq 7$.

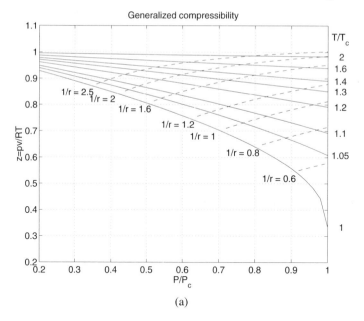

(a)

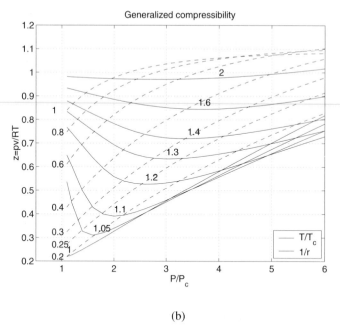

(b)

FIGURE 6.30
Generalized compressibility; (a) $0 \le p/p_c \le 1$, (b) $1 \le p/p_c \le 6$.

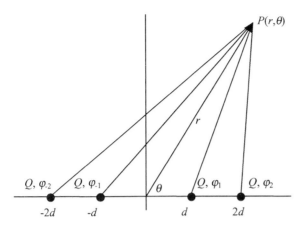

FIGURE 6.31
Linear array of acoustic sources.

$$y = 0.001x^5 + 0.01x^4 + 0.2x^3 + x^2 + 4x - 5$$

Plot only its positive values. Force the values of y at the first and last points of each segment to be (almost) equal to zero. [Hint: Use find.]

6.14 Write a script that creates Figure 5.14 of Exercise 5.6.

6.15 Consider a linear array of N pairs of acoustic sources shown in Figure 6.31, which are vibrating at a frequency ω and amplitude Q. The total acoustic pressure at a distance r from the array is

$$P(r,\theta) = Z_o \left[\sum_{m=1}^{N} \left(1 + \frac{md}{r}\cos\theta\right) \exp\left[j\left(-\varphi_m + mdk\cos\theta\right)\right] \right.$$
$$\left. + \sum_{m=1}^{N} \left(1 - \frac{md}{r}\cos\theta\right) \exp\left[j\left(-\varphi_{-m} - mdk\cos\theta\right)\right] \right]$$

where

$$Z_o = \frac{j\rho ckQ}{4\pi r} e^{j(\omega t - kr)}$$

and ρ is the density of the medium, c is the wave speed in the medium, $k = 2\pi\omega/c$ is the wave number, $\varphi_{\pm m}$ are the phase angles with respect to $\varphi_1 = 0$, $d/r \ll 1$, and $dk \ll 1$.
For the case where $N = 1$, $\varphi_1 = 0$, and $\varphi_{-1} = \pi$, the above simplifies to

$$P(r,\theta) = 2Z_o \left[jdk + \frac{d}{r} \right] \cos\theta$$

which is the expression for the far field pressure of an acoustic dipole.

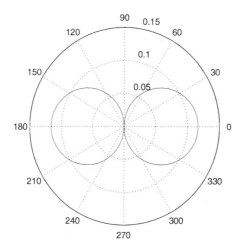

FIGURE 6.32
Radiation pattern of an acoustic dipole.

Compute $|P(r,\theta)/Z_o|$ as a function of θ and plot the results for $0 \le \theta \le 2\pi$ using `polar` for $d/r = 0.05$, $dk = 0.03$, $\varphi_{-1} = \pi$, and $\varphi_1 = 0$. The results should look like those shown in Figure 6.32. Use the formula for the general case of a linear array. Also plot the percentage difference between the exact solution and the numerically reduced solution for the dipole. Exclude the first point, $\theta = 0$, from this plot. First create a function to compute the magnitude of the pressure as a function of an arbitrary number of pairs of sources, their phase relationships and spacing, and the far field position in space.

6.16 The probability density function of a time-varying signal is used to relate the probability that over a period of time T the signal's amplitude has a value between x and $x + dx$. In other words, it is used to obtain a measure of the percentage of time the signal spends within this amplitude range. The probability density function can be approximated by

$$P(x) = \lim_{\substack{\Delta x \to 0 \\ T \to \infty}} \left[\sum_i \Delta t_i \bigg/ T\Delta x \right]$$

where the terms in this expression are shown for one period of a sine wave in Figure 6.33. The probability density function $P(x)$ of a sine wave of amplitude A_o is given by

$$P(x) = \frac{1}{\pi\sqrt{A_o^2 - x^2}} \qquad |x| \le A_o$$

$$= 0 \qquad\qquad |x| > A_o$$

Estimate the probability density function for

$$y = A_o \sin t$$

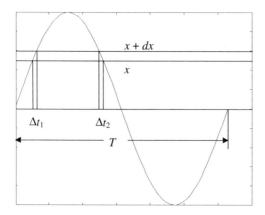

FIGURE 6.33
Determination of the amount of time a sine wave spends between x and $x + dx$.

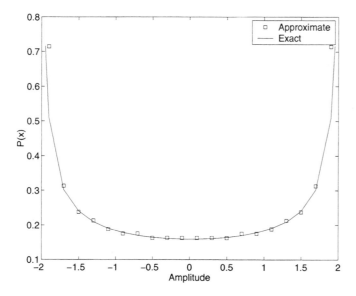

FIGURE 6.34
Probability density function of a sine wave.

for $-\pi \leq t \leq \pi$ and compare the results to the exact values. Let $A_o = 2$, the number of amplitude bins equal 20, and the number data points in the time interval equal 400. Plot the estimated values of $P(x)$ and the exact values. The results should look like those shown in Figure 6.34, where the legend has been moved manually.

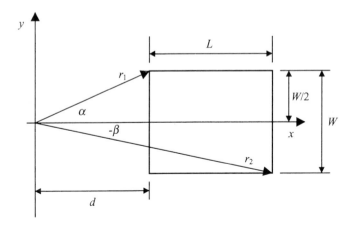

FIGURE 6.35
Description of a rectangle for Exercise 6.17.

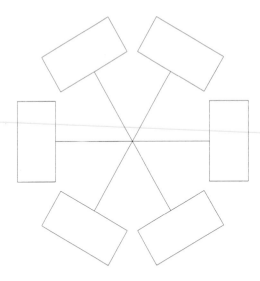

FIGURE 6.36
Replicated non-overlapping rectangles.

6.17 Consider the rectangle shown in Figure 6.35, where it is seen that

$$r_1 = \sqrt{d^2 + (W/2)^2} \qquad \alpha = \tan^{-1}(W/2d)$$
$$r_2 = \sqrt{(d+L)^2 + (W/2)^2} \qquad \beta = \tan^{-1}(W/2(d+L))$$

If the values of L, W, and d are given, then create a script that generates the maximum number of non-overlapping replicated rectangles as shown in Figure 6.36. The values of $L = 1$, $W = 2$, and $d = 2$ were used to generate Figure 6.36. The maximum number of rectangles can be determined from $\text{floor}(\pi/\alpha)$. This script can be written without using a `for` loop.

C H A P T E R   7

3D GRAPHICS

Edward B. Magrab

7.1	LINES IN 3D
7.2	SURFACES

The implementation of a wide selection of three-dimensional plotting capabilities is presented.

7.1 LINES IN 3D

The 3D version of the `plot` is

    plot3(u1,v1,w1,c1,u2,v2,w2,c2,...)

where u_j, v_j, and w_j are the (x,y,z) coordinates, respectively, of a point or a series of points. They are either a triplet of numbers, vectors of the same length, matrices of the same order, or expressions that, when evaluated, result in one of these three quantities. The quantity c_j is a string of characters, where one character specifies the color, one character specifies the point characteristics, and up to two characters specify the line type. See the introductory discussion to `plot` in Section 6.2.

Suppose that we want to draw a set of n unconnected lines whose end points are (x_{1n}, y_{1n}, z_{1n}) and (x_{2n}, y_{2n}, z_{2n}). To accomplish this, we create six vectors:

$$
\begin{aligned}
x_j &= [x_{j1}\ x_{j2}\ \dots\ x_{jn}] \\
y_j &= [y_{j1}\ y_{j2}\ \dots\ y_{jn}] \qquad j = 1,\,2 \\
z_j &= [z_{j1}\ z_{j2}\ \dots\ z_{jn}]
\end{aligned}
$$

Then the `plot3` instruction is

    plot3([x1;x2],[y1;y2],[z1;z2])

where [x1;x2], [y1;y2] and [z1;z2] are each $(2 \times n)$ matrices. This is the 3D counterpart to the way it is done with `plot`.

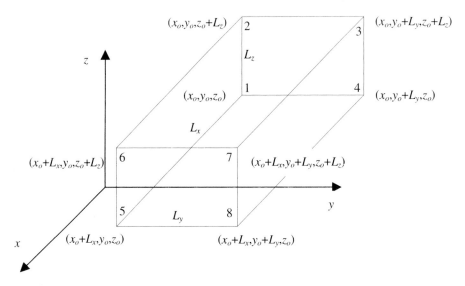

FIGURE 7.1
Coordinates of a box.

All annotation procedures discussed for 2D drawings in Section 6.2 are applicable to the 3D curve- and surface-generating functions, except that `text3` is used instead of `text` and `zlabel` is used to label the z-axis.

Example 7.1 Wire frame box

Consider the box of dimensions $L_x \times L_y \times L_z$ shown in Figure 7.1. We create the following function *BoxPlot3* to draw the four edges of each of the six surfaces of the box. The location and orientation of the box are determined by the coordinates of its two diagonally opposing corners: $\mathbf{P}(x_o, y_o, z_o)$ and $\mathbf{P}(x_o \pm L_x, y_o \pm L_y, z_o \pm L_z)$

```
function BoxPlot3(x0,y0,z0,Lx,Ly,Lz)
x = [x0      x0      x0      x0      x0+Lx   x0+Lx   x0+Lx   x0+Lx];
y = [y0      y0      y0+Ly   y0+Ly   y0      y0      y0+Ly   y0+Ly];
z = [z0      z0+Lz   z0+Lz   z0      z0      z0+Lz   z0+Lz   z0   ];
index = zeros(6,5);
index(1,:) = [1 2 3 4 1];
index(2,:) = [5 6 7 8 5];
index(3,:) = [1 2 6 5 1];
index(4,:) = [4 3 7 8 4];
index(5,:) = [2 6 7 3 2];
index(6,:) = [1 5 8 4 1];
for k = 1:6
  plot3(x(index(k,:)),y(index(k,:)),z(index(k,:)))
```

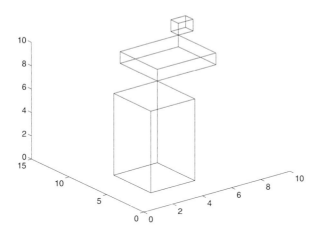

FIGURE 7.2
Wire frame boxes.

```
    hold on
end
```

Consider the following script that generates three boxes with the following dimensions and locations of one of its corners.

Box #1

Size: 3×5×7
Location: (1,1,1)

Box #2

Size: 4×5×1
Location: (3,4,5)

Box #3

Size: 1×1×1
Location: (4.5,5.5,6)

The script to create and display these wire frame boxes is

```
BoxPlot3(1,1,1,3,5,7)
BoxPlot3(4,6,8,4,5,1)
BoxPlot3(8,11,9,1,1,1)
```

which, upon execution, gives Figure 7.2.

7.2 SURFACES

A more powerful set of 3D plotting functions are those that create surfaces, contours, volumes, and variations and specialization of these basic forms. The basic surface plotting functions are

    surf

and

    mesh

The function surf draws a surface composed of colored patches, whereas mesh draws white surface patches that are defined by their boundary. In surf, the colors of the patches are determined by the magnitude of z, whereas it is the colors of the lines in mesh that are determined by the magnitude of z.

A surface is defined by the expression

$$z = f(x, y)$$

where x and y are the coordinates in the xy plane and z is the resulting height. The generation of a surface is then accomplished with

    surf(x,y,z)

The surf function has already been used to generate Figure 2.3 and mesh to generate Figure 2.6. We will further illustrate the use of these functions as well as several others with the plotting of the surface created by

$$z(x_1, x_2) = x_1^4 + 3x_1^2 + x_2^2 - 2x_1 - 2x_2 - 2x_1^2 x_2 + 6$$

over the range $-3 < x_1 < 3$ and $-3 < x_2 < 13$. The script to plot this surface is:

```
xx1 = linspace(-3,3,15);                    % (1×15)
xx2 = linspace(-3,13,17);                   % (1×17)
[x1,x2] = meshgrid(xx1,xx2);                % (17×15)
z = x1.^4+3*x1.^2-2*x1+6-2*x2.*x1.^2+x2.^2-2*x2; % (17×15)
surf(x1,x2,z)
```

The meshgrid function creates two (17×15) matrices so that z can be evaluated at all combinations of x_1 and x_2. This evaluation of all combinations of x_1 and x_2 is performed by the indicated dot operations in the evaluation of the expression for $z = z(x_1, x_2)$.

The execution of this script results in Figure 7.3. To see a projection of several contours of this surface projected onto the $z = 0$ plane, we replace surf with surfc and get the result shown in Figure 7.4. The arguments of surfc are the same as those for surf.

To draw a line from each of the four corners of the surface to the $z = 0$ plane, we first note that the coordinates of these corner points are

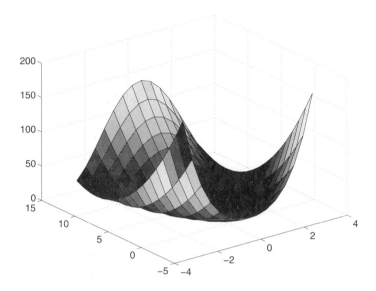

FIGURE 7.3
Surface generated with `surf`.

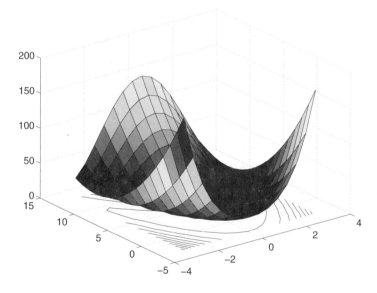

FIGURE 7.4
Surface and contours generated with `surfc`.

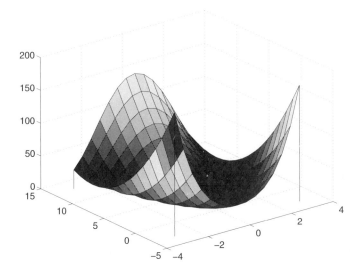

FIGURE 7.5
Surface with lines drawn to its corners.

$$[-3, -3, z(-3,-3)]$$
$$[-3, 13, z(-3,13)]$$
$$[3, 13, z(3,13)]$$
$$[3, -3, z(3,-3)]$$

The script is

```
xx1 = linspace(-3,3,15);
xx2 = linspace(-3,13,17);
[x1,x2] = meshgrid(xx1,xx2);
z = x1.^4+3*x1.^2-2*x1+6-2*x2.*x1.^2+x2.^2-2*x2;
surf(x1,x2,z)
x11 = [-3 -3 3 3];
x22 = [-3 13 13 -3];
z2 = x11.^4+3*x11.^2-2*x11+6-2*x22.*x11.^2+x22.^2-2*x22;
hold on
plot3([x11;x11],[x22;x22],[zeros(1,4);z2],'b')
```

Execution of this script results in Figure 7.5. The fourth line is hidden from view.

As mentioned previously, the colors of the patches are generated automatically with surf according to their z-value. Similarly, the colors of the lines generated automatically with mesh vary according to their z-value. The colors of either the patches or the lines can be changed to a constant value using

```
colormap(c)
```

where c is a three-element vector whose values vary between 0 and 1. The first element corresponds to the intensity of red, the second to the intensity of green, and the third to the intensity of blue. See `colormap` in the *Help* file. Some commonly used combinations are

$c = [0\ 0\ 0] \rightarrow$ black
$c = [1\ 1\ 1] \rightarrow$ white
$c = [1\ 0\ 0] \rightarrow$ red
$c = [0\ 1\ 0] \rightarrow$ green
$c = [0\ 0\ 1] \rightarrow$ blue
$c = [1\ 1\ 0] \rightarrow$ yellow
$c = [1\ 0\ 1] \rightarrow$ magenta
$c = [0\ 1\ 1] \rightarrow$ cyan
$c = [0.5\ 0.5\ 0.5] \rightarrow$ gray

To show the distinction between `surf` and `mesh` and to illustrate the use of `colormap`, we replace `surf` in the previous script with

```
mesh(x1,x2,z)
colormap([0 0 1])
```

and obtain Figure 7.6, in which all the lines of the surface mesh are now blue.
The function

```
grid off
```

removes the grid lines in these figures. To put them back we use

```
grid on
```

In addition, we can place a box around the figure using

```
box on
```

Thus, we modify Figure 7.6 by removing its grid lines and placing a box around it. The script is

```
xx1 = linspace(-3,3,15);
xx2 = linspace(-3,13,17);
[x1,x2] = meshgrid(xx1,xx2);
z = x1.^4+3*x1.^2-2*x1+6-2*x2.*x1.^2+x2.^2-2*x2;
mesh(x1, x2,z)
colormap([0 0 1])
```

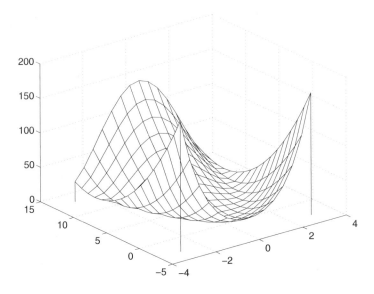

FIGURE 7.6
Surface generated with mesh with its colors changed with colormap.

```
x11 = [-3 -3 3 3];
x22 = [-3 13 13 -3];
z2 = x11.^4+3*x11.^2-2*x11+6-2*x22.*x11.^2+x22.^2-2*x22;
hold on
plot3([x11;x11],[x22;x22],[zeros(1,4);z2],'b')
grid off
box on
```

The execution of this script generates Figure 7.7. On the other hand, if we turn off the grid lines with grid off, remove the box and axes with

```
box off
```

and

```
axis off
```

respectively, we obtain Figure 7.8.

There are several other ways to visually enhance the surfaces appearing in Figures 7.3 through 7.8. These are summarized in Figures 7.9 to 7.13. Figure 7.9 is obtained with the following script:

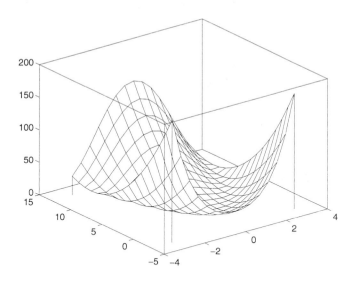

FIGURE 7.7
Figure 7.6 with grid off and box on.

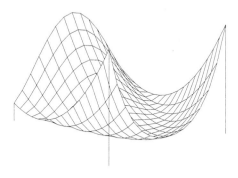

FIGURE 7.8
Figure 7.6 with grid off, box off, and axis off.

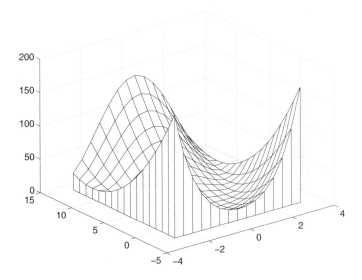

FIGURE 7.9
Surface generated with meshz.

```
xx1 = linspace(–3,3,15);
xx2 = linspace(–3,13,17);
[x1,x2] = meshgrid(xx1,xx2);
z = x1.^4+3*x1.^2–2*x1+6–2*x2.*x1.^2+x2.^2–2*x2;
meshz(x1,x2,z)
colormap([0 0 1])
```

Figure 7.10 is obtained by replacing meshz in the above script with

```
waterfall
```

The arguments for waterfall are the same as those for meshz.
      The surfaces can also be transformed into various contour plots using either

```
contour
```

for 2D contour plots,

```
contour3
```

for 3D contour plots and

```
contourf
```

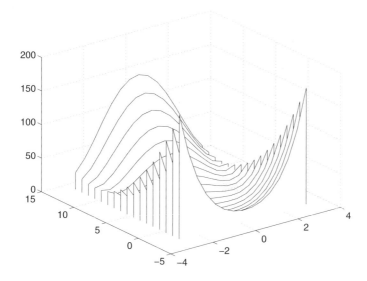

FIGURE 7.10
Surface generated with waterfall.

for filled contour plots. The contour and contour3 functions can be labeled by following either of these expressions with

        clabel

Contourf can be annotated using

        colorbar

which places a bar of colors and their corresponding numerical values adjacent to the figure. We now illustrate the application of these functions.

To obtain only the 2D contours of the surface shown in Figure 7.4, we have

        xx1 = linspace(−3,3,15);
        xx2 = linspace(−3,13,17);
        [x1,x2] = meshgrid(xx1,xx2);
        z = x1.^4+3*x1.^2−2*x1+6−2*x2.*x1.^2+x2.^2−2*x2;
        h = contour(x1,x2,z);
        clabel(h)

The execution of this script results in Figure 7.11. The expression h = contour(...) is required when clabel is used. If clabel is not used—that is, the contour lines are displayed without their numerical values—then only contour(...) is used. If we replace

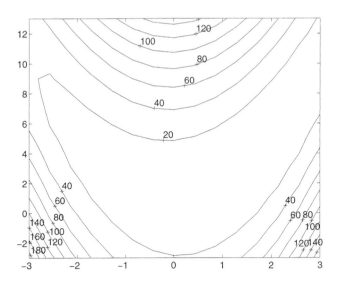

FIGURE 7.11
Labeled contour plot using `contour` and `clabel`.

`contour` with `contour3` we obtain Figure 7.12. The arguments for `contour` and `contour3` are the same.

To obtain a filled colored contour map we use `contourf` and `colorbar` as follows:

```
xx1 = linspace(-3,3,15);
xx2 = linspace(-3,13,17);
[x1,x2] = meshgrid(xx1,xx2);
z = x1.^4+3*x1.^2-2*x1+6-2*x2.*x1.^2+x2.^2-2*x2;
contourf(x1,x2,z);
colorbar('vert')
```

where `vert` tells `colorbar` to display the color bar vertically. Execution of this script gives the results shown in Figure 7.13.

One can also use a 2D curve as a generator to create surfaces of volumes of revolution using

```
cylinder
```

To illustrate this consider the curve

$$y = 1.1 + \sin(z) \qquad 0 \le z \le 2\pi$$

which is rotated 360° about the z-axis. The script is

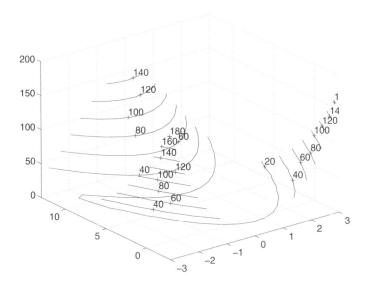

FIGURE 7.12
Labeled 3D contour plot using `contour3` and `clabel`.

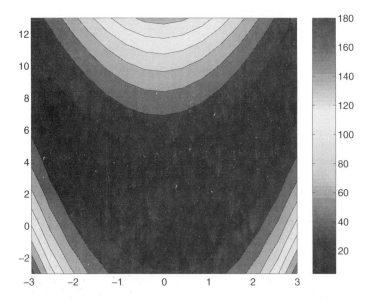

FIGURE 7.13
The application of `contourf` and `colorbar`.

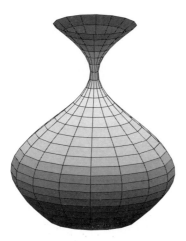

FIGURE 7.14
Application of cylinder.

```
[x,y,z] = cylinder(1.1+sin(0:0.25:2*pi),16);
surf(x,y,z)
axis off
```

which, upon execution, gives the results shown in Figure 7.14.

In Figure 7.14, the viewing angles are the default values. There are instances, though, when one wants to change the default viewing angle of the 3D image because either (1) it does not display the features of the surface that are of interest, (2) it is desirable to display several different views of the surface using subplot, or (3) one wants to explore the surface from many different views before deciding on the final orientation. MATLAB provides a straightforward way to determine the viewing direction using rotate3d and view. In Figure 7.15, the viewing angles were determined in the following manner. In the MATLAB command window the statement rotate3d is typed or the rotation icon is clicked in the figure window. This activates the left mouse button. In the figure window the left mouse button is depressed and held while the mouse is moved so that the axes are reoriented to another position that seems to improve the view. The mouse button is released and the 3D drawing observed. If the view is not satisfactory, then the process is repeated until a suitable orientation is found. After a suitable orientation is found, we return to the MATLAB command window and type

```
[az,elev] = view
```

FIGURE 7.15
Figure 7.14 after use of `rotate3d` and `view`.

Two numbers are displayed, the first for *az* and the second for *elev* (any variable names can be used). Then, in the script file, one inserts after the surface-generating function

    view(n,m)

where *n* is the *numerical* value for *az* and *m* is the *numerical* value *elev*. Using this procedure it was found that $az = -35.5$ and $elev = -34$; hence, the revised script is

    [x,y,z] = cylinder(1+sin(0:0.25:2*pi),16);
    surf(x,y,z)
    view(−35.5,−34)
    axis off

which, upon execution, gives Figure 7.15.
Multiple surfaces on one figure can also be generated. Consider the surface

$$z(r,\theta) = r^3 \cos(3\theta)$$

where $0 \le r \le 1$ and $0 \le \theta \le 2\pi$. It is assumed that this surface intersects two parallel discs of radius 1 located at $z = \pm 0.5$. The script to generate these surfaces is

    nr = 12; nth = 50;
    r = linspace(0,1,nr);
    theta = linspace(0,2*pi,nth);
    [R,T] = meshgrid(r,theta);

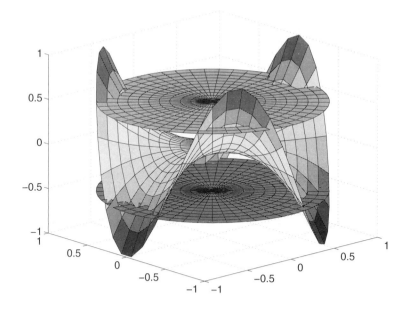

FIGURE 7.16
Intersection of two discs with a surface.

```
x = cos(theta')*r;
y = sin(theta')*r;
surf(x,y,R.^3.*cos(3*T))
hold on
z0 = repmat(0.5,size(x));
surf(x,y,z0)
surf(x,y,-z0)
view(-42.5,20)
```

which, upon execution, gives Figure 7.16.

Example 7.2 Generation of planes

When three points in space, $\mathbf{P}_o(x_o,y_o,z_o)$, $\mathbf{P}_1(x_1,y_1,z_1)$, and $\mathbf{P}_2(x_2,y_2,z_2)$, have been specified, the parametric representation of any point in a plane containing these three points is given by

$$\mathbf{P} = \mathbf{P}_o + s\mathbf{v} + t\mathbf{w}$$

where

$$\mathbf{P} = x\mathbf{i} + y\mathbf{j} + z\mathbf{k}$$
$$\mathbf{P}_o = x_o\mathbf{i} + y_o\mathbf{j} + z_o\mathbf{k}$$
$$\mathbf{v} = v_1\mathbf{i} + v_2\mathbf{j} + v_3\mathbf{k} = (x_1 - x_o)\mathbf{i} + (y_1 - y_o)\mathbf{j} + (z_1 - z_o)\mathbf{k}$$

$$\mathbf{w} = w_1\mathbf{i} + w_2\mathbf{j} + w_3\mathbf{k} = (x_2 - x_o)\mathbf{i} + (y_2 - y_o)\mathbf{j} + (z_2 - z_o)\mathbf{k}$$

and $0 \le s \le 1$ and $0 \le t \le 1$. Thus,

$$x = x_o + sv_1 + tw_1 = x_o + s(x_1 - x_o) + t(x_2 - x_o)$$
$$y = y_o + sv_2 + tw_2 = y_o + s(y_1 - y_o) + t(y_2 - y_o)$$
$$z = z_o + sv_3 + tw_3 = z_o + s(z_1 - z_o) + t(z_2 - z_o)$$

If it is assumed that we can adequately display the plane as a surface using a 5×5 grid of patches, then we can create a function called *PlanarSurface* that creates and displays this planar surface.

```
function PlanarSurface(P0,P1,P2)
v = P1–P0;
w = P2–P0;
S = 0:0.2:1;
[s,t] = meshgrid(S,S);
xx = P0(1)+s*v(1)+t*w(1);
yy = P0(2)+s*v(2)+t*w(2);
zz = P0(3)+s*v(3)+t*w(3);
surf(xx,yy,zz)
hold on
```

where P_o, P_1 and P_2 are each three-element vectors containing the coordinates of the points on the plane. Thus, if we enter the following expression in the MATLAB command window,

PlanarSurface([0 0 0],[2 6 3],[7 1 5])

we obtain the results shown in Figure 7.17.

To project this surface onto the three orthogonal coordinate reference planes, we take the appropriate dot products. Thus, to project the planar surface onto the *xy*-plane we have

$$\mathbf{P}\cdot(\mathbf{i} + \mathbf{j} + 0\mathbf{k})$$

which is equivalent to setting all the *z*-coordinates of the points comprising the plane to the minimum value of the display's *z*-coordinate. Similarly, we have for the projection onto the *yz*-plane

$$\mathbf{P}\cdot(0\mathbf{i} + \mathbf{j} + \mathbf{k})$$

which is equivalent to setting all the *x*-coordinates of the points comprising the plane to the maximum value of the display's *x*-coordinate. For the projection onto the *xz*-plane we have

$$\mathbf{P}\cdot(\mathbf{i} + 0\mathbf{j} + \mathbf{k})$$

which is equivalent to setting all the *y*-coordinates of the points comprising the plane to the maximum value of the display's *y*-coordinate. Thus, we can modify *SurfacePlanar* to include the option to include these projections.

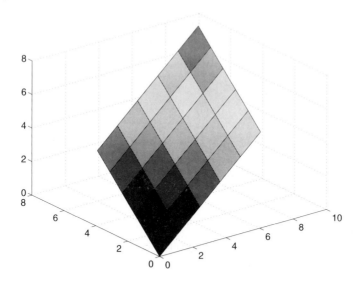

FIGURE 7.17
Generation of a planar surface.

```
function PlanarSurface(P0,P1,P2,projection)
v = P1−P0;
w = P2−P0;
S = 0:0.2:1; L = length(S);
[s,t] = meshgrid(S,S);
xx = P0(1)+s*v(1)+t*w(1);
yy = P0(2)+s*v(2)+t*w(2);
zz = P0(3)+s*v(3)+t*w(3);
surf(xx,yy,zz)
hold on
if nargin>3
 a = axis;
 c(1:L,1:L,1:3) = zeros(L,L,3);
 c(:,:,1) = 1;
 c(:,:,2) = 1;
 c(:,:,3) = 0;
 surf(xx,yy,a(5)*ones(L,L),c)
 surf(xx,a(4)*ones(L,L),zz,c)
 surf(a(2)*ones(L,L),yy,zz,c)
end
```

where *projection* is any number. The array c is defined such that the projections are
displayed in yellow. The first two indices of array c must be of the same order as *xx*, *yy*, and

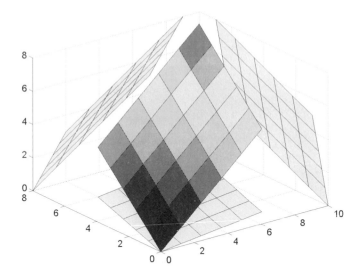

FIGURE 7.18
Projection of a plane onto its coordinate reference planes.

zz. The last index must represent exactly three elements, each of which can have a value from zero to one. These last three elements specify the color of each patch at each combination of the first two indices. If we enter in the MATLAB command window

PlanarSurface([0 0 0],[2 6 3],[7 1 5],1)

we obtain the results shown in Figure 7.18. Although there is an illusion that the projections do not appear to be in their designated planes, the use of `rotate3d` will confirm that they are.

Example 7.3 Generation of boxes

We now use the results of Example 7.2 to create rectangular parallelepipeds (boxes) whose dimensions are $L_x \times L_y \times L_z$. Referring to Figure 7.1, we see that the boxes are composed of six planes, each of which has the following three sets of points to define it.

Surfaces perpendicular to *yz*-plane

$\mathbf{P}_o(x_o,y_o,z_o)$, $\mathbf{P}_1(x_o,y_o,z_o+L_z)$, $\mathbf{P}_2(x_o,y_o+L_y,z_o)$
$\mathbf{P}_o(x_o+L_x,y_o,z_o)$, $\mathbf{P}_1(x_o+L_x,y_o,z_o+L_z)$, $\mathbf{P}_2(x_o+L_x,y_o+L_y,z_o)$

Surfaces perpendicular to *xz*-plane

$\mathbf{P}_o(x_o,y_o,z_o)$, $\mathbf{P}_1(x_o,y_o,z_o+L_z)$, $\mathbf{P}_2(x_o+L_x,y_o,z_o)$
$\mathbf{P}_o(x_o,y_o+L_y,z_o)$, $\mathbf{P}_1(x_o,y_o+L_y,z_o+L_z)$, $\mathbf{P}_2(x_o+L_x,y_o+L_y,z_o)$

Surfaces perpendicular to *xy*-plane

$\mathbf{P}_o(x_o,y_o,z_o)$, $\mathbf{P}_1(x_o+L_x,y_o,z_o)$, $\mathbf{P}_2(x_o,y_o+L_y,z_o)$
$\mathbf{P}_o(x_o,y_o,z_o+L_z)$, $\mathbf{P}_1(x_o+L_x,y_o,z_o+L_z)$, $\mathbf{P}_2(x_o,y_o+L_y,z_o+L_z)$

We use these relations in the following function called *BoxSurface*

```
function BoxSurface(P0,L)
PlanarSurface(P0,P0+[0 0 L(3)],P0+[0 L(2) 0])
PlanarSurface(P0+[L(1) 0 0],P0+[L(1) 0 L(3)],P0+[L(1) L(2) 0])
PlanarSurface(P0,P0+[0 0 L(3)],P0+[L(1) 0 0])
PlanarSurface(P0+[0 L(2) 0],P0+[0 L(2) L(3)],P0+[L(1) L(2) 0])
PlanarSurface(P0,P0+[L(1) 0 0],P0+[0 L(2) 0])
PlanarSurface(P0+[0 0 L(3)],P0+[L(1) 0 L(3)],P0+[0 L(2) L(3)])
```

where $\mathbf{P}_o = [x_o,y_o,z_o]$, $L = [L_x,L_y,L_z]$, and *PlanarSurface* is given in Example 7.2.

Consider the following script that generates three boxes with the following dimensions and locations of one of its corners.

Box #1

Size: 3×5×7
Location: (1,1,1)

Box #2

Size: 4×5×1
Location: (3,4,5)

Box #3

Size: 1×1×1
Location: (4.5,5.5,6)

The script to create and display these boxes is

```
BoxSurface([1,1,1],[3,5,7])
BoxSurface([3,4,5],[4,5,1])
BoxSurface([4.5,5.5,6],[1,1,1])
view(29.5,44)
```

which, upon execution, gives Figure 7.19.

Example 7.4 Rotation and translation of 3D objects: a car chassis

The rotation and translation of a point $p(x,y,z)$ to another location $P(X,Y,Z)$ is given by[1]

---

[1] W. Gellert, H. Kustner, M. Hellwich, and H. Kastner, *The VNR Concise Encyclopedia of Mathematics*, Van Nostrand Reinhold, New York, 1975, pp. 534–535.

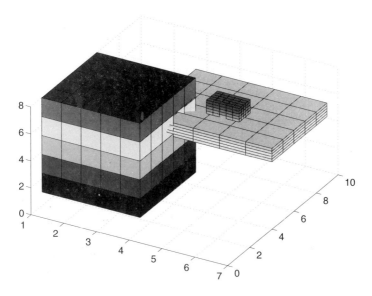

FIGURE 7.19
Three boxes.

$$X = L_x + a_{11}x + a_{12}y + a_{13}z$$
$$Y = L_y + a_{21}x + a_{22}y + a_{23}z$$
$$Z = L_z + a_{21}x + a_{22}y + a_{23}z$$

where L_x, L_y, and L_z are the (x,y,z) components of the translation, respectively, and a_{ij} are the elements of

$$a = \begin{bmatrix} \cos\psi\cos\chi & -\cos\psi\sin\chi & \sin\psi \\ \cos\phi\sin\chi + \sin\phi\sin\psi\cos\chi & \cos\phi\cos\chi - \sin\phi\sin\psi\sin\chi & -\sin\phi\cos\psi \\ \sin\phi\sin\chi - \cos\phi\sin\psi\cos\chi & \sin\phi\cos\chi + \cos\phi\sin\psi\sin\chi & \cos\phi\cos\psi \end{bmatrix}$$

The quantities ϕ, ψ, and χ are the ordered rotation angles (Euler angles) of the coordinate system about the origin: ϕ about the x-axis, then ψ about the y-axis, and finally χ about the z-axis. In general, (x,y,z) can be scalars, vectors of the same length, or matrices of the same order.

Before we apply these relations, we create the following function to implement them:

```
function [Xrt, Yrt, Zrt] = EulerAngles(psi,chi,phi,Lx,Ly,Lz,x,y,z)
R = [cos(psi)*cos (chi), −cos(psi)*sin(chi), sin(psi);
    cos(phi)*sin(chi)+sin(phi)*sin(psi)*cos(chi),
    cos(phi)*cos(chi)−sin(phi)*sin(psi)*sin(chi), −sin(phi)*cos(psi);
```

Torus

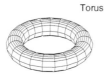

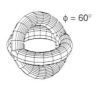

$\phi = 60°$

$\psi = 60°$

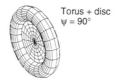

Torus + disc
$\psi = 90°$

FIGURE 7.20
Rotations of a torus and a torus and interior disc.

```
      sin(phi)*sin(chi)-cos(phi)*sin(psi)*cos(chi),
      sin(phi)*cos(chi)+cos(phi)*sin(psi)*sin(chi), cos(phi)*cos(psi)];
Xrt = R(1,1)*x+R(1,2)*y+R(1,3)*z+Lx;
Yrt = R(2,1)*x+R(2,2)*y+R(2,3)*z+Ly;
Zrt = R(3,1)*x+R(3,2)*y+R(3,3)*z+Lz;
```

We now illustrate the use of these transformation equations with the manipulation of a torus, which will be used to represent a car tire. It is expressed as

$$z = \pm\sqrt{a^2 - \left(\sqrt{x^2 + y^2} - b\right)^2}$$

where

$$x = r\cos\theta$$
$$y = r\sin\theta$$

and $b - a \le r \le b + a$, $0 \le \theta \le 2\pi$, and $b > a$.

First we plot the torus by itself, then we plot the torus rotated 60° about the x-axis only ($\phi = 60°$) and then rotated 60° about the y-axis only ($\psi = 60°$). Finally, we place a disc that is originally in the $z = 0$ plane inside the torus and rotate both of them 90° about the about y-axis ($\psi = 90°$). The results are shown in Figure 7.20. Before creating the script, we first create two additional functions. The first describes the torus.

```
function [X,Y,Z] = CarTire(a,b)
r = linspace(b–a,b+a,10);
th = linspace(0,2*pi,22);
x = r'*cos(th);
y = r'*sin(th);
z = real(sqrt(a^2–(sqrt(x.^2+y.^2)–b).^2));
X = [x x];
Y = [y y];
Z = [z –z];
```

where `real` is used to eliminate any small imaginary parts caused by numerical round-off. The second function generates the disc.

```
function [XD,YD,ZD] = CarDisc(a,b)
discr = linspace(0,b–a,7);
th = linspace(0,2*pi,16);
XD = discr'*cos(th);
YD = discr'*sin(th);
ZD = zeros(7,16);
```

For $a = 0.2$ and $b = 0.8$, the script is

```
a = 0.2; b = 0.8;
[X Y Z] = CarTire(a,b);
[XD YD ZD] = CarDisc(a,b);
Lx = 0; Ly = 0; Lz = 0;
for k = 1:4
 subplot(2,2,k)
 switch k
 case 1
  mesh(X,Y,Z)
  v = axis;
  axis([v(1) v(2) v(3) v(4) –1 1])
  text(0.5,–0.5,1,'Torus')
 case 2
  psi = 0; chi = 0; phi = pi/3;
  [Xr Yr Zr] = EulerAngles(psi,chi,phi,Lx,Ly,Lz,X,Y,Z);
  mesh(X,Y,Z)
  hold on
  mesh(Xr,Yr,Zr)
  text(0.5,–0.5,1,'\phi = 60\circ')
 case 3
  psi = pi/3; chi = 0; phi = 0;
```

```
 [Xr Yr Zr] = EulerAngles(psi,chi,phi,Lx,Ly,Lz,X,Y,Z);
 mesh(X,Y,Z)
 hold on
 mesh(Xr,Yr,Zr)
 text(0.5,-0.5,1,'\psi = 60\circ')
case 4
 psi = pi/2; chi = 0; phi = 0;
 [Xr Yr Zr] = EulerAngles(psi,chi,phi,Lx,Ly,Lz,X,Y,Z);
 [Xd Yd Zd] = EulerAngles(psi,chi,phi,Lx,Ly,Lz,XD,YD,ZD);
 mesh(Xd,Yd,Zd)
 hold on
 mesh(Xr,Yr,Zr)
 text(0.5,-0.5,0.7,'\psi = 90\circ')
 text(0.5,-0.5,1,'Torus + disc')
 end
 colormap([0 0 1])
 axis equal
 axis off
 grid off
end
```

We shall now use the torus and interior disc and create a car chassis and its tires as shown in Figure 7.21. To do this, we also need to create a cylinder whose description is given by

$$x = r\cos\theta$$
$$y = r\sin\theta$$
$$z = z$$

It assumed that the cylinder's diameter is $0.3(b - a)$ and that is has various lengths depending on what element it represents. To make the script more readable, we create an additional function, which generates a shaft of length $2L_2$.

```
function [XC,YC,ZC] = CarShaft(a,b,L2)
th = linspace(0,2*pi,16);
[XC,ZC] = meshgrid(0.3*(b-a)*cos(th), [-L2 L2]);
YC = meshgrid(0.3*(b-a)*sin(th), [-L2 L2]);
```

The script is

```
a = 0.2; b = 0.8;
[X Y Z] = CarTire(a,b);
[XD YD ZD] = CarDisc(a,b);
psi = [pi/2 pi/2 pi/2 pi/2]; chi = [0 0 0 0]; phi = [0 0 0 0];
```

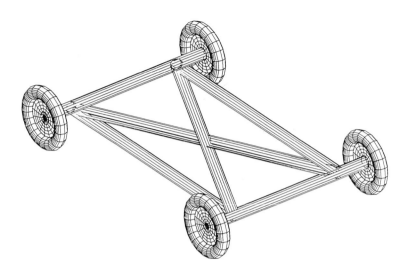

FIGURE 7.21
Car chassis.

```
Lx = [3 –3 3 –3]; Ly = [0 0 8 8]; Lz = [0 0 0 0];
for k = 1:4
  [Xr Yr Zr] = EulerAngles(psi(k),chi(k),phi(k),Lx(k),Ly(k),Lz(k),X,Y,Z);
  [Xd Yd Zd] = EulerAngles(psi(k),chi(k),phi(k),Lx(k),Ly(k),Lz(k),XD,YD,ZD);
  mesh(Xd,Yd,Zd)
  hold on
  mesh(Xr,Yr,Zr)
end
psi = [pi/2 pi/2 0 0 atan(0.5) –atan(0.5)];
chi = [0 0 0 0 0 0];
phi = [0 0 pi/2 pi/2 pi/2 pi/2];
Lx = [0 0 2 –2 0 0]; Ly = [0 8 4 4 4 4]; Lz = [0 0 0 0 0 0];
for k = 1:6
 switch k
 case {1,2}
   [XC,YC,ZC] = CarShaft(a,b,[–3 3]);
 case {3,4}
   [XC,YC,ZC] = CarShaft(a,b,[–4 4]);
 case{5,6}
   [XC,YC,ZC] = CarShaft(a,b,[–4.4721 4.4721]);
 end
 [Xc Yc Zc] = EulerAngles(psi(k),chi(k),phi(k),Lx(k),Ly(k),Lz(k),XC,YC,ZC);
```

```
mesh(Xc,Yc,Zc)
end
colormap([0 0 1])
axis equal
axis off
```

EXERCISES

7.1 Plot the following three-dimensional curves.[2] Use `axis equal`.

<u>Spherical helix</u> ($c = 5.0$, $0 \le t \le 10\pi$)

$$x = \sin(t/2c)\cos(t)$$
$$y = \sin(t/2c)\sin(t)$$
$$z = \cos(t/2c)$$

<u>Sine wave on cylinder</u> ($a = 10.0$, $b = 1.0$, $c = 0.3$, $0 \le t \le 2\pi$)

$$x = b\cos(t)$$
$$y = b\sin(t)$$
$$z = c\cos(at)$$

<u>Sine wave on sphere</u> ($a = 10.0$, $b = 1.0$, $c = 0.3$, $0 \le t \le 2\pi$)

$$x = \cos(t)\sqrt{b^2 - c^2\cos^2(at)}$$
$$y = \sin(t)\sqrt{b^2 - c^2\cos^2(at)}$$
$$z = c\cos(at)$$

<u>Toroidal spiral</u> ($a = 0.2$, $b = 0.8$, $c = 20.0$, $0 \le t \le 2\pi$)

$$x = \left[b + a\sin(ct)\right]\cos(t)$$
$$y = \left[b + a\sin(ct)\right]\sin(t)$$
$$z = a\cos(ct)$$

7.2 Plot the surfaces of the following solids.[3] Use the vector form of the coordinate transformation $x = r\cos(\theta)$ and $y = r\sin(\theta)$ or $x = a\cos(\theta)$ and $y = b\sin(\theta)$ as appropriate in (a) thru (f), and let r (or a and/or b) be of length 10 and θ of length 22. Exercise (g) requires `meshgrid`. All of these shapes require `axis equal`.

<u>Sphere</u> ($r = 1$, $0 \le \theta \le 2\pi$)

$$z = \sqrt{1 - x^2 - y^2}$$

[2] D. von Seggern, *CRC Standard Curves and Surfaces*, CRC Press, Inc., Boca Raton, FL, 1993.
[3] D. von Seggern, *ibid*.

Ellipsoid ($a = 1.0$, $b = 1.5$, $c = 2.0$)

$$z = c\sqrt{1 - x^2/a^2 - y^2/b^2}$$

Oblate spheroid (Ellipsoid with $a = b > c$: $a = b = 1.0$, $c = 0.5$)

Prolate spheroid (Ellipsoid with $a = b < c$: $a = b = 1.0$, $c = 1.2$)

Cone ($-2 \leq x \leq 2$, $-2 \leq y \leq 2$) [Must use surf twice.]

$$z = \pm\sqrt{x^2 + y^2}$$

where $x = r\cos\theta$ and $y = r\sin\theta$ for $0 \leq r \leq 2$ and $0 \leq \theta \leq 2\pi$.

Cornucopia ($a = 0.3$, $b = 0.5$, $0 \leq u \leq 2\pi$, $-3 \leq v \leq 3$) [Use rotate3d to explore the surface.]

$$x = e^{bv}\cos(v) + e^{av}\cos(u)\cos(v)$$
$$y = e^{bv}\sin(v) + e^{av}\cos(u)\sin(v)$$
$$z = e^{av}\sin(u)$$

7.3 Plot the following surfaces[4] and use rotate3d to explore them.

a) ($a = b = 1$, $c = 0.5$, $-3 \leq x \leq 3$, $-3 \leq y \leq 3$)

$$z = c\left((x/a)^4 \pm (y/b)^4\right)$$

b) ($a = 3$, $c = 0.25$, $-1 \leq x \leq 1$, $-1 \leq y \leq 1$)

$$z = c\sin\left(2\pi a\sqrt{x^2 + y^2}\right)$$

c) ($a = 3$, $c = 0.25$, $-1 \leq x \leq 1$, $-1 \leq y \leq 1$)

$$z = c\sin(2\pi axy)$$

d) ($c = 0.2$, $-1 \leq x \leq 1$, $-1 \leq y \leq 1$; $x \neq 0$, $y \neq 0$)

$$z = c\ln(|xy|)$$

e) Catenoid ($1 \leq u \leq 5$, $0 \leq v \leq 2\pi$)

$$x = u\cos(v)$$
$$y = u\sin(v)$$
$$z = \cosh^{-1}(u)$$

f) Right helicoid ($c = 1/2\pi$, $-0.5 \leq u \leq 0.5$, $-2\pi \leq v \leq 2\pi$)

$$x = u\cos(v)$$
$$y = u\sin(v)$$
$$z = cv$$

---

[4] D. von Seggern, *ibid.*

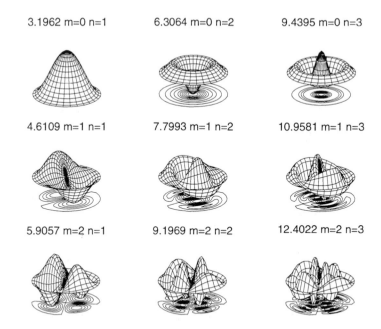

FIGURE 7.22
Mode shapes of a circular plate.

7.4 The mode shape of a solid circular plate clamped along its outer boundary $r = b$ is[5]

$$w_{mn}(r,\theta) = \left[C_{mn}J_m(\Omega_{mn}r/b) + I_m(\Omega_{mn}r/b)\right]\cos(m\theta)$$

where $m = 0, 1, 2, \ldots$, $J_m(x)$ is the Bessel function of the first kind of order m and $I_m(x)$ is the modified Bessel function of the first kind of order m,

$$C_{mn} = -\frac{I_m(\Omega_{mn})}{J_m(\Omega_{mn})}$$

and Ω_{mn} are the solutions to

$$J_m(\Omega_{mn})I_{m+1}(\Omega_{mn}) + I_m(\Omega_{mn})J_{m+1}(\Omega_{mn}) = 0$$

and have already been obtained in Exercise 5.2(f).

Using the results of Exercise 5.2(f) in which the lowest three natural frequency coefficients for $m = 0, 1, 2$ have been determined, plot the corresponding nine mode shapes with `surfc` on one figure using `subplot`, and place at the top of each figure the value of m, n, and the frequency coefficient. Do not draw the x and y axes. The first row is for $m = 0$, and so on. Normalize each mode shape using the `max` function twice (because the displacement field is a matrix) so that the maximum amplitude is 1. It is suggested that the number of radial divisions (r/b) be 15 and those for the angular divisions be

---

[5] E. B. Magrab, *Vibration of Elastic Structural Members*, Sijthoff & Noordhoff, The Netherlands, 1979, p. 252.

30. The results should look like those shown in Figure 7.22, which has been obtained with `meshc` for clarity upon reproduction.

7.5 Consider a slab of thickness $2L$ in the x-direction and of very large dimensions in the y- and z-directions. If the slab, which is initially at a uniform constant temperature T_i at $t = 0$, is suddenly exposed to a convective environment of temperature T_∞, then the temperature distribution as a function of time and position within the slab is[6]

$$\frac{\theta}{\theta_i} = 2\sum_{n=1}^{\infty} \frac{\sin\delta_n \cos(\delta_n \eta)}{\delta_n + \sin\delta_n \cos(\delta_n)} \exp(-\delta_n^2 \tau)$$

where $\theta = \theta(\eta, \tau) = T - T_\infty$, $T = T(\eta, \tau)$ is the temperature in the slab, $\theta_i = T_i - T_\infty$, $\eta = x/L$, $\tau = \alpha^2 t/L^2$ is the nondimensional time (sometimes called the Fourier modulus), α is the thermal diffusivity, and δ_n are the solutions of

$$\cot\delta_n = \frac{\delta_n}{B_i}$$

where $B_i = \bar{h}L/k$ is the Biot number, $\bar{h}$ is the average heat transfer coefficient for convection from the entire surface and k is the thermal conductivity of the slab.

Find the lowest 20 values of δ_n for $B_i = 0.7$, and use them to plot the surface $\theta(\eta, \tau)/\theta_i$ for $0 \le \eta \le 1$ and $0 \le \tau \le 2$. Then use the `rotate3d` function interactively to obtain an acceptable view of the surface. Label the axes and title the figure. Also add vertical lines as shown in Figure 7.5 to aid further in the visualization of the surface.

7.6 Plot the following mode shape and its contours for a square membrane clamped on its outer boundary using 25 grid points in each direction for $0 \le x \le 1$ and $0 \le y \le 1$:

$$w_{23}(x, y) = \sin(2\pi x)\sin(3\pi y)$$

7.7 The mean Nusselt number for turbulent flow over a plate of length l is[7]

$$Nu = \frac{0.037\,\text{Re}^{0.8}\,\text{Pr}}{1 + 2.443\,\text{Re}^{-0.1}\left(\text{Pr}^{2/3} - 1\right)} \qquad 5\times10^5 \le \text{Re} \le 10^7 \quad 0.6 \le \text{Pr} \le 2000$$

where Re is the Reynolds number and Pr is the Prandtl number. Plot the $\log_{10}(Nu)$ as a surface that is a function of the $\log_{10}(\text{Re})$ and $\log_{10}(\text{Pr})$ over the ranges indicated. Connect vertical lines from the boundary plane of the figure to the corners of the surface as shown in Figure 7.5.

7.8 The location of the neutral axis of a steel reinforced concrete beam shown in Figure 7.23 is determined by the parameter k as defined below[8]

$$k = -\rho n + \sqrt{(\rho n)^2 + 2\rho n}$$

[6] D. R. Pitts and L. E. Sissom, *Theory and Practice of Heat Transfer*, Schaum's Outline Series, McGraw-Hill, New York, 1977, p. 79.
[7] W. Beitz and K. H. Kuttner, Eds., *Handbook of Mechanical Engineering*, Springer-Verlag, New York, 1994, p. C31.
[8] L. Spiegal and G. F. Limbrunner, *Reinforced Concrete Design*, 3rd ed., Prentice Hall, Upper Saddle River, NJ, 1992, p. 196.

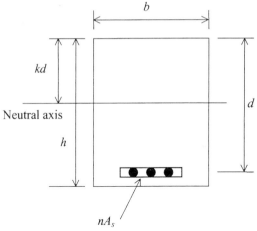

FIGURE 7.23
Section of a steel reinforced concrete beam.

where $\rho = A_s/bd$ and $n = E_s/E_c$, which is the ratio of the Young's modulus of the steel and concrete, respectively. Plot a surface of k as a function of n and ρ for ten values of n for $6 \leq n \leq 12$ and for nine values of ρ for $0.001 \leq \rho \leq 0.009$ plus another ten values for $0.01 \leq \rho \leq 0.1$.

7.9 The maximum nondimensional principal shear stress τ' in a rectangular beam subjected to a torsion T is obtained from[9]

$$\tau'^2 = \tau'^2_{xz} + \tau'^2_{yz}$$

where

$$\tau'_{xz} = \frac{\tau_{xz}J}{Ta} = -\frac{16}{\pi^2}\sum_{n=0}^{\infty}\frac{(-1)^n}{(2n+1)^2}\frac{\sinh(k_n\xi)}{\cosh(k_n b/a)}\cos(k_n\eta)$$

$$\tau'_{yz} = \frac{\tau_{yz}J}{Ta} = 2\eta - \frac{16}{\pi^2}\sum_{n=0}^{\infty}\frac{(-1)^n}{(2n+1)^2}\frac{\cosh(k_n\xi)}{\cosh(k_n b/a)}\sin(k_n\eta)$$

and J is the torsional constant, $\eta = x/a$ $(-1 \leq \eta \leq 1)$, $\xi = y/b$ $(-1 \leq \xi \leq 1)$ and $k_n = (2n+1)\pi/2$. Generate a surface of $\tau'^2(\eta,\xi)$ for $b/a = 1$, a square cross section, and in a separate figure a contour plot of $\tau'^2(\eta,\xi)$ with 30 contour lines. Use `rotate3d` to explore the surface. The results should look like those shown in Figures 7.24 and 7.25.

7.10 Consider the data in Table 7.1, which are the deviations of the output of a process about its mean value $z = 0$ for the given inputs x_1 and x_2. Use the `stem3` plotting function to obtain Figure 7.26. You will have to plot the plane at $z = 0$ with a separate command. Use `view(-30,7)` to obtain the orientation shown. (The 2D version is `stem`.)

---

[9] C. T. Wang, *Applied Elasticity*, McGraw-Hill, New York, 1953, p. 89.

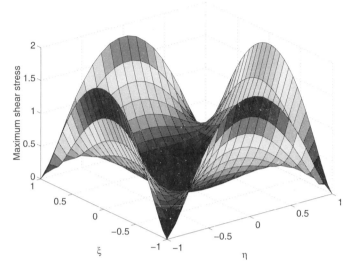

FIGURE 7.24
Square of the maximum shear stress from the torsion of a beam of square cross section.

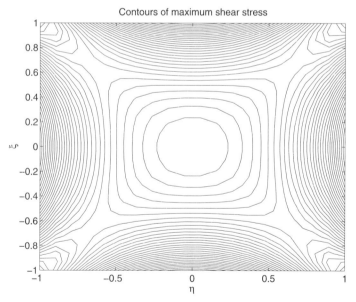

FIGURE 7.25
Contour representation of the maximum shear stress shown in Figure 7.24.

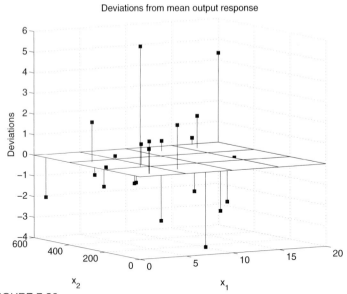

FIGURE 7.26
Deviations from the plane $z = 0$ using stem3.

TABLE 7.1
Deviations From Process Norms

x_1	x_2	z	x_1	x_2	z
2	50	1.5713	2	360	−0.6023
8	110	−1.1460	4	205	5.8409
11	120	−2.2041	4	400	−0.3620
10	550	−1.5968	20	600	4.3341
8	295	−2.8937	1	585	−2.0368
4	200	1.1136	10	540	−1.5415
2	375	1.9297	15	250	0.0302
2	52	1.1962	15	290	−2.1809
9	100	−3.8650	16	510	1.5587
8	300	−0.4763	17	590	0.3222
4	412	−1.3223	6	100	2.1478
11	400	−0.4619	5	400	0.1537
12	500	0.4911			

C H A P T E R   8

DESIGN OF MACHINE ELEMENTS

Edward B. Magrab

Various methods to analyze different types of machine elements are illustrated.

8.1 VECTORS, FORCES, AND THE EQUILIBRIUM OF RIGID BODIES

Consider the vector

$$\mathbf{a} = a_1\mathbf{i} + a_2\mathbf{j} + a_3\mathbf{k}$$

Its dot product is defined as

$$\mathbf{a} \bullet \mathbf{a} = a_1^2 + a_2^2 + a_3^2 \qquad (8.1)$$

and its magnitude is obtained from

$$a = |a| = \sqrt{\mathbf{a} \bullet \mathbf{a}} = \sqrt{a_1^2 + a_2^2 + a_3^2} \qquad (8.2)$$

If **a** is given by

a = [a1 a2 a3]

then the dot product is obtained from

adot = dot(a,a)

and its magnitude from either

maga = sqrt(dot(a,a))

or

maga = norm(a)

The direction cosines of **a** are

$$\cos(\alpha_j) = \frac{a_j}{|\mathbf{a}|} \quad j = 1,2,3 \qquad (8.3)$$

which are the components of a unit vector $\mathbf{u}_a$ in the direction of **a**; that is,

$$\mathbf{u}_a = \cos\alpha_1 \mathbf{i} + \cos\alpha_2 \mathbf{j} + \cos\alpha_3 \mathbf{k} = \frac{a_1}{|\mathbf{a}|}\mathbf{i} + \frac{a_2}{|\mathbf{a}|}\mathbf{j} + \frac{a_3}{|\mathbf{a}|}\mathbf{k} \qquad (8.4)$$

Therefore,

$$\mathbf{a} = |\mathbf{a}|\mathbf{u}_a \qquad (8.5)$$

and

$$\mathbf{u}_a \bullet \mathbf{u}_a = \cos^2\alpha_1 + \cos^2\alpha_2 + \cos^2\alpha_3 = \frac{a_1^2}{|\mathbf{a}|^2} + \frac{a_2^2}{|\mathbf{a}|^2} + \frac{a_3^2}{|\mathbf{a}|^2} = 1$$

where

$$\alpha_j = \cos^{-1}\frac{a_j}{|\mathbf{a}|} \quad j = 1,2,3 \qquad (8.6)$$

The unit vector $\mathbf{u}_a$ in the direction of $\mathbf{a}$ is obtained from

ua = a/norm(a)

and the values of the angles of its direction cosines in radians are

alpha = acos(a/norm(a))

and in degrees

alphadeg = acos(a/norm(a))*180/pi

If we have another vector

$$\mathbf{b} = b_1\mathbf{i} + b_2\mathbf{j} + b_3\mathbf{k}$$

then, if $\mathbf{c} = \mathbf{a} \pm \mathbf{b}$

$$\mathbf{c} = (a_1 \pm b_1)\mathbf{i} + (a_2 \pm b_2)\mathbf{j} + (a_3 \pm b_3)\mathbf{k} \qquad (8.7)$$

The addition and subtraction of vectors are

c = a+b

and

c = a–b

The cross-product of two vectors $\mathbf{a}$ and $\mathbf{b}$ is defined as

$$\mathbf{c} = \mathbf{a} \times \mathbf{b} = \begin{vmatrix} \mathbf{i} & \mathbf{j} & \mathbf{k} \\ a_1 & a_2 & a_3 \\ b_1 & b_2 & b_3 \end{vmatrix} = (a_2 b_3 - a_3 b_2)\mathbf{i} + (a_1 b_3 - a_3 b_1)\mathbf{j} + (a_1 b_2 - a_2 b_1)\mathbf{k} \qquad (8.8)$$

where $\mathbf{c}$ is perpendicular to the plane containing $\mathbf{a}$ and $\mathbf{b}$. The cross-product can be obtained from

c = cross(a,b)

To determine the magnitude of the cross-product in the direction specified by a unit vector $\mathbf{u}_a$, we use the triple scalar product to obtain

$$c_a = \mathbf{u}_a \bullet \mathbf{a} \times \mathbf{b} \qquad (8.9)$$

where c_a is a scalar. Then,

ca = dot(ua,cross(a,b))

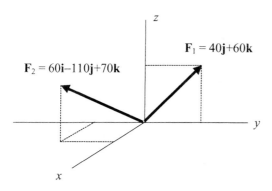

FIGURE 8.1
Orientation of forces for Example 8.1.

These results are now used to determine the solutions to a range of problems in the analysis of forces and moments on rigid members.

Example 8.1 Summation of forces

Consider the system of forces shown in Figure 8.1. We shall determine the magnitude of **F** and the values of the angles of the direction cosines α_i of the resultant force. Thus,

$$\mathbf{F}_R = \mathbf{F}_1 + \mathbf{F}_2$$

and from Eq. (8.6)

$$\alpha_i = \cos^{-1}\frac{F_{Ri}}{|\mathbf{F}_R|}$$

The script is

```
F1 = [0 40 60]; F2 = [60 –110 70];
resultant = norm(F2+F1)
angles = acos((F2+F1)/resultant)*180/pi
```

When the script is executed, we obtain $|\mathbf{F}| = resultant = 159.3738$ and $\alpha = angles = [67.8846\ 116.0541\ 35.3441]$, which are in degrees.

Example 8.2 Components of a force

Consider the force shown in Figure 8.2. We shall determine the components of the force $\mathbf{F}_C$ acting at C using Eqs. (8.4) and (8.5) and values of the angles of the direction cosines α_C of this force using Eq. (8.6). The script is

```
r = [24 –16 –48];
```

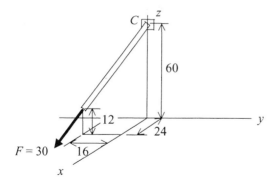

FIGURE 8.2
Orientation of force for Example 8.2.

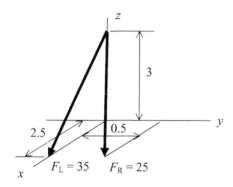

FIGURE 8.3
Orientation of forces for Example 8.3.

```
ur = r/norm(r);
Fcomps = 30*ur
angles = acos(ur)*180/pi
```

When the script is executed, we obtain $\mathbf{F}_C$ = *Fcomps* = [12.8571 −8.5714 −25.7143] and α_C = *angles* = [64.6231 106.6015 148.9973], which are in degrees.

Example 8.3 Magnitude of a resultant force

Consider the system of forces shown in Figure 8.3. We shall determine the components and magnitude of the resultant of forces $\mathbf{F}_L$ and $\mathbf{F}_R$, which is

$$\mathbf{F} = \mathbf{F}_L + \mathbf{F}_R$$

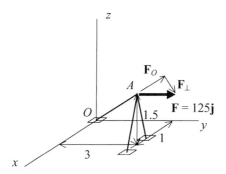

FIGURE 8.4
Orientation of force for Example 8.4

Using Eqs. (8.4), (8.5), and (8.2) the script is

```
rl = [2.5 0 –3]; rr = [2.5 0.5 –3];
F = 35*rl/norm(rl)+ 25*rr/norm(rr)
resultant = norm(F)
```

When the script is executed, we obtain $|\mathbf{F}|$ = *resultant* = 59.8818. The components of
F are *F* = [38.2815 3.1750 –45.9378].

Example 8.4 Magnitude of force components in specified directions

Consider the force shown in Figure 8.4. We shall determine the magnitude of the
components of **F** in a direction parallel ($\mathbf{F}_{OA}$) and perpendicular ($\mathbf{F}_\perp$) to member *OA* and the
magnitude of $\mathbf{F}_\perp$. Using Eqs. (8.4), (8.5), and (8.2) and noting that

$$\mathbf{F} = \mathbf{F}_{OA} + \mathbf{F}_\perp$$

the script is

```
r = [1 3 1.5]; F = [0 125 0];
ur = r/norm(r);
FoaPar = dot(F,ur)*ur
FoaPerp = F–FoaPar
FoaPerpMag = norm(FoaPerp)
```

When the script is executed, we obtain $\mathbf{F}_{OA}$ = *FoaPar* = [30.6122 91.8367 45.9184],
$\mathbf{F}_\perp$ = *FoaPerp* = [–30.6122 33.1633 –45.9184], and $|\mathbf{F}_\perp|$ = *FoaPerpMag* = 64.3848.

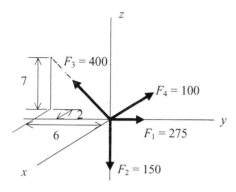

FIGURE 8.5
Orientation of forces for Example 8.5.

Example 8.5 Equilibrium force

Consider the system of forces shown in Figure 8.5. We shall determine the components, magnitude, and values of the angles of the direction cosines α of the force required to keep this system in equilibrium:

$$\mathbf{F} = -(\mathbf{F}_1 + \mathbf{F}_2 + \mathbf{F}_3 + \mathbf{F}_4)$$

Using Eqs. (8.4), (8.5), (8.2), and (8.6) the script is

```
F1 = [0 275 0]; F2 = [0 0 –150];
F4 = [–100 0 0]; r = [–2 –6 7];
F3 = 400*r/norm(r);
Fequil = –(F1+F2+F3+F4)
FequilMag = norm(Fequil)
angles = acos(Fequil/FequilMag)*180/pi
```

When the script is executed, we obtain $\mathbf{F}$ = *Fequil* = [184.7998 –20.6005 –146.7994], $|\mathbf{F}|$ = *FequilMag* = 236.9080 and α = *angles* = [38.7350 94.9885 128.2904], which are in degrees.

Example 8.6 Force magnitudes

Consider the system of forces shown in Figure 8.6. We shall determine the magnitude of $\mathbf{F}_1$, $\mathbf{F}_2$, and $\mathbf{F}_3$ when $\mathbf{W} = -85\mathbf{k}$. We first determine the components $\mathbf{F}_j = |\mathbf{F}_j|\mathbf{u}_j$, where $\mathbf{u}_j$ is the unit vector in the $\mathbf{r}_j = r_{j1}\mathbf{i} + r_{j2}\mathbf{j} + r_{j3}\mathbf{k}$ direction, $j = 1, 2, 3$, and is determined from Eqs. (8.4) and (8.5). Thus,

$$\mathbf{F}_1 + \mathbf{F}_2 + \mathbf{F}_3 + \mathbf{W} = 0$$

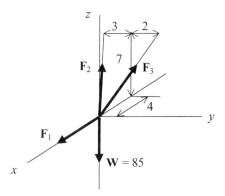

FIGURE 8.6
Orientation of forces for Example 8.6.

or

$$H_1\mathbf{i} + H_2\mathbf{j} + H_3\mathbf{k} = 85\mathbf{k}$$

$$H_n = \sum_{m=1}^{3} |F_m/r_m| r_{mn} \qquad n = 1,2,3$$

This can be rewritten in matrix form as

$$\begin{bmatrix} r_{11}/|\mathbf{r}_1| & r_{21}/|\mathbf{r}_2| & r_{31}/|\mathbf{r}_3| \\ r_{12}/|\mathbf{r}_1| & r_{22}/|\mathbf{r}_2| & r_{32}/|\mathbf{r}_3| \\ r_{13}/|\mathbf{r}_1| & r_{23}/|\mathbf{r}_2| & r_{33}/|\mathbf{r}_3| \end{bmatrix} \begin{bmatrix} /\mathbf{F}_1| \\ |\mathbf{F}_2| \\ |\mathbf{F}_3| \end{bmatrix} = \begin{bmatrix} 0 \\ 0 \\ 85 \end{bmatrix}$$

The script is

```
r1 = [1 0 0]; r2 = [–4 –3 7]; r3 = [–4 2 7];
u1 = r1/norm(r1);
u2 = r2/norm(r2);
u3 = r3/norm(r3);
Fmag123 = [u1' u2' u3']\[0 0 85]'
```

When the script is executed, we obtain $|\mathbf{F}_j| = Fmag123 = [48.5714\ 41.7827\ 60.5197]'$; that is, $|\mathbf{F}_1| = Fmag123(1) = 48.5714$, $|\mathbf{F}_2| = Fmag123(2) = 41.7827$ and $|\mathbf{F}_3| = Fmag123(3) = 60.5197$.

Example 8.7 Moment computation

Consider the force shown in Figure 8.7. We shall determine the magnitude of the moment created by $\mathbf{F}$ acting on member OA about point O. If $\mathbf{r}_a$ is the position vector from O to A

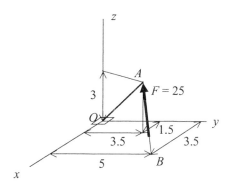

FIGURE 8.7
Orientation of force for Example 8.7.

and r_b is the position vector from O to B, then the components of $\mathbf{F}$ in the direction BA is $|\mathbf{F}|\mathbf{u}_f$, where $\mathbf{u}_f$ is the unit vector of $\mathbf{r}_a - \mathbf{r}_b$. Then, from Eq. (8.8) the moment is

$$\mathbf{M} = \mathbf{r}_a \times (|\mathbf{F}|\mathbf{u}_f)$$

and its magnitude is obtained from Eq. (8.2). The script is

    ra = [1.5 3.5 3]; rb = [3.5 5 0];
    F = 25*(ra–rb)/norm(ra–rb);
    FaboutA = cross(ra,F);
    Mmag = norm(FaboutA)

When the script is executed, we obtain $|\mathbf{M}| = Mmag = 121.0968$.

Example 8.8 Moment due to several forces

Consider the system of forces shown in Figure 8.8, which are acting on a structural member OAB. We shall determine the magnitude of the moment $\mathbf{M}$ created by $\mathbf{F}_1$, $\mathbf{F}_2$ and $\mathbf{F}_3$ about O and the angles α of its direction cosines. Thus,

$$\mathbf{M} = \mathbf{r}_a \times \mathbf{F}_1 + \mathbf{r}_a \times \mathbf{F}_2 + \mathbf{r}_b \times \mathbf{F}_3$$

where $\mathbf{r}_a$ is the position vector OA and $\mathbf{r}_b$ is the position vector OB. The script is

    ra = [0 11 0]; rb = [9 11 0];
    F1 = [–55 45 30]; F2 = [0 20 0]; F3 = [70 40 –50];
    Mro = cross(ra,F1)+cross(ra,F2)+cross(rb,F3);
    MroMag = norm(Mro)
    angles = acos(Mro/MroMag)*180/pi

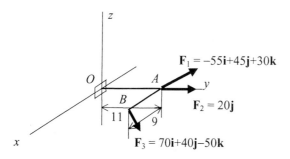

FIGURE 8.8
Orientation of forces for Example 8.8.

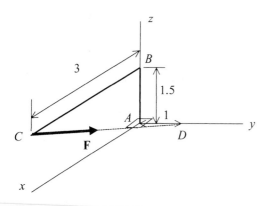

FIGURE 8.9
Orientation of force for Example 8.9.

When the script is executed, we obtain $|\mathbf{M}| = MroMag = 537.5174$ and $\alpha = angles =$ [114.1602 33.1563 68.7290], which are in degrees.

Example 8.9 Moment causing rotation about an axis

Consider the system of forces shown in Figure 8.9, where

$$\mathbf{F} = -30\mathbf{i} + 10\mathbf{j} - 15\mathbf{k}$$

is acting on the structural member *ABC*. We shall determine the moment produced by $\mathbf{F}$ that would rotate member *AB* about its axis, if it were not prevented from doing so. Thus,

$$|\mathbf{M}_{AB}| = \mathbf{u}_b \bullet \mathbf{r}_d \times \mathbf{F}$$

and

$$\mathbf{M}_{AB} = |\mathbf{M}_{AB}|\mathbf{u}_b$$

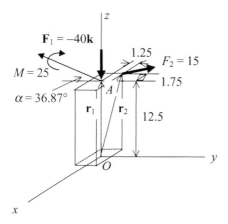

FIGURE 8.10
Orientation of forces for Example 8.10.

where $\mathbf{u}_b$ is the unit vector in the direction of AB and $\mathbf{r}_d$ is the vector in the direction of AD. The script is

    rb = [0 0 1.5]; rd = [0 1 0]; F = [−30 10 −15];
    ub = rb/norm(rb);
    Mab = dot(ub,cross(rd,F))
    MabVec = Mab*ub

When the script is executed, we obtain $|\mathbf{M}_{AB}| = Mab = 30$ and $\mathbf{M}_{AB} = MabVec = [0\ 0\ 30]$.

Example 8.10 Equivalent forces and moments

Consider the system of forces shown in Figure 8.10, where M is the moment acting about the line shown. We shall replace the forces and moment by an equivalent resultant force $\mathbf{F}_O$ and couple $\mathbf{M}_O$ acting through point O. Thus, if $\mathbf{r}_{AF}$ is a position vector representing the direction of M from A ($\alpha = 36.87°$ indicates a 3-4-5 triangle) and $\mathbf{r}_{21} = \mathbf{r}_2 - \mathbf{r}_1$, then

$$\mathbf{F}_2 = F_2\mathbf{r}_{21}/|\mathbf{r}_{21}|$$
$$\mathbf{M} = M\mathbf{r}_{AF}/|\mathbf{r}_{AF}|$$
$$\mathbf{F}_O = \mathbf{F}_1 + \mathbf{F}_2$$

and

$$\mathbf{M}_O = \mathbf{M} + \mathbf{r}_1 \times \mathbf{F}_1 + \mathbf{r}_2 \times \mathbf{F}_2$$

The script is

    r1 = [0 0 12.5]; r2 = [−1.75 1.25 12.5];

```
rAF = [0 −4 3]; F1 = [0 0 −40];
r21 = r2−r1;
F2 = 15*r21/norm(r21);
M = 25*rAF/norm(rAF);
FatO = F1+F2
MatO = M+cross(r1,F1)+cross(r2,F2)
```

When the script is executed, we obtain $\mathbf{F}_O = FatO = [−12.2060\ 8.7186\ −40.0000]$ and $\mathbf{M}_O = MatO = [−108.9822\ −172.5750\ 15.0000]$.

8.2 STRESSES AND DEFLECTIONS IN BEAMS, COLUMNS, AND SHAFTS

8.2.1 Statically Determinate Beams

The nondimensional equation governing the transverse displacement $w(x)$ of beams of constant cross section, length L, Young's modulus E, moment of inertia of its cross section I, and loading per unit length $P_o q(x)$ is

$$\frac{d^4 y}{d\eta^4} = q(\eta) \tag{8.10}$$

where $\eta = x/L$, $y = y(\eta) = w/h_o$, $h_o = P_o L^4/EI$, and P_o is a constant representing the maximum value of q. The slope θ_d, bending moment M_d about the beam's neutral axis, and shear V_d are expressed in terms of the non dimensional displacement y as follows:

$$\theta = \frac{\theta_d}{P_o L^3 / EI} = \frac{dy}{d\eta}$$

$$M = \frac{M_d}{P_o L^2} = \frac{d^2 y}{d\eta^2} \tag{8.11}$$

$$V = \frac{V_d}{P_o L} = \frac{d^3 y}{d\eta^3}$$

Using these nondimensional quantities we can generate numerical solutions that are explicitly independent of the beam's geometric and physical properties and the magnitude of the loading, and are just a function of the boundary conditions and shape of the load along the beam.

The maximum shear and bending stresses in the beam are, respectively,

$$\tau = \frac{\alpha V}{A} \quad \text{and} \quad \sigma = \frac{Mc}{I}$$

where A is the area of the beam's cross section, α is a factor that is a function of the shape of the beam's cross section and c is the distance from the neutral axis to the top (or bottom, if asymmetrical) edge of the beam's cross section. When the cross section is a solid circle $\alpha = 4/3$, when a rectangle $\alpha = 3/2$, and when a circular annulus $\alpha = 2$.

Rather than obtain a general analytical solution to Eq. (8.10) and solve it for different combinations of the boundary conditions and loading we propose to solve it only numerically using `ode45` and `fsolve`, which were discussed in Sections 5.5.4 and 5.5.5, respectively.

To convert Eq. (8.10) into the form acceptable to `ode45` we reformulate it into four first order equations. Thus, if

$$y_1 = y \qquad y_2 = \frac{dy}{d\eta}$$

$$y_3 = \frac{d^2 y}{d\eta^2} \qquad y_4 = \frac{d^3 y}{d\eta^3}$$

then Eq. (8.10) becomes

$$\frac{dy_1}{d\eta} = y_2 \qquad \frac{dy_2}{d\eta} = y_3$$

$$\frac{dy_3}{d\eta} = y_4 \qquad \frac{dy_4}{d\eta} = q \tag{8.12}$$

We recall from Section 5.5.4 that the output of `ode45` is a column vector representing the n values of η and an ($n \times 4$) array (which we denote yy) in which

$$yy(:,1) = y \qquad\qquad yy(:,3) = d^2 y/d\eta^2 = M$$
$$yy(:,2) = dy/d\eta = \theta \qquad yy(:,4) = d^3 y/d\eta^3 = V$$

The boundary conditions in terms of yy at each end of the beam, $\eta = 0$ and $\eta = 1$, for the three most common types of boundary conditions are given in Table 8.1.

In using `ode45` one can only specify the boundary conditions at $\eta = 0$. For a fourth order equation we have to specify four boundary conditions. Thus, we can only specify two at $\eta = 0$, because we also have to specify two boundary conditions at $\eta = 1$. Therefore, we pose the question: what values do the two unspecified boundary conditions at $\eta = 0$ have to have in order for the two boundary at $\eta = 1$ to be satisfied. The answer can be obtained approximately numerically using `fsolve`, which attempts to solve the nonlinear equations $F(x) = 0$. In our case $F(x)$ represents the two boundary conditions at $\eta = 1$ as determined from the `ode45` solution to Eqs. (8.12). The independent parameters in the search process are the two unspecified boundary conditions at $\eta = 0$.

The numerical procedure goes as follows. We guess at the values of the two unspecified boundary conditions at $\eta = 0$, solve Eq. (8.12) using `ode45`, and see if the boundary conditions at $\eta = 1$ are satisfied. If they aren't, then `fsolve` selects another set of values for the two unspecified boundary conditions at $\eta = 0$ and `ode45` again obtains a solution to Eq. (8.12). The process is repeated until an acceptable approximation to the boundary conditions at $\eta = 1$ is obtained.

TABLE 8.1
Common Boundary Conditions for Beams and Their Relationship to ode45

		From ode45[√]	
Type	Requirements	$\eta = 0$	$\eta = 1$
Simply supported $(y = M = 0)$	$y = d^2y/d\eta^2 = 0$	$yy(1,1) = yy(1,3) = 0$	$yy(\text{end},1) = yy(\text{end},3) = 0$
Clamped $(y = \theta = 0)$	$y = dy/d\eta = 0$	$yy(1,1) = yy(1,2) = 0$	$yy(\text{end},1) = yy(\text{end},2) = 0$
Free $(M = V = 0)$	$d^2y/d\eta^2 = d^3y/d\eta^3 = 0$	$yy(1,3) = yy(1,4) = 0$	$yy(\text{end},3) = yy(\text{end},4) = 0$

[√] $yy(:,1) = y;\quad yy(:,2) = dy/d\eta = \theta;\quad yy(:,3) = d^2y/d\eta^2 = M;\quad yy(:,4) = d^3y/d\eta^3 = V.$

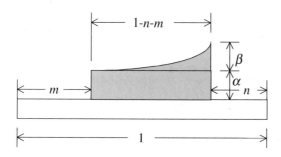

FIGURE 8.11
Nomenclature for a general loading on the beam.

We will now illustrate this with a series of examples. Before doing so, however, we will create several functions that will permit us a degree of flexibility. First we create two distinct loading distributions, one for a point load and the other for a continuous load. Referring to Figure 8.11 we assume for the continuous loading that

$$q(\eta) = \left[\alpha + \beta\left(\frac{\eta - m}{1 - n - m}\right)^k\right]\left[u(\eta - m) - u(\eta - 1 + n)\right] \tag{8.13}$$

where $u(x)$ is the unit step function, $k > 0$, $1 \geq n + m \geq 0$, $m \geq 0$, $n \geq 0$, $\alpha = 0$ or 1, and $\beta \geq 0$. For a point load at $\eta = \xi$, $0 \leq \xi \leq 1$,

$$q(\eta) = 1/2\varepsilon \quad \xi - \varepsilon < \eta < \xi + \varepsilon \tag{8.14}$$

where 2ε is the increment between adjacent values of η specified in ode45.

If we call the function that computes the loading *BeamLoad*, then the implementation of Eqs. (8.13) and (8.14) is

```
function lod = BeamLoad(eta,alpha,m,n,k,beta,xi,flag)
lod = 0;
if flag == 0
  if (eta>xi−.012)&(eta<xi+.012)
    lod = 1;
  end
else
  if (eta>=m)&(eta<=1−n)
    lod = alpha+beta*((eta−m)/(1−n−m))^k;
  end
end
```

where $eta = \eta$, $alpha = \alpha$, $m = m$, $n = n$, $k = k$, $beta = \beta$, $xi = \xi$, and $flag$ = 0 or 1. When $flag$ = 0 we have a point load and when $flag$ = 1 we have a distributed load. We will be incrementing η by 0.02, therefore we set ε = 0.012 so that 2ε = 0.024 is slightly greater than 0.02.

A function that is required by ode45 is the column vector that represents the four first order equations given by Eq. (8.12). Recall Section 5.5.4. We shall call this function *StaticBeam*. Thus,

```
function sb = StaticBeam(eta,w,d,alpha,m,n,k,beta,xi,flag)
sb = [w(2);w(3);w(4);BeamLoad(eta,alpha,m,n,k,beta,xi,flag)];
```

where $w(2) = y_2$, $w(3) = y_3$, $w(4) = y_4$, *BeamLoad* = q, which is given by Eqs. (8.13) and (8.14) and d is required by ode45, but is not used in this case.

We will plot and display the numerical results with a function called *BeamPlot*. This function will

- Plot the displacement, slope, moment, and shear along the length of the beam
- Display the values of shear and slope at each end of the beam
- Display the maximum values of the displacement, slope, moment, and shear and the locations at which they occur.

The function will do this for two different cases:[1]

1. When *over* = 0, we have the case for statically determinate beams given in this section
2. When *over* = 1, we have the case for beams with an overhang as discussed in Section 8.2.2

---

[1] This plotting function is used to plot the results from both this section and those from Section 8.2.2, which considers beams with overhangs. The discussion of the case when *over* = 1 can be left until after that section has been read.

The quantity *lenover* is the length of the over hanging portion of the beam and *rho*, *alpha_over, m_over, n_over, k_over, beta_over, xi_over,* and *flag_over* are analogous to *eta, alpha, m, n, k, beta, xi,* and *flag,* respectively, except that they pertain to the loading on the overhung portion of the beam. When *over* = 0 *ic* is a four element vector containing the four boundary conditions at η = 0, two of which were specified and two of which were determined by fsolve.

When we consider the overhung beam, the left end of the beam is considered only simply supported. Therefore, when *over* ≠ 0 the first two elements of *ic* contain the slope and shear found at η = 0 by fsolve. The last two elements are the moment and shear at the left-hand portion of the overhung beam at ρ = 0 (η = 1; see Figure 8.16), which has also been determined by fsolve. The quantities *lbc* and *rbc* are strings that identify the boundary conditions at the left and right ends of the beam, respectively. When the beam is overhung *rbc* pertains to the right end of the overhung portion of the beam. Lastly, for plotting purposes we have scaled the displacements by 100 and the quantity *den* = 2ε = 0.024. Thus,

```
function BeamPlot(alpha,m,n,k,beta,xi,flag,ic,lbc,rbc,over,lenover,...
                  alpha_over,m_over,n_over,k_over,beta_over, xi_over,...
                  flag_over)
if over == 0
  [eta,y] = ode45('StaticBeam',[0:0.02:1],ic',[],alpha,m,n,k,beta,xi,flag);
else
  [eta,y] = ode45('StaticBeam',[0:0.02:1],[0 ic(1) 0 ic(2)]',[],alpha,m,n,k,beta,xi,flag);
  [zeta,z] = ode45('StaticBeam',[0:0.02:lenover],[0 y(end,2) ic(3) ic(4)]',[],...
                  alpha_over,m_over,n_over,k_over,beta_over, xi_over, flag_over);
  eta = [eta;1+zeta];
  y = [y;z];
end
y = -y; den = 1;
if flag == 0, den = 0.024; end
subplot(2,2,1)
plot(eta,y(:,1)*100/den,'k-',[0 1+lenover],[0 0],'k--')
if over == 0
  if flag == 0
  title(['Point load at \xi =' num2str(xi,2)])
else
  title(['Load: \alpha=' num2str(alpha,2) ' m=' num2str(m,2) ' n=' ...
        num2str(n,2) ' k=' num2str(k,2) ' \beta=' num2str(beta,2)])
end
ylabel('displacement (\times10^{-2})')
xlabel('\eta')
[ymax,index] = max(abs(y(:,1))/den);
disp(['max displacement =' num2str(ymax,3) ' at eta =' num2str(eta(index),3)])
subplot(2,2,2)
plot(eta,y(:,2)/den,'k-',[0 1+lenover],[0 0],'k--')
ylabel('slope')
```

```
xlabel('\eta')
title(['left bc: ' lbc ' right bc: ' rbc])
[tmax,index] = max(abs(y(:,2))/den);
disp('slope:')
disp(['  ' num2str(y(1,2)/den,3) ' at eta = 0' ])
disp(['  ' num2str(y(end,2)/den,3) ' at eta = 1'])
disp(['max slope = ' num2str(tmax,3) ' at eta = ' num2str(eta(index),3)])
subplot(2,2,3)
plot(eta,y(:,3)/den,'k-',[0 1+lenover],[0 0],'k--')
ylabel('moment')
xlabel('\eta')
[mmax,index] = max(abs(y(:,3))/den);
disp(['max moment = ' num2str(mmax,3) ' at eta = ' num2str(eta(index),3)])
subplot(2,2,4)
plot(eta,y(:,4)/den,'k-',[0 1+lenover],[0 0],'k--')
ylabel('shear')
xlabel('\eta')
[vmax,index] = max(abs(y(:,4))/den);
disp('shear:')
disp(['  ' num2str(y(1,4)/den,3) ' at eta = 0'])
disp(['  ' num2str(y(end,4)/den,3) ' at eta = 1'])
disp(['max shear = ' num2str(vmax,3) ' at eta = ' num2str(eta(index),3)])
```

We now illustrate the procedure with several examples.

Example 8.11 Simply supported beam with uniform load

Consider a beam that is simply supported at both ends and subjected to a uniform load along its entire length. The boundary conditions are given in the first row of Table 8.1, and the loading is described by $\alpha = 1$, $m = n = k = \beta = \xi = 0$, and $flag = 1$. The script is

```
alpha = 1; m = 0; n = 0; k = 0; beta = 0; xi = 0; flag = 1;
alpha_over = 0; m_over = 0; n_over = 0; k_over = 0;
beta_over = 0;  xi_over = 0; flag_over = 0;
over = 0; lenover = 0;
options = optimset('display','off');
x = fsolve('BeamSolveSSSS',[.2 .5],options,alpha,m,n,k,beta,xi,flag);
BeamPlot(alpha,m,n,k,beta,xi,flag,[0 x(1) 0 x(2)],'ss','ss',over,lenover, ...
         alpha_over,m_over,n_over,k_over,beta_over, xi_over, flag_over);
```

where the function *BeamSolveSSSS* is

```
function d = BeamSolveSSSS(bc,alpha,m,n,k,beta,xi,flag)
[eta,y] = ode45('StaticBeam', [0:.02:1],[0 bc(1) 0 bc(2)]',[],alpha,m,n,k,beta,xi,flag);
d = [y(end,1);y(end,3)];
```

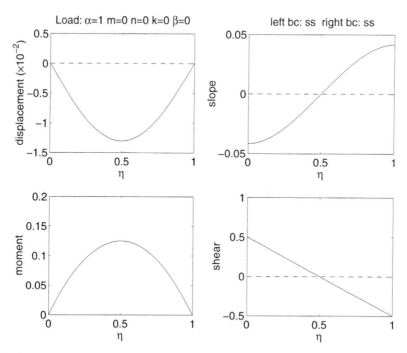

FIGURE 8.12
Simply supported beam subjected to a uniform load along its length.

The execution of the script results in Figure 8.12 and the following information being displayed to the MATLAB command window.

```
max displacement = 0.013 at eta = 0.5
slope:
  -0.0417 at eta = 0
   0.0417 at eta = 1
max slope = 0.0417 at eta = 1
max moment = 0.125 at eta = 0.5
shear:
0.5 at eta = 0
-0.5 at eta = 1
max shear =  0.5 at eta = 0
```

The analytical solution[2] to this problem yields the same results as those above.

---

[2] R. L. Norton, *Design of Machinery*, McGraw-Hill, New York, 1992, p. 1,003.

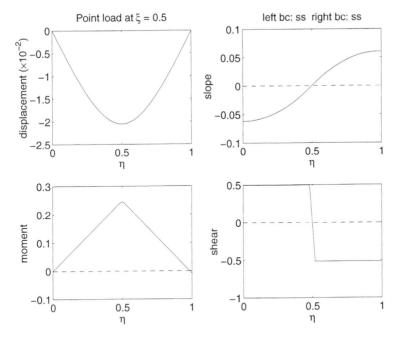

FIGURE 8.13
Simply supported beam subjected to a point load at $\eta = 0.5$.

Example 8.12 Simply supported beam with point load

Consider a beam that is simply supported at both ends and subjected to a point load acting at $\eta = 0.5$. The boundary conditions are given in the first row of Table 8.1, and the loading is described by $\alpha = m = n = k = \beta = 0$, $\xi = 0.5$, and *flag* = 0. The script is

```
alpha = 0; m = 0; n = 0; k = 0; beta = 0; xi = 0.5; flag = 0;
alpha_over = 0; m_over = 0; n_over = 0; k_over = 0;
beta_over = 0;  xi_over = 0; flag_over = 0;
over = 0; lenover = 0;
options = optimset('display','off');
x = fsolve('BeamSolveSSSS',[.2 .5],options,alpha,m,n,k,beta,xi,flag);
BeamPlot(alpha,m,n,k,beta,xi,flag,[0 x(1) 0 x(2)],'ss','ss',over,lenover, ...
         alpha_over,m_over,n_over,k_over,beta_over, xi_over, flag_over);
```

The execution of this script results in Figure 8.13 and the following information being displayed to the MATLAB command window.

max displacement = 0.0206 at eta = 0.5

slope:
  -0.0618 at eta = 0
  0.0602 at eta = 1
max slope = 0.0618 at eta = 0
max moment = 0.245 at eta = 0.5
shear:
  0.496 at eta = 0
  -0.514 at eta = 1
max shear = 0.514 at eta = 1

The analytical solution[3] to this problem yields $y_{max}(\eta = 0.5) = 0.0208$, $\theta_{max}(\eta = 1) = 0.0625$, $M_{max}(\eta = 0.5) = 0.250$, and $V_{max}(\eta = 0) = 0.500$.

Example 8.13 Cantilever beam with uniform load

Consider a beam that is clamped at $\eta = 0$ and free at $\eta = 1$. This type of beam is called a cantilever beam. The beam is subjected to a uniform load acting from $\eta = 0.5$ to $\eta = 1$. The boundary conditions at $\eta = 0$ are given in the second row of Table 8.1 and the boundary conditions at $\eta = 1$ are in the third row. The loading is described by $\alpha = 1$, $m = 0.5$, $n = k = \beta = 0 = \xi = 0$, and *flag* = 1. The script is

```
alpha = 1; m = 0.5; n = 0; k = 0; beta = 0; xi = 0; flag = 1;
alpha_over = 0; m_over = 0; n_over = 0; k_over = 0;
beta_over = 0;  xi_over = 0; flag_over = 0;
over = 0; lenover = 0;
options = optimset('display','off');
x = fsolve(' BeamSolveCant',[.2 .5],options,alpha,m,n,k,beta,xi,flag);
BeamPlot(alpha,m,n,k,beta,xi,flag,[ 0 0 x(1) x(2)],'clamped','free',over,lenover, ...
         alpha_over,m_over,n_over,k_over,beta_over, xi_over, flag_over);
```

where the function *BeamSolveCant* is

```
function d = BeamSolveCant(bc,alpha,m,n,k,beta,xi,flag)
[eta,y] = ode45('StaticBeam', [0:.02:1],[0 0 bc(1) bc(2)]',[],alpha,m,n,k,beta,xi,flag);
d = [y(end,3);y(end,4)];
```

The execution of the script results in Figure 8.14 and the following information being displayed to the MATLAB command window.

max displacement = 0.108 at eta = 1
slope:
  0 at eta = 0
  -0.147 at eta = 1

---

[3] R. L. Norton, *ibid.*, p. 1,003.

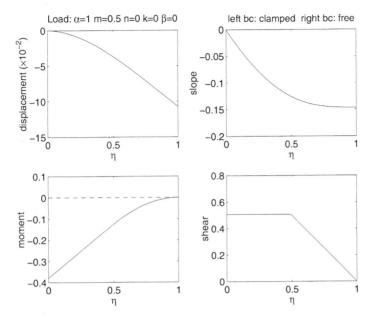

FIGURE 8.14
Cantilever beam subjected to a uniform load from $\eta = 0.5$ to $\eta = 1$.

> max slope = 0.147 at eta = 1
> max moment = 0.379 at eta = 0
> shear:
>   0.508 at eta = 0
>   5.97e-009 at eta = 1
> max shear = 0.508 at eta = 0

The analytical solution[4] to this problem yields $y_{max}(\eta = 1) = 0.1068$, $\theta_{max}(\eta = 1) = 0.1458$, $M_{max}(\eta = 0) = 0.375$, and $V_{max}(\eta = 0) = 0.500$.

Example 8.14 Cantilever beam with point load

Consider a beam that is clamped at $\eta = 0$, free at $\eta = 1$, and subjected to a point load acting at $\eta = 0.5$. The boundary conditions at $\eta = 0$ are given in the second row of Table 8.1, and the boundary conditions at $\eta = 1$ are in the third row. The loading is described by $\alpha = m = n = k = \beta = 0$, $\xi = 0.5$ and *flag* = 0. The script is

```
alpha = 0; m = 0; n = 0; k = 0; beta = 0; xi = 0.5; flag = 0;
alpha_over = 0; m_over = 0; n_over = 0; k_over = 0;
beta_over = 0; xi_over = 0; flag_over = 0;
```

---

[4] R. L. Norton, *ibid.*, p. 1,002.

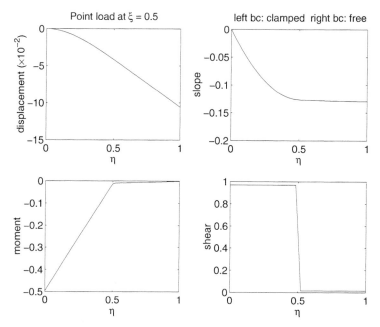

FIGURE 8.15
Cantilever beam subjected to a point load at $\eta = 0.5$.

```
over = 0; lenover = 0;
options = optimset('display','off');
x = fsolve('BeamSolveCant',[.2 .5],options,alpha,m,n,k,beta,xi,flag);
BeamPlot(alpha,m,n,k,beta,xi,flag,[ 0 0 x(1) x(2)],'clamped','free',over,lenover,...
         alpha_over,m_over,n_over,k_over,beta_over, xi_over, flag_over);
```

The execution of the script results in Figure 8.15 and the following information being displayed to the MATLAB command window.

```
max displacement = 0.106 at eta = 1
slope:
  0 at eta = 0
  -0.13 at eta = 1
max slope = 0.13 at eta = 1
max moment = 0.496 at eta = 0
shear:
  0.97 at eta = 0
  0.0162 at eta = 1
max shear =  0.97 at eta = 0
```

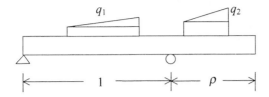

FIGURE 8.16
Beam with an overhang.

The analytical solution[5] to this problem yields $y_{max}(\eta = 1) = 0.1042$, $\theta_{max}(\eta = 0.5$ to $\eta = 0.5) = 0.1250$, $M_{max}(\eta = 0) = 0.500$, and $V_{max}(\eta = 0) = 1.000$.

8.2.2 Beams With Overhangs

We extend the numerical procedure described in Section 8.2.1 to obtain the approximate numerical solutions to a beam with an overhang shown in Figure 8.16. The first step is to consider the beam as two beams: one whose nondimensional displacement is denoted $y(\eta)$ for which η varies from 0 to 1, and another beam whose nondimensional displacement is denoted $z(\xi)$, for which ξ varies from 0 to ρ, where $\rho > 0$. If we assume that the overhanging portion extends beyond the right ($\eta = 1$) support, then the following conditions must be satisfied:

1. Two boundary conditions for y at $\eta = 0$.
2. The free end boundary conditions for z at $\xi = \rho$ (the right end of the overhung portion of the beam) — that is,

$$d^2z(\rho)/d\xi^2 = d^3z(\rho)/d\xi^3 = 0$$

3. The continuity of the displacements and slopes where the two beams meet—that is,

$$y(1) = z(0) = 0$$
$$dy(1)/d\eta = dz(0)/d\xi$$

4. The equality of the moments where the two beams meet—that is,

$$d^2z(0)/d\xi^2 = d^2y(1)/d\eta^2$$

Thus, there are two sets of equations that have to be satisfied in an iterative manner. The first set involving $y(\eta)$ requires that the magnitudes of the two remaining boundary conditions at $\eta = 0$ are such that at $\eta = 1$

$$y(1) = 0$$
$$dy^2(1)/d\eta^2 - dz^2(0)/d\xi^2 = 0$$

[5] R. L. Norton, *ibid.,* p. 1,002.

The second set involving $z(\xi)$ requires that the magnitudes of $d^2z(0)/d\xi^2$ and $d^3z(0)/d\xi^3$ are such that at $\xi = \rho$

$$d^2z(\rho)/d\xi^2 = d^3z(\rho)/d\xi^3 = 0$$

and $\xi = 0$

$$dy(1)/d\eta = dz(0)/d\xi.$$

We now illustrate this procedure.

Example 8.15 Uniformly loaded simply supported beam with an overhang

Consider a beam that is simply supported at both ends, except that the end $\eta = 1$ has an overhang of length 0.5—that is, $\rho = 0.5$. Both the beam and its overhang are subjected to a uniform load along their entire lengths. The loading on the supported portion of the beam is described by $\alpha = 1$, $m = n = k = \beta = \xi = 0$, and *flag* = 1. The loading on the overhung portion of the beam is also described by $\alpha = 1$, $m = n = k = \beta = \xi = 0$, and *flag* = 1. The script is

```
alpha = 1; m = 0; n = 0; k = 0; beta = 0; xi = 0; flag = 1;
alpha_over = 1; m_over = 0; n_over = 0; k_over = 0;
beta_over = 0;  xi_over = 0; flag_over = 1;
over = 1; lenover = 0.5;
options = optimset('display','off');
x = fsolve('BeamSolveOver',[0.5 0.5 0.5 0.5],options,alpha,m,n,k,beta,xi,flag,...
           alpha_over,m_over,n_over,k_over,beta_over, xi_over, flag_over,lenover);
BeamPlot(alpha,m,n,k,beta,xi,flag,[x(1) x(2) x(3) x(4)],'ss','overhung',over,lenover,...
           alpha_over,m_over,n_over,k_over,beta_over, xi_over, flag_over);
```

where the function *BeamSolveOver* is given by

```
function d = BeamSolveOver(bc,alpha,m,n,k,beta,xi,flag,...
              alpha_over,m_over,n_over,k_over,beta_over, xi_over, flag_over,...
              lenover)
[eta,y] = ode45('StaticBeam', [0:.02:1],[0 bc(1) 0 bc(2)]',[],alpha,m,n,k,beta,xi,flag);
[zeta,z] = ode45('StaticBeam',[0:.02:lenover],[0 y(end,2) bc(3) bc(4)], [],...
              alpha_over,m_over,n_over,k_over,beta_over, xi_over, flag_over);
d = [y(end,1);y(end,3)–z(1,3);z(end,3);z(end,4)];
```

The execution of this script results in Figure 8.17 and the following information being displayed to the MATLAB command window

```
max displacement = 0.00781 at eta = 1.5
slope:
  -0.0208 at eta = 0
  -0.0208 at eta = 1
max slope = 0.0208 at eta = 1.5
```

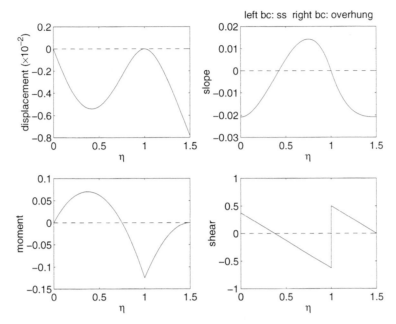

FIGURE 8.17
Simply supported beam with overhang uniformly loaded on both spans with $\rho = 0.5$.

max moment = 0.125 at eta = 1
shear:
0.375 at eta = 0
1.23e-006 at eta = 1
max shear = 0.625 at eta = 1

The analytical solution[6] to this problem yields $y_{max}(\eta = 1.5) = 0.0078$.

8.2.3 Buckling of Columns

Consider a structural column of length L, cross-sectional area A, Young's modulus E, moment of inertia I, and yield strength S_y that is subjected to an axial compressive load P that is concentric with the column's axis and passes through the centroid of A. The critical value of P, denoted P_{cr}, that can cause the column to buckle is estimated by

$$S_r > \pi \sqrt{2E/S_y}$$

$$P_{cr} = \frac{\pi^2 AE}{S_r^2}$$

---

[6] R. L. Norton, *ibid.*, p. 1,004.

$$S_r \leq \pi \sqrt{2E/S_y}$$

$$P_{cr} = A \left[S_y - \frac{1}{E} \left(\frac{S_y S_r}{2\pi} \right)^2 \right]$$

where $S_r = L_{eff}/k$, $k = \sqrt{I/A}$ is the radius of gyration of the cross section and $L_{eff} = 2.1L$ for a cantilevered column, $L_{eff} = L$ for a pinned-pinned column, $L_{eff} = 0.8L$ for a fixed-pinned column, and $L_{eff} = 0.65L$ for a fixed-fixed column.

For a solid rectangular cross section $k = h/2\sqrt{3}$, where h is the depth of the cross section, and for a solid circular cross section $k = r/2$, where r is the radius of the circle. For a circular tube of inner radius r_i and outer radius r_o,

$$k = 0.5\sqrt{r_o^2 + r_i^2}$$

or, if $r_o = r_i + t$, then

$$k = 0.5\sqrt{r_o^2 + (r_o - t)^2}$$

If a factor of safety F_s is used, then $P = P_{cr}/F_s$.

When P is eccentrically loading the column by an offset e, then

$$P_{cr} = AS_y \left[1 + \frac{ec}{k^2} \sec\left(\frac{l_{eff}}{k} \sqrt{\frac{P_{cr}}{4AE}} \right) \right]^{-1}$$

where c is the distance from the centroid of A to the outer perimeter of A. This relationship is valid for $ec/k^2 \leq 0.025$. When the cross section is circular $c = r_o$. We see that P_{cr} appears on both sides of the equation and, therefore, must be solved by interation (i.e., using fzero).

We now illustrate these relationships with two examples.

Example 8.16 Determination of column diameter

A 13-foot cantilevered steel column is to withstand a 150,000-lb. compressive axial load. If the column's cross section is a circular tube whose wall thickness is 0.75 inches, then we shall determine the minimum outside diameter when $E = 3 \times 10^7$ psi, $S_y = 55,000$ psi, and $F_s = 3$.

We shall use fzero to obtain the estimate of d. Thus, we first create a function called *ColumnBuckling*:

```
function Pcr = ColumnBuckling(r,P,Sy,E,Leff,Fs,t)
Sr = 2*Leff/sqrt(r^2+(r-t)^2);
if Sr>pi*sqrt(2*E/Sy)
Pcr = P-(pi^3*(r^2-(r-t)^2)*E/Sr^2)/Fs;
```

```
else
  Pcr = P−pi*((Sy−((Sy*Sr)/(2*pi))^2/E)*(r^2−(r−t)^2))/Fs;
end
```

The script is

```
options = optimset('display','off');
diam = 2*fzero('ColumnBuckling',5,options,1.5e+5,5.5e+4,3e+7,2.1*12*13,3,0.75)
```

which, when executed, gives $d = 8.9392$ inches. This corresponds to $P_{cr} = 450,000$ lb.

Example 8.17 Determination of diameter of an eccentrically loaded column

Consider again the previous example, except that the column is now eccentrically loaded at e = 0.6 inches. For this case we have to create two functions, one to evaluate P_{cr} at a given value of r and the other to determine the value of r that satisfies $P = P_{cr}/F_s$. The first function is

```
function Pest = SecColumnBuckling(Pcr,r,t,Sy,E,Leff,ecc)
a = (r^2−(r−t)^2)*pi;
k = 0.5*sqrt(r^2+(r−t)^2);
Pest = Pcr−a*Sy/(1+((ecc*r/k)^2)*sec(Leff/k*sqrt(Pcr/4/E/a)));
```

and the second

```
function Pcr = EccenColumnBuckling(r,p,Sy,E,Leff,Fs,t,ecc)
options = optimset('display','off');
Pcr = p−fzero('SecColumnBuckling',50000,options,r,t,Sy,E,Leff,ecc)/Fs;
```

The script is

```
options = optimset('display','off');
diam = 2*fzero('EccenColumnBuckling',6,options,15e4,55e3,3e7, ...
               2.1*12*13,3,.75,0.6)
```

which, when executed, gives $diam = d = 10.9539$ inches. This corresponds to $P_{cr} = 450,000$ lb.

8.2.4 Shafts Subjected to Alternating Loads

Consider a solid circular steel shaft subjected to a fully reversed alternating torque and bending moment T_a and M_a, respectively; a mean torque and bending moment T_m and M_m, respectively; and no axial load. Its diameter can be estimated from[7]

---

[7] R. L. Norton, *ibid., p.* 575.

$$d = \sqrt[3]{\frac{32F_s}{\pi}} \sqrt[3]{\sqrt{(k_f M_a)^2 + 0.75(k_{fs} T_a)^2} \Big/ S_f + \sqrt{(k_{fm} M_m)^2 + 0.75(k_{fsm} T_m)^2} \Big/ S_{ut}} \qquad (8.15)$$

where F_s is the factor of safety, S_{ut} is the ultimate strength of the material, S_f is the corrected fatigue strength, and k_α are the various stress concentration factors. This relationship is valid when M_a/M_m and T_a/T_m are constants. As will be seen subsequently, many of the quantities are themselves a function of d and are defined as follows.

Corrected Fatigue Strength—S_f

$$S_f = C_{size} C_{surf} C_{rel} S_{fu}$$

where, for circular shafts,

$C_{size} = 1$ $\qquad\qquad\qquad\qquad$ $d < 0.3$ in
$C_{size} = 0.869 d^{-0.097}$ $\qquad$ $0.3 \le d \le 10$ in
$C_{size} = 0.6$ $\qquad\qquad\qquad$ $d > 10$ in

For machined surfaces $C_{surf} = 2.7(S_{ut})^{-0.265}$ and for 99% reliability $C_{rel} = 0.814$. In the absence of published data the following rough approximation for the uncorrected fatigue strength S_{fu} can be used for steels: $S_{fu} = 0.5 S_{ut}$, for $S_{ut} < 200,000$ psi. With these assumptions we obtain

$$S_f = 1.0989 C_{size} S_{ut}^{0.735}$$

Stress Concentration Factors—k_α

The fatigue stress concentration factor k_f is estimated from

$$k_f = 1 + q(k_t - 1) \qquad (8.16)$$

where k_t is the theoretical static stress concentration factor and q is the notch sensitivity, which is a function of the Neuber constant a (recall Section 5.6.1)

$$q = \left(1 + \sqrt{a/r}\right)^{-1}$$

where r is the radius of the notch.

The quantity k_t is a function of the loading and geometry. Consider the case of a shaft changing abruptly from a diameter D to a smaller diameter d as shown in Figure 8.18, the value for the bending fatigue stress concentration factor can be approximated by[8]

$$k_t = 1 + \left[A t_r^{-k} + B \left[\frac{1 + a_r}{a_r^{3/2}} \right]^l + \frac{C a_r}{(a_r + t_r) t_r^m} \right]^{-1/2} \qquad (8.17)$$

where

---

[8] W. Beitz, and K. H. Kuttner, Eds., *Handbook of Mechanical Engineering*, Springer-Verlag, New York, 1994, p. D78.

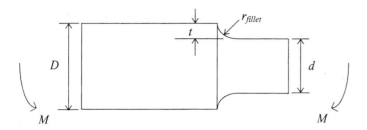

FIGURE 8.18
Geometry and loading for the determination of the stress concentration factor.

TABLE 8.2
Values for the Constants of the Theoretical Stress Concentration Factor k_t

Constant	Bending	Torsion
A	0.40	0.40
B	6.00	25.0
C	0.80	0.20
k	0.40	0.45
l	2.75	2.25
m	1.50	2.00

$$t_r = t/r_{fillet} \qquad a_r = d/(2r_{fillet})$$

$r_{fillet} < (D - d)/2$, and A, B, C, k, l, and m are given in Table 8.2 for bending and for torsion. The quantity k_{fm} is determined as follows:

$k_f|\sigma_{max}| < S_y$

$$k_{fm} = k_f$$

$k_f|\sigma_{max}| > S_y$

$$k_{fm} = (S_y - k_f\sigma_a)/|\sigma_m|$$

$k_f|\sigma_{max} - \sigma_{max}| > 2S_y$

$$k_{fm} = 0$$

where k_f is determined from Eqs. (8.16) and (8.17) for bending. The stresses appearing in the above equation are determined from

$$\sigma_{max} = \frac{M_{max} r_{shaft}}{I} \qquad \sigma_{min} = \frac{M_{min} r_{shaft}}{I}$$

$$\sigma_a = \frac{M_a r_{shaft}}{I} \qquad \sigma_m = \frac{M_m r_{shaft}}{I}$$

where $r_{shaft} = d/2$, $I = \pi d^4/64$ is the moment of inertia of the cross section of the circular shaft, M_{max} is the maximum bending moment, M_{min} is the minimum bending moment, and

$$M_a = (M_{max} - M_{min})/2$$
$$M_m = (M_{max} + M_{min})/2$$

The quantity k_{fsm} is determined as follows:

$k_{fs}|\tau_{max}| < S_s$

$$k_{fsm} = k_{fs}$$

$k_{fs}|\tau_{max}| > S_s$

$$k_{fsm} = (S_s - k_{fs}\tau_a)/|\tau_m|$$

$k_{fs}|\tau_{max} - \tau_{max}| > 2S_s$

$$k_{fsm} = 0$$

where k_{fs} is determined from Eqs. (8.16) and (8.17) for torsion. The quantity S_s is the shear yield strength, which may be approximated by

$$S_s \approx 0.58 S_y$$

The stresses appearing in the above equations are given by

$$\tau_{max} = \frac{T_{max} r_{shaft}}{J} \qquad \tau_{min} = \frac{T_{min} r_{shaft}}{J}$$

$$\tau_a = \frac{T_a r_{shaft}}{J} \qquad \tau_m = \frac{T_m r_{shaft}}{J}$$

where $J = \pi d^4/32$ is the polar moment of inertia of the cross section of the shaft, T_{max} is the maximum torque, T_{min} is the minimum torque, and

$$T_a = (T_{max} - T_{min})/2$$
$$T_m = (T_{max} + T_{min})/2$$

We now illustrate these relationships with an example.

Example 8.18 Diameter of a shaft subjected to alternating loads

Consider a machined steel circular shaft subjected to a maximum and minimum bending moment of 4000 lb.-in and 1000 lb.-in, respectively and a maximum and minimum torque of 1600 lb.-in and 250 lb.-in, respectively. In addition, the factor of safety is 2.5, the yield strength of the material is 40,000 psi, its ultimate strength 70,000 psi, and the notch radius is 0.03 in. We shall determine the minimum diameter of the shaft for the case where D is 15% larger than d, the fillet radius is 10% of d and the reliability is at the 99% level.

Since many of the quantities in Eq. (8.15) are themselves a function of the shaft diameter, we must create several functions for those quantities that vary with d and use fzero to estimate d. These will be:

neuber, computes q (see Section 5.6.1)

StressConcenB, computes k_f and k_{fs}

StressConcenM, computes k_{fm} and k_{fsm}

SsubF, determines the corrected fatigue stress S_f

FatigueDiameter, computes the diameter d

The *neuber* function for steel is

```
function q = neuber(r,Su)
ncs = [50, .13; 70, .092; 90, .072; 110, .057; 130, .046; 150, .037; ...
       170, .028; 190, .020; 210, .015; 230, .010; 250, .007];
q = 1/(1+polyval(polyfit(ncs(:,1),ncs(:,2),4),Su)/sqrt(r));
```

where the values for *ncs* are given in Table 5.1.

Function *StressConcenB* is

```
function [kf,kfs] = StressConcenB(d,rfillet,dout,rnotch,Su)
A = [0.4 0.4]; B = [6 25]; C = [0.8 0.2];
k = [0.4 0.45]; l = [2.75 2.25]; m = [1.5 2];
dod = dout/d;
rd = rfillet/d;
tr = (dout−d)/2/rfillet;
ar = d/rfillet/2;
for n = 1:2
 t1 = A(n)/(tr)^k(n);
 t2 = B(n)*((1+ar)/(ar*sqrt(ar)))^l(n);
 t3 = C(n)*ar/(ar+tr)/(tr)^m(n);
 alpha(n) = 1+1/sqrt(t1+t2+t3);
end
kf = 1+neuber(rnotch,Su)*(alpha(1)−1);
kfs = 1+neuber(rnotch,Su)*(alpha(2)−1);
```

Function *StressConcenM* is

```
function [kfm,kfsm] = StressConcenM(d,Mmax,Mmin,Tmax,Tmin,Sy,kf,kfs)
roj = 16/pi/d^3;
roi = 2*roj;
Smax = Mmax*roi;
```

```
Smin = Mmin*roi;
if kf*abs(Smax)<=Sy
 kfm = kf;
else
 kfm = (Sy−kf*roi*(Mmax−Mmin)/2)/abs(roi*(Mmax+Mmin)/2);
end
if kf*abs(Smax−Smin)>2*Sy; kfm = 0; end
Tmax = Tmax*roj;
Tmin = Tmin*roj;
if kf*abs(Tmax)<=0.58*Sy
 kfsm = kfs;
else
 kfsm = (.58*Sy−kfs*roj*(Tmax−Tmin)/2)/abs(roj*(Tmax+Tmin)/2);
end
if kf*abs(Tmax−Tmin)>1.16*Sy; kfsm = 0; end
```

Function *SsubF* is

```
function Sf = SsubF(d,Su)
csize = 0.869*d^(−0.097);
if d<3; csize = 1;end
if d>10; csize = 0.6; end
Sf = 1.0989*csize*Su^(0.735);
```

Function *FatigueDiameter* is

```
function diam = FatigueDiameter(d,Mmax,Mmin,Tmax,Tmin,Sy,Su,...
                  prfillet,pDod,rnotch,fs)
Sf = SsubF(d,Su);
dout = pDod*d;
rfill = prfillet*d;
[kf,kfs] = StressConcenB(d,rfill,dout,rnotch,Su);
[kfm,kfsm] = StressConcenM(d,Mmax,Mmin,Tmax,Tmin,Sy,kf,kfs);
p1 = sqrt((kf*(Mmax−Mmin)/2)^2+0.75*(kfs*(Tmax−Tmin)/2)^2)/Sf;
p2 = sqrt((kfm*(Mmax+Mmin)/2)^2+0.75*(kfsm*(Tmax+Tmin)/2)^2)/Su;
diam = d−(32/pi*fs*(p1+p2))^(1/3);
```

where *prfillet* = r_{fillet}/d and *pDod* = D/d.
    The script is

```
options = optimset('display','off');
d = fzero('FatigueDiameter',3,options,4e3,1e3,1.6e3,250,4e4,7e4,0.1,1.15,0.03,2.5)
```

which, upon execution, gives $d = 2.2376$ inches.

8.3 STRESSES IN SPUR GEARS

The bending stress on a gear tooth subjected to a uniform (nonvarying) tangentially transmitted load F_t is given by

$$\sigma_b = \frac{K_v K_H F_t}{mbJ_K} \quad \text{N/mm}^2$$

where b is the face width of the gear tooth, m is the module, J_K is the geometry factor for bending strength, K_v is a dynamic factor that is a function of the quality of the gear tooth and the operating pitch circle's tangential velocity v_t, and K_H is a load distribution factor.

The tangential load can be found from

$$F_t = \frac{9.549 \times 10^6 P}{nR_p} = \frac{1000T}{R_p} \quad \text{N}$$

where P is the power in kW, T is the torque in Nm, n is the rotational speed in rpm of the smaller of the two gears (pinion), and R_p is the operating pitch of the smaller of the two gears in mm.

The dynamic load factor can be estimated from

$$K_v = \left(\frac{A + \sqrt{200v_t}}{A} \right)^B$$

where

$$v_t = \frac{2\pi R_p n}{60000} \quad \text{m/s}$$
$$A = 50 + 56(1 - B)$$
$$B = 0.25(12 - Q_v)^{2/3}$$

and Q_v is a quality factor for the gear and is represented by an integer in the range $5 \le Q_v \le 11$. The upper limit is for precision gears and the lower limit for the least precise gears. The operating pitch radius R_p is in mm and n is the rotational speed in rpm. For each value of Q_v there is a recommended maximum value for v_t, which is given by

$$v_{t\max} = (A + Q_v - 3)^2 / 200 \quad \text{m/s}$$

For stiff gear designs having gears mounted between bearings and relatively free from externally caused deflections, the load distribution factor can be estimated from

$$K_H = 1 + K_{Hpf} + K_{Hma}$$

where K_{Hpf} is a pinion proportion factor and K_{Hma} is a mesh alignment factor. The pinion proportion factor is estimated from:

TABLE 8.3
Constants A, B and C[†]

Type Number	Type of Gearing	A	B	C
1	Open	0.247	0.657×10^{-3}	-1.186×10^{-7}
2	Enclosed	0.127	0.622×10^{-3}	-1.69×10^{-7}
3	Precision enclosed	0.0675	0.504×10^{-3}	-1.44×10^{-7}
4	Extra precision enclosed	0.0380	0.402×10^{-3}	-1.27×10^{-7}

[†] From AGMA Standard 2101-C95.

$\underline{b \leq 25 \text{ mm}}$

$$K_{Hpf} = k_o - 0.025$$

$\underline{25 < b \leq 432 \text{ mm}}$

$$K_{Hpf} = k_0 - 0.0375 + 0.000492b$$

$\underline{432 < b \leq 1020 \text{ mm}}$

$$K_{Hpf} = k_o - 0.1109 + 0.000815b - 0.353 \times 10^{-6} b^2$$

where for $k_o \geq 0.05$

$$k_o = 0.05b/R_p$$

and for $k_o < 0.05$

$$k_o = 0.05$$

The quantity R_p is the operating pitch radius of the smaller of the two gears.

The mesh alignment factor is estimated from

$$K_{Hma} = A + Bb + Cb^2$$

where the empirical constants A, B and C are given in Table 8.3.

The determination of the geometry factor is very tedious; however, the AGMA provides a graphical procedure. We will follow, instead, the analytical procedure given by Colbourne[9] who uses the same underlying theory that AGMA uses to determine the geometry factor J_K for spur gears, and differs only in the way in which the critical section of the gear tooth fillet is found.

The procedure requires a very large number of terms and expressions. These have been listed in Tables 8.4 and 8.5 and illustrated in Figures 8.19 and 8.20. Referring to these tables and the figures the geometry factor can be estimated from

[9] J. R. Colbourne, *The Geometry of Involute Gears*, Springer-Verlag, New York, 1987.

TABLE 8.4
Definition of Quantities Used to Determine the Geometry Factor of a Spur Gear J_K

Quantity	Symbol/Formula
Module	m
Number of gear teeth	N
Base pitch	$p_b = m\pi\cos(\varphi_s)$
Circular pitch	$p_s = m\pi$
Diametral pitch	$p_d = 1/m$
Standard pitch radius	$R_s = Np_s/2\pi = Nm/2$
Base circle radius	$R_b = R_s\cos(\varphi_s) = Np_b/2\pi = (Nm/2)\cos(\varphi_s)$
Gear tooth tip radius (gear blank radius)	R_T
Addendum	$a = R_T - R_s$
(Standard addendum for full-depth teeth)	$(a = m)$
Radius of a point on a tooth profile	R
Operating pitch radius	$R_{p_1} = C/(1 + N_2/N_1),\ R_{p_2} = C/(1 + N_1/N_2)$
Root radius	R_{root}
Distance between gear centers	$C = R_{p_1} + R_{p_2}$
Gear pressure angle	φ_s
Rack pressure angle	$\varphi_r\ (= \varphi_s)$
Operating pressure angle	φ
Tooth thickness at R_s	t_s
Tooth thickness at R (See Figure 8.19)	$t_R = 2R\theta_R$
Tooth fillet radius	r_f
Rack addendum[*]	a_r
Tip radius of rack cutter[*]	r_{rT}
Distance between reference line and cutting pitch line. [The reference line is where tooth thickness is equal to space width ($= m\pi/2$). See Figure 8.20.]	e
Involute function	$\mathbf{inv}(\varphi) = \tan(\varphi) - \varphi$

[*] The values of a_r and r_{rT} are chosen so that h, which is defined in Table 8.5, is approximately equal to m.

$$J_K = \frac{\cos\varphi}{mK_J \cos\gamma_w}$$

where

TABLE 8.5
Geometric Quantities Used in the Computation of $J_K{}^{\dagger}$

$$e = \frac{t_s - m\pi/2}{2\tan\varphi_s} \qquad\qquad m_c = \left[\sqrt{R_{T_1}^2 - R_{b_1}^2} - \sqrt{R_{T_2}^2 - R_{b_2}^2} - \left(R_{b_1} + R_{b_2}\right)\tan\varphi\right]\Big/ p_b$$

$$r_f = r_{rT} + \frac{\left(a_r - e - r_{rT}\right)^2}{mN_1/2 + a_r - e - r_{rT}} \qquad R_w^2 = R_b^2 + \left[\sqrt{R_T^2 - R_b^2} - (m_c - 1)p_b\right]^2$$

$$R_{b_j} = N_j\pi\cos\varphi_s \qquad j = 1,2 \qquad \varphi_w = \cos^{-1}\left(R_b/R_w\right)$$

$$\varphi = \cos^{-1}\left(\frac{R_{b_1} + R_{b_2}}{C}\right) \qquad \theta_w = \frac{t_s}{Nm} + \mathbf{inv}\,\varphi_s - \mathbf{inv}\,\varphi_w$$

$$\gamma_w = \varphi_w - \theta_w$$

$$x_r' = -a_r + r_{rT} \qquad\qquad x_D = R_w\cos\theta_w - R_w\sin\theta_w\tan\gamma_w$$

$$y_r' = m\pi/4 + h\tan\varphi_s + r_{rT}\cos\varphi_s \qquad u_{r_{min}} = \frac{e + x_r'}{\tan\varphi_s} - y_r'$$

$$h = a_r - r_{rT} + r_{rT}\sin\varphi_s$$

$$u_{r_{max}} = -y_r'$$

† The subscript "1" denotes the gear for which J_K is to be determined and the subscript "2" refers to the mating gear. The absence of either number refers only to the gear for which J_K is being computed.

$$K_J = K_f\left[\frac{1.5(x_D - x)}{y^2} - \frac{\tan\gamma_w}{2y}\right]_{max}$$

$$K_f = k_1 + \left(\frac{2y}{r_f}\right)^{k_2}\left(\frac{2y}{x_D - x}\right)^{k_3}$$

and

$$k_1 = 0.3054 - 0.00489\varphi_s - 0.000069\varphi_s^2$$
$$k_2 = 0.3620 - 0.01268\varphi_s + 0.000104\varphi_s^2$$
$$k_3 = 0.2934 + 0.00609\varphi_s + 0.000087\varphi_s^2$$

where φ_s is one of the following gear pressure angles *expressed in degrees*: either 14.5°, 20° or 25°. The quantity $[\ldots]_{max}$ indicates that K_J is the maximum value, which is determined by varying x and y. The values of x and y are obtained by varying u_r in the formulas given below between the limits given in Table 8.5—that is,

$$u_{r_{min}} \le u_r \le u_{r_{max}}$$

The values of x and y are given by

$$x = R\cos\theta_R$$
$$y = R\sin\theta_R$$

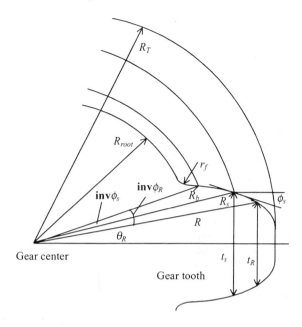

FIGURE 8.19
Nomenclature for a gear tooth.

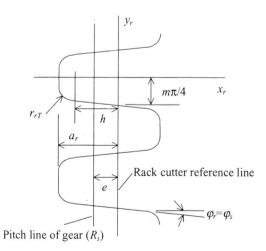

FIGURE 8.20
Nomenclature for a gear tooth rack cutter.

where

$$R = \sqrt{(N_1m/2+\xi)^2 + \eta^2}$$

$$\theta_R = \tan^{-1}\left(\frac{\eta}{N_1m/2+\xi}\right) - \frac{u_r - m\pi/2}{N_1m/2}$$

$$\xi = s\xi' \qquad \eta = s\eta'$$

$$s = 1 + \frac{r_rT}{\sqrt{\xi'^2 + \eta'^2}}$$

$$\xi' = e + x_r' \qquad \eta' = u_r + y_r'$$

Once the stress σ_b has been computed the permissible stress σ_F must be determined, and verified that it is greater than that caused by F_t—that is, $\sigma_b \le \sigma_F$, where the permissible stress is

$$\sigma_F = \frac{\sigma_{FP}Y_N}{F_S Y_Z}$$

for oil or gear temperatures less than 120 °C. The quantity F_S is the factor of safety, Y_N is the bending stress cycle factor, and Y_Z is the reliability factor. The reliability factor has the following values: $Y_Z = 1$ for less than 1 failure in 100, $Y_Z = 1.25$ for less than 1 failure in 1,000, and $Y_Z = 1.5$ for less than 1 failure in 10,000.

If n_L is the number of unidirectional tooth load cycles, then the bending stress cycle factor Y_N for steel gears at the 99% reliability level is estimated from:

$\underline{n_L \le 3 \times 10^3}$

$$Y_N = f(B_H)$$

where

$$f(B_H) = -9.2592 \times 10^{-6}(B_H - 160)^2 + 0.009722(B_H - 160) + 1.6 \qquad 160 \le B_H \le 400$$

and B_H is the Brinell hardness number.

$\underline{3 \times 10^3 \le n_L \le 3 \times 10^6}$

$$Y_N = Dn_L^E$$

where

$$D = f(B_H)10^{0.8628C_1}$$
$$E = -0.2876C_1$$
$$C_1 = \log_{10}[f(B_H)] - 0.0169$$

$\underline{n_L > 3 \times 10^6}$

$$Y_N = 1.638n_L^{-0.0323}$$

which is independent of B_H.

The number of cycles is obtained from

$$n_L = 60nL$$

where L is the gear's life in hours, n is the rotation speed of the gear in rpm, and it is assumed there is one contact per revolution on the tooth.

The value for the allowable bending stress number for Grade 1 hardened steel gears is

$$\sigma_{FP} = 0.533B_H + 88.3 \quad \text{N/mm}^2$$

Before presenting an example it is first necessary to create the following functions to compute the various factors:

GearKofV, computes K_v

GearKofH, computes K_H

involute, computes the involute of an angle

GearParameters, computes the quantities appearing in Table 8.5

GearKofF, computes K_f

GearKofJ, computes K_J

GearJofK, computes J_K

GearYofN, computes Y_N

Function *GearKofV* is

```
function Kv = GearKofV(Rp,n,Qv)
vt = 2*pi*Rp*n/60000;
B = 0.25*(12-Qv)^(2/3);
A = 50+56*(1-B);
vtmax = (A+Qv-3)^2/200;
if vt>vtmax
  error('Maximum tangential velocity exceeded for given Qv')
end
Kv = ((A+sqrt(200*vt))/A)^B;
```

Function *GearKofH* is

```
function Kh = GearKofH(b,typeg,Rp)
class = [0.247 0.127 0.0675 0.0380; ...
        0.657e-3 0.622e-3 0.504e-3 0.402e-3;...
        -1.186e-7 -1.69e-7 -1.44e-7 -1.27e-7];
Khma = class(1,typeg)+class(2,typeg)*b+class(3,typeg)*b^2;
ko = 0.05*b/Rp;
if ko<0.05, ko = 0.05; end
if b<=25
  Khpf = ko-0.025;
```

```
elseif b<=432
  Khpf = ko–0.0375+0.000492*b;
else
  Khpf = ko–0.1109+0.000815*b–0.353e–6*b^2;
end
Kh = 1+Khpf+Khma;
```

Function *involute* is

```
function inv = involute(angle)
inv = tan(angle)–angle;
```

Function *GearParameters* is

```
function [urmin,urmax,e,xD,rf,xrp,yrp,gammaw,phi] =
        GearParameters(m,phis,ar,rrT,ts,N1,N2,C,Rt1,Rt2)
xrp = –ar+rrT;
h = ar–rrT+rrT*sin(phis);
yrp = –pi*m/4+h*tan(phis)+rrT*cos(phis);
e = (ts–pi*m/2)/tan(phis)/2;
urmin = (e+xrp)/tan(phis)–yrp;
urmax = –yrp;
Pb = m*pi*cos(phis);
Rb1 = N1*m/2*cos(phis);
Rb2 = N2*m/2*cos(phis);
phi = acos((Rb1+Rb2)/C);
mc = (sqrt(Rt1^2–Rb1^2)+sqrt(Rt2^2–Rb2^2)–(Rb1+Rb2)*tan(phi))/Pb;
Rw = sqrt(Rb1^2+(sqrt(Rt1^2–Rb1^2)–(mc–1)*Pb)^2);
phiw = acos(Rb1/Rw);
thetaw = ts/m/N1+involute(phis)–involute(phiw);
gammaw = phiw–thetaw;
xD = Rw*cos(thetaw)–Rw*sin(thetaw)*tan(gammaw);
rf = rrT+(ar–e–rrT)^2/(N1*m/2+ar–e–rrT);
```

Function *GearKofF* is

```
function Kf = GearKofF(phis,rf,xD,x,y)
d = phis*180/pi;
k1 = 0.3054–0.00489*d–0.000069*d^2;
k2 = 0.362–0.01268*d+0.000104*d^2;
k3 = 0.2934+0.00609*d+0.000087*d^2;
Kf = k1+(2*y/rf)^k2*(2*y/(xD–x))^k3;
```

Function *GearKofJ* is

```
function KJ = GearKofJ(ur,m,rf,e,rrT,N1,xrp,yrp,phis,xD,gammaw)
xip = e+xrp;
etap = ur+yrp;
s = 1+rrT/sqrt(xip^2+etap^2);
xi = s*xip;
eta = s*etap;
thetaR = atan(eta/(N1*m/2+xi))–(ur–pi*m/2)/(N1*m/2);
R = sqrt((N1*m/2+xi)^2+eta^2);
x = R*cos(thetaR);
y = R*sin(thetaR);
Kf = GearKofF(phis,rf,xD,x,y);
KJ = –m*cos(gammaw)*Kf*(1.5*(xD–x)/y^2–0.5*tan(gammaw)/y);
```

See the discussion of *GearJofK* for the reason for the minus sign in the last line.
Function *GearJofK* is

```
function JK = GearJofK(m,phis,ar,rrT,ts,N1,N2,C,rT1,rT2)
[urmin,urmax,e,xD,rf,xrp,yrp,gammaw,phi] = ...
                    GearParameters(m,phis,ar,rrT,ts,N1,N2,C,rT1,rT2);
options = optimset('display','off');
ur = fminbnd('GearKofJ',urmin,urmax,options,m,rf,e,rrT,N1,xrp,yrp, ...
                    phis,xD,gammaw);
JK = –cos(phi)/GearKofJ(ur,m,rf,e,rrT,N1,xrp,yrp,phis,xD,gammaw);
```

This function makes use of $fminbnd$ to determine the maximum value of K_J as a function of u_r. In order for $fminbnd$ to work properly, we have to change the sign of the value of *GearKofJ* in this function; hence, we have to change the sign of J_K and do so by inserting the minus sign in the last line of the function *GearJofK*.
Function *GearYofN* is

```
function YN = GearYofN(BH,n,L)
nL = 60*n*L;
fBH = –9.2592e–6*(BH–160)^2+0.009722*(BH–160)+1.6;
if nL<=1e3
  YN = fBH;
elseif nL<=3e6
  D = 0.8628*(log10(fBH)–0.0169);
  E = –0.2876*(log10(fBH)–0.0169);
  YN = (fBH*10^D)* nL.^E;
else
  YN = 1.683*nL^(–0.0323);
end
```

We now use these functions in an example.

Example 8.19 Bending strength of a gear tooth

Consider the following pair of gears and the geometric attributes of the rack cutter that made them.

$$m = 10 \text{ mm} \qquad a_r = 12.5 \text{ mm} \qquad R_{T_1} = 153.9 \text{ mm}$$
$$\varphi_s = 20° \qquad r_{rT} = 3.8 \text{ mm}$$
$$N_1 = 28 \qquad b = 45 \text{ mm} \qquad R_{T_2} = 391.1 \text{ mm}$$
$$N_2 = 75 \qquad C = 525 \text{ mm} \qquad n_1 = 1800 \text{ rpm}$$
$$T = 2500 \text{ Nm} \qquad t_s = 18.51 \text{ mm} \qquad B_H = 260$$

We note that $h = 10 = m$, which is within the recommended limits. We also assume that the factor of safety is 1.2, that the gear will be used for 4000 hours, and that the desired reliability is less than one failure in 100, which means that $Y_Z = 1.0$. Furthermore, we assume $Q_v = 8$ and that the gears will be in an enclosed unit, that is, type 2 in Table 8.3.

The script that will determine the bending stress and the permissible stress is as follows.

```
m = 10; phis = 20*pi/180; ar = 12.5; rrT = 3.8; ts = 18.51;
C = 525; N1 = 28; N2 = 75; rT1 = 153.9; rT2 = 391.1; torque = 2400;
BH = 260; fs = 1.2; YZ = 1.0; b = 45; n = 1800; Qv = 8; typeg = 2; L = 4000;
Rp = C/(1+N2/N1);
Ft = 1000*torque/Rp;
JK = GearJofK(m,phis,ar,rrT,ts,N1,N2,C,rT1,rT2);
Kv = GearKofV(Rp,n,Qv);
KH = GearKofH(b,typeg,Rp);
sigmab = Kv*KH*Ft/m/b/JK;
sigmafp = 0.533*BH+88.3;
YN = GearYofN(BH,n,L);
sigmaf = sigmafp*YN/fs/YZ;
disp(['The bending stress is ' num2str(sigmab,5) ' N/mm^2'])
disp(['The permissible level is ' num2str(sigmaf,5) ' N/mm^2'])
```

When this script is executed, the following is displayed to the MATLAB command window.

```
The bending stress is 149.64 N/mm^2
The permissible level is 167.41 N/mm^2
```

8.4 KINEMATICS OF A FOUR-BAR LINKAGE

8.4.1 Position and Velocity of the Links

Consider the linkage shown in Figure 8.21. When the angles θ_1 and θ_2 are given, θ_3 and θ_4 are obtained from

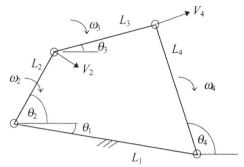

FIGURE 8.21
Nomenclature for a four-bar linkage.

$$L_2 \cos\theta_2 + L_3 \cos\theta_3 - L_4 \cos\theta_4 - L_1 \cos\theta_1 = 0$$
$$L_2 \sin\theta_2 + L_3 \sin\theta_3 - L_4 \sin\theta_4 - L_1 \sin\theta_1 = 0 \qquad (8.18)$$

For convenience we set $\theta_1 = 0$. If the angular velocity of link 2 is given, then the angular velocities of links 3 and 4 are, respectively,

$$\omega_3 = \frac{L_2\omega_2 \sin(\theta_4 - \theta_2)}{L_3 \sin(\theta_3 - \theta_4)} \qquad \omega_4 = \frac{L_2\omega_2 \sin(\theta_2 - \theta_3)}{L_4 \sin(\theta_4 - \theta_3)}$$

where θ_3 and θ_4 are those obtained from Eq. (8.18). The linear velocity at the end of link 2 is $V_2 = L_2\omega_2$, and that at the end of link 4 is

$$V_4 = L_4\omega_4 = V_2 \frac{\sin(\theta_2 - \theta_3)}{\sin(\theta_4 - \theta_3)}$$

Each of these velocities is perpendicular to its respective L_j in the direction of ω_j.
The angular accelerations of links 3 and 4 are[10]

$$\alpha_3 = \frac{-L_2\alpha_2 \sin(\theta_4 - \theta_2) + L_2\omega_2^2 \cos(\theta_4 - \theta_2) + L_3\omega_3^2 \cos(\theta_4 - \theta_3) - L_4\omega_4^2}{L_3 \sin(\theta_3 - \theta_4)}$$

$$\alpha_4 = \frac{L_2\alpha_2 \sin(\theta_3 - \theta_2) - L_2\omega_2^2 \cos(\theta_3 - \theta_2) + L_4\omega_4^2 \cos(\theta_3 - \theta_4) - L_3\omega_3^2}{L_4 \sin(\theta_3 - \theta_4)}$$

Algebraic solutions to obtain expressions for θ_3 are θ_4 from Eq. (8.18) are straightforward, but tedious. We shall, instead, solve these equations numerically using `fsolve`.

---

[10] A. G. Erdman and G. N. Sandor, *Mechanism Design: Analysis and Synthesis*, 2nd ed., Prentice Hall, Upper Saddle River, NJ, 1991, p. 231.

Example 8.20 Visualization of four-bar mechanism's position, velocity, and acceleration

We shall plot the orientation of link #3 for the case where $L_1 = 0.8$, $L_2 = 2$, $L_3 = 2$, and $L_4 = 3$. In separate graphs, we shall present the velocity ratio V_4/V_2, and the acceleration α_4 for $\omega_2 = 4$ rad/s and $\alpha_2 = 5$ rad/s^2. We first create the function *FourBarPosition*, from which fsolve will determine θ_3 and θ_4. Thus,

```
function t = FourBarPosition(th,th2,L2,L3,L4,L1)
t = [L2*cos(th2)+L3*cos(th(1))–L4*cos(th(2))–L1; ...
    L2*sin(th2)+L3*sin(th(1))–L4*sin(th(2))];
```

where $th(1) = \theta_3$ and $th(2) = \theta_4$.

The script to display various positions of link #3, the velocity of the end of link #4, and the accelerations of link #4 is

```
L2 = .8; L3 = 2; L4 = 2; L1 = 3;th1 = 0;
th2 = [1/6:1/6:2]*pi;
th34 = zeros(length(th2),2);
options = optimset('display','off');
for m = 1:length(th2)
  th34(m,:) = fsolve('FourBarPosition',[5 5],options,th2(m),L2,L3,L4,L1);
end
y = L2*sin(th2)+L3*sin(th34(:,1)');
x = L2*cos(th2)+L3*cos(th34(:,1)');
xx = [L2*cos(th2)];
yy = [L2*sin(th2)];
figure(1)
plot([x;xx],[y;yy],'k',[0 L1],[0 0],'k--^',x,y,'ko',xx,yy,'ks')
title('Several positions of the connecting link of a four-bar mechanism')
xlabel('Horizontal position')
ylabel('Vertical position')
axis equal
th2 = [0:.05:2]*pi;
th34 = zeros(length(th2),2);
for m = 1:length(th2)
  th34(m,:) = fsolve('FourBarPosition',[5 5],options,th2(m),L2,L3,L4,L1);
end
figure(2)
y = sin(th2–th34(:,1)')./sin(th34(:,2)'– th34(:,1)');
plot(180*th2/pi,y)
v = axis;
v(2) = 360;
axis(v)
xlabel('\theta_2 (degrees)')
```

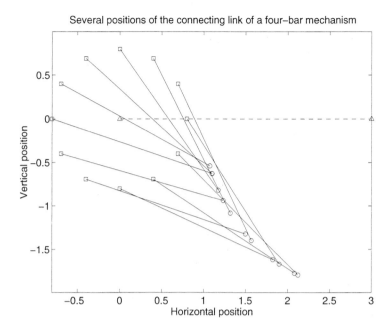

FIGURE 8.22
Several positions of link #3.

```
ylabel('V_4/V_2')
title('Velocity ratio of tip of link #4')
w2 = 4; alph2 = 5;
w3 = (L2*w2*sin(th34(:,2)–th2')).⁄(L3*sin(th34(:,1)–th34(:,2)));
w4 = (L2*w2*sin(th2'–th34(:,1))).⁄(L4*sin(th34(:,2)–th34(:,1)));
s32 = th34(:,1)–th2';
s34 = th34(:,1)–th34(:,2);
alph4 = (L2*alph2*sin(s32)–L2*w2^2*cos(s32)+L4*w4.^2.*cos(s34)–...
        L3*w3.^2).⁄(L4*sin(s34));
figure(3)
plot(180*th2/pi,alph4)
v = axis;
v(2) = 360;
axis(v)
xlabel('\theta_2 (degrees)')
ylabel('\alpha_4')
title('Angular acceleration of link #4')
```

The execution of the script results in Figures 8.22, 8.23, and 8.24.

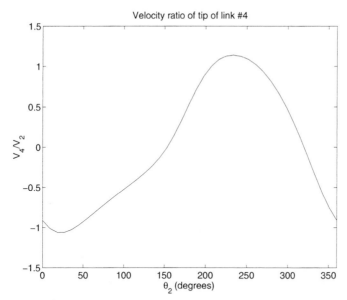

FIGURE 8.23
Velocity of the tip of link #4.

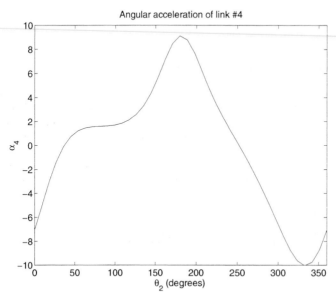

FIGURE 8.24
Angular acceleration of link #4.

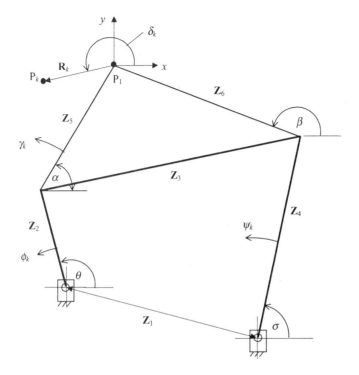

FIGURE 8.25
Nomenclature for three-position synthesis.

8.4.2 Synthesis of a Four-Bar Linkage

Synthesis of a four-bar linkage has as one of its objective the determination of the linkage lengths so that a specified point on the floating bar passes through three prescribed points. Consider the mechanism shown in Figure 8.25. The objective is to determine the lengths Z_k and their initial orientations so that point P passes through points P_1, P_2, and P_3. We shall assume that point P_1 is located at the origin of the coordinate system so that $R_1 = 0$.

The equations from which the six link lengths can be determined are given in terms of the two dimensional vectors, which are most easily expressed as complex numbers. The lengths and orientation of the six vectors can be determined from[11]

$$\mathbf{Z}_2 = \frac{1}{\mathbf{D}} \begin{vmatrix} \mathbf{R}_1 & \mathbf{d}_{12} \\ \mathbf{R}_2 & \mathbf{d}_{22} \end{vmatrix} \qquad \mathbf{Z}_5 = \frac{1}{\mathbf{D}} \begin{vmatrix} \mathbf{d}_{11} & \mathbf{R}_1 \\ \mathbf{d}_{21} & \mathbf{R}_2 \end{vmatrix}$$

---

[11] A. G. Erdman and G. N. Sandor, *ibid.*, pp. 530-2.

$$\mathbf{Z}_4 = \frac{1}{E}\begin{vmatrix} \mathbf{R}_1 & e_{12} \\ \mathbf{R}_2 & e_{22} \end{vmatrix} \qquad \mathbf{Z}_6 = \frac{1}{E}\begin{vmatrix} e_{11} & \mathbf{R}_1 \\ e_{21} & \mathbf{R}_2 \end{vmatrix}$$

$$\mathbf{Z}_3 = \mathbf{Z}_5 - \mathbf{Z}_6 \qquad \mathbf{Z}_1 = \mathbf{Z}_2 + \mathbf{Z}_3 - \mathbf{Z}_4$$

$$D = \begin{vmatrix} d_{11} & d_{12} \\ d_{21} & d_{22} \end{vmatrix} = \begin{vmatrix} e^{j\phi_1} - 1 & e^{j\gamma_1} - 1 \\ e^{j\phi_2} - 1 & e^{j\gamma_2} - 1 \end{vmatrix}$$

$$E = \begin{vmatrix} e_{11} & e_{12} \\ e_{21} & e_{22} \end{vmatrix} = \begin{vmatrix} e^{j\psi_1} - 1 & e^{j\gamma_1} - 1 \\ e^{j\psi_2} - 1 & e^{j\gamma_2} - 1 \end{vmatrix}$$

where

$$\mathbf{R}_k = |\mathbf{R}_k| e^{j\delta_k}$$

Comparing Figure 8.21 with Figure 8.25 we see that $|\mathbf{Z}_1| = L_1$, $|\mathbf{Z}_2| = L_2$, $|\mathbf{Z}_3| = L_3$, and $|\mathbf{Z}_4| = L_4$.

It is standard practice to assume values for $\mathbf{R}_k$, ϕ_k, γ_k, and ψ_k, $k = 1,2$. In this case we can then determine the lengths of the six links and their original orientation angles α, β, σ, and θ. First we create the following function that can be used to evaluate the pairs $\mathbf{Z}_2$ and $\mathbf{Z}_5$ and $\mathbf{Z}_4$ and $\mathbf{Z}_6$.

```
function z = FourBarSynth(phi,gama,R)
coeff = [exp(j*phi(1))-1 exp(j*gama(1))-1; exp(j*phi(2))-1 exp(j*gama(2))-1];
D = det(coeff);
z1 = det([R(1) coeff(1,2); R(2) coeff(2,2)])/D;
z2 = det([coeff(1,1) R(1); coeff(2,1) R(2)])/D;
z = [z1 z2];
```

We now illustrate these results.

Example 8.21 Synthesis of a four-bar linkage

We assume the following values:

$\phi_1 = 340°$	$\gamma_1 = -48°$	$\delta_1 = -31°$
$\phi_2 = 325°$	$\gamma_2 = 9°$	$\delta_2 = -15°$
$\psi_1 = 31°$	$|\mathbf{P}_1| = 2.7$	
$\psi_2 = 81°$	$|\mathbf{P}_2| = 3.9$	

The script is

```
c = pi/180; phi = [340.0 325.0]*c; gama = [-48 9.0]*c;
R = [2.7*exp(-31.0*j*c) 3.9*exp(-15.0*j*c)];
z25 = FourBarSynth(phi,gama,R);
disp(['Z2 = ' num2str(abs(z25(1)))' theta = '...
```

```
          num2str(angle(z25(1))/c)'degrees'])
disp(['Z5 = 'num2str(abs(z25(2)))' alpha = '...
          num2str(angle(z25(2))/c)'.degrees'])
psi = [31 80]*c;
z46 = FourBarSynth(psi,gama,R);
disp(['Z4 = 'num2str(abs(z46(1)))' sigma = '...
          num2str(angle(z46(1))/c)'degrees'])
disp(['Z6 = 'num2str(abs(z46(2)))' beta = '...
          num2str(angle(z46(2))/c)'degrees'])
Z3 = z25(2)−z46(2);
Z1 = z25(1)+Z3−z46(1);
disp(['Z3 = 'num2str(abs(Z3))])
disp(['Z1 = 'num2str(abs(Z1))])
```

which, upon execution, displays to the MATLAB command window

```
Z2 = 6.7143   theta = 90.5276 degrees
Z5 = 1.2378   alpha = 24.8126 degrees
Z4 = 3.1762   sigma = -143.832 degrees
Z6 = 1.2774   beta = 95.0336 degrees
Z3 = 1.447
Z1 = 8.6814
```

The visualization of these results is shown in Figure 8.26; however, the script used to generate this figure has been left for Exercise 8.7.

8.5 CAM PROFILES AND SYNTHESIS

8.5.1 Cam Displacement

Cams are devices for transforming one motion into another. A cam has either a curved or a grooved surface that mates with a follower and imparts motion to it. The cam's motion, usually rotational, is transformed into oscillation, translation or both. We shall consider the case of cycloidal motion for the displacement profile for the follower, which is created in two types of followers: a translating flat-face follower and an offset translating roller follower. The objective is to determine the cam's profile and the coordinates of the cutter of given radius that would be used to manufacture the cam's profile.

We define the base circle of a cam r_b as the smallest circle that can be drawn tangent to the cam's surface, and is concentric to the cam's axis of rotation. The motion of the follower is

$$L(\varphi) = r_b + s(\varphi)$$

where, for cycloidal motion,

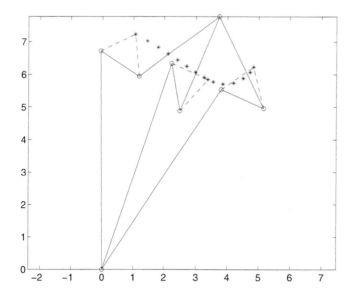

FIGURE 8.26
Path of point P of the synthesized four-bar linkage.

$$s(\varphi) = h\left(\frac{\varphi}{\beta} - \frac{1}{2\pi}\sin(2\pi\,\varphi/\beta)\right) \qquad 0 \le \varphi \le \beta$$

$$s(\varphi) = h - h\left(\frac{\varphi - \beta}{\beta} - \frac{1}{2\pi}\sin(2\pi\,(\varphi - \beta)/\beta)\right) \qquad \beta \le \varphi \le 2\beta$$

$$s(\varphi) = 0 \qquad 2\beta \le \varphi \le 2\pi$$

is the follower's displacement profile, h is the maximum displacement of the follower, and $0 \le \beta \le \pi$.

If we assume that the rotational speed of the cam $\omega = d\varphi/dt$ is a constant, then the velocity v, acceleration a and jerk j (the time-derivative of acceleration) of the follower are, respectively:

Velocity

$$v(\varphi) = \frac{\omega h}{\beta}\left(1 - \cos(2\pi\,\varphi/\beta)\right) \qquad 0 \le \varphi \le \beta$$

$$v(\varphi) = -\frac{\omega h}{\beta}\left(1 - \cos(2\pi\,(\varphi - \beta)/\beta)\right) \qquad \beta \le \varphi \le 2\beta$$

$$v(\varphi) = 0 \qquad 2\beta \le \varphi \le 2\pi$$

Acceleration

$$a(\varphi) = \frac{2\pi\omega^2 h}{\beta^2} \sin(2\pi \varphi/\beta) \qquad 0 \le \varphi \le \beta$$

$$a(\varphi) = -\frac{2\pi\omega^2 h}{\beta^2} \sin(2\pi (\varphi-\beta)/\beta) \qquad \beta \le \varphi \le 2\beta$$

$$a(\varphi) = 0 \qquad 2\beta \le \varphi \le 2\pi$$

Jerk

$$j(\varphi) = \frac{4\pi^2\omega^3 h}{\beta^3} \cos(2\pi \varphi/\beta) \qquad 0 \le \varphi \le \beta$$

$$j(\varphi) = -\frac{4\pi^2\omega^3 h}{\beta^3} \cos(2\pi (\varphi-\beta)/\beta) \qquad \beta \le \varphi \le 2\beta$$

$$j(\varphi) = 0 \qquad 2\beta < \varphi < 2\pi$$

We define the nondimensional displacement $S = s/h$, the nondimensional velocity $V = v/\omega h$, the nondimensional acceleration $A = a/h\omega^2$, and the nondimensional jerk $J = j/h\omega^3$. Then, if $\beta = 60°$, the following script obtains the results shown in Figure 8.27.

```
beta = 60*pi/180;
phi = linspace(0,beta,40);
phi2 = [beta+phi];
ph = [phi phi2]*180/pi;
arg = 2*pi*phi/beta;
arg2 = 2*pi*(phi2-beta)/beta;
s = [ phi/beta-sin(arg)/2/pi 1-(arg2-sin(arg2))/2/pi];
v = [(1-cos(arg))/beta -(1-cos(arg2))/beta];
a = [2*pi /beta^2*sin(arg) 2*pi /beta^2*sin(arg2)];
j = [4*pi^2/beta^3*cos(arg) 4*pi^2/beta^3*cos(arg2)];subplot(2,2,1)
plot(ph,s,'k')
xlabel('Cam angle (degrees)')
ylabel('Displacement (S)')
g = axis; g(2) = 120; axis(g)
subplot(2,2,2)
plot(ph,v,'k',[0 120],[0 0],'k--')
xlabel('Cam angle (degrees)')
ylabel('Velocity (V)')
g = axis; g(2) = 120; axis(g)
subplot(2,2,3)
plot(ph,a,'k',[0 120],[0 0],'k--')
xlabel('Cam angle (degrees)')
ylabel('Acceleration (A)')
```

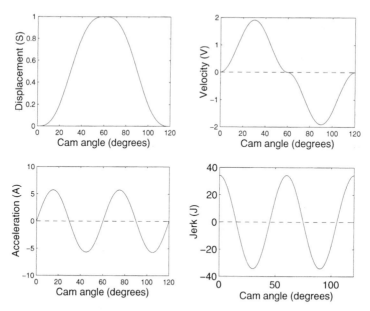

FIGURE 8.27
Normalized displacement, velocity, acceleration, and jerk for a cycloidal cam profile.

```
g = axis;
g(2) = 120;
axis(g)
subplot(2,2,4)
plot(ph,j,'k',[0 120],[0 0],'k--')
xlabel('Cam angle (degrees)')
ylabel('Jerk (J)')
g = axis;
g(2) = 120;
axis(g)
```

We now shift our attention to two specific cam configurations: a translating flat-face follower and an offset translating roller follower.

8.5.2 Translating Flat-Face Follower

Referring to Figure 8.28 we have the following relationships[12] for the (x,y) coordinates R_x and R_y of the cam's profile and the cutter's coordinates C_x and C_y:

---

[12] See, for example, A. G. Erdman and G. N. Sandor, *ibid.*, pp. 385–387 and H. A. Rothbart, *Cams: Design, Dynamics, Accuracy*, John Wiley & Sons, New York, 1956, pp. 122–124.

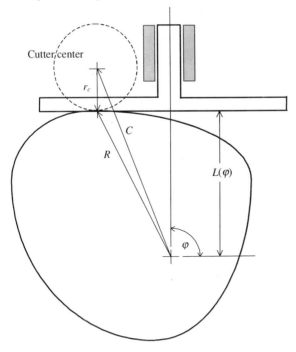

FIGURE 8.28
Cam with translating flat-face follower.

$$R_x = R\cos(\theta + \varphi) \qquad R_y = R\sin(\theta + \varphi)$$
$$C_x = C\cos(\gamma + \varphi) \qquad C_y = C\sin(\gamma + \varphi)$$

where

$$R = \frac{L}{\cos\theta} \qquad \theta = \tan^{-1}\left(\frac{1}{L}\frac{dL}{d\varphi}\right)$$

$$C = \frac{L + r_c}{\cos\gamma} \qquad \gamma = \tan^{-1}\left(\frac{dL/d\varphi}{L + r_c}\right)$$

and r_c is the radius of the cutter and $dL/d\varphi = v(\varphi)/\omega$.

In order to display these results, which are shown in Figure 8.29, we first create the functions *CamProfile*, which computes $L(\varphi)$ and $dL/d\varphi$, and *ContourFlat*, which computes R_x, R_y, C_x, and C_y.

```
function [L,dLdphi] = CamProfile(phi,rb,h,beta)
arg = 2*pi*phi/beta;
L = rb+h*(phi/beta−sin(arg)/2/pi);
```

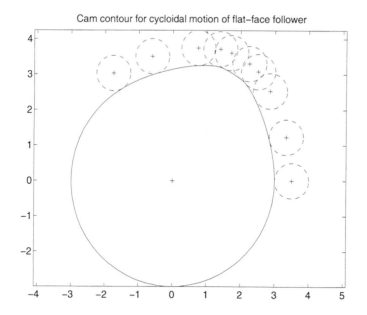

FIGURE 8.29
Cam contour for cycloidal motion of flat-face follower and several of its cutter's positions.

```
dLdphi = (h/beta)*(1−cos(arg));
L = [L fliplr(L)];
dLdphi  = [dLdphi −dLdphi];
```

Function *ContourFlat* is

```
function [Rx,Ry,Cx,Cy] = ContourFlat(phi,rb,h,beta,rc)
[L,dLdphi] = CamProfile(phi,rb,h,beta);
theta = atan2(dLdphi,L);
R = L./cos(theta);
ph = [phi beta+phi];
Ry = R.*sin(theta+ph);
Rx = R.*cos(theta+ph);
gama = atan(dLdphi./(L+rc));
C = (L+rc)./cos(gama);
Cy = C.*sin(gama+ph);
Cx = C.*cos(gama+ph);
```

If we let $\beta = 60°$, $r_b = 3.0$, and $h = 0.5$, then the script is

```
beta = 60*pi/180; rb = 3; h = 0.5; rc = 0.5; n = 23;
phi = linspace(0,beta,n);
ph = [phi beta+phi];
[Rx,Ry,Cx,Cy] = ContourFlat(phi,rb,h,beta,rc);
ang = linspace(2*beta,2*pi,40);
plot(Rx,Ry,'k',rb*cos(ang),rb*sin(ang),'k',0,0,'k+',Cx(1:5:2*n),Cy(1:5:2*n),'k+')
axis equal
phd = linspace(0,2*pi,50);
[x,phx] = meshgrid(Cx(1:5:2*n),phd);
y = meshgrid(Cy(1:5:2*n),phd);
hold on
plot(x+rc.*cos(phx),y+rc.*sin(phx),'k--')
title('Cam contour for cycloidal motion of flat-face follower')
```

8.5.3 Translating Offset Roller Follower

Referring to Figure 8.30 we have the following relationships[13] for the (x,y) coordinates R_x and R_y of the cam's profile and the cutter's coordinates C_x and C_y:

$$R_x = R\cos(\psi + \varphi + \gamma) \qquad R_y = R\sin(\psi + \varphi + \gamma)$$
$$C_x = C\cos(\psi + \varphi + \delta) \qquad C_y = C\sin(\psi + \varphi + \delta)$$

where

$$R^2 = (F - r_f\cos\alpha)^2 + r_f^2\cos^2\alpha \qquad \psi = \tan^{-1}(m/L)$$

$$C^2 = c_x^2 + c_y^2 \qquad \alpha = \tan^{-1}\left(\frac{LdL/d\varphi}{F^2 - m\,dL/d\varphi}\right)$$

$$c_x = F + (r_c - r_f)\cos\alpha \qquad \gamma = \tan^{-1}\left(\frac{F - r_f\cos\alpha}{r_f\sin\alpha}\right)$$

$$c_y = (r_c - r_f)\sin\alpha \qquad \delta = \tan^{-1}(c_y/c_x)$$

$$F^2 = m^2 + L^2$$

The base circle radius of the cam is

$$L(0) = r_b = \sqrt{R_x^2(\varphi = 0) + R_y^2(\varphi = 0)}$$

which starts at $\varphi = 2\beta + \Delta$, where

$$\Delta = \tan^{-1}\left(\frac{R_y(\varphi = 0)}{R_x(\varphi = 0)}\right)$$

---

[13] See, for example, A. G. Erdman, and G. N. Sandor, *ibid.*, pp. 389–393 and H. A. Rothbart, *ibid.*, pp. 120–122.

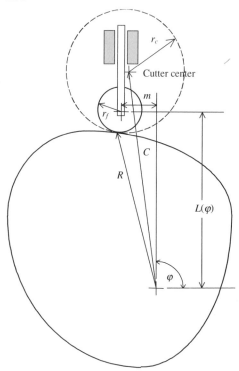

FIGURE 8.30
Cam with an offset translating roller follower.

In order to display these results we first create the function *ContourRoller*, which computes R_x, R_y, C_x, and C_y.

```
function [Rx,Ry,Cx,Cy] = ContourRoller(phi,rb,h,beta,rc,m,rf)
[L,dLdphi] = CamProfile(phi,rb,h,beta);
F2 = m^2+L.^2;
F = sqrt(F2);
psi = atan2(m,L);
alpha = atan2(L.*dLdphi,F2−m*dLdphi);
gamma = atan2(rf*sin(alpha),F−rf*cos(alpha));
ph = [phi beta+phi];
R = sqrt((F−rf*cos(alpha)).^2+(rf*sin(alpha)).^2);
Ry = R.*sin(psi+gamma+ph);
Rx = R.*cos(psi+gamma+ph);
cx = F+(rc−rf)*cos(alpha);
cy = (rc−rf)*sin(alpha);
delta = atan2(cy,cx);
C = sqrt(cx.^2+cy.^2);
```

```
Cy = C.*sin(psi+delta+ph);
Cx = C.*cos(psi+delta+ph);
```

If we let $\beta = 60°$, $r_b = 3.0$, and $h = 0.5$, $r_c = 0.5$, $r_f = 0.375$, and $m = 0.375$, then the script is

```
beta = 60*pi/180; rb = 3; h = 0.5; rc = 0.5; rf = 0.375; m = .375; n = 23;
phi = linspace(0,beta,n);
ph = [phi beta+phi];
[Rx,Ry,Rx,Ry] = ContourRoller(0,rb,h,beta,rc,m,rf);
rb = sqrt(Rx(1)^2+Ry(1)^2);
delta = atan2(Ry(1),Rx(1));
[Rx,Ry,Cx,Cy] = ContourRoller(phi,rb,h,beta,rc,m,rf);
ang = linspace(2*beta+delta,2*pi+delta,40);
plot(Rx,Ry,'k',Rx(1)*cos(ang),Rx(1)*sin(ang),'k',0,0,'k+',Cx(1:5:2*n), ...
    Cy(1:5:2*n),'k+')
axis equal
phd = linspace(0,2*pi,50);
[x,phx] = meshgrid(Cx(1:5:2*n),phd);
y = meshgrid(Cy(1:5:2*n),phd);
hold on
plot(x+rc.*cos(phx),y+rc.*sin(phx),'k--')
title('Cam contour for cycloidal motion of an offset roller follower')
```

When executed this script produces the results shown in Figure 8.31.

8.5.4 Cam Radius of Curvature

The radius of curvature of the cam profile is given by

$$\rho = \frac{\left[(L(\varphi))^2 + (dL(\varphi)/d\varphi)^2\right]^{3/2}}{(L(\varphi))^2 + 2(dL(\varphi)/d\varphi)^2 - L(\varphi)d^2L(\varphi)/d\varphi^2}$$

A cam's profile should be such that the radius of curvature of a follower is always greater than the minimum radius of curvature of the profile. Thus, the quantity of interest is the minimum radius of curvature. Using the definitions in Section 8.5.1 for the nondimensional displacement, velocity, acceleration and jerk, the radius of curvature can be written as

$$\rho/h = \frac{\left[(r_b/h+S)^2 + V^2\right]^{3/2}}{(r_b/h+S)^2 + 2V^2 - (r_b/h+S)A}$$

To determine the minimum (nondimensional) radius of curvature we first create the function *CamCurvature*, which uses the fact that the radius of curvature is symmetrical about β.

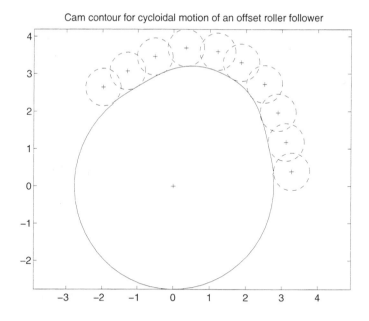

Cam contour for cycloidal motion of an offset roller follower

FIGURE 8.31
Cam contour for cycloidal motion of offset roller follower and its cutter coordinates.

```
function RadiusCurve = CamCurvature(phi,beta,rbh)
arg = 2*pi*phi/beta;
S = phi/beta−sin(arg)/2/pi;
V = (1−cos(arg))/beta;
A = 2*pi /beta^2*sin(arg);
RadiusCurve = ((rbh+S)^2+V^2)^1.5/((rbh+S)^2+2*V^2−(rbh+S)*A);
```

which is valid for $0 \leq \varphi \leq \beta$.

Then, for any value of r_b/h and β the script is

```
rbh = input('Enter ratio rb/h: ');
beta = input('Enter angle beta (degrees): ')*pi/180;
options = optimset('display','off');
phimin = fminbnd('CamCurvature',0,beta,options,beta,rbh);
rmin = CamCurvature(phimin,beta,rbh);
disp(['When beta = ' num2str(beta*180/pi) ' degrees and rb/h = ' ...
            num2str(rbh) 'the minimum radius of curvature for a'])
disp(['cycloidal cam profile is = ' num2str(rmin) 'h, which occurs at ' ...
            num2str(phimin*180/pi) ' degrees.'])
```

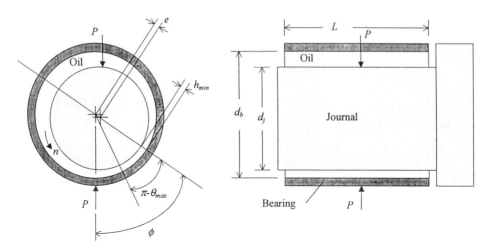

FIGURE 8.32
Hydrodynamic journal bearing nomenclature.

When this script is executed, we have displayed to the MATLAB command window

Enter ratio rb/h: 4
Enter angle beta (degrees): 80
When beta = 80 degrees and rb/h = 4 the minimum radius of curvature for a
cycloidal cam profile is = 2.9777h, which occurs at 58.8421 degrees.

where the user entered the values of 4 and 80.

8.6 HYDRODYNAMIC BEARINGS

Consider the short journal bearing shown in Figure 8.32. If $c_d = (d_b - d_j)$, then the radial clearance $c_r = c_d/2$ is the maximum value of e, the eccentricity. The eccentricity ratio is defined as $\varepsilon = e/c_r$. However, in practice this quantity is usually obtained from the following relationship, which has been obtained from experiments:

$$\varepsilon \rightarrow \varepsilon_x = 0.21394 + 0.38517 \log_{10} O_N - 0.0008(O_N - 60)$$

where O_N is the load factor, or Ocvirk number, given by

$$O_N = \frac{P}{nLd\eta}\left(\frac{d}{L}\right)^2\left(\frac{c_d}{d}\right)^2 = 4\pi K_\varepsilon$$

where η is the absolute viscosity of the oil and n is the rotational speed of the journal in revolutions per second. A desirable design goal is to keep $O_N < 30$.

The minimum film thickness is given by

$$h_{min} = c_r(1 - \varepsilon_x)$$

which should be a factor of three to four times greater than the surface finish of the bearing and journal in order to greatly minimize the chance of contact of the surfaces.

The load that the bearing can support is given by

$$P = 4\pi K_\varepsilon \eta n d L^3 / c_d^2$$

and the torque needed to rotate the journal is

$$T_r = \frac{\pi^2 d^3 L n \eta}{c_d \sqrt{\left(1 - \varepsilon_x^2\right)}} + 0.5 P \varepsilon_x c_d \sin\phi$$

where the first term on the right hand side is the stationary torque and

$$\phi = \tan^{-1}\left(\frac{\pi\sqrt{1 - \varepsilon_x^2}}{4\varepsilon_x}\right)$$

The coefficient of friction between the journal and the bearing is

$$\mu = \frac{2T_r}{Pd}$$

and the temperature rise in the oil in °F is given by

$$\Delta T = \frac{2\pi n T_r}{6600 \rho c_p Q_H}$$

where

$$Q_H = \pi d n L \varepsilon_x c_d / 2$$

is the hydrodynamic oil flow in in^3/s, c_p is the heat capacity of the lubricant and ρ is its density. For lubricating oils, we have the approximate values $c_p = 0.48$ Btu/(lb.-°F) and $\rho = 0.031$ lb/in^3. The temperature rise assumes that the oil is at an inlet temperature of T_{in}. However, since η (see below), and therefore T_r, is a function of temperature, this equation has to be solved iteratively. Using these values for c_p and ρ we have

$$\Delta T = \frac{0.0640 n T_r}{Q_H}$$

The absolute viscosity of the oil in reyn (lb-s/in^2) can be estimated within ±10% from the relationship

$$\eta = 10^{C-7}$$

where

TABLE 8.6
Constants Used to Determine η

SAE Number	j	A_j	B_j
10	1	9.1209	3.5605
20	2	9.1067	3.5385
30	3	8.9939	3.4777
40	4	8.9133	3.4292
50	5	8.5194	3.2621
60	6	8.3666	3.1884

$$C = 10^{A_j - B_j \log_{10} T_o}$$

and $T_o = 255.2 + 5/9T$ K, where T is the temperature of the oil in °F, and A_j and B_j are given in Table 8.6 as a function of the oil's SAE number. (See Exercise 6.7.)

Before we illustrate these results with an example we create three functions:

AbsViscosity, computes the absolute viscosity η

Ocvirk, computes the Ocvirk number O_N

TempRise, computes the temperature rise ΔT

Function *AbsViscosity* is

```
function absvis = AbsViscosity(tempF,SAE)
AandB = [9.1209 3.5605; 9.1067 3.5385; 8.9939 3.4777; 8.9133 3.4292;...
         8.5194 3.2621; 8.3666 3.1884];
SAEn = SAE/10;
absvis = 10^(10^(AandB(SAEn,1)−AandB(SAEn,2)*log10(255.2+5/9*tempF))−7);
```

Function *Ocvirk* is

```
function [ex,ocv] = Ocvirk(vis,L,d,cd,n,P)
ocv = 60*P/n/L/d/vis*(cd/L)^2;
ex = 0.21394+0.38517*log10(ocv)−0.0008*(ocv−60);
```

Function *TempRise* is

```
function deltaT = TempRise(temp,n,d,cd,ex,L,P,SAE)
QH = pi*d*(n/60)*L*ex*cd/2
phi = atan(pi*sqrt(1−ex^2)/4/ex);
vis = AbsViscosity(temp,SAE);
Tr = pi^2*d^3*L*(n/60)*vis/cd/sqrt(1−ex^2)+0.5*P*ex*cd*sin(phi);
deltaT = (0.0640)*Tr*(n/60)/QH;
```

Example 8.22 Load carrying capacity of a hydrodynamic journal bearing

Consider the following specification of a hydrodynamic journal bearing:

Oil inlet temperature = 120 °F

SAE 30 oil

Shaft rotational speed = 3000 rpm

Shaft diameter = 2.0 inches

Journal length = 1.1 inches

Radial clearance = 0.0013 inches

Let us determine the maximum load that the bearing can support such that the Ocvirk number is less than 25, and the corresponding temperature rise, minimum oil film thickness, and value for the absolute viscosity.

We first create a function called *JournalLoad,* which, for a given value of the load, computes the temperature rise in the oil, the absolute viscosity of the oil and the Ocvirk number. This function is then used by `fzero` to find a value of the load for which the Ocvirk number is equal to 25.

```
function [Omax,absvis,ex,temp] = JournalLoad(P,Tin,SAE,n,d,cd,L)
temp = Tin; Told = 0;
while abs(temp–Told)>0.1
  Told = temp;
  absvis = AbsViscosity(temp,SAE);
  ex = Ocvirk(absvis,L,d,cd,n,P);
  deltaT = TempRise(temp,n,d,cd,ex,L,P,SAE);
  temp = Tin+deltaT;
end
absvis = AbsViscosity(temp,SAE);
[ex,ocv] = Ocvirk(absvis,L,d,cd,n,P);
Omax = 25–ocv;
```

Then the script is

```
Tin = 120; SAE = 30; n = 3000; d = 2; cd = .0026; L = 1.1;
options = optimset('display','off');
P = fzero('JournalLoad',1000,options,Tin,SAE,n,d,cd,L);
[Omax,absvis,ex,temp] = JournalLoad(P,Tin,SAE,n,d,cd,L);
disp(['Maximum load = ' num2str(P) ' lb.'])
disp(['Temperature rise = ' num2str(temp-Tin) ' degrees F'])
disp(['Absolute viscosity = ' num2str(absvis) ' reyn'])
disp(['Minimum oil film thickness = ' num2str(0.5*cd*(1-ex)) ' inches'])
```

When executed, the script displays to the MATLAB command window

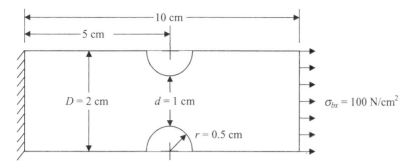

Thickness = 0.2 cm

FIGURE 8.33
Notched plate under tension.

Maximum load = 1078.3427 lb.
Temperature rise = 58.6577 degrees F
Absolute viscosity = 2.1907e-006 reyn
Minimum oil film thickness = 0.0002855 inches

8.7 PDE TOOLBOX AND THE STRESS CONCENTRATION FACTOR FOR NOTCHES IN A THIN PLATE[14]

MATLAB's partial differential equation (PDE) toolbox and its associated graphical user interface (GUI) is used to analyze several classes of two-dimensional field equations. One such class is the plane stress problem. Plane stress problems are approximations that are used to determine the stresses, strains, and displacements in thin plates of arbitrary shape and thickness h. For these plates it is assumed that the stress (σ_z) normal to the plate's surface at $z = \pm\, h/2$ and the shear stresses (σ_{xz}, σ_{yz}) on this surface are zero, and that the remaining stresses are independent of z.

We shall demonstrate the procedure for using this toolbox and GUI by determining the stress concentration factor in a rectangular steel plate in which two semicircular notches have been cut from opposing edges at the plate's middle. The plate's geometry and dimensions are shown in Figure 8.33. The plate is clamped at its left end and subjected to a force per unit length $F_x = 20$ N/cm acting in the positive x-direction at its right end. If the plate's thickness is 0.2 cm, then the stress in the positive x-direction at this edge is 100 N/cm². The Young's modulus for steel in the current units is 200×10^5 N/cm².

The PDE toolbox requires that one describe the boundary conditions on each edge comprising its shape. There are two types of boundary conditions that are usually considered in plane stress problems: (1) the displacement is either zero or specified, and (2) the surface stress is either zero or specified. The specification of the displacements is denoted in the

---

[14] See Section 11.3.3 for an application of the PDE Toolbox to flow visualization and Section 12.1 for an application to heat transfer.

GUI as the *Dirichlet* boundary condition, and those for the stresses is denoted the *Neumann* boundary condition.

Consider the two components of the stress acting on a boundary segment that is at some arbitrary orientation with respect to the (x,y) coordinate system. Using the notation of the GUI, if the component of the stress acting in the x-direction is g_1 and that in the y-direction g_2, then

$$g_1 = n_x \sigma_{bx} + n_y \sigma_{bxy}$$
$$g_2 = n_y \sigma_{by} + n_x \sigma_{bxy}$$

where σ_{bx} is the stress on the boundary in the x-direction, σ_{by} is the stress on the boundary in the y-direction and σ_{bxy} is the shear stress on the boundary. In addition, n_x and n_y are the direction cosines with respect to the x- and y-axis, respectively. Thus, on a boundary segment that is parallel to the x-axis $n_x = 0$ and $n_y = \pm 1$ (+1 is in the positive y-direction) and we specify the surface stresses as

$$g_1 = \pm \sigma_{bxy}$$
$$g_2 = \pm \sigma_{by}$$

If the shear stress on the boundary segment is zero—that is $\sigma_{bxy} = 0$—then $g_1 = 0$; conversely, if the normal stress $\sigma_{by} = 0$, then $g_2 = 0$. When the boundary segment is stress-free, then $g_1 = g_2 = 0$.

When we are dealing with a curved boundary segment (the arc of a circle or an ellipse), then one specifies the boundary conditions as

$$g_1 = N*nx$$
$$g_2 = N*ny$$

where nx and ny are interpreted by the GUI as the direction cosines with respect to the x and y axes, respectively, and N is the *numerical* value for the magnitude of the stress normal to the curved boundary segment.

The process of using the PDE GUI to determine the stresses, strains, and displacements requires the following steps:

1. Set up the drawing area.
2. Specify the appropriate PDE—plane stress in this case.
3. Draw (create) the 2D shape.
4. Specify the boundary conditions.
5. Specify the physical constants.
6. Generate the mesh.
7. Obtain the solution.
8. Display results.
9. Export arrays of numerical values generated by the GUI to the MATLAB command window, if further analysis is desired.

We shall now give the detailed procedure for implementing each of these steps. At any step during this process one can return to any of the previously completed steps and make changes. Then the previously completed subsequent steps must be implemented again. To access the GUI we type in the MATLAB command window

```
pdetool
```

which is a MATLAB function.

Set up the drawing area. Based on the dimensions of the plate shown in Figure 8.33, we create a plotting area that is 12×4 units, where 1 unit = 1 cm. In addition, we show the grid lines and engage the snap-to-grid-points option by clicking on *Snap*. Thus, we click on the *Options* menu several times. The first time we click on *Grid* so that a check (✓) appears. We then do the same with *Snap*. Next we click on *Axis Limits*. In the menu window for *X-axis range* we enter

[0 12]

and for the *Y*-axis range

[0 4]

Then we click on *Apply* and then *Close*. Prior to clicking on *Apply* make sure that the *Auto* boxes are blank. Lastly, we click on *Grid Spacing* and enter for *X-axis linear spacing*

0:0.5:12

and for *Y*-axis linear spacing

0:0.5:4

Leave the areas for the extra tick marks blank, and make sure that the *Auto* boxes are also blank. Click on *Apply* and then on *Done*.

Specify the PDE. To specify the PDE we go to the right hand side of the toolbar, click on the arrowhead adjacent to the descriptor *Generic Scalar*, which appears when `pdetool` is first opened, and select *Structural Mech., Plane Stress*.

Draw (create) the 2D shape. The drawing routines use constructive solid geometry procedures to create a planar shape by performing either Boolean additions or subtractions on any combination of rectangles (squares), ellipses (circles) and *n*-sided polygons. Each of these entities can be placed anywhere within the drawing area previously created, and can have any dimensions that do not exceed the bounds of the drawing area. The location of the cross hairs of the cursor is given in the upper right hand corner of the GUI window. One selects one of the entities that is to be drawn by clicking on the appropriate icon in the left hand corner just above the drawing area. Then one places either a corner or the center of the entity, depending on which form has been selected, by depressing the mouse button. Then, with the button depressed, the cursor is moved to the next location and the mouse button is released.   The engagement of the *Snap* option was selected to simplify this placement process.

After each entity is placed, an alphanumeric indicator appears both interior to the entity just created and in the data entry window above the drawing area and to the right of the denotation *Set formula*.   The convention is *R* for a rectangle, *SQ* for a square, *E* for an ellipse, *C* for a circle, and *P* for a polygon.   When an entity is placed, the sign of its alphanumeric indicator is assumed positive (+).   To remove (subtract) an entity from another entity one goes into this data area and changes the sign(s) of the appropriate entities to minus (−).   After changing the sign(s), press *Enter* from the keyboard.

We now illustrate the steps needed to create the plate shown in Figure 8.33.   First we click on the toolbar symbol with the open rectangle.   Then we place the cursor at the coordinates (1,1), click and, while still holding the mouse button down, drag the cursor to the coordinates (11,3).   Release of the mouse button produces a rectangle that is 10×2.   If the placement or size is not what is desired, then go to *Edit* and select *Clear* or depress *Del* on the keyboard.   When more than one entity has been placed, one must first click on the entity that is to be deleted; otherwise all entities may be deleted.   The entity selected will have a black border.

Next we select the centered ellipse (circle) and place the cursor at (6,1), click the mouse button and, while still depressing it, move the cursor until a circle of diameter 1 appears.   On the drawing area it will appear elliptical because the axes are unequal.   The process is repeated with another circle centered at (6,3).   The final result looks like that shown in Figure 8.34.

In the *Set formula* area we change

$R1+C1+C2$

to

$R1-C1-C2$

and hit *Enter*.

We also turn of the grid lines, as they are no longer needed.

Specify the boundary conditions.   Before we specify the boundary conditions on each boundary segment, we must instruct the GUI to perform the set operations.   Thus, we first go to *Boundary* and select *Boundary Mode*.   The results of this operation produce Figure 8.35.   This places the figure in the drawing area in the boundary selection mode.

Next we work our way around each of these boundary segments, which are identified as that portion of the boundary that starts from the tip of one arrowhead to the tip of an adjacent one.   The boundary conditions can be specified on each segment in any order; however, it is suggested that one traverse the boundary in either a clockwise or counterclockwise direction so as to minimize the possibility of missing a segment.   We start at segment #1 and proceed clockwise around the boundary.

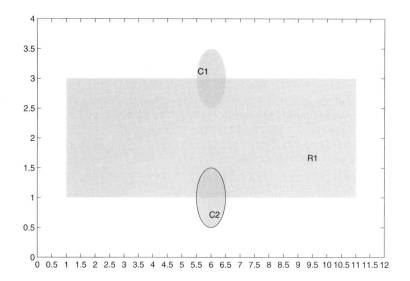

FIGURE 8.34
Result from drawing one rectangle and two circles.

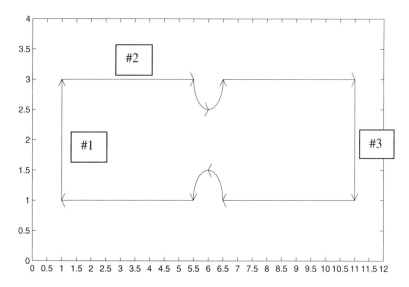

FIGURE 8.35
Result from set operations in *Boundary Mode*. (Note: Numbers on figure are not part of the display.)

When we click on segment #1 it changes color from red to black. Then we double-click on the segment to bring up the *Boundary Conditions* window for that segment only. This edge is fixed and, therefore, will have zero displacements. As mentioned previously, the specification for the displacements is denoted the Dirichlet type of boundary condition. Thus, under *Condition type* we select *Dirichlet*. Since the displacements are zero we can use the default conditions: $h_{11} = h_{22} = 1$ and $h_{12} = h_{21} = r_1 = r_2 = 0$. Remember that the displacement symbol shown at the top of the menu window, u, represents two vector components: one is the displacement in the x-direction, and the other a displacement in the y-direction. Thus, r_1 is associated with the displacement in the x-direction and r_2 with the displacement in the y-direction. Click *OK* to close the boundary condition window. Notice that the color of the line segment remains red.

Since the remaining boundary segments are either stress-free or have a known stress applied to it (segment #3), they are all of the Neumann type. Thus, for segment #2 and all of the other stress-free boundary segments we employ the following procedure. Again, we double-click on the segment and for *Condition type*, we select *Neumann* and leave all the values at their default values, which are zeros. Click *OK* to close the boundary condition window. Notice that the line segment is now blue. This procedure is repeated for the remaining line segments, except segment #3. For segment #3 we again select Neumann. However, for the value of $g1$ we enter the value 100, which stands for 100 (N/cm^2). The remaining default values are left as they are.

Specify the physical constants. To specify the physical constants for the plate, we go to *PDE* and select *PDE Specification*. For the value of E we enter 200e5 and accept the default values of $nu = 0.3$ (Poisson's ratio) and $rho = 1$ (mass density). Since this is a static problem, density is not used. Then click *OK*.

Generate the mesh. To have the system generate the mesh we select *Initialize Mesh* from the *Mesh* menu. This results in Figure 8.36. If the mesh appears to be too coarse, then we return to the *Mesh* menu and select *Refine Mesh*. This results in Figure 8.37. Each time *Refine Mesh* is selected, the size of the mesh triangles becomes smaller.

Obtain the solution. To obtain the solution, either select *Solve PDE* from the *Solve* menu or click on the "=" icon.

Display results. To display the various results in a form that best illustrates them, one goes to the *Plot* menu and selects *Parameters*. The selections are reasonably self-explanatory. The distribution of σ_{xx} is shown in Figure 8.38. This was created by selecting *Color* and *Contour* under *Plot type* and by selecting x *stress* in the first selection box under *Property*.

Figures 8.34 to 8.37 were saved as encapsulated postscript level 2 files with a "tiff" image that was used to view the figures in an MS Word document. This was done in the following manner. In the *File* menu, *Print* was selected. In the *Device option* data area, we entered

```
-deps2 -tiff
```

and pressed Enter. In the *Send to* area, we selected *File* and then clicked on *Save*. This opens a typical *Save As* window and the directories and file name are selected in the usual

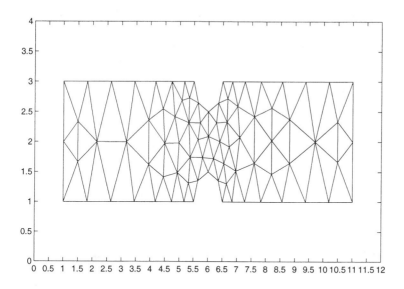

FIGURE 8.36
Result from *Initialize Mesh*.

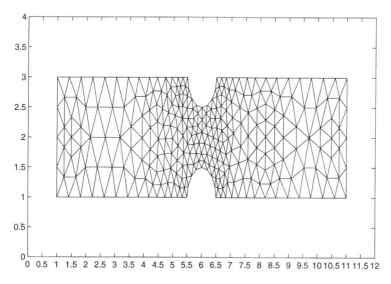

FIGURE 8.37
Result from *Refine Mesh* used one time.

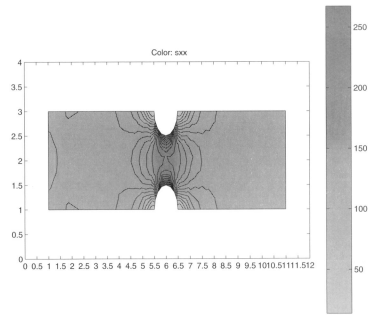

FIGURE 8.38
Stress contours and color bar for σ_{xx}.

manner. The file name should end with the suffix ".eps." For other options see the help file for `print`.

To transfer the figure to the Windows clipboard, we use, instead

```
-dmeta
```

and then select *Printer*.

Export arrays of numerical values generated by the GUI to the MATLAB command window. To determine the stress concentration factor, we need the value of the maximum stress σ_{xx}. Therefore, we must first transfer (export) the appropriate results to the MATLAB command window. In this window we use

StressX = `pdesmech(p,t,c,u,'tensor','sxx');`

to obtain an array of values for σ_{xx}, and then use `max` to find the maximum value. Here p gives the coordinates of the points in the mesh, e describes the edges of the mesh triangles, t describes the triangles, and u is the solution. See the help file for `initmesh`. All of these quantities are exported from the GUI in the following manner. It is recalled that to use the results in the MATLAB command window they must have a variable name. One can use the names provided by MATLAB, which are the names appearing in the argument list in the function statement above, or one can change them if they conflict with previously defined global variables. If they are changed, then they must also be changed in the argument list of pdesmech.

The parameters p and t are exported to the MATLAB command window by going to the *Mesh* menu and selecting *Export Mesh*. When the window appears with the variable names click *OK*. If one were to now go to the MATLAB command window and type p (and Enter), an array of values would appear. (This is not recommended, however, since these arrays can be quite large.) If one or more of the variable names were to be changed, they would be renamed at this time and then *OK* would be clicked.

The parameter c is exported to the MATLAB command window by going to the *PDE* menu and selecting *Export PDE Coefficients*. Lastly, to export the solution array u, we go to the *Solve* menu and select *Export Solution*.

Now that the necessary variables have been exported to the MATLAB command window, we employ the following two expressions to determine the maximum stress in the *x*-direction.

StressX = pdesmech(p,t,c,u,'tensor','sxx');
MaxSxx = max(StressX)

which gives *MaxSxx* = 301.4699 (N/cm^2).

To estimate the stress concentration factor, we compare σ_{xx} in an unnotched plate of cross-sectional area $0.2d$ to the maximum stress determined above. The stress in the unnotched plate σ_{xu} is approximately equal to

$$\sigma_{xu} = \frac{(100)(0.2)D}{0.2d} = 200 \quad \text{N/cm}^2$$

since $D/d = 2$. Then the stress concentration factor S_{cc} is approximately

$$S_{cc} = \frac{301.4699}{200} \cong 1.50$$

This value compares favorably[15] with 1.37, which was obtained experimentally, and with 1.45, which was obtained from Nueber's nomograph.

A note of caution: prior to using the pdetool to solve another problem, one should use clear to remove the variables p, t, c, and a. However, if new names will be assigned to these variables, then clear does not have to be used.

EXERCISES

8.1 Referring to Figure 8.39 express the forces F_1, F_2, and F_3, and their resultant as vectors. Determine the magnitude of the resultant and the angles of its direction cosines in degrees. [Answer: $\mathbf{F}_1$ = [56.5685 −42.4264 −70.7107]; $\mathbf{F}_2$ = [−26.9489 −33.6861 −67.3722]; $\mathbf{F}_3$ = [28.6401 66.8268 −95.4669]; $\mathbf{R} = \mathbf{F}_1 + \mathbf{F}_2 + \mathbf{F}_3$ = [58.2597 −9.2857 −233.5497], $|\mathbf{R}|$ = 240.8856; α_R = [76.0039 92.2092 165.8235].]

---

[15] A. P. Boresi, R. J. Schmidt, and O. M. Sidebottom, *Advanced Mechanics of Materials*, 5th ed., John Wiley & Sons, New York, 1993, pp. 582–584.

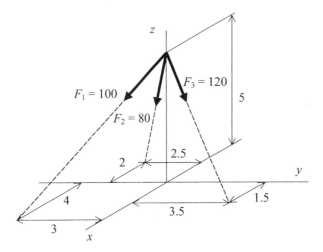

FIGURE 8.39
Orientation of forces for Exercise 8.1.

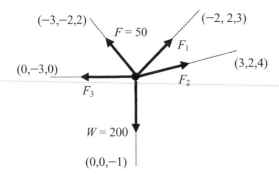

FIGURE 8.40
Orientation of forces for Exercise 8.2.

8.2 The system of ropes in Figure 8.40 are attached at the coordinate locations indicated. What are the magnitudes of $\mathbf{F}_1$, $\mathbf{F}_2$, and $\mathbf{F}_3$ and their respective components. [Answer: $\mathbf{F}_1 = [-44.9080\ 44.9080\ 67.3620]$; $|\mathbf{F}_1| = 92.5802$; $\mathbf{F}_2 = [81.2883\ 54.1922\ 108.3844]$; $|\mathbf{F}_2| = 145.9170$; $\mathbf{F}_3 = [0\ -74.8467\ 0]$; $|\mathbf{F}_3| = 74.8467$.]

8.3 Referring to the oscillating flat-faced follower shown Figure 8.41, we have the following relationships[16] for the (x,y) coordinates R_x and R_y of the cam's profile and the cutter's coordinates C_x and C_y:

---

[16] A. G. Erdman, and G. N. Sandor, *ibid.*, pp. 387–389.

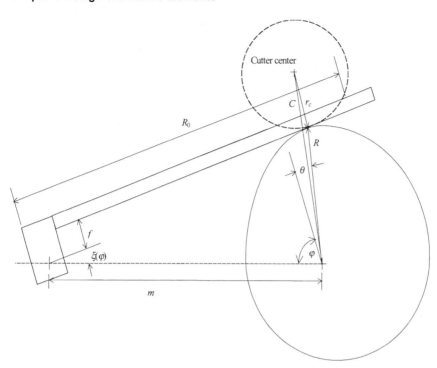

FIGURE 8.41
Oscillating flat-faced follower.

$$R_x = R\cos(\theta + \varphi + \xi_0) \qquad\qquad R_y = R\sin(\theta + \varphi + \xi_0)$$
$$C_x = C\cos(\theta + \varphi + \xi_0 - \gamma_0) \qquad C_y = C\sin(\theta + \varphi + \xi_0 - \gamma_0)$$

where

$$R = \frac{f + m\sin(\xi)}{\cos(\theta)} \qquad \theta = \tan^{-1}\left[\left(\frac{d\xi/d\varphi}{1 - d\xi/d\varphi}\right)\frac{m\cos(\xi)}{f + m\sin(\xi)}\right]$$

$$C = \sqrt{c_x^2 + c_y^2} \qquad c_x = r_c\sin(\theta) \qquad c_y = R + r_c\cos(\theta)$$

$$\gamma_0 = \tan^{-1}\left(\frac{c_y}{c_x}\right) \qquad \xi_0 = \sin^{-1}\left(\frac{r_b - f}{m}\right) \qquad \xi = \xi(\varphi) = \xi_0 + s(\varphi)/R_0$$

For cycloidal motion of the point R_0, $s(\varphi)$ is given in Section 8.5.1. Obtain a graph similar to those shown in Figures 8.29 and 8.31 when $\beta = 60°$, $r_b = 3.25$, $h = 0.5$, $r_c = 0.5$, $f = 0.5$, $m = 5$, and $R_0 = 9$.

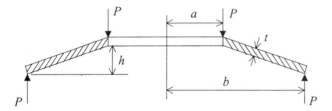

FIGURE 8.42
Cross section of a Belleville conical spring.

8.4 Consider the Belleville conical spring shown in Figure 8.42. The nondimensional load P', nondimensional spring rate (spring constant) k' and nondimensional maximum compressive stress σ' as a function of the spring deflection δ are given by,[17] respectively,

$$P' = \frac{P}{P_0} = C_1 C_2 \qquad\qquad P_0 = \frac{Et^4}{(1-v^2)b^2}$$

$$k' = \frac{k}{k_0} = C_2\left[1 + 1.5d_t^2 - 3d_t h_t + h_t^2\right] \qquad k_0 = \frac{P_0}{t}$$

$$\sigma'_{max} = \frac{\sigma_{max}}{\sigma_0} = -d_t\left[C_3\left(h_t - 0.5d_t\right) + C_4\right] \qquad \sigma_0 = \frac{P_0}{t^2}$$

where

$$C_1 = 0.5d_t^3 - 1.5h_t d_t^2 + (1 + h_t^2)d_t$$

$$C_2 = \pi\left(\frac{\alpha+1}{\alpha-1} - \frac{2}{\ln(\alpha)}\right)\left(\frac{\alpha}{\alpha-1}\right)^2$$

$$C_3 = \frac{\alpha^2}{(\alpha-1)^2}\left(\frac{\alpha-1}{\ln(\alpha)} - 1\right)$$

$$C_4 = \frac{\alpha^2}{2(\alpha-1)}$$

and v is Poisson's ratio, E is Young's modulus, $\alpha = b/a$, $h_t = h/t$, $d_t = \delta/t$. The maximum compressive stress occurs at the inner boundary a on the upper surface of the cone and is usually stipulated as $\sigma_{max} = \sigma_p/F_s$, where σ_p is the maximum permissible stress and F_s is the factor of safety.

Find the values of α and h_t and the corresponding value of k' when $d_t = 0.6667h_t$, $P' = 2.0$ and $\sigma'_{max} = -4.5$. [Answer: $\alpha = 2.2693$, $h_t = 1.4846$ and $k' = 0.3598$.]

8.5 Referring to Example 8.20 and Figure 8.22, determine the values of θ_2 that make θ_4 a maximum and minimum value. [Hint: To find the two values of θ_2, one for which θ_4 is a minimum and one for which θ_4 is a maximum, use two search ranges: $\pi/2$ to π and $3\pi/2$ to 2π. In the second search range the sign of θ_4 must be changed.] [Answer: $\theta_2 = 153.4345°$ and $\theta_4 = 195.5639°$; $\theta_2 = 319.8489°$ and $\theta_4 = 244.5329°$.]

---

[17] A. H. Burr and J. B. Cheatham, *Mechanical Analysis and Design*, 2nd ed., Prentice Hall, Upper Saddle River, NJ, 1995, pp. 652–656.

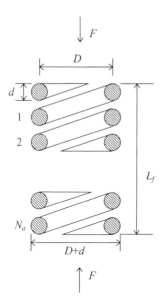

FIGURE 8.43
Nomenclature for a helical spring.

8.6 Referring to Figure 8.43, the sizing of helical compression springs that are subjected to cyclic loading is governed by the following equations. The first is the factor of safety F_s due to stresses in the spring coils

$$F_s = \frac{S_{eL}(S_u - \sigma_L)}{S_{eL}(\sigma_m - \sigma_L) + S_u \sigma_a} > 1$$

where

$$\sigma_L = K_s F_{min} K_1 \qquad K_1 = \frac{8C}{\pi d^2} \qquad C = \frac{D}{d}$$

$$\sigma_m = K_s F_m K_1 \qquad F_m = 0.5(F_{max} + F_{min})$$

$$\sigma_a = K_w F_a K_1 \qquad F_a = 0.5(F_{max} - F_{min})$$

$$K_s = 1 + \frac{1}{2C} \qquad K_w = \frac{4C-1}{4C-4} + \frac{0.615}{C}$$

$$S_u = 0.67 A d^b \qquad S_e = \frac{0.707 S_{eL} S_u}{S_u - 0.707 S_{eL}}$$

and F_{max} is the maximum load and F_{min} is the minimum load that is applied to the spring, S_{eL} is the endurance limit for infinite life, S_e is the endurance limit for fully reversed loading, S_u is the ultimate shear strength, D is the mean diameter of the spring, and d is the diameter of the wire. The constants A and b for cold drawn wire are $A = 141,040$ psi and $b = -0.1822$. For peened spring-steel wire, where $d < 0.4$ inches, $S_{eL} = 67,500$ psi.

The second equation determines the spring rate (constant) k, which is given by

$$k = \frac{dG}{8N_a C^3}$$

where G is the shear modulus of the material and N_a is the number of active coils of the spring. For steel $G = 11.5 \times 10^6$ psi.

The last equation ensures that the unloaded spring length L_f, the coil diameter d and the maximum applied load F_{max} are such that the steel spring doesn't buckle. Then, for both ends hinged,

$$\frac{F_{max}}{kL_f} = 0.8125\left[1 - \sqrt{1 - 6.865(Cd/L_f)^2}\right]$$

where $Cd = D$ and

$$L_f = d(N_a + 2) + 1.15 F_{max}/k - 0.15 F_{min}/k$$

which provides for 15% clash allowance.

For the peened spring-steel with $N_a = 7$, $F_{max} = 200$ lb., $F_{min} = 40$ lb., $F_s = 1.4$ and $k = 125$ lb/inch, determine D and d. Will the spring buckle? [Answer: $d = 0.251$ inches, $D = 1.8682$ inches and $C = 7.4432$. The spring will not buckle.]

8.7 Using the results of Example 8.21 draw the three positions of the links and indicate the path of point P_1 as shown in Figure 8.26. The path of P_1 is determined using fsolve to obtain ψ and γ for 16 equally spaced values of ϕ ($\theta \le \phi \le \theta + \phi_2$) from the following equation:

$$\mathbf{Z}_2\left(e^{j\phi} - 1\right) - \mathbf{Z}_4\left(e^{j\psi} - 1\right) + \left(\mathbf{Z}_5 - \mathbf{Z}_6\right)\left(e^{j\gamma} - 1\right) = 0$$

The two required equations for fsolve are obtained by setting the real and imaginary parts of the above equation to zero. Do this numerically—that is, do not solve algebraically.

8.8 The torque required by a power-driven screw to raise a load W is

$$T_{raise} = \frac{Wd_p}{2}\left[\frac{\mu + \tan(\lambda)\cos(\alpha)}{\cos(\alpha) - \mu\tan(\lambda)} + \mu_c \frac{d_c}{d_p}\right]$$

where λ is the lead angle obtained from

$$\tan(\lambda) = \frac{L}{\pi d_p}$$

and μ is the coefficient of friction of the threads, μ_c is the coefficient of friction of the collar (nut), d_p is the pitch diameter of the thread, d_c is the mean diameter of the collar, $L = mp$ is the lead, $p = 1/N_t$ is the pitch, N_t is the number of threads per inch, and m is the number of start threads. The angle α is the thread angle, which is 14.5° for an Acme thread. Also for Acme threads $1.9° < \lambda < 6°$. The efficiency e of the thread and collar is

$$e = \frac{WL}{2\pi T_{raise}} = \tan(\lambda)\left[\frac{\mu + \tan(\lambda)\cos(\alpha)}{\cos(\alpha) - \mu\tan(\lambda)} + \mu_c \frac{d_c}{d_p}\right]^{-1}$$

When $\mu_c = 0$ (recall Exercise 6.3),

$$e = \frac{\cos(\alpha) - \mu \tan(\lambda)}{\cos(\alpha) + \mu \cot(\lambda)}$$

The horsepower required to raise the load at a rate of v_r feet per minute is

$$hp = \frac{v_r T_{raise}}{2626 d_p}$$

where T_{raise} is in in-lb.

For a single-start ($m = 1$) Acme thread whose pitch diameter is 1.0 inch and lead is 4°, find the torque and horsepower required to raise 800 lb. at a rate of 15 feet per minute when the mean diameter of the collar is 1.25 inches. The coefficient of friction for the thread is 0.13 and that for the collar 0.04. What is the efficiency of the system. [Answer: T_{raise} = 99.8583 in-lb, e = 25.501%, and hp = 0.5704.]

8.9 The power limitation based on the fatigue strength of the link plates in a link chain is

$$hp = K_s N_1^{1.08} n_1^{0.9} p^{3-0.07/p}$$

where N_1 is the number of teeth in the smaller sprocket, n_1 is the rotational speed in rpm of the smaller sprocket, p is the pitch, which the distance between the pin centers of the links, and $K_s = 0.004$ for regular weight chains. Find the pitch when $N_1 = 21$ teeth, $n_1 = 1750$ rpm, and $hp = 10$. [Answer: $p = 0.47881$.]

8.10 The contact stress on a gear tooth subjected to a uniform (non-varying) tangentially transmitted load F_t is given by[18]

$$\sigma_c = Z_E \sqrt{\frac{K_v K_H F_t}{d_w b Z_I}} \quad \text{N/mm}^2$$

where Z_I is the geometry factor for pitting resistance, $d_w = 2R_{p_1}$ is the operating pitch diameter of the pinion (gear 1) and R_{p_1} is defined in Table 8.4, and Z_E is the elastic coefficient. The remaining quantities are defined in Section 8.3.

The elastic coefficient is given by

$$\frac{1}{Z_E} = \sqrt{\pi \left[\frac{1 - v_1^2}{E_1} + \frac{1 - v_2^2}{E_2} \right]}$$

where v_1 and v_2 are the Poisson's ratio for the pinion and gear, respectively, and E_1 and E_2 are the Young's modulus of the pinion and gear, respectively. When both the pinion and the gear are steel $Z_E = 190$ (N/mm²)$^{1/2}$.

The geometry factor for pitting resistance is given by

$$Z_I = \frac{\rho_1 \rho_2 \cot(\varphi)}{C d_p}$$

$$\rho_1 = \sqrt{R_{T_1}^2 - R_{b_1}^2} - m\pi \cos(\varphi_s)$$

$$\rho_2 = \left(R_{b_1} + R_{b_2} \right) \tan(\varphi) - \rho_1$$

---

[18] J. R. Colbourne, *ibid.*, 1987.

where $d_p = N_1 m$ is the diameter of the pinion pitch circle and the remaining quantities are defined in Tables 8.4 and 8.5.

Once the contact stress σ_c has been computed, the permissible stress σ_H must be determined and verified that it is greater than that caused by F_r—that is, $\sigma_c \leq \sigma_H$, where the permissible contact stress is

$$\sigma_H = \frac{\sigma_{HP} Z_N Z_w}{F_{Sc} Y_Z}$$

for oil or gear temperatures less than 120 °C. The quantity F_{Sc} is the factor of safety for pitting, Y_Z is the reliability factor defined in Section 8.3, Z_N is the pitting resistance stress cycle factor, σ_{HP} is the allowable contact stress number for pitting, and Z_w is the hardness ratio factor for pitting resistance.

The allowable contact stress number for pitting of through-hardened steel gears is estimated from

$$\sigma_{HP} = 2.41 B_H + 237$$

for Grade 2 steel and from

$$\sigma_{HP} = 2.22 B_H + 200$$

for Grade 1 steel for Brinell hardness in the range $180 \leq B_H \leq 400$.

The pitting resistance stress cycle factor is given by

$$Z_N = 1.4723 \qquad n_L < 10^4$$
$$Z_N = 2.466 n_L^{-0.056} \qquad n_L \geq 10^4$$

where n_L is the number of unidirectional tooth load cycles.

The hardness ratio factor for pitting resistance for surfaced hardened pinions driving through-hardened gears is estimated from

$$Z_w = 1 + 0.00075 e^{-0.448 R_z} \left(450 - B_{H_2}\right) \qquad R_z \leq 1.6$$
$$Z_w = 1 \qquad R_z > 1.6$$

where R_z is the surface finish of the pinion in μm and B_{H_2} is the Brinell hardness of the gear in the range $180 \leq B_{H_2} \leq 400$.

Consider the following pair of steel gears:

$m = 10$ mm	$b = 45$ mm	$n = 1800$ rpm	$B_{H_2} = 260$
$N_1 = 28$	$\varphi_s = 20°$	$T = 2500$ Nm	
$N_2 = 75$	$C = 525$ mm	$R_{T_1} = 153.9$ mm	

Determine the contact stress and the permissible contact stress when

The factor of safety is 1.2.

The number of unidirectional loading cycles is 4×10^8.

A grade 2 steel is used.

The surface finish of the pinion is 1.1 μm.

Less than 1 failure in 100 is desired.

$Q_v = 8$.

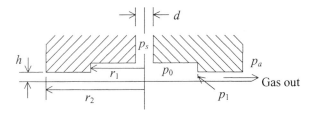

FIGURE 8.44
Air bearing geometry.

The gear will be a type 2 gear as defined in Table 8.3.

[Answer: $\sigma_c = 857.2436$ N/mm^2 and $\sigma_H = 636.2982$ N/mm^2.]

8.11 Using the techniques of Section 8.2.1, plot the nondimensional deflection, slope, moment, and shear over the length of the beam, and give the maximum values and their locations for the following combinations of boundary conditions and loading.

(a) Clamped at $\eta = 0$ and $\eta = 1$. Loading: Uniform across the length of the beam. [The analytical solution[19] to this set of conditions yields $y_{max}(\eta = 0.5) = -1/384$; $\theta_{max}(\eta = 0.2113$ or $0.7887) = -0.0080$; $M_{max}(\eta = 0$ or $1) = -1/12$; and $V_{max}(\eta = 0$ or $1) = 0.500$.]

(b) Simply supported at $\eta = 0$ and clamped at $\eta = 1$. Loading: Uniform across the length of the beam. [The analytical solution[20] to this set of conditions yields $y_{max}(\eta = 0.4215) = -1/185$; $\theta_{max}(\eta = 0) = -1/48$; $M_{max}(\eta = 1) = -1/8$; and $V_{max}(\eta = 1) = 5/8$.]

(c) Clamped at $\eta = 0$ and $\eta = 1$. Loading: Triangular, 0 at $\eta = 0$ and 1 at $\eta = 1$. [The analytical solution[21] to this set of conditions yields $y_{max}(\eta = 0.525) = -1/764$; $\theta_{max}(\eta = 0.8077) = 0.00427$; $M_{max}(\eta = 1) = -1/20$; and $V_{max}(\eta = 1) = -7/20$.]

8.12 Consider an externally pressurized central recess thrust air bearing shown in Figure 8.44. Using the definitions given in Table 8.7, the normalized mass flow through the bearing for a given P_s is[22]

$$m' = P_s \sqrt{\left(\frac{P_1}{P_s}\right)^{2/k} - \left(\frac{P_1}{P_s}\right)^{(k+1)/k}}$$

where $m' = m/m_o$, $P_1 = p_1/p_a$, $P_s = p_s/p_a$, and P_1 is the solution to

$$P_1 = \sqrt{1 + BP_s^{(k-1)/2k} P_1^{1/k} \sqrt{P_s^{(k-1)/k} - P_1^{(k-1)/k}}}$$

when $P_1/P_s = p_1/p_s > P_c = [2/(k+1)]^{k/(k-1)}$ and P_1 is the solution to

$$P_1 = \sqrt{1 + BP_s P_c^{1/k} \sqrt{1 - P_c^{(k-1)/k}}}$$

[19] W. Beitz, and K. H. Kuttner, *ibid.*, p. B24.
[20] W. Beitz, and K. H. Kuttner, *ibid.*, p. B23.
[21] W. Beitz, and K. H. Kuttner, *ibid.*, p. B24.
[22] W. A. Gross, *Gas Film Lubrication*, John Wiley & Sons, New York, 1962, Chapter 5.

TABLE 8.7
Definition of Quantities in Gas Bearing Formulas

Quantity	Definition
C_D	Discharge coefficient
$A_o = \pi d^2/4$	Restrictor area
p_s	Supply pressure
p_o	Recess pressure
p_1	Inlet pressure
p_a	Ambient pressure
h	Gas film thickness
μ	Viscosity of gas
k	Ratio of specific heats ($= 1.4$ for air)
R	Gas constant (universal gas constant divided by molecular weight)
θ	Temperature (absolute scale)
$B = \dfrac{12 C_D \mu A_o}{h^3 p_a \pi} \ln\left(\dfrac{r_2}{r_1}\right) \sqrt{\dfrac{(k-1)R\theta}{2k}}$	Bearing parameter
$m_o = \dfrac{1}{C_D A_o p_a} \sqrt{\dfrac{(k-1)R\theta}{2k}}$	Mass flow parameter
m	Mass flow
W	Bearing load

when $P_1/P_s \le P_c$, which is the region wherein the flow is choked (the Mach number is equal to 1). The normalized load that the bearing can support is

$$W' = \frac{\sqrt{\pi}}{2} \frac{r_1^2}{r_2^2} A_2 \exp\left(P_1^2/A_2^2\right)\left[\mathrm{erf}\left(\frac{P_1}{A_2}\right) - \mathrm{erf}\left(\frac{1}{A_2}\right)\right]$$

where $W' = W/(\pi r_2^2 p_a)$, erf is the error function and

$$A_2 = \sqrt{\frac{1 - P_1^2}{2\ln(r_1/r_2)}}$$

(a) Determine the values of P_1 when $B = 2$ and (i) $P_s = 2$ and (ii) $P_s = 10$. In using `fzero`, set the search range to $[0.1\ P_s]$. [Answer: (i) $P_1 = 1.4016$; (ii) $P_1 = 2.4852$.]

(b) Determine the values of m' and W' when $r_1/r_2 = 0.1$, $B = 2$ and (i) $P_s = 2$ and (ii) $P_s = 10$. [Answer: (i) $m' = 0.4822$, $W' = 0.0954$; and (ii) $m' = 2.5880$, $W' = 0.4147$.]

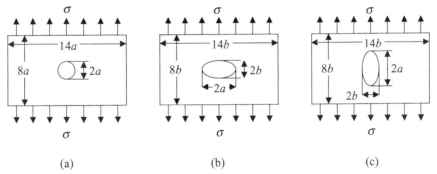

(a)   (b)   (c)

FIGURE 8.45
(a) Plate with circular hole; (b) plate with elliptical hole and load perpendicular to major axis; (c) plate with elliptical hole and load perpendicular to minor axis.

8.13 Using the procedure outlined in Section 8.7 determine estimates for the maximum stress for the cases of circular and elliptical holes in a plate. The three cases are shown in Figure 8.45. The boundaries of the holes are stress-free. For these three cases, let $\sigma = 1$ in the positive y-direction and $\sigma = -1$ in the negative y-direction. Also, let the Young's modulus equal 200×10^3. Use *Refine Mesh* once. For case (a), let $a = 1$ (unit); for cases (b) and (c), let $b = 1$ (unit) and $a = 2$.

[Answers:

Case (a): For the case of the circular hole, the analytically obtained[23] maximum stress ratio is $\sigma_{yy}/\sigma = 3$; the PDE solution gives 2.9122, or 2.9 % lower.

Case (b): For an elliptical hole with the load perpendicular to the major axis, the analytical solution[24] is $\sigma_{yy}/\sigma = 1 + 2a/b$, which for our case gives $\sigma_{yy}/\sigma = 5$. The PDE solution gives $\sigma_{yy}/\sigma = 4.2264$, or 15.5 % lower.

Case (c): For an elliptical hole with the load perpendicular to the minor axis, the analytical solution[25] is $\sigma_{yy}/\sigma = 1 + 2b/a$, which for our case gives $\sigma_{yy}/\sigma = 2$. The PDE solution gives $\sigma_{yy}/\sigma = 2.3552$, or 17.8 % higher.]

BIBLIOGRAPHY

"Fundamental Rating Factors and Calculation Methods for Involute Spur and Helical Gear Teeth," AGMA Standard ANSI/AGMA 2002-C95, American Gear Manufacturers Association, 1500 King Street, Alexandria VA, 22314.

W. Beitz and K. H. Kuttner, Eds., *Handbook of Mechanical Engineering*, Springer-Verlag, New York, 1994.

S. R. Bhonsle and L. J. Weinmann, *Mathematical Modeling for the Design of Machine Components*, Prentice Hall, Upper Saddle River, NJ, 1999.

---

[23] Boresi, et al., *ibid.*, pp. 566–567, 569.
[24] Boresi, et al., *ibid.*, pp. 568–569.
[25] Boresi, et al., *ibid.*, p. 570.

A. H. Burr and J. B. Cheatham, *Mechanical Analysis and Design*, 2nd ed., Prentice Hall, Upper Saddle River, NJ, 1995.

J. R. Colbourne, *The Geometry of Involute Gears*, Springer-Verlag, New York, 1987.

A. D. Dimarogonas, *Computer Aided Machine Design*, Prentice Hall, Upper Saddle River, NJ, 1989.

A. G. Erdman and G. N. Sandor, *Mechanical Design: Analysis and Synthesis*, 2nd ed., Prentice Hall, Upper Saddle River, NJ, 1991.

R. C. Hibbeler, *Engineering Mechanics, Statics*, 8th ed., Prentice Hall, Upper Saddle River, NJ, 1998.

P. J. Jensen, *Cam Design and Manufacture*, 2nd ed., Marcel Dekker, Inc., New York, 1987.

R. L. Norton, *Design of Machinery*, McGraw-Hill, Inc., New York, 1992.

R. L. Norton, *Machine Design, An Integrated Approach*, Prentice Hall, Upper Saddle River, NJ, 1996.

H. A. Rothbart, *Cams: Design, Dynamics and Accuracy*, John Wiley & Sons, New York, 1956.

J. E. Shigley and C. R. Mischke, *Mechanical Engineering Design*, 5th ed., McGraw-Hill, New York, 1989.

A. H. Slocum, *Precision Machine Design*, Prentice Hall, Upper Saddle River, NJ, 1992.

M. F. Spotts and T. E. Shoup, *Design of Machine Elements*, Prentice Hall, Upper Saddle River, NJ, 1998.

C. E. Wilson, *Computer Integrated Machine Design*, Prentice Hall, Upper Saddle River, NJ, 1997.

B C H A P T E R   9

DYNAMICS AND VIBRATIONS

Balakumar Balachandran

Various methods are presented to analyze the dynamics of rigid bodies, the free and forced oscillations of linear and nonlinear systems with one and more degrees of freedom, and the vibrations of thin beams.

9.1 ORBITAL MOTIONS

Consider a system of two bodies in a gravitational field, shown in Figure 9.1, where the mass m_2 is fixed and the mass m_1 orbits m_2 in a plane. The coordinates describing the orbiting mass are the radial distance variable r and the angular variable θ.

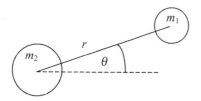

FIGURE 9.1
A two-body system.

For a satellite orbiting about the earth, m_2 is the mass of the earth, m_1 is the mass of the satellite, and r is the radial distance between their centers. The governing equations of motion are given by[1,2]

$$\frac{d^2r}{d\tau^2} - r\left(\frac{d\theta}{d\tau}\right)^2 = -\frac{4\pi^2}{r^2}$$

$$r\frac{d^2\theta}{d\tau^2} + 2\frac{dr}{d\tau}\frac{d\theta}{d\tau} = 0$$

(9.1)

In Eqs. (9.1), t is time, P_c is the period of a circular orbit at the earth's surface, and $\tau = t/P_c$. At the surface of m_2, r can be approximated by the radius of the earth; that is $r = 6.373 \times 10^6$ m.

Although a closed-form solution of the nonlinear system given by Eqs. (9.1) is available,[3] numerical solutions will be sought for a given set of initial conditions:

$$r(0), \quad dr(0)/d\tau, \quad \theta(0), \quad d\theta(0)/d\tau$$

For compactness, this set of initial conditions will be written sometimes as

$$(r(0), dr(0)/d\tau, \theta(0), d\theta(0)/d\tau)$$

Equations (9.1), which provide an example of a differential dynamical system, describe the evolution of states r and θ with respect to τ. In general, a differential dynamical system is a set of differential equations that describes the evolution of the considered states with respect to an independent variable, such as time. When a dynamical system consists of ordinary-differential equations, such as that given by Eqs. (9.1), a solution of these equations for a given set of initial conditions can be determined through numerical integration with respect to the independent variable. To this end, we use ode45, which first requires that Eqs. (9.1) be rewritten as a set of first-order equations.

Introducing the new variables or states,

$$x_1 = r, \qquad\qquad x_3 = \theta,$$

[1] D. T. Greenwood, *Principles of Dynamics*, 2nd ed., Prentice Hall, Englewood Cliffs, NJ, 1988, Chapter 5.
[2] F. C. Moon, *Applied Dynamics with Applications to Multibody and Mechatronic Systems*, John Wiley & Sons, New York, 1998, Chapter 7.
[3] D. T. Greenwood, *ibid*.

TABLE 9.1
Three Sets of Initial Conditions

Set	$x_1(0)$	$x_2(0)$	$x_3(0)$	$x_4(0)$	Orbit type
1	2.0	0.0	0.0	1.5	Elliptical
2	1.0	0.0	0.0	2π	Circular
3	2.0	0.0	0.0	4.0	Hyperbolic

$$x_2 = \frac{dr}{d\tau}, \qquad x_4 = \frac{d\theta}{d\tau}$$

we rewrite Eqs. (9.1) as the following set of four first-order differential equations.

$$\frac{dx_1}{d\tau} = x_2$$

$$\frac{dx_2}{d\tau} = x_1 x_4^2 - \frac{4\pi^2}{x_1^2}$$

$$\frac{dx_3}{d\tau} = x_4$$

$$\frac{dx_3}{d\tau} = -\frac{2x_2 x_4}{x_1}$$

(9.2)

We express Eqs. (9.2) with the function called *orbit*.

```
function xdot = orbit(t,x)
xdot = [x(2); x(1)*x(4)^2–4.0*pi^2/x(1)^2; x(4); –2.0*x(2)*x(4)/x(1)];
```

This function will now be used by `ode45` to determine the orbits of mass m_1 for the three sets of initial conditions shown in Table 9.1. Although the type of orbit realized in each case is not known *a priori*, the orbit type that was determined after analyzing the numerical results is also shown in the table. The orbits are determined and then plotted with the following script.

```
initcond = [2.0 0.0 0.0 1.5; 1.0 0.0 0.0 2.0*pi; 2.0 0.0 0.0 4.0];
tspan = linspace(0,5,1000);
options = odeset('RelTol',1e–6,'AbsTol',[1e–6 1e–6 1e–6 1e–6]);
lintype = ['- ' '-.' '-.'];
for i = 1:3
   [t,x] = ode45('orbit',tspan,[initcond(i,:)]',options);
   polar(x(:,3),x(:,1),lintype(2*(i–1)+1:2*i));
   hold on
end
```

text(0.50,−1.20,'Elliptical orbit');
text(−1.20,1.00,'Circular orbit');
text(1.75,2.00,'Hyperbolic orbit');

The three sets of initial conditions are provided in the array labeled *initcond*. A conservative spacing of 1,000 equally spaced locations is used in the specified time interval to minimize numerical errors that may lead to spurious solutions. In addition, odeset is used to set the relative tolerance to 10^{-6} and the absolute tolerance for each of the four states—namely, x_j, $j = 1,2...4$.

Execution of the script results in Figure 9.2. The first set of initial conditions leads to an elliptical orbit, the second set of initial conditions leads to a circular orbit, and the third set of initial conditions leads to a hyperbolic orbit. This orbit, which is an open orbit, is associated with unbounded motion.[4] Open orbits represent escape trajectories from earth and are not considered for satellite motions.

When systems, such as those given by Eqs. (9.1), are numerically integrated, one has to be aware that spurious solutions may be obtained during the integration. Usually, in problems such as the present one, there is a constant of motion (here, the angular momentum per unit mass $r^2 d\theta/d\tau$) that does not change with time. If a spurious solution were obtained, this constant would vary with time. For other systems without damping one can determine whether or not the sum of the kinetic energy and potential energy remains constant during the numerical integration. It is good practice, therefore, to determine whether a different result is obtained when the step size and/or the tolerances are changed (see Exercise 9.1).

9.2 SINGLE-DEGREE-OF-FREEDOM SYSTEMS

9.2.1 Introduction

Consider a spring-mass-damper system with a mass m, a spring with linear spring constant k and nonlinear spring coefficient α, and a damper with damping coefficient c. The mass is subjected to an excitation $F(t) = X_o k f(t)$. This system, which is illustrated in Figure 9.3, is a prototypical model used to study mechanical systems ranging from washing machines to vehicles.[5]

If x describes the displacement of the system, then the governing equation of motion is of the form

$$\frac{d^2x}{d\tau^2} + 2\zeta \frac{dx}{d\tau} + x + \hat{\alpha}x^3 = X_o f(\tau) \qquad (9.3)$$

where $\tau = \omega_n t$ is the nondimensional time and the damping factor ζ is given by

---

[4] D. T. Greenwood, *ibid*, p. 211.
[5] D. J. Inman, *Engineering Vibration*, Prentice Hall, Englewood Cliffs, NJ, 1994; S. S. Rao, *Mechanical Vibrations*, 3rd ed., Addison-Wesley, Reading, MA, 1995; B. H. Tongue, *Principles of Vibration*, Oxford University Press, New York, 1996.

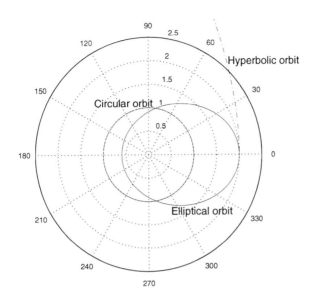

FIGURE 9.2
Orbits from Eq. (9.1) for three sets of initial conditions given in Table 9.1.

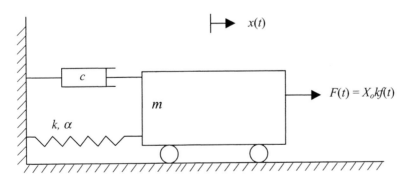

FIGURE 9.3.
Spring-mass-damper system.

$$\zeta = \frac{c}{2m\omega_n} \qquad (9.4)$$

In Eq. (9.4), the natural frequency ω_n is given by

$$\omega_n = \sqrt{k/m} \tag{9.5}$$

and the coefficient of the nonlinearity $\hat{\alpha}$ is given by

$$\hat{\alpha} = \frac{\alpha}{m\omega_n^2} \tag{9.6}$$

The nonlinear system given by Eq. (9.3) is said to have a softening spring when $\hat{\alpha}$ has a negative value and a hardening spring when $\hat{\alpha}$ has a positive value.[6]

Equation (9.3) is put into state-space form by introducing the new variables, or states:

$$x_1 = x$$

$$x_2 = \frac{dx}{d\tau}$$

Then Eq. (9.3) becomes

$$\frac{dx_1}{d\tau} = x_2$$

$$\frac{dx_2}{d\tau} = -2\zeta x_2 - x_1 - \hat{\alpha}x_1^3 + X_o f(\tau) \tag{9.7}$$

Before considering several solutions to Eq. (9.7), we create a function *FreeOscillation* in a form that can be used by `ode45`. Thus,

```
function xdot = FreeOscillation(t,x,dummy,zeta,AlphaHat)
xdot = [x(2); –2*zeta*x(2)–x(1)–AlphaHat*x(1)^3];
```

When the function is used for a linear system, *AlphaHat* = $\hat{\alpha}$ = 0.

9.2.2 Free Oscillations of Linear Systems

When $\hat{\alpha} = F(\tau) = 0$, we have the free motion of a linear system. Then, Eq. (9.3) becomes

$$\frac{d^2x}{d\tau^2} + 2\zeta\frac{dx}{d\tau} + x = 0 \tag{9.8}$$

The characteristic equation of this system is

$$\lambda^2 + 2\zeta\lambda + 1 = 0 \tag{9.9}$$

When $\zeta = 0.1$, then the values of λ can be found from

lambda = `roots([1 0.2 1])`

---

[6] A. H. Nayfeh and B. Balachandran, *Applied Nonlinear Dynamics: Analytical, Computational, and Experimental Methods*, John Wiley & Sons, New York, 1995.

which gives $\lambda_1 = -0.1000 + 0.9950i$ and $\lambda_2 = -0.1000 - 0.9950i$, where $i = \sqrt{-1}$. The real parts of both the roots are negative, indicating that the system is stable; this is characteristic of underdamped systems.[7] For an underdamped system,

$$\left|\text{Re}(\lambda_j)\right| = \zeta \quad \text{and} \quad |\lambda_1| = |\lambda_2| = 1$$

We now determine the free response of the linear spring-mass-damper system given by Eq. (9.8) for the initial conditions

$$x(0) = x_o$$
$$\frac{dx(0)}{d\tau} = v_o$$

and for three values of the damping factor ζ: (1) $\zeta = 0.1$, an underdamped case; (2) $\zeta = 1$, the critically damped case; and (3) $\zeta = 5.0$, an overdamped case. The system is set in motion from the initial conditions $x_o = 1$ and $v_o = 1$.

To determine the free response over the range $0 \le \tau \le 40$, the script is

```
zeta = [0.1 1.0 5.0]; AlphaHat = [0.0 0.0 0.0];
tspan = linspace(0,40,400);
lintyp = ['- ' '--' '- '];
for i = 1:3
  [t,x] = ode45('FreeOscillation',tspan,[1 1]',[],zeta(i),AlphaHat(i));
  subplot(2,1,1);
  plot(t,x(:,1),lintyp(2*(i-1)+1:2*i));
  hold on
  subplot(2,1,2);
  plot(x(:,1),x(:,2),lintyp(2*(i-1)+1:2*i));
  hold on
end
subplot(2,1,1)
xlabel('Time (\tau)');
ylabel('Displacement x(\tau)');
title('Displacement as a function of \tau');
axis([0 40 -2.0 2.0]);
text(2.7,-1.3,'\zeta = 0.1');
text(3.6,-0.1,'1.0');
text(3.6,1.0,'5.0');
subplot(2,1,2)
xlabel('Displacement');
ylabel('Velocity');
title('Phase portrait');
```

---

[7] D. J. Inman, *ibid.*, p. 19; S. S. Rao, *ibid.*, p. 130; B. H. Tongue, *ibid.*, p. 25.

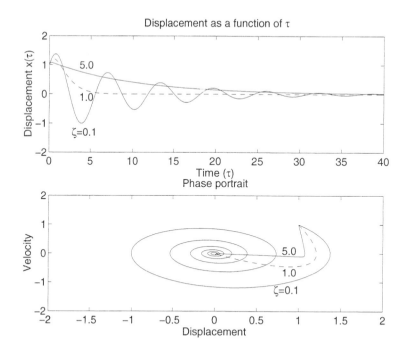

FIGURE 9.4
Displacement histories and phase portraits for the free oscillations of a damped, linear oscillator.

```
axis([-2.0 2.0 -2.0 2.0]);
text(0.7,-1.25,'\zeta = 0.1');
text(0.8,-0.65,'1.0');
text(0.8,0.1,'5.0');
```

Execution of the script produces the graphs shown in Figure 9.4. The displacement responses are shown in the top figure, and the displacements-versus-velocity plots are shown in the bottom figure. The space $(x, \dot{x})$, which is formed using the displacement and velocity coordinates, is called the phase space. The collections of trajectories that are initiated in this space from different sets of initial conditions constitute a phase portrait. The equilibrium position of the linear system given by Eq. (9.8) corresponds to the location $x_1 = 0$ and $x_2 = 0$ [or (0.0,0.0)] in the phase space. It is seen from the time histories that there are oscillations only in the underdamped case, which correspond to the spiral trajectory in the phase portrait. As time unfolds this trajectory is attracted to the location (0.0,0.0), which is the equilibrium position, and is an example of a point attractor. No oscillations are observed as the system approaches the equilibrium position in the critically damped and overdamped cases. When the system is critically damped, it is seen that it reaches the equilibrium position in the shortest time.

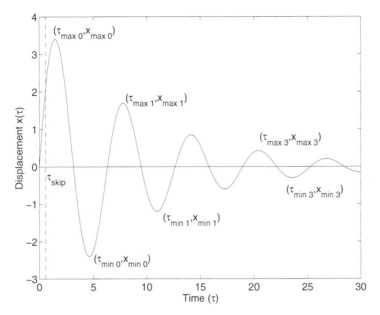

FIGURE 9.5
Free response of an underdamped system.

We now estimate the damping factor ζ from the displacement response of an underdamped system on the basis of the logarithmic decrement δ, which is given by[8]

$$\delta = \frac{1}{n} \ln\left(\frac{x_j}{x_{j+n}}\right) \tag{9.10}$$

The damping is related to δ by

$$\zeta = \frac{\delta^2}{\sqrt{4\pi^2 + \delta^2}} \tag{9.11}$$

The x_j and x_{j+n} are the displacements at t_j and $t_j + nT$, respectively, where T is the period of the underdamped oscillation. One way to determine δ is to determine the magnitudes the various maxima (minima) and then determine the period T from the times at which they occur. From these results, the x_j are determined. Referring to Figure 9.5, which is the free response of an underdamped system, the following function is used to estimate the system's damping coefficient:

---

[8] D. J.Inman, *ibid*, p. 44; S. S. Rao, *ibid*, p. 136.

```
function [pspace,tref] = period(tdata,xdata,n,nskip)
[xmin0,tmin0] = min(xdata((1+nskip):length(xdata)));
[xmax0,tmax0] = max(xdata((1+nskip):length(xdata)));
tmin0 = tmin0+nskip; tmax0 = tmax0+nskip;
m = fix(length(tdata)/(abs(tmin0-tmax0)*2.0));
while n>m
 n = n-1;
end
pspace = zeros(n,1);
tref = zeros(n+1,1);
for j = 1:n
 if  tmin0 < tmax0
  tref(1) = tmin0;
  if j == 1
   [xmin1,tmin1] = min(xdata(tmax0:length(xdata)));
   pspace(j) = (tmax0-tmin0)+tmin1;
   tref(j+1) = tref(j)+pspace(j);
  else
   [xmaxj,tmaxj] = max(xdata(tref(j):length(xdata)));
   [xminj,tminj] = min(xdata(tref(j)+tmaxj:length(xdata)));
   pspace(j) = tmaxj+tminj;
   tref(j+1) = tref(j)+pspace(j);
  end
 else
  tref(1) = tmax0;
  if j == 1
   [xmax1,tmax1] = max(xdata(tmin0:length(xdata)));
   pspace(j) = (tmin0-tmax0)+tmax1;
   tref(j+1) = tref(j)+pspace(j);
  else
   [xminj,tminj] = min(xdata(tref(j):length(xdata)));
   [xmaxj,tmaxj] = max(xdata(tref(j)+tminj:length(xdata)));
   pspace(j) = tmaxj+tminj;
   tref(j+1) = tref(j)+pspace(j);
  end
 end
end
```

The input quantities to *period* are the time *tdata*, the corresponding response *xdata*, the number of cycles *n*, and the number of initial data points to skip *nskip*. The output from *period* comprises the arrays *pspace* and *tref*, which are, respectively, the index spacing between the peaks (or valleys) and the corresponding time indices. The functions max and min are used to determine the times at which the peaks (maxima) and the valleys (minima) occur and the time between them. The second and third lines of the function are used to determine the location of the first valley and the first peak, respectively. Since `gradient` is not used to ascertain the presence of extrema, errors can be made in ascertaining the extrema—in particular, the first extremum. For example, in the data shown in Figure 9.5, the first data point can be mistaken for the first minimum if the `min` function is used on the data starting from $\tau = 0$. To avoid this, the input parameter called *nskip* has been provided to specify the starting point of the data set.

The spacing between a maximum (minimum) and a subsequent minimum (maximum) corresponds to a half period of the damped oscillation. This fact is made use of in the fifth line to estimate the total number of cycles *m* in *xdata*. If the number of specified input cycles *n* is larger than *m*, then *n* is set to a value that is less than or equal to *m*. Following the initialization of the arrays *pspace* and *tref* in the ninth line, the spacing between the extrema (either maximum or minimum) is determined within the `for` loop. Logic has been provided within this the loop to distinguish between cases where the first extremum is a minimum and cases where the first extremum is a maximum. In the latter case, the index spacing between the peaks and the associated time indices are determined. For the other cases, the index spacing between the valleys and the associated time indices are determined. The extrema determined by *period* can be used as a basis to determine the period of damped oscillation over different cycles.

Although for a linear system the period of damped oscillation does not change over different cycles, this is not so for nonlinear systems. In the script provided next, the output from *period* is used with Eq. (9.10) to obtain an estimate of the logarithmic decrement from the response of a system given by Eq. (9.8). The system parameters are $\zeta = 0.3$ and $\hat{\alpha} = 0.0$, and the response is initiated from $x_0 = 0.0$ and $v_0 = -10.0$.

```
zeta = 0.3; AlphaHat = 0.0;
tspan = linspace(0.0,40.0,400);
[t,x] = ode45('FreeOscillation',tspan,[0 –10]',[],zeta,AlphaHat);
n = input(' Enter number of cycles ');
nskip = input(' Enter number of initial points to skip ');
[pspace,tref] = period(t(:,1),x(:,1),n,nskip);
zeta = zeros(length(pspace),1);
fprintf(1,'Cycle Number  Damping Factor\n')
for  j = 1:length(pspace)
  logdec = log(x(tref(j),1)/x(tref(j+1),1));
  zeta(j) = sqrt(logdec^2/(4.0*pi^2+logdec^2));
  fprintf(1,'  %3d            %6.4f\n',j,zeta(j))
end
```

The first two lines of the script are used to generate uniformly spaced data for the system given by Eq. (9.8). The function *period* is then called to determine the damping factor. Equations (9.10) and (9.11) are implemented in the tenth and eleventh lines, respectively. When one executes this script with $n = 4$ and *nskip* = 4, the following results are displayed to the MATLAB command window.

```
Enter number of cycles  4
Enter number of initial points to skip  4
Cycle Number   Damping Factor
     1               0.3008
     2               0.3006
     3               0.2992
     4               0.3004
```

As expected, for a linear system in which energy is dissipated through viscous damping, the decay is exponential, and the logarithmic decrement remains constant over each cycle of the damped oscillation.

The script discussed above illustrates one approach that can be used to estimate the damping factor. This script can be modified to include logic that excludes data points toward the end of a time history and to determine whether or not the data correspond to an underdamped system. The above approach can lead to errors as the damping factor approaches one. The following script gives an alternative approach using graphical input.

```
zeta = 0.3; AlphaHat = 0.0;
tspan = linspace(0.0,40.0,400);
[t,x] = ode45('FreeOscillation',tspan,[0 –10]',[],zeta,AlphaHat);
plot(t(:,1),x(:,1));
disp(['Choose the location of the first peak (valley)']);
[tj xj] = ginput(1);
disp(['Choose the location of the next peak (valley)']);
[tjn xjn] = ginput(1);
n = input('Enter number of cycles between chosen peaks (valleys) ');
logdec = log(xj/xjn)/n;
disp(['Estimated zeta = ' num2str(sqrt(logdec^2/(4.0*pi^2+logdec^2)))])
```

The function `ginput` is used to determine the (t,x) coordinates of a user selected point from the plot. Recall Section 6.3.7.

9.2.3 Free Oscillations of Nonlinear Systems

We shall now explore the oscillations of two nonlinear systems. In the first system there is a nonlinear cubic spring that is described by Eq. (9.3) when $F(\tau) = 0$ and $\hat{\alpha} \neq 0$. In the second system there is nonlinear damping.

System with Nonlinear Spring. The motion of the system given by Eq. (9.3) is examined for the three cases presented in Table 9.2. The first case corresponds to a linear system, while the second and third cases correspond to a nonlinear system with a softening spring. The initial conditions are the same in the first two cases and different for the third case.

The function *FreeOscillation* created in Section 9.2.1 is used to describe the system given by Eq. (9.3). The following script generates the responses for the three cases. In

TABLE 9.2
Parameters and Initial Conditions for Three Cases

Case	System type	$\hat{\alpha}$	ζ	$x(0) = x_o$	$dx(0)/d\tau = v_o$
1	Linear	0.00	0.20	−2.00	2.00
2	Nonlinear	−0.25	0.20	−2.00	2.00
3	Nonlinear	−0.25	0.20	−2.00	2.31

addition, the period of each cycle of the response is determined along with an estimate of its damping factor.

```
zeta = 0.20; AlphaHat = [0.00 −0.25 −0.25];
xo = [−2.00 −2.00 −2.00]; vo = [ 2.00 2.00 2.31];
tspan = linspace(0.0,40.0,401);
lintyp = ['- ' '--' '- '];
options = odeset('RelTol',1e−8,'AbsTol',[1e−8 1e−8]);
for i = 1:3
[t,x] = ode45('FreeOscillation',tspan,[xo(i) vo(i)]',options,zeta,AlphaHat(i));
subplot(2,1,1)
plot(t,x(:,1),lintyp(2*(i−1)+1:2*i))
hold on
subplot(2,1,2)
plot(x(:,1),x(:,2),lintyp(2*(i−1)+1:2*i))
hold on
fprintf(1,'\n\n Case %3d\n',i)
[pspace,tref] = period(t,x(:,1),3,8);
zetaest = zeros(length(pspace),1);
fprintf(1, '\n Cycle No.      Period      Damping Factor\n')
  for j = 1:length(pspace)
    per(j) = t(tref(j+1))−t(tref(j));
    logdec = log(x(tref(j),1)/x(tref(j+1),1));
    zetaest(j) = sqrt(logdec^2/(4.0*pi^2+logdec^2));
    fprintf(1,'  %3d       %8.3f       %6.4f\n',j,per(j),zetaest(j))
  end
end
subplot(2,1,1)
xlabel('Time {\tau}');
ylabel('Displacement x(\tau)');
title('Displacement histories');
axis([0.0 40.0 −3.0 3.0]);
text(4.0,−1.15,'Case 1: Linear system');
text(4.0,2.2,'Case 3: Nonlinear system');
```

```
subplot(2,1,2)
xlabel('Displacement');
ylabel('Velocity');
title('Phase portraits');
axis([-3.0 3.0 -3.0 3.0]);
text(0.85,-1.45,'Case 1');
text(0.85,0.0,'Case 2');
text(2.0,0.0,'Case 3');
```

Tolerances used during the integration are specified in the fifth line and they are provided to ensure that numerical errors do not lead to spurious solutions.

The logarithmic decrement is not strictly applicable for estimating the damping factor of a nonlinear system. Here, it is used to illustrate that its application can lead to errors when estimating the damping factor based on "large" motions of a nonlinear system, and to reasonable values when estimating the damping factor based on "small" motions of a nonlinear system. In addition, the results are used to illustrate that the period of oscillation of a nonlinear system can depend upon the response amplitude. When this script is executed, the output to the Matlab command window consists of the damping factor estimate over the different cycles of oscillation in each case.

Case 1		
Cycle No.	Period	Damping Factor
1	6.500	0.2005
2	6.400	0.1999
3	6.400	0.1999
Case 2		
Cycle No.	Period	Damping Factor
1	7.300	0.2328
2	6.400	0.2008
3	6.400	0.2000
Case 3		
Cycle No.	Period	Damping Factor
1	9.000	0.2592
2	6.500	0.2026
3	6.400	0.1998

Graphs of the free oscillations for these three cases are shown in Figure 9.6.

In Case 1, which corresponds to the linear system, the period of the damped oscillation remains essentially constant over each cycle. In Cases 2 and 3, which correspond to a nonlinear system, both the period of the damped oscillation and the damping factor estimated from the first cycle are significantly different from those estimated from the subsequent cycles of motion. The effect of the nonlinearity is typically pronounced when the amplitudes of motion are "large," as it is in the first cycle of oscillation in Case 3. The behavior of the

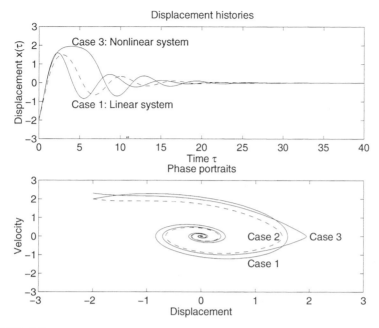

FIGURE 9.6
Displacement histories and phase portraits for the free responses of a damped, nonlinear oscillator.

systems in Cases 2 and 3 approaches that of the linear system (Case 1) as the amplitudes of motion become "smaller."

As in the corresponding linear case, the orbits of the nonlinear system initiated from these sets of the initial conditions are attracted towards the stable equilibrium position (0.0,0.0) in the phase portrait. The spirals in the phase portrait indicate that the corresponding motions of the nonlinear system are underdamped. For "small" oscillations around the stable equilibrium position, the nonlinear system should behave like a linear system. Examining the responses initiated from the two sets of initial conditions, the feature observed for Case 3 around the first extremum in the time history is not typical of the response of a linear system. In this case, the trajectory comes "close" to the unstable equilibrium position (2.00,0.00) of the system and the system motion is affected. Unlike a linear system, a nonlinear system can have multiple equilibrium positions, not all of which are necessarily stable.[9]

System with Nonlinear Damping We now consider a spring-mass system with dry friction shown in Figure 9.7. This system is governed by

$$\frac{d^2x}{d\tau^2} + x + d \ \text{signum}(dx/x\tau) = 0 \tag{9.12}$$

[9] A. H. Nayfeh and B. Balachandran, *ibid*.

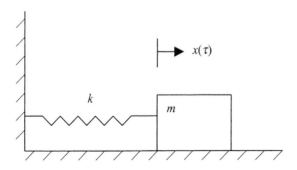

FIGURE 9.7
Spring-mass system with dry friction.

where the constant $d = \mu mg/k$, μ is the friction coefficient, mg is the weight of the object, and k is the spring constant of the linear spring restraining the mass m. The dry friction force, which is a piecewise constant function of the velocity, is described with signum in Eq. (9.12). It has a value of $+1$ when the velocity is positive and a value of -1 when the velocity is negative. Since the dry friction force varies nonlinearly with respect to velocity, the system is nonlinear. When the system is set into motion, the system comes to rest when the spring force is no longer able to overcome the dry friction force. This means that the system will stop when

$$\frac{dx}{d\tau} = 0 \ \text{ and } \ |x| \le d \qquad\qquad (9.13)$$

The nonlinear system described by Eq. (9.12) has multiple equilibria, and the locus of these equilibria in the phase space is the straight line joining the points $(-d,0)$ and $(d,0)$.

A closed-form solution of Eq. (9.12) can be obtained from the fact[10] that the system is linear in the region $dx/d\tau > 0$ and linear in the region $dx/d\tau < 0$. However, we shall obtain its numerical solution using ode45. First, Eq. (9.12) is rewritten in a state-space form by introducing the variables

$$x_1 = x$$
$$x_2 = \frac{dx}{d\tau}$$

This results in the following system of first-order equations:

$$\frac{dx_1}{d\tau} = x_2$$
$$\frac{dx_2}{d\tau} = -x_1 - d\,\text{signum}(x_2) \qquad\qquad (9.14)$$

A function called *FreeOscillation2* is created to represent Eqs. (9.13) and (9.14).

---

[10] D. J. Inman, *ibid.*, Section 2.7; S. S. Rao, *ibid.*, Section 2.7.

```
function xdot = FreeOscillation2(t,x,dummy,d)
if  abs(x(1)) <= d & x(2) == 0.0
  xdot = [0 0]';
else
  xdot = [x(2) –d*sign(x(2))–x(1)]';
end
```

The numerical solutions of Eq. (9.12) are obtained when $d = 0.86$ and for the following two sets of initial conditions: (a) (3.0,0.0) and (b) (5.0,0.0). The script is

```
d = 0.86;
xo = [3.0 5.0];
vo = [0.0 0.0];
tspan = linspace(0,12,120);
options = odeset('AbsTol',[1e–3 1e–3]);
lintyp = ['--' '- ' ];
for i = 1:2
  [t,x] = ode45('FreeOscillation2',tspan,[xo(i) vo(i)]',options,d);
  subplot(2,1,1);
  plot(t,x(:,1),lintyp(2*(i–1)+1:2*i));
  hold on
  subplot(2,1,2);
  plot(x(:,1),x(:,2),lintyp(2*(i–1)+1:2*i));
  hold on
end
subplot(2,1,1)
xlabel('Time (\tau)');
ylabel('Displacement x(\tau)');
title('Displacement histories');
axis([0.0 12.0 –4.0 6.0]);
subplot(2,1,2)
xlabel('Displacement');
ylabel('Velocity');
title('Phase portraits');
text(2.5,0.5,'(3.0,0.0)');
text(4.5,0.5,'(5.0,0.0)');
axis([–4.0 6.0 –6.0 4.0]);
```

The absolute tolerance specified for each state is larger than the default value of 1.0e–6 to speed up the computations. Execution of the script produces the results shown in Figure 9.8.

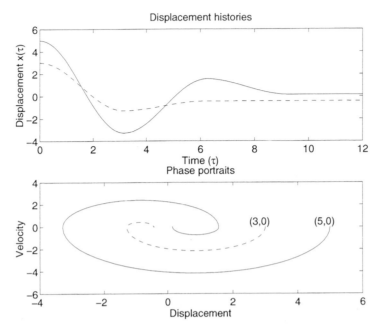

FIGURE 9.8
Displacement histories and phase portraits for the free response of an oscillator with dry friction.

The systems come to rest at two different positions, and the respective rest positions are reached at two different times. This example illustrates the fact that the long time response of a nonlinear system depends upon the initial conditions. By contrast, the asymptotic response of a damped linear system is independent of the initial conditions.

9.2.4 Forced Oscillations of Linear and Nonlinear Systems

Responses of linear and nonlinear systems to harmonic excitations will be determined in the time domain using `ode45`. The corresponding information in the frequency domain will be determined with `fft`. Recall Section 5.6.4.

Consider the system given by Eq. (9.3). Let the forcing be harmonic—that is,

$$F(\tau) = X_o \cos(\Omega \tau) \tag{9.15}$$

where Ω is the nondimensional excitation frequency and X_o is a measure of the forcing amplitude. For a selected excitation frequency and excitation amplitude, we determine the steady-state response of the system given by Eq. (9.3)—that is,

$$\lim_{t \to \infty} x(t)$$

and examine the spectral content of this response for the following cases: (1) $\hat{\alpha} = 0$ (linear system) and (2) $\hat{\alpha} \neq 0$ (nonlinear system). To this end we create the following function:

```
function xdot = ForcedOscillator1 (t,x,dummy,zeta,AlphaHat,Omega,Xo)
xdot = [x(2); -2*zeta*x(2)-x(1)-AlphaHat*x(1)^3+ Xo*cos(Omega*t)];
```

Equation (9.3) is numerically integrated by ode45 for the forcing function given by Eq. (9.15) and the following parameters: (1) the initial conditions (0,0); (2) $\zeta = 0.4$; (3) $\hat{\alpha} = 1.5$ (in the nonlinear case); (4) $\Omega = 3.0$; and (5) $X_o = 5.0$. The excitation frequency Ω has been chosen to be three times the natural frequency of the system. The data from this analysis is saved for use in the subsequent example. The script is

```
zeta = 0.4; AlphaHat = [0 1.5];
Omega = 3.0; Xo = 50.0;
tspan = linspace(0,30,6000);
sampint = tspan(2);
options = odeset('RelTol',1e-8,'AbsTol',[1e-8 1e-8]);
for m = 1:2
  [t,x] = ode45('ForcedOscillator1',tspan,[0 0]',options,zeta,AlphaHat(m),Omega,Xo);
  if m == 1
    subplot(2,1,1);
    plot(t,x(:,1));axis([0 30 -8 8]);
    xlabel('\tau');
    ylabel('x(\tau)');
    title('Response of a linear system');
    yy = x(:,1);
    save 'c:\path\ForcedOscLin.txt' yy -ascii;
  else
    subplot(2,1,2);
    plot(t, x(:,1));
    axis([0 30 -8 8]);
    xlabel('\tau');
    ylabel('x(\tau)');
    title('Response of a nonlinear system');
    yy = x(:,1);
    save 'c:\path\ForcedOscNonLin.txt' yy -ascii;
  end
end
```

where *path* is defined by the user.

Execution of the script results in Figure 9.9, where it is seen that the responses of both the linear and nonlinear systems reach steady state when $\tau \geq 8$. This time corresponds to an index $N_{start} = 1600$. Although both of the steady-state responses have a period equal to the period of the harmonic forcing function, they have different characteristics that can be more clearly distinguished in the frequency domain.

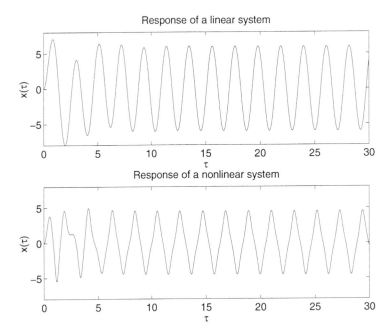

FIGURE 9.9
Response of a linear system and a nonlinear system.

To obtain the information in the frequency domain, we will use `fft` on portions of the linear and nonlinear time histories saved in *ForcedOscLin.txt* and *ForcedOscNonLin.txt*, respectively. Then, using the results in Section 5.6.4 the amplitude spectrum of each signal for $\tau \geq 8$ is computed in the following function *AmplitudeSpectrum*.

```
function [f,amplitude] = AmplitudeSpectrum(AmplData,SamplingFreq,Nstart,N);
f = (SamplingFreq*(0:N−1)/N)*2.0*pi;
amplitude = abs(fft(AmplData(Nstart:Nstart+N),N))/N;
```

The sampling rate at which the data in *ForcedOscLin.txt* and *ForcedOscNonLin.txt* are acquired is $\tau_s = 30/6000 = 0.005$. Therefore, the (dimensionless) sampling frequency is $f_s = 1/\tau_s = 200$. This is far in excess of what is necessary to sample the response based on the excitation frequency $\Omega = 3$. The consequences are that we have to truncate the spectrum plot; thus, we shall display only the first 40 values. Also, we let $N_{start} = 3200$ and $N = 2^{11} = 2048$. The script is

```
load 'c:\path\ForcedOscLin.txt';
load 'c:\path\ForcedOscNonLin.txt';
N = 2048; Nstart = 3200; Fs = 200;
[fLin,AmpLin] = AmplitudeSpectrum(ForcedOscLin,Fs,Nstart,N);
```

```
[fNonLin,AmpNonLin] = AmplitudeSpectrum(ForcedOscNonLin,Fs,Nstart,N);
subplot(2,1,1)
semilogy(fLin(1:40),2*AmpLin(1:40));
xlabel('Frequency');
ylabel('Amplitude');
title('Response spectrum of a linear system');
text(3.1,10^4.5,'\Omega');
subplot(2,1,2);
semilogy(fNonLin(1:40),2*AmpNonLin(1:40));
v = axis;
xlabel('Frequency');
ylabel('Amplitude');
title('Response spectrum of a nonlinear system');
text(3.1,.5*v(4),'\Omega');
text(9.1,.2*v(4),'3\Omega');
```

where *path* is defined by the user.

The execution of the script results in Figure 9.10, where it is seen that the amplitude spectrum of the displacement response in the nonlinear case shows spectral peaks at the forcing frequency Ω and integer multiples of it. The additional peaks are due to the cubic nonlinearity of the spring. In the linear case, there is only one spectral peak, which corresponds to the excitation frequency. The above example illustrates that the response of a nonlinear system can have spectral components different from the excitation frequency.

9.2.5 Frequency Response and the Response to Step and Impulse Excitations

We now illustrate how to compute and display the frequency response curves for linear systems. Although the material of this section does not differ in principle from that presented in Section 9.2.4, it is presented to demonstrate the use of the functions

`bode, tf, step, impulse, damp`

from the Controls Toolbox. The transfer function of a linear time-invariant system (i.e., a system described by a differential equation with constant coefficients) can be represented in the form

$$G(s) = \frac{N(s)}{D(s)}$$

where $N(s)$ and $D(s)$ are polynomials in the complex variable s. The function

sys = tf(N,D)

is used to specify the system's transfer function when the arrays of coefficients for $N(s)$ and $D(s)$ are known.

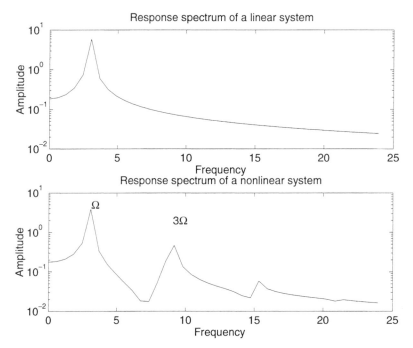

FIGURE 9.10
Fourier analysis of the responses of a linear and a nonlinear system.

The frequency response function

$$G(s = i\omega)$$

can be computed and plotted with

bode(tf(N,D),w)

which plots the magnitude and phase of $G(i\omega)$, or with

[magnitude,phase] = bode(tf(N,D),w)

which provides arrays of numerical values for the magnitude and phase. The array w is either a two-element cell that specifies the minimum and maximum values of the frequency range of interest or an array of radian frequency values.

The functions impulse and step can be used to determine the impulse and step responses, respectively, of linear time-invariant systems set into motion from rest. Thus,

impulse(tf(N,D))

plots the impulse response of the system described by `tf` and

    step(tf(N,D))

plots the response of a system to a unit step function applied at $t = 0$. See Chapter 10 for additional applications of these functions.
The function

    [wn,zeta] = damp(tf(N,D))

is used to determine the damping factors ζ and natural frequencies ω_n of a linear time-invariant system from its transfer function.
To illustrate these functions consider again the system described by Eq. (9.3) with $\hat{\alpha} = 0$. Taking the Laplace transform,[11] the (nondimensional) transfer function for this system is

$$\frac{\bar{x}(s)}{X_o f(s)} = G(s) = \frac{1}{s^2 + 2\zeta s + 1} \tag{9.16}$$

Thus

$$N(s) = 1$$
$$D(s) = s^2 + 2\zeta s + 1$$

and the arrays defining N and D are, respectively,

    N = [0 0 1];
    D = [1 2*zeta 1];

Frequency Response—Bode Plots. The transfer function given by Eq. (9.16) is now used to construct the frequency-response curves using `tf` and `bode`. The script is

```
zeta = 0.2:0.2:1.0;
omega = 0.0:0.01:3.0;
for i = 1:length(zeta)
  sys = tf([0 0 1],[1 2*zeta(i) 1]);
  [mag,phas] = bode(sys,omega);
  subplot(2,1,1)
  plot(omega,mag(1,:));
  hold on;
  subplot(2,1,2)
  plot(omega,phas(1,:));
  hold on;
end
```

---

[11] L. Meirovitch, *ibid.*, Appendix B.

```
subplot(2,1,1)
xlabel('Frequency');
ylabel('Magnitude');
title('Amplitude response');
text(0.8,2.7,'\zeta = 0.2');
text(0.8,1.55,'\zeta = 0.4');
text(0.8,0.4,'\zeta = 1.0');
hold on;
plot([0.0 3.0],[1.0 1.0],'--');
subplot(2,1,2)
xlabel('Frequency');
ylabel('Phase(degrees)');
title('Phase response');
text(0.7,-15.0,'\zeta = 0.2');
text(0.5,-80.0,'\zeta = 1.0');
hold on;
plot([0.0 3.0],[-90 -90],'--');
plot([1.0 1.0],[-200 0],'--');
```

The execution of this script results in Figure 9.11. The magnitude of the nondimensional transfer function is sometimes referred to as the magnification factor.

Impulse Response. We determine the impulse response of the system described by Eq. (9.16) for $\zeta = 0.1$, 1.0, and 3.0, which represent an underdamped system, a critically damped system, and an overdamped system, respectively. The script is

```
zeta = [0.2 1.0 3.0]; tfinal = 30;
tdata = linspace(0,tfinal, 100);
for i = 1:length(zeta)
 xdata = impulse([0 0 1],[1 2*zeta(i) 1],tdata);
  plot(tdata,xdata);
  hold on;
end
axis([0.0 30.0 -0.5 1.0]);
xlabel('Time \tau');
ylabel('x(\tau)');
title('Impulse response');
text(1.5,0.8,'\zeta = 0.2');
text(10.5,0.08,'\zeta = 3.0');
```

The results, which are shown in Figure 9.12, can also be obtained from the free-vibration response by integrating the time domain counterpart of Eq. (9.16) from the set of initial conditions (0,1).

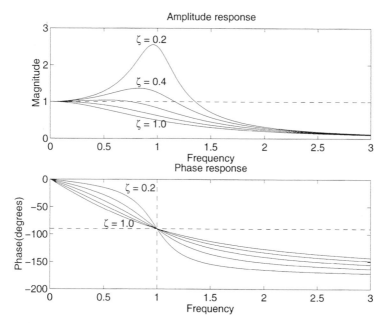

FIGURE 9.11.
Amplitude and phase responses for a directly excited spring-mass-damper system.

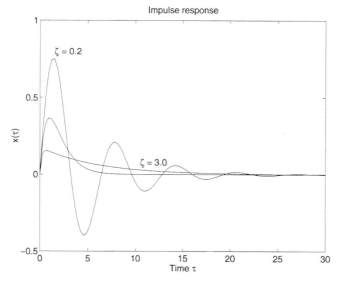

FIGURE 9.12
Impulse responses of underdamped, critically damped, and overdamped systems.

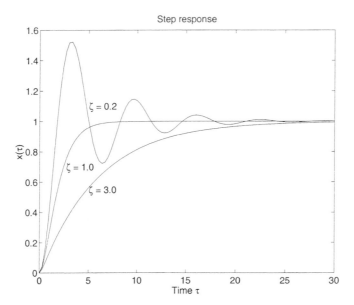

FIGURE 9.13.
Step responses of underdamped, critically damped, and overdamped systems.

Step response. We determine the step response of the system described by Eq. (9.16) for $\zeta =$ 0.2, 1.0, and 3.0, which represent an underdamped system, a critically damped system, and an overdamped system, respectively. The script is

```
zeta = [0.2 1.0 3.0];tfinal = 30;
tdata = linspace(0,tfinal, 100);
for i = 1:length(zeta)
 xdata = step([0 0 1],[1 2*zeta(i) 1],tdata);
 plot(tdata,xdata);
 hold on;
end
xlabel('Time \tau');
ylabel('x(\tau)');
title('Step response');
text(5.0,1.10,'\zeta = 0.2');
text(2.7,0.70,'\zeta = 1.0');
text(5.0,0.55,'\zeta = 3.0');
```

The results are shown in Figure 9.13. The response of the underdamped system oscillates about the steady-state position before settling down, while the responses in the critically damped and overdamped cases are not oscillatory. In the critically damped case, the system settles to the steady-state position in the shortest amount of time.

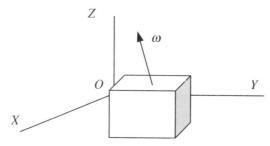

FIGURE 9.14.
Rotation of a rigid body in a frame with Cartesian axes.

Estimation of ω_n and ζ We shall determine the natural frequency and the damping for the system described by Eq. (9.16) for $\zeta = 0.3$. First we model the system with $\zeta = 0.3$, and then we use damp to determine this value. The function damp determines the damping factors and associated natural frequencies from the poles of the transfer function. The script is

```
sys = tf([0 0 1],[1 2*0.3 1]);
[w,zeta] = damp(sys)
```

which, upon execution, gives $\omega_n = 1$ and $\zeta = 0.3$.

Although, thus far, the illustrations of the uses of these functions have been made only for single-degree-of-freedom systems, they can be used to study multi-degree-of-freedom systems, as illustrated in Section 9.3.

9.3 MULTI-DEGREE-OF-FREEDOM SYSTEMS

9.3.1 Free Oscillations

We shall consider three different classes of problems that require the determination of the system's eigenvalues:

1. Principal moments of inertia

2. Stability of a rotating rigid body

3. Natural frequencies of a multi-degree-of-freedom system

Principal Moments of Inertia. Consider the rigid body shown in Figure 9.14, which has three rotational degrees of freedom. The associated rotational inertia matrix has the form

$$I_{rot} = \begin{bmatrix} I_{xx} & I_{xy} & I_{xz} \\ I_{yx} & I_{yy} & I_{yz} \\ I_{zx} & I_{zy} & I_{zz} \end{bmatrix} \tag{9.17}$$

where the various moments of inertia are defined with respect to the coordinate system shown in Figure 9.14.

We shall determine a new set of orthogonal axes such that the inertia matrix is diagonal. These axes are called the principal axes, and the associated moments of inertia are called the principal moments of inertia. The eigenvalues of Eq. (9.17) provide the principal moments of inertia, and the associated eigenvectors define the principal axes.[12] These two quantities are determined with `eig` as shown below. We also note that the sum of the eigenvalues of a matrix is equal to the trace of the matrix. The trace of a matrix is the sum of the diagonal elements of the matrix, and it is determined with `trace`. Furthermore, let

$$[I] = \begin{bmatrix} 150 & 0 & -100 \\ 0 & 250 & 0 \\ -100 & 0 & 500 \end{bmatrix} \text{kg m}^2 \tag{9.19}$$

The script is

```
Irot = [150 0 –100; 0  250 0; –100 0 500];
[PrincipalDirections PrincipalMoments] = eig(Irot)
TraceIrot = trace(Irot)
TracePM = trace(PrincipalMoments)
```

which, upon execution, produces

```
PrincipalDirections =
      0 -0.9665  -0.2567
 -1.0000      0      0
      0 -0.2567   0.9665
PrincipalMoments =
 250.0000      0       0
      0 123.4436       0
      0       0 526.5564
TraceIrot =
  900
TracePM =
  900
```

Although the first eigenvector corresponds to the first eigenvalue, the second eigenvector corresponds to the second eigenvalue, and so forth, the eigenvalues (principal moments, in this case) are not in any particular order. This is typical of the results obtained from `eig`. When the inertia matrix is examined, it is found that in this case, the y-axis is a principal axis and hence one of the eigenvalues is equal to I_{yy}. The matrix of principal directions defines a direction cosine matrix that can be used to transform the (x,y,z) axes to the principal axes.

---

[12] D. T. Greenwood, *ibid.*

Stability of a Rigid Body. Consider the rigid body shown in Figure 9.14. Let I_1, I_2, and I_3, respectively, represent the second mass moments of inertia about the x-, y-, and z-axes that are chosen to be along the respective principal axes of the body—that is, the principal moments of inertia in the previous example. Let ω_1, ω_2, and ω_3 represent the respective angular velocities about these axes, and let M_1, M_2, and M_3 represent the respective external moments about these axes. The equations of motion, which are known as Euler's equations, are of the form[13]

$$I_1\dot{\omega}_1 + (I_3 - I_2)\omega_2\omega_3 = M_1$$
$$I_2\dot{\omega}_2 + (I_1 - I_3)\omega_3\omega_1 = M_2 \qquad (9.19)$$
$$I_3\dot{\omega}_3 + (I_2 - I_1)\omega_1\omega_2 = M_3$$

where

$$\dot{\omega}_j = \frac{d\omega_j}{dt} \qquad j = 1,2,3$$

In the moment-free case—that is, when $M_1 = M_2 = M_3 = 0$—there are three types of solutions where ω_j are constant with respect to time. These solutions, which are called the constant solutions, are as follows:

1. $(\omega_{10} \neq 0,\ \omega_{20} = 0,\ \omega_{30} = 0)$

2. $(\omega_{10} = 0,\ \omega_{20} \neq 0,\ \omega_{30} = 0)$

3. $(\omega_{10} = 0,\ \omega_{20} = 0,\ \omega_{30} \neq 0)$

Each of these solutions corresponds to pure rotational motions about one of the principal axes. We are interested in determining the stability of these three types of motions. To this end, we let ξ_j, $j = 1,2,3$, represent the disturbances provided to the system about the respective axes – that is,

$$\omega_1(t) = \omega_{10} + \xi_1(t)$$
$$\omega_2(t) = \omega_{20} + \xi_2(t) \qquad (9.20)$$
$$\omega_3(t) = \omega_{30} + \xi_3(t)$$

After substituting Eqs. (9.20) into Eqs. (9.19) and assuming that the magnitudes of the disturbances are "small," one can linearize[14] Eqs. (9.19) and study the associated eigenvalue problem. This results in the following system of equations:

$$\begin{bmatrix} 0 & (I_3 - I_2)\omega_{30}/I_1 & (I_3 - I_2)\omega_{20}/I_1 \\ (I_1 - I_3)\omega_{30}/I_2 & 0 & (I_1 - I_3)\omega_{10}/I_2 \\ (I_2 - I_1)\omega_{20}/I_3 & (I_2 - I_1)\omega_{10}/I_3 & 0 \end{bmatrix} \begin{Bmatrix} \xi_1 \\ \xi_2 \\ \xi_3 \end{Bmatrix} = \lambda \begin{Bmatrix} \xi_1 \\ \xi_2 \\ \xi_3 \end{Bmatrix} \qquad (9.21)$$

---

[13] D. T. Greenwood, *ibid.*, p. 392; F. C. Moon, *ibid.*, p. 192.
[14] A. H. Nayfeh and B. Balachandran, *ibid.*

If one or more of the three eigenvalues of Eqs. (9.21) has a positive real part, then the disturbances will grow in magnitude and the associated motion will be unstable. Since the trace of Eq. (9.21) is zero, the sum of its eigenvalues will also be zero. Let us consider a rigid body with $I_1 = 150$ kg m^2, $I_2 = 50$ kg m^2, and $I_3 = 300$ kg m^2 and determine the stability of each of the three constant solutions. The script shown next will be used to determine the eigenvalues λ for disturbances provided to the rotational motions along the axis of maximum inertia, the axis of minimum inertia, and the other axis.

```
I = [150 50 300];
omega10 = [1 0 0];
omega20 = [0 1 0];
omega30 = [0 0 1];
for i = 1:length(omega10)
  A = [0  (I(3)–I(2))*omega30(i)/I(1) (I(3)–I(2))*omega20(i)/I(1); ...
        (I(1)–I(3))*omega30(i)/I(2) 0  (I(1)–I(3))*omega10(i)/I(2); ...
        (I(2)–I(1))*omega20(i)/I(3) (I(2)–I(1))*omega10(i)/I(3)  0];
  fprintf(1,'\nCase %3d: Eigenvalues\n',i);
  lambda = eig(A)
  SumLambda = sum(lambda)
end
```

Execution of the script displays the following to the MATLAB command window

```
Case  1: Eigenvalues
lambda =
     1
    -1
     0
sum_lambda =
     0
Case  2: Eigenvalues
lambda =
     0 + 0.7454i
     0 - 0.7454i
     0
sum_lambda =
0
Case  3: Eigenvalues
lambda =
     0 + 2.2361i
     0 - 2.2361i
     0
sum_lambda =
     0
```

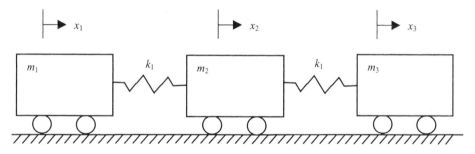

FIGURE 9.15.
System with three degrees of freedom.

In each of the three cases, one of the eigenvalues is always zero and the sum of the eigenvalues is always zero. In the first case, where the initial rotational motion is along the axis with the intermediate value of inertia, one of the eigenvalues has a positive real part indicating that the motion is unstable. The associated physical motions are wobbly. In the second case, which corresponds to an initial rotational motion about the axis of minimum rotational inertia, two of the eigenvalues form a purely imaginary pair. In the third case, which corresponds to an initial rotational motion about the axis of maximum rotational inertia, two of the eigenvalues form a purely imaginary pair. In the second and third cases, the respective disturbances to the system do not grow because none of the eigenvalues has a positive real part. Hence, the motions in this case are stable. If one further explores the solutions of Eqs. (9.19) by numerically integrating the last two cases, it will be found that the motions correspond to circular orbits in the three-dimensional space defined by the three states ω_1, ω_2, and ω_3. These orbits lie on an ellipsoid called Poinsot's ellipsoid.[15]

Natural frequencies and mode shapes of a three-degree-of-freedom system. Consider the system shown in Figure 9.15. Let the displacements x_1, x_2, and x_3 be measured from the static-equilibrium position of the system. The governing system of equations is given by

$$\begin{bmatrix} m_1 & 0 & 0 \\ 0 & m_2 & 0 \\ 0 & 0 & m_3 \end{bmatrix} \begin{Bmatrix} \ddot{x}_1 \\ \ddot{x}_2 \\ \ddot{x}_3 \end{Bmatrix} + \begin{bmatrix} k_1 & -k_1 & 0 \\ -k_1 & (k_1+k_2) & -k_2 \\ 0 & -k_2 & k_2 \end{bmatrix} \begin{Bmatrix} x_1 \\ x_2 \\ x_3 \end{Bmatrix} = \begin{Bmatrix} 0 \\ 0 \\ 0 \end{Bmatrix} \tag{9.22}$$

where

$$\ddot{x}_j = \frac{d^2 x_j}{dt^2}$$

The associated eigenvalue problem has the following form:

[15] D. T. Greenwood, *ibid.*, Section 8.4.

$$
\begin{bmatrix} k_1 & -k_1 & 0 \\ -k_1 & (k_1 + k_2) & -k_2 \\ 0 & -k_2 & k_2 \end{bmatrix} \begin{Bmatrix} v_1 \\ v_2 \\ v_3 \end{Bmatrix} = \lambda \begin{bmatrix} m_1 & 0 & 0 \\ 0 & m_2 & 0 \\ 0 & 0 & m_3 \end{bmatrix} \begin{Bmatrix} v_1 \\ v_2 \\ v_3 \end{Bmatrix} \qquad (9.23)
$$

where $\lambda = \omega^2$.

We assume that $k_1 = 100$ N/m, $k_2 = 50$ N/m, and $m_1 = m_2 = m_3 = 100$ Kg. The script that determines the eigenvalues and associated eigenvectors is

```
k = [100 –100 0; –100 150 –50; 0 –50 50];
m = [100 0 0; 0 100 0; 0 0 100];
[VibrationModes, Eigenvalues] = eig(k,m)
```

Execution of the script gives

```
VibrationModes =
   0.5774    0.5774   -0.5774
  -0.7887    0.5774   -0.2113
   0.2113    0.5774    0.7887
Eigenvalues =
   2.3660        0        0
        0   0.0000        0
        0        0   0.6340
```

When the system shown in Figure (9.15) is examined, it is found that, since the masses at each end are not restrained, a rigid-body mode in which all masses move in the same direction by the same amount is possible. This is reflected in the corresponding vibration mode, which is depicted by the second column of the matrix of vibration modes. The springs are neither stretched nor compressed in this case. This motion is associated with the zero eigenvalue.

When a square matrix has a zero eigenvalue, the determinant of the matrix is zero. In order to ascertain whether or not a matrix has zero eigenvalues, the rank of a matrix can be determined. The rank of a matrix, which is the order of the largest square matrix for which the determinant is nonzero, can be determined from

```
rank
```

The script for determining whether or not the stiffness matrix in Eqs. (9.22) has a zero eigenvalue is

```
k = [100 –100 0; –100 150 –50; 0 –50 50];
rnk = rank(k);
[m n] = size(k);
disp(['Number of zero eigenvaules is ' num2str(m–rnk,2)])
```

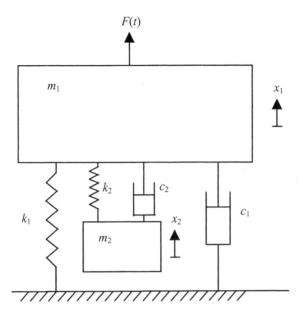

FIGURE 9.16.
A two-degree-of-freedom system subjected to an external force $F(t)$.

Execution of the script produces the following output

> Number of zero eigenvaules is 1

Here, the rank of the stiffness matrix is two, indicating that one can form a (2×2) matrix with a nonzero determinant from the (3×3) stiffness matrix.

9.3.2 Forced Oscillations and the Vibration Absorber

A two-degree-of-freedom system subjected to a forcing function $F(t)$ is shown in Figure 9.16, where the mass m_2, the spring k_2, and the damper c_2 comprise the secondary system, and the mass m_1, the spring k_1, and the damper c_1 comprise the primary system. When the secondary system is added to the forced primary system to attenuate its motions, it is called an absorber.

The transfer functions for this system are given by

$$\frac{\bar{x}_1(s)}{F(s)} = \frac{m_2 s^2 + c_2 s + k_2}{D(s)}$$

$$\frac{\bar{x}_2(s)}{F(s)} = \frac{c_2 s + k_2}{D(s)} \tag{9.24}$$

where

$$D(s) = m_1 m_2 s^4 + \left[(c_1 + c_2)m_2 + c_2 m_1\right]s^3 + \left[(k_1 + k_2)m_2 + k_2 m_1 + c_1 c_2\right]s^2$$
$$+ (k_1 c_2 + k_2 c_1)s + k_1 k_2 \tag{9.25}$$

Since these two transfer functions will be used several times, the following function called *Transferab* is created:

```
function sys = Transferab(m,k,c)
N = {[m(2) c(2) k(2)]; [c(2) k(2)]};
D = [m(1)*m(2) ((c(1)+c(2))*m(2)+c(2)*m(1))...
    ((k(1)+k(2))*m(2)+k(2)*m(1)+c(1)*c(2)) ...
    (k(1)*c(2)+c(1)*k(2)) k(1)*k(2)];
sys = tf(N,D);
```

Impulse response. Assume that

$m_1 = 50$ kg	$k_1 = 200$ N/m	$c_1 = 10$ Ns/m
$m_2 = 10$ kg	$k_2 = 40$ N/m	$c_2 = 6$ Ns/m

We determine the responses of masses m_1 and m_2 when an impulse of unit magnitude is applied at time $t = 0$ to mass m_1. The script is

```
m = [50 10];
k = [200 40];
c = [10 6];
[y,t] = impulse(Transferab(m,k,c),20);
subplot(2,1,1);
plot(t,y(:,1,1));
ylabel('x_1(t)');
title('Impulse response of m_1');
subplot(2,1,2);
plot(t,y(:,2,1));
xlabel('Time t');
ylabel('x_2(t)');
title('Impulse response of m_2');
```

The execution of the script results in Figure 9.17, where it is seen that the initial transient motions of both the masses are different. Although the impulse is applied to mass m_1, the response amplitude of the secondary mass m_2 is initially larger than that of m_1. After the first seven seconds or so, the two masses appear to be oscillating with the same period.

The step responses of the system can be obtained in a similar manner by replacing impulse with step.

Vibration Absorber. We now determine the frequency-response functions for the displacement responses of masses m_1 and m_2 when a forcing is applied to mass m_1. This type

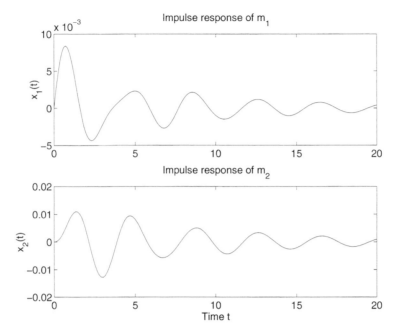

FIGURE 9.17.
Impulse responses of a two-degree-of-freedom system, when the impulse is applied to m_1.

of analysis is used to design vibration absorbers, whose purpose is to attenuate the displacement response of the primary mass at the disturbance frequency.[16] Using the same system parameters as in the previous example, the script is

```
m = [50 10];
k = [200 40];
c = [10 6];
omega = 0.0:0.005:4;
for i = 1:2
  if i == 1
    sys = tf([1],[m(1) c(1) k(1)]);
    [mag phas] = bode(sys,omega);
  plot(omega,mag(1,:),'--');
    hold on;
  else
    sys = Transferab(m,k,c);
    [mag, phas] = bode(sys,omega);
    plot(omega,mag(1,:));
```

[16] D. J. Inman, *ibid.*; Section 5.3; S. S. Rao, *ibid.*, Section 9.10; B. H. Tongue, *ibid.*, Section 4.4.

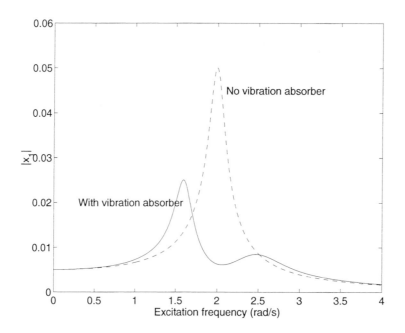

FIGURE 9.18.
Magnitude of response of primary mass with and without an absorber.

```
  end
end
xlabel('Excitation frequency (rad/s)');
ylabel('|x_1|');
text(2.1,0.045,'No vibration absorber');
text(0.3,0.02,'With vibration absorber');
```

Executing the script produces Figure 9.18. It is seen that the response of m_1 is attenuated in the frequency range around 2 rad/s, which is the undamped natural frequency of the primary system—that is, when $m_2 = 0$. In the system with the absorber, there are two degrees of freedom and the associated system behavior indicates the presence of two resonance frequencies. No attempt has been made to obtain an optimal set of parameters.

9.4 VIBRATIONS OF THIN BEAMS[17]

9.4.1 Beams with Uniform Cross Section

The governing nondimensional equation of motion for the transverse deflection $w'(x,t)$ of a beam of length L, cross-sectional area A, moment of inertia I, density ρ, and Young's modulus E subjected to a dynamic force $F(x,t)$ is

$$\frac{\partial^4 w}{\partial u^4} + \frac{\partial^2 w}{\partial \tau^2} = F_o(u,\tau) \tag{9.26}$$

where $u = x/L$, $\tau = c_0 t$, $w(u,\tau) = w'(x/L, c_0 t)/L$, $F_o(u,\tau) = F(x/L, c_0 t)L^3/EI$, $c_0 = rc_b/L^2$, $r^2 = I/A$, and $c_b^2 = E/\rho$.

Assume that the beam has the following general boundary conditions:

$\underline{u = 0}$

$$\frac{\partial^3 w}{\partial u^3} = -\alpha_1 w$$
$$\frac{\partial^2 w}{\partial u^2} = \gamma_1 \frac{\partial w}{\partial u} \tag{9.27a}$$

$\underline{u = 1}$

$$\frac{\partial^3 w}{\partial u^3} = \alpha_2 w + \frac{M_o}{m_o} \frac{\partial^2 w}{\partial \tau^2}$$
$$\frac{\partial^2 w}{\partial u^2} = -\gamma_2 \frac{\partial w}{\partial u} \tag{9.27b}$$

where M_o is the magnitude of an attached mass, $m_o = \rho A L$ is the mass of the beam,

$$\alpha_j = \frac{k_j L^3}{EI} \qquad \gamma_j = \frac{\beta_j L}{EI} \qquad j = 1,2$$

are the nondimensional linear and torsion spring constants, respectively, k_j is the linear spring constant, and β_j is the torsion spring constant.

Assuming that the initial conditions are zero, the solution to Eq. (9.26), subject to the general boundary conditions Eqs. (9.27a,b), is

$$w(u,\tau) = \sum_{n=1}^{\infty} \frac{W_n(u)}{\Omega_n^2 N_n} \int_0^1 \int_0^\tau F(u,\tau') W_n(u) \sin[\Omega_n(\tau - \tau')] d\tau' du \tag{9.28}$$

---

[17] This section was written by Edward B. Magrab and is adapted, in part, from E. B. Magrab, *Vibrations of Elastic Structural Members*, Sijthoff & Noordhoff, The Netherlands, 1979, Chapter IV.

where

$$W_n(u) = A'_n U(\Omega_n u) + B'_n V(\Omega_n u) + C'_n S(\Omega_n u) + D'_n T(\Omega_n u) \tag{9.29}$$

is the modal function corresponding to Ω_n,

$$U(u) = [\cos(u) + \cosh(u)]/2$$
$$V(u) = [\sin(u) + \sinh(u)]/2$$
$$S(u) = [\cosh(u) - \cos(u)]/2$$
$$T(u) = [\sinh(u) - \sin(u)]/2$$

and

$$N_n = \frac{1}{4\Omega_n}\{G_1 + \cosh 2\Omega_n (G_2 \tanh 2\Omega_n + G_3) + \cosh \Omega_n [(G_4 + G_6)\tanh \Omega_n$$
$$+ G_5 + G_7]\} + \frac{M_0}{m_0}W_n^2(1) \tag{9.30}$$

In Eqs. (9.30)

$$G_1 = \Omega_n(A'^2_n + C'^2_n - 2B'_n D'_n) + B'_n C'_n - 3A'_n D'_n + 0.25[(A'_n - C'_n)^2 - (B'_n - D'_n)^2]\sin 2\Omega_n$$
$$- 0.5(B'_n - D'_n)(A'_n - C'_n)\cos 2\Omega_n$$
$$G_2 = 0.25[(A'_n + C'_n)^2 + (B'_n + D'_n)^2]$$
$$G_3 = 0.5(B'_n + D'_n)(A'_n + C'_n)$$
$$G_4 = (A'^2_n - C'^2_n + D'^2_n - B'^2_n)\cos \Omega_n$$
$$G_5 = (A'^2_n - C'^2_n - D'^2_n + B'^2_n)\sin \Omega_n$$
$$G_6 = 2(A'_n B'_n - C'_n D'_n)\sin \Omega_n$$
$$G_7 = 2(A'_n D'_n - C'_n B'_n)\cos \Omega_n$$

In addition, the frequency coefficient $\Omega_n = \sqrt{\omega_n/c_0}$, where $\omega_n = 2\pi f_n$ is the radian natural frequency, is a root of

$$\Lambda(\Omega_n) = z_1[\cos \Omega_n \tanh \Omega_n + \sin \Omega_n] + z_2[\cos \Omega_n \tanh \Omega_n - \sin \Omega_n]$$
$$- 2z_3 \sin \Omega_n \tanh \Omega_n + z_4(\cos \Omega_n - 1/\cosh \Omega_n) \tag{9.31}$$
$$+ z_5(\cos \Omega_n + 1/\cosh \Omega_n) + 2z_6 \cos \Omega_n = 0$$

where

$$z_1 = [b_{1n}b_{2n}(a_{1n} + a_{2n}) + (b_{1n} - b_{2n})]$$
$$z_2 = [a_{1n}a_{2n}(b_{1n} - b_{2n}) - (a_{1n} + a_{2n})]$$
$$z_3 = (a_{1n}a_{2n} + b_{1n}b_{2n})$$

TABLE 9.3
Definition of the Coefficients A_n', B_n', C_n' and D_n'.

Case	a_{1n}	b_{1n}	A_n'	B_n'	C_n'	D_n'
1	$0 \le a_{1n} < \infty$	$0 \le b_{1n} < \infty$	E_n	1	b_{1n}	$-a_{1n}E_n$
2	$0 < a_{1n} \le \infty$	$0 \le b_{1n} < \infty$	$-E_n/a_{1n}$	1	b_{1n}	E_n
3	$0 \le a_{1n} < \infty$	$0 < b_{1n} \le \infty$	E_n	$1/b_{1n}$	1	$-a_{1n}E_n$
4	$0 < a_{1n} \le \infty$	$0 < b_{1n} \le \infty$	$-E_n/a_{1n}$	$1/b_{1n}$	1	E_n

Case	E_n
1	$\dfrac{a_{2n}V(\Omega_n)+(a_{2n}b_{1n}-1)S(\Omega_n)-b_{1n}T(\Omega_n)}{V(\Omega_n)-(a_{1n}+a_{2n})U(\Omega_n)+a_{1n}a_{2n}T(\Omega_n)}$
2	$\dfrac{a_{2n}V(\Omega_n)+(a_{2n}b_{1n}-1)S(\Omega_n)-b_{1n}T(\Omega_n)}{-(1/a_{1n})V(\Omega_n)+(a_{2n}/a_{1n}+1)U(\Omega_n)-a_{2n}T(\Omega_n)}$
3	$\dfrac{a_{2n}/b_{1n}V(\Omega_n)+(a_{2n}-1/b_{1n})S(\Omega_n)-T(\Omega_n)}{V(\Omega_n)-(a_{2n}+a_{1n})U(\Omega_n)+a_{1n}a_{2n}T(\Omega_n)}$
4	$\dfrac{a_{2n}/b_{1n}V(\Omega_n)+(a_{2n}-1/b_{1n})S(\Omega_n)-T(\Omega_n)}{-(1/a_{1n})V(\Omega_n)+(a_{2n}/a_{1n}+1)U(\Omega_n)-a_{2n}T(\Omega_n)}$

$$z_4 = (1 - a_{1n}a_{2n}b_{1n}b_{2n})$$
$$z_5 = (a_{2n}b_{2n} - a_{1n}b_{1n})$$
$$z_6 = (a_{1n}b_{2n} - a_{2n}b_{1n})$$

and

$$a_{1n} = \frac{\alpha_1}{\Omega_n^3} \qquad\qquad b_{1n} = \frac{\gamma_1}{\Omega_n}$$

$$a_{2n} = \frac{\alpha_2}{\Omega_n^3} - \frac{M_0}{m_0}\Omega_n \qquad\qquad b_{2n} = -\frac{\gamma_2}{\Omega_n}$$

The expressions for A_n', B_n', C_n', and D_n' are given in Table 9.3. These expressions are a function of the boundary conditions, which have been chosen so that numerous special cases can be considered. These special cases are obtained by setting the quantities a_{1n}, a_{2n}, b_{1n}, and b_{2n} either to 0 or to ∞ as the case may be. Several of the more common sets of boundary conditions are summarized in Table 9.4, along with their corresponding relations for A_n', B_n', C_n', D_n', and $\Lambda(\Omega_n)$.

When the beam is subjected to an impulse load at $u = \xi$ $(0 < \xi < 1)$—that is,

TABLE 9.4
Several Special Cases of the General Solution Given in Table 9.3

Boundary
conditions[†]

$u=0$	$u=1$	M_0	a_{1n}	b_{1n}	a_{2n}	b_{2n}	A'_n	B'_n	C'_n	D'_n
ss	ss	0	∞	0	∞	0	0	1	0	-1
c	c	0	∞	∞	∞	∞	0	0	1	$-S(\Omega_n)/T(\Omega_n)$
c	f	M_0	∞	∞	$-(M_0/m_0)\Omega_n$	0	0	0	1	$-\dfrac{T(\Omega_n)+(\Omega_n M_0/m_0)S(\Omega_n)}{U(\Omega_n)-(\Omega_n M_0/m_0)T(\Omega_n)}$
c	f	0	∞	∞	0	0	0	0	1	$-T(\Omega_n)/U(\Omega_n)$
c	ss	0	∞	∞	∞	0	0	0	1	$-S(\Omega_n)/T(\Omega_n)$

Boundary
conditions[†]

$u=0$	$u=1$	$\Lambda(\Omega_n)$	Case No. Table 9.3
ss	ss	$\sin(\Omega_n)$	2
c	c	$\cos(\Omega_n)\cosh(\Omega_n)-1$	4
c	f	$(M_0/m_0)\Omega_n[\cos(\Omega_n)\sinh(\Omega_n)$ $-\sin(\Omega_n)\cosh(\Omega_n)]+\cos(\Omega_n)\cosh(\Omega_n)+1$	4
c	f	$\cos(\Omega_n)\cosh(\Omega_n)+1$	4
c	ss	$\tanh(\Omega_n)-\tan(\Omega_n)$	4

[†] ss = simply supported; c = clamped; f = free.

$$F_o(u,\tau) = \delta(u-\xi)\delta(\tau)$$

then Eq. (9.28) becomes

$$w(u,\tau) = \sum_{n=1}^{\infty} \frac{W_n(u)W_n(\xi)}{\Omega_n^2 N_n}\sin(\Omega_n\tau) \tag{9.32}$$

Since the quantities a_{1n}, a_{2n}, b_{1n}, and b_{2n} can each have values that vary from 0 to ∞, there are 16 combinations of these four quantities at their extreme values that have to be considered. Since MATLAB cannot be used to take the limits, each of these 16 combinations requires that Eq. (9.31) be algebraically manipulated to obtain the proper form of each of these expressions. Thus, the following scheme shown in Table 9.5 has been used to identify each of these 16 cases, and at the same time provide a means to locate the name of the function that contains the appropriate expression. Each of the four digits identified as b2, a2, b1, and a1 is appended to the string 'beam'. Thus, the file name is ['beam' 'b2' 'a2' 'b1' 'a1'],

TABLE 9.5
Function Naming Scheme for the 16 Special Cases of Eq. (9.35)

b_2	0	0	0	0	0	0	0	0
a_2	0	0	0	0	∞	∞	∞	∞
b_1	0	0	∞	∞	0	0	∞	∞
a_1	0	∞	0	∞	0	∞	0	∞
$b_2a_2b_1a_1$	0000	0001	0010	0011	0100	0101	0110	0111
b_2	∞	∞	∞	∞	∞	∞	∞	∞
a_2	0	0	0	0	∞	∞	∞	∞
b_1	0	0	∞	∞	0	0	∞	∞
a_1	0	∞	0	∞	0	∞	0	∞
$b_2a_2b_1a_1$	1000	1001	1010	1011	1100	1101	1110	1111

where b2, a2, b1, and a1 have the values of either 0 or 1. The value of 1 signifies that the quantity can increase from a value greater than zero up to a very large value, and the value of 0 means that the quantity can increase from zero to a very large value that is $< \infty$. The *beamxxxx* functions, which are given in Appendix B at the end of the chapter, are the 16 expressions for $\Lambda(\Omega_n) = 0$ used to determine the natural frequency coefficients Ω_n. In the same manner, we must determine the appropriate $W_n(u)$ and the name of the file in which it resides. However, since b_{2n} doesn't appear in these expressions we have only eight functions. Therefore, the functions that compute the mode shapes are accessed by ['mode' '0' 'a2' 'b1' 'a1']. Hence, a total of 24 functions have to be created. Furthermore, since we have determined the values for A_n', B_n', C_n', and D_n' for each of these special cases, we also compute N_n in the functions *mode0xxx*. The functions *beamxxxx* and *mode0xxx* are given in Appendix B at the end of this chapter.

Example 9.1 Display of the normal modes and impulse response

Let us create a script and its supporting functions with the following features:

1. Permits the user to select a wide combination of boundary conditions at each end of the beam

2. Computes the first 20 natural frequency coefficients and displays the first four normalized mode shapes and their corresponding values of Ω_n/π.

3. Uses these 20 natural frequency coefficients to compute and display the beam's displacement at 8 values of τ from 0.1 to 0.8 when an impulse force is applied at $\xi = 0.4$.

To implement this script we create three functions in addition to the 24 given in Appendix B at the end of this chapter. The first is *GetBC*, which solicits from the user the boundary conditions. The second is *BeamEqn*, which converts the boundary conditions selected into the file names that access the appropriate $\Lambda(\Omega_n)$ and $W_n(u)$. The third is Nn, which computes N_n. These three functions are given in Appendix B. For convenience we also use the multiple root-finding function *ManyZeros*, which has been described in Section 4.3.2 and in Figure 5.1. It is given below for completeness.

```
function nRoots = ManyZeros(FileName, n, xstart, toler, increment, g)
x = xstart;
dx = increment;
for m = 1:n
 s1 = sign(feval(FileName, x, g));
 while dx/x >toler
   if s1 ~= sign(feval(FileName, x+dx, g ))
     dx = dx/2;
   else
     x = x+dx;
   end
 end
 nRoots(m) = x;
 dx = increment;
 x = 1.05*x;
end
```

The script is:

```
nfnum = 20; u = 0:0.02:1; xi = 0.4;
tau = 0.1:.1:.8;
gg = GetBC;
[nffile,modefile] = BeamEqn(gg(7:10));
nfcoeff = ManyZeros(nffile,nfnum, 0.4, 1e–6, .4, gg(1:6));
lit = ['First ','Second','Third ','Fourth'];
for j = 1:nfnum
 wnx(j) = feval(modefile, nfcoeff(j),gg(1:6),xi);
 [mode,c] = feval(modefile, nfcoeff(j),gg(1:6),u);
 wnu(j,:) = mode;
 nn(j) = c;
 if j <= 4
   subplot(2,2,j)
   plot(u,mode/max(abs(mode)),'k',[0,1],[0,0],'k-')
   axis([0,1,–1,1])
   xlabel('Beam position')
   ylabel('Relative amplitude')
   title([lit(j*6–5:j*6),' mode: \Omega/\pi = ' num2str(nfcoeff(j)/pi,6)])
 end
end
wtau = (wnu'.*repmat(wnx./(nn.*nfcoeff.^2),length(u),1))*sin(nfcoeff*tau);
figure(2)
```

```
for k = 1:8
 if k<5
  subplot(4,2,2*k−1)
 else
  subplot(4,2,2*k−8)
 end
 plot(u',−wtau(:,k))
 if k == 4|k == 8
  xlabel('Beam position')
 end
 text(.1,.15,['\tau = ' num2str(tau(k),3)])
 axis([0 1 −.2 .2])
end
```

When we execute this script for the case of a beam clamped at $u = 0$ and free at the end $u = 1$, but with $M_o/m_o = 0.2$, we obtain Figures 9.19 and 9.20. In addition, the following interaction first takes place in the MATLAB command window:

Enter one of the following numbers to select the bc at x = 0:
  [1] clamped (w = dw/dx = 0)
  [2] simply supported (w = d^2w/dx^2 = 0)
  [3] linear spring (d^2w/dx^2 = 0 and d^3w/dx^3 = kw)
  [4] torsion spring (d^2w/dx^2 = bdw/dx and w = 0)
  [5] linear spring and torsion spring (d^2w/dx^2 = bdw/dx and
      d^3w/dx^3 = kw)
Enter number for bc at x = 0: 1

where the user entered the value of 1. Then the following is displayed to the screen:

Enter one of the following numbers to select the bc at x = L:
  [1] clamped (w = dw/dx = 0)
  [2] simply supported (w = d^2w/dx^2 = 0)
  [3] vertically constrained slider with or without mass(dw/dx = 0 and
      d^3w/dx^3 = 0 or d^3w/dx^3 = mw
  [4] linear spring with or without attached mass (d^2w/dx^2 = 0 and
      d^3w/dx^3 = kw)
  [5] free with or without attached mass (d^2w/dx^2 = 0 and d^3w/dx^3 = 0 or
      d^3w/dx^3 = mw)
  [6] torsion spring (d^2w/dx^2 = bdw/dx and w = 0)
  [7] linear spring with or without attached mass and torsion spring
      (d^2w/dx^2 = bdw/dx and d^3w/dx^3 = kw)
Enter number for bc at x = L 5

where the user entered the selection of 5. This is followed by

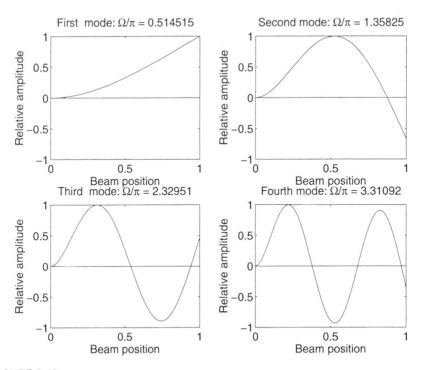

FIGURE 9.19
First four mode shapes of a beam clamped at one end and free at the other end with $M_o/m_o = 0.2$.

Enter ratio of attached mass to mass of beam (0 to 10000).
If no mass then enter zero. 0.2

where the value of 0.2 was entered by the user.

The results shown in Figure 9.20 can also be animated with the following script, in which we have selected τ to vary from 0 to $2\pi/\Omega_1$ in increments of 0.05. This interval is approximately equal to one period for $M_o/m_o = 0.2$: $2\pi/\Omega_1 \cong 3.9$.

```
nfnum = 20; u = 0:0.02:1; xi = 0.4; M = 2;
tau = 0.1:0.05:3.9;
gg = GetBC;
[nffile,modefile] = BeamEqn(gg(7:10));
nfcoeff = ManyZeros(nffile,nfnum, 0.4, 1e–6, .4, gg(1:6));
for j = 1:nfnum
  wnx(j) = feval(modefile, nfcoeff(j),gg(1:6),xi);
  [mode,c] = feval(modefile, nfcoeff(j),gg(1:6),u);
  wnu(j,:) = mode;
  nn(j) = c;
```

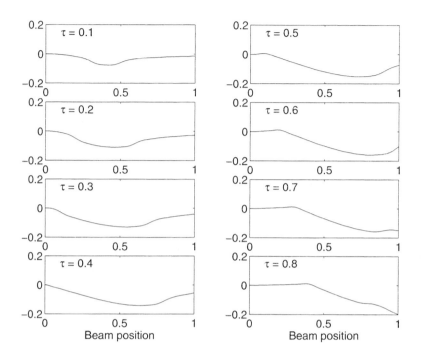

FIGURE 9.20
Response of a beam clamped at one end and free at the other end with $M_o/m_o = 0.2$ when an impulse is applied at $\xi = 0.4$.

```
end
wtau = (wnu'.*repmat(wnx./(nn.*nfcoeff.^2),length(u),1))*sin(nfcoeff*tau);
set(gca,'nextplot','replacechildren')
for j = 1:length(tau)
 plot(u',-wtau(:,j))
 axis([0 1 -.2 .2])
 BeamFrame(j) = getframe;
end
movie(BeamFrame,M)
```

The set command is used to prevent the plot function from resetting itself each time it is called. The getframe command returns a pixel snapshot of the current picture window. The movie function displays sequentially all the members of *BeamFrame M* = 2 times.

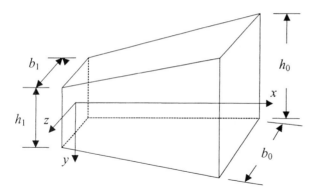

FIGURE 9.21
Nomenclature for a tapered beam.

9.4.2 Beams With Variable Cross Section

The nondimensional equation of motion of a beam of variable cross section shown in Figure 9.21 undergoing free harmonic oscillations in the z-direction is

$$\frac{d^2}{du^2}\left[I(u)\frac{d^2w}{du^2}\right] - \Omega'^4 A(u)w = 0 \tag{9.33}$$

where

$$I(u) = [\alpha + (1-\alpha)u]^3[\beta + (1-\beta)u^{n-1}]$$

$$A(u) = [\alpha + (1-\alpha)u][\beta + (1-\beta)u^{n-1}]$$

$$\Omega'^4 = \omega^2 L^4 / c_b^2 r_0^2$$

and r_0 is the radius of gyration of the cross section at $u = 1$, $\alpha = h_1/h_0 \le 1$ is the depth taper ratio, $\beta = b_1/b_0 \le 1$ is the thickness taper ratio, and n is a positive constant. This type of beam is called a double-tapered beam. When $\beta = 0$, the beam tapers to a point at $u = 0$ in the xz-plane, and when $\alpha = 0$, the beam tapers to a point at $u = 0$ in the yz-plane. When $\beta = \alpha = 1$, we have a beam of constant cross section. When the thickness taper ratio and the depth taper ratio are linearly proportional to u, then $n = 2$. When the beam has constant thickness ($\beta = 1$), then $n = 1$. When the thickness and depth taper ratios are equal, then $\beta = \alpha$.

We shall confine the discussion to a double-tapered beam for which $\beta = \alpha$ and $n = 2$. Then Eq. (9.33) can be written as

$$\frac{d^2}{d\varphi^2}\left[\varphi^4 \frac{d^2w}{d\varphi^2}\right] - \lambda^4 \varphi^2 w = 0 \tag{9.34}$$

where

$$\varphi = [\alpha + (1-\alpha)u]$$
$$\lambda = \Omega'\alpha/(1-\alpha)$$

The solution of Eq. (9.34) is

$$w(\varphi) = \varphi^{-1}\left[AJ_2(2\lambda\sqrt{\varphi}) + BY_2(2\lambda\sqrt{\varphi}) + CI_2(2\lambda\sqrt{\varphi}) + DK_2(2\lambda\sqrt{\varphi})\right] \tag{9.35}$$

where $J_2(z)$ and $Y_2(z)$ and $I_2(z)$ and $K_2(z)$ are the Bessel functions and the modified Bessel functions of the first and second kind of order 2, respectively.

The boundary conditions can be obtained from Eqs. (9.27a,b) by replacing $\partial/\partial u$ with $[(1-\alpha)/\alpha]d/d\varphi$.

Example 9.2 Three lowest natural frequencies of a double-tapered cantilever beam

We shall determine the lowest three natural frequency coefficients for a cantilever beam that is clamped at $u = 1$ and free at $u = 0$ for a range of values of α. The boundary conditions are:

$\underline{u = 1}$ ($\varphi = 1$)

$$w = 0 \qquad \frac{dw}{d\varphi} = 0 \tag{9.36a}$$

$\underline{u = 0}$ ($\varphi = \alpha$)

$$\frac{d^2w}{d\varphi^2} = 0 \qquad \frac{d^3w}{d\varphi^3} = 0 \tag{9.36b}$$

Substituting Eq. (9.35) into Eqs. (9.36a,b) yields the following equation from which the natural frequency coefficients λ_n can be determined.

$$\begin{vmatrix} J_5(2\lambda\sqrt{\alpha}) & Y_5(2\lambda\sqrt{\alpha}) & -I_5(2\lambda\sqrt{\alpha}) & K_5(2\lambda\sqrt{\alpha}) \\ J_4(2\lambda\sqrt{\alpha}) & Y_4(2\lambda\sqrt{\alpha}) & I_4(2\lambda\sqrt{\alpha}) & K_4(2\lambda\sqrt{\alpha}) \\ J_2(2\lambda) & Y_2(2\lambda) & I_2(2\lambda) & K_2(2\lambda) \\ J_3(2\lambda) & Y_3(2\lambda) & -I_3(2\lambda) & K_3(2\lambda) \end{vmatrix} = 0 \tag{9.37}$$

To obtain Eq. (9.37), we used the fact that

$$\frac{d}{d\varphi}\left[\varphi^{-n/2}J_n(2\lambda\sqrt{\varphi})\right] = -\lambda\varphi^{-(n+1)/2}J_{n+1}(2\lambda\sqrt{\varphi})$$

$$\frac{d}{d\varphi}\left[\varphi^{-n/2}Y_n(2\lambda\sqrt{\varphi})\right] = -\lambda\varphi^{-(n+1)/2}Y_{n+1}(2\lambda\sqrt{\varphi})$$

$$\frac{d}{d\varphi}\left[\varphi^{-n/2}I_n(2\lambda\sqrt{\varphi})\right] = \lambda\varphi^{-(n+1)/2}I_{n+1}(2\lambda\sqrt{\varphi})$$

$$\frac{d}{d\varphi}\left[\varphi^{-n/2}K_n(2\lambda\sqrt{\varphi})\right] = -\lambda\varphi^{-(n+1)/2}K_{n+1}(2\lambda\sqrt{\varphi})$$

The solution for the special case when $\beta = \alpha = 1$ is obtained from the execution of the script given in Example 9.1 for the case of a cantilever beam—that is, the solution to the equation given in the fourth row of Table 9.4 under the column labeled $\Lambda(\Omega_n)$. The results are $\lambda_1 = \Omega_1 = 1.8751$, $\lambda_2 = \Omega_2 = 4.6941$, and $\lambda_3 = \Omega_3 = 7.8548$.

To obtain the solution of Eq. (9.37), we first create the function *TaperedBeam*.

```
function r = TaperedBeam(x,alpha)
a1 = 2*x;
a2 = a1*sqrt(alpha);
r = det([besselj(5,a2) bessely(5,a2) -besseli(5,a2) besselk(5,a2);...
         besselj(4,a2) bessely(4,a2) besseli(4,a2) besselk(4,a2);...
         besselj(2,a1) bessely(2,a1) besseli(2,a1) besselk(2,a1);...
         besselj(3,a1) bessely(3,a1) -besseli(3,a1) besselk(3,a1)]);
```

The script is

```
c = [1 1.2 1.4 1.6 1.8 2 2.5 3 3.5 4 5 6 7 8 9 10];
a = 1./c;
for k = 2:length(a)
  b(k,:) = ManyZeros('TaperedBeam', 3, 0.4, 1e-6, 0.4, a(k))*(1-a(k))/a(k);
end
b(1,:) = [1.8751 4.6941 7.8548];
semilogy(c,b,'k')
xlabel('1/\alpha')
ylabel('Natural frequency coefficient (\lambda)')
title('Double-tapered cantilever beam')
text(8.5,20,'first')
text(8.5,32, 'second')
text(8.5,45,'third')
```

Execution of this script results in Figure 9.22.

9.4.3 Beam Carrying a Concentrated Mass

The nondimensional equation of motion of a beam undergoing free harmonic oscillations and carrying a concentrated mass M_0' at $u = \xi$ is

$$\frac{d^4w}{du^4} - \Omega^4[1 + \frac{M_0'}{m_0}\delta(u - \xi)]w = 0 \tag{9.38}$$

where $w = w(u)$. The boundary conditions are those given by Eq. (9.27a,b). The general solution to Eq. (9.38) is

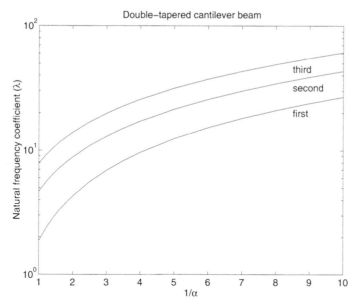

FIGURE 9.22
First three natural frequency coefficients for a double-tapered cantilever beam.

$$w(u)/w(\xi) = AU(\Omega u) + BV(\Omega u) + CS(\Omega u) + DT(\Omega u) +$$
$$\frac{M_0'}{m_0}\Omega T(\Omega(u-\xi))H(u-\xi) \tag{9.39}$$

where $H(u-\xi)$ is the unit step function: $H(u-\xi < 0) = 0$ and $H(u-\xi > 0) = 1$. The frequency coefficients Ω_n are determined from Eq. (9.39) evaluated at $u = \xi$. Thus,

$$1 = AU(\Omega_n\xi) + BV(\Omega_n\xi) + CS(\Omega_n\xi) + DT(\Omega_n\xi) \tag{9.40}$$

since $T(0) = 0$. The constants $A, \ldots, D$ are determined from the substitution of Eq. (9.39) into the boundary conditions given by Eqs. (9.27a,b). The corresponding mode shape is

$$w_n(u) = A_nU(\Omega_n u) + B_nV(\Omega_n u) + C_nS(\Omega_n u) + D_nT(\Omega_n u)$$
$$+\frac{M_0'}{m_0}\Omega_n T(\Omega_n(u-\xi))H(u-\xi) \tag{9.41}$$

We now illustrate these results with an example.

Example 9.3 Mode shapes of a simply supported beam carrying a mass

We determine and plot the first three natural frequency coefficients of a beam simply supported at both ends as the position of the mass ξ varies from 0.05 to 0.5 and M_0'/m_0 has the three values: 0.1, 1, and 10. Since the beam's boundary conditions are the same at each end, the values of Ω_n will be symmetrical around $\xi = 0.5$. In addition, we plot the mode shapes and compare them to those of a beam simply supported at both ends without the attached mass.

The boundary conditions are

$$w(0) = \frac{d^2 w(0)}{du^2} = 0$$

$$w(1) = \frac{d^2 w(1)}{du^2} = 0 \tag{9.42}$$

Substituting Eq. (9.39) into Eq. (9.42), we find that $A = C = 0$ and

$$B = \frac{M_0' \Omega}{G_0 m_0} [T(\Omega) V(\Omega \varepsilon) - V(\Omega) T(\Omega \varepsilon)]$$

$$D = \frac{M_0' \Omega}{G_0 m_0} [T(\Omega) T(\Omega \varepsilon) - V(\Omega) V(\Omega \varepsilon)] \tag{9.43}$$

$$G_0 = V^2(\Omega) - T^2(\Omega)$$

where $\varepsilon = 1 - \xi$. Then Eq. (9.40) becomes

$$V^2(\Omega_n) - T^2(\Omega_n) - \frac{M_0'}{m_0} \Omega_n \{ V(\Omega_n \xi)[T(\Omega_n)V(\Omega_n \varepsilon) - V(\Omega_n)T(\Omega_n \varepsilon)]$$

$$+ T(\Omega_n \xi)[T(\Omega_n)T(\Omega_n \varepsilon) - V(\Omega_n)V(\Omega_n \varepsilon)]\} = 0 \tag{9.44}$$

Using Eq. (9.44) in Eq. (9.41), the mode shape is

$$w_n(u) = B_n V(\Omega_n u) + D_n T(\Omega_n u) + \frac{M_0'}{m_0} \Omega_n T(\Omega_n(u - \xi)) H(u - \xi) \tag{9.45}$$

where B_n and D_n are given by Eq. (9.43) with $\Omega = \Omega_n$.

For a simply supported beam without an attached mass we use the first row of Table 9.4 and find that $\Omega_n = n\pi$ and $w_n(u) = \sin(n\pi u)$.

First we create the following function to represent Eq. (9.44):

```
function nf = BeamMass(om,v)
ee = 1–v(1);
p1 = Vvib(om)^2–Tvib(om)^2;
p2 = Vvib(om*v(1))*(Tvib(om)*Vvib(om*ee)–Vvib(om)*Tvib(om*ee));
p3 = Tvib(om*v(1))*(Tvib(om)*Tvib(om*ee)–Vvib(om)*Vvib(om*ee));
nf = p1–v(2)*om*(p2+p3);
```

where $v(1) = \xi$, $v(2) = M_0'/m_0$, and *Vvib* and *Tvib* are given in the Appendix B at the end of the chapter.

Next we create a function to compute the mode shape given by Eq. (9.45). Hence,

```
function [modeshape,uu] = BeamMassMode(om,xi)
ee = 1-xi;
p1 = Vvib(om)^2-Tvib(om)^2;
p2 = (Tvib(om)*Vvib(om*ee)-Vvib(om)*Tvib(om*ee))/p1;
p3 = (Tvib(om)*Tvib(om*ee)-Vvib(om)*Vvib(om*ee))/p1;
u1 = 0:0.01:xi;
modeshape1 = Vvib(om*u1)*p2+Tvib(om*u1)*p3;
u = xi+0.01:0.01:1;
modeshape2 = Vvib(om*u)*p2+Tvib(om*u)*p3+Tvib(om*(u-xi));
modeshape = [modeshape1 modeshape2];
modeshape = modeshape/max(abs(modeshape));
uu = [u1 u];
```

The script is

```
mo = [.1 1 10];
xi = linspace(0.05,.5,10);
for m = 1:length(mo)
  for k = 1:length(xi)
    coeff(m,k,:) = ManyZeros('BeamMass', 3, 0.4, 1e-6, 0.4, [xi(k), mo(m)])/pi;
  end
end
lab = ['first ';'second';'third '];
figure(1)
for kk = 1:3
  plot(xi,coeff(1,:,kk),'k-', xi,coeff(2,:,kk),'k--',xi,coeff(3,:,kk),'k:')
  hold on
  plot([0.05 0.1],[kk kk+.2],'k-')
  text(0.1,kk+.2,'M/m = 0')
  text(.4,kk+.1,lab(kk,:))
end
axis([0.05 .5 0 3.5])
xlabel('Mass position')
ylabel('\Omega/\pi')
title('Simply supported beam with attached mass')
legend(['M/m = ' num2str(mo(1))],['M/m = ' num2str(mo(2))],...
       ['M/m = ' num2str(mo(3))],3)
figure(2)
sig = 1;
lab = ['First  mode';'Second mode';'Third  mode'];
for k = 1:3
  if k == 3, sig = -1;end;
  for kk = 1:3
    subplot(3,3,3*(k-1)+kk)
    [shape,u] = BeamMassMode(coeff(kk,2,k)*pi,xi(8));
```

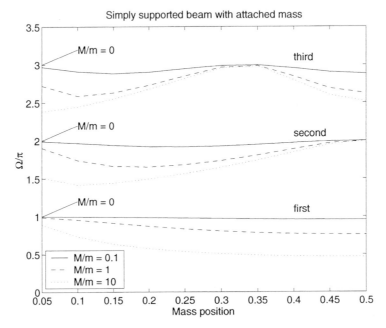

FIGURE 9.23
Natural frequency coefficients of a beam simply supported at each end as a function of the position and magnitude of the attached mass.

```
    plot(u,shape,'k-',u,sig*sin(k*u*pi),'k--',[0 1],[0 0],'k-')
    axis([0 1 -1 1])
    if k == 1, title([' M/m = ' num2str(mo(kk))]), end;
    if kk == 1, ylabel(lab(k,: )),end;
  end
end
```

Execution of this script results in Figures 9.23 and 9.24.

EXERCISES

9.1 For the two-mass system given by Eqs. (9.1), numerically determine the corresponding orbit in the (r,θ) plane for the initial conditions $r(0) = 2.0$, $dr(0)/dt = 0.0$, $\theta(0) = 0.0$, and $d\theta(0)/dt = 0.5$. Use ode45 with the following parameter values: (a) time span of 20 units, step size of 20/400, relative tolerance of 10^{-3}, and absolute tolerance of 10^{-3} for each of the states; and (b) time span of 20 units, step size of 20/4000, relative tolerance of 10^{-6}, and absolute tolerance of 10^{-6} for each of the states.

   Determine whether or not the angular momentum per unit mass $r^2\dot\theta$ is conserved in each case throughout the time span of 20 units and display graphs of the following: (i) orbits; and (ii) angular momentum per unit mass versus time.

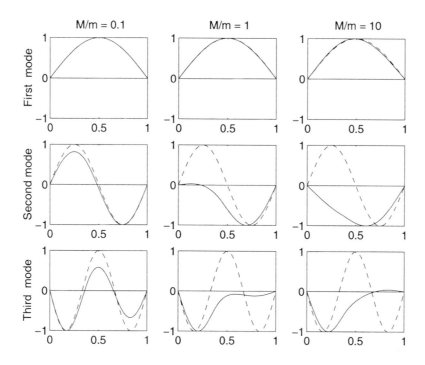

FIGURE 9.24
Mode shapes of a beam simply supported at each end with a mass attached at $\xi = 0.4$: solid line—beam with mass; dashed line—beam without mass.

9.2 For the free response of a spring-mass-damper system given by Eq. (9.8), use the function *freeosc.m* to numerically determine the responses for selected underdamped, overdamped, and critically damped cases. Compare these responses with those computed from the following equations:[18]

Underdamped

$$x(\tau) = e^{-\zeta\tau}\{x_o \cos(\sqrt{1-\zeta^2}\,\tau) + \frac{v_o + \zeta x_o}{\sqrt{1-\zeta^2}}\sin(\sqrt{1-\zeta^2}\,\tau)\}$$

Critically damped

$$x(\tau) = [x_o + (v_o + x_o)\tau]e^{-\tau}$$

Overdamped

$$x(\tau) = C_1 e^{(-\zeta+\sqrt{\zeta^2-1})\tau} + C_2 e^{(-\zeta-\sqrt{\zeta^2-1})\tau}$$

---

[18] D. J. Inman, *ibid.*, Section 1.3; S. S. Rao, *ibid.*, Section 2.6.

where $\tau = \omega_n t$ and

$$C_1 = \frac{x_o(\zeta + \sqrt{\zeta^2 - 1}) + v_o}{2\sqrt{\zeta^2 - 1}}$$

$$C_2 = \frac{-x_o(\zeta - \sqrt{\zeta^2 - 1}) - v_o}{2\sqrt{\zeta^2 - 1}}$$

9.3 A mass m slides along a rough rod of length l, which is pivoted at the end O. The angular orientation of the rod with respect to the horizontal is given by $\theta(t)$, and the location of the mass along the rod from its pivot point is given by r. When the rod rotates in the horizontal plane with a constant angular speed $d\theta/dt = \omega$, the equation of motion of mass m is

$$\ddot{r} + 2\mu \omega \dot{r} - \omega^2 r = 0$$

where μ is the coefficient of friction between the rod and the mass. For $\mu = 0.2$, $l = 3.0$ m, $\omega = 6$ rad/s, and initial conditions $r(0) = 1.0$ m and $\dot{r}(0) = 0.0$ m/s, graph the path of the mass in the (r, θ) plane until it leaves the rod.

9.4 The ratio of the measured amplitude to the true acceleration amplitude for an accelerometer is

$$\frac{A_m}{A_t} = \frac{1}{\sqrt{(1 - r^2)^2 + 4\zeta^2 r^2}}$$

where $r = \omega/\omega_n$, ω is the acceleration frequency, ω_n is the accelerometer's natural frequency, and ζ is the accelerometer's damping factor. Obtain the following:

(a) A plot of A_m/A_t as a function of r and ζ.

(b) The damping factor of an accelerometer with a mass $m = 0.01$ kg and natural frequency of 150 Hz that is to measure accelerations at 6000 rpm with an error e

$$e = 100\left(1 - \frac{A_m}{A_t}\right) \%$$

of $\pm 2.0\%$.[19]

9.5 The ratio of the measured amplitude to the true displacement amplitude of a seismometer is[20]

$$\frac{d_m}{d_t} = \frac{r^2}{\sqrt{(1 - r^2)^2 + 4\zeta^2 r^2}}$$

where $r = \omega/\omega_n$, ω is the acceleration frequency, ω_n is the seismometer's natural frequency, and ζ is the seismometer's damping factor. Obtain the following:

(a) A plot of d_m/d_t as a function of r and ζ.

---

[19] D. J. Inman, *ibid.*, Section 2.6; S. S. Rao, *ibid.*, Section 10.3.
[20] S. S. Rao, *ibid.*, Section 10.3.

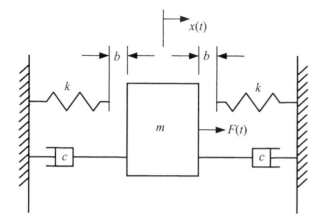

FIGURE 9.25
Spring-mass-damper system with dead zone.

(b) determine the maximum natural frequency of the seismometer to measure vibrations in the range of 500 rpm to 1500 rpm with an error less than ±2.0 %.

9.6 A single-degree-of-freedom system is shown in Figure 9.25 with a dead zone of width $2b$ centered on its equilibrium position. The governing equations of the system are

$$m\ddot{x} + k(x+b) + 2c\dot{x} = F(t) \quad x < -b$$
$$m\ddot{x} + 2c\dot{x} = F(t) \quad -b \leq x \leq b$$
$$m\ddot{x} + k(x-b) + 2c\dot{x} = F(t) \quad x > b$$

Determine the free response of a system with $m = 10.0$ kg, $k = 150 \times 10^3$ N/m and $c = 50$ Ns/m when the motion is initiated from $x(0) = 0$ and $dx(0)/dt = 20$ m/s in the following cases: (a) dead zone $b = 0.5 \, \mu m$; and (b) dead zone $b = 5.0 \, \mu m$. Also determine the forced response of the system when $F(t) = 20\cos(12t)u(t)$ N, where $u(t)$ is the unit step function.

9.7 The transfer function for a mechanical system shown in Figure 9.26 when subjected to base excitation $x_b(t)$ is

$$G(s) = \frac{x_m(s)}{x_b(s)} = \frac{2\zeta\omega_n s + \omega_n^2}{s^2 + 2\zeta\omega_n s + \omega_n^2}$$

Use bode to determine the amplitude and phase response of this system. Compare these results with those obtained from the analytical solution:

$$G(\omega) = \sqrt{\frac{\omega_n^4 + (2\zeta\omega\omega_n)^2}{(\omega_n^2 - \omega^2)^2 + (2\zeta\omega\omega_n)^2}}$$

$$\phi(\omega) = \tan^{-1}\left(\frac{2\zeta\omega}{\omega_n}\right) - \tan^{-1}\left(\frac{2\zeta\omega\omega_n}{\omega_n^2 - \omega^2}\right)$$

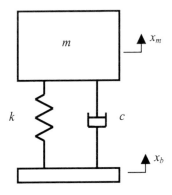

FIGURE 9.26
Spring-mass-damper system excited at its base.

9.8 Consider the vibration absorber discussed in Section 9.3.2 for the undamped case—that is, when c_1 = c_2 = 0. Let the ratio of the secondary mass to the primary mass be 0.2 and the ratio of the natural frequency of the secondary mass to the natural frequency of the primary mass be 1.0. Plot the nondimensional frequency-response functions for mass m_1 and mass m_2 and verify the following features: (a) that the resonance (pole) locations coincide in both plots and (b) that there is an anti-resonance (zero) in the response curve of mass m_1 at the absorber natural frequency.

9.9 Consider the vibration absorber discussed in Section 9.3.2. Set c_1 = 0 and fix the ratio of the secondary mass to the primary mass at 0.05. Let the ratio of natural frequency of the absorber to the natural frequency of the primary mass be 1.0. For various values of the absorber's damping factor, plot the frequency-response curves for the primary mass and verify that the different graphs intersect at two frequency locations. What should be the ratio of the natural frequency of the absorber to the natural frequency of the primary mass if the response amplitudes at the aforementioned frequency locations are the same? Determine the corresponding value of ζ for this absorber, which is often referred to as the optimally tuned vibration absorber.[21]

9.10 An overhead crane's trolley is carrying, via a cable, a load of mass m as shown in Figure 9.27. When the trolley is moved with an acceleration $b(t)$, the governing equation of motion of the crane load is

$$L\frac{d^2\theta}{dt^2} + g\sin\theta = -b(t)\cos\theta$$

where g = 9.8 m/s^2 is the gravity constant. If the cable length is 2 m, then graph the swing motion $\theta(t)$ for the following accelerations of the trolley over the time interval $0 \le t \le 10$ s:

(a) $b(t) = 5u(t)$ m/s^2, $\theta(0)$ = 0.2 rad and $d\theta(0)/dt$ = 0 rad/s.

(b) $b(t) = 0.2u(t)$ m/s^2, $\theta(0)$ = 0.2 rad and $d\theta(0)/dt$ = 0 rad/s, where $u(t)$ is the unit step function.

9.11 A model that is frequently used to study the bounce-pitch motion of a vehicle is shown in Figure 9.28. The equations governing the free oscillations of the undamped system are

---

[21] S. S. Rao, *ibid.*, Section 9.10.

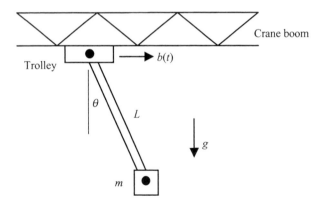

FIGURE 9.27
Trolley on an overhead crane carrying a swinging load m.

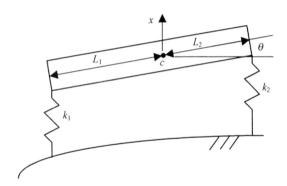

FIGURE 9.28
Two-degree-of-freedom model of a vehicle.

$$m\frac{d^2x}{dt^2}+(k_1+k_2)x+(L_2k_2-L_1k_1)\theta=0$$

$$I_c\frac{d^2\theta}{dt^2}+(k_1L_1^2+k_2L_2^2)\theta+(L_2k_2-L_1k_1)x=0$$

If k_1 = 1000 lb./ft, k_2 = 1500 lb./ft, L_1 = 5 ft, L_2 = 4 ft, m = 50 slug, and I_c = 1000 slug·ft², then by using the associated eigenvalue problem find the natural frequencies, mode shapes, and node locations.

9.12 A vehicle suspension system can be modeled as shown in Figure 9.29. The governing equations of this system are

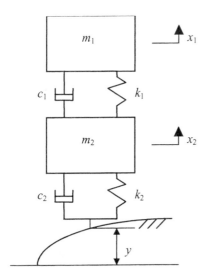

FIGURE 9.29
One-quarter car model of a vehicle suspension system.

$$m_1 \frac{d^2 x_1}{dt^2} + c_1 \left(\frac{dx_1}{dt} - \frac{dx_2}{dt} \right) + k_1 (x_1 - x_2) = 0$$

$$m_2 \frac{d^2 x_2}{dt^2} + c_1 \left(\frac{dx_2}{dt} - \frac{dx_1}{dt} \right) + k_1 (x_2 - x_1) + k_2 x_2 + c_2 x_2 = k_2 y + c_2 \frac{dy}{dt}$$

Determine the free response of the system when its initial conditions are $x_1(0) = 0.5$ m, $dx_1(0)/dt = 0$ m/s, $x_2(0) = 0.2$ m, and $dx_2(0)/dt = 0$ m/s. Let $m_1 = 1$ kg, $m_2 = 2$ kg, $c_1 = 1$ N/m/s, $c_2 = 5$ N/m/s, $k_1 = 10$ N/m, and $k_2 = 30$ N/m. Also, take the Laplace transform the equations of motion and, assuming that the initial conditions are zero, plot the frequency response curves for the system.

9.13 Consider a spinning rigid circular shaft that is elastically supported at each end as shown in Figure 9.30. The rotor is spinning at an angular speed of ω rad/s about its axis. Furthermore, the rotor has a polar moment of inertia J_p about the axis of rotation, a transverse moment of inertia J_t about any axis in the plane of rotation, and support stiffnesses k_1 and k_2 in their respective horizontal directions. The free whirling speeds Ω can be determined from the solution to the eigenvalue problem

$$K^* w = \lambda M^* w$$

where

$$K^* = \begin{bmatrix} KM^{-1}K & KM^{-1}G \\ G'M^{-1}K & K + G'M^{-1}G \end{bmatrix} \quad M^* = \begin{bmatrix} K & 0 \\ 0 & M \end{bmatrix}$$

and

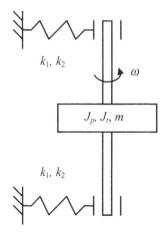

FIGURE 9.30
Rigid spinning rotor on an elastic support.

$$M = \begin{bmatrix} m & 0 & 0 & 0 \\ 0 & J_t & 0 & 0 \\ 0 & 0 & m & 0 \\ 0 & 0 & 0 & J_t \end{bmatrix} \qquad G = \begin{bmatrix} 0 & 0 & 0 & 0 \\ 0 & 0 & 0 & -J_p\omega \\ 0 & 0 & 0 & 0 \\ 0 & J_p\omega & 0 & 0 \end{bmatrix}$$

$$K = \begin{bmatrix} k_1 & 0 & 0 & 0 \\ 0 & k_2 & 0 & 0 \\ 0 & 0 & k_1 & 0 \\ 0 & 0 & 0 & k_2 \end{bmatrix}$$

and $\lambda = \Omega^2$.

If m = 10 kg, J_p = 2 kg m^2, J_t = 1.2 kg m^2, $k_1 = k_2$ = 2.5×10^6 N/m, then plot the value of Ω as a function of ω in the range $0 \le \omega \le 1500$ rad/s. This graph is an example of a Campbell diagram.[22] The speed at which $\Omega = \omega$ is called the critical speed. The results should look like those shown in Figure 9.31.

BIBLIOGRAPHY

D. T. Greenwood, *Principles of Dynamics*, 2nd ed., Prentice Hall, Englewood Cliffs, NJ, 1988.

F. J. Hale, *Introduction to Space Flight*, Prentice Hall, Englewood Cliffs, NJ, 1994.

D. J. Inman, *Engineering Vibration*, Prentice Hall, Englewood Cliffs, NJ, 1994.

E. B. Magrab, *Vibrations of Elastic Structural Members*, Sijthoff & Noordhoff, The Netherlands, 1979.

---

[22] G. Genta, *Vibration of Structures and Machines: Practical Aspects*, Springer-Verlag, New York, 1993, Section 4.3.

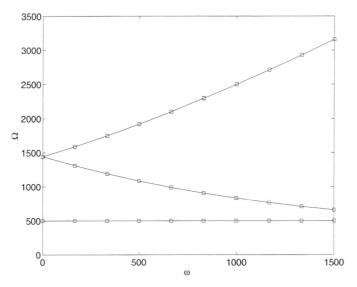

FIGURE 9.31
Campbell diagram for a spinning rigid rotor on an elastic support.

L. Meirovitch, *Elements of Vibration Analysis*, McGraw Hill, New York, 1986.

F. C. Moon, Applied Dynamics with Applications to Multibody and Mechatronic Systems, John Wiley & Sons, New York, 1998.

A. H. Nayfeh and B. Balachandran, *Applied Nonlinear Dynamics: Analytical, Computational, and Experimental Methods*, John Wiley & Sons, New York, 1995.

S. S. Rao, *Mechanical Vibrations*, 3rd ed., Addison-Wesley, Reading, MA, 1995.

B. H. Tongue, *Principles of Vibration*, Oxford University Press, New York, 1996.

APPENDIX B

Beam Functions Used in Section 9.4

The functions that are used to compute the natural frequencies and mode shapes of uniform beams under a wide variety of boundary conditions are given below. They are used in support of Example 9.1. We evaluate Eq. (9.31) with the function *lambda* as follows:

```
function GammaOmega = lambda(x,z1,z2,z3,z4,z5,z6)
if x>20;
 ch = 0;
 tt = 1;
else
 ch = 1/cosh(x);
 tt = tanh(x);
end
ct = cos(x)*tt;
st = sin(x)*tt;
GammaOmega = z1*(ct+sin(x))+z2*(ct−sin(x))−2*z3*st+ ...
             z4*(cos(x)−ch)+z5*(cos(x)+ch)+2*z6*cos(x);
```

We now define the 16 functions *beamxxxx* used to provide the input to lambda, which will be used to determine the values of Ω_n that satisfy $\Lambda(\Omega_n) = 0$. Referring to Eqs. (9.27a,b), the functions use the following definitions:

$$v(1) = \gamma_2$$
$$v(2) = \alpha_2$$
$$v(3) = \gamma_1$$
$$v(4) = \alpha_1$$
$$v(5) = M_0/m_0$$
$$x = \Omega$$

and the naming scheme described in Table 9.5.

Function *beam0000*

```
function c = beam0000(x,v)
b2 = −v(1)/x;
a2 = v(2)/(x^3)−v(5)*x;
b1 = v(3)/x;
a1 = v(4)/(x^3);
z1 = b1*b2*(a1+a2)+(b1−b2);
z2 = a1*a2*(b1−b2)−(a1+a2);
z3 = a1*a2+b1*b2;
z4 = 1−a1*a2*b1*b2;
```

```
z5 = a2*b2−a1*b1;
z6 = a1*b2−a2*b1;
c = lambda(x,z1,z2,z3,z4,z5,z6);
```

Function *beam0001*

```
function c = beam0001(x,v)
b2 = −v(1)/x;
a2 = v(2)/(x^3)−v(5)*x;
b1 = v(3)/x;
a1 = v(4)/(x^3);
z1 = b1*b2;
z2 = a2*(b1−b2)−1;
z3 = a2;
z4 = a1*b1*b2;
z5 = −b1;
z6 = b2;
c = lambda(x,z1,z2,z3,z4,z5,z6);
```

Function *beam0010*

```
function c = beam0010(x,v)
b2 = −v(1)/x;
a2 = v(2)/(x^3)−v(5)*x;
a1 = v(4)/(x^3);
z1 = b2*(a1+a2)+1
z2 = a1*a2;
z3 = b2;
z4 = −a1*a2*b2;
z5 = −a1;
z6 = −a2;
c = lambda(x,z1,z2,z3,z4,z5,z6);
```

Function *beam0011*

```
function c = beam0011(x,v)
b2 = −v(1)/x;
a2 = v(2)/(x^3)−v(5)*x;
z1 = b2;
z2 = a2;
z3 = 0;
z4 = −a2*b2;
z5 = −1;
z6 = 0;
```

```
c = lambda(x,z1,z2,z3,z4,z5,z6);
```

Function *beam0100*

```
function c = beam0100(x,v)
b2 = -v(1)/x;
b1 = v(3)/x;
a1 = v(4)/(x^3);
z1 = b1*b2;
z2 = a1*(b1-b2)-1;
z3 = a1;
z4 = -a1*b1*b2;
z5 = b2;
z6 = -b1;
c = lambda(x,z1,z2,z3,z4,z5,z6);
```

Function *beam0101*

```
function c = beam0101(x,v)
b2 = -v(1)/x;
b1 = v(3)/x;
z1 = 0;
z2 = b1-b2;
z3 = 1;
z4 = -b1*b2;
z5 = 0;
z6 = 0;
c = lambda(x,z1,z2,z3,z4,z5,z6);
```

Function *beam0110*

```
function c = beam0110(x,v)
b2 = -v(1)/x;
a1 = v(4)/(x^3);
z1 = b2;
z2 = a1;
z3 = 0;
z4 = -a1*b2;
z5 = 0;
z6 = -1;
c = lambda(x,z1,z2,z3,z4,z5,z6);
```

Function *beam0111*

```
function c = beam0111(x,v)
```

```
b2 = -v(1)/x;
z1 = 0;
z2 = 1;
z3 = 0;
z4 = -b2;
z5 = 0;
z6 = 0;
c = lambda(x,z1,z2,z3,z4,z5,z6);
```

Function *beam1000*

```
function c = beam1000(x,v)
a2 = v(2)/(x^3)-v(5)*x;
b1 = v(3)/x;
a1 = v(4)/(x^3);
z1 = b1*(a1+a2)-1;
z2 = -a1*a2;
z3 = b1;
z4 = -a1*a2*b1;
z5 = a2;
z6 = a1;
c = lambda(x,z1,z2,z3,z4,z5,z6);
```

Function *beam1001*

```
function c = beam1001(x,v)
a2 = v(2)/(x^3)-v(5)*x;
b1 = v(3)/x;
z1 = b1;
z2 = -a2;
z3 = 0;
z4 = -a2*b1;
z5 = 0;
z6 = 1;
c = lambda(x,z1,z2,z3,z4,z5,z6);
```

Function *beam1010*

```
function c = beam1010(x,v)
a2 = v(2)/(x^3)-v(5)*x;
a1 = v(4)/(x^3);
z1 = a1+a2;
z2 = 0;
z3 = 1;
z4 = -a1*a2;
```

```
z5 = 0;
z6 = 0;
c = lambda(x,z1,z2,z3,z4,z5,z6);
```

Function *beam1011*

```
function c = beam1011(x,v)
a2 = v(2)/(x^3)–v(5)*x;
z1 = 1;
z2 = 0;
z3 = 0;
z4 = –a2;
z5 = 0;
z6 = 0;
c = lambda(x,z1,z2,z3,z4,z5,z6);
```

Function *beam1100*

```
function c = beam1100(x,v)
b1 = v(3)/x;
a1 = v(4)/(x^3);
z1 = b1;
z2 = –a1;
z3 = 0;
z4 = –a1*b1;
z5 = 1;
z6 = 0;
c = lambda(x,z1,z2,z3,z4,z5,z6);
```

Function *beam1101*

```
function c = beam1101(x,v)
b1 = v(3)/x;
z1 = 0;
z2 = –1;
z3 = 0;
z4 = –b1;
z5 = 0;
z6 = 0;
c = lambda(x,z1,z2,z3,z4,z5,z6);
```

Function *beam1110*

```
function c = beam1110(x,v)
a1 = v(4)/(x^3);
```

```
z1 = 1;
z2 = 0;
z3 = 0;
z4 = –a1;
z5 = 0;
z6 = 0;
c = lambda(x,z1,z2,z3,z4,z5,z6);
```

Function *beam1111*

```
function c = beam1111(x,v)
z1 = 0;
z2 = 0;
z3 = 0;
z4 = –1;
z5 = 0;
z6 = 0;
c = lambda(x,z1,z2,z3,z4,z5,z6);
```

The eight functions *mode0xxx* are given below. They are used to determine $W_n(\eta)$, which are given by Eq. (9.29), and to determine N_n, which are given by Eq. (9.30). In these functions, $En = E_n$ and $Nn = N_n$.

Function *mode0000*

```
function [mode,c] = mode0000(x,v,eta)
a2 = v(2)/(x^3)–v(5)*x;
b1 = v(3)/x;
a1 = v(4)/(x^3);
En = (a2*Vvib(x)+(a2*b1–1)*Svib(x)–b1*Tvib(x))/(Vvib(x)–(a1+a2)*Uvib(x)+ ...
      a2*a1*Tvib(x));
mode = En*(Uvib(x*eta)–a1*Tvib(x*eta))+Vvib(x*eta)+b1*Svib(x*eta);
c = Nn(x,En,1,b1,–a1*En,v(5));
```

Function *mode0001*

```
function [mode,c] = mode0001(x,v,eta)
a2 = v(2)/(x^3)–v(5)*x;
b1 = v(3)/x;
En = (a2*Vvib(x)+(a2*b1–1)*Svib(x)–b1*Tvib(x))/(Uvib(x)–a2*Tvib(x));
mode = En*Tvib(x*eta)+Vvib(x*eta)+b1*Svib(x*eta);
c = Nn(x,0,1,b1,En,v(5));
```

Function *mode0010*

```
function [mode,c] = mode0010(x,v,eta)
```

```
a2 = v(2)/(x^3)−v(5)*x;
a1 = v(4)/(x^3);
En = (a2*Svib(x)−Tvib(x))/(Vvib(x)−(a1+a2)*Uvib(x)+a1*a2*Tvib(x));
mode = En*(Uvib(x*eta)−a1*Tvib(x*eta))+ Svib(x*eta);
c = Nn(x,En,1,0,−a1*En,v(5));
```

Function *mode0011*

```
function [mode,c] = mode0011(x,v,eta)
a2 = v(2)/(x^3)−v(5)*x;
En = (a2*Svib(x)−Tvib(x))/(Uvib(x)−a2*Tvib(x));
mode = En*Tvib(x*eta)+Svib(x*eta);
c = Nn(x,0,0,1,En,v(5));
```

Function *mode0100*

```
function [mode,c] = mode0100(x,v,eta)
b1 = v(3)/x;
a1 = v(4)/(x^3);
En = (Vvib(x)+b1*Svib(x))/(−Uvib(x)+a1*Tvib(x));
mode = En*(Uvib(x*eta)−a1*Tvib(x*eta))+Vvib(x*eta)+b1*Svib(x*eta);
c = Nn(x,En,1,b1,−a1*En,v(5));
```

Function *mode0101*

```
function [mode,c] = mode0101(x,v,eta)
b1 = v(3)/x;
En = (Vvib(x)+b1*Svib(x))/(−Tvib(x));
mode = En*Tvib(x*eta)+Vvib(x*eta)+b1*Svib(x*eta);
c = Nn(x,0,1,b1,En,v(5));
```

Function *mode0110*

```
function [mode,c] = mode0110(x,v,eta)
a1 = v(4)/(x^3);
En = (Svib(x))/(−Uvib(x)+a1*Tvib(x));
mode = En*(Uvib(x*eta)−a1*Tvib(x*eta))+ Svib(x*eta);
c = Nn(x,En,0,1,−a1*En,v(5));
```

Function *mode0111*

```
function [mode,c] = mode0111(x,v,eta)
En = −Svib(x)/Tvib(x);
mode = En*Tvib(x*eta)+Svib(x*eta);
```

```
c = Nn(x,0,0,1,En,v(5));
```

and N_n is determined from function *Nn* as follows:

```
function nn = Nn(x,a,b,c,d,mo)
c1 = x*(a^2+c^2-2*b*d)+c*b-3*a*d+0.25*((a-c)^2-(b-d)^2)*sin(2*x)-...
     0.5*(b-d)*(a-c)*cos(2*x);
c2 = 0.25*((b+d)^2+(a+c)^2);
c3 = 0.5*(b+d)*(a+c);
c4 = (a^2-c^2+d^2-b^2)*cos(x);
c5 = (a^2-c^2-d^2+b^2)*sin(x);
c6 = 2*(a*b-c*d)*sin(x);
c7 = 2*(a*d-c*b)*cos(x);
test1 = c2*tanh(2*x)+c3;
test2 = (c4+c6)*tanh(x)+c5+c7;
nn = (0.25./x)*(c1+cosh(2*x)*test1+cosh(x)*test2);
if mo ~= 0
  nn = nn+mo*(a*Uvib(x)+b*Vvib(x)+c*Svib(x)+d.*Tvib(x))^2;
end
```

and

```
function ux = Uvib(x)
ux = 0.5*(cos(x)+cosh(x));

function sx = Svib(x)
sx = 0.5*(cosh(x)-cos(x));

function vx = Vvib(x)
vx = 0.5*(sinh(x)+sin(x));

function tx = Tvib(x)
tx = 0.5*(sinh(x)-sin(x));
```

The boundary conditions at each end of the beam are selected by the user, who is queried by the following function *GetBC*.

```
function g = GetBC
disp('Enter one of the following numbers to select the bc at x = 0:')
disp(' [1]  clamped (w = dw/dx = 0)')
disp(' [2]  simply supported (w = d^2w/dx^2 = 0)')
disp(' [3]  linear spring (d^2w/dx^2 = 0 and d^3w/dx^3 = kw)')
disp(' [4]  torsion spring (d^2w/dx^2 = bdw/dx and w = 0)')
disp(' [5]  linear spring and torsion spring (d^2w/dx^2 = bdw/dx and
             d^3w/dx^3 = kw)')
```

```
lhn = input('Enter number for bc at x = 0: ');
alpha1 = 0; beta1 = 0;
switch lhn
 case 1
  g1 = -1; a1 = -1;
 case 2
  g1 = 0; a1 = -1;
case 3
  alpha1 = input('Enter dimensionless linear spring constant (0.01 to 100,000): ');
  g1 = 0; a1 = 0;
 case 4
  beta1 = input('Enter dimensionless torsion spring constant (0.01 to 100,000): ');
  g1 = 0; a1 = -1;
 case 5
  alpha1 = input('Enter dimensionless linear spring constant (0.01 to 100,000): ');
  beta1 = input('Enter dimensionless torsion spring constant (0.01 to 100,000): ');
  g1 = 0; a1 = 0;
end
mo = 0; rhn = -1;
disp(' ')
disp('Enter one of the following numbers to select the bc at x = L:')
disp(' [1] clamped (w = dw/dx = 0)')
disp(' [2] simply supported (w = d^2w/dx^2 = 0)')
disp(' [3] vertically constrained slider with or without mass(dw/dx = 0 and ...
         d^3w/dx^3 = 0')
disp('     or d^3w/dx^3 = mw')
disp(' [4] linear spring with or without attached mass (d^2w/dx^2 = 0 and ...
         d^3w/dx^3 = kw)')
disp(' [5] free with or without attached mass (d^2w/dx^2 = 0 and d^3w/dx^3 = 0 ...
         or ')
disp('      d^3w/dx^3 = mw)')
disp(' [6] torsion spring (d^2w/dx^2 = bdw/dx and w = 0)')
disp(' [7] linear spring with or without attached mass and torsion spring ...
         d^2w/dx^2 = bdw/dx')
disp('     and d^3w/dx^3 = kw)')
rhn = input('Enter number for bc at x = L ');
alpha2 = 0; beta2 = 0;
switch rhn
 case 1
   g2 = -1; a2 = -1;
 case 2
   g2 = 0; a2 = -1;
 case 3
   mo = -1;
```

```
    disp('Enter ratio of attached mass to mass of beam (0 to 10000).')
    mo = input('  If no mass then enter zero.  ');
    g2 = -1; a2 = 0;
  case 4
    alpha2 = input('Enter dimensionless linear spring constant (0.01 to 100,000): ');
    mo = -1;
    disp('Enter ratio of attached mass to mass of beam (0 to 10000).')
    mo = input('  If no mass then enter zero.  ');
    g2 = 0; a2 = 0;
  case 5
    mo = -1;
    disp('Enter ratio of attached mass to mass of beam (0 to 10000).')
    mo = input('  If no mass then enter zero.  ');
    g2 = 0; a2 = 0;
  case 6
    beta2 = input('Enter dimensionless torsion spring constant (0.01 to 100,000): ');
    g2 = 0; a2 = -1;
  case 7
    alpha2 = input('Enter dimensionless linear spring constant (0.01 to 100,000): ');
    mo = -1;
    disp('Enter ratio of attached mass to mass of beam (0 to 10000).')
    mo = input('  If no mass then enter zero.  ');
    beta2 = input('Enter dimensionless torsion spring constant (0.01 to 100,000): ');
    g2 = 0; a2 = 0;
end
g = [beta2 alpha2 beta1 alpha1 mo 0 g2 a2 g1 a1];
```

The file names that access the appropriate functions to evaluate $\Lambda(\Omega_n)$ and $W_n(u)$ are obtained from the function *BeamEqn*:

```
function [nf,mo] = BeamEqn(g)
if g(1) == -1; d4 = '1'; else; d4 = '0'; end;
if g(2) == -1; d3 = '1'; else; d3 = '0'; end;
if g(3) == -1; d2 = '1'; else; d2 = '0'; end;
if g(4) == -1; d1 = '1'; else; d1 = '0'; end;
nf = ['beam' d4 d3 d2 d1];
mo = ['mode' '0' d3 d2 d1];
```

where $g(1)$, $g(2)$, $g(3)$, and $g(4)$ represent the limiting cases of b_2, a_2, b_1, and a_1, respectively.

C H A P T E R   1 0

CONTROL SYSTEMS

Gregory C. Walsh

The representation, design, and evaluation of control systems using MATLAB's Controls Toolbox and SIMULINK are presented.

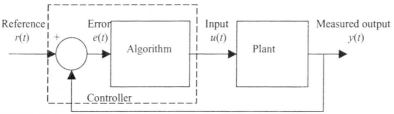

FIGURE 10.1
Schematic diagram of a feedback loop.

10.1 INTRODUCTION TO CONTROL SYSTEM DESIGN

Consider the system shown in Figure 10.1. We find that, typically, control systems involve a device modeled with differential equations (the plant), with one or more operator-controlled variables (the inputs $u(t)$) and one or more outputs $y(t)$. For all of the systems, there is an algorithm (the controller) which, using both the operator's commands (the reference $r(t)$) and the plant outputs, computes the controlled variables. Figure 10.1 represents schematically a cascade-control system in a block diagram. In a cascade control system the controller takes the difference between the reference and the output, forming the error signal $e(t) = r(t) - y(t)$. The error signal is then used in the algorithm to produce the input to the plant, $u(t)$. The controller is typically a computer, though in some (older) systems, analog circuits or mechanical devices may be found.

   In control systems, one knows from the outset how he or she wants the system to behave. The control design problem involves, therefore, changing the physical system so that the desired behavior occurs. This requires not only the ability to predict what will happen to a given model of the system, but also what changes in the system model are needed to obtain the desired behavior. Thus, control system design is an inverse problem.

   The control design problem is usually addressed by using feedback. Feedback is the natural idea of using the output of the system as a correction to the input. In addition to the obvious advantage of making a system work without human intervention, feedback also can be used to reduce nonlinearity, increase system robustness, and enhance stability. Feedback is the most powerful (but not the only) tool in the control engineer's toolbox.

   In this chapter, we emphasize how one uses the many tools available in MATLAB for solving classes of control problems. In Section 10.2, we detail how control systems are represented in MATLAB, using transfer functions, block diagrams, and state space models. In Section 10.3, methods for computing the response of control systems are explained, and in Section 10.4, design tools such as Bode plots, the root locus, and LQR/LQG are detailed. The last section, Section 10.5, is devoted to design examples.

10.1.1 Tools for Controller Design

Controller design demands a good understanding of the solutions of ordinary differential equations, which are required to describe the behavior of physical systems. Prior to the advent of computational tools like MATLAB, this understanding had to be gained by solving hundreds of differential equations. Linear, time-invariant ordinary differential equations are represented in three different formats in MATLAB:

1. State-space equations
2. Transfer-functions
3. Block diagrams

State-space representations are time-domain based and use matrices. Transfer functions are Laplace-domain based and use polynomials of the complex variable *s*. Block-diagram representations, available through the SIMULINK toolbox in MATLAB, visually depict the input and output connections. Conversion between the various representations is facilitated by built-in functions provided by MATLAB.

Control design objectives typically fall into three categories:

1. Transient
2. Steady state
3. Stability

Transient design requirements focus on the short-term behavior of the system and address concerns such as responsiveness and stiffness. Steady-state requirements focus on the long-term behavior of the system, answering questions about how the system will perform over long periods of time. Standard input signals such as steps, ramps, and sinusoids are applied to test whether or not the system meets transient and steady-state design requirements. MATLAB provides functions for finding the response of systems to the standard test signals. Feedback has the potential to both remove and introduce instability into otherwise well-behaved physical processes, and instability must always be avoided. Transient and steady-state design requirements are typically in conflict, forcing one to make a design trade-off.

Graphical tools used to solve control problems include Bode plots, Nyquist plots, and root locus plots. Linear algebra-based tools are used in more advanced design techniques such as LQG (linear quadratic Gaussian), H∞, and *μ*-synthesis. For most single-input, single-output control designs, one of five controllers that are presented will solve the design problem.

10.1.2 Naming and File Conventions

In the course of this chapter, we use a standard set of naming conventions. Because the description of even a simple differential equation requires multiple vectors and matrices, MATLAB has provided a method for gathering the necessary matrices and vectors under a single name. These collections of matrices, vectors, and even strings are called systems. We will use the name *Plant* to label systems whose structure is fixed during the controller design and the name *Control* to label the part we will be able to choose. The final closed-loop system consisting of the *Plant* connected with the *Control* we will label *clSys*. If the feedback connection is broken, we will call the resulting system *olSys*. The MATLAB functions used in this chapter to assemble and analyze control systems take systems as arguments, instead of vectors and matrices.

Several example systems are considered in this chapter. For convenience, we will create function files that return these model systems. The functions will return a system object. The examples covered include:

- A permanent magnet motor with a load (*MotorSS.m*)
- A pointer with a flexible shaft (*Pointer.m*)
- A magnetic levitator (*MagLev.m*)
- An inverted pendulum (*Pend.m*)
- A flywheel (*Fly.m*).

Controllers such lead, lag, PI, and PD are generated as needed.

10.2 REPRESENTATION OF SYSTEMS IN MATLAB

The input to a control system is described by a real-valued function of time $r(t)$. This quantity typically represents some physical variable under control, such as a force, voltage, or temperature. The output of a control system is also described by a real-valued function of time $y(t)$. The value of this function is some measured quantity, such as angle, pressure, or velocity. The relationship between the input function $u(t)$ and the output function $y(t)$ in control systems is represented by a linear time-invariant ordinary differential equation, which has the general form

$$a_n \frac{d^n y(t)}{dt^n} + a_{n-1} \frac{d^{n-1} y(t)}{dt^{n-1}} + \ldots + a_0 y(t) = b_m \frac{d^m u(t)}{dt^m} + b_{m-1} \frac{d^{m-1} u(t)}{dt^{m-1}} + \ldots + b_0 u(t) \quad (10.1)$$

where $n \geq m$. The coefficients of the equation, a_j and b_j, are constant real-valued numbers. System models in MATLAB are stored as objects, and much like the graphics objects of Chapters 6 and 7, the properties of these models are accessible though the use of `get` and `set`. Introductory control topics typically focus on differential equations of the form shown in Eq. (10.1), and MATLAB provides three classes to represent this type of input-output relationship:

- Transfer function representation (class `tf`)
- State-space representation (class `ss`)
- Zero-pole-gain representation (class `zpk`).

Discrete-time linear systems are also of great practical interest, since control loops are often implemented on computers. All three representations also have discrete time versions, where the additional information concerning the sampling time is appended. Having the system models encapsulated as objects allows the user to attach auxiliary data to the representation. Examples of data fields attached to system objects include `InputName`, `OutputName`, and even `Notes`.

To illustrate the three primary representations, consider a simple model of a DC permanent-magnet servomotor shown in Figure 10.2. The input voltage $v(t)$ is applied to the windings of the motor producing electrical current $i(t)$. The current in the windings produces a torque on the rotor that is proportional to its magnitude. The effective inertia J is the sum of the load inertia J_l and the rotor inertia J_m. The rotor with angle $\theta(t)$ acts like a generator,

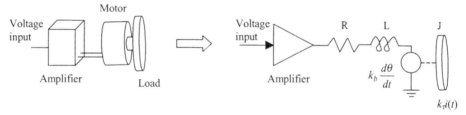

Figure 10.2
A common electric servomotor.

producing a back voltage proportional to the angular velocity of the rotor. A torque balance and circuit analysis yields the following coupled linear ordinary differential equations[1] describing the relationship between the input voltage $v(t)$ and the output angle $\theta(t)$:

$$L\frac{di(t)}{dt} + k_b\frac{d\theta(t)}{dt} + Ri(t) = v(t)$$

$$J\frac{d^2\theta(t)}{dt^2} + b\frac{d\theta(t)}{dt} - k_\tau i(t) = 0$$

(10.2)

The electrical constants are R, L, k_τ, and k_b, where R is the motor resistance, L is the winding inductance, k_τ is the conversion factor from current to torque, and k_b is the back emf generator constant. The total inertia J is usually dominated by the load inertia J_l. The motor friction b is generally small if there is no gearbox. We shall now convert these equations into the three system representations.

10.2.1 State-Space Models

State-space models gained popularity with the widespread use of computers, since they are more numerically reliable than transfer functions. State-space models are first-order-coupled differential equations. The model of the motor in Eqs. (10.2) is not first order. In particular, there is a second time derivative of $\theta(t)$. In order to represent the motor as a state-space model, we first have to convert the equations to first order as was done in Section 5.5.4. Let

$$x_1(t) = \theta(t)$$

$$x_2(t) = \frac{d\theta(t)}{dt} = \omega(t)$$

$$x_3(t) = i(t)$$

Then Eqs. (10.2) become

---

[1] D. K. Anand and R. B. Zmood, *Introduction to Control Systems*, 3rd ed., Butterworth-Heinemann Ltd, Oxford, England, 1995.

$$\frac{dx_1}{dt} = x_2$$

$$\frac{dx_2}{dt} = -\frac{b}{J}x_2 + \frac{k_\tau}{J}x_3$$

$$\frac{dx_3}{dt} = -\frac{k_b}{L}x_2 - \frac{R}{L}x_3 + \frac{v(t)}{L}$$

If we let

$$x(t) = [x_1(t), x_2(t), x_3(t)]'$$
$$u(t) = v(t)$$
$$y(t) = \theta(t) = x_1(t)$$

then the state-space representation for the motor system is

$$\frac{dx(t)}{dt} = Ax(t) + Bu(t) \tag{10.3}$$

$$y(t) = Cx(t) + Du(t)$$

where

$$A = \begin{bmatrix} 0 & 1 & 0 \\ 0 & -b/J & k_r/J \\ 0 & -k_b/L & -R/L \end{bmatrix}$$

$$B = \begin{bmatrix} 0 & 0 & 1/L \end{bmatrix}'$$

$$C = \begin{bmatrix} 1 & 0 & 0 \end{bmatrix}$$

$$D = [0]$$

The matrices A, B, C, and D are the essential data needed to describe the differential equations in MATLAB.

We are now ready to enter this model into MATLAB. To simplify matters, we create a function *MotorSS*, which will return a state-space system model of a motor. The values assumed for the constants are $L = 5$ mH (motor inductance), $R = 5\ \Omega$ (motor resistance), $k_b = 0.125$ V/rad/s (back emf constant), $k_\tau = 15$ Nm/A (motor torque constant), $J = 0.03$ kg·m^2 (rotor inertia), and $B = 0.01$ Nm/rad/s (rotor friction).

```
function Plant = MotorSS(Jl)
if nargin < 1, Jl = 0; end;
L = 5e-3; R = 5; kb = 12.5e-2;
ki = 15; J = 3e-2 + Jl; b = 1e-2;
A = [0 1 0; 0 -b/J ki/J; 0, -kb/L -R/L];
B = [0; 0; 1/L];
C = [1 0 0];
D = 0;
Plant = ss(A,B,C,D);
```

```
set(Plant,'InputName','volts','OutputName','\theta');
set(Plant,'StateName',{'\theta','\omega','i'});
set(Plant,'Notes','Small DC servomotor');
```

The function `ss` collects the matrices A, B, C, and D into a single system object. Typing

```
MotorSS
```

in the MATLAB command window displays

```
a =
            \theta    \omega        i
   \theta     0         1          0
   \omega     0      -0.33333      500
       i      0        -25       -1000
b =
            volts
   \theta     0
   \omega     0
       i     200
c =
            \theta    \omega        i
   \theta     1         0          0
d =
            volts
   \theta     0
Continuous-time model.
```

The input is labeled by default $u1$, the output $y1$ and the interior states $x1$, $x2$, and $x3$. We preferred to label these, which was done using `set`. Thus we have named the state-space variables θ, ω, and i. In addition, we have included a note to remind us what the model represents. Without the labeling the model, the following would have been printed to the MATLAB command window

```
a =
            x1        x2         x3
   x1        0         1          0
   x2        0      -0.33333      500
   x3        0        -25       -1000
b =
            u1
   x1        0
   x2        0
   x3       200
```

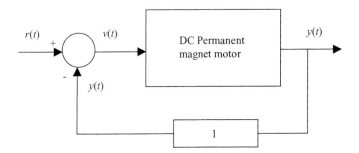

FIGURE 10.3
A simple unity gain feedback control system for controlling the servomotor.

```
c =
                 x1      x2      x3
          y1      1       0       0
d =
                 u1
          y1      0
Continuous-time system.
```

When the function is called, only the system object is returned, and not any of the constants. If we wish to recover the matrices A, B, C, and D, then we use

   [A,B,C,D] = ssdata(MotorSS)

which returns the system matrices A, B, C, and D.

   MATLAB provides built-in functions that take system objects such as *MotorSS* as an argument. Suppose we wish to examine the behavior of the motor when it is connected in a simple feedback configuration as shown in Figure 10.3. From the schematic we have

$$v(t) = r(t) - y(t) = r(t) - Cx(t)$$

and consequently Eq. (10.3) becomes

$$\frac{dx(t)}{dt} = (A - BC)x(t) + Br(t)$$
$$y(t) = Cx(t) + Dr(t)$$

which amounts to replacing A in Eq. (10.3) with $A - BC$. MATLAB provides a function for the operation we have just described mathematically. The command is

   clSys = feedback(MotorSS,1);

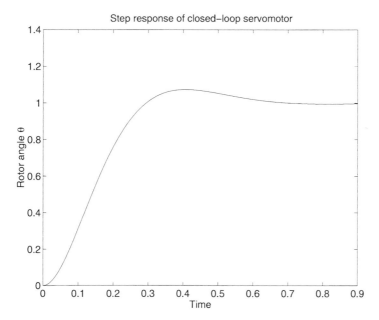

FIGURE 10.4
Step response of the servomotor control system.

which returns the closed-loop system. The number 1 in the second argument describes the transfer function of the feedback loop, which we have assumed is 1. Note that *A* of *clSys* is equal to *A − BC* of *MotorSS*. One can check this by typing

```
clSys = feedback(MotorSS,1);
Plant = MotorSS;
clSys.a − (Plant.a − Plant.b*Plant.c)
```

which returns a (3×3) matrix of zeros.

The MATLAB function `feedback` performed the algebra necessary to connect the motor system into a new configuration. Other MATLAB functions, which take systems as arguments, solve the differential equations when inputs are applied. For example, the following script uses `step` to compute the response of the system to a step input signal, which results in Figure 10.4.

```
[y,t] = step(feedback(MotorSS,1));
plot(t,y);
xlabel('Time');
ylabel('Rotor angle \theta');
title('Step response of closed-loop servomotor');
```

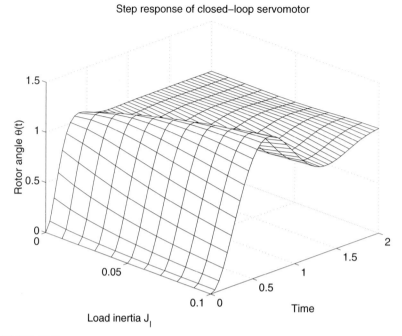

FIGURE 10.5
Response of the closed-loop servomotor to a step command in position as a function of load inertia.

The following script generates the step response of the servomotor for a variety of load inertias. The results are shown in Figure 10.5. The response overshoots the goal more as the load inertia J_{load} is increased. In Section 10.3, we shall develop a similar set of expectations for system responses as a function of pole and zero locations.

```
t = 0:0.05:2;
Jload = 0:0.01:0.1;
data = zeros(length(t),length(Jload));
for i = 1:length(Jload)
  data(:,i) = step(feedback(MotorSS(Jload(i)),1),t);
end;
mesh(Jload,t,data);
view([45,30]);
xlabel('Load inertia J_l');
ylabel('Time');
zlabel('Rotor angle \theta(t)')
title('Step response of closed-loop servomotor')
```

which are the closed-loop poles of the simple control system. The function `tzero` returns the transmission zeros of a plant. Thus

    z = tzero(feedback(MotorTF,1));

sets *z* to an empty matrix — that is, the system has no zeros. Both `pole` and `tzero` may be applied to state-space systems as well. The transfer function is related to the state-space model through the equation

$$H(s) = C(sI - A)^{-1}B$$

where *I* is the unit matrix. From this equation, it is seen that the roots of the denominator equation, the poles, are equal to the roots of the determinant of $(sI - A)$, which are the eigenvalues of the matrix *A*. The concepts of poles, zeros, and eigenvalues are frequently used to develop understanding of the behavior of a control system.

One representation of a transfer function is the zero-pole-gain format, which is parameterized by the poles and zeros. In general, because the transfer function is a rational polynomial function, its numerator and denominator can both be factored to give

$$H(s) = k \frac{(s - z_1)(s - z_2)\dots(s - z_m)}{(s - p_1)(s - p_2)\dots(s - p_n)} \tag{10.6}$$

The transfer function is uniquely defined by its list of poles and zeros together with the constant gain *k*. We now generate a zero-pole-gain model of the closed-loop control system shown in Figure 10.3. First we generate the lists of the poles and zeros and set the gain to 1 by dividing by the DC gain. The script is

    Poles = pole(feedback(MotorTF,1));
    Z = tzero(feedback(MotorTF,1));
    PlantZPK = zpk(Z,Poles,1);
    PlantZPK = dcgain(feedback(MotorTF,1))/dcgain(PlantZPK)*PlantZPK;
    step(PlantZPK);

which, upon execution, also yields Figure 10.4. The commands `feedback`, `pole`, and `tzero` also apply to this model.

10.2.3 Discrete-Time Models

Discrete-time versions of the state-space, transfer-function, and zero-pole-gain models can be generated using

    c2d

In the script below, we convert a continuous-time model into a discrete-time model with a sampling time of 1 ms. For clarity in the graphical output of the script, we plot the results

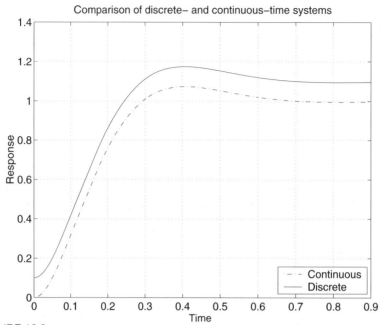

FIGURE 10.6
Comparison of the discrete-time step response and the continuous-time step response. (A vertical shift of 0.1 in the discrete time response has been arbitrarily introduced.)

with a small offset added to the continuous system response to separate it from the discrete-time response.

```
[ydiscrete,time] = step(feedback(c2d(MotorSS,0.001),1));
ycontinous = step(feedback(MotorSS,1),time);
plot(time,ycontinous,'b-.',time,ydiscrete+0.1,'b-');
grid;
xlabel('Time');
ylabel('Response');
legend('Continuous','Discrete',4)
title('Comparison of discrete- and continuous-time systems');
```

The result of this script is shown in Figure 10.6. Since the sampling time chosen was so small, there is no observable difference between the two step responses.

The function c2d uses, by default, the zero-order-hold approximation. Functions such as step, impulse, and feedback support discrete-time system models. The sampling time of the various components must be the same when combining elements. If

```
c2d(MotorSS,0.001)
```

is typed in the MATLAB command window, the following system description is displayed:

```
a =
            \theta      \omega        i
    \theta     1    0.00099818  0.00018374
    \omega     0      0.99507     0.31535
        i      0     -0.015768    0.36458
b =
            volts
    \theta   1.3203e-05
    \omega  0.036748
        i    0.12617
c =
            \theta      \omega        i
    \theta     1          0          0
d =
            volts
    \theta     0
```

Note that the matrices a and b of the discrete-time model are substantially different from those of the continuous time models. The state equations for discrete-time models evolve using difference equations, not differential equations. In the case of state-space models we have, for time indexed by k,

$$x[k+1] = A_d x[k] + B_d u[k]$$
$$y[k] = Cx[k] + Du[k]$$

which are matrix multiplications. These matrix multiplications match the behavior of the continuous-time differential equations given by Eq. (10.3) at sample times $t = k\Delta$, where Δ is the sampling interval as long as the matrices A_d and B_d are chosen properly. With a zero-order hold approximation, we have[3]

$$A_d = e^{A\Delta}$$
$$B_d = \int_0^\Delta e^{A(\Delta-\tau)} B d\tau$$

which maps all left-half complex plane eigenvalues into the unit circle. The triangle approximation, the bilinear approximation (Tustin), the pre-warped Tustin approximation, and the matched approximation are also available in MATLAB.

---

[3] See, for example, T. Kailith, *Linear Systems Theory*, Prentice Hall, Englewood Cliffs, NJ, 1980; or K. Astrom and B. Wittenmark, *Computer Controlled Systems*, 3rd ed., Prentice Hall, Upper Saddle River, NJ, 1997.

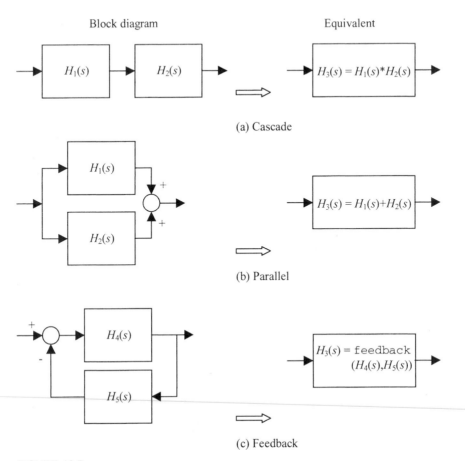

Block diagram   Equivalent

(a) Cascade

(b) Parallel

(c) Feedback

FIGURE 10.7
The most common block-diagram algebra operations: (a) series (cascade); (b) parallel; (c) feedback.

10.2.4 Block Diagrams and SIMULINK

A typical control system is composed of several distinct units, such as the plant and the controller. More complicated structures involving many distinct subsystems are often studied, and these input-output maps are sketched by system designers using block diagrams, the basic elements of which are shown in Figure 10.7. MATLAB has provided a collection of built-in functions and operators to compute their transfer functions, a process referred to as block-diagram algebra. MATLAB supplies standard operators +, −, *, / and provides `feedback`, `series`, and `connect`, among others, so that from the command line the block diagrams may be implemented and simulated. The SIMULINK toolbox provides a graphical user interface from which one can literally sketch the block diagram and simulate the characteristics of the resulting system.

The cascade connection of two systems shown in Figure 10.7a can be determined using the multiplication operator. For example, if system objects H1 and H2 represent the transfer functions $H_1(s)$ and $H_2(s)$, respectively, then the resulting cascaded system $H_3(s)$ can be obtained by

H3 = H1*H2

Division is also supported, but is applicable only to strictly proper models and will not be considered here.

The parallel connection of two systems illustrated in Figure 10.7b can be found using the addition and subtraction operators. If systems *H1* and *H2* are connected in parallel, then the resulting system is

H3 = H1 + H2

Subtraction is obtained by changing the sign in the above equation to minus.

The feedback connection shown in Figure 10.7c differs from the other two operations in that a function, instead of an operator, implements the operation. If systems *H4* and *H5* are connected in feedback, then the resulting closed loop system is given by

H3 = feedback(H4,H5);

Negative feedback is assumed; if positive feedback is desired, then $H_3(s)$ is obtained from

H3 = feedback(H4,H5,+1);

One common control configuration is called cascade feedback, which was shown in Figure 10.1. This configuration is the combination of Figure 10.7a, the cascade, with Figure 10.7c, feedback. In this case, the output of the *Plant* (H_2) is subtracted from the input, and the resulting error signal is fed to the *Controller* (H_1). To build the closed loop model we set

H4 = Controller*Plant

and

H5 = 1

The closed-loop system *clSys* is then obtained from

clSys = feedback(Controller*Plant,1);

The functions feedback and series and the operators *, +, and – also support multiple-input, multiple-output (MIMO) systems by allowing vector-valued inputs and outputs. In addition, matrix operations allow the quick construction of MIMO systems. For example, a

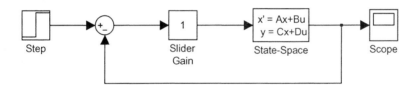

FIGURE 10.8
A block diagram model of a DC servomotor created in SIMULINK.

two-input, one-output system *H3* can be created from two single-input, single-output (SISO) plants, *H1* and *H2*, using

H3 = [H1, H2]

A one-input, two-output system can be created with

H3 = [H1; H2]

The subsystems *H1* and *H2* can be extracted from *H3* using the same operations used to extract submatrices discussed Section 2.4. Cascade, parallel, and feedback connections require specifications as to which inputs are connected to which outputs when working with MIMO systems. The functions `series` and `parallel` are provided for these purposes. More complicated MIMO structures may be formed using `star` and `connect`. We consider SISO control systems almost exclusively.

If the system objects *H1* and *H2* are different types, then an implicit conversion is performed so that the resulting model is homogeneous. MATLAB favors state-space models above all others and, therefore, if any one of the models in a computation is a state-space model, the result will be in state-space form. Between transfer-function and zero-pole-gain models, transfer-function models are favored.

SIMULINK. SIMULINK allows a designer to model and simulate systems by constructing them from a large library of components. The components are selected from the library, dragged to a modeling window, and connected, and their individual parameters are specified. Then the model is run and the results displayed.

SIMULINK is invoked by typing

```
simulink
```

at the MATLAB command line. Variables defined in the MATLAB command window are accessible from the SIMULINK window.

We shall illustrate how to model the DC servomotor with SIMULINK. The final result is shown in Figure 10.8. To generate the plant model, we first define it in the MATLAB command window and extract the system matrices. Then we start SIMULINK. Thus,

```
[A,B,C,D] = ssdata(MotorSS);
simulink
```

This brings up the SIMULINK library browser window, which displays a list of four main libraries: *Simulink, Control System Toolbox, Neural Network Blockset,* and *Simulink Extras.* First, we click on the new page icon (white rectangle) to open a SIMULINK modeling window. Then, we return to the browser window and double-click on *Simulink,* which displays the directory of SIMULINK component libraries:

Continuous
Discrete
Functions & Tables
Math
Nonlinear
Signals & Systems
Sinks
Sources

To open the components (blocks) of any of these libraries, one double-clicks on the library name of interest. We start by displaying the *Continuous* library. Next, we click on *State-Space* and, keeping the mouse button depressed, drag a copy of this library component to the modeling window. We place the component at its desired location and release the mouse button. Next, we go to the *Math* library and sequentially select *Slider Gain* and *Sum* and drag them one at a time to the model window, placing each, respectively, to the left of the *State-Space* component. Then, we go to the *Sources* library and select *Step* and place it in the modeling window to the left of all components placed so far. The last component we select is *Scope* from the *Sinks* library. It is placed to the right of all components selected.

The next steps are to specify the parameters of the components. We start with the *State-Space* block and double-click on it. This brings up a *State-Space* parameter window with five places to enter data: *A, B, C, D,* and *Initial condition.* Since these matrices have been defined in the MATLAB command window, we type *A, B, C,* and *D,* respectively, for each of the four quantities. Had we selected different names in the MATLAB command window, we would have entered those names in their appropriate places. We leave the initial condition at 0. The signs of the summation are changed in the same manner; the second sign is changed to negative. The range of gains for the slider may also be selected. A range of 0 for the smallest and 15 for the largest is recommended. The center selection of 1 is left as is. We use the default values for the *Step* block except for *Step time* (time offset or delay), which we set to 0. Double-clicking on *Scope* brings up a simulation of an oscilloscope display. There are no parameters to select at this point.

We now connect the components to form a feedback control system. Each of the components in the project window may be moved and resized using the mouse, if desired. Connections are made at the small protrusions on the exterior of the blocks; by default, inputs are on the left and outputs on the right. Connections are made using the mouse and dragging a line from an output to an input. Place the crosshairs at the output of the *Step* block and, with the left button depressed, move the crosshairs to the plus (+) input of the *Sum* component. Continue this process until the connected block diagram looks like that shown in Figure 10.8. The line that goes from the middle of the *State-Space* block and the

Scope to the negative input of the summing device is created as follows. Place the cursor (arrowhead) on the existing line between these two blocks and, while maintaining this position, depress the *Ctrl* key on the keyboard and then the left mouse button. While holding both of these down, move the crosshairs to the negative input of the summing device and release the mouse and *Ctrl* key. To adjust the line, simply click on it and, with the mouse button depressed, move it up or down to its desired position.

The placement and size of each component is not material, only the connections. There will be models in which, prior to making these connections, we will have to flip one or more of the blocks around so that the inputs are on the right and the outputs on the left. This operation is performed by selecting (clicking on) the block and then going to the *Format* pull-down menu and selecting *Flip Block*. Also from the format menu one can suppress the display of the block identifier beneath the block. Select the block and then select *Hide Name*. To put the identifier back, select the block and then select *Show Name*. These two choices do not appear together.

To run the simulation, we go to the *Simulation* menu and select *Start*. After the simulation has executed, double-click on *Scope* to see the results. Use the *x*- and *y*-axis zoom icons to obtain the desired resolution for the image. Note that under the *Simulation* menu, one may adjust the parameters of the simulation, such as the integration method used, by selecting *Parameters*. If the diagram is not completely or correctly connected, the simulation will not run, and MATLAB will send error messages to that effect to the MATLAB command window and to a special pop-up window. When rendered as indicated in Figure 10.8, the results shown in *Scope* are those given in Figure 10.4.

10.2.5 Conversion Between Representations

MATLAB provides functions for converting between the three representations using the system constructor functions `ss`, `tf` and `zpk`. For example, the transfer-function model can be generated from the state-space model by using the state-space model *MotorSS* in `tf`.

> PlantTF = `tf`(MotorSS)

Slight differences in the coefficients of system models result from numerical errors in the conversion process.

The state-space model can be generated from the transfer function model by using `ss`. Thus

> PlantSS = `ss`(PlantTF)

The resulting system matrices A, B, C, and D are not the same matrices that were defined in *MotorSS*, which points out that unlike the transfer-function model, there is no unique state-space representation for a given system. One typically uses

> `ssbal`

to scale the input, state, and output quantities to make the simulation as well-conditioned as possible. Thus

> PlantBal = ssbal(PlantSS)

attempts to find the best-conditioned representation of the system.

The zero-pole-gain model can also be converted from state-space or transfer-function models. For example, the zero-pole-gain model could have been generated from the state-space model using

> PlantZ = zpk(PlantSS)

This, and the other conversion methods, make use of the numerical root-finding algorithms within MATLAB and are sometimes subject to large numerical errors, especially for systems of order 10 and higher.[4] In practical situations, it is recommended that one resist changing representations too often.

10.3 RESPONSE OF SYSTEMS

In this section, we illustrate the use of a number of tools available for computing the response of a system. Functions applicable to all three representations include step, impulse, initial, and lsim. The SIMULINK toolbox also supplies a number of built-in signal sources that simplify simulation when using block diagrams.

The locations of the poles and zeros, either in a transfer-function or state-space representation, are a shorthand notation that control engineers use to estimate the responses of a system. Many design specifications can be translated into pole and zero location constraints. The controller design problem often becomes one of designing feedback so that the closed loop poles lie in desired regions of the complex plane. Zeros can not be moved by feedback.

10.3.1 Simulation

The response of a control system to a step input is the most commonly used benchmark to compare different controller designs. The MATLAB function step computes the step response and, if the return values are not requested, plots it as well. The function automatically determines a suitable range of times in which to compute the simulation. Thus, the script

```
[theta,t] = step(MotorSS);
plot(t,theta)
title('Step response of a motor')
xlabel('Time')
```

---

[4] N. E. Leonard and W. S. Levine, *Using MATLAB to Analyze and Design Control Systems*, Benjamin/Cummings, Redwood City, CA, 1992.

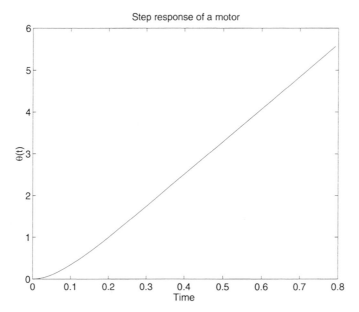

FIGURE 10.9
Step response of the motor without feedback.

```
ylabel('\theta(t)')
```

provides the numerical values used to obtain Figure 10.9. From this figure it is seen that the
step response of the motor is a ramp, because if a constant voltage is applied to the windings,
eventually a constant speed will be reached.

On the other hand, we can specify the range of times t rather than accept what `step`
provides. In this case, we would replace the first line of the previous script with the
following two expressions:

```
t = linspace(0,100,100);
theta = step(MotorSS,t);
```

where time now spans $0 \le t \le 100$.

The MATLAB function `impulse` is used in the same manner as `step`, except that it
computes the response of the system to an impulse.

MATLAB does not supply functions for all standard test inputs. However, it does
provide the capability of determining the response of a system to an arbitrary input using

```
lsim (sys,u,t)
```

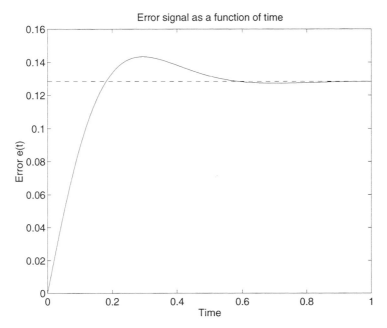

FIGURE 10.10
Tracking error of a control system as a function of time.

where *sys* is the system under consideration, and *u* is a vector representing the amplitude of the input as a function of time, *t*. The lengths of *u* and *t* must be equal.

We now determine the steady-state tracking error of the motor control system. The steady-state tracking error is the eventual difference between the desired position and the actual position when the input is a ramp. We will use a ramp with a slope of 1 over the range $0 \le t \le 1$. For the DC servomotor the error is $e(t) = \theta(t) - t$ for $0 \le t \le 1$. The script is

```
t = linspace(0,1,100);
theta = lsim(feedback(MotorSS,1),t,t);
plot(t,t'–theta);
error = t(end) – theta(end);
hold on;
plot([0,t(end)],[error,error],'r--');
xlabel('Time');
ylabel('Error e(t)');
title('Error signal as a function of time')
```

which, upon execution, generates Figure 10.10. Note that after an initial transient, the error settles to approximately 0.13. A control system design objective could be to reduce this value to less than 0.05.

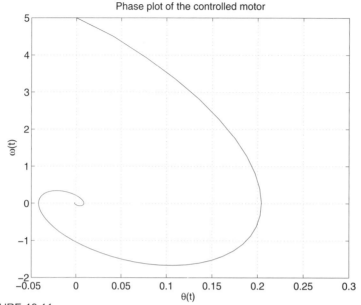

FIGURE 10.11
Phase plot of the rotor with an initial angular velocity $\omega(t) = 5$ rad/s.

For a state-space system, the MATLAB function

```
initial(sys,x0)
```

runs a simulation with non-zero initial conditions, where *sys* is the system under consideration and *x0* is a vector of initial conditions. Consider the DC motor with an initial position $\theta(0) = 0$, an initial current $i(0) = 0$, and an initial angular velocity of $\omega(0) = 5$ rad/s. In addition, we assume a gain of 2. If the voltage across the windings is kept at zero (possibly by shorting them), the following script will compute the response of the motor to these initial conditions.

```
x0 = [0; 5; 0];
[theta,t,x] = initial(feedback(2*MotorSS,1),x0);
plot(x(:,1),x(:,2));
grid on;
xlabel('\theta(t)');
ylabel('\omega(t)');
title('Phase plot of the controlled motor');
```

where $x(:,1) = \theta(t)$, $x(:,2) = \omega(t)$, and $x(:,3) = i(t)$. The result of executing this script is shown in Figure 10.11.

10.3.2 Estimating Response from Poles and Zeros

When using MATLAB to solve control problems, it is important to have a qualitative understanding of the solution of differential equations. Since controller design is an inverse process, having this qualitative understanding allows one to know what the system should be like in order to achieve some desired behavior. MATLAB can be used to help develop this important qualitative understanding of the solutions to differential equations by solving many equations of particular types.

In this section, we shall compute the step response to a number of systems characterized by their pole and zero locations. First we consider a first-order system with one pole and no zeros. We assume that the pole is located at $-\sigma$; therefore, the transfer function is

$$H(s) = \frac{\sigma}{s + \sigma}$$

The numerator is set to σ to keep the DC gain of the system at 1. The following script generates a series of step responses for pole locations ranging from slow ($\sigma = 0.1$) to quick ($\sigma = 2$).

```
t = 0:0.1:10;
polevect = 0.1:0.1:2;
hold on;
for i = 1:length(polevect)
  y = step(tf([polevect(i)],[1 polevect(i)]),t);
  plot(t,y);
end;
xlabel('Time');
ylabel('Step response');
title('Step response for a variety of pole locations');
text(0.2,0.95,'p = 2');
text(3,0.1,'p = 0.1  (\Deltap = 0.1)')
```

The results from executing this script are shown in Figure 10.12.

As the pole of a first-order system approaches the imaginary axis (that is, as σ becomes small), the control system becomes more sluggish. Sluggishness is usually not a good characteristic of a control system, but sometimes, if the slow response is with respect to some disturbance that needs to be rejected, this slowness is a good characteristic. The best location of the system poles will depend on the objective of the control system.

If two first-order systems are cascaded, then the system becomes a second-order one. Many mechanical systems are second order, so that a good understanding of second-order systems is important. Consider the following second-order system:

$$H(s) = \frac{\sigma^2 + \omega^2}{s^2 + 2s\sigma + \sigma^2 + \omega^2} \tag{10.7}$$

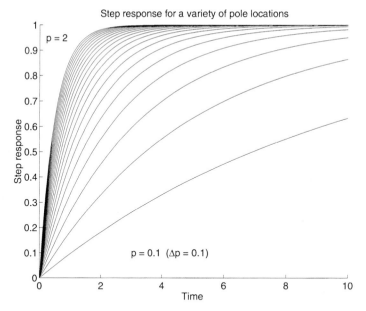

FIGURE 10.12
Response of a first-order system for a variety of pole locations p.

The system has complex poles located at $-\sigma \pm j\omega$, where σ is the real part of the pole locations and ω is the complex part. In general, σ represents the amount of damping in the system and ω specifies the strength of the storage mechanism, or spring. However, since we are interested in relating the system's response to the location of the pole, the transfer function is parameterized by the pole location. Below is a script that explores the response of the system to a variety of pole locations. First, we plot the step response as a function of σ with $\omega = 1.0$. Then, we plot the step response as a function of ω with $\sigma = 0.5$. We also sketch the locus of pole locations next to each response plot.

```
t = 0:0.4:10; sigma = linspace(0.05,1.0,10);
data = zeros(length(t),length(sigma));
omega = 1.0;
for i = 1:length(sigma)
  data(:,i) = step(tf([sigma(i)^2 + omega^2], ...
                   [1 2*sigma(i) sigma(i)^2+omega^2]), t);
end;
subplot(2,2,1);
mesh(t,-sigma,data');
ylabel('\sigma');
xlabel('Time');
zlabel('Response');
```

```
title('Response as a function of \sigma: \omega = 1.0');
data = zeros(length(t),length(omega));
sigma = 0.5; omega = linspace(0.3,2.0,10);
for i = 1:length(omega)
  data(:,i) = step(tf([sigma^2 + omega(i)^2],[1 2*sigma sigma^2+omega(i)^2]), t);
end;
subplot(2,2,3);
mesh(t,omega,data');
ylabel('\omega');
xlabel('Time');
zlabel('Response');
title('Response as a function of \omega: \sigma = 0.5');
subplot(2,2,2);
hold on;
plot([-0.1,-0.1],[1.0,-1],'x');
plot([-0.1,-1],[1.0,1.0]);
plot([-0.1,-1],[-1.0,-1.0]);
plot ([-1,-1],[1.0,-1],'<');
plot ([-2 1],[0 0],'k');
plot ([0 0],[-2 2],'k');
axis([-2 1 -2 2]);
xlabel('Real axis');
ylabel('Imaginary axis');
title('Pole location');
subplot(2,2,4);
hold on;
plot ([-0.5,-0.5],[0.3,-0.3],'x');
plot ([-0.5,-0.5],[0.3,1.5]);
plot ([-0.5,-0.5],[-0.3,-1.5]);
plot ([-0.5],[1.5],'^');
plot ([-0.5],[-1.5],'v');
plot ([-2 1],[0 0],'k');
plot ([0 0],[-2 2],'k');
axis([-2 1 -2 2]);
xlabel('Real axis');
ylabel('Imaginary axis');
title('Pole location');
```

The results from executing this script are shown in Figure 10.13.

Like the first-order system, the steady-state response is $H(0) = 1$. As seen in Figure 10.13, when σ is fixed and ω is increased, the system response becomes less damped. When ω is held constant and σ is increased, the response becomes more damped. If the real part of

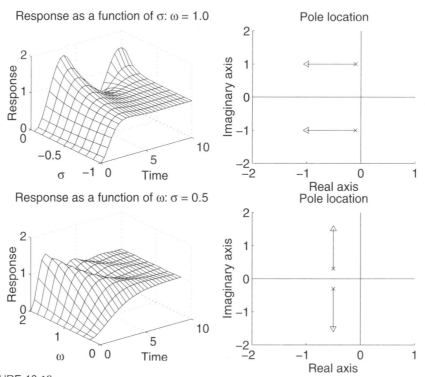

FIGURE 10.13
Response of a second-order system as a function of pole location.

the pole approaches the imaginary axis, then the system become less damped. If the pole crosses into the right half of the complex plane, then the response becomes unbounded.

Systems of higher order, like the electric motor, often behave like a second- and sometimes a first-order system. The system poles with the greatest real part dominate the input-output behavior of the system if they are much greater than the real part of the closest poles, as long as there are no transmission zeros near them. This allows the designer to approximate the closed-loop behavior of a system with that of either a first- or second-order system. To understand why this is true, consider the velocity control of a DC permanent magnet motor. The equations of motion are the same as Eq. (10.2), except the output is now rotor angular velocity $d\theta(t)/dt = \omega(t)$, instead of rotor angle $\theta(t)$. The following script makes the needed changes.

```
PlantRPM = MotorSS;
PlantRPM.c = [0 1 0];
PlantRPM = minreal(PlantRPM);
set(PlantRPM,'OutputName','\omega');
```

The first line of the script creates a system *PlantRPM* and then sets the readout matrix *C* to select $\omega(t)$ instead of $\theta(t)$. Since the rotor angle $\theta(t)$ is now unobservable, `minreal` is called to eliminate that state from the equations. Typing

```
pole(PlantRPM)/(2*pi)
```

in the MATLAB command window returns the poles of the system: one fast pole at nearly 160 Hz, which is related to the electronic coil, and one slow pole at approximately 2 Hz, which is related to the rotor dynamics. The slow pole due to the rotor dynamics dominates the open-loop response of the system, since the fast pole is more than 10 times the speed of the slow pole. The following script runs simulations with initial conditions for the rotor speed $\omega(t)$ and coil current *i* ranging between −1 and 1, and plots the results together in a phase plot − that is, a graph of $\omega(t)$ versus $i(t)$. Time is not explicitly marked in a phase-plot, so a circle is placed on the trajectory when 5% of the total trajectory time has passed.

```
PlantRPM = MotorSS;
PlantRPM.c = [0 1 0];
PlantRPM = minreal(PlantRPM);
set(PlantRPM,'OutputName','\omega');
t = linspace(0,0.05,500);
hold on;
for i = 0:13;
  x0 = [−1.4+0.2*i,1];
  [y,t,x] = initial(PlantRPM,x0,t);
  plot(x(:,2),x(:,1));
  k = floor(0.05*length(t));
  plot(x(k,2),x(k,1),'ro');
end;
for i = 0:13;
  x0 = [−1+0.2*i,−1];
  [y,t,x] = initial(PlantRPM,x0,t);
  plot(x(:,2),x(:,1));
  k = floor(0.05*length(t));
  plot(x(k,2),x(k,1),'ro');
end;
plot([1 −1],[0 0],'k--');
plot([0 0],[1 −1],'k--');
axis([−1 1 −1 1]);
ylabel('i(t)');
xlabel('\omega(t)');
title('Phase portrait of DC motor');
```

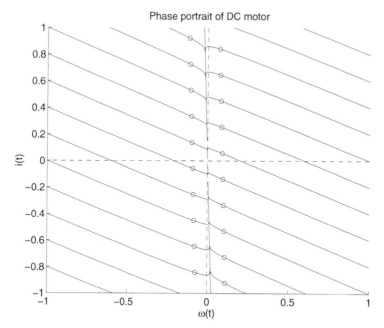

FIGURE 10.14
Phase portrait of a DC electric motor.

The resulting phase portrait of the system is shown in Figure 10.14. Note that the vast majority of the time for every trajectory is spent about a one-dimensional subspace. The subspace is associated with the slow pole. In general, those poles with the larger real part will dominate the step response of a system.

Although zeros can not be moved by feedback, the effect of their positions can be profound if they are near poles or near the imaginary axis. Consider the second-order plant

$$H(s) = \frac{-(s-z)}{z(s^2 + 0.5s + 1)}$$

where z is the location of the zero. The step response of a family of plants with a zero approaching and crossing the imaginary axis is shown in Figure 10.15, which is obtained with the execution of the following script. The zeros are stable when at $z = -5$ and $z = -1$; however, for the cases where $z = 1$ and $z = 5$, the zero is unstable.

```
t = linspace(0,25,200);
Z = [-5 -1 1 5];
Den = [1 0.5 1];
y = zeros(length(t),length(Z));
for i = 1:length(Z)
  y(:,i) = step(-1/Z(i)*tf([1 -Z(i)],Den),t);
```

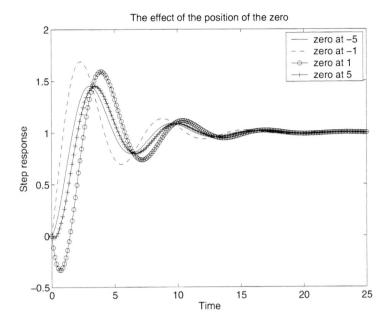

FIGURE 10.15
Effect of a zero approaching and crossing the imaginary axis.

```
end
plot(t,y(:,1));
hold on;
plot(t,y(:,2),'k--');
plot(t,y(:,3),'r-o');
plot(t,y(:,4),'g-+');
legend('zero at -5','zero at -1', 'zero at 1', 'zero at 5');
xlabel('Time');
ylabel('Step response');
title('The effect of the position of the zero');
```

Although unstable zeros do not destabilize a system, they limit the amount of feedback that can be applied. The hallmark of an unstable zero is the system's tendency to go the wrong way initially, as seen with the plot with the zero at 1. A system with one or more unstable zeros is called non-minimum phase.

Zeros can also serve to mask modal dynamics, either from observation or from excitation. Consider the first- through fourth-order systems given by

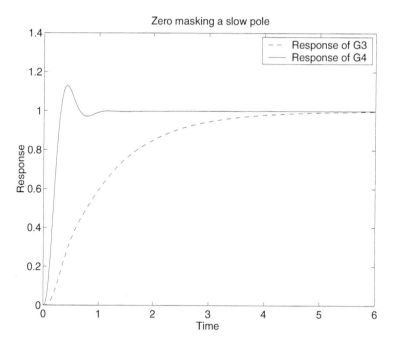

FIGURE 10.16
Effect of hiding a system's slow dynamics with a zero.

$$G_1 = \frac{1}{s+1} \qquad G_3 = G_1(s) * G_2(s)$$

$$G_2 = \frac{100}{s^2 + 10s + 100} \qquad G_4 = \frac{19.8s + 20}{s + 20} G_3(s)$$

The step response of the plant G_3 is very similar to the response of the first-order plant G_1, because the pole at -1 dominates the complex poles, as discussed previously. However, if a zero were near the pole -1, then that pole would no longer dominate. The system given by G_4 places at zero near the dominant pole at -1 in G_3, masking its effect. However, this is not generally practical to do, since in order to force G_3 to move quickly, G_4 will initially produce a large output, which may saturate or damage the actuators. This can be observed in the step response of G_4. The step responses of G_3 and G_4 are shown in Figure 10.16 and are obtained from the following script:

```
G1 = tf([1],[1 1]);
G2 = tf([100],[1 10 100]);
G3 = G1*G2;
G4 = tf([19.8 20],[1 20])*G3;
t=linspace(0,6,200);
```

```
yG3=step(G3,t);
yG4=step(G4,t);
plot(t,yG3,'k--',t,yG4,'k-')
legend('Response of G3','Response of G4')
xlabel('Time')
ylabel('Response')
title('Zero masking a slow pole')
```

The distance between a zero and a pole measures how perpendicular the input or output matrices are to the mode eigenvector. If a zero is directly on top of a pole, then the mode is either not excitable or not seeable in the output. The terms controllability and observability are also used to describe this phenomena.

10.4 DESIGN TOOLS

In this section, we consider design tools in MATLAB and the criteria by which designs are evaluated. Many design techniques are graphical, as they were developed before computers were in general use. The graphical design tools include

bode—creates Bode plots
nyquist—creates Nyquist plots
rlocus—creates root locus plots

A computer-based modern design tool employing lqr and lqe is also introduced.

Having a trusted model of the plant is very important in the design process. Much of the effort in designing a control system is spent developing and refining the model of the plant. The modeling process, however, is outside the scope of this chapter; MATLAB does provide the ident toolbox, which takes experimental data and finds the best model that fits it.

Design criteria for control systems involve three requirements:

- Stability
- Transient
- Steady state

The need for stability is clear when solving the differential equations. Each root of the denominator polynomial corresponds to a component of the solution, and any root with a positive real part will contribute a term that grows exponentially. A system with a pole on the imaginary axis is labeled marginally stable. The other two categories of design criteria assume that the system is stable. Transient requirements look at the short-term response of the system to the unit step. Steady-state requirements look at the long-term error in tracking either a step, a ramp, or, on rare occasion, a parabola. The stability criteria must always be met; some systems are initially unstable and must be stabilized. Examples of such systems include an inverted pendulum and a magnetic bearing. Many systems can be destabilized by

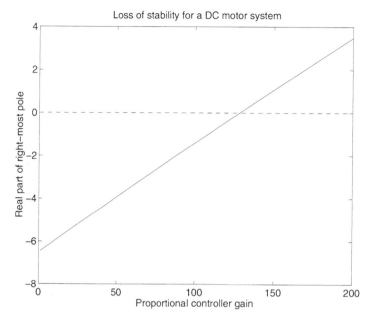

FIGURE 10.17
Real part of the right-most system pole of the closed-loop system as a function of controller gain.

the application of feedback. Stability of a closed-loop control system can easily be checked using `root` on the denominator of the closed-loop transfer function. Any roots with a positive real part indicate instability of the closed-loop system.

10.4.1 Design Criteria

We return to the DC motor to study design tools, and consider the stability of a closed-loop system with the DC motor as the plant. A proportional controller, which takes the error between the desired position and the actual position and multiplies it by its gain, is used. The designer using the proportional controller must choose which gain to use. The following script generates Figure 10.17, which is a plot of the real part of the right-most pole as a function of the design parameter gain, which ranges from 1 to 200.

```
gains = linspace(1,200,50); y = [];
for i = 1:length(gains)
 y = [y, max(real(pole(feedback(gains(i)*MotorSS,1))))];
end;
plot(gains,y,[0 200],[0 0],'r--');
xlabel('Proportional controller gain');
ylabel('Real part of right-most pole');
title('Loss of stability for a DC motor system');
```

and peak time are in conflict with the next criteria, overshoot. Percentage overshoot is the amount by which the system overshoots its goal. Settling time is typically defined as the amount of time it takes for the system to come to and stay within a 2% envelope of the final value. These quantities are calculated in *Transient* given below. The function returns [−1, −1, −1] if the system is not stable.

```
function criteria = transient(system)
criteria = [−1 −1 −1];
maxP = max(real(pole(system)));
if maxP >= 0
 return
end
MaxTime = −6*(1/maxP);
Time = linspace(0,MaxTime,500);
Response = step(system,Time);
[ResponseMax,IndexMax] = max(Response);
FinalValue = Response(end);
TimeLow = interp1(Response(1:IndexMax),Time (1:IndexMax),0.1*FinalValue);
TimeHigh = interp1(Response(1:IndexMax),Time (1:IndexMax),0.9*FinalValue);
criteria(1) = TimeHigh − TimeLow;
k = length(Time);
while (k>0)& (0.02 > abs((FinalValue − Response(k))/FinalValue));
 k = k−1;
end;
criteria(2) = Time(k);
criteria(3) = 100*(max(Response) − FinalValue)/FinalValue;
```

where *criteria*(1) = rise time, *criteria*(2) = settling time, and *criteria*(3) = percentage overshoot.

We use this function to evaluate controllers for the DC motor. Thus

```
transient(feedback(MotorSS,1));
```

displays the vector [0.1935 0.6080 7.6136], where 0.1935 is the rise time, 0.6080 the settling time, and 7.6136 the percentage overshoot.

10.4.2 Design Tools

For the design criteria discussed in Section 10.4.1, we introduce a collection of design tools and illustrate their application to the motor controller. Typically, one of three different tools will be applied:

- Frequency-based
- Root locus

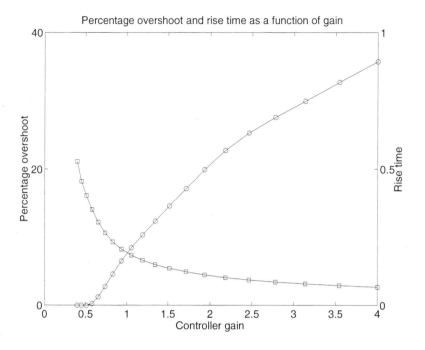

FIGURE 10.20
Percentage overshoot (circles) and rise time (squares) as a function of controller gain.

- LQG based

Frequency-based design does not require an explicit model, only the results from a collection of experiments. The last two methods require very good models of the plant.

The problem we now consider is the motor controller. The design criteria require that we keep the overshoot under 20%; thus, many of the design gains shown in Figure 10.19 are unacceptable. Furthermore, we want the closed-loop system to be very quick, having a rise time under 0.05 s. Using a straight proportional controller, we see that we are in a deadlocked situation. To obtain a rise time under 0.05 s, a gain greater than 3 must be used. To have an overshoot under 20%, a gain smaller than 2 must be used. The following script generates Figure 10.20, which graphs the overshoot and rise time as functions of gain for the proportional controller.

```
kp = 0.4*logspace(0,1,20); result = [];
for i = 1:length(kp)
 result = [result; transient(feedback(kp(i)*MotorSS,1))];
end;
[ax,h1,h2] = plotyy(kp, result(:,3),kp, result(:,1));
```

```
xlabel('Controller gain');
ylabel('Percent overshoot');
v = axis;
text(v(2)*1.06,v(3)+(v(4)−v(3))/2.4,'Rise time','rotation',90);
set(h2,'Marker','s');
set(h1,'Marker','o');
title('Percentage overshoot and rise time as a function of gain');
```

First we attempt a frequency-based design. The overshoot requirement can be translated into a phase-margin minimum. For this system, a phase margin of $45°$ is needed to meet the overshoot requirements. Looking at the Bode plot in Figure 10.18, we see that at a phase of $−135°$ (= $45°$ phase margin), a gain of approximately 2.0 is allowed. In order to compute the gain more precisely, we can use fzero with *transient*. First we create the function *PEcontrol*.

```
function s=PEcontrol(gain)
rval = transient(feedback(gain*MotorSS,1));
s = rval(3)−20;
```

We then use

```
options = optimset('display','off');
gain = fzero('PEcontrol',2,options)
```

to obtain *gain* = 1.9384 for a 20% overshoot. Using the command

```
transresp=transient(feedback(1.9384*MotorSS,1))
```

gives that *transresp*(1) = rise time = 0.1111 s, more than twice as slow as the design specification.

A lead controller is typically used to improve the transient response of a system. A properly designed lead controller increases the phase for a short range of frequencies; this boost in phase allows more gain to be applied. The zero of the lead controller is chosen to be at $−15$, just to the left of the second open-loop pole at $−13$. This ensures that the lead controller's phase boost starts about where the phase of the DC motor starts to roll off. The lead controller pole is at $−100$, nearly 10 times the zero location. In theory, the further to the left the better, but having the pole very far to the left makes the controller sensitive to noise. As a rule of thumb, the pole cannot be located further left than 10 times the location of the zero. The resulting controller transfer function is

$$C(s) = \frac{100}{15} \frac{s+15}{s+100} = \frac{6.667s+100}{s+100}$$

where we have multiplied the transfer function by 100/15 to set the DC gain to 1.

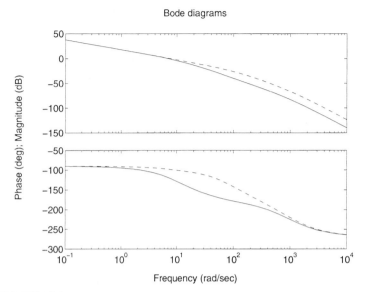

FIGURE 10.21

Bode plot of the lead compensated system (dashed line) and that of the uncompensated system (solid line).

The following script generates Figure 10.21, which compares the frequency response of the uncompensated and compensated system:

```
Control = tf([6.667 100],[1 100]);
bode(MotorSS,'k-',Control*MotorSS,'k--')
```

Note how the phase roll-off is delayed to higher frequencies. Again, we use the Bode plot to find a initial guess for the correct feedback gain, approximately 10. To compute the exact gain at which an overshoot of 20% is reached we create the function *LDcontrol*.

```
function s = LDcontrol(gain)
rval = transient(feedback(gain*tf([6.667 100],[1 100])*MotorSS,1));
s = rval(3)–20;
```

We then use

```
options = optimset('display','off');
gain = fzero('LDcontrol',[10],options)
```

to determine that *gain* = 13.0108 for a 20% overshoot. Using

```
transresp = transient(feedback(13.0108*tf([6.667 100],[1 100])*MotorSS,1))
```

we find that *transresp*(1) = rise time = 0.0170 s, nearly three times faster than the target value. The graphs of the step responses for both the proportional and lead-controlled systems are shown subsequently in Figure 10.24.

Using the lead compensator, one is able to meet both the overshoot and the rise-time requirements. Frequency-based design requires data from a Bode plot, but does not depend on an explicit model. The other frequency-based tools include the Nyquist plot and the Nichols plot, which are used in a similar manner.

The root locus is another commonly applied tool. The same lead compensator may be applied, but the approach differs. Given that the complex poles subtend an angle ξ from the imaginary axis and have radius ω_n, we have[5]

$$M_p = \exp\left(-\frac{\pi\xi}{\sqrt{1-\xi^2}}\right)$$

$$T_r \approx \frac{1}{\omega_n}(1+1.4\xi)$$

where M_p is the peak magnitude and T_r is the rise time. Inverting these formulas constrains where the closed loop poles may be located in the complex plane in order to meet the transient design requirements. Hence, an overshoot requirement of less than 20% constrains ξ, requiring that the dominant poles be located within a 120° wedge centered along the negative imaginary axis. A 0.05 s rise time corresponds roughly to a minimum pole radius ω_n of 20. These formulas are rules of thumb, but they serve as a good starting point. In the following script, we first shade the region of the complex plane in which all closed loop poles must lie. Then we plot the root locus to see if this condition is met at any gain.

```
theta = linspace(-2/3*pi,-4/3*pi,15);
X = [20*cos(theta) 200*cos(-4/3*pi) 200*cos(-2/3*pi) 20*cos(-2/3*pi)];
Y = [20*sin(theta) 200*sin(-4/3*pi) 200*sin(-2/3*pi) 20*sin(-2/3*pi)];
hold on;
fill(X,Y,'y');
sgrid;
rlocus(MotorSS);
axis(100*[-1 0 -1 1]);
ylabel('Imaginary axis');
xlabel('Real axis');
title('Root locus of proportional-controlled motor');
```

The resulting plot is shown in Figure 10.22a. A similar plot can be generated for the lead-controlled system using

```
theta = linspace(-2/3*pi,-4/3*pi,15);
```

---

[5] D. K. Anand and R. B. Zmood, *Ibid.*, 1995.

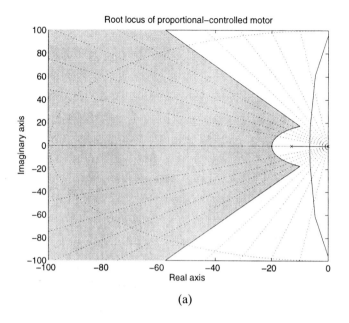

(a)

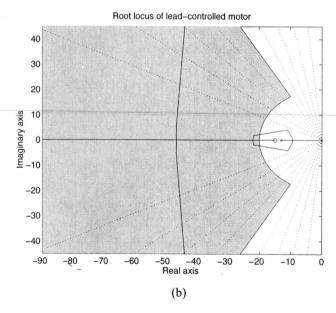

(b)

FIGURE 10.22
Root-locus plots of both the (a) proportional- and the (b) lead-controlled motor positioning system.

```
X = [20*cos(theta) 200*cos(-4/3*pi) 200*cos(-2/3*pi) 20*cos(-2/3*pi)];
Y = [20*sin(theta) 200*sin(-4/3*pi) 200*sin(-2/3*pi) 20*sin(-2/3*pi)];
hold on;
fill(X,Y,'y');
sgrid;
rlocus(MotorSS*tf([6.667,100],[1 100]));
axis(90*[-1 0 -0.5 0.5]);
ylabel('Imaginary axis');
xlabel('Real axis');
title('Root locus of lead-controlled motor');
```

Notice that the controller and plant, *MotorSS*, have had their order switched. In theory, this produces the same root-locus plot. However, when the root-locus command with the lead controller precedes the plant, the calculations run much slower and may cause some systems to lock. This is due to the controller's zero being near the plant pole. The transformation to controller form, which simplifies the computation of the closed loop poles, is nearly singular when the lead controller precedes the plant—that is, the cascade is nearly uncontrollable. By switching the order, we make the system nearly unobservable and do not compromise the transformation.

Execution of the script results in the graph shown in Figure 10.22b. Notice that for the proportional controller, there is no gain where all of the closed loop roots are located in the acceptable region. The net effect of the lead controller is to bend the root-locus lines back into the acceptable region.

To find the correct gain, we use

```
rlocus(MotorSS*tf([6.667 100],[1 100]))
[k,p] = rlocfind(MotorSS*tf([6.667 100],[1 100]))
```

and place the crosshairs where the root locus crosses the edge of the acceptable region. The function `rlocus` precedes `rlocfind` because `rlocfind` does not draw the root locus. This procedure yields a gain of 12. These regions are approximate, so it is a good practice to fine-tune the gain by simulation. Thus, from a simulation it will be found that a gain as high as 13 can be applied.

In the root-locus design, the objective is to place the poles of the closed loop system into the acceptable region. With the linear-algebra tools developed for state-space models, such a problem can be solved by directly placing the poles in the desired locations. The two methods introduced here are pole placement with

```
place
```

and

```
acker
```

and LQG design with

```
lqr
lqe
```

and

```
reg
```

In order to meet the design specifications, we choose the pole locations −30, −20+30*i*, −20−30*i*. These pole locations are arbitrarily chosen, but are safely inside the acceptable shaded region of Figures 10.22. The following script uses place to compute the gain matrix *K* so that the matrix *A* − *BK* has eigenvalues in the desired locations. The quantities *A* and *B* are those in Eq. (10.3).

```
DesiredPoles = [−30, −20+30*i, −20−30*i];
[A,B,C,D] = ssdata(MotorSS);
K = place(A,B,DesiredPoles)
```

The execution of the script gives *K* = [0.3900 −0.1002 −4.6517]. The feedback needed is then *u* = *Kx*, which assumes we have available the internal state of the system given by *x*. Since only the output is available, a state estimator needs to be designed. A complete script computing both the controller and the observer is listed below.

```
DesiredPoles = [−30, −20+30*i, −20−30*i];
[A,B,C,D] = ssdata(MotorSS);
K = place(A,B,DesiredPoles);
L = (place(A',C',3*DesiredPoles))';
ControlSS = reg(MotorSS,K,L);
clSys = feedback(MotorSS,ControlSS,+1);
clSys = 1/dcgain(clSys)*clSys;
step(clSys);
```

The result of this script is plotted subsequently in Figure 10.24 as the state-space controller. The first three lines of the script generate the feedback gain matrix *K*. Using duality through the transpose between observability and controllability, place is used to compute the observer feedback gain matrix *L*. This matrix depends on the system matrices *A* and *C* and a set of desired observer pole locations, which we set to 3 times the feedback pole locations. The function reg then creates the estimator which, using the plant output, estimates the internal state and outputs the corrective command. Since the command signal has the correct sign, we employ positive feedback in feedback.

Pole locations in the previous example were chosen to satisfy the transient requirements. These requirements are inequalities in nature, so a range of pole locations is acceptable; we arbitrarily chose a set of pole locations within the acceptable region. The linear quadratic Gaussian controller design method follows similar steps, but offers the designer a systematic method for assigning pole locations. Poles are chosen to minimize the integral[6]

$$J = \int \left[x'(t)Qx(t) + u'(t)Ru(t) \right] dt \qquad (10.8)$$

where $x(t)$ is the internal system state at time t, $u(t)$ is the input vector at time t, Q is a positive semidefinite matrix, and R is a positive definite matrix. The matrix Q is often chosen as $C'C$, so that the first term reduces to the square of the output error.

The designer may adjust the relative importance of the state error to the input by modifying the relative magnitudes of Q and R. In our particular case, the plant has only one input, so R is a positive scalar. With $Q = C'C$, the following script plots the location of the optimal poles as a function of R and, in addition, the region in which the poles must lie to satisfy the transient design requirements.

```
[A,B,C,D] = ssdata(MotorSS);
clPoles = [];
R = logspace(–4,1,60);
for i = 1:length(R)
  [K,S,E] = lqr(A,B,C'*C,R(i));
  clPoles = [clPoles, E];
end;
theta = linspace(–2/3*pi,–4/3*pi,15);
X = [20*cos(theta) 200*cos(–4/3*pi) 200*cos(–2/3*pi) 20*cos(–2/3*pi)];
Y = [20*sin(theta) 200*sin(–4/3*pi) 200*sin(–2/3*pi) 20*sin(–2/3*pi)];
fill(X,Y,'c');
hold on;
plot(real(clPoles),imag(clPoles),'x');
axis(40*[–1 0 –0.5 0.5]);
sgrid;
title('Optimal root locus for motor system');
ylabel('Imaginary axis');
xlabel('Real axis');
```

Figure 10.23 shows the resulting root locus, which plots discrete root location with an 'x', instead of using lines. For large values of R, the cost of the input is large relative to the cost of the output error, and, consequently, little control effort is applied. The closed-loop poles are close to the open-loop poles. As the cost of the input is made less expensive, the optimal closed-loop poles move further into the left half of the complex plane. More control action is being applied, and the response of the system is much faster. Since we want to meet both an optimality condition and the transient requirements, we must select R so that the optimal closed-loop poles lie within the shaded region.

---

[6] T. Kailith, *Ibid.*, 1980.

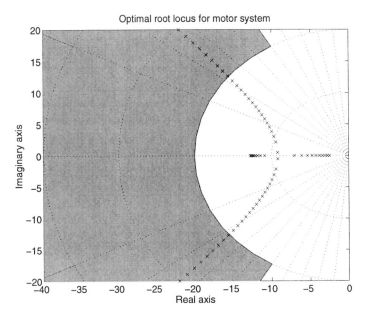

FIGURE 10.23
Closed-loop poles of the optimal controller as a function of the input cost weight R.

The step responses of the three major controller designs discussed so far are generated in the following script and are compared in Figure 10.24. The proportional controller fails to meet the rise-time design criteria. Using pole placement, both the lead controller and the state-space controller meet the design criteria. The state-space controller has the additional benefit of having almost no overshoot.

```
t = linspace(0,1,200);
yp = step(feedback(1.9416*MotorSS,1),t);
yl = step(feedback(13.0108*tf([6.667 100],[1 100])*MotorSS,1),t);
DesiredPoles = [-30, -20+30*i, -20-30*i];
[A,B,C,D] = ssdata(MotorSS);
K = place(A,B,DesiredPoles);
L = (place(A',C',3*DesiredPoles))';
ControlSS = reg(MotorSS,K,L);
clSys = feedback(MotorSS,ControlSS,+1);
clSys = clSys/dcgain(clSys);
ys = step(clSys,t);
plot(t,yp,'k-',t,yl,'k--',t,ys,'k-.');
xlabel('Time');
ylabel('Step response');
title('Step response of proportional-, lead-, and state-space controllers');
```

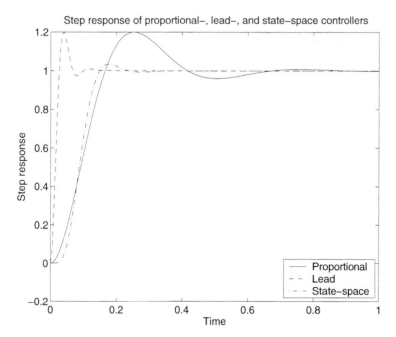

FIGURE 10.24
Comparison of a proportional-, lead-, and state-space controller to a step input.

    legend('Proportional','Lead','State-space',4);

10.5 DESIGN EXAMPLES

In this section we shall use MATLAB tools to design controllers for four different physical systems:

- DC motor with flexible shaft—design a notch controller in order not to excite the flexible shaft's vibration mode.
- Single axis magnetic suspension system—design a PID controller to keep the mass positioned at its equilibrium location.
- Inverted pendulum—design multi-input single output controller to keep a pendulum vertical.
- Magnetically suspended flywheel—design a multi-input, multi-output controller to keep a flywheel suspended.

There are four steps in the controller design process:

1. Specify the controller requirements.

2. Develop a model of the plant.
3. Design the controller to meet the requirements.
4. Simulate and test the controller design.

Plant models in the following sections are derived from first principles, but are not tested against experimental data. It can not be overemphasized that validating and refining the model is a step that is of great importance in controller design and one that must not be ignored. The latter three plant models described above are nonlinear, but only slightly; each can be linearized about an operating point, which is stabilized. Frequency-based design using open-loop data from Bode plots is possible only for the DC motor with flexible shaft, since all the other systems are open-loop unstable.

Controllers used in the subsequent sections include

*   Lead (Lag)
*   Notch
*   PID
*   LQG

With each of these methods, the root locus is the primary design tool. In practice, the PID controller is by far the most common type of controller used for single-input, single-output control systems.

10.5.1 Notch Control of a Flexible Pointer

Consider the read-write head on a hard-disk drive. The objective is for the head to move as fast as possible to a desired location, and once there, to provide a steady platform for the read or write operation. With limited actuation, typically a voice coil, the way to go faster is to remove material from the swing arm holding the read-write head. Removing material tends to reduce the stiffness of the arm, and hence moving quickly will more likely excite the vibration modes of the arm.

As a model of this design, we consider the DC motor mounted with a flexible shaft as shown in Figure 10.25. The user specifies a desired angle θ_d and the control system, measuring the angle of inclination of the rod θ attempts to match the command in as quick a manner as possible. However, if the pointer gets to the desired position and then oscillates for a long time, the head will not function properly.

The equations of motion for the flexible pointer are[7]:

$$L\frac{di(t)}{dt} + k_b\frac{d\theta(t)}{dt} + Ri = v(t)$$

$$J_m\frac{d^2\theta(t)}{dt^2} - k_\tau i(t) = b\left(\frac{d\phi(t)}{dt} - \frac{d\theta(t)}{dt}\right) + k[\phi(t) - \theta(t)] \qquad (10.9)$$

---

[7] R. C. Dorf and R. H. Bishop, *Modern Control Systems*, Addison Wesley, Reading, MA, 1998.

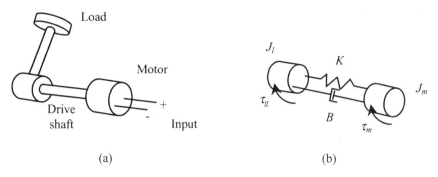

FIGURE 10.25
(a) Pointer with a flexible drive shaft; and (b) its equivalent model.

$$J_l \frac{d^2\phi(t)}{dt^2} = -b\left(\frac{d\phi(t)}{dt} - \frac{d\theta(t)}{dt}\right) - k[\phi(t) - \theta(t)]$$

where θ is the angle of the rotor, ϕ is the orientation of the pointer, $J_m = 0.03$ kg·m^2 is the rotor inertia, $J_l = 0.015$ kg·m^2 is the load inertia, $b = 0.01$ Nm/rad/s is the flexible shaft damping, and $k = 10$ Nm/rad is the flexible shaft spring constant. The values for the inductance L, resistance R, back emf constant k_b, and the motor torque constant k_τ are defined in Section 10.2.1.

The coupled second order differential equations can be converted to linear coupled first-order equations by introducing the state variables

$$x_1 = \theta \qquad x_4 = \phi$$
$$x_2 = \frac{d\theta}{dt} \qquad x_5 = \frac{d\phi}{dt}$$
$$x_3 = i$$

Then Eqs. (10.9) become

$$\frac{dx_1}{dt} = x_2$$

$$\frac{dx_2}{dt} = -\frac{k}{J_m}x_1 - \frac{b}{J_m}x_2 + \frac{k_2}{J_m}x_3 + \frac{k}{J_m}x_4 + \frac{b}{J_m}x_5$$

$$\frac{dx_3}{dt} = -\frac{k_b}{L}x_2 - \frac{R}{L}x_3 + v$$

$$\frac{dx_4}{dt} = x_5$$

$$\frac{dx_5}{dt} = \frac{k}{J_l}x_1 + \frac{b}{J_l}x_2 - \frac{k}{J_l}x_4 - \frac{b}{J_l}x_5$$

The following function *Pointer* computes the system matrices for the coupled first-order equations and returns a state-space system object model.

```
function Plant = Pointer
L = 5e-3; R = 5; kb = 0.125;
ki = 15; Jm = 3e-2;
Jl = 0.5*Jm; k = 10; b = 0.01;
A = [0 1 0 0 0;
     -k/Jm -b/Jm  ki/Jm k/Jm b/Jm;
     0 -kb/L -R/L 0 0;
     0 0 0 0 1;
     k/Jl b/Jl 0 -k/Jl -b/Jl];
B = [0; 0; 1/L; 0; 0];
C = [0 0 0 1 0];
D = 0;
Plant = ss(A,B,C,D);
```

The output of the system is the angular position of the pointer $\phi(t)$. Typing

```
pole(Pointer)
```

in the MATLAB command window gives

```
1.0e+002 *
  -9.8734
  -0.0248 + 0.3104i
  -0.0248 - 0.3104i
   0.0000
  -0.0871
```

which shows that the flexible pointer system has five poles, three of which are on the real axis: one at the origin, one at nearly -1000 rad/s due to the motor coil electronics, and a pole at -8.7 rad/s due to the rotor dynamics. The flexible attachment adds a pair of complex poles at $-2.5 \pm 31.0i$. As before, a lead controller could be applied to improve the transient response; however, the poorly damped poles will frustrate this approach.

To illustrate the limitation of lead control for this system we shall generate the root locus of the proportional and lead-controlled systems. We place the lead zero at -6, which is just to the right of the first stable pole. The lead pole is placed at -50, nearly ten times the location of the zero. Then the transfer function is

$$H(s) = \frac{s+6}{s+50}$$

The script is

```
rlocus(Pointer);
axis(70*[−1 1 −0.5 0.5]);
sgrid;
xlabel('Real axis');
ylabel('Imaginary axis');
title('Root locus for proportional control');
figure(2);
rlocus(tf([1 6],[1 50])*Pointer);
axis(70*[−1 1 −0.5 0.5]);
sgrid;
xlabel('Real axis');
ylabel('Imaginary axis');
title('Root locus for lead control');
```

The result of executing this script is shown in Figure 10.26. The allowable gain for both designs is limited not by the real-axis open-loop poles, as it was in the case of the DC motor, but by the complex poles due to the flexible shaft. The performance of the lead controller will be only a little better than the performance of the proportional controller. By entering

```
rlocus(tf([1 6],[1 50])*Pointer)
[k,p] = rlocfind(tf([1 6],[1 50])*Pointer)
```

in the MATLAB command window, we can pick the best gains for the lead-controlled system and, similarly, the proportional-controlled system. The crosshairs must be placed near the complex poles that are due to the flexible shaft, because they primarily limit the gain. A gain of 3 for each is stable and has fair performance, as shown subsequently by their closed-loop step responses in Figure 10.28. The undamped complex poles block further performance improvement because standard controllers will unwittingly excite the flexible mode.

Not exciting the flexible mode is the key to further improving the closed-loop performance. Recall from Section 10.3.2 that if a zero happens to be near a pole, then that mode is difficult to excite. We will use a notch controller whose zeros are chosen close to the flexible mode locations at $-3 \pm 30i$. To keep the transfer strictly proper, we choose both notch poles at -60. There is no realistic hope of being directly on top of the poles and canceling them, for to be close requires a good model that has most likely been derived from a set of experiments on the system.

The following script plots the root locus of the notch-controlled system.

```
Notch = zpk([−3+30i,−3−30i],[−60,−60],1);
rlocus(tf([1 6],[1 50])*Notch*Pointer);
axis(70*[−1 1 −0.5 0.5]);
sgrid;
xlabel('Real axis');
ylabel('Imaginary axis');
```

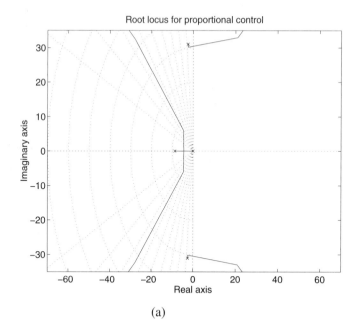

(a)

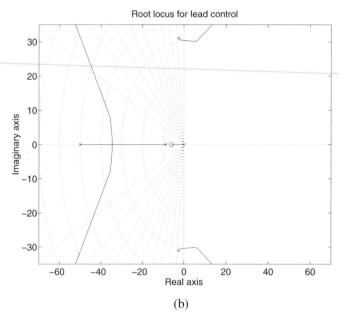

(b)

FIGURE 10.26
Root locus of the flexible pointer under (a) proportional control, and (b) lead control.

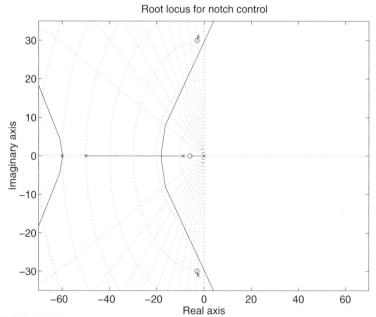

FIGURE 10.27
Root locus of the notch-lead compensated flexible pointer.

        title('Root locus for notch control');

The result of executing this script is shown in Figure 10.27. The zeros are very close to the poles due to the flexible mode, and the root-locus plot is very similar to a system without the flexible modes.
    Using

        rlocus(tf([1,6],[1,50])*Notch*Pointer)
        rlocfind(tf([1,6],[1,50])*Notch*Pointer)

a gain of 40.0 is found to produce a stable closed-loop system. The crosshairs are placed along the root-locus lines that cross the imaginary axis. Placing them inside a 120° wedge centered about the negative real axis will yield good transient performance.
    The following script computes the step response of all three types of control schemes previously described.

        Lead = tf([1 6],[1 50]);
        Notch = zpk([−3+30i,−3−30i],[−60,−60],1);
        t = linspace(0,3,200);
        yp = step(feedback(3.0*Pointer,1),t);

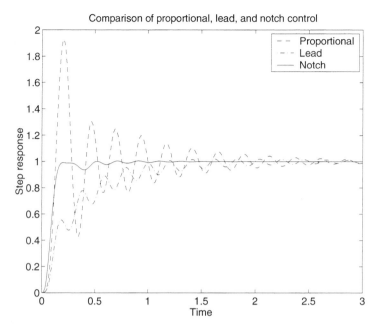

FIGURE 10.28
Comparison of the step response of the proportional, lead, and notch controllers.

```
yl = step(feedback(3.0*Lead*Pointer,1),t);
yn = step(feedback(40.0*Notch*Lead*Pointer,1),t);
plot(t,yp,'k--',t,yl,'k-.',t,yn,'k-');
legend('Proportional','Lead','Notch');
xlabel('Time');
ylabel('Step response');
title('Comparison of proportional, lead, and notch control');
```

The results of executing this script are shown in Figure 10.28. The notch controller has the rise time of the proportional controller but doesn't excite the flexible mode of the shaft.

The controllers resulting from the preceding design are analog; however, the final controller will most likely be implemented using an embedded controller, which is a small, inexpensive computer. The embedded controller, using perhaps an optical encoder, periodically measures the position of the pointer and compares to its desired position. After some computation, a digital-to-analog converter or a pulse-width modulator sets the effective amplifier voltage. In the following example, the computer reads the encoder and updates the output of the voltage amplifier one hundred times a second. Because of the small sampling interval, the computation done at every sampling instance must be kept to a minimum. The following script designs the controller for the discretized version of the plant and then compares the digital design to that obtained from the previous continuous notch design. The zeros of the digital notch filter are set at $0.92 \pm 0.3i$, close to the poles of the discretized version of the plant, and the poles are placed at 0.6. A digital transfer function does not have to be strictly proper to be implemented. The zero of the digital lead is placed at 0.95, just to the right of the first stable pole of the discretized plant, the pole at 0.5. Using

```
rlocus(DNotch*DLead*c2d(Pointer,Ts))
rlocfind(DNotch*DLead*c2d(Pointer,Ts))
```

one places the crosshairs on the root-locus line that leaves the unit circle and finds a gain of 15.

```
Ts = 1/100;
DNotch = zpk([0.92+0.3i,0.92−0.3i],[0.6 0.6],1,Ts);
DLead = tf([1 −0.95],[1 −0.5],Ts);
rlocus(DNotch*DLead*c2d(Pointer,Ts));
axis(1.2*[−1 1 −1 1]);
zgrid;
figure(2);
[yd,t]= step(feedback(15*DNotch*DLead*c2d(Pointer,Ts),1));
Lead = tf([1 6],[1 50]);
Notch = zpk([−3+30i,−3−30i],[−60,−60],1);
yn = step(feedback(40.0*Notch*Lead*Pointer,1),t);
plot(t,yd,'k-',t,yn,'k:');
legend('Discrete control','Continuous control',4);
title('Comparison of discrete (100 Hz) and continuous control');
xlabel('Time');
ylabel('Step response');
axis(1.2*[0 1 0 1]);
```

The results from executing this script are shown in Figure 10.29.

10.5.2 PID Control of a Magnetic Suspension System

Consider the magnetic suspension system[8] shown in Figure 10.30. The objective is to keep the ball floating at a desired height when it is subjected to external disturbances. The height of the ball is $h(t)$, and the current in the coil is $i(t)$. The equations of motion for the magnetic suspension are

$$m\frac{d^2h(t)}{dt^2} = mg - k\left(\frac{i(t)}{h(t)}\right)^2$$

$$L\frac{di(t)}{dt} = v(t) - Ri(t)$$

(10.10)

---

[8] B. Friedland, *Advanced Control System Design*, Prentice Hall, Englewood Cliffs, NJ, 1996.

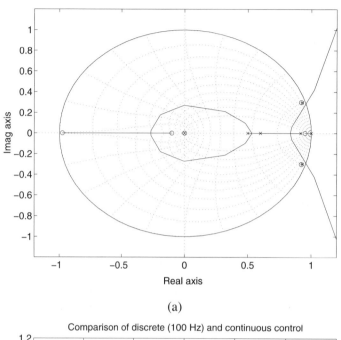

(a)

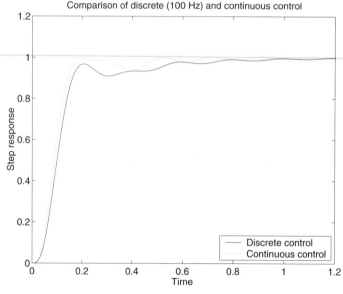

FIGURE 10.29   (b)
Digital implementation of the flexible pointer system: (a) root locus and (b) step response.

Electromagnet k

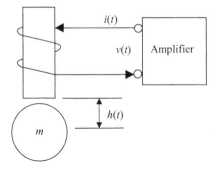

FIGURE 10.30
A magnetic suspension system.

where m is the mass of the ball, g is the gravitational constant, L is the inductance of the coil, R the coil resistance, and k the coupling factor between the magnetic fields and the ball. The input to the system is the coil voltage $v(t)$, and the measured output is the height of the ball $h(t)$. The equations are nonlinear.

The magnetic fields are stronger the closer the ball is to the electromagnet, which tends to destabilize the system. Ideally, the ball is located far enough away so that the magnetic force cancels the pull of gravity. If the ball drops too far, then the magnetic fields are weaker and the ball drops away completely. If the ball is too close to the magnet, then the magnetic fields are stronger and the ball will be pulled to the magnet. Our first step is to compute the point where the gravitational pull equals the attractive magnetic force. This point is called an equilibrium point. Given a desired position h_0, the current that is required to maintain that position can be found by setting the acceleration equal to zero. Hence,

$$i_0^2 = \frac{mg}{k} h_0^2$$

Knowing the equilibrium point the model can be linearized about it. This linearization simplifies Eq. (10.10) to give a set of linear equations.

First we introduce the state variables

$$x_1 = h \quad x_2 = \frac{dh}{dt} \quad x_3 = i$$

Then Eqs. (10.10) become

$$\frac{dx_1}{dt} = x_2$$

$$\frac{dx_2}{dt} = g - \frac{k}{m}\left(\frac{x_3}{x_1}\right)^2 \tag{10.11}$$

$$\frac{dx_3}{dt} = \frac{v}{L} - \frac{R}{L}x_3$$

Equations (10.11) can be linearized by taking a Taylor's series expansion around the operating points $x_3 = i_0$ and $x_1 = h_0$. The linearization results in dx_2/dt being modified. The linearized result is

$$\begin{bmatrix} dx_1/dt \\ dx_2/dt \\ dx_3/dt \end{bmatrix} = \begin{bmatrix} 0 & 1 & 0 \\ \dfrac{2k}{m}\dfrac{i_0^2}{h_0^3} & 0 & \dfrac{-2k}{m}\dfrac{i_0}{h_0^2} \\ 0 & 0 & -R/L \end{bmatrix} \begin{bmatrix} x_1 \\ x_2 \\ x_3 \end{bmatrix} + v \begin{bmatrix} 0 \\ 0 \\ 1/L \end{bmatrix}$$

We assume the mass of the ball is 100 gm, the resistance of the coil is 5 Ω, the inductance of the coil is 40 mH, the coupling constant is 0.01 Nm²/A, and the desired height is 2 cm. We first create the function *MagLev* to represent the state-space model of the system.

```
function Plant = MagLev
m = 0.1; g = 9.82; R = 5;
L = 0.04; k = 0.01; h0 = 0.02;
i0 = h0*sqrt(m*g/k);
A = [0 1 0; 2*k*i0^2/(m*h0^3) 0 −2*k*i0/(m*h0^2); 0 0 −R/L];
B = [0;0;1/L];
C = [1 0 0];
D = 0;
Plant = ss(A,B,C,D)
```

Typing in the MATLAB command window

MagPoles = pole(MagLev)

we obtain

```
MagPoles =
   31.3369
  -31.3369
 -125.0000
```

Thus, the poles of the linearized system are located at ±31.3 for the suspension and −125 for the amplifier. Thus, a proportional derivative (PD) controller to stabilize the system is needed. Theoretically, the transfer function for a PD controller is given by

$$C_0(s) = k_p + sk_d$$

where k_p is the proportional gain and k_d is the derivative gain. The controller output involves the derivative of the input, which is hard to realize in practice because of high-frequency noise. Typically, the derivative is approximated and then filtered to remove the noise, resulting in

$$C_1(s) = k_p + k_d \frac{s}{\tau_f s + 1} = k_p \frac{\left(\tau_f + k_d/k_p\right)s + 1}{\tau_f s + 1}$$

The transfer function $C_1(s)$ is equivalent to a lead controller with the zero time constant $\tau_f + k_d/k_p$ and the pole (filter) time constant τ_f. The controller is a lead controller because the zero is always slower than the pole. We select the controller zero at −20, which is just to the right of the first stable pole of the magnetic levitation system, and the filter pole at −50, which results in $\tau_f = 20$ ms. This system requires positive feedback to be stabilized, so we include the sign change in the controller. Thus, the transfer function is

$$C_1(s) = -\frac{s + 20}{s + 50}$$

The script is

```
PD = tf(−1*[1 20],[1 50]);
rlocus(PD*MagLev);
sgrid
title('Root locus of PD controlled magnetic levitator');
xlabel('Real axis');
ylabel('Imaginary axis');
```

The resulting root locus plot is shown in Figure 10.31.

The plot shows that at some low gain, the unstable pole is pulled into the left half plane, and at a higher gain, a complex conjugate pair cross over into the right half plane. A stabilizing gain can be determined from this figure by typing

```
rlocus(tf(−1*[1 20],[1 50])*MagLev)
rlocfind(tf(−1*[1 20],[1 50])*MagLev)
```

in the MATLAB command window and then placing the crosshairs on the real axis root-locus line between the unstable pole and the controller zero. A point approximately halfway between the imaginary axis and the controller zero yields a gain of 150. Hence $k_p = -60$, $k_d = -1.8$, and the filter time constant is 20 ms, which is equal to 1/50.

Measurement and modeling errors are likely to result in errors in determining $v_0 = Ri_0$. This will cause a steady-state error in the position of the ball, $h(t)$. While the PD portion of the control shapes the instability and transient behavior of the system, the PI portion is typically used to improve the steady-state behavior. Consider the PI controller

$$C_2(s) = k_p + \frac{k_i}{s} = \frac{k_p}{k_i} \frac{s + k_i/k_p}{s}$$

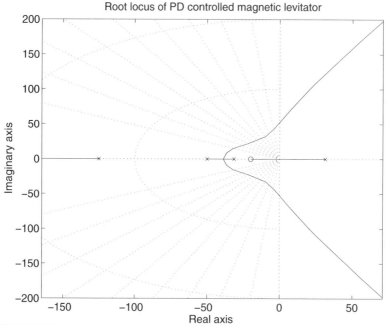

FIGURE 10.31
Root-locus plot of the PD-cascade control magnetic-levitation system.

with parameters k_p and k_i. The PI controller has one pole at the origin and a zero at $-k_i/k_p$. If the zero is close to the pole relative to the locations of the other poles and zeros of the system, then the effect of the PI controller on the closed-loop transient behavior is negligible when it is cascaded with the PD controller to form a PID controller. Hence, the feedback gain of 150 may still be used. The effect of the PI controller on the steady-state error is large. For this control system, we choose $k_p = k_i = 1$. The following script simulates the impulse response of the closed-loop system with the linearized model of the magnetic levitator.

```
PD = tf(−1*[1 20],[1 50]);
PI = tf([1 1],[1 0]);
[y,t] = impulse(feedback(150*PI*PD*MagLev,1));
plot(t,y);
grid;
xlabel('Time');
ylabel('Impulse response');
title('Impulse response of a magnetic levitator');
```

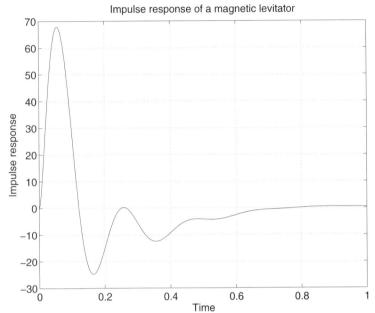

FIGURE 10. 32
Impulse response of the linear approximation to the magnetic-levitation system.

The result of executing this script is shown in Figure 10.32. The result returns the closed-loop system of the linearized plant model. However, determining the stability of the system with the nonlinear model in the loop is of far greater interest.

The nonlinear system will now be simulated using SIMULINK. We will require a block called *S-Function*, which is a user-defined function. We will call this user-defined function *MagModel*. There are four parameters to be passed to *MagModel* in the following order specified by SIMULINK's *S-Function*: time t, state variables x, inputs u, and an integer *flag*. Hybrid models with both discrete and continuous states may be constructed using *S-Function*; we consider those parts that enable continuous nonlinear models. SIMULINK queries the user function to determine everything about the nonlinear model; *flag* determines the purpose of the query. When *flag* = 1, the function returns the derivatives of x using time t, states x, and input u given by Eq. (10.11). When *flag* = 3, the function returns the outputs. Finally, when *flag* = 0, the function returns a vector *sys* whose components are, in order, the number of continuous states, the number of discrete states, the number of outputs, the number of inputs, the number of roots, and a final flag that is set to 1 if the system has direct feedthrough. In the case of the magnetic levitator, *sys* = [3 0 1 1 0 0], which indicates three continuous states, no discrete states, one input, one output, no roots, and no feedthrough. When *flag* = 0, we also return the initial conditions of the continuous states—that is, the state of the system when it is first started. The equilibrium of the system is $x(0) = [h(0)\ 0\ i(0)]'$. We will start the system near, but not at the equilibrium position, by setting the initial value $h(0)$ 10% larger than the equilibrium value. With such an initial condition, the controller must take action or the ball will drop away from the magnet. The deviation for the equilibrium position must be small, because the controller is based on a linearized model of the system.

```
function [sys,x0] = MagModel(t,x,u,flag)
m = 0.1; g = 9.82; R = 5; L = 0.040;
k = 0.01; h0 = 0.02;
i0 = h0*sqrt(m*g/k);
switch flag
 case 1
   xdot = zeros(3,1);
   xdot(1) = x(2);
   xdot(2) = m*g – k*x(3)^2/x(1)^2;
   xdot(3) = –R/L*x(3) + 1/L*u(1);
   sys = xdot;
 case 3
   sys = x(1);
 case 0
   sys = [3 0 1 1 0 0];
   x0 = [h0+0.1*h0; 0; i0];
 otherwise
   sys = [];
end
```

The controller will be specified using variable names rather than numerical values; therefore, these variables must be defined in the MATLAB command window prior to running the simulation in SIMULINK. To generate these variables and start SIMULINK, we run the following script:

```
PD = tf(–1*[1 20],[1 50]);
PI = tf([1 1],[1 0]);
v0 = 0.991; h0 = 0.02;
[num,den] = tfdata(150*PD*PI,'v');
simulink;
```

The values of $v0$ and $h0$ were computed from the values given.

We now use SIMULINK to generate the block diagram shown in Figure 10.33. From the *Math* library, we use *Sum* and *Gain*. From the *Functions & Tables* library, we use *S-Function*, which, in turn, will use *MagModel*. This assignment is done by double-clicking on the *S-Function* block in the modeling window and entering *MagModel* for the *S-Function* name.

From the *Continuous* library, we use *Transfer Fnc*. Then we double-click on this block and, in our case, enter the variable names *num* and *den* for the numerator and denominator, respectively, since these two quantities have been specified in the third line in the script we ran prior to entering SIMULINK.

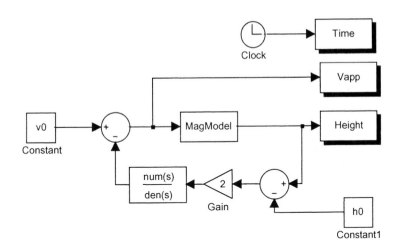

FIGURE 10.33
SIMULINK block diagram for the nonlinear magnetic-levitation system.

From the *Sources* library, we use *Constant* to enter a voltage offset and a height offset. These quantities are used to represent errors. Their values are defined by double-clicking on the block and entering either numerical values or variable names, if the variable names have been or will be assigned numerical values in the MATLAB command window. We choose the latter method since $v0$ and $h0$ have been defined in our previously run script.

Lastly, we use *To Workspace* from the *Sinks* library to record the bearing's height (*Height*) and the magnitude of the magnet's coil voltage (*Vapp*) as a function of time. The values of time are stored in the array *Time* by *Clock*, which is from the *Sources* library. The shadows around these three blocks are obtained using *Show Drop Shadow* from the *Format* pull-down menu. The quantities *Vapp* and *Height* are saved to the workspace each time the simulation is run and can then be displayed with `plot`. Figure 10.34 shows the quantities *Vapp* and *height* as a function of *Time*, which were obtained with the following script run in the MATLAB command window. The values of *Height* have been scaled by a factor of 50.

```
plot(Time,50*Height,'k-',Time,Vapp,'k-.')
legend('50h(t)','v(t)')
text(1,1.5,'Initial conditions')
text(1.2,1.45,'h(0) = 0.022 m')
text(1.2,1.4,'v(0) = 0.991 V')
xlabel('Time (s)')
ylabel('V_{app} and h(t)')
axis([0 4 .7 1.6])
```

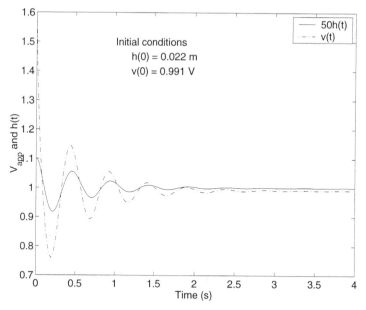

FIGURE 10.34

Response under PID control of the nonlinear magnetic suspension system to initial conditions and modeling errors.

10.5.3 Lead Control of an Inverted Pendulum

We shall design a lead controller for an inverted pendulum using root-locus techniques. Consider an inverted pendulum mounted on a disk as shown in Figure 10.35. The objective of the control system is to command the position of the disk while keeping the pendulum upright. Both the angle of the disk ψ and the angle of the pendulum θ are measured. The equations of motion are

$$ml^2 \frac{d^2\theta}{dt^2} + mrl\cos(\theta)\frac{d^2\psi}{dt^2} = mgl\sin(\theta) + b_1\frac{d\theta}{dt}$$

$$mrl\cos(\theta)\frac{d^2\theta}{dt^2} + (J + mr^2)\frac{d^2\psi}{dt^2} = mrl\sin(\theta)\left(\frac{d\theta}{dt}\right)^2 + b_2\frac{d\psi}{dt} + \tau_m \tag{10.12}$$

where m is the mass of the bob, l the length of the pendulum, r is the radius of the disk (which is also the radius of the bob attachment), d is the thickness of the disk, $J = \rho\pi dr^4/4$ is the inertia of the disk, b_1 is the friction coefficient of the revolute joint of the pendulum, b_2 is the friction in the revolute joint of the disk, and τ_m is the torque applied by the motor attached to the base of the disk. As with the magnetic bearing, the equations of motion may be linearized about the operating point when θ and $d\theta/dt$ are very small.

We define the elements of the state vector x as

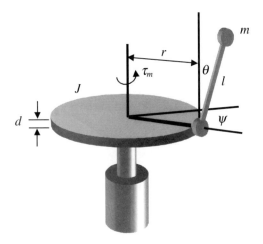

FIGURE 10.35
Inverted pendulum on a disk.

$$x_1(t) = \theta(t) \qquad x_3(t) = \frac{d\theta}{dt}$$

$$x_2(t) = \psi(t) \qquad x_4(t) = \frac{d\psi}{dt}$$

Substituting these equations into Eq. (10.12) and assuming that θ and $d\theta/dt$ are very small and, hence, we can neglect all terms of order 2 and higher, we obtain

$$\frac{dx_1}{dt} = x_3$$

$$\frac{dx_2}{dt} = x_4$$

$$ml^2 \frac{dx_3}{dt} + mlr \frac{dx_4}{dt} = mglx_1 + b_1 x_3$$

$$mlr \frac{dx_3}{dt} + \left(J + mr^2\right)\frac{dx_4}{dt} = b_2 x_4 + \tau_m$$

or in matrix form

$$M\dot{x} = Qx + Wu$$

where

$$W = \begin{bmatrix} 0 & 0 & 0 & 1 \end{bmatrix}' \qquad x = \begin{bmatrix} x_1 & x_2 & x_3 & x_4 \end{bmatrix}' \qquad \dot{x} = dx/dt$$

$$
M = \begin{bmatrix} 1 & 0 & 0 & 0 \\ 0 & 1 & 0 & 0 \\ 0 & 0 & ml^2 & mlr \\ 0 & 0 & mlr & J+mr^2 \end{bmatrix} \quad Q = \begin{bmatrix} 0 & 0 & 1 & 0 \\ 0 & 0 & 0 & 1 \\ mgl & 0 & b_1 & 0 \\ 0 & 0 & 0 & b_2 \end{bmatrix} \quad u = \tau_m
$$

The upright position corresponding to $x(t) = 0$ is an equilibrium point of the system at which $u = \tau_m = 0$. The linearized equations of the inverted pendulum system about the upright position are represented as a state-space system in the following function called *Pendulum*. This system has the angle of the pendulum θ and the angle of the disk ψ as the outputs. Therefore, the output *Plant* of *Pendulum* is a system with two outputs and one input, which can be accessed as follows: *Plant*(1,1) is the transfer function from τ_m to θ and *Plant*(2,1) is the transfer function from τ_m to ψ. We assume the length of the pendulum is 30 cm, the mass of the bob 0.2-kg, the radius of the disk 15-cm, the thickness of the disk 1 cm, and its density 2500 kg/m^3. The friction in the systems is set to zero; thus, $b_1 = b_2 = 0$.

```
function Plant = Pendulum
l = 0.3; g = 9.81; m = 0.2; r = 0.15;
d = 0.01; rho = 2500; b1 = 0; b2 = 0;
J = 0.25*pi*rho*d*r^4;
M = [1 0 0 0; 0 1 0 0; 0 0 m*l^2 m*r*l; 0 0 m*r*l J+m*r^2];
Q = [0 0 1 0; 0 0 0 1; m*g*l 0 b1 0; 0 0 0 b2];
W = [0;0;0;1];
A = inv(M)*Q;
B = inv(M)*W;
C = [1 0 0 0;0 1 0 0];
D = [0];
Plant = ss(A,B,C,D);
```

Recall Example 5.2.
    The poles of the system are found by typing

```
pole(Pendulum)
```

in the MATLAB command window. This displays

```
0
0
6.8923
-6.8923
```

Thus, there are two poles at the origin and a pair on the real axis mirrored about the imaginary axis at ±6.9 rad/s. The system is, therefore, open-loop unstable. The transmission zeros of the inverted pendulum from the perspective of θ, the angle of the pendulum, is found by typing in the MATLAB command window

Plant = Pendulum;
tzero(Plant(1,1))

which displays two zeros. The system with only the first output θ and first input τ_m may be addressed using matrix notation; hence, the (1,1) subscript on *Plant*. Thus, there are two zeros right on top of the poles. This indicates that using only the output θ to control the inverted pendulum will ignore some of the dynamics. In particular, the angle of the pendulum contains insufficient information to discern the position and velocity of the disk. Thus, the outputs of a sensor measuring this angular motion can be zero even when the disk is rotating at a uniform angular velocity. The dynamics, which are not at rest while the output is zero, are sometimes referred to as zero dynamics. These (unobservable) zero dynamics will not be stabilized by feedback from θ alone. The zeros of the pendulum from the perspective of the disk angle ψ are found by typing

Plant = Pendulum;
tzero(Plant(2,1))

in the MATLAB command window. Since the plant has two outputs, we address the subsystem with the second output and the first input with the subscript (2,1). It is found from these results that the zeros are located at ± 5.7, which are close to the open-loop poles of the pendulum, which are ± 6.9. This indicates that while the behavior of the pendulum is observable from the disk position, it is just barely so. A single-input, single-output (SISO) controller designed using either output will perform badly.

A multiple-input, single-output (MISO) controller that is dependent on both outputs would perform much better than a SISO controller and, thus, this will be the focus of the rest of our effort. We shall design this controller shown in Figure 10.36 in two steps. First we shall design a controller using the output θ to keep the pendulum upright. Wrapped around this control loop will be a controller that uses ψ to keep the angle of the disk at the commanded position.

We start the design process with a lead controller that keeps the pendulum upright. Such a controller will use the output θ to determine which correction to apply. Recall that the open-loop poles are located at ± 6.9. We put the lead zero at -5, just to the right of the stable pole in the pair in order to pull the unstable pole into the left half of the complex plane. The lead pole is placed at -10. Hence,

$$C_\theta(s) = -\frac{s+5}{s+10}$$

Since positive feedback is required a negative sign appears in $C_\theta(s)$.

The following script generates the root-locus plot of the θ control loop. MATLAB automatically picks a range of gains to apply, but in this case we select a range of $0.1 \leq \theta \leq 10$ equally spaced on a logarithmic scale.

Plant = Pendulum;
PlantTheta = minreal(Plant(1,1));

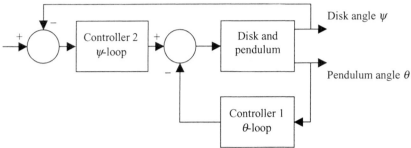

FIGURE 10.36
Block diagram for the inverted pendulum control system.

```
ControlTheta = tf(−1*[1 5],[1 10]);
rlocus(ControlTheta*PlantTheta,logspace(−1,1,60));
sgrid;
xlabel('Real axis');
ylabel('Imaginary axis');
title('Root locus of \theta control loop');
```

Executing the script results in Figure 10.37a.
    A suitable gain can be found with

```
rlocus(ControlTheta*PlantTheta)
rlocfind(ControlTheta*PlantTheta)
```

Placing the crosshairs on the real axis between the imaginary axis and the lead zero, we find that a gain of 4 stabilizes the θ-loop. The resulting closed-loop poles of the theta control system are found from the following script.

```
Plant = Pendulum;
PlantTheta = minreal(Plant(1,1));
ControlTheta = tf(−1*[1 5],[1 10]);
pole(feedback(4*ControlTheta*PlantTheta,1))
```

It is found from the execution of this script that the closed-loop poles are approximately −4, $-3 \pm 11i$, which, although stable, are not well damped.
    Now we design the outer feedback loop for the disk position ψ. The outer feedback loop is designed with the inner θ loop in place, so we first form the closed-loop system by wrapping the first controller inside a loop employing θ. We do this with the following script.

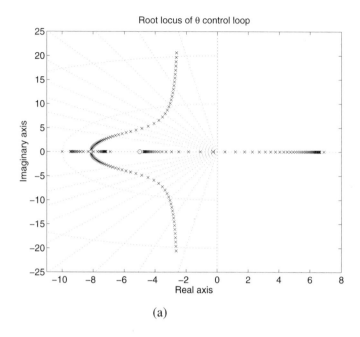

(a)

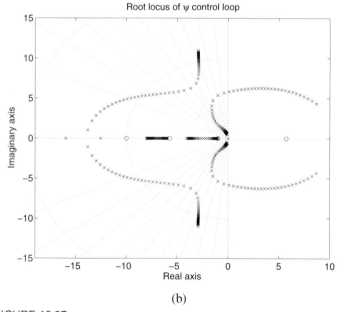

(b)

FIGURE 10.37
Root locus of the control loops in feedback for (a) the θ control loop, and (b) the ψ control loop.

```
ControlTheta = tf(-1*[1 5],[1 10]);
PlantPsi = feedback(Pendulum,4*ControlTheta,[1],[1]);
pole(PlantPsi)
tzero(PlantPsi)
```

Note that we have to specify which inputs and outputs to use since the plant is MIMO and the controller is SISO. The results show that *PlantPsi* has two additional poles at the origin, which is representative of a double integrator. These need to be moved to the left; however, complicating that objective is an unstable zero. The inverted pendulum is an example of a system that is non-minimum phase. In order to move the disk, the controller first must move in the opposite direction to keep the pendulum upright during the transition from its current position to the desired position. The unstable zero attracts one of the poles of the double integrator. To solve this problem, we again use a lead controller whose zero is just inside the left half of the complex plane. The following script plots the root locus of the ψ control loop.

```
ControlTheta = tf(-1*[1 5],[1 10]);
PlantPsi = feedback(Pendulum,4*ControlTheta,[1],[1]);
ControlPsi = tf(-1*[1 1],[1 8]);
k = 0.35*logspace(-1,1,60);
rlocus(ControlPsi*PlantPsi(2,1),k);
sgrid;
xlabel('Real axis');
ylabel('Imaginary axis');
title('Root locus of \psi control loop');
```

The execution of this script results in Figure 10.37b. To find the appropriate gain we type

```
rlocus(ControlPsi*PlantPsi)
rlocfind(ControlPsi*PlantPsi)
```

in the MATLAB command window and place the crosshairs near the lower half of the root locus lines that loop into the complex plane. It is found that a gain of 0.3 places all the poles inside the left-half complex plane.

The step response of the final control system is computed from the following script:

```
ControlTheta = tf(-1*[1 5],[1 10]);
PlantPsi = feedback(Pendulum,4*ControlTheta,[1],[1]);
ControlPsi = tf(-1*[1 1],[1 8]);
[y,t] = step(feedback(0.3*ControlPsi*PlantPsi,1,[1],[2]));
plot(t,y(:,1),'k-',t,y(:,2),'k--');
xlabel('Time');
```

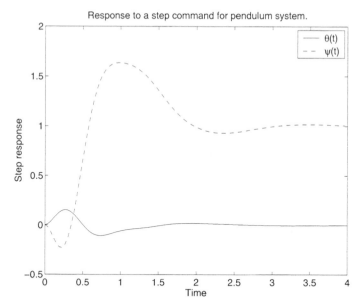

FIGURE 10.38
Step response of the inverted pendulum.

```
ylabel('Step response');
title('Response to a step command for pendulum system.');
legend('\theta(t)','\psi(t)');
```

The resulting step-response plot is shown in Figure 10.38, which reveals the non-minimum phase behavior of the controller and the plant.

10.5.4 Control of a Magnetically Suspended Flywheel

Consider the magnetically suspended flywheel system shown in Figure 10.39. Magnetic coils are used to float the wheel so that the wheel can be run at high speeds without the losses associated with friction. The objective of the control system is to keep the wheel suspended. Like the magnetic suspension described in Section 10.5.2, the system is naturally unstable. There are four distances that are measured as outputs. These distances correspond to the x and y positions of the top and bottom shafts as measured in the inertial frame. Four coil currents may be selected to control the magnetic fields about the shaft; these coils are co-located with the sensors.

$$\frac{d^2 x_{cm}}{dt^2} = \frac{f_1 + f_3}{m}$$

$$\frac{d^2 y_{cm}}{dt^2} = \frac{f_2 + f_4}{m}$$

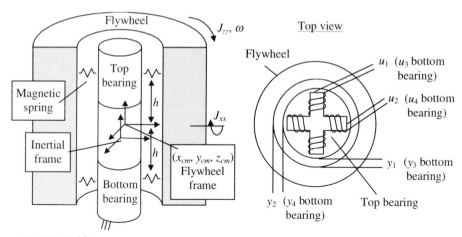

FIGURE 10.39
A magnetically suspended flywheel.

The linearized equations of motion are

$$\frac{d^2\phi}{dt^2} = -\beta\omega\frac{d\psi}{dt} + \frac{h}{J_{xx}}(f_4 - f_2)$$

$$\frac{d^2\psi}{dt^2} = \beta\omega\frac{d\phi}{dt} + \frac{h}{J_{xx}}(f_1 - f_3)$$

where x_{cm} and y_{cm} are the location of the center of mass of the flywheel as measured in the inertial frame, (ϕ, ψ) give the orientation of the flywheel frame with respect to the inertial frame using roll (ϕ), pitch (ψ), and yaw orientation,[9] m is the mass of the flywheel, J_{xx} is the rotational inertia of the flywheel about the nonspinning axis, $\beta = J_{zz}/J_{xx}$, and h is the distance from the center of mass to the actuators. The inputs f_i are the forces applied by the magnetic bearings and obey the following relationships

$$f_i = k_1 y_i + k_2 u_i$$

where y_i is the distance from the wheel to the actuator and is the system's output. The bearings are composed of a permanent magnet surrounded by coils. The negative spring constant k_1 is due to the permanent magnet, and the gain k_2 is due to the field generated by the current u_i in the coils. The operating speed of the wheel is ω rad/s.

The output values y_i for small ϕ and ψ are given by

$$y_1 = x_{cm} + h\psi$$
$$y_2 = y_{cm} - h\phi$$
$$y_3 = x_{cm} + h\psi$$

[9] R. M. Murray, X. Li, and S. S. Sastry, *A Mathematical Introduction to Robotic Manipulation*, CRC Press, Boca Raton, FL, 1994.

$$y_4 = y_{cm} - h\phi$$

If we let

$$q(t) = [x_{cm}, y_{cm}, \phi(t), \psi(t)]'$$

and

$$u(t) = [u_1 \ u_2 \ u_3 \ u_4]'$$

then the linearized equations can be written as

$$\ddot{q} = \omega P_a \dot{q} + k_1 B_a C_a q + k_2 B_a u$$
$$y = C_a q$$

where

$$P_a = \begin{bmatrix} 0 & 0 & 0 & 0 \\ 0 & 0 & 0 & 0 \\ 0 & 0 & 0 & \beta \\ 0 & 0 & -\beta & 0 \end{bmatrix}$$

$$B_a = \begin{bmatrix} 1/m & 0 & 1/m & 0 \\ 0 & 1/m & 0 & 1/m \\ 0 & -h/J_{xx} & 0 & h/J_{xx} \\ h/J_{xx} & 0 & -h/J_{xx} & 0 \end{bmatrix} \qquad (10.13)$$

$$C_a = \begin{bmatrix} 1 & 0 & 0 & h \\ 0 & 1 & -h & 0 \\ 1 & 0 & 0 & -h \\ 0 & 1 & h & 0 \end{bmatrix}$$

Hence, if we set

$$z = \begin{bmatrix} q \\ \dot{q} \end{bmatrix}$$

we have the following matrix equations

$$\dot{z} = \begin{bmatrix} 0 & I \\ k_1 B_a C_a & \omega P_a \end{bmatrix} z + \begin{bmatrix} 0 \\ k_2 B_a \end{bmatrix} u$$
$$y = [C_a \ \ 0] z + [0] u$$

where I is the unit matrix.

The following function *Flywheel* generates the linearized model as a function of rotational speed in revolutions per minute (rpm) and is used in the subsequent design evaluations. If no arguments are supplied to this function, it is assumed the operating speed is 0 rpm. For the flywheel under consideration, the rotational inertia about the x and y body-axes of the flywheel is 1.563×10^{-4} Nm·s^2, and the rotational inertia about the z-axis is 1.141×10^{-4} Nm·s^2. The dimensionless shape factor β is approximately 1. The mass of the wheel is 340 gm, and the height from the center of mass is 3 cm. The coil constants are $k_1 = 4.8 \times 10^4$ N/m and $k_2 = 3.75$ N/A.

```
function Plant = Flywheel(rpm)
if nargin < 1, rpm = 0; end;
Jxx = 1.563e-4;
Jzz = 1.141e-4;
beta = Jzz/Jxx;
m = 0.34;
h = 0.03;
k1 = 4.8e4;
k2 = 3.75;
omega = rpm/60*2*pi;
Pa = [zeros(1,4); zeros(1,4); 0 0 0 -beta; 0 0 beta 0];
Ba = [1/m 0 1/m 0; 0 1/m 0 1/m; 0 -h/Jxx 0 h/Jxx; h/Jxx 0 -h/Jxx 0];
Ca = [1 0 0 h; 0 1 -h 0; 1 0 0 -h; 0 1 h 0];
A = [zeros(4), eye(4); k1*Ba*Ca, omega*Pa];
B = [zeros(4); k2*Ba];
C = [Ca zeros (4)];
D = [zeros(4)];
Plant = ss(A,B,C,D);
```

The open-loop poles change as a function of *rpm*. Execution of the following script plots the open-loop poles for a range of typical operating speeds.

```
rpm = [0:100:16000 16100:10:20000];
result = zeros(8,length(rpm));
for j = 1:length(rpm);
 result(:,j) = pole(Flywheel(rpm(j)));
end
plot(real(result(:,1)),imag(result(:,1)),'x');
hold on;
for j = 1:8;
x=real(result(j,:));
 y=imag(result(j,:));
 plot(x,y);
end;
grid;
xlabel('Real axis');
ylabel('Imaginary axis');
title('RPM root locus of the flywheel');
```

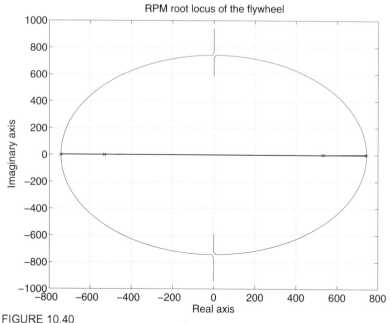

FIGURE 10.40
Root locus as a function of operating speed from 0 to 20,000 rpm.

The result of executing this script is shown in Figure 10.40. There are two sets of poles (but no zeros) mirrored about the imaginary axis. One set, located at ±530 rad/s (85 Hz), is due to the translational modes and does not change with operating speed. The other set, located at ±740 rad/s (120 Hz), is due to the two rotational modes and is affected by the gyroscopic coupling.

In summary, there are four unstable and four stable poles, and half of the poles change location with the operating speed. From an examination of Eq. (10.13) we see that at $\omega = 0$ rpm, P does not affect the solution. This suggests that the flywheel at 0 rpm may be statically decoupled, resulting in two rotational and two translational SISO systems. Thus, traditional lead-control design techniques, such as a root locus, can now be used to generate a stabilizing controller. Consider the matrix T, which forms the sums and differences between input channels.

$$T = \begin{bmatrix} 1 & 0 & 0 & 1 \\ 0 & 1 & -1 & 0 \\ 1 & 0 & 0 & -1 \\ 0 & 1 & 1 & 0 \end{bmatrix}$$

Note that the matrix T diagonalizes the input and output matrices of Eqs. (10.13) as shown in the following.

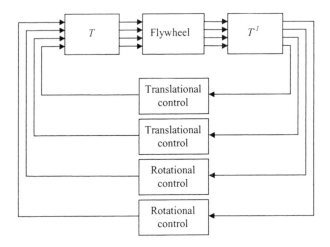

FIGURE 10.41
Static decoupling of the flywheel

$$BT = \begin{bmatrix} 2/m & 0 & 0 & 0 \\ 0 & 2/m & 0 & 0 \\ 0 & 0 & 2h/J_{xx} & 0 \\ 0 & 0 & 0 & 2h/J_{xx} \end{bmatrix}$$

$$T^{-1}C = \begin{bmatrix} 1 & 0 & 0 & 0 \\ 0 & 1 & 0 & 0 \\ 0 & 0 & h & 0 \\ 0 & 0 & 0 & h \end{bmatrix}$$

After performing a static decoupling using T, we can perform our lead design on the four resulting SISO plants. Figure 10.41 shows how the matrices T would be inserted in practice. The following script generates the decoupled SISO plants and computes a root locus of the result.

```
T = [1 0 0 1;0 1 –1 0;1 0 0 –1;0 1 1 0];
decoupFly = inv(T)*Flywheel(0)*T;
transFly = minreal(decoupFly(1,1));
rotFly = minreal(decoupFly(3,3));
Lead = tf([1 400],[1 1000]);
rlocus(Lead*transFly);
sgrid;
xlabel('Real axis');
ylabel('Imaginary axis');
```

```
title('Root locus of translational component');
figure(2);
rlocus(Lead*rotFly);
sgrid;
xlabel('Real axis');
ylabel('Imaginary axis');
title('Root locus of rotational component');
```

The result of executing this script is shown in Figure 10.42.
The commands

```
rlocus(Lead*transFly)
rlocfind(Lead*transFly)
```

are used to find a stabilizing gain for the translational system, and the commands

```
rlocus(Lead*rotFly)
rlocfind(Lead*rotFly)
```

are used similarly for the rotational system. By design, the same gain (5) stabilizes both the translational and rotational components of the system. Since the gain for the translational and rotational control is the same, the controllers are identical, and decoupling is not needed in the implementation because the matrix T commutes with the transfer function of the controller. This fact makes the implementation easier.

We now design an LQG controller for the flywheel. The design involves choosing the appropriate penalty R for the cost function. The following script computes the optimal closed-loop poles for $10^{-10} \leq R \leq 10^{-6}$. The result of its execution is shown in Figure 10.43.

```
[A,B,C,D] = ssdata(Flywheel);
clPoles = [];
R = logspace(-10,-6,60);
for i = 1:length(R)
  [K,S,E] = lqr(A,B,C'*C,R(i)*eye(4));
  clPoles = [clPoles, E];
end;
plot(real(clPoles),imag(clPoles),'kx');
sgrid;
title('Optimal root locus for the Flywheel system');
ylabel('Imaginary axis');
xlabel('Real axis');
text(-700,0,'R = 10^{-10}');
text(-1000,1000,'R = 10^{-6}');
```

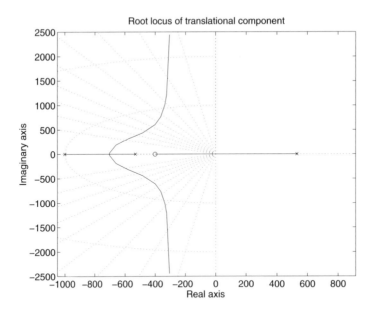

(a)

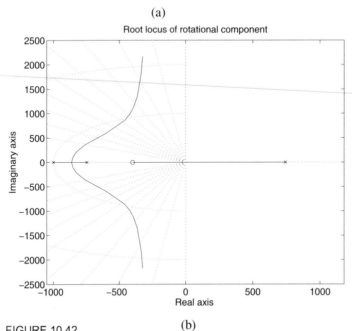

(b)

FIGURE 10.42
Root locus of the control loops for (a) the translational and (b) the rotational motion.

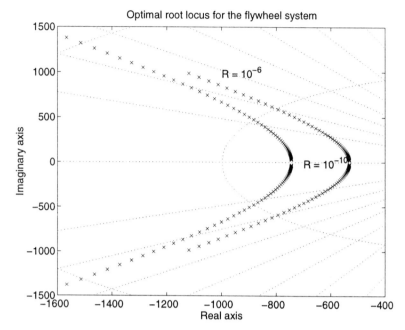

FIGURE 10.43
Optimal root locus for the flywheel for $10^{-10} \le R \le 10^{-6}$.

To compare the two different control schemes, the following script computes the response of the two different controllers with the same initial conditions. The initial conditions are all zero, except that the flywheel is slightly tilted such that $\phi(0) = 0.001$ radians. The flywheel spins at 10,000 rpm, even though the controllers were designed for 0 rpm. The LQG controller is designed with penalty factor $R = 10^{-6}$.

```
Control = 4e4*eye(4)*tf([1 400],[1 1000]);
x0 = zeros(12,1);  x0(3) = 1e−3;  t = linspace(0,0.25,1000);
yl = initial(feedback(Flywheel(10000),Control),x0,t);
[A,B,C,D] = ssdata(Flywheel);
K = lqr(A,B,C'*C,1e−6*eye(4));
L = (lqr(A',C',B*B',1e−6*eye(4)))';
ControlSS = reg(Flywheel,K,L);
x0 = zeros(16,1); x0(3) = 1e−3;
ys= initial(feedback(Flywheel(10000),ControlSS,+1),x0,t);
plot(1000*yl(:,1),1000*yl(:,2),'k-',1000*ys(:,1),1000*ys(:,2),'k-.');
grid;
xlabel('x upper bearing');
ylabel('y upper bearing');
```

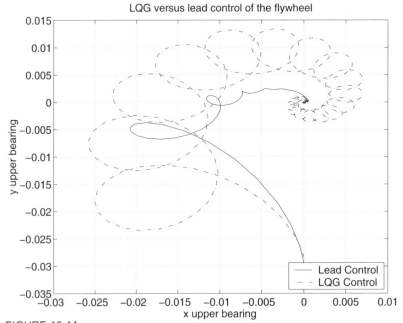

FIGURE 10.44
Phase response of the state-space and lead-controlled flywheels.

> title('LQG versus lead control of the flywheel')
> legend('Lead Control','LQG Control',4)

The results from the execution of the script are the phase plots shown in Figure 10.44. Both controllers keep the flywheel suspended with comparable levels of performance.

EXERCISES

10.1 The suspension system[10] shown in Figure 10.45 has the level of the road surface as the input $y(t)$ and absolute position of m_1 as the output $x(t)$. The transfer function of the system is

$$\frac{y(s)}{r(s)} = \frac{sbk_2 + k_1k_2}{m_1m_2s^4 + b(m_1 + m_2)s^3 + k_1(m_1 + m_2)s^2 + k_2m_1s^2 + k_2bs + k_1k_2}$$

Assume that $m_1 = 500$ kg, $m_2 = 100$ kg, $b = 1000$ Ns/m, $k_1 = 2000$ N/m, and $k_2 = 10^4$ N/m.

(a) A washboard-like road surface can be approximated by

$$r(t) = \varepsilon \sin \omega t$$

---

[10] U. Ozguner, H. Goktas, and H. Chan, "Automotive Suspension Control Through a Computer Communication Network," *Proceedings of 1st IEEE Conference on Control Application*, Vol. 2, 1992, pp. 895–900.

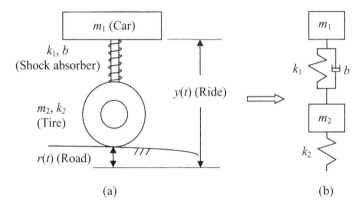

FIGURE 10.45
(a) A simplified model of an automotive wheel suspension; (b) mass and spring equivalent.

Determine the value of ω such that the amplitude of the induced response amplitude of the ride $y(t)$ is 10% of the amplitude of $r(t)$.

(b) Depending on its usage, the mass of the car may double. Generate a meshed surface of the magnitude of the Bode plot as a function of m_1 for $500 \le m_1 \le 1000$ kg.

(c) Plot the value of ω for which the attenuation of the road variation $r(t)$ is 90% as a function of b and m_1.

10.2 Construct a fifth-order system with five equally spaced poles on a circle of radius $2\pi k$ in the left half of the complex plane, and five zeros in the right-half plane at the mirror-image locations. Set the DC gain to one and $k = 1$.

(a) Cascade the fifth-order system with a simple first-order plant with a pole at -1 and a DC gain of 1. Plot the step response of the system for 4 s and the step response of the plant without the fifth-order system on the same graph.

(b) Compute the percentage overshoot and the rise time.

(c) Repeat parts (a) and (b) for $k = 0.5$ and $k = 2.0$. Notice how the response delay grows with increasing k.

(d) Repeat parts (a) and (b) for 3 and 7 equally spaced poles. Notice how the oscillations increase with an increase in the number of poles.

10.3 Suppose a controller is designed using a simple nominal plant model such as[11]

$$G_0(s) = \frac{1}{s+1}$$

The plant may not be accurately modeled. For each of the following alternate models, plot the open-loop step response of the nominal plant $G_0(s)$ with the open-loop step response of the alternate plant. Also plot the closed-loop step response of both systems with proportional error control and a gain of

---

[11] R. Jurgen, *Electronic Engine Control Technologies*, SAE International, Troy, MI, 1999.

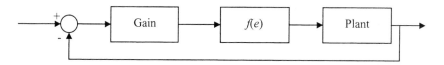

FIGURE 10.46
Block diagram for simple system with a nonlinear input.

20. Use a maximum time of 2 s. Notice that while the open-loop responses are very different, the closed-loop responses are nearly identical.

(a)

$$G_1(s) = \frac{3.7}{0.75s + 0.6}$$

(b)

$$G_2(s) = \frac{1.63}{0.94s + 0.92}$$

(c)

$$G_3(s) = \frac{0.7s^2 + 7s + 17}{s^3 + 2s^2 + 5.2s + 4}$$

10.4 Consider the flexible drive-shaft system discussed in Section 10.5.1 with configuration shown in Figure 10.25. As mentioned in that section, it is difficult to know the exact frequency of the resonant mode. The question is whether it is better to overestimate or underestimate this frequency. To investigate this, plot together the Bode plots of the uncompensated pointer with the following two compensators:

$$\text{Notch Filter \#1:} \ \frac{(s+3+28i)(s+3-28i)}{(s+60)^2}$$

$$\text{Notch Filter \#2:} \ \frac{(s+3+34i)(s+3-34i)}{(s+60)^2}$$

Set the gain of each notch filter to one before plotting and draw your conclusions from the plotted results.

10.5 The appearances of nonlinear characteristics in systems are very common in practice. Consider a feedback system with an input nonlinearity as shown in Figure 10.46. The nonlinearity obeys the relationship $u(t) = f(e(t))$ where $e(t)$ is the input signal and $u(t)$ is the nonlinear output signal. The plant is given by

$$G_0(s) = \frac{1}{s+1}$$

Find the steady-state response of the system as a function of the magnitude of a step input signal for the three controller gains $k = 1$, $k = 10$, and $k = 100$ for the following nonlinear functions.

(a)

$$f(e) = 0.2\left(e^3 - e\right)$$

(b)

$$f(e) = e + \sin(e) \quad |e| > 1$$
$$= 0 \quad |e| \le 1$$

(c)

$$f(e) = \tan^{-1}(e)$$

10.6 Consider the guided missile in Figure 10.47. The lateral force of the air rotates a missile about its center of gravity. The force applied by the air can be considered a point force applied to the center of pressure. If this center of pressure is ahead of the center of mass, the guided missile is unstable.

The input to the system is the angle of thrust $\psi(t)$ and the output of the system is $\theta(t)$. The force applied by the air drag can be modeled as $F_d = k_d\sin(\theta)$, where k_d depends on the shape and velocity of the rocket. The off-axis force applied by the rocket engines is given by $F_r\sin(\psi)$. The other relevant parameters are l_1, the distance from the rocket engine to the center of mass of the missile; l_2, the distance from the center of mass of the missile to the center of pressure; and J, the rotational inertia of the rocket.

For a fixed k_d and F_r the effective transfer function from ψ to θ, when ψ to θ are small, is[12]

$$G(s) = \frac{l_1 F_r / J}{s^2 - l_2 k_d / J}$$

Assume that $l_1 F_r / J = l_2 k_d / J = 9$ is an operating point of interest.

(a) Using a lead-control structure

$$C(s) = k\frac{s+z}{z+p}$$

find the values of k, z, and p such that the closed-loop system response is stable.

(b) As the velocity of the rocket changes, k_d changes. The operating speed changes enormously over the life of the rocket, effectively changing k_d. For the fixed controller designed in (a), use a root-locus plot to determine the range of k_d for which the system remains stable.

10.7 Consider the design of a cruise controller for an automobile. The car is modeled as a mass with a damper that limits the forward motion. The open-loop transfer function $G(s)$ from the engine throttle angle to the car's velocity is

$$G(s) = \frac{1}{ms + b}$$

The controller $C(s)$ is PI, with transfer function

$$C(s) = k_p + k_i / s$$

---

[12] M. Driels, *Linear Control Systems*, McGraw-Hill, New York, 1996.

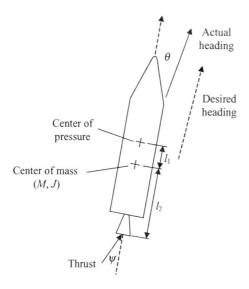

FIGURE 10.47
Attitude control of a missile.

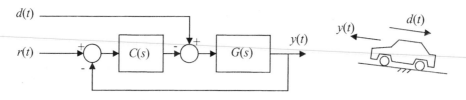

FIGURE 10.48
Block diagram of the automobile cruise control.

Assume that the car's mass m is 1,200 kg and the friction coefficient b is 70 Ns/m. The grade (slope) of the road acts as a disturbance into the plant. The block diagram for this system is shown in Figure 10.48. The desired speed is $r(t)$, the input for the motor (a throttle angle) is $u(t)$, and the speed of the vehicle is $y(t)$ as measured by a speedometer. The disturbance $d(t)$ represents the effect of the road grade.

(a) The transfer function from the disturbance $d(t)$ to the speed $y(t)$ is

$$G_{CL}(s) = \frac{G(s)}{1 + C(s)G(s)}$$

where $G(s)$ is the open-loop response and $C(s)$ is the PI transfer function defined previously. Plot the step response of the open-loop system and closed-loop system on the same figure for $k_p = 100$ and $k_i = 0$. Note that as the gain is increased the disturbance is reduced.

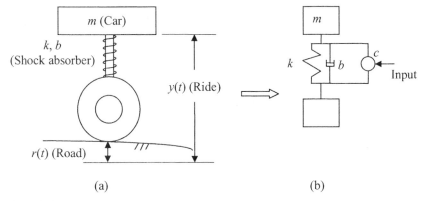

FIGURE 10.49
(a) A simplified model of the quarter-car model with an active suspension, and (b) its mass and spring equivalent.

(b) The transfer function from the velocity command $r(t)$ to speed $y(t)$ is

$$G_{ry}(s) = \frac{C(s)G(s)}{1 + C(s)G(s)}$$

Plot the step response for $k_p = 100$ and $k_i = 0$.

(c) Plot the steady-state output for the systems in (a) and (b) to a step response as a function of the proportional gain P in the range 50 to 150. It is seen that the integrator eliminates the steady-state error, and its speed is determined by the gain k_i.

10.8 An automotive suspension is typically passive, being composed of springs and dampers. To improve the suspension of cars, active suspensions systems have been proposed. Figure 10.49 depicts a simplified model of an active automobile suspension system in which $y(t)$ represents the input of the road surface and $x(t)$ is the vertical position of the passenger compartment. Assume that the mass of the tire is negligible and that velocity feedback is used so that $u(t) = Cdx(t)/dt$. The actuator applies a force to the rod and the passenger compartment that is proportional to their relative velocity: $C(dx/dt - dy/dt)$. The velocity transfer function from the road $y(t)$ to the ride $r(t)$ is

$$G(s) = \frac{(c+b)s + k}{ms^2 + (c+b)s + k}$$

(a) Use `rlocus` and `rlocfind` to determine the value of c needed to set the damping ratio to 1—that is, to make the system critically damped. To use `rlocus`, notice that the denominator can be written as $ms^2 + bs + k + cs$. Hence, it is now in standard from for `rlocus`, with the numerator [1 0] and the denominator [m b k]. The value determined by `rlocfind` will be c. Place the crosshairs at the point where the closed loop poles first cross the real axis.

(b) Plot the step response and Bode diagrams for the system with and without active control ($c = 0$). Assume that $m = 5000$ kg, $k = 8\times10^5$ N/m and $b = 12000$ Ns/m.

(c) In this problem, the spring is accounted for in k. Using the design in (b), and for k ranging between 4×10^5 to 10×10^5 N/m, create a meshed surface of the step response. Which car would you prefer to ride in?

10.9 Consider the task of designing an autopilot for a large, slowly moving ship in which the output of a compass provides the feedback. The controller sends commands to a rudder mechanism, which, with delay, turns it to the desired position, thereby turning the ship. The following equations have been linearized from Nomoto's equation[13] for a ship at cruising speed. The open-loop transfer function of the steering system without the controller is[14]:

$$G(s) = \frac{s + 0.03}{s(s + 0.09)(s + 0.04)(s - 0.0004)}$$

(a) The plant has an unstable pole. Plot the root locus of the steering system.

(b) Using the lead-control structure

$$C(s) = k\frac{s + z}{z + p}$$

find the values of k, z, and p that stabilize the closed-loop system response while maintaining less than 30% overshoot.

(c) Using a new sensor that provides velocity information one can now use PD control. Thus,

$$C(s) = k_p + sk_d$$

Find k_p and k_d such that the closed-loop response is stable, has less than 5% overshoot, and has a settling time less than 275 s.

10.10 A recent-model automobile has a catalytic converter to meet the exhaust-emission-performance standards. The catalytic converter requires tight control of the engine air/fuel ratio (A/F), the ignition-spark timing, and exhaust-gas recirculation. We consider the air/fuel ratio regulation task. The transfer function of the carburetor with the effective A/F ratio as output is[15]

$$G(s) = \frac{4e^{-T_d s}}{s + 4}$$

where the time delay T_d is 0.2 s. The function pade may be used to generate an approximation of the time delay, or one may set the output delay property of the transfer function to 0.2. However, using pade is less difficult, because it is one of MATLAB's few functions that supports time delay.

(a) Suppose that the time delay is neglected in the design of the controller and we let the controller be a PI controller so that

$$C(s) = k_p + \frac{k_i}{s}$$

Set $k_i = 2$ and select the value of k_p so that the rise time for the unit-step response is smaller than 0.4 s. Determine the step response of the system.

(b) Consider feeding a time-delayed signal back into the controller as shown in Figure 10.50. The extra compensation element in the controller contains a model of the plant and its time delay and is called a Smith predictor. Using a lead-control structure

[13] M. Driels, *ibid*.
[14] C. L. Phillips and R. D. Harbor, *Feedback Control Systems*, 3rd ed., Prentice Hall, Englewood Cliffs, NJ, 1996.
[15] B. Kuo, *Automatic Control Systems*, 7th ed., Prentice Hall, Englewood Cliffs, NJ, 1995, p. 815.

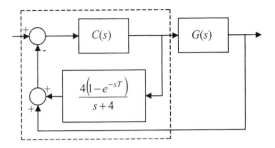

FIGURE 10.50
Exhaust emission control system using a Smith predictor.

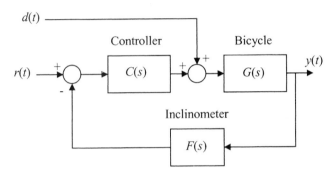

FIGURE 10.51
Block diagram of an automatic motorized bicycle.

$$C(s) = k\frac{s+z}{z+p}$$

find the values of k, z, and p that stabilize the closed loop system response while having no overshoot and a rise time less than 0.2 s. Compare the results to the PI controller in (a).

(c) Suppose that the time delay and the plant are not modeled correctly. Determine the step responses for system time delays of 0.3 and 0.1 s with the controller generated in (b) and a plant model with a DC gain of 1.2 and a pole at −5 instead of −4. From the results, is it better to overestimate or underestimate the time delay?

10.11 Consider an automatic motorized bicycle whose block diagram is shown in Fig. 10.51. An inclinometer detects the angle of the bicycle body from vertical, $y(t)$. The inclinometer's output is compared to the desired angle from vertical $r(t)$ and the error is input to the controller to generate a steering signal. Any disturbances to the system $d(t)$ are modeled as entering with the input to the bicycle. The transfer functions for the blocks shown in Figure 10.51 are

$$G(s) = \frac{9}{s^2 + 9}$$

$$F(s) = \frac{\omega^2}{s^2 + 2\xi\omega s + \omega^2}$$

$$C(s) = k\frac{s + z}{s + p}$$

where $C(s)$ is a lead controller.

(a) A micro-machined inclinometer has a settling time of 0.2 s and a bandwidth of 125 Hz. The sensor's parameters are $\omega = 250\pi$ and $\xi = 20/\omega$. Find k, z, and p such that the overshoot for unit step response is no more than 20% and the setting time is less than 4 s.

(b) Suppose that there is another type of inclinometer to choose, one that is based on the principle of a pendulum. Its resonant frequency is 7.4 Hz ($\omega = 14.8\pi$) and its damping coefficient $\xi = 0.4$. Can this inclinometer also be used?

BIBLIOGRAPHY

D. K. Anand and R. B. Zmood, *Introduction to Control Systems*, Butterworth and Heinmann, Ltd., Oxford, England, 1995.

E. Chowanietz, *Automobile Electronics*, SAE International, Troy, MI, 1995.

R. Dorf and R. Bishop, *Modern Control Systems*, Addison-Wesley Publishing, Reading, MA, 1997.

M. Driels, *Linear Control System Engineering*, McGraw-Hill, New York, 1996.

G. Franklin, J. Powell, and A. Emami-Naeini, *Feedback Control of Dynamic Systems*, 3rd ed., Addison-Wesley, Reading, MA, 1994.

B. Friedland, *Advanced Control System Design*, Prentice Hall, Englewood Cliffs, NJ, 1996.

R. Jurgen, Electronic Engine Control Technologies, SAE International, Troy, MI, 1999.

B. Kuo, Automatic Control Systems, Prentice Hall, Englewood Cliffs, NJ, 1995.

W. Levine, *The Control Handbook*, CRC Press, Boca Raton, FL, 1996.

N. Nise, *Control Systems Engineering*, Addison-Wesley, Reading, MA, 1995.

U. Ozguner, H. Goktas, and H. Chan, "Automotive Suspension Control Through a Computer Communication Network," *Proceedings of 1st IEEE Conference on Control Application*, vol. 2, 1992, pp. 895–900.

C. Phillips and R. Harbor, *Feedback Control Systems*, Prentice Hall, Englewood Cliffs, NJ, 1996.

C H A P T E R   1 1

FLUID MECHANICS

James H. Duncan

Several classes of problems in fluid mechanics are analyzed, and several flow fields are presented using a variety of visualization techniques.

11.1 HYDROSTATICS

In hydrostatics, the pressure is constant on any surface of constant height in a single fluid, and the pressure varies with height according to

$$\frac{dP}{dz} = -\rho g \tag{11.1}$$

where $\rho = \rho(z)$ is the density distribution, g is the acceleration of gravity (9.81 m/s^2), P is the pressure, and z is the vertical Cartesian coordinate, with positive being up. We now use Eq. (11.1) to solve two hydrostatics problems.

TABLE 11.1
Temperature of the Standard Atmosphere as a Function of Elevation

Elevation (m)	Temperature (°C)
0.0	15.0
11,000.0	−56.5
20,100.0	−56.5
32,200.0	−44.5
47,300.0	−2.5

11.1.1 Pressure Distribution in the Standard Atmosphere

The temperature distribution in the standard atmosphere is a piecewise linear distribution that is specified by a set of temperatures at various elevations. These are tabulated in Table 11.1. It is assumed that the temperature varies linearly between these elevations. If the atmosphere is a perfect gas, then

$$\rho = P/(RT)$$

where $R = 287.13$ J/(kg K) is the perfect gas constant, and T is the temperature in degrees Kelvin. With this assumption, Eq. (11.1) can be integrated to obtain:

$$P(z) = P_0 \exp\left[-\frac{g}{R} \int_0^z \frac{dz}{T} \right] \qquad (11.2)$$

where $P_0 = 101,330$ Pa is the pressure at $z = 0$.

Although Eq. (11.2) is easily integrated analytically, we shall do the evaluation numerically. A script that integrates Eq. (11.2) and plots both P and T as a function of z is given below. We use interp1 to perform the linear interpolation between the temperature values given in Table 11.1. The results are shown in Figure 11.1.

```
gravity = 9.81; p0 = 101330; R = 287.13;
tempC = [15 −56.5 −56.5 −44.5 −2.5];
z = [0 11000 20100 32200 47300];
inversetemp = 1./(tempC+273.15);
np = 18;
goverR = gravity/R;
elevation = linspace(0,z(end),np);
pressure = zeros(1,np);
intarg = inline('interp1(z,inversetemp,elevation)','elevation','z','inversetemp');
for i = 1:np
  pressure(i) = p0*exp(−goverR*quad8(intarg,0,elevation(i),[],[],z,inversetemp));
end
subplot(1,2,1)
```

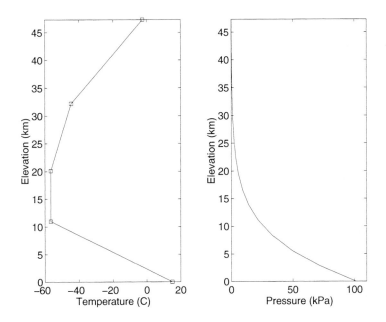

FIGURE 11.1
The standard atmosphere: (a) temperature from Table 11.1 versus elevation and (b) pressure from Eq.
(11.2) versus elevation.

```
plot(tempC,z/1000.0,'k-s')
axis([−60 20 0 elevation(end)/1000.0])
xlabel('Temperature (C)')
ylabel('Elevation (km)')
subplot(1,2,2)
plot(pressure/1000.0, elevation/1000.0,'k')
axis([0 110 0 elevation(end)/1000.0])
ylabel('Elevation (km)')
xlabel('Pressure (kPa)')
```

11.1.2 Force on a Planar Gate

Consider the reservoir shown in Figure 11.2. One wall of the reservoir is a tiltable metal
gate that is hinged at the bottom and has weight W and length L. The width of the reservoir
in the direction normal to the page is B. Initially, the gate is vertical and the water level
reaches the top of the gate. The total volume of water is $V_w = aLB$. A rod holds the gate
closed, and the force of the rod on the gate F_{rod} is directed along the rod. A stop holds the
opposite end of the rod in place. This stop can be moved to the right, thus letting the gate
rotate clockwise about its hinge. For gate angles θ less than or equal to some critical angle

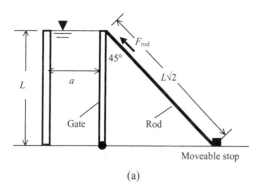

(a)

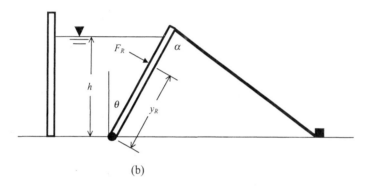

(b)

FIGURE 11.2
Reservoir with tiltable gate: (a) gate vertical; (b) gate opened to an angle θ.

θ_{max}, the water level is at or below the top of the gate; however, for $\theta > \theta_{max}$, the water spills over the top.

The volume bounded by the bottom, the fixed walls, the gate, and a level surface at the top of the gate is

$$\frac{V}{V_w} = \cos\theta + \frac{L}{2a}\cos\theta \sin\theta \qquad (11.3)$$

The water will spill over the dam when

$$\frac{V}{V_w} < 1.0$$

An equation for the water level h versus θ is obtained by equating V_w to an equation for the water volume at any θ. Thus,

$$\frac{V_w}{B} = aL = ah + 0.5h^2 \tan\theta \qquad (11.4)$$

The magnitude of F_{rod} is obtained by taking moments about the hinge. Thus,

$$F_{rod} = \frac{F_R y_R + 0.5WL\sin\theta}{L\sin\alpha} \tag{11.5}$$

where F_R is the total force of the water on the gate, y_R is the distance from the hinge to the center of pressure, and the angle α is shown in Figure 11.2b and is given by

$$\alpha = \theta + \cos^{-1}\left(\cos\theta/\sqrt{2}\right)$$

From the hydrostatics equations we find that

$$F_R = \frac{B\rho g h^2}{2\cos\theta}$$

$$y_R = \frac{h}{2\cos\theta} - \frac{2I_{xx}\cos^2\theta}{Bh^2}$$

where

$$I_{xx} = \frac{Bh^3}{12\cos^3\theta}$$

is the moment of inertia about the hinge of the submerged portion of the gate. Thus, Eq. (11.5) becomes

$$F_{rod} = \frac{1}{L\sin\alpha}\left[\frac{B\rho g h^3}{6\cos^2\theta} + \frac{WL}{2}\sin\theta\right] \tag{11.6}$$

In the following script, we shall determine θ_{max} and plot the depth of the water h and F_{rod} for $0 \le \theta \le \theta_{max}$. The results are shown in Figure 11.3. We assume that $L = 10$ m, $a = 5$ m, $B = 10$ m, and $W = 100,000$ N. In addition, V/V_w is computed from Eq. (11.3) and plotted versus θ. The MATLAB function fzero is used to determine θ_{max}, the location of which is denoted in Figure 11.3a. In the computation of θ_{max}, the inline function *MaxTheta*, which returns $1 - V/V_w$, is created. To obtain a graph of h as a function of θ, the quadratic equation in h given by Eq. (11.4) is solved using roots. Only the positive root is used. It is also of interest to determine the value of θ for which the reservoir is capable of holding the most water. This is obtained from fminbnd, which also calls *MaxTheta*. The script to determine these values and to display the results, including F_{rod} versus θ shown in Figure 11.4, is

```
a = 5.0; L = 10.0; B = 10.0;
rho = 1000.0; grav = 9.81 ; W = 100000.0;
ratio = L/a;
theta = linspace(0.0,pi/2.0);
VoverVw = cos(theta)+0.5*ratio*cos(theta).*sin(theta);
options = optimset('display','off');
figure(1)
```

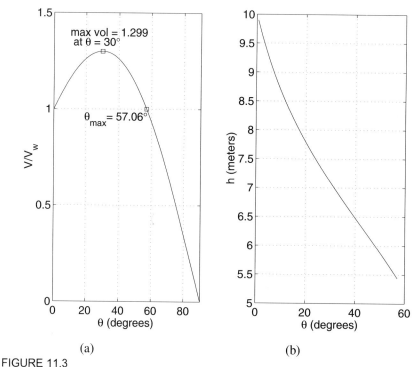

(a)   (b)

FIGURE 11.3

Results for the hinged gate configuration: (a) V/V_w versus θ; (b) h versus θ.

```
subplot(1,2,1)
plot(theta*180/pi,VoverVw,'k')
axis([0.0,90.0,0.0,1.5])
ylabel('V/V_w')
xlabel('\theta (degrees)')
grid on
hold on
MaxTheta =
inline('1−(cos(theta)+0.5*ratio*cos(theta).*sin(theta))','theta','ratio');
ThetaMaxDeg = fzero(MaxTheta,[0.01,pi/2.0],options,ratio)*180/pi;
plot(ThetaMaxDeg,1.0,'sk')
text(19, 0.95, ['\theta_{max}= ',num2str(ThetaMaxDeg,4) '\circ'])
ThetaMaxVol = fminbnd(MaxTheta,0.0,ThetaMaxDeg*pi/180,options,ratio);
MaxVol = 1−MaxTheta(ThetaMaxVol,ratio);
plot(ThetaMaxVol*180/pi,MaxVol,'ks')
text(10, MaxVol+0.1,['max vol = ' num2str(MaxVol,4) ])
text(10, MaxVol+0.05,[' at \theta = ' num2str(ThetaMaxVol* 180/pi,4) '\circ'])
subplot(1,2,2)
```

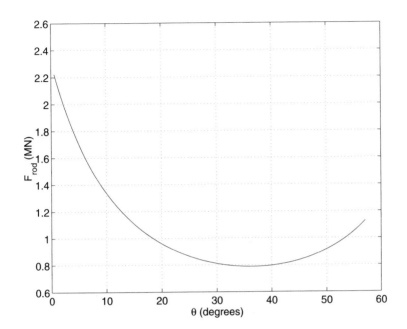

FIGURE 11.4
Force needed to keep the gate closed versus θ.

```
theta = linspace(0.01,ThetaMaxDeg*pi/180);
h = zeros(1,length(theta));
for i = 1:length(theta)
 r = roots([tan(theta(i))*0.5, a, -a*L]);
 h(i) = r(2);
end
plot(theta*180.0/pi,h)
ylabel('h (meters)')
xlabel('\theta (degrees)')
grid on
figure(2)
Frod = ((B*rho*grav*h.^3)./(6*cos(theta).^2)+0.5*W*L*sin(theta))./...
       (L*sin(theta+acos(cos(theta)/ sqrt(2))));
plot(theta*180.0/pi,Frod*1e−6)
ylabel('F_{rod} (MN)')
xlabel('\theta (degrees)')
grid on
```

11.2 INTERNAL VISCOUS FLOW

There is a large class of problems that concern laminar and turbulent viscous flow in pipes and ducts. The solutions to several of these problems are given below. For low Reynolds numbers, the flow is laminar, and the PDE toolbox is used to compute the flow field and the pressure drop along the pipe. For higher Reynolds numbers, the flow is turbulent, and the flow and pressure drop are computed with the aid of the Colebrook equation.[1]

11.2.1 Laminar Flow in a Horizontal Pipe with Various Cross Sections

With the MATLAB PDE toolbox, it is relatively straightforward to compute the fully developed laminar flow field in a horizontal pipe with various cross-sectional shapes. The analytical solution for a circular pipe is available in most textbooks.[2] Therefore, we begin by computing this flow field and comparing the computed maximum and average velocities to the analytically determined values. We assume that the pipe radius is $R = 5.0$ mm, the dynamic viscosity of the fluid is $\mu = 0.38$ N s/m^2, and the pressure gradient in the axial direction is $dP/dz = 1.0 \times 10^8$ Pa/m.

The differential equation for the axial flow field is

$$\frac{\partial^2 u}{\partial y^2} + \frac{\partial^2 u}{\partial z^2} = \frac{1}{\mu} \frac{dP}{dx} \tag{11.7}$$

where $u(y,z)$ is the axial velocity in the x-direction and y and z are the Cartesian coordinates of the pipe cross-section, with the point $(0,0)$ being at the center of the pipe. The (y,z) coordinates of wall of the pipe are given by

$$y^2 + z^2 = R^2$$

and the no-slip boundary condition on the wall requires that $u = 0$.

We shall solve the problem using `pdetool`.[3] Once in `pdetool`, we create a circle of radius 1.0 centered at $(0,0)$. This implies that we have created the dimensionless coordinates $y' = y/R$ and $z' = z/R$, and Eq. (11.7) becomes

$$\frac{\partial^2 u}{\partial y'^2} + \frac{\partial^2 u}{\partial z'^2} = \frac{R^2}{\mu} \frac{dP}{dx} = f$$

In `pdetool`, we select the *Boundary Mode* from the *Boundary* pull-down menu and specify the Dirichlet boundary conditions ($u = 0$) on each of the four arcs comprising the circle. We then select the elliptic partial differential equation with the parameters $c = 1$, $a = 0$, and $f = 6578.95$ m/s ($= (0.005^2/0.38) \times 10^8$). Next, we initialize the mesh and refine it two times. The resulting solution is plotted in contour form in Figure 11.5.

---

[1] C. E. Colebrook, "Turbulent flow in pipes with particular reference to the transition region between smooth and rough pipe laws," *Journal of the Institute of Civil Engineers*, London, Vol. 11, 1939, pp. 133–156.

[2] B. R. Munson, D. F. Young, and T. H. Okiishi, *Fundamental of Fluid Mechanics*, John Wiley & Sons, New York, 1998.

[3] See Section 8.7 for more details on how to use `pdetool`.

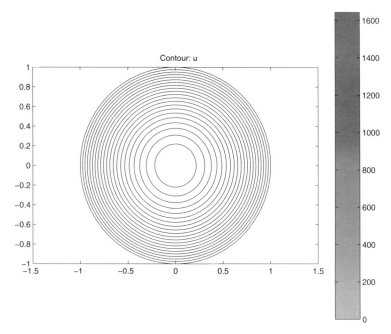

FIGURE 11.5
Axial flow field in a circular pipe. The value of the innermost contour is 1,600.

To obtain additional quantitative data from the solution, we export the solution u and the mesh descriptors p, e, and t to the MATLAB command window. The maximum value of the velocity occurs at the center of the pipe cross-section and can be found by typing

umax = max(u)

in the MATLAB command window. The result is $umax$ = 1643.5, which is very close to the theoretically predicted value of 1644.74.

The flux of volume Q is given by

$$Q = \iint_A u\,dA \approx \sum_{i=1}^{N_t} u_i \Delta A_i$$

where A is the cross-sectional area of the pipe, N_t is the number of triangles in the mesh, u_i is the value of the velocity at the center of each triangular grid, and ΔA_i is the area of each triangle. In the following script, u_i is determined by pdeintrp and ΔA_i is determined by pdetrg.

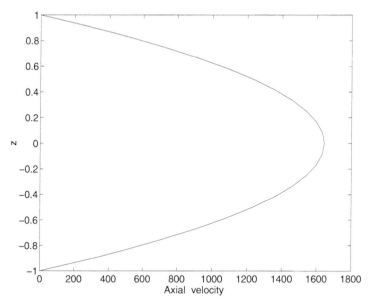

FIGURE 11.6
Axial flow velocity versus the radial position inside a pipe.

```
ui = pdeintrp(p,t,u);
DeltaAi = pdetrg(p,t);
Q = sum(DeltaAi.*ui)
```

Executing this script—after exporting u, p, e, and t to the MATLAB window—gives Q = 2580.6. The resulting average velocity is $u_{ave} = Q/A = 2580.6/\pi = 821.4$, which is very close to the theoretical value of one-half the maximum velocity, or $1644.74/2 = 822.37$. Further refinement of the mesh will bring the computed and theoretical values to closer agreement.

It is also possible to plot the velocity as a function of distance along a pipe diameter: y' = 0 and $-1 \leq z' \leq 1$. To do this, it is first necessary to use `tri2grid` to interpolate the triangular mesh data onto points that lie on a diameter of the pipe cross section. The result is shown in Figure 11.6, and has the parabolic profile that is obtained from the theory. The script is

```
z = linspace(-1, 1, 25);
uyz = tri2grid(p,t,u,0,z);
plot(uyz,z)
axis([0,1800,-1.0,1.0])
ylabel('z')
xlabel('Axial velocity')
```

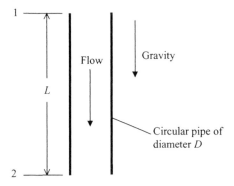

FIGURE 11.7
Flow in a vertically oriented pipe of diameter D.

11.2.2 Downward Flow in a Vertical Pipe

Consider a vertically oriented smooth pipe of length L and diameter $D = 4.0$ cm in which water of density $\rho = 1000.0$ Kg/m^3 and kinematic viscosity $v = 1.2 \times 10^{-6}$ m^2/s is flowing downward, as shown in Figure 11.7. We shall find the flow rate for which the pressure drop due to the downward flow is balanced by the pressure gain due to gravity—that is, the flow rate for which the static pressure in the pipe is independent of the distance along the pipe.

The head loss equation is:

$$\frac{P_1}{\rho g} + \frac{V_1^2}{2g} + z_1 = \frac{P_2}{\rho g} + \frac{V_2^2}{2g} + z_2 + \frac{\lambda L V^2}{2gD} \tag{11.8}$$

where P is the pressure, V is the average flow speed, z is the height, and λ is the friction factor. In the present problem, $P_1 = P_2$, $V_1 = V_2$, and $z_1 - z_2 = L$; therefore, Eq. (11.8) reduces to

$$\lambda = \frac{2gD^3}{v^2 R_e^2} \tag{11.9}$$

where R_e is the Reynolds number defined as

$$R_e = \frac{VD}{v} \tag{11.10}$$

The Colebrook formula for λ versus R_e in pipes of varying roughness factors k/D is given by (recall Exercise 5.5)

$$\frac{1}{\sqrt{\lambda}} = -2\log_{10}\left(\frac{2.51}{R_e\sqrt{\lambda}} + \frac{k/D}{3.7}\right) \qquad R_e \geq 4000 \tag{11.11}$$

In the present case, $k = 0$. Eliminating λ between Eqs. (11.9) and (11.10) yields a transcendental equation for the Reynolds number of the pipe flow and, therefore, the desired flow rate. The Colebrook expression is evaluated in *ColebrookFriction*, which is given by

```
function value = ColebrookFriction(Re,nu,kOverD,gravity,diameter)
lambda = 2*gravity*diameter^3/(nu*Re)^2;
value = 1/sqrt(lambda)+2*log10(kOverD/3.7+2.51/(Re*sqrt(lambda)));
```

The script is

```
diameter = 0.04; gravity = 9.81;
nu = 1.2e-6; kOverD = 0.000;
options = optimset('display','off');
Re = fzero('ColebrookFriction',[1e3,1e7],options,nu,kOverD,gravity,diameter);
disp(['Re = ', num2str(Re)])
disp(['Flow Rate = ' num2str(pi*diameter*Re*nu/4) ' m^3/s'])
```

which, when executed, gives

```
Re = 240405.8408
Flow Rate = 0.0090631 m^3/s
```

where the flow rate $Q = \pi D^2 V/4$.

11.2.3 Three-Reservoir Problem

Consider the classical three-reservoir problem[4] in which three reservoirs of different elevations are connected to a common junction at location J as shown in Figure 11.8. If we are given the length L_j, diameter d_j, and roughness k_j of the pipes meeting at J and the elevations of each reservoir h_j, then we can determine the corresponding flow rates Q_j and direction of flow in each pipe. The method is as follows. If an open-ended tube were installed at the junction, then the water's elevation in the tube would rise to the elevation h_p, which is unknown. The difference between the elevations at P and J is the pressure head at the junction. Secondly, at J the sum of the flows from each pipe must be zero—that is

$$\sum_{j=1}^{3} Q_j = 0 \quad j = 1,2,3 \tag{11.12}$$

with a positive value of Q_j indicating flow towards the junction and a negative value indicating flow out of the junction.

The flow in each pipe is determined from

$$Q_j = 0.25\pi d_j^2 V_j s_j \quad j = 1,2,3$$

[4] N. H. C. Hwang and C. E. Hita, *Fundamentals of Hydraulic Engineering Systems*, 2nd ed., Prentice-Hall, Englewood Cliffs, NJ, 1987, pp. 106–110.

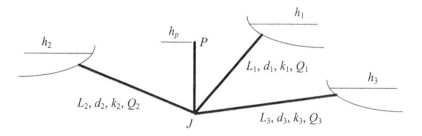

FIGURE 11.8
Pipes connecting three reservoirs at junction J.

where

$$V_j = \sqrt{\frac{2gd_j|\Delta h_j|}{\lambda_j L_j}} \qquad \Delta h_j = h_j - h_p \qquad j = 1,2,3$$

and s_j is the sign of Δh_j, $g = 9.81$ m/s² is the gravity constant, and λ_j is the pipe friction coefficient as determined from Eq. (11.11) and is a function of R_{ej}—that is, (recall Eq. (11.10))

$$R_{ej} = \frac{V_j d_j}{\nu} \qquad j = 1,2,3$$

where $\nu = 1.002 \times 10^{-6}$ m²/s is the kinematic viscosity of water at 20 °C. Thus, the objective is to determine the value of h_p that satisfies Eq. (11.12).

The solution is obtained as follows. We assume a value for h_p, which we know lies somewhere between the minimum and maximum values of h_j. Then we compute a value for each V_j by first assuming a value for λ_j that is obtained from Eq. (11.11) for very large Re:

$$\lambda_j = \left[2\log_{10}\left(3.7\frac{d_j}{k_j} \right) \right]^{-2}$$

We use these values of V_j to determine values for R_{ej}, which are then used to determine λ_j from the general Colebrook formula given by Eq. (11.11). We continue this process until the values of V_j are within an acceptable tolerance.

After each V_j has been determined, we compute each Q_j and determine whether or not Eq. (11.12) has been satisfied. If it hasn't, then another value of h_p is selected, and new values of V_j are computed as just described. It should be noted that when $\Delta h_j = 0$, $Q_j = 0$ and the value of λ_j cannot be computed since $R_{ej} = 0$. In the scripts and functions that implement this procedure, we use nested applications of `fzero`, an inner one to determine V_j and an outer one to determine h_p.

Using the solution method described above we shall determine the flow rates for the values are given in Table 11.2.

TABLE 11.2
Parameters for Reservoir in Figure 11.8

Reservoir	d_j (m)	L_j (m)	k_j (m)	h_j (m)
1	0.30	1000	0.00060	120
2	0.50	4000	0.00060	100
3	0.40	2000	0.00060	80

We now create three functions. The first one determines Q_j and evaluates Eq. (11.12) and is called *ReservoirSumQ*. The second function, called *PipeFrictionCoeff*, evaluates Eq. (11.11). The third function, called *ResFriction*, evaluates Eq. (11.11) at each V_j. These three functions are given below. Function *ReservoirSumQ* is

```
function [sq,q] = ReservoirSumQ(hg,d,el,k,h)
cv = 2*9.81*d./el;
ro = d/1.002e-6;
dk = d./k;
qd = 0.25*pi*d.^2;
frictguess = (2*log10(3.7*dk)).^-2;
hh = h-hg;
options = optimset('display','off');
for n = 1:length(d)
 if hh(n) == 0
   q(n) = 0;
 else
   lambda = fzero('ResFriction',frictguess(n),options,dk(n),hh(n),cv(n),ro(n));
   q(n) = sign(hh(n))*sqrt(cv(n)*abs(hh(n))/lambda)*qd(n);
 end
end
sq = sum(q);
```

Function *PipeFrictionCoeff* is

```
function x = PipeFrictionCoeff(el,re,dk)
if dk>100000|dk == 0
 x = el-(2*log10(re*sqrt(el)/2.51))^-2;
else
 x = el-(2*log10(2.51/re/sqrt(el)+0.27/dk))^-2;
end
```

Function *ResFriction* is

```
function lamb = ResFriction(lambda,dk,dh,cv,ro)
ren = sqrt(cv*abs(dh)/lambda)*ro;
```

lamb = PipeFrictionCoeff(lambda,ren,dk);

The script is

d = [0.3 0.5 0.4];
el = [1000 4000 2000];
k = [0.6 0.6 0.6]*1e−3;
h = [120 100 80];
options = optimset('display','off');
hg = fzero('ReservoirSumQ',110,options,d,el,k,h);
[sq,q] = ReservoirSumQ(hg,d,el,k,h);
disp(['Elevation h_sub_p = 'num2str(hg)' m'])
disp(['Q1 = 'num2str(q(1))' m^3/s Q2 = 'num2str(q(2))' m^3/s Q3 = '...
num2str(q(3))' m^3/s'])

Execution of the script gives

Elevation h_sub_p = 98.904 m
Q1 = 0.16185 m^3/s   Q2 = 0.068728 m^3/s   Q3 = -0.23058 m^3/s

11.3 EXTERNAL FLOW

11.3.1 Boundary Layer on an Infinite Plate Started Suddenly from Rest

Consider a layer of liquid of thickness $h = 10.0$ cm that extends to infinity in the x-z plane and is bounded by a rigid plate at $y = 0$ and a free surface at $y = h$. The plate and the fluid are initially at rest. At $t = 0$, the plate is instantaneously accelerated to a speed U in the positive x-direction. The resulting fluid motion is only in the x-direction, and is a function only of time and the y coordinate. We shall determine $u = u(y,t)$ for $U = 5.0$ cm/s and a fluid with kinematic viscosity $v_{vis} = 1.0$ cm^2/s.

The solution is obtained by solving for the x-component of the Navier-Stokes equations, which in the present case reduces to

$$\frac{\partial u}{\partial t} = v_{vis} \frac{\partial^2 u}{\partial y^2} \tag{11.13}$$

The initial condition is

$$u(y,0) = 0$$

The boundary condition at the surface of the plate is the no-slip condition,

$$u(0,t) = U$$

while the boundary condition at the free surface, $y = 10.0$ cm, is zero shear stress—that is,

$$\left.\frac{du}{dy}\right|_{y=10.0} = 0$$

We shall solve this problem with `pdetool`. In the `pdetool` window we use the *Axes Limits* in the *Options* menu to create a window with dimensions −1.5 to 1.5 in the *x*-direction and 0.0 to 10.0 in the *y*-direction. Then we create a rectangle extending from −0.25 to 0.25 in the *x*-direction and from 0.0 to 10.0 in the *y*-direction. The PDE Toolbox solves equations in the (*x,y*) domain, whereas the present computation will be independent of *x*. Thus, the computation time is decreased if, as we have done above, the *x* dimension of the computational domain is a small fraction of the total dimension of the *y*-direction.

The boundary conditions on the rectangle are set as follows. On the bottom of the rectangle, which is the surface of the plate, the Dirichlet boundary condition is $u = U = 5.0$ ($h = 1$, $r = 5$). On the top of the rectangle, which is the free surface, the Neumann boundary condition is $\partial u/\partial x = 0$ ($q = g = 0$). The Neumann boundary conditions $\partial u/\partial x = 0$ are also used on the two vertical boundaries of the rectangle to make the solution independent of *x*. The solution was obtained with a mesh that was refined twice. To specify Eq. (11.13) in `pdetool`, we use the *Parabolic* option in the *PDE Specification* window of the *PDE* pull-down menu. For this choice, we set $c = 1$, $a = 0$, $f = 0$, and $d = 1$. Finally, to select times for which the solution will be displayed, we use the *Parameters* option from the *Solve* pull-down menu. In the input area for *Time*, we enter 0:0.5:10. After solving the equation, we export the solution *u* and the mesh parameters *p*, *e*, and *t* to the M_{ATLAB} command window. The size of the solution array *u* is ($n_m \times n_t$), where n_m is the number of mesh points and n_t is the number of times for which the solution is given, in this case $n_t = 21$. The following script extracts the data along the line *x* = 0 and produces the plot given in Figure 11.9, where the Δt between the contours is 0.5 s.

```
ymin = 0.0; ymax = 10.0;
y = linspace(ymin, ymax, 30);
[nm,nt] = size(u);
for i = 1:nt
 plot(tri2grid(p,t, u(:,i),0,y),y)
 hold on
end
axis([0,5,ymin,ymax])
ylabel('y (cm)')
xlabel('Horizontal velocity (cm/s)')
text(1.5,5,'t=10.0 s')
```

11.3.2 Blasius Boundary Layer

The incompressible flow field in a laminar boundary layer on a flat plate is given by the solution to the boundary layer equations

$$\frac{\partial u}{\partial x} + \frac{\partial v}{\partial y} = 0 \qquad\qquad\qquad (11.14)$$

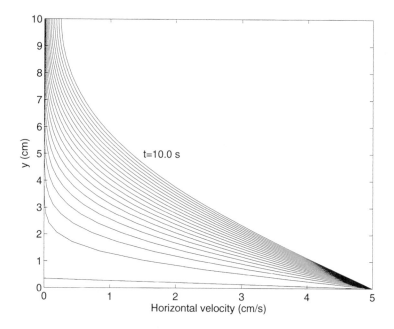

FIGURE 11.9
Horizontal velocity in a fluid layer of depth 10.0 cm that is suddenly accelerated to a speed $U = 5.0$ cm/s.

$$u\frac{\partial u}{\partial x} + v\frac{\partial v}{\partial y} = v_{vis}\frac{\partial^2 u}{\partial y^2}$$

where x and y are the coordinates parallel to and perpendicular to the plate surface, respectively, u and v are the corresponding fluid velocity components, respectively; and v_{vis} is the kinematic viscosity. The boundary conditions are that both u and v are zero on the plate surface and that $u \rightarrow U$ and $v \rightarrow 0$ as $y \rightarrow \infty$.

A similarity solution is proposed where

$$\frac{df}{d\eta} = \frac{u}{U} \tag{11.15a}$$

and

$$\eta = y\sqrt{\frac{U}{xv_{vis}}} \tag{11.15b}$$

The quantity f is proportional to the stream function of the flow, and $d^2f/d\eta^2$ is proportional to the shear. The similarity solution transforms the boundary layer equation into the ordinary nonlinear differential equation

$$2\frac{d^3 f}{d\eta^3} + f\frac{d^2 f}{d\eta^2} = 0 \tag{11.16}$$

where at $\eta = 0$

$$f = 0 \qquad \frac{df}{d\eta} = 0 \tag{11.17a}$$

and as $\eta \to \infty$

$$\frac{df}{d\eta} \to 1 \tag{11.17b}$$

In order to solve Eq. (11.16), we reduce it to three first-order equations using the definitions

$$f_1 = f$$
$$f_2 = \frac{df}{d\eta} \tag{11.18}$$
$$f_3 = \frac{d^2 f}{d\eta^2}$$

to obtain

$$\frac{df_1}{d\eta} = f_2$$
$$\frac{df_2}{d\eta} = f_3 \tag{11.19}$$
$$\frac{df_3}{d\eta} = -0.5 f_1 f_3$$

The boundary conditions at $\eta = 0$ become

$$f_1(0) = f_2(0) = 0 \tag{11.20a}$$

and as $\eta \to \infty$

$$f_2(\eta \to \infty) \to 1 \tag{11.20b}$$

To solve Eqs. (11.19) subject to the boundary conditions given by Eqs. (11.20), an iterative method is used. In this method, the values of $f_1(0)$ and $f_2(0)$ are given by Eq. (11.20a), and a guess for the wall shear stress $f_3(0)$ is assumed. Then the differential equations Eqs. (11.19) are integrated using ode45 to find f_2 at the outer boundary at $\eta =$

η_{max}: $f_2(\eta_{max})$. For the correct value of $f_3(0)$, $f_2(\eta_{max}) \rightarrow 1.0$ when η_{max} is sufficiently large (see Eq. (11.20b)). In the script, the correct value of $f_3(0)$ is determined by iteration using fzero. The function *Blasius* is used by ode45 to evaluate Eqs. (11.19). The function *Blasius2* is called by fzero to perform the iteration to find the value of $f_3(0)$ that produces $f_2(\eta_{max} \rightarrow \infty) \rightarrow 1.0$. This function also calls *Blasius*. These functions are given below.

The function *Blasius* is

```
function F = Blasius(x,y)
F = [y(2); y(3); -0.5*y(1)*y(3)];
```

and the function *Blasius2* is

```
function fn = Blasius2(fp0,EtaMax)
[eta ff] = ode45('Blasius', [0 EtaMax], [0 0 fp0]');
fn = 1.0-ff(end,2);
```

The script is

```
EtaMax = 20.0;
options = optimset('display','off');
shear0 = fzero('Blasius2', 0.3, options, EtaMax);
disp(['The shear stress at eta = 0 is: ' num2str(shear0)]);
[eta ff] = ode45('Blasius', [0 EtaMax], [0 0 shear0]');
plot(ff(:,1),eta,'k-',ff(:,2),eta,'k-.',ff(:,3),eta,'k--.')
axis([0 3 0 4])
ylabel('\eta')
xlabel('f, df/d\eta, d^2f/d\eta^2')
legend('f','df/d\eta','d^2f/d\eta^2',4)
```

When this script is executed we find that the shear stress is 0.33203 at $\eta = 0$, and we obtain the results shown in Figure 11.10.

11.3.3 Potential Flow

In incompressible potential flows, the velocity fields $\vec{u}$ are governed by

$$\nabla \cdot \vec{u} = 0$$

and

$$\nabla \times \vec{u} = 0$$

These conditions dictate that the velocity can be expressed as the gradient of a potential field, ϕ,

$$\vec{u} = \nabla \phi$$

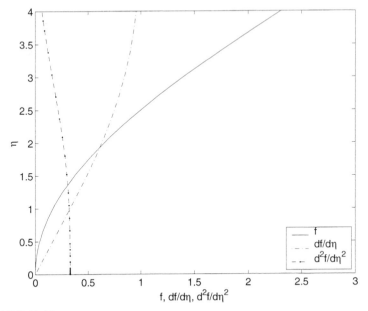

FIGURE 11.10.
Blasius boundary layer profiles of the stream function f_1, streamwise component of velocity f_2, and the shear f_3.

where ϕ satisfies Laplace's equation,

$$\nabla^2 \phi = 0 \qquad\qquad (11.21)$$

An alternative mathematical description for two-dimensional flows is obtained using the stream function ψ, where

$$u = \frac{\partial \psi}{\partial y}$$

$$v = -\frac{\partial \psi}{\partial x}$$

The stream function also satisfies Laplace's equation. Boundary conditions consist of the Neumann conditions, where the component of the velocity normal to a boundary is specified, or the Dirichlet conditions, where the value of ϕ is specified. At solid boundaries, the Neumann condition is $\vec{u} \cdot \hat{n} = 0$, where $\hat{n}$ is the unit normal to the boundary. In the following text, several methods for obtaining flow fields for two-dimensional potential flows are discussed. In two of these methods, the flows are constructed by adding together known potentials or stream functions. We now give four such quantities.

Sources and sinks

$$\phi_M = \frac{m}{2\pi} \ln r_M \qquad\qquad \psi_M = \frac{m}{2\pi} \theta_M$$

$$r_M^2 = (x - x_M)^2 + (y - y_M)^2 \qquad \theta_M = \tan^{-1} \frac{y - y_M}{x - x_M}$$

where (x_M, y_M) is the location of the source or sink and m is the source strength.

Doublets (dipoles)

$$\phi_K = \frac{K \cos\theta}{r_K} \qquad\qquad \psi_K = -\frac{K \sin\theta}{r_K}$$

$$r_K^2 = (x - x_K)^2 + (y - y_K)^2 \qquad \theta_K = \tan^{-1} \frac{y - y_K}{x - x_K}$$

where (x_K, y_K) is the location of the dipole and K is the dipole strength.

Vortices

$$\phi_\Gamma = \frac{\Gamma}{2\pi} \theta_\Gamma \qquad\qquad \psi_\Gamma = -\frac{\Gamma \ln r_\Gamma}{2\pi}$$

$$r_\Gamma^2 = (x - x_\Gamma)^2 + (y - y_\Gamma)^2 \qquad \theta_\Gamma = \tan^{-1} \frac{y - y_\Gamma}{x - x_\Gamma}$$

where (x_Γ, y_Γ) is the location of the vortex and Γ is the vortex strength;

Uniform flow field

$$\phi_U = Ux \qquad\qquad \psi_U = Uy$$

where U is the flow speed.

Thus, in general, one can form an additive combination of these different stream functions to simulate different flows around different shapes. Then, if ψ_s is the new streamline function,

$$\psi_s = \psi_M + \psi_K + \psi_\Gamma + \psi_U$$

Method 1: Determining the Streamline Pattern with contour. The first and easiest method of determining the streamline pattern of a flow is to plot the streamlines with contour. The following script plots the streamline ψ_s for a flow consisting of a uniform flow of speed U, a dipole of strength K located at (x_K, y_K), and a vortex of strength Γ located at (x_Γ, y_Γ). To illustrate this result, we choose the location of the dipole and vortex at $(-1, -1)$ and give the strengths of each of these quantities the following values:

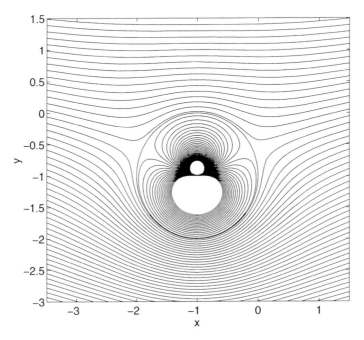

FIGURE 11.11
Streamlines for a cylinder with circulation in cross flow. Obtained from a contour plot of ψ_s.

$K = 5.0$ $(x_K, y_K) = (-1, -1)$
$\Gamma = 8\pi$ $(x_\Gamma, y_\Gamma) = (-1, -1)$
$U = 5.0,$

As illustrated in Figure 11.11, the resulting streamlines show flow about a cylinder with circulation. The main difficulty in obtaining these results is how to choose the contour levels to obtain a complete description of the flow. This can be accomplished using the value of ψ_s at the lower left corner of the domain for the minimum value and the value of ψ_s at the top middle of the domain for the maximum value. In Figure 11.11, the surface of a cylinder, which is also a streamline, has been superimposed on the streamlines.

```
nx =100; xmin = –3.5; xmax = 1.5;
ny = 100; ymin = –3.0; ymax = 1.5;
[x y] = meshgrid(linspace(xmin, xmax, nx),linspace(ymin, ymax, ny));
U0 = 5.0;
Gamma = 8*pi; xGamma = –1.0; yGamma = –1.0;
K = 5.0; xK = –1.0; yK = –1.0;
radius = inline('sqrt((x–x1).^2+(y–y1).^2)','x','y','x1','y1');
```

```
PsiK = K*sin(atan2(y-yK,x-xK))./radius(x,y,xK,yK);
PsiGamma = Gamma*log(radius(x,y,xGamma,yGamma))/2/pi;
StreamFunction = U0*y-PsiGamma -PsiK;
levmin = StreamFunction(1,nx);
levmax = StreamFunction(ny,nx/2);
levels = linspace(levmin,levmax,50)';
contour(x,y,StreamFunction,levels)
hold on
theta = linspace (0,2*pi);
plot(xGamma+cos(theta),yGamma+sin(theta),'k')
axis equal
axis([xmin xmax ymin ymax])
ylabel('y')
xlabel('x')
```

Method 2: Direct Calculation of Streamlines. A second method to obtain flow patterns is to use `fzero` to find specific streamlines. As an example we assume that the flow consists of a uniform stream of $U = 1$ in the positive y-direction, a source of strength $m = 4.0$ at $(0,-1)$, and a source of strength $m = -4.0$ at $(0,1)$. Thus,

$$\psi_{oval} = +\psi_U + \psi_{M_1} + \psi_{M_2}$$

These components produce a uniform flow over an oval-shaped body given by[5]

$$\frac{2x}{x^2 + y^2 - a^2} = \tan\frac{xU}{m/2\pi} \tag{11.22}$$

where U is the flow speed, m is the source strength, and a is a characteristic dimension.

A difficulty in using `fzero` in this example is the need to find a good starting guess. In the following script, this is done by finding the value of the stream function ψ at a set of x locations along $y = -2.0a$. Given this initial data, a streamline is computed by marching along it, starting at $y = -2.0a$. At each successive y location, `fzero` uses function *StreamFun* to determine the x location of the stream function; the value of x at the previous y location is used as the initial guess. A plot from the output of the script is given in Figure 11.12, where we have assumed that $a = 1$. The graph has been rotated 90° so that the flow is horizontal, which is traditional way of presenting it. The streamline that coincides with the boundary of the oval was not computed in this manner; it is plotted directly from Eq. (11.22). The script is

```
U = 1.0;a = 1.0;m = 4.0; co = m/(2*pi);
nPsi = 15; n = 30; yStart = -2.0*a;
xStart = linspace(0,2*a,nPsi);
y = linspace(-2*a,2*a,n);
x = zeros(1,n);
```

---

[5] L. M. Milne-Thomson, *Theoretical Hydrodynamics*, Dover, Mineola, NY, 1996, p. 216.

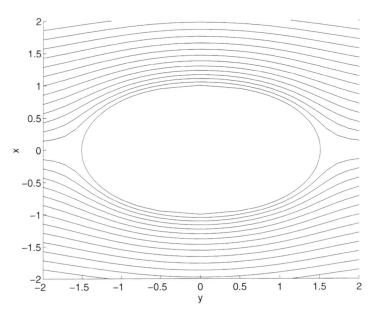

FIGURE 11.12
Streamlines for the oval given by Eq. (11.22).

```
StreamFun = inline('-U*x-co*(atan2(x,y+a)-atan2(x,y-a))- psi',...
                    'x','y','psi','U','co','a');
Psi = StreamFun(xStart,yStart,0,U,co,a);
options = optimset('display','off');
for j = 1:nPsi
  guess = xStart(j);
  for i = 1:n
    x(i) = fzero(StreamFun,guess,options,y(i),Psi(j),U,co,a);
    guess = x(i);
  end
  if j>1
    plot(y,x,'b',y,-x,'b')
  end
  hold on
end
axis([-2*a,2*a,-2*a,2*a])
ylabel('x')
xlabel('y')
xx = linspace(-1,1,40);
yy = sqrt(1-xx.^2+2*xx./tan(xx/co));
plot(yy,xx,'k',-yy,xx,'k')
```

where *nPsi* is the number of streamlines and *n* is the number of points computed along each streamline.

Method 3: Solving for the Flow Field with `pdetool`. A third method to obtain potential flow solutions is to use `pdetool` to solve Eq. (11.21) directly. Let us compute the flow field for a cylinder of diameter 1.0 that is placed in the center of a duct in which the flow speed is 10.0. In the `pdetool` window we select the axes of the window to extend from −3.5 to 3.5 in *x*-direction and from −2.5 to 2.5 in *y*-direction. We then create a circle (*C1*) of radius 1.0 centered at (0,0) and a rectangle (*R1*) of dimensions 6.0 wide by 5.0 high centered at (0,0). We alter the *Set Formula* to *R1−C1* and then select the *Boundary Mode*.

We then select *Specify Boundary Conditions*, and on the circle and the top and bottom boundaries of the rectangle we select the Neumann boundary condition $\hat{n} \cdot \nabla \phi = 0$. To achieve this specification we set $c = 1$, $q = 0$, and $g = 0$. On the left side of the rectangle we select the Neumann boundary condition $\hat{n} \cdot \nabla \phi = 10$—that is, we set $c = 1$, $q = 0$, and $g = 10$. On the right side we set $\hat{n} \cdot \nabla \phi = -10$—that is, we set $c = 1$, $q = 0$, and $g = -10$. This makes the mean flow go from left to right, since the unit normal $\hat{n}$ to the boundary in `pdetool` is directed from the boundary toward the flow domain.

Next we initialize the mesh and refine it twice. The partial differential equation is specified by selecting *elliptic* from *PDE Specification* in the *PDE* pull-down menu. Our equation is $\nabla^2 u = 0$, where in the present case the MATLAB variable *u* represents ϕ; therefore, we set $c = 1$, $a = 0$, and $f = 0$. We solve for *u* and produce a vector plot of the velocity ∇u on top of a contour plot of *u* as shown in Figure 11.13.

To obtain more detailed results, we export the solution *u* and the mesh coordinates *p*, *e*, and *t* to the MATLAB command window. A plot of the velocity along any vertical or horizontal line can be obtained in the following manner. Consider the horizontal velocity along the vertical line $x = 0$ extending from the top of the cylinder to the top of the rectangle. To obtain a plot of this velocity distribution, the script given below is used. In the script we first create a rectangular grid in the area of interest, say $-0.5 \leq x \leq 0.5$ ($n_x = 9$ points) and $0.5 \leq y \leq 2.5$ ($n_y = 25$ points) with `tri2grid`. We then use `gradient` to obtain the difference field. Finally, the horizontal component of the gradient is obtained along the line $x = 0$ by dividing the appropriate differences by the grid spacing in the *x*-direction. The resulting array of velocities is called *ux* in the script. A plot of *ux* versus *y* is given in Figure 11.14. For a cylinder in an infinite flow field, the maximum velocity, which occurs on the top and bottom of the cylinder ($\pm 90°$ from the flow direction), is $2U$. In the present case, the cylinder is in a duct created by the top and bottom of the rectangle. The maximum velocity is again at the $90°$ position on the cylinder, and the value is $ux(1) = 2.264U$.

```
nx = 9; xmin = −0.5; xmax = 0.5;
x = linspace(xmin, xmax, nx);
ny = 25; ymin = 0.5; ymax = 2.5;
y = linspace(ymin, ymax, ny);
uxy = tri2grid(p,t,u,x,y);
[DX,DY] = gradient(uxy);
ux = −DX(:,(nx−1)/2)/((xmax−xmin)/(nx−1));
plot(ux,y)
```

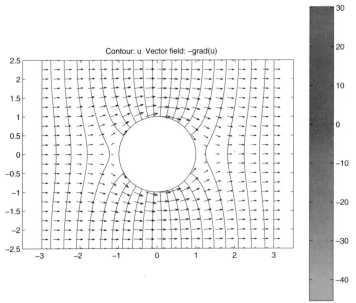

FIGURE 11.13
Velocity potential (contours) and velocity vectors from the direct solution of Eq. (11.21).

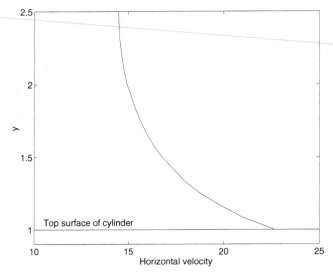

FIGURE 11.14
Horizontal velocity distribution along a vertical line extending from the top surface of a cylinder.

```
axis([10,25,0.9,2.5])
ylabel('y')
xlabel('Horizontal velocity')
hold on
plot([10,25],[1,1])
text(10.5,1.05,'Top surface of cylinder')
ux1 = max(ux)
```

EXERCISES

11.1 Obtain the flow fields in two ducts with the same cross-sectional area, but with one whose cross-sectional shape is square and one whose shape is rectangular. The rectangular shaped cross section has the length of one side four times that of the other. Compare the volume flow rates of the two ducts using pdetool. The governing equation is that given by Eq. (11.7). Assume that the right-hand side of Eq. (11.7) is the same for each duct, say 1.0—that is, they have the same fluid and pressure gradient. Also, the boundary condition at the duct wall is $u = 0$. Export each solution to the MATLAB command window and use the procedure illustrated in Section 11.2.1 to obtain

$$Q_{sq}/Q_{rect} \approx 2$$

where Q is the flow rate.

11.2 The flow about a thin symmetric airfoil can be approximated by potential flow theory.[6] The chord of the airfoil extends along the x axis from $x = 0$ to $x = c$, and is represented by a vortex sheet whose strength $\gamma(x)$ is given by

$$\gamma(\theta) = 2\alpha V_\infty \frac{1+\cos\theta}{\sin\theta}$$

where

$$x = \frac{c}{2}(1-\cos\theta) \qquad 0 \le \theta \le \pi$$

α is the angle of attack (in radians) of the incoming flow relative to the x axis, and V_∞ is the flow speed. Consider the vortex sheet to be approximated by a set of N discrete vortices separated by a distance $\Delta x = c/N$ with strength $\Gamma_i = \gamma(\theta_i)\Delta x$. Using Method 1 of Section 11.3.3, draw the streamlines of this flow for $\alpha = 10°$, $c = 2$ m, and $V_\infty = 100$ m/s. The results should look like those shown in Figure 11.15.

11.3 Consider the flow field around a cylinder in a duct as shown in Figure 11.16. Assume potential flow and use pdetool to compute the streamlines. Export the mesh and solution variables to the MATLAB command window and compute the velocity distribution along the bottom wall of the channel. The results should look like those presented in Figure 11.17.

11.4 Consider a potential flow over a cylinder that is placed near a wall as shown in Figure 11.18. Represent the flow over the cylinder and wall with a uniform flow of speed $U = 1.0$ m/s and two dipoles located at $(x,y) = (0,0.25D)$ and $(0,-0.25D)$. The velocity potential for each dipole is

$$\phi = \frac{UD^2}{4r}\cos\theta$$

---

[6] See, for example, J. D. Anderson, *Fundamentals of Aerodynamics*, McGraw-Hill, New York, 1991, Chapter 4.

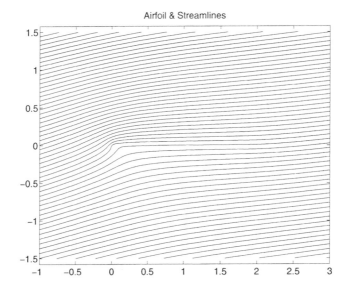

FIGURE 11.15
Stream lines for a thin airfoil with a 2-m chord and an angle of attack of 10 degrees. The flow is from left to right and the foil extends horizontally from (0,0) to (2,0).

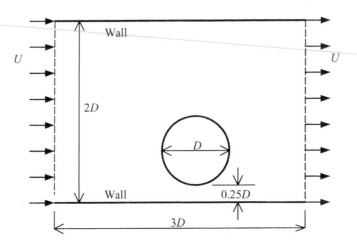

FIGURE 11.16
The flow enters the duct on the left and leaves the duct on the right with a uniform horizontal velocity profile of $U = 1$ m/s. The cylinder has a diameter of $D = 1.0$ m and its center is located at $(x,y) = (0.0, 0.75)$ m.

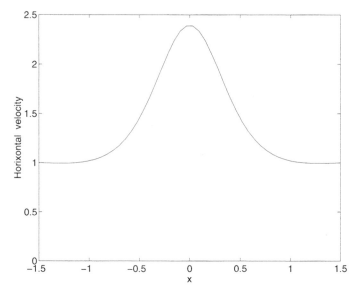

FIGURE 11.17
Horizontal velocity along the bottom wall of the duct.

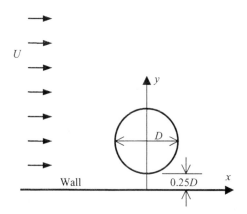

FIGURE 11.18
Cylinder near wall with uniform horizontal flow upstream.

where r and θ are cylindrical coordinates centered on the dipole. Plot the streamline pattern. Note that the closed streamline around each dipole is not circular. Plot the velocity distribution along the wall and compare it to the solution obtained in Exercise 11.3.

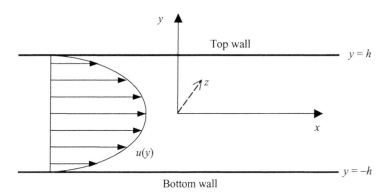

FIGURE 11.19
A channel extending from ±∞ in the z-direction. (For the duct, two additional vertical walls are placed at $z = \pm 2h$.)

11.5 Consider laminar, steady, pressure-driven flow in a channel of height $2h$ as depicted in Figure 11.19. The velocity is given by

$$u(y) = -\frac{h^2}{2\mu}\frac{dP}{dx}\left(1 - \frac{y^2}{h^2}\right)$$

where dP/dx is the pressure gradient and μ is the dynamic viscosity of the fluid. Using `pdetool` compare this velocity distribution to the velocity distribution along the center plane of a duct with the same height as the channel and a width that is twice the height. Assume the same pressure gradient and viscosity. The differential equation to be solved is given by Eq. (11.7). The results should look like those presented in Figure 11.20.

11.6 Consider the laminar, steady, fully developed, pressure-driven flow of oil in a duct shown in Figure 11.21. The duct has a rectangular cross section, which is 1 cm high and 0.5 cm wide. The right wall is moving at a velocity of 0.5 m/s in the direction of the flow driven by the pressure gradient (out of the plane of the page in Figure 11.21) while the other three walls are stationary. Assume that the pressure gradient is 10 kPa/m and that the dynamic viscosity of the oil is 0.1 kg/m·s. Using `pdetool` plot the distributions of velocity along the horizontal and vertical center planes of the duct. The differential equation to be solved is given by Eq. (11.7). The results should look like those shown in Figures 11.22 and 11.23.

11.7 Consider a viscous fluid with $\mu = 0.02$ kg/m·s and $\rho = 800$ kg/m^3 in a rectangular duct with dimensions 0.2 cm by 0.3 cm. The fluid is initially at rest. At $t = 0$, a pressure gradient of magnitude 10 kPa/m in the direction along the axis of the duct is turned on. For times from 0 to 0.04 s in steps of 0.005 s, plot the velocity profile across the center plane connecting the 0.3-cm-long walls of the duct. The results should look like those shown in Figure 11.24.

11.8 Consider the viscous, fully developed flow along a duct with a square cross section of dimensions a by a. At $t = 0$, the velocity distribution is uniform with magnitude 1 m/s over the cross section. For

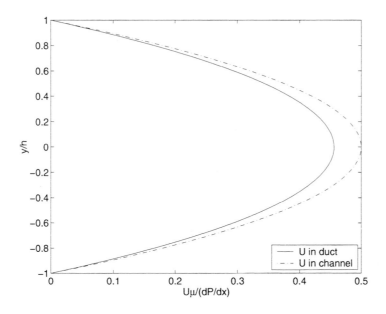

FIGURE 11.20
Comparison of the velocity distribution along centerline of duct and velocity distribution in channel of same height.

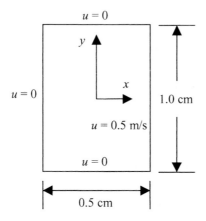

FIGURE 11.21
Duct cross section for Exercise 11.6.

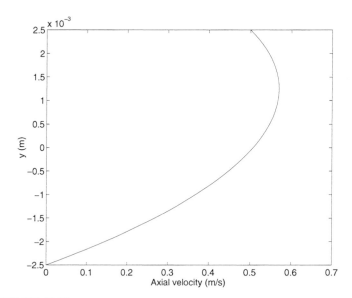

FIGURE 11.22
Axial velocity in the center plane connecting the stationary and moving 1-cm-long walls.

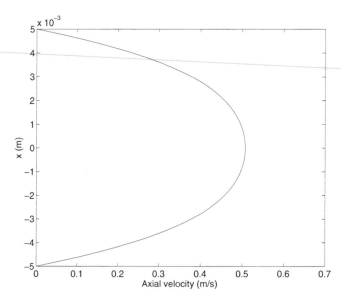

FIGURE 11.23
Axial velocity in the center plane connecting the two stationary 0.5-cm-long walls.

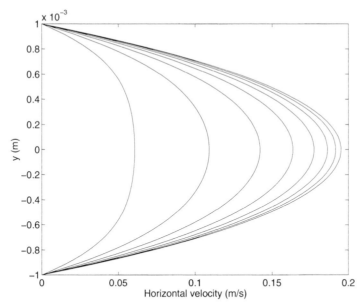

FIGURE 11.24
Axial velocity in the center plane connecting the two 0.3-cm-long walls.

$t > 0$, the no-slip boundary condition at the walls is applied and an axial pressure gradient dP/dx is imposed[7] such that the final steady flow rate Q_f attained after a long time is equal to the flow rate Q_0 at $t = 0$:

$$\frac{dP}{dx} = \frac{28.46\mu Q_0}{a^4}$$

where μ is the dynamic viscosity of the fluid. Assume that $a = 1$ cm and that the fluid is an oil with $\mu = 0.2$ kg/m·s and $\rho = 800$ kg/m^3. Use the results from pdetool to plot the distribution of axial velocity across one of the center planes of the duct at various times and the flow rate in the duct versus time. The results should look like those in Figures 11.25 and 11.26, respectively.

11.9 Water is to flow from reservoir A to reservoir B through the piping system shown in Figure 11.27. The flow rate when the valve is completely open is to be 0.003 m^3/s. The generalized head loss equation is

$$\frac{P_1}{\rho g} + \frac{V_1^2}{2g} + z_1 = \frac{P_2}{\rho g} + \frac{V_2^2}{2g} + z_2 + \frac{\lambda L V^2}{2gD} + \sum_{m=1}^{5} K_{Lm} \frac{V^2}{2g}$$

where K_{Lm} are the minor loss coefficients at the locations shown in Figure 11.27, λ is the pipe friction coefficient and $V = 4Q/\pi D^2$ is the average velocity in the pipe. If $v_{vis} = 1.3 \times 10^{-6}$ m^2/s and $\rho = 1,000$ kg/m^3, then determine the pipe diameter. [Answer: $D = 0.051$ m.]

---

[7] F. M. White, *Fluid Mechanics*, 4th ed., McGraw-Hill, New York, 1999, p. 365.

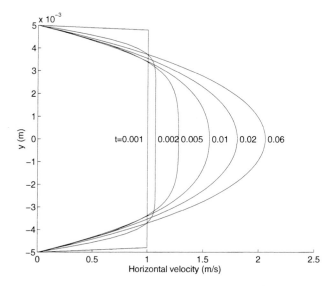

FIGURE 11.25
Distribution of the axial velocity over the center plane of the duct at various times.

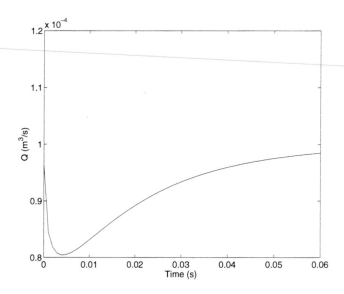

FIGURE 11.26
Flow rate in the duct versus time.

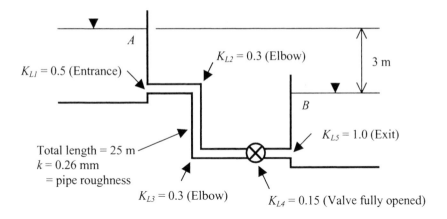

FIGURE 11.27
Piping system between two reservoirs.

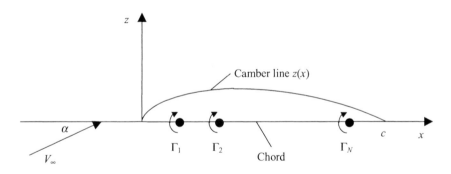

FIGURE 11.28
Placement of a vortex sheet on the chord line.

11.10 The flow about a thin cambered airfoil shown in Figure 11.28 can be approximated by potential flow theory.[8] The chord of the airfoil extends along the x-axis from $x = 0$ to $x = c$ and is represented by a vortex sheet placed along the chord. The strength $\gamma(x)$ of this vortex sheet is given by

$$\gamma(\theta) = 2V_\infty \left(A_0 \frac{1 + \cos\theta}{\sin\theta} + \sum_{n=1}^\infty A_n \sin(n\theta) \right)$$

where

$$\frac{x}{c} = \frac{1}{2}(1 - \cos\theta) \qquad 0 \le \theta \le \pi$$

[8] J. D. Anderson, *ibid.*

α is the angle of attack (in radians) of the incoming flow relative to the x axis, and V_∞ is the flow speed. The constants A_n are given by

$$A_0 = \alpha - \frac{1}{\pi} \int_0^\pi \frac{dz}{dx} d\theta_o$$

$$A_n = \frac{2}{\pi} \int_0^\pi \frac{dz}{dx} \cos(n\theta_o) d\theta_o$$

where $z(x)$ is the vertical distance between the chord line and the camber line.

Let the camber line be

$$\frac{z}{c} = 2.6595 \frac{x}{c} \left[\left(\frac{x}{c}\right)^2 - 0.6075 \frac{x}{c} + 0.1147 \right] \quad 0 \le x/c \le 0.2025$$

$$= 0.02208 \left(1 - \frac{x}{c}\right) \quad 0.2025 \le x/c \le 1.0$$

where the distance z is normal to the chord. Compute A_n for $n = 0, 1, ... 20$. As in Exercise 11.2, let the vortex sheet be approximated by a set of N_v discrete vortices (see Section 11.3.3) along the x-axis in the region $0 \le x/c \le 1$. The vortices are separated by a distance $\Delta x = c/N$ and have the strengths $\Gamma_i = \gamma(\theta_i)\Delta x$. Use contour to draw the streamlines of this flow for $\alpha = 10°$, $c = 2$ m, and $V_\infty = 100$ m/s. The results should look like those shown in Figure 11.29. [Partial answers: $A_0 = 0.0412$, $A_1 = 0.0955$, $A_2 = 0.0792$, $A_3 = 0.0568$.]

11.11 The oscillations caused by a suddenly released fluid from a height Z that separates the fluid levels in two rectangular prismatic reservoirs connected by a long pipeline of length L shown in Figure 11.30 can be determined from[9]

$$\frac{d^2 Z}{dt^2} + \text{signum}(dZ/dt) p \left(\frac{dZ}{dt}\right)^2 + qZ = 0$$

where

$$p = \frac{f A_1 A_2 L_e}{2 D a L (A_1 + A_2)} \qquad q = \frac{g a (A_1 + A_2)}{A_1 A_2 L}$$

and it has been assumed that the motion of the liquid is mostly turbulent so that the head loss is proportional to the square of the velocity. The quantity L_e is the equivalent length of the pipe incorporating minor losses, g is the gravitational constant, f is the friction coefficient in the pipe, A_1 and A_2 are the surface areas of the two reservoirs, a is the area of the pipeline, and D is its diameter.

If $p = 0.375$ m^{-1}, $q = 7.4 \times 10^{-4}$ s^{-2} and the initial conditions are $Z(0) = Z_n$ m and $dZ(0)/dt = 0$ m/s, then determine the value of the first occurrence of t_n for which $Z(t_n) = 0$ when $Z_n = 5, 10, ..., 50$. Plot the results, which should look like those shown in Figure 11.31. Use interp1 to determine t_n.

[9] D. N. Roy, *Applied Fluid Mechanics*, Ellis Horwood Limited, Chichester, England, 1988, pp. 290–293.

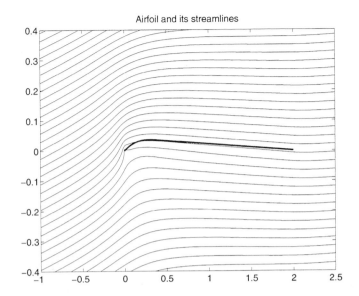

FIGURE 11.29
Streamlines of a cambered airfoil.

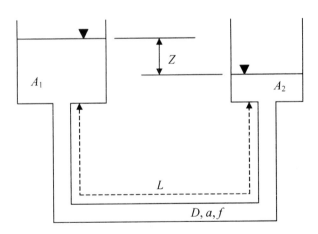

FIGURE 11.30
Interconnected reservoirs.

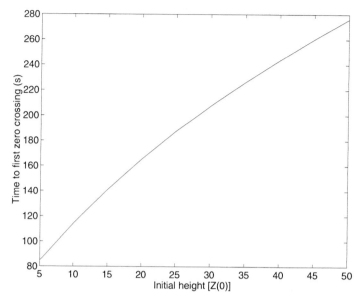

FIGURE 11.31
Values of the first occurrence of t_n for which $Z(t_n) = 0$ as a function of $Z(0) = Z_n$.

BIBLIOGRAPHY

B. R. Munson, D. F. Young, and T. H. Okiishi, *Fundamentals of Fluid Mechanics*, 3rd ed., John Wiley & Sons, New York, 1998.

J. D. Anderson, *Fundamentals of Aerodynamics*, 2nd ed., McGraw-Hill, New York, 1991.

V. L. Streeter, E. B. Wylie, and K. W. Bedford, *Fluid Mechanics*, 9th ed., McGraw-Hill, New York, 1998.

R. W. Fox and A. McDonald, *Introduction to Fluid Mechanics*, 5th ed., John Wiley & Sons, New York, 1998.

C H A P T E R   1 2

HEAT TRANSFER

Keith E. Herold

Several techniques for analyzing and visualizing conduction, convection, and radiation heat transfer are presented.

12.1 HEAT CONDUCTION

12.1.1 Transient Heat Conduction in a Semi-Infinite Slab with Surface Convection

The transient temperature distribution in a semi-infinite solid that is initially at a uniform temperature and that has convection at the boundary surface $\eta = 0$ is given by[1]

$$\theta(\eta,\tau) = \text{erfc}\left[\frac{\eta}{2\tau}\right] - \exp\left[\eta + \tau^2\right]\text{erfc}\left[\frac{\eta}{2\tau} + \tau\right]$$

where erfc is the complementary error function,

$$\theta(\eta,\tau) = \frac{T(\eta,\tau) - T_\infty}{T_\infty - T_i}$$

$$\tau = \frac{h}{k}\sqrt{\alpha t}$$

$$\eta = \frac{hx}{k}$$

and x is the spatial coordinate, t is time, h is the heat-transfer coefficient, k is the thermal conductivity of the solid, T_∞ is the ambient air temperature, and α is the thermal diffusivity of the solid.

We shall plot the temperature in the solid over the range $0 \le \eta \le 5$ and $0.01 \le \tau \le 3$, and then plot the temperature as a function of τ for $0.01 \le \tau \le 4$ at six different locations: $\eta = 0, 1, ..., 5$. The script is

```
tau = linspace(0.01,3,30); eta = linspace(0,5,20);
[x,t] = meshgrid(eta,tau);
theta = inline('erfc(0.5*x./t)-exp(x+t.^2).*erfc(0.5*x./t+t)','x','t');
figure(1)
mesh(x,t,theta(x,t))
xlabel('\eta')
ylabel('\tau')
zlabel('\theta')
figure(2)
eta = linspace(0,5,6);
tau = linspace(0.01,4,40);
for k = 1:6
   thet = theta(eta(k),tau);
   plot(tau,thet)
   text(.92*4,1.02*thet(end),['\eta = ' num2str(eta(k))])
```

---

[1] F. P. Incropera and D. P. DeWitt, *Fundamentals of Heat and Mass Transfer*, 4th ed., John Wiley & Sons, New York, 1996, p. 239.

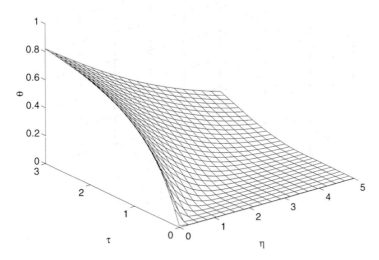

FIGURE 12.1

Temperature in a semi-infinite solid as a function of position η and time τ.

```
  hold on
end
xlabel('\tau')
ylabel('\theta')
```

When this script is executed, we obtain Figures 12.1 and 12.2.

12.1.2 Transient Heat Conduction in an Infinite Solid Cylinder with Convection

The transient temperature distribution in an infinitely long solid circular cylinder, which is initially at a uniform temperature and has convection at the surface, is given by[2]

$$\theta(\xi,\tau) = \sum_{n=1}^{\infty} C_n \exp(-\zeta_n^2 \tau) J_0(\zeta_n \xi)$$

where

$$\theta(\xi,\tau) = \frac{T(\xi,\tau) - T_\infty}{T(\xi,0) - T_\infty}$$

---

[2] F. P. Incropera and D. P. DeWitt, *ibid.*, p. 229.

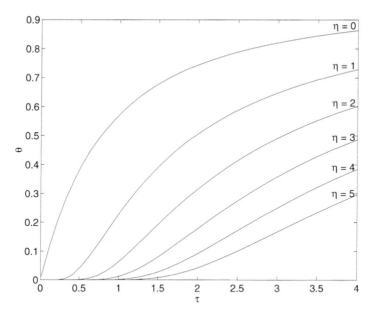

FIGURE 12.2.
Temperature in a semi-infinite solid as a function of time τ at several locations η.

and

$$C_n = \frac{2}{\zeta_n} \frac{J_1(\zeta_n)}{J_0^2(\zeta_n) + J_1^2(\zeta_n)}$$

The quantity $J_m(x)$ is the Bessel function of the first kind of order m, $\tau = \alpha t/a^2$, α is the thermal diffusivity, a is the radius of the cylinder, t is time, $\xi = r/a$, r is the radial location in the cylinder, T_∞ is the ambient air temperature, and ζ_n are the positive roots of

$$\frac{J_1(\zeta_n)}{J_0(\zeta_n)} - \frac{Bi}{\zeta_n} = 0$$

where $Bi = ha/k$ is the Biot number, h is the heat-transfer coefficient, and k is the thermal conductivity of the cylinder.

We shall plot $\theta(\xi, \tau)$ for $0 \le \xi \le 1$, $0 \le \tau \le 1.5$, and $Bi = 0.5$ using the lowest 15 positive roots of ζ_n. The script is

```
Bi = .5; nroots = 15; r = zeros(1,nroots);
guess = 0.01;
CylinderRoots = inline('x.*besselj(1,x)–Bi*besselj(0,x)','x','Bi');
options = optimset('display','off');
```

```
for k = 1:nroots
  r(k) = fzero(CylinderRoots,[guess guess+1.1*pi],options,Bi);
  guess = 1.05*r(k);
end
tau = linspace(0,1.5,20);
[t,rt] = meshgrid(tau,r);
Fn = exp(-t.*rt.^2);
cn = 2*besselj(1,r)./(r.*(besselj(0,r).^2+besselj(1,r).^2));
ccn = meshgrid(cn,tau);
pro = ccn'.*Fn;
rstar = linspace(0,1,20);
[R,rx] = meshgrid(rstar,r);
Jo = besselj(0,rx.*R);
the = Jo'*pro;
[rr,tt] = meshgrid(rstar,tau);
mesh(rr,tt,the')
xlabel('\xi')
ylabel('\tau')
zlabel('\theta')
view(49.5,-34)
```

where the values of *guess* are determined from a plot of *CylinderRoots*. Execution of this script results in Figure 12.3.

12.1.3 Transient One-Dimensional Conduction with a Heat Source

One-dimensional, transient conduction is governed by

$$\frac{1}{\alpha}\frac{dT}{dt} = \frac{d^2T}{dx^2} + \frac{q}{k}$$

where T is the temperature, t is time, x is the spatial coordinate, α is the thermal diffusivity, k the thermal conductivity, and q the volumetric heat source. We convert this equation to a dimensionless form by introducing the following nondimensional quantities

$$\xi = \frac{x}{L} \qquad \tau = \frac{\alpha t}{L^2} \qquad Bi = \frac{hL}{k}$$

$$\theta = \frac{T-T_\infty}{T_i - T_\infty} \qquad \Sigma = \frac{L^2 q}{k(T_i - T_\infty)} \qquad \chi = \frac{-q''L}{k(T_i - T_\infty)}$$

where L is the length of the domain, T_i is an arbitrary temperature that usually represents the initial temperature, q'' is the heat flux, and T_∞ is the fluid temperature for a convective boundary. For cases where a convective boundary condition is not used, T_∞ is an arbitrary

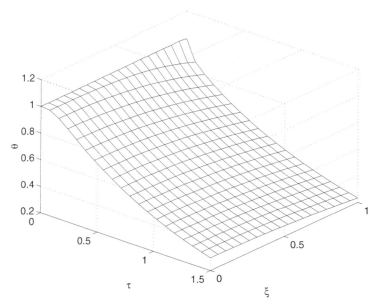

FIGURE 12.3
Temperature distribution in a cylinder as a function of time τ and radial position ξ.

temperature with the requirement that it must be different from T_i. In terms of these variables, the governing equation becomes

$$\frac{\partial \theta}{\partial \tau} = \frac{\partial^2 \theta}{\partial \xi^2} + \Sigma$$ (12.1)

Typical boundary conditions at each end of the domain are:

Fixed temperature

$$\theta = \theta_w$$

Specified flux

$$\frac{\partial \theta}{\partial \xi} = \chi_w$$

Convective

$$\frac{\partial \theta}{\partial \xi} = -Bi\theta_w$$

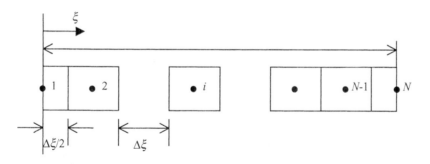

FIGURE 12.4
Finite-difference geometry.

where the negative sign in the convective condition is correct for the left boundary and the subscript w represents the wall values.

Equation (12.1) is a partial differential equation of the parabolic type with one spatial dimension. One method of solution, applicable to a restricted set of boundary conditions, is separation of variables. An example of this type of solution was used to obtain the result given in Section 12.1.2. The Partial Differential Equation (PDE) toolbox provides another solution method. Unfortunately, it is not designed to solve for only one spatial variable and, therefore, is cumbersome to use for this type of problem.

Thus, we formulate a finite-difference solution, which is implicit in time and which utilizes the MATLAB matrix/vector capabilities to solve the spatial aspects of the problem. The spatial derivatives of the problem are calculated from a finite-difference formulation shown in Figure 12.4. A uniformly spaced grid of N temperatures is assumed, which divides the region into N one-dimensional subdomains in which a temperature is calculated. The length of each interior subdomain is $\Delta\xi = 1/(N-1)$, whereas on each end of the system the length is $\Delta\xi/2$. The difference equation for each interior subdomain then becomes

$$\frac{d\theta_i}{d\tau} = \frac{\theta_{i-1} - 2\theta_i + \theta_{i+1}}{\Delta\xi^2} + \Sigma \qquad i = 2,\ldots,N-1$$

For those subdomains in which one end is a boundary of the region we have three possible relationships:

Fixed wall temperature

$$\frac{d\theta_i}{d\tau} = 0 \qquad i = 1 \text{ or } N$$

Fixed flux

$$\frac{d\theta_i}{d\tau} = \frac{2}{\Delta\xi^2}(\theta_I - \theta_i) + \Sigma - \frac{2\chi_w}{\Delta\xi} \qquad i = 1 \text{ or } N$$

TABLE 12.1
Boundary and Initial Conditions to Obtain Figure 12.5

Parameter	Value
Boundary Conditions and Source	
Dimensionless source strength, Σ	1
Left boundary Biot number	0.1
Right boundary dimensionless temperature, $\theta(1)$	0.55
Initial Conditions	
Left boundary, $\theta_i(0)$	1
Linear distribution between $\theta_i(0) = 1$ and $\theta_i(1) = 0.55$	
Finite Difference Parameters	
Number of elements	5
Extent of integration (dimensionless time)	1

Convective

$$\frac{d\theta_i}{d\tau} = -\frac{2 Bi\theta_i}{\Delta\xi} + \frac{2}{\Delta\xi^2}(\theta_I - \theta_i) + \Sigma \qquad i = 1 \text{ or } N$$

where θ_I is an adjacent interior point: $I = 2$ at a left boundary and $I = N - 1$ at a right boundary.

We first create a function *FiniteDiffCond* to calculate the time-derivative vector for each of the subdomains in the finite difference formulation. In this function, a convective boundary condition is used on the left side and a fixed temperature condition on the right side.

```
function dTdtau = FiniteDiffCond(t,T,flag,N,sigma,Bi)
dTdtau = zeros(N,1);
dx = 1/(N–1);
dTdtau(1,1) = –2*Bi*T(1)/dx+2/dx^2*(T(2)–T(1))+sigma;
for i = 2:N–1
  dTdtau(i,1) = (–2*T(i)+T(i–1)+T(i+1))/dx^2+sigma;
end
dTdtau(N,1) = 0;
```

We now consider the case in which the system is subjected to the boundary and initial conditions stated in Table 12.1. The script is

```
D = 5; Sigma = 1; Bi = 0.1;
Tright = 0.55; Tleft = 1; tmax = 1;
Tp = linspace(Tleft,Tright,D)';
[t T] = ode15s('FiniteDiffCond',[0 1],Tp,[],D,Sigma,Bi);
```

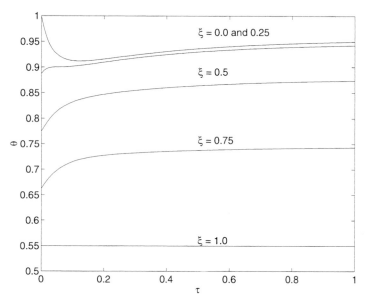

FIGURE 12.5
One-dimensional heat conduction using the data in Table 12.1.

```
plot(t,T,'k')
axis([0 1 0.5 1])
xlabel('\tau')
ylabel('\theta')
text(0.5,1.02*T(end,5),'\xi = 1.0')
text(0.5,1.02*T(end,4),'\xi = 0.75')
text(0.5,1.02*T(end,3),'\xi = 0.5')
text(0.5,1.02*T(end,1),'\xi = 0.0 and 0.25')
```

The execution of the script results in Figure 12.5. The script utilizes `ode15s` to integrate over dimensionless time τ. The temperatures in the adjacent elements are strongly coupled such that they represent a stiff system of equations. Attempts to solve the problem using `ode45` will lead to instabilities. The function `ode15s` is designed to handle such stiff systems, and it produces a smooth (stable) result.

12.2 SIZING OF SHELL AND TUBE HEAT EXCHANGERS

Using the definitions in Table 12.2 and Figure 12.6, we have the following equations that govern the characteristics of shell and tube heat exchangers.

The energy balance on a heat exchanger can be written as

TABLE 12.2
Definitions of Terms in Heat-Exchanger Relations

Symbol	Units	Description
c_p	J/(kg K)	Specific heat at constant pressure
d_o	m	Tube outside diameter
d_i	m	Tube inside diameter
f		Tube flow friction factor
f_s		Friction factor shell side
h_o	W/(m^2 K)	Heat-transfer coefficient inside tube
h_i	W/(m^2 K)	Heat-transfer coefficient outside tube
k	W/(m K)	Thermal conductivity of fluids
k_{tube}	W/(m K)	Thermal conductivity of tubes
$\dot{m}_t$	kg/s	Tube side mass flow rate
$\dot{m}_s$	kg/s	Shell side mass flow rate
Δp_s	Pa	Shell side pressure drop
Δp_t	Pa	Tube side pressure drop
u_t	m/s	Mean axial velocity of fluid in tube ($= \dot{m}_t / \rho A_t$)
A_o	m^2	Tube outside surface area per pass($= \pi d_o L N_T / N_P$)
A_i	m^2	Tube inside surface area per pass ($= \pi d_i L N_T / N_P$)
A_s	m^2	Cross-flow area at or near shell centerline
A_t	m^2	Total cross-sectional area of tubes per pass $\left(= \pi d_i^2 N_T / (4 N_P)\right)$
B	m	Baffle spacing
C	m	Clearance between adjacent tubes. (See Figure 12.7.)
C_L		Tube layout constant
C_{TP}		Tube count calculation constant
D_e	m	Equivalent diameter of shell
D_s	m	Shell inside diameter
F		LMTD correction factor for counter flow arrangements
L	m	Tube length
N_b		Number of baffles ($=$ Integer(L/B))
N_T		Number of tubes
N_p		Number of tube passes
P_T	m	Pitch size (See Figure 12.7)

TABLE 12.2 (CONTINUED)
Definitions of Terms in Heat-Exchanger Relations

Symbol	Units	Description
P_P	W	Pumping power of fluid in tubes
Pr		Prandtl number
Q	W	Heat transfer rate
R_{fo}	(m² K)/W	Fouling resistance on outside of tube
R_{fi}	(m² K)/W	Fouling resistance on inside of tube
Re_b		Reynolds number at T_b
Re_s		Shell side Reynolds number at T_b
ΔT_m	°C, K	Log mean temperature difference (LMTD)
T_{h1}	°C, K	Inlet temperature of hot fluid
T_{h2}	°C, K	Outlet temperature of hot fluid
T_{c1}	°C, K	Inlet temperature of cold fluid
T_{c2}	°C, K	Outlet temperature of cold fluid
T_b	°C, K	Bulk temperature
T_w	°C, K	Wall temperature
U	W/(m² K)	Average overall heat-transfer coefficient based on A
η_p		Pump efficiency ($0.80 \le \eta_p \le 0.85$)
ϕ_s		Viscosity correction factor
μ	kg/(s m)	Dynamic viscosity
μ_b	kg/(s m)	Dynamic viscosity at T_b
μ_w	kg/(s m)	Dynamic viscosity at T_w
ρ	kg/m³	density

$$Q = UAF\Delta T_m = \left(\dot{m}c_p\right)_h \left(T_{h1} - T_{h2}\right) = \left(\dot{m}c_p\right)_c \left(T_{c2} - T_{c1}\right)$$

where the subscript 1 denotes the temperature of the fluid entering and the subscript 2 the fluid leaving, the subscript h denotes the hot fluid and the subscript c the cold fluid, and

$$\Delta T_m = \frac{\Delta T_1 - \Delta T_2}{\ln\left(\Delta T_1/\Delta T_2\right)}$$
$$\Delta T_1 = T_{h1} - T_{c2}$$
$$\Delta T_2 = T_{h2} - T_{c1}$$

is the log mean temperature difference, assuming a counterflow arrangement.

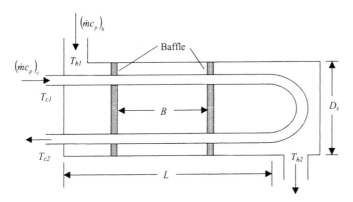

Note: The choice of which fluid to place on the shell side is
arbitrary and is usually governed by other design considerations.

FIGURE 12.6
Typical one-shell, two-tube-pass, heat exchanger arrangement.

For one shell pass and 2, 4, … tube passes[3]

$$F = R_s C_o \left[\log_{10} \frac{C_1 + R_s}{C_1 - R_s} \right]^{-1}$$

and for two shell passes and 4, 8, … tube passes

$$F = 0.5 R_s C_o \left[\log_{10} \frac{C_1 + C_2 + R_s}{C_1 + C_2 - R_s} \right]^{-1}$$

where

$$R_s = \sqrt{R^2 + 1} \qquad P = \frac{T_{c2} - T_{c1}}{T_{h1} - T_{c1}} \qquad R = \frac{T_{h1} - T_{h2}}{T_{c2} - T_{c1}}$$

$$C_1 = \frac{2}{P} - 1 - R \qquad C_2 = \frac{2}{P} \sqrt{(1 - P)(1 - PR)}$$

$$C_o = \frac{1}{R - 1} \log_{10} \frac{1 - P}{1 - PR} \qquad R \neq 1$$

$$= \frac{P}{2.3(1 - P)} \qquad R = 1$$

The overall heat-transfer coefficient U is given by

---

[3] R. A. Bowman, A. C. Mueller, and W. M. Nagle, "Mean Temperature Difference in Design," *Trans. ASME*, Vol. 62, May, 1940, pp. 283–293.

$$U = \left[\frac{d_o}{d_i} \frac{1}{h_i} + \frac{d_o}{d_i} R_{fi} + \frac{d_o}{2k_{tube}} \ln \frac{d_o}{d_i} + R_{fo} + \frac{1}{h_o} \right]^{-1}$$

The value of the heat-transfer coefficient inside the tube is approximated from

$$h_i = \frac{k}{d_i} Nu_b$$

where, for fully developed turbulent forced convection through a circular pipe with constant properties,[4]

$$Nu_b = \frac{0.125 f (Re_b - 1000) Pr_b}{1 + 12.7 \sqrt{0.125 f} \left((Pr_b)^{2/3} - 1 \right)} \qquad 0.5 < Pr_b < 2000 \quad 3000 < Re_b < 5 \times 10^6$$

The subscript b indicates that the quantities are evaluated at the average temperature of the fluid inside the pipe, which is called the bulk temperature.

The quantity f is the friction factor for flow in smooth pipes given by

$$f = (0.790 \ln Re_b - 1.64)^{-2} \qquad 3000 \le Re_b \le 10^6$$

For rough tubes, the results of Exercise 5.5 are used with $\lambda = f$.

The Reynolds number Re_b is given by

$$Re_b = \frac{\rho u_t d_i}{\mu} = \frac{4 \dot{m}_t}{\pi d_i \mu N_T / N_P}$$

since

$$u_t = \dot{m}_t / \left(0.25 \rho \pi d_i^2 N_T / N_p \right)$$

and Pr_b is the Prandtl number given by

$$Pr_b = \frac{c_p \mu}{k}$$

The shell side heat-transfer coefficient is estimated from

$$h_o = 0.36 \frac{k \phi_s}{D_e} (Re_s)^{0.55} (Pr)^{1/3} \qquad 2000 < Re_s < 10^6$$

$$\phi_s = \left(\frac{\mu_b}{\mu_w} \right)^{0.14} \qquad T_w = (T_{c1} + T_{c2} + T_{h1} + T_{h2}) / 4$$

where the quantities are evaluated at the average temperature of the shell side fluid, except for ϕ_s; where μ_w is evaluated at T_w. The equivalent diameter D_e of the shell with tubes laid out on a square pitch, as shown in Figure 12.7, is given by

---

[4] F. P. Incropera and D. P. DeWitt, *ibid.*, p. 424.

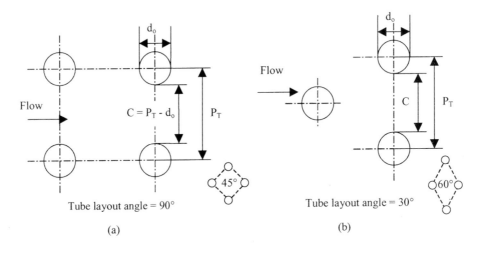

FIGURE 12.7
Two tube layouts: (a) layout angle equals 90°; (b) layout angle equal 30°.

$$D_e = 4\left(P_T^2 - \pi d_o^2 / 4\right)/\pi d_o$$

and for tubes on a triangular pitch by

$$D_e = 8\left(P_T^2 \sqrt{3}/4 - \pi d_o^2/8\right)/\pi d_o$$

The shell side Reynolds number Re_s is given by

$$Re_s = \frac{\dot{m}_s D_e}{A_s \mu}$$

$$A_s = 1.128 CB\sqrt{\frac{N_T C_L}{C_{TP}}} = \frac{D_s CB}{P_T}$$

where D_s is the shell inside diameter given by

$$D_s = 1.128 P_T \sqrt{\frac{N_T C_L}{C_{TP}}}$$

Suggested values for C_{TP} are

One-tube pass ($N_P = 1$):	$C_{TP} = 0.93$
Two-tube pass ($N_P = 2$):	$C_{TP} = 0.90$
Three-tube pass ($N_P = 3$):	$C_{TP} = 0.85$

and for C_L (see Figure 12.7)

$C_L = 1$ for $90°$ and $45°$

$C_L = 0.87$ for $30°$ and $60°$

There are standard tube layout tables that tabulate the number of tubes (N_T) that are used with a given shell inside diameter (D_s) as a function of the tube outside diameter (d_o), tube pitch (square or triangular), and number of tube passes (N_P).[5] Therefore, the appropriate results from the numerical calculations are usually adjusted to assume a value nearest to these standard values.

The shell side pressure drop is given by

$$\Delta p_s = \frac{f_s \dot{m}_s^2 (N_b + 1) D_s}{2 A_s^2 \rho D_e \phi_s}$$

where

$$f_s = \exp(0.576 - 0.19 \ln \mathrm{Re}_s)$$

and the properties are evaluated at T_b. The tube side pressure drop is given by

$$\Delta p_t = f \left(\frac{L N_p}{d_i} \right) \left(\frac{\rho u_t^2}{2} \right)$$

where the properties are evaluated at T_b and the effects of any tube bends have been neglected, which is a good assumption for low speed flow of liquids.

The pumping power is

$$P_P = \frac{\dot{m}_t \Delta p_t}{\rho \eta_p}$$

We now illustrate these results with an example.

Example 12.1 Determining tube length and pressure drops

A preliminary analysis was performed to size a one-shell, two-pass, water-to-water heat exchanger to remove approximately 800 kW. Cold water is in the tubes and the hot water is on the shell side. The results of the preliminary analysis are summarized in Table 12.3. The objective is to determine whether the length of the heat exchanger is less than 4.5 m and that both the shell side and tube side pressure drops are less than 4000 Pa. Rearrangement of several of the preceding equations results in the following equations that govern this analysis.

$$T_{h_2} = T_{h_1} - \frac{(\dot{m} c_p)_t}{(\dot{m} c_p)_s} (T_{c_2} - T_{c_1})$$

---

[5] See, for example, S. Kakaç and H. Liu, *Heat Exchangers: Selection, Rating and Thermal Design*, CRC Press, Boca Raton, FL, 1998, pp. 258–261.

TABLE 12.3
Parameters from a Preliminary Analysis of a Heat Exchanger

Geometric	Physical
$D_s = 0.39$ m	$T_{c_1} = 18\ °C$
$N_T = 124$	
$N_P = 2$	$T_{c_2} = 42\ °C$
$P_T = 0.024$ m	$T_{h_1} = 65\ °C$
$B = 0.5$ m	
$N_b = 4$	$\dot{m}_s = \dot{m}_h = 14$ kg/s
$d_i = 16$ mm (0.016 m)	$\dot{m}_t = \dot{m}_c = 8.5$ kg/s
$d_o = 19$ mm (0.019 m)	$R_{fi} = 0.00015$
$k_{tube} = 60$ W/m^2 K (carbon steel)	$R_{fo} = 0.00015$
90 ° tube layout	
Tubes are on a square pitch	
Tubes are smooth	

$$\Delta p_t = C_o \frac{f \dot{m}_t^3}{UF\Delta T_m}$$

$$\Delta p_s = \frac{f_s \dot{m}_s^2 (N_b + 1) D_s}{2 A_s^2 \rho D_e \phi_s}$$

$$L = \frac{(\dot{m}c_p)_t (T_{c_2} - T_{c_1})}{\pi d_o N_T UF\Delta T_m}$$

where

$$C_o = \frac{N_P (T_{c_2} - T_{c_1})(c_p)_t}{2\pi d_i d_o N_T \rho_t A_t^2}$$

$$A_t = \frac{\pi d_i^2}{4} \frac{N_T}{N_P}$$

Before evaluating these quantities, we first create the following functions:

LMTDcorrFactor, computes F

TubeFF, computes f for smooth pipes

WaterProperties, computes k, ρ, μ, c_p, and Pr at a temperature between 0 and 100 °C

LMTD, computes the log mean temperature difference

TABLE 12.4
Thermophysical Properties of Water

T (K)	k (W/m K)	ρ (kg/m^3)	μ (N s/m^2)	c_p (J/kg K)	Pr
273	0.569	1000.0	1750×10^{-6}	4217	12.99
285	0.590	1000.0	1225×10^{-6}	4189	8.81
300	0.613	998.0	855×10^{-6}	4179	5.83
315	0.634	991.1	631×10^{-6}	4179	4.16
330	0.650	984.3	489×10^{-6}	4184	3.15
345	0.668	976.6	389×10^{-6}	4191	2.45
360	0.674	967.1	324×10^{-6}	4203	2.02
373	0.680	957.9	279×10^{-6}	4217	1.76

hTubeOutside, computes h_o and Δp_s

hTubeInside, computes h_i

PressureDropLength, computes Δp_t and L

T2HotSide, computes T_{h_2} using `fzero`

WaterProperties determines the various physical properties from the data given
in Table 12.4.

Function *LMTDcorrFactor* is

```
function F = LMTDcorrFactor(Tc1,Tc2,Th1,Th2,NP)
P = (Tc2–Tc1)/(Th1–Tc1);
R = (Th1–Th2)/(Tc2–Tc1);
C1 = 2/P–1–R;
C2 = 2*sqrt((1–P)*(1–P*R))/P;
Rs = sqrt(R^2+1);
if R == 1
 Co = P/2.3/(1–P);
else
 Co = log10((1–P)/(1–P*R))/(R–1);
end
if NP == 1
 F = Rs*Co/log10((C1+Rs)/( C1–Rs));
else
 F = 0.5*Rs*Co/log10((C1+C2+Rs)/( C1+C2–Rs));
end
```

Function *TubeFF* is

```
function f = TubeFF(Re)
f = 1/(0.79*log(Re)–1.64)^2;
```

Function *WaterProperties* is

```
function [cp,mu,k,rho,Pr] = WaterProperties(Temp)
Temp = Temp+273;
T = [273 285 300 315 330 345 360 373];
cpp = [4217 4189 4179 4179 4184 4191 4203 4217];
muu = [1750 1225 855 631 489 389 324 279]*1e–6;
kk = [569 590 613 634 650 668 674 680]*0.001;
rhoo = [ 1000 1000 998 991.1 984.3 976.6 967.1 957.9];
Prr = [12.99 8.81 5.83 4.16 3.15 2.45 2.02 1.76];
cp = spline(T,cpp,Temp);
mu = spline(T,muu,Temp);
k = spline(T,kk,Temp);
rho = spline(T,rhoo,Temp);
Pr = spline(T,Prr,Temp);
```

Function *LMTD* is

```
function Tm = LMTD(Tc1,Tc2,Th1,Th2)
DT1 = Th1–Tc2;
DT2 = Th2–Tc1;
Tm = (DT1–DT2)/log(DT1/DT2);
```

Function *hTubeInside* is

```
function hi = hTubeInside(Reb,Prb,kb,di)
f = TubeFF(Reb);
Nub = 0.125*f*(Reb–1000)*Prb/(1+12.7*sqrt(0.125*f)*(Prb^(2/3)–1));
hi = Nub*kb/di;
```

Function *hTubeOutside* is

```
function [ho, DeltaPs] = hTubeOutside(Tb,Tw,ms,Ds,C,B,PT,do,pitch,Nb)
[cpb,mub,kb,rhob,Prb] = WaterProperties(Tb);
[cpw,muw,kw,rhow,Prw] = WaterProperties(Tw);
phis = (mub/muw)^0.14;
if pitch == 'square'
  De = 4*(PT^2–pi*do^2/4)/pi/do;
else
  De = 8*(PT^(sqrt(3)/4)–pi*do^2/8)/pi/do;
end
```

```
As = Ds*C*B/PT;
Res = ms*De/mub/As;
ho = 0.36*kb*phis*Res^0.55*Prb^(1/3)/De;
fs = exp(0.576-0.19*log(Res));
DeltaPs = fs*ms^2*(Nb+1)*Ds/(2*As^2*rhob*De*phis);
```

The function *T2HotSide* is

```
function Th = T2HotSide(Th2,mt,ms,Tc1,Tc2,Th1)
cph = WaterProperties((Th2+Th1)/2);
cpc = WaterProperties((Tc1+Tc2)/2);
Th = Th1-mt*cpc*(Tc2-Tc1)/ms/cph-Th2;
```

The function *PressureDropLength* is

```
function [DeltaPt,DeltaPs,L] = PressureDropLength(mt,Tc1,Tc2,Th1,Th2,ms,...
                           di,do,NT,NP,Ds,C,B,PT,pitch,kTube,Rfi,Rfo)
Tcb = (Tc1+Tc2)/2;
[cpc,muc,kc,rhoc,Prc] = WaterProperties(Tcb);
[cph,muh,kh,rhoh,Prh] = WaterProperties((Th1+Th2)/2);
Th2 = Th1-mt*cpc*(Tc2-Tc1)/ms/cph;
Thb = (Th1+Th2)/2;
At = 0.25*pi*di^2*NT/NP;
Co = 2*NP*(Tc2-Tc1)*cpc/pi/di/do/NT/rhoc/At^2;
Tm = LMTD(Tc1,Tc2,Th1,Th2);
F = LMTDcorrFactor(Tc1,Tc2,Th1,Th2,NP);
Tw = (Th1+Th2+Tc1+Tc2)/4;
[ho, DeltaPs] = hTubeOutside(Thb,Tw,ms,Ds,C,B,PT,do,pitch,Nb);
Rec = 4*mt*NP/pi/di/muc/NT;
hi = hTubeInside(Rec,Prc,kc,di);
U = 1/(do/di/hi+do*Rfi/di+do/2/kTube*log(do/di)+Rfo+1/ho);
f = TubeFF(Rec);
DeltaPt = Co*f*mt^3/U/F/Tm;
Q = mt*cpc*(Tc2-Tc1);
L = Q/pi/do/NT/U/F/Tm;
```

The script is

```
Ds = 0.39; NT = 124; NP = 2; B = 0.5; PT = 0.024;
di = 0.016; do = 0.019; kTube = 60;
Rfi = 0.00015; Rfo = 0.00015;
pitch = 'square'; C = PT-do; ms = 14; mt = 8.5;
Tc1 = 18; Tc2 = 42; Th1 = 65; Nb = 4;
options = optimset('display','off');
```

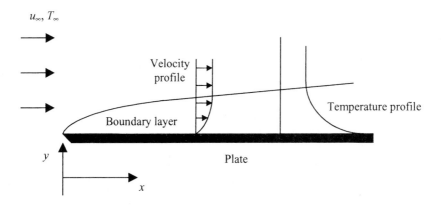

FIGURE 12.8
Flow over a flat plate.

```
Th2 = fzero('T2HotSide',Th1+15,options,mt,ms,Tc1,Tc2,Th1);
[DeltaPt, DeltaPs,L] = PressureDropLength(mt,Tc1,Tc2,Th1,Th2,ms,...
                            di,do,NT,NP,Ds,C,B,PT,pitch,kTube,Rfi,Rfo,Nb);
disp(['Shell side exit temperature = ' num2str(Th2) ' deg C'])
disp(['Tube side pressure drop = ' num2str(DeltaPt) ' Pa'])
disp(['Shell side pressure drop = ' num2str(DeltaPs) ' Pa'])
disp(['Tube length = ' num2str(L) ' m'])
```

Execution of the script displays the following results to the MATLAB command window:

```
Shell side exit temperature = 50.4487 deg C
Tube side pressure drop = 3568.8913 Pa
Shell side pressure drop = 1799.4813 Pa
Tube length = 4.232 m
```

We see that our design limits have been met.

12.3 CONVECTION HEAT TRANSFER

12.3.1 Thermal Boundary Layer on a Flat Plate—Similarity Solution

The determination of the velocity profiles for laminar boundary layer flow over a flat plate shown in Figure 12.8 are obtained from the solution of the following Blasius equation:[6]

---

[6] F. P. Incropera and D. P. DeWitt, *ibid.*, pp. 350–352.

$$\frac{d^3 f}{d\eta^3} + \frac{f}{2}\frac{d^2 f}{d\eta^2} = 0$$

where f is a modified stream function

$$f = \frac{\psi}{u_\infty \sqrt{v_{vis} x / u_\infty}}$$

The stream function ψ is defined such that

$$u = \partial\psi / \partial y$$
$$v = -\partial\psi / \partial x$$

where u and v are the velocities in the x and y directions, respectively, and η is the similarity variable

$$\eta = y\sqrt{u_\infty / v_{vis} x}$$

The free stream velocity is u_∞, and v_{vis} is the kinematic viscosity of the fluid. Solution of the Blasius equation gives the velocity at any location within the boundary layer. A numerical solution of the Blasius equation is described in Section 11.3.2.

Under conditions of constant fluid properties and certain boundary layer assumptions, the thermal energy equation for the fluid can be expressed in terms of the similarity variable as[7]

$$\frac{d^2 T^*}{d\eta^2} + \Pr\frac{f}{2}\frac{dT^*}{d\eta} = 0$$

where T^* is a dimensionless temperature

$$T^* = \frac{T - T_s}{T_\infty - T_s}$$

T is the fluid temperature, T_s is the plate surface temperature, T_∞ is the fluid free stream temperature, and the Prandtl number is $\Pr = v_{vis}/\alpha$ where α is the thermal diffusivity of the fluid. Note that T^* is coupled to the velocity solution through the presence of f in the energy equation.

The boundary conditions are

$$f(0) = 0 \qquad \frac{df}{d\eta}\bigg|_{\eta=0} = 0 \qquad \frac{df}{d\eta}\bigg|_{\eta\to\infty} \to 1$$

$$\frac{dT^*}{d\eta}\bigg|_{\eta=0} = 0 \qquad T^*(\eta \to \infty) \to 1$$

---

[7] F. P. Incropera and D. P. DeWitt, *ibid.*

The method used to solve this extended Blasius formulation is similar to that used to solve the Blasius equation in Section 11.3.2. In this case, `fsolve` is used to determine the unknown boundary conditions at $\eta = 0$ so that the boundary conditions as $\eta \to \infty$ are approximately satisfied. The two, coupled nonlinear equations are decomposed into a set of five coupled first-order ordinary differential equations by introducing the following set of dependent variables

$$y_1 = f \qquad\qquad y_4 = T^*$$

$$y_2 = \frac{df}{d\eta} \qquad\qquad y_5 = \frac{dT^*}{d\eta}$$

$$y_3 = \frac{d^2 f}{d\eta^2}$$

where y_1 represents the stream function, y_2 the velocity, y_3 the shear, y_4 the temperature, and y_5 the heat flux. These quantities are governed by the five first-order differential equations

$$\frac{dy_1}{d\eta} = y_2 \qquad\qquad \frac{dy_4}{d\eta} = y_5$$

$$\frac{dy_2}{d\eta} = y_3 \qquad\qquad \frac{dy_5}{d\eta} = -\frac{\text{Pr}}{2} y_1 y_5$$

$$\frac{dy_3}{d\eta} = -\frac{1}{2} y_1 y_3$$

with the corresponding boundary conditions

$$y_1(0) = 0 \qquad\qquad y_4(\eta \to \infty) \to 1$$

$$y_2(0) = 0 \qquad\qquad y_5(0) = 0$$

$$y_2(\eta \to \infty) \to 1$$

The `ode45` function requires that all boundary conditions must be specified at a particular value of η; in this case $\eta = 0$. The two boundary conditions where $\eta \to \infty$ must be replaced by an appropriate pair of corresponding boundary conditions at $\eta = 0$. These are

$$y_3(0) = a$$

$$y_4(0) = b$$

The values of a and b are determined through an iterative process using `fsolve` such that the conditions as $\eta \to \infty$ are approximately satisfied.

The function *Blasius* was introduced in Section 11.3.2 to solve for the velocity of the flow over a flat plate. The same function is used here for the extended formulation that includes the solution of the energy equation. Since this function was described earlier, it is presented here without further discussion.

```
function F = Blasius(x,y)
F = [y(2);y(3);-0.5*y(1)*y(3)];
```

We now create *BlasiusT* to evaluate the y_i, which is used by ode45 during integration. This function calls *Blasius* as a part of the evaluation process.

```
function F = BlasiusT(x,y,flag,Pr)
F = [Blasius(x,y(1:3)); y(5); -Pr*0.5*y(1)*y(5)];
```

Finally, we create a function called *BlasiusT2* to call ode45 to integrate the five ordinary differential equations. Inputs to the function include the Prandtl number Pr and the two-element vector x of trial values for the unknown boundary conditions a and b. The system is integrated to a sufficiently high value of η such that it adequately approximates the approach to infinity (η_{max}). The appropriate value of η_{max} depends on the Prandtl number and the accuracy required. In general, a low value of Pr requires a larger value of η_{max}. The output of *BlasiusT2* is a two-dimensional vector representing the values of $1-y_2(\eta_{max})$ and $1-y_4(\eta_{max})$, respectively. This vector is driven toward zero by fsolve during the iteration process.

```
function fn = BlasiusT2(x,Pr,eta_max)
xspan = [0 eta_max];
y0 = [0 0 x(1) 0 x(2)];
[eta ff] = ode45('BlasiusT', xspan,y0,[],Pr);
fn = [1-ff(end,2), 1-ff(end,4)];
```

The script to obtain the solution is given below. Solutions for Pr = 0.07, 0.7, and 7.0 are shown in Figures 12.9 to 12.11, respectively. A value of η_{max} = 8 is used for Pr = 0.7 and 7.0, and a value of η_{max} = 20 is used for Pr = 0.07.

```
Pr = [0.07 .7 7]; etaMax = [15 8 8]; xm = [15 5 5];
x0 = [.3 .3];
options = optimset('display','off');
for k = 1:3
  figure(k)
  slopeW = fsolve('BlasiusT2',x0,options,Pr(k),etaMax(k));
  y0 = [0 0 slopeW(1) 0 slopeW(2)];
  xspan = [0 etaMax(k)];
  [eta ff] = ode45('BlasiusT',xspan,y0,[],Pr(k));
  subplot(2,1,1)
  plot(eta,ff(:,1),':k',eta,ff(:,2),'-k',eta,ff(:,3),'--k')
  legend('Stream function','Velocity','Shear')
  axis([0 xm(k) 0 2])
  xlabel('\eta')
  ylabel('y_i (i = 1, 2, 3)')
```

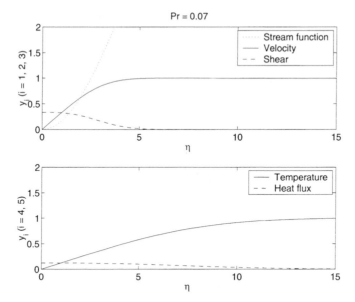

FIGURE 12.9
Extended Blasius solution for Pr = 0.07.

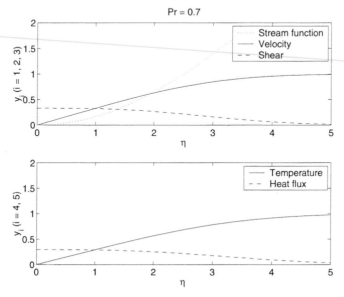

FIGURE 12.10
Extended Blasius solution for Pr = 0.7.

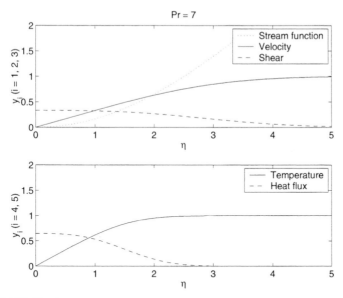

FIGURE 12.11
Extended Blasius solution for Pr = 7.

```
title(['Pr = ' num2str(Pr(k))])
subplot(2,1,2)
plot(eta,ff(:,4),'-',eta,ff(:,5),'--')
axis([0 xm(k) 0 2])
legend('Temperature','Heat flux')
xlabel('\eta')
ylabel('y_i (i = 4, 5)')
end
```

12.3.2 Natural Convection Similarity Solution

Natural convection along a heated vertical plate in contact with a cooler fluid is shown in Figure 12.12. The bulk fluid is quiescent, but the heat transfer from the plate causes buoyancy-driven flow. This flow is described by the following two coupled nonlinear ordinary differential equations[8]

$$\frac{d^3 f}{d\eta^3} + 3f \frac{d^2 f}{d\eta^2} - 2\left(\frac{df}{d\eta}\right)^2 + T^* = 0$$

$$\frac{d^{2} T^*}{d\eta^2} + 3\mathrm{Pr}\, f \frac{dT^*}{d\eta} = 0$$

[8] F. P. Incropera and D. P. DeWitt, *ibid.*, pp. 487–490.

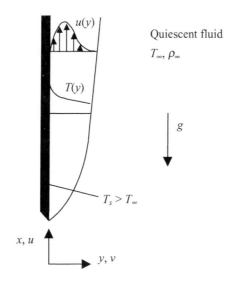

FIGURE 12.12
Natural convection plume along a heated plate.

where f is the modified stream function

$$f = \frac{\psi}{4v_{vis}\left(Gr_x/4\right)^{0.25}}$$

The stream function ψ is defined such that

$$u = \partial\psi/\partial y$$
$$v = -\partial\psi/\partial x$$

where u and v are the velocities in the x and y directions, respectively. The quantity η is the similarity variable

$$\eta = \frac{y}{x}\left(\frac{Gr_x}{4}\right)^{0.25}$$

defined in terms of the Grashof number

$$Gr_x = g\beta\left(T_s - T_\infty\right)x^3/v_{vis}^2$$

where g is the acceleration of gravity, β is the coefficient of thermal expansion

$$\beta = \frac{-1}{\rho}\left(\frac{\partial\rho}{\partial T}\right)_p$$

and v_{vis} is the kinematic viscosity. The quantity Pr is the Prandtl number defined previously, and the quantity T^* is the dimensionless temperature given by

$$T^* = \frac{T - T_\infty}{T_s - T_\infty}$$

The boundary conditions for this system are:

$$\eta = 0: \quad f = 0 \quad \frac{df}{d\eta} = 0 \quad \text{and} \quad T^* = 1$$

$$\eta \to \infty: \quad \frac{df}{d\eta} \to 0 \quad \text{and} \quad T^* \to 0$$

This system can be decomposed into a system of five first-order equations by introducing the following set of dependent variables:

$$y_1 = f \qquad y_4 = T^*$$
$$y_2 = \frac{df}{d\eta} \qquad y_5 = \frac{dT^*}{d\eta}$$
$$y_3 = \frac{d^2 f}{d\eta^2}$$

The differential equations in terms of these new variables are

$$\frac{dy_1}{d\eta} = y_2 \qquad\qquad \frac{dy_4}{d\eta} = y_5$$

$$\frac{dy_2}{d\eta} = y_3 \qquad\qquad \frac{dy_5}{d\eta} = -3\, \text{Pr}\, y_1 y_5$$

$$\frac{dy_3}{d\eta} = 2y_2^2 - 3 y_1 y_3 - y_4$$

The corresponding boundary conditions are

$$y_1(0) = 0 \qquad\qquad y_4(0) = 1$$
$$y_2(0) = 0 \qquad\qquad y_4(\eta \to \infty) \to 0$$
$$y_2(\eta \to \infty) \to 0$$

The complication in obtaining the solution to these equations is that the boundary conditions are not all defined at $\eta = 0$. Therefore, we use a procedure similar to that used to obtain a solution to the Blasius equation. Here we find the values of a and b in the following equations

$$y_3(0) = \left.\frac{d^2 f}{d\eta^2}\right|_{\eta=0} = a \qquad y_5(0) = \left.\frac{dT^*}{d\eta}\right|_{\eta=0} = b$$

such that

$$\eta \to \infty: \quad y_2 = \frac{df}{d\eta} \to 0 \quad \text{and} \quad y_4 = T^* \to 0$$

We create the function *NaturalConv* to evaluate each of the five dependent variables y_i, which is then used by ode45 to obtain the solution.

function ff = NaturalConv(x,y,flag,Pr)
ff = [y(2); y(3); –3*y(1)*y(3)+2*y(2)^2–y(4); y(5); –3*Pr*y(1)*y(5)];

Next we create the function *NaturalConv2* which calls ode45 to integrate the five first-order ordinary differential equations. Inputs to the function include the Prandtl number Pr, a two-element vector *x* of trial values for the unknown initial conditions *a* and *b*, and the integration limit for η, called η_{max}. The appropriate value of η_{max} depends on the Prandtl number, with larger Prandtl numbers requiring smaller values of η_{max}. An accurate solution is found only when the solution becomes independent of the choice of η_{max} as η_{max} increases. The output of the function is a two-dimensional vector representing the values of $y_2(\eta_{max})$ and $y_4(\eta_{max})$. This vector is driven toward zero by fsolve during the iteration process.

function fn = NaturalConv2(x,Pr,etaMax)
xspan = [0 etaMax];
y0 = [0 0 x(1) 1 x(2)];
[eta ff] = ode45('NaturalConv', xspan,y0,[],Pr);
fn = [ff(end,2), ff(end,4)];

The script to obtain the solution is given below. Results are obtained for three values of Prandtl number—0.07, 0.7, and 7.0—and are shown in Figures 12.13 to 12.15, respectively. The solution of this system is sensitive to the initial guesses for the values *a* and *b*.

Pr = [0.07 0.7 7]; etaMax = [20 20 5]; xm = [15 5 5];
x01 = [0.9 0.7 0.5]; x02 = [–0.2 –0.5 –1]; ym = [2 0.8 0.5];
options = optimset('display','off');
for k = 1:3
  x0 = [x01(k) x02(k)];
  slopeW = fsolve('NaturalConv2',x0,options,Pr(k),etaMax(k));
  y0 = [0 0 slopeW(1) 1 slopeW(2)]
  xspan = [0 etaMax(k)];
  [eta ff] = ode45('NaturalConv',xspan,y0,[],Pr(k));
  figure(k)
  subplot(2,1,1)
  plot(eta,ff(:,1),':k',eta,ff(:,2),'-k',eta,ff(:,3),'--k')
  legend('Stream function','Velocity','Shear')

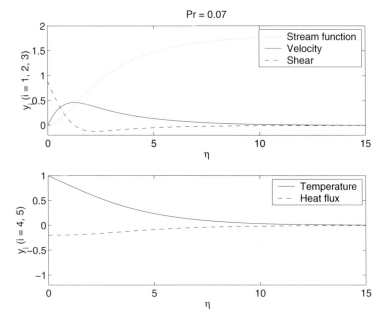

FIGURE 12.13
Natural convection solution for Pr = 0.07.

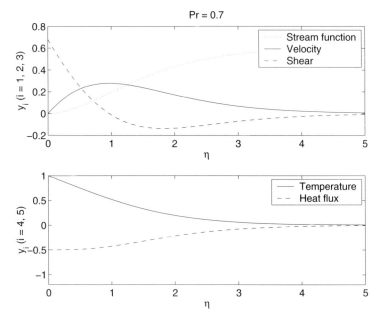

FIGURE 12.14
Natural convection solution for Pr = 0.7.

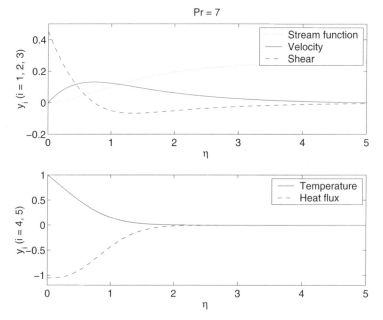

FIGURE 12.15
Natural convection solution for Pr = 7.

```
      axis([0 xm(k) –0.2 ym(k)])
      xlabel('\eta')
      ylabel('y_i (i = 1, 2, 3)')
      title(['Pr = ' num2str(Pr(k))])
      subplot(2,1,2)
      plot(eta,ff(:,4),'-',eta,ff(:,5),'--')
      axis([0 xm(k) –1.2 1])
      legend('Temperature','Heat flux')
      xlabel('\eta')
      ylabel('y_i (i = 4, 5)')
  end
```

One must experiment with the solution to determine the integration limit on η that can be considered infinite for a particular Prandtl number. For the cases run here, the integration was done from $0 < \eta < \eta_{max} = 20$ for Pr = 0.07 and 0.7 and for $0 < \eta < \eta_{max} = 5$ for Pr = 7. The values of the unknown variables at the wall, determined from these three runs, are given in Table 12.5 to assist the reader in running cases for other Prandtl numbers.

Referring to Figures 12.13 to 12.15, which are for Prandtl numbers 0.07, 0.7, and 7.0, respectively, we see that in all three cases, there is a wall plume where the velocity attains a maximum around a value of $\eta = 1$. The shear stress in the fluid in a direction parallel to the wall is

TABLE 12.5
Computed Values for $y_3(0)$ and $y_5(0)$

Pr	$y_3(0) = df^2/d\eta^2 = a$	$y_5(0) = dT^*/d\eta = b$
0.07	0.885	−0.197
0.7	0.68	−0.50
7.0	0.45	−1.05

$$\tau_s = \frac{\sqrt{2}v^2\rho}{x^2} Gr_x^{3/4} \frac{d^2f}{d\eta^2}$$

which goes to zero at the location where the velocity is maximum.

The thermal effects drive the flow. As a result, the thickness of the temperature and velocity boundary layers is approximately equal and independent of the Prandtl number. This is different from the result obtained for the corresponding case for forced flow over a flat plate in Section 12.3.1. Here it is seen that the relative thickness of the two boundary layers is independent of the Prandtl number.

The maximum value of the stream function is a measure of the pumping action provided by the heating of the fluid, which is a strong function of Pr. High values of Pr yield low values of the modified stream function f. The maximum value of the modified stream function is related to the total volumetric flow rate in the plume. However, to interpret this for a particular fluid, one must compute the dimensional stream function using

$$\psi(x, y) = 4f(\eta)v\left(\frac{Gr_x}{4}\right)^{0.25}$$

When this is done, it is found that the volumetric flow rate for air, at the same temperature difference, is significantly greater than it is for water.

Since the flow carries energy away from the surface, a similar analysis is of interest for the heat flux, which is determined from

$$q''_s = -\frac{k(T_s - T_\infty)}{x}\left(\frac{Gr_x}{4}\right)^{0.25} \frac{dT^*}{d\eta}\bigg|_{\eta=0}$$

When the heat flux is computed for both air and water, it is found that the heat flux for water is on the order of 100 times greater than that for air. This is primarily due to the roles of thermal conductivity, specific heat, and density, which determine the magnitude of the heat flux. At atmospheric pressure and 300 K, the thermal conductivity is approximately 30 times greater for water as compared with air, the specific heat is 4 times greater, and the density is 1,000 times greater. Thus, even though the volumetric flow rate in the plume is larger for air, the heat flux is larger for water.

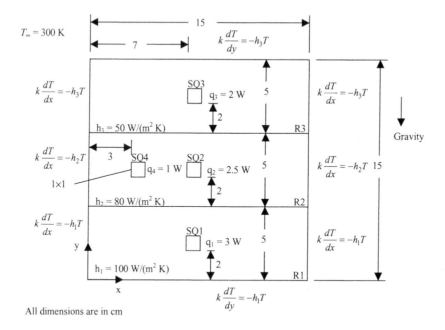

All dimensions are in cm

FIGURE 12.16
Geometry and constants describing a printed circuit board.

12.3.3 Temperature Distribution in a Printed Circuit Board[9]

Consider the printed circuit board shown in Figure 12.16, which has had placed on it four flush-mounted electronic devices that dissipate energy in the amounts indicated in the figure. The board is mounted in a rack such that the y-axis is vertical. In such situations, the heat-transfer coefficient h varies in the y-direction. To simplify the model somewhat, we assume that the heat-transfer coefficient is constant in the x-direction. In order to approximate the variation of the heat-transfer coefficient in the y-direction, the board is considered composed of three equal-sized contiguous boards, each having different heat-transfer coefficients, as shown in Figure 12.16. However, the thermal conductivity k of the boards and components is assumed to be the same and independent of location. For simplification, it is also assumed that the four heating elements have the same thermal conductivity as the board on which they are placed.

The governing equation for each of the three boards and electronic components is

$$\nabla(k\nabla T) + q'' - H(T - T_\infty) = 0$$

―――――――――――――
[9] Problem suggested by Professor Yogendra Joshi, Department of Mechanical Engineering, University of Maryland, College Park, MD.

TABLE 12.6
Numerical Values Used in the Description of the Printed Circuit Board and Their Corresponding
`pdetool` Notation

	Region						
	R1	R2	R3	SQ1	SQ2	SQ3	SQ4
Boundary Conditions							
Left							
g	0	0	0	—	—	—	—
$q \to h$ (W/cm^2 K)	0.01	0.008	0.005	—	—	—	—
Right							
g	0	0	0	—	—	—	—
$q \to h$ (W/cm^2 K)	0.01	0.008	0.005	—	—	—	—
Top							
g	—	—	0	—	—	—	—
$q \to h$ (W/cm^2 K)	—	—	0.005	—	—	—	—
Bottom							
g	0	—	—	—	—	—	—
$q \to h$ (W/cm^2 K)	0.01	—	—	—	—	—	—
PDE Specification							
$k \to k$ (W/cm K)	0.003	0.003	0.003	0.003	0.003	0.003	0.003
$Q \to Q$ (W/cm^3)	0	0	0	30	25	20	10
$h \to H$ (W/cm^3 K)	0.1	0.08	0.05	0.1	0.08	0.05	0.08
$Text \to T_\infty$ (K)	300	300	300	300	300	300	300

where q''' is the power per unit volume of the heat source (W/m^3), $H = 2h/t$ (W/m^3 K), t is the thickness of the board, and T_∞ is the ambient temperature of the surroundings. The factor of 2 in the definition of H is because the heat is convected from both sides of the board.

We shall determine an estimate of the temperature distribution throughout the board using the PDE Toolbox. First we create the appropriate drawing environment by going to the *Options* menu and setting the *Axis Limits* to [0 17] with the grid spacing of 1 for both axes, and then selecting *Snap*. Next we change *Generic Scalar* to *Heat Transfer*. Then, we draw three rectangles and four squares with the dimensions and locations shown in Figure 12.16. This results in the set formula *R1 + R2 + R3 + SQ1 + SQ2 + SQ3 + SQ4*. Each of these regions will be governed by the heat-conduction equation. However, we have to specify boundary conditions only for the edges of the rectangular regions indicated in Table 12.6. This is because the combination of the plus (+) signs in the set formula and the fact that each *SQn* resides completely within a previously defined region (*Rn*) indicates to the PDE tool that no new boundaries have been created. Notice that the units for k, h, and Q are

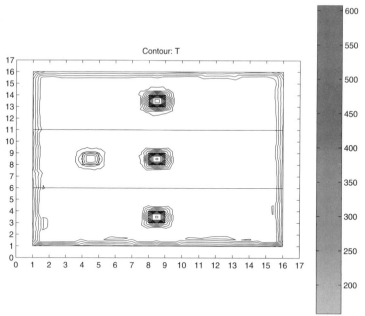

FIGURE 12.17
Temperature distribution in the printed circuit board shown in Figure 12.16.

converted to W/(cm K), W/(cm^2 K), and W/cm^3, respectively, to be consistent with the units of the dimensions of the board.

Next, we go the *Boundary Mode* and then *Specify Boundary Conditions*. The boundary conditions on the edges that are indicated in Table 12.6 are each of the Neumann type. These boundaries appear as red lines terminated by an arrowhead. After double-clicking each line, the values given in Table 12.6 are entered in the appropriate places. The *PDE Mode* is then selected. Placing the cursor in one of the seven regions and double-clicking brings up the *PDE Specification* window. In each of the seven appearances of this window, the appropriate values from Table 12.6 are entered.

The mesh is initialized and refined once. Then the solution is obtained, and both the temperature distribution and the heat flux are plotted. The results are shown in Figures 12.17 and 12.18, respectively.

12.4 RADIATION HEAT TRANSFER

12.4.1 Radiation View Factor—Differential Area to Arbitrary Rectangle in Parallel Planes

The computation of radiation view factors is required when analyzing the radiation in enclosures with diffuse surfaces. There are numerous techniques for evaluating these

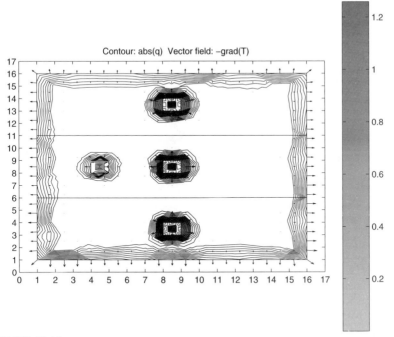

FIGURE 12.18
Heat flux in the printed circuit board shown in Figure 12.16.

factors, many of which apply to specific geometries. A more general approach is to start from the relations that define the view factor and integrate them numerically. Consider first the general expression[10] for the view factor between a differential area element dA_1 and a finite area A_2.

$$dF_{2-d_1} = \frac{dA_1}{A_2} \int_{A_2} \frac{\cos\theta_1 \cos\theta_2}{\pi S^2} dA_2 \qquad (12.2)$$

where S is the line-of-sight distance between dA_1 and some position on A_2 as shown in Figure 12.19. The angles θ_j, $j = 1,2$ are measured between the normal to the surface and S. The reciprocity relation for the view factors is

$$A_2 dF_{2-d_1} = dA_1 F_{d_1-2} \qquad (12.3)$$

Thus, F_{d_1-2} can be written as

[10] R. Siegel and J. R. Howell, *Thermal Radiation Heat Transfer*, 3rd ed., Hemisphere Pub., Washington, 1992, pp. 189–252.

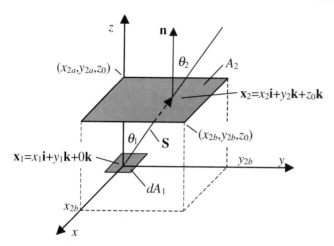

FIGURE 12.19
Geometry when the differential area and the finite rectangle are in parallel planes.

$$F_{d_1-2} = \int_{A_2} \frac{\cos\theta_1 \cos\theta_2}{\pi S^2} dA_2 \qquad (12.4)$$

We shall perform the integration numerically. Consider the case where dA_1 and A_2 are in parallel planes and A_2 is a rectangle. Both of these restrictions could be removed with additional programming effort. For this case, Eq. (12.4) can be written as

$$F_{d_1-2} = \frac{1}{\pi} \int_{y_{2a}}^{y_{2b}} \int_{x_{2a}}^{x_{2b}} \frac{\cos\theta_1 \cos\theta_2}{S^2} dx_2 dy_2$$

where the line-of-sight vector $\mathbf{S}$ is

$$\mathbf{S} = \mathbf{x}_2 - \mathbf{x}_1 = (x_2 - x_1)\mathbf{i} + (y_2 - y_1)\mathbf{j} + (z_2 - z_1)\mathbf{k}$$

and

$$S = |\mathbf{S}|$$

The angles can be expressed in terms of the line-of-sight vector and a normal vector to the rectangle $\mathbf{n} = \mathbf{k}$:

$$\cos\theta_1 = \cos\theta_2 = \frac{\mathbf{n} \cdot \mathbf{S}}{|\mathbf{S}|}$$

Since the two surfaces are parallel, $\theta_1 = \theta_2 = \theta$. Then

$$F_{d_1-2} = \frac{1}{\pi} \int_{y_{2a}}^{y_{2b}} I_{x2}(y_2)\,dy_2$$

where

$$I_{x2}(y_2) = \int_{x_{2a}}^{x_{2b}} f(x_2, y_2)\,dx_2$$

and

$$f(x_2, y_2) = \frac{\cos^2\theta}{|\mathbf{S}|^2} = \frac{(\mathbf{n}\cdot\mathbf{S})^2}{|\mathbf{S}|^4}$$

We first create a function called *kernel* to evaluate $f(x_2,y_2)$ at any location on surface A_2. The inputs to the function are the x_2, y_2 and $z_2 = z_0$ coordinates of the point on A_2. The function uses a vector-based formulation to determine the length S and $\cos\theta$. It is noted that for compatibility with quad8, *kernel* must return a vector whose length equals the length of the input vector x. This allows quad8 to minimize the number of calls to the integrand function while still providing the needed data. This capability is implemented in *kernel* by using length to determine the number of elements in x.

```
function f = kernel(x,y,z,xp1)
L = length(x);
S = [x-xp1(1);ones(1,L)*y-xp1(2);ones(1,L)*z-xp1(3)];
f = dot(repmat([0 0 1]',1,L),S).^2./dot(S,S).^2;
```

We now create a function *Intx2* to integrate over x for a given value of y. The integration is performed by quad8. *Intx2* is itself called by quad8 since the formulation involves a double integration and thus, *Intx2* must be written to allow the variable y to be a vector of arbitrary length. Just as for *kernel*, *Intx2* is written to compute a vector whose length equals the length of the input vector y.

```
function Int = Intx2(y,xp1,x2a,x2b,z)
Int = zeros(1,length(y));
for i = 1:length(y)
  Int(i) = quad8('kernel',x2a,x2b,[],[],y(i),z,xp1);
end
```

We now use these functions in two examples. The geometry for both examples and the computed view factor are given in Table 12.7. We obtain the two view factors in the table with the following script:

```
x21 = -1; y21 = -1;
x22 = 0; y22 = 0;
```

TABLE 12.7.
Example Configurations and View Factor Results

Parameter	Set #1	Set #2
Geometry of A_2		
X coordinate of first corner point, x_{2a}	−1	−1
Y coordinate of first corner point, y_{2a}	−1	−1
X coordinate of opposite corner point, x_{2b}	0	1
Y coordinate of opposite corner point, y_{2b}	0	1
Separation distance between planes, z_0	5	1
Computed View Factor, F_{d_1-2}	0.0121	0.5541

```
x1 = [0 0 0];
Fd12Set1 = quad8('Intx2',y21,y22,[],[],x1,x21,x22,5)/pi
x22 = 1;y22 = 1;
Fd12Set2 = quad8('Intx2',y21,y22,[],[],x1,x21,x22,1)/pi
```

In addition, we plot the view factor as a function of the separation distance for Set #1 given in Table 12.7. The script is

```
x21 = −1; y21 = −1;
x22 = 0; y22 = 0;
x1 = [0 0 0]; nz = 20;
z = linspace(0.1,5,nz);
for i = 1:nz
  Fd12(i) = quad8('Intx2',y21,y22,[],[],x1,x21,x22,z(i))/pi;
end
plot(z,Fd12)
xlabel('Separation of surfaces')
ylabel('View factor')
text(1.8,.2,'Areas are in parallel planes')
text(1.8,.19,'Finite area is 1 x 1 (arbitrary length units)')
text(1.8,.18,'Differential area is aligned with a corner')
title('Radiation view factor - differential to finite area')
```

which, upon execution, gives the result shown in Figure 12.20. It is interesting to note that F_{d_1-2} goes to a limiting value of 0.25 as the separation distance between the two parallel planes goes to zero. This is because the point dA_1 is aligned with one of the corners of the square area A_2. Thus, as the two parallel planes approach each other, A_2 cuts off one-quarter of the total hemispherical view from dA_1. In the geometry of Set #2, dA_1 is aligned with the center point of A_2 and the limiting value on F_{d_1-2} as the planes approach each other is 1.0.

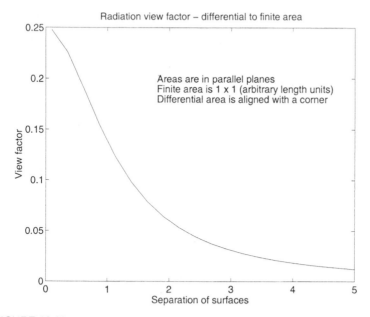

FIGURE 12.20
Configuration factor versus separation distance between two parallel planes for the geometry shown in Figure 12.19.

It is noted that the function dblquad has a capability to evaluate double integrals, but it does not have the ability to accept additional arguments that are needed in the present formulation.

12.4.2 View Factor Between Two Rectangles in Parallel Planes

The view factor computed previously was from an infinitesimal area to a finite area. The infinitesimal area can be integrated over a second finite area to obtain the view factor between two finite areas. The equation defining such a view factor is

$$F_{2-1} = \frac{1}{\pi A_2} \int_{A_1}\int_{A_2} \frac{\cos\theta_1 \cos\theta_2}{S^2} \, dA_2 dA_1 = \frac{1}{\pi A_2} \int_{y_{1a}}^{y_{1b}}\int_{x_{1a}}^{x_{1b}}\int_{y_{2a}}^{y_{2b}}\int_{x_{2a}}^{x_{2b}} \frac{\cos\theta_1 \cos\theta_2}{S^2} \, dx_2 dy_2 dx_1 dy_1 \qquad (12.5)$$

where the variables are defined similarly to those discussed in the previous section. Variables specific to this quadruple integral are defined in Figure 12.21. There are numerous methods to evaluate this integral. The approach used here is again direct integration. Since the two plates are in parallel planes and their edges are parallel, Eq. (12.5) can be written as

$$F_{2-1} = \frac{1}{\pi A_2} \int_{y_{1a}}^{y_{1b}} I_{x1}(y_1) dy_1$$

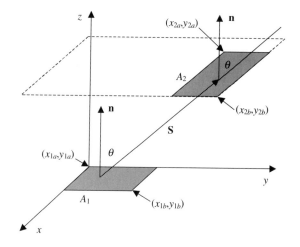

FIGURE 12.21
Geometry for the determination of the view factors between two finite rectangles in parallel planes.

where

$$I_{x1}(y_1) = \int_{x_{1a}}^{x_{1b}} I_{y2}(x_1, y_1) dx_1$$

$$I_{y2}(x_1, y_1) = \int_{y_{2a}}^{y_{2b}} I_{x2}(x_1, y_1, y_2) dy_2$$

$$I_{x2}(x_1, y_1, y_2) = \int_{x_{2a}}^{x_{2b}} f(x_1, y_1, x_2, y_2) dx_2$$

$$f(x_1, y_1, x_2, y_2) = \frac{\cos^2 \theta}{|S|^2} = \frac{(n \cdot S)^2}{|S|^4}$$

$$S = (x_1 - x_2)i + (y_1 - y_2)j + (z_1 - z_2)k$$

and $n = k$, $z_1 = 0$, and $z_2 = z_0$.

Although direct integration works well, it is computationally very lengthy since MATLAB uses an adaptive approach in its numerical integration algorithms.

The solution of the quadruple integral requires four functions. Two of them have already been created in Section 12.4.1: *kernel* and *Intx2*, which calls *kernel*. We now create two more functions. The first is *Inty2*, which computes I_{y2} and calls *Intx2*.

```
function Int = Inty2(x1,y1,XY2,z)
Int = zeros(1,length(x1));
for i = 1:length(x1);
```

TABLE 12.8
Data Used to Compute the View Factor

Parameter	Set #1	Set #2
Geometry of A_1		
X coordinate of first corner point, Area 1, x_{1a}	-1	-2
Y coordinate of first corner point, Area 1, y_{1a}	-1	-2
X coordinate of opposite corner point, Area 1, x_{1b}	1	0
Y coordinate of opposite corner point, Area 1, y_{1b}	1	0
Geometry of A_2		
X coordinate of first corner point, Area 2, x_{2a}	-1	2
Y coordinate of first corner point, Area 2, y_{2a}	-1	2
X coordinate of opposite corner point, Area 2, x_{2b}	1	0
Y coordinate of opposite corner point, Area 2, y_{2b}	1	0
Separation distance between planes	2	2
Computed View Factor (F_{2-1})	0.1998	0.0433

```
    xp1 = [x1(i) y1 0];
    Int(i) = quad8('Intx2',XY2(1,2),XY2(2,2),[],[],xp1,XY2(1,1),XY2(2,1),z);
end
```

The second function is *Intx1*, which computes I_{x1} and calls *Inty2*.

```
function Int = Intx1(y1,x1a,x1b,XY2,z)
Int = zeros(1,length(y1));
for i = 1:length(y1);
  Int(i) = quad8('Inty2',x1a,x1b,[],[],y1(i),XY2,z);
end
```

We now compute the view factor between two arbitrarily located rectangles in parallel planes for the data listed as Set #1 in Table 12.8. The data listed for Set #2 is computed in a similar manner, with the obvious changes to the data. The script is

```
x1a = -1; y1a = -1; x2a = -1; y2a = -1;
x1b = 1; y1b = 1; x2b = 1; y2b = 1;
z = 2;
A2 = abs(x2a-x2b)*abs(y2a-y2b);
XY2 = [x2a,y2a;x2b,y2b];
Ff = quad8('Intx1',y1a,y1b,[],[],x1a,x1b,XY2,z)/A2/pi
```

12.4.3 Enclosure Radiation with Diffuse Gray Walls

A common problem in radiation heat transfer is to determine the temperatures and heat-transfer rates due to radiation in an enclosure with diffuse, gray surfaces enclosing a nonparticipating medium. These situations occur in ovens, rooms, and other enclosed spaces. Making the diffuse, gray surface assumptions considerably reduces the complexity of the model compared with the general radiation model. The diffuse specification means that the intensity of the radiation leaving and arriving at all surfaces is independent of direction. The gray specification means that the emissivity and absorptivity are independent of wavelength. However, even with these simplifications, enclosure problems still require considerable effort to set up and solve. Such problems are naturally expressed in matrix notation, and, thus, MATLAB provides an ideal environment for their formulation and solution. The equations that result from such an analysis are[11]

$$\frac{Q_k}{A_k} = q_k = \frac{\varepsilon_k}{1 - \varepsilon_k}\left(\sigma T_k^4 - q_{0,k}\right) \tag{12.6}$$

$$\frac{Q_k}{A_k} = q_k = q_{0,k} - \sum_{j=1}^{N} F_{k-j} q_{0,j} = \sum_{j=1}^{N} F_{k-j}\left(q_{0,k} - q_{0,j}\right) \tag{12.7}$$

where Q_k is the heat transfer rate from surface k, A_k is its area, q_k is its heat flux, $q_{0,k}$ is its radiosity, F_{k-j} is the view factor representing the fraction of the energy leaving surface k that is intercepted by surface j, N is the number of surfaces in the enclosure, and $\sigma = 5.67 \times 10^{-8}$ W/(m^2 K^4) is the Stefan-Boltzmann constant. The formulation of these equations assumes that both the incoming and the outgoing radiation from each of the surfaces is uniform over that surface, and that the intensity is independent of direction. This assumption should be evaluated for a given problem by subdividing the surfaces of the enclosure until results are obtained that are independent of the area subdivision scheme.

For a general enclosure problem one must specify either the heat-transfer rate or the temperature of each of the surfaces. Once such a specification has been made, Eqs. (12.6) and (12.7) yield a single independent relation for each surface. For a specified temperature, Eqs. (12.6) and (12.7) are equated to yield

$$q_{0,k} - \sum_{j=1}^{N} F_{k-j} q_{0,j} = \frac{\varepsilon_k}{1 - \varepsilon_k}\left(\sigma T_k^4 - q_{0,k}\right) \tag{12.8}$$

When the heat transfer rate is specified, Eq. (12.8) is written as

$$\frac{Q_k}{A_k} = q_{0,k} - \sum_{j=1}^{N} F_{k-j} q_{0,j} \tag{12.9}$$

These equations can be written in matrix form as

---

[11] R. Siegel and J. R. Howell, *ibid.*, pp. 189–252.

$$\begin{bmatrix} d_1 - F_{1-1} & -F_{1-2} & \cdots & -F_{1-N} \\ -F_{2-1} & d_2 - F_{2-2} & & -F_{1-2} \\ \vdots & & & \vdots \\ -F_{N-1} & -F_{N-2} & & d_N - F_{N-N} \end{bmatrix} \begin{bmatrix} q_{0,1} \\ q_{0,2} \\ \vdots \\ q_{0,N} \end{bmatrix} = \begin{bmatrix} b_1 \\ b_2 \\ \vdots \\ b_N \end{bmatrix}$$

where, when the temperatures are specified

$$d_k = 1/(1 - \varepsilon_k)$$

$$b_k = \frac{\varepsilon_k}{1 - \varepsilon_k} \sigma T_k^4$$

and when the heat-transfer rates are specified

$$d_k = 1$$

$$b_k = \frac{Q_k}{A_k}$$

Each row of the matrix represents one surface whose form depends on whether the temperature or the heat-transfer rate is specified for that surface. In either case, the radiosity associated with the surface is the unknown. Thus, the resulting system of equations consists of N equations in the N unknown radiosities. Once the radiosities are known, the unknown temperature or heat-transfer rate for a given surface can be determined from either Eqs. (12.6) or (12.7). Equation (12.6) is somewhat simpler to evaluate except for the special case where the emmissivity equals one, in which case Eq. (12.7) is used.

To illustrate these results, consider the following example. The geometry is a rectangular cross-section oven, which is assumed to be infinitely long into the plane of the page. The geometry is defined in Figure 12.22. The view factors are defined in Table 12.9. These factors can be computed using Hottel's crossed-string method.[12] The values shown in boldface were those chosen and the remaining values were computed from view-factor algebra based on these chosen values and the areas.

The following script makes use of an identifier c_k, $k = 1, 2...N$, which equals 0 when the temperature is given and equals 1 when the heat-transfer rate is given. It is then used to select the appropriate values for d_k and b_k. Furthermore, all vectors must be of length N and the matrix F is ($N \times N$). The script is

```
sigma = 5.6693e–8; N = 4;
A = [3 5 3 5]; epsilon = [0.7 0.3 0.85 0.45];
T = [550 700 650 600];
F = –[0 0.3615 0.277 0.3615;...
      0.2169 0 0.2169 0.5662;...
      0.277 0.3615 0 0.3615;...
      0.2169 0.5662 0.2169 0];
Q = [0 0 0 0];
```

---

[12] R. Siegel and J. R. Howell, *ibid.*

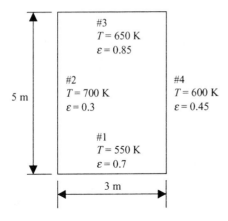

FIGURE 12.22
Enclosure geometry and surface properties for radiation in an enclosure with gray walls.

TABLE 12.9
View Factors F_{i-j} for the Enclosure Shown in Figure 12.22

i\j	1	2	3	4
1	**0**	**0.3615**	**0.2770**	0.3615
2	0.2169	**0**	**0.2169**	0.5662
3	0.2770	0.3615	**0**	0.3615
4	0.2169	0.5662	0.2169	0

```
c = [0 0 0 0];
b = sigma*epsilon./(1−epsilon).*(1−c).*T.^4+c.*Q./A;
d = (1−c).*1./(1−epsilon)+c;
for k = 1:N
  F(k,k) = d(k)+F(k,k);
end
q0 = F\b';
Q = A.*epsilon./(1−epsilon).*(1−c).*(sigma*T.^4−q0')
T = c.*((Q./A.*(1−epsilon)./epsilon+q0')/sigma).^(1/4)
q = Q./A
```

Execution of the script gives $Q = [-8627.9\ 8061.1\ 4525.9\ -3959.1]$ W and $q = [-2876\ 1612.2\ 1508.6\ -791.8]$ W/m^2. It is seen that the heat-transfer rates Q correctly sum to zero.

12.4.4 Transient Radiation Heating of a Plate in a Furnace[13]

Consider a vertically suspended flat plate in a furnace. One wall of the furnace that is parallel to the plate's surface contains heating elements. The furnace and the plate are initially at room temperature. The amount of heating power Q required in the heating elements to raise the plate's temperature to T_e in time t_h can be determined from energy balances on the plate and the furnace walls, which yield the following coupled equations:

$$\frac{dT_w}{dt} = P_1 Q - P_2 \left(T_w^4 - T_p^4 \right)$$

$$\frac{dT_p}{dt} = -P_3 \left(T_p^4 - T_w^4 \right)$$

where the plate and wall are modeled as lumped masses, T_w is the temperature of the wall, and T_p is the temperature of the plate. If we assume that this setup can be modeled as a two-surface enclosure with gray diffuse surfaces, then[14]

$$P_1 = \frac{1}{m_w c_w}$$

$$P_2 = \frac{\sigma}{m_w c_w} \left[\frac{1-\varepsilon_p}{\varepsilon_p A_p} + \frac{1}{A_w F_{wp}} + \frac{1-\varepsilon_w}{\varepsilon_w A_w} \right]^{-1}$$

$$P_3 = \frac{\sigma}{m_p c_p} \left[\frac{1-\varepsilon_p}{\varepsilon_p A_p} + \frac{1}{A_p F_{pw}} + \frac{1-\varepsilon_w}{\varepsilon_w A_w} \right]^{-1}$$

where m_p and m_w are the masses of the plate and wall, respectively; c_p and c_w are the specific heats of the plate and wall, respectively; ε_p and ε_w are the emissivities of the plate and wall, respectively; A_p and A_w are the areas of the plate and wall, respectively; F_{pw} and F_{wp} are the view factors; and $\sigma = 5.67 \times 10^{-8}$ W/(m^2 K^4) is the Stefan-Boltzmann constant.

Let us assume that for a certain configuration we have determined that $P_1 = 1.67 \times 10^{-5}$ K/J, $P_2 = 8.8 \times 10^{-14}$ s^{-1}K^{-3}, and $P_3 = 6.3 \times 10^{-13}$ s^{-1}K^{-3}. We want to determine the value of Q required by the heating elements to raise the plate's temperature to $T_e = 1100$ K in $t_h = 10$ minutes (600 s). It is assumed that both the plate and the furnace are initially at 300 K. We first need to create two functions, one that will be used by ode45 to solve the two coupled first-order ordinary differential equations and the other that will be used by fzero to determine the value of Q. We shall call the former one *RadTemp* and the latter *QGen*. For *RadTemp* we have

```
function dTdt = RadTemp(t,T,flag,P1,P2,P3,Q)
dTdt = [P1*Q−P2*(T(1)^4−T(2)^4);−P3*(T(2)^4−T(1)^4)];
```

---

[13] Problem suggested by Professor Yogendra Joshi, Department of Mechanical Engineering, University of Maryland, College Park, MD.

[14] F. P. Incropera and D. P. DeWitt, *ibid.*, Chapter 13.

where $T(1) = T_w(t)$ and $T(2) = T_p(t)$. For $QGen$ we have

```
function PlateTempDev = QGen(Q,Te,th,P1,P2,P3,T1o,T2o,tend)
[t,T] = ode45('RadTemp',[0,tend],[T1o;T2o],[],P1,P2,P3,Q);
PlateTempDev = Te-interp1(t,T(:,2),th,'spline');
```

where $T1o = T_w(0)$, and $T2o = T_p(0)$ and we have used `interp1` to locate the time at which the temperature $T_e = Te = 1,100$ K.

The script that determines Q and plots the temperatures of the wall and plate as a function of time is

```
P1 = 1.67e-5; P2 = 8.8e-14; P3 = 6.3e-13; Qguess = 100000;
Te = 1100; th = 600; tend = 660; T1o = 300; T2o = 300;
options = optimset('display','off');
Q = fzero('Qgen',Qguess,options,Te,th,P1,P2,P3,T1o,T2o,tend);
[t,T] = ode45('RadTemp',[0,tend],[T1o;T2o],[],P1,P2,P3,Q);
plot(t,T(:,1),'k-',t,T(:,2),'k--')
z = axis;
hold on
plot([0,z(2)],[Te,Te],'k',[th,th],[z(3),z(4)],'k')
xlabel('Time (s)')
text(0.05*z(2),0.85*z(4),['Q = ' num2str(Q,6) ' W'])
ylabel('Temperature (K)')
legend('Wall temperature','Plate temperature',2)
```

When executed, this script produces Figure 12.23.

EXERCISES

12.1 One-dimensional conduction in a plane wall can be represented by

$$k(T)\frac{dT}{dx} = q$$

where q is the heat flux, $k(T)$ is the temperature dependent thermal conductivity, T is the temperature, and x is the spatial coordinate. If we assume that the wall is composed of mineral wool insulation, then the thermal conductivity varies as

$$k(T) = -A + BT \qquad 240 < T < 365 \text{ K}$$

where $A = 0.408$, $B = 0.00032$, k is in W/m·K, and T is in K. Determine the temperature at $x = 0$ when the heat flux is $q = 12.5$ W/m^2, the wall thickness is 0.1 m, and the temperature of the surface at $x = 0.1$ m is 300 K. Compare the results with the analytical solution

$$A(T - T_1) + \frac{B}{2}(T^2 - T_1^2) = qx$$

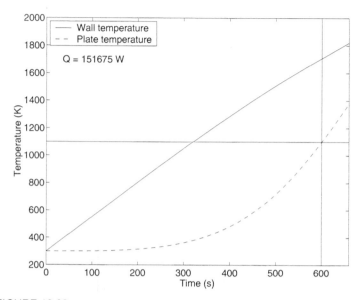

FIGURE 12.23
Temperature as a function time in the plate and in the furnace.

where $T(0) = T_1$. It is noted that the heat flux computed from an average value of the thermal conductivity will give an excellent prediction of true value.

12.2 A standard plastic milk jug can be represented as a lumped capacitance for the purpose of estimating the time required to heat (or cool) the milk. The governing equation for such a situation is

$$\frac{dT}{dt} = \frac{Q}{mc_v}$$

where $Q = hA(T_{amb}-T)$ is the heat transfer to the jug from the surroundings, m is the mass of the jug, and c_v is the specific heat. For a simple radiation model

$$Q = A\sigma\varepsilon(T^4 - T_{amb}^4)$$

where $\sigma = 5.667\times10^{-8}$ W/m²·K⁴ is the Stephan-Boltzmann constant, ε is the emissivity, A is the surface area, T is the jug temperature, and T_{amb} is the ambient temperature.

Determine the time constant for this system with and without radiation. The time constant τ is the time required for the temperature difference between the jug's temperature and the ambient temperature to decrease by 63.2 % from its initial value—that is,

$$\frac{T_{amb} - T(\tau)}{T_{amb} - T(0)} = 0.368$$

With no radiation, assume natural convection from the jug surface with a heat-transfer coefficient of h = 2 W/K·m², T_{amb} = 30 °C, and $T(0)$ = 5 °C. With radiation, assume that ε = 0.5, m = 3.5 kg, c_v = 4.2

J/g·K, $A = 0.3$ m^2, $T(0) = 5$ °C, and $T_{amb} = 30$ °C. [Answers: For the case without radiation $\tau = 6.8$ hr ($= mc_v/(hA)$); with radiation present $\tau = 2.78$ hr, and is a function of the initial temperature.]

12.3 The heat loss by convection from the outer surface of the insulation of an insulated pipe is determined from

$$q = \frac{2\pi L (T_i - T_\infty)}{\frac{1}{k}\ln(r_o/r_i) + \frac{1}{r_o h}}$$

where L is the pipe length, r_o is the outer diameter of the insulation, r_i its inner diameter, k its thermal conductivity and h the heat-transfer coefficient. For small values of r_o, additional insulation has the effect of increasing the heat-transfer rate. Demonstrate this effect by plotting q as a function of r_o for a range of r_o that spans $r_o = k/h$. Let $h = 5$ W/m^2·K, $k = 0.1$ W/m·K, $r_i = 0.01$ m, and $L = 1$ m. Although one's usual experience is that adding insulation reduces the heat-transfer rate, this is an example of an exception.

12.4 A temperature sensor is used to measure the temperature of a flowing fluid. The sensor is mounted on a small diameter cylindrical probe that protrudes through a duct wall into the flow normal to the direction of flow. The probe can be modeled as a fin whose temperature distribution is given by

$$\frac{T(x) - T_\infty}{T_b - T_\infty} = \frac{\cosh m(L-x)}{\cosh mL}$$

where

$$m^2 = \frac{hP}{kA_c}$$

and T_b is the wall temperature, T_∞ is the fluid temperature, $P = \pi d$ is the perimeter of the probe of diameter d, $A_c = \pi d^2/4$ is the cross-sectional area, k is the thermal conductivity, h is the heat-transfer coefficient, and L is the length of the probe.

The error e in the sensed temperature due to conduction along the probe is, therefore,

$$e = T(L) - T_\infty = \frac{T_b - T_\infty}{\cosh ml}$$

Plot the error as a function of probe length for $0.005 \leq L \leq 0.1$ m for several values of k in the range $20 \leq k \leq 400$ W/m·K. Assume that the fluid temperature is 100 °C and the wall temperature is 80°C. The heat-transfer coefficient between the fluid and the probe is 25 W/m^2·K.

12.5 Because of the nonlinear nature of radiation heat transfer, the placement of shields in the radiation path reduces heat transfer. Thus, for insulation applications, the use of radiation shields is important. The effect of radiation shields can be illustrated by considering the heat transfer between two infinite parallel plates at temperatures T_1 and T_2 that are separated by an evacuated space. When the surfaces radiate as black bodies, the heat-transfer rate q with no shield is obtained from

$$q = \sigma(T_1^4 - T_2^4)$$

When we have one shield the heat transfer rate is determined from

TABLE 12.10
Answers to Exercise 12.7

Pr	δ_u	δ_T	δ_u/δ_T	$Pr^{1/3}$
0.07	5.0526	15.0261	0.3363	0.4122
0.7	4.9684	5.7243	0.8679	0.8879
7.0	4.9177	2.5046	1.9635	1.9128

$$q = \sigma(T_1^{\,4} - T_m^{\,4})$$
$$q = \sigma(T_m^{\,4} - T_2^{\,4})$$

where T_m is the temperature of the shield. The heat-transfer rate with two shields is obtained from

$$q = \sigma(T_1^{\,4} - T_{m1}^{\,4})$$
$$q = \sigma(T_{m1}^{\,4} - T_{m2}^{\,4})$$
$$q = \sigma(T_{m2}^{\,4} - T_2^{\,4})$$

where $\sigma = 5.667 \times 10^{-8}$ W/m^2·K^4 is the Stephan-Boltzmann constant and T_{m1} and T_{m2} are the temperatures of shields 1 and 2, respectively. If the temperatures of the two plates are 100 °C and 20 °C, then determine the heat-transfer rate with no shield, one shield, and two shields. [Answers: With no shield, $q = 680$ W/m^2; with one shield, $q = 340.1$ W/m^2 and $T_m = 340.15$ K; and with two shields, $q = 226.7$ W/m^2, $T_{m1} = 352.2$ K and $T_{m2} = 326.7$ K.]

12.6 The Planck distribution represents the power spectral density of black-body radiation at a particular temperature and is given by

$$E_{\lambda,b}(\lambda,T) = \frac{C_1}{\lambda^5 \left[\exp(C_2/\lambda T) - 1\right]}$$

where λ is the wavelength, T is the temperature, $E_{\lambda,b}$ is the spectral emissive power, and $C_1 = 3.742 \times 10^8$ W·μm^4/m^2, and $C_2 = 1.439 \times 10^4$ μm·K. A common need in radiation calculations is to integrate this function over some range of wavelengths. When integrated over all wavelengths, we have that

$$\int_0^\infty E_{\lambda,b}\,d\lambda = \sigma T^4$$

where $\sigma = 5.667 \times 10^{-8}$ W/m^2·K^4 is the Stephan-Boltzmann constant. Perform this integration numerically for $T = 300$, 400, and 500 K and compare the result with the exact value. A note of caution: both integration limits give considerable difficulty numerically. Approximate the integral by using a very small nonzero lower limit, such as 0.5 μm. For the upper limit, start with a value of 150 μm, which will vary depending on the value of T.

12.7 Use the solution method introduced in Section 12.3.1 to determine the thickness of the temperature and velocity boundary layers for $Pr = 0.07$, 0.7, and 7.0. In the notation of Section 12.3.1,

TABLE 12.11
Answers to Exercise 12.11

Pr	0.07	0.7	7.0
η_{max}	1.2672	0.9535	0.6911
δ_u	13.309	5.8009	4.8762
δ_T	13.455	4.5372	1.8259

the boundary layer thickness for the temperature δ_T is defined as that value of η for which $y_4 = T^*(\eta = \delta_T) = 0.99$, and the boundary layer thickness for the velocity δ_u is defined as that value of η for which $y_2 = u(\eta = \delta_u) = 0.99$. At each value of the Prandtl number, compare the ratio δ_u/δ_T to that predicted by the relation $Pr^{1/3}$. [Answers are given in Table 12.10.]

12.8 Consider air flowing over a flat plate at $u_\infty = 1$ m/s for which $Pr = 0.7$ and $v_{vis} = 1.5 \times 10^{-5}$ m/s². Use the formulation of Section 12.3.1 to compute $T(x,y)$ over the full laminar domain $0 < x < x_{crit}$ and $0 < y < 10x_{crit}/(Re_{crit})^{1/2}$ where

$$Re_{crit} = \frac{u_\infty x_{crit}}{v_{vis}} = 5 \times 10^{-5}$$

Create a contour plot of $T(x,y)$ over this domain. In the notation of Section 12.3.2, $T(x,y) = y_4$ and

$$\eta = y\sqrt{u_\infty/v_{vis}x}$$

12.9 For the same conditions defined in Exercise 12.8, create a contour plot of the stream function

$$\psi = fu_\infty\sqrt{\frac{v_{vis}x}{u_\infty}}$$

12.10 For the natural convection solution of Section 12.3.2, find the value of η at which the velocity u is a maximum for $Pr = 0.07$, 0.7, and 7.0. In the notation of Section 12.3.2 $u = y_2$. Use fminbnd on the negative of u and select the search region based on the curves in Figures 12.13 to 12.15. [Answer: For $Pr = 0.7$, $u_{max} = 0.2784$ at $\eta_{max} = 0.9535$.]

12.11 For the natural convection solution of Section 12.3.2, determine the thickness of the thermal and velocity boundary layers for $Pr = 0.07$, 0.7 and 7.0. In the notation of Section 12.3.2, the boundary layer thickness for the temperature δ_T is defined as that value of η for which $y_4 = T^*(\eta = \delta_T) = 0.01$, and the boundary layer thickness for the velocity δ_u is defined as that value of η for which $y_2 = u(\eta = \delta_u)/u_{max} = 0.01$, where u_{max} are those values found in Exercise 12.4. [Answers are given in Table 12.11.]

12.12 Consider the natural convection of air over a heated plate as described in Section 12.3.2. The dimensional velocities can be expressed in terms of the dimensionless solution as

$$u = \frac{2v_{vis}}{x}Gr_x^{1/2}\frac{df}{d\eta}$$

$$v = \frac{v_{vis}}{x}\left(\frac{Gr_x}{4}\right)^{1/4}\left(\eta\frac{df}{d\eta} - 3f\right)$$

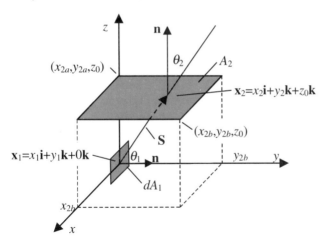

FIGURE 12.24
Geometry when the differential area and the finite rectangle are in perpendicular planes.

For quiescent air at 300 K, compute the velocity components $u(x,y)$ and $v(x,y)$ over the domain $0 < x < 1$ m and $0 < y < 0.25$ m. Plot u and v at a series of five evenly spaced x locations. Refer to Figure 12.12 for the definition of x and y.

12.13 The steam function was defined in Section 12.3.2 as

$$\psi = 4vf \left(\frac{Gr_x}{4} \right)^{1\backslash 4}$$

For air at 300 K, create a contour plot of the stream function over the domain $0 < x < 1$ m and $0 < y < 0.25$ m. Refer to Figure 12.12 for the definition of x and y.

12.14 Based on the analysis given in Section 12.4.1, alter the formulation for the view factors to evaluate the case where the rectangles are in two perpendicular planes. As shown in Figure 12.24, the differential area element is located a distance from a perpendicular plane in which a finite rectangular area exists. For simplicity, we consider only the case where the differential element can see the entire finite rectangle. In other words, the line of intersection of the perpendicular planes cannot pass through the finite rectangle. Using data given in Table 12.12, determine the view factor for the surfaces shown in Figure 12.24. Note that in this case, $\cos\theta_1 \neq \cos\theta_2$.

12.15 Based on the enclosure analysis of Section 12.4.3, recalculate the example given with surface #4 split into two equal size surfaces—that is, the system will now have five surfaces. Assume that the surface properties are the same as those used in the original example. Calculate the heat-transfer rate from each of the surfaces and compare it with the more coarse calculation done originally. Using the surface numbering scheme given in Section 12.4.3, surface 4 is now split in two, and surface #4 refers to the upper half and surface #5 to the lower half. The view factors for this geometry were calculated and are given in Table 12.13. These values were obtained from Hottel's crossed-string method. The results of the enclosure calculation are summarized in Table 12.14.

TABLE 12.12
Parameters and Answers for Exercise 12.14

Parameter	Set #1
Geometry of finite rectangle	
X coordinate of first corner point	−1
Y coordinate of first corner point	−1
X coordinate of opposite corner point	0
Y coordinate of opposite corner point	0
Separation distance between the differential element and the perpendicular plane	5
Computed View Factor (F_{d_1-2})	0.0012

TABLE 12.13
View Factors for Exercise 12.15

i\j	1	2	3	4	5
1	**0**	**0.3615**	**0.2770**	**0.0957**	0.2658
2	0.2169	**0**	**0.2169**	**0.2831**	0.2831
3	0.2770	0.3615	**0**	**0.2658**	0.0957
4	0.1148	0.5662	0.3190	**0**	0
5	0.3190	0.5662	0.1148	0	0

TABLE 12.14
Answers to Exercise 12.15

Surface #	1	2	3	4	5
Q (kW)	−8560	8064	4451	−2373	−1582
T (K)	550	700	650	600	600
q (kW/m^2)	−2853	1613	1484	−949	−633

It is noted that the energy balance is satisfied—that is, the Q's sum to zero. Comparing these results with those in the text, it is seen that the heat-transfer rates (Q) and the fluxes (q) are similar between the two calculations for surfaces 1–3. However, for the surface that was split, it is seen that the flux varies considerably over the length. It is interesting to note that the overall heat-transfer rate (the sum for surfaces #4 and #5) matches reasonably closely with the originally calculated heat-transfer rate.

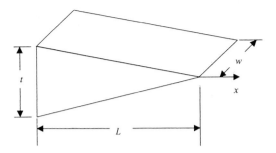

FIGURE 12.25
Triangular fin geometry.

12.16 The transient temperature distribution in a solid sphere, which is initially at a uniform temperature and has convection at the boundary surface, is given by[15]

$$\theta(\xi,\tau) = \sum_{n=1}^{\infty} C_n \exp(-\zeta_n^2 \tau) \frac{\sin(\zeta_n \xi)}{\zeta_n \xi}$$

where

$$\theta(\xi,\tau) = \frac{T(\xi,\tau) - T_\infty}{T(\xi,0) - T_\infty}$$

and $\tau = \alpha t/a^2$, α is the thermal diffusivity, a is the radius of the sphere, t is time, $\xi = r/a$, r is the radial location in the sphere, T_∞ is the ambient air temperature,

$$C_n = \frac{4[\sin\zeta_n - \zeta_n \cos\zeta_n]}{2\zeta_n - \sin 2\zeta_n}$$

and ζ_n are the positive roots of

$$1 - \zeta_n \cot\zeta_n = Bi$$

where $Bi = ha/k$ is the Biot number, h is the heat transfer coefficient, and k is the thermal conductivity of the sphere.

Plot $\theta(\xi,\tau)$ as a function of ξ and τ for $0 \le \xi \le 1$, $0 \le \tau \le 1.5$ and $Bi = 0.5$.

12.17 The steady-state temperature distribution in a triangular fin shown in Figure 12.25 is determined from

$$(1-\eta)\frac{d^2\theta}{d\eta^2} - \frac{d\theta}{d\eta} - M^2\theta = 0$$

where $\eta = x/L$,

---

[15] F. P. Incropera and D. P. DeWitt, *ibid.*, p. 229.

$$\theta(\eta) = \frac{T(\eta) - T_\infty}{T_b - T_\infty}$$

$$M^2 = \frac{2hL^2}{kt} \sqrt{1 + \left(\frac{t}{2L}\right)^2}$$

h is the heat-transfer coefficient, k is the thermal conductivity, and it is assumed that $t/w \ll 1$.
Assume that the boundary condition at $\eta = 0$ is $T(0) = T_b$—that is,

$$\theta(0) = 1$$

and that at $\eta = 1$ the boundary condition is

$$\left.\frac{d\theta}{d\eta}\right|_{\eta=1} = 0$$

The fin efficiency η_f for this fin is obtained from

$$\eta_f = \frac{-1}{M^2} \left.\frac{d\theta}{d\eta}\right|_{\eta=0}$$

Determine the fin efficiency for ten (10) logarithmically equally spaced values from $0.01 < M^2 < 100$
and plot the results using `semilogx`. Compare these results with those from the analytically obtained
expression[16]

$$\eta_f = \frac{1}{M} \frac{I_1(2M)}{I_0(2M)}$$

where $I_n(x)$ in the modified Bessel function of the first kind of order n and is determined from
`besseli`.

BIBLIOGRAPHY

J. P. Holman, *Heat Transfer*, 7th ed. McGraw Hill, New York, 1990.

F. P. Incropera and D.P. DeWitt, *Fundamentals of Heat and Mass Transfer*, 4th ed. John Wiley &
Sons, New York, 1996.

S. Kakaç and H. Liu, *Heat Exchangers: Selection, Rating and Thermal Design*, CRC Press, Boca
Raton, FL, 1998.

F. Krieth and M. S. Bohn, *Principles of Heat Transfer*, 5th ed. West Publishing Co., New York, 1993.

A. F. Mills, *Heat Transfer*, Irwin, Boston, 1992.

R. Siegel and J. R. Howell, *Thermal Radiation Heat Transfer*, 3rd ed. Hemisphere Publishing Co.,
Washington, DC, 1992.

N. V. Suryanarayana, *Engineering Heat Transfer*, West Publishing Co., New York, 1995.

---

[16] F. P. Incropera and D. P. DeWitt, *ibid.*, p. 125.

C H A P T E R   1 3

OPTIMIZATION

Shapour Azarm

Representative examples from a range of engineering optimization problems are solved using MATLAB's Optimization toolbox.

13.1 DEFINITION, FORMULATION, AND GRAPHICAL SOLUTIONS

13.1.1 Introduction

Optimization in engineering refers to the process of finding the "best" possible values for a set of variables for a system while satisfying various constraints. The term "best" indicates that there is one or more design objectives that the decisionmaker wishes to optimize by either minimizing or maximizing. For example, one might want to design the best possible product by maximizing its reliability while minimizing its weight and cost. In an optimization process, variables are selected to describe the system (e.g., size, shape, material type, operational characteristics). An objective refers to a quantity that the decisionmaker wants to be made as high (a maximum) or as low (a minimum) as possible. A constraint refers to a quantity that indicates a restriction or limitation on an aspect of the system's technological capabilities.

Generally speaking, an optimization problem involves minimizing one or more objective functions subject to some constraints, and is stated as

$$\underset{x \in D}{\text{minimize}} \ \{f_1(x), f_2(x), \ldots, f_m(x)\} \tag{13.1}$$

where f_i, $i = 1, \ldots, m$, is a scalar objective function that maps a variable vector x into the objective space. The n-dimensional design variable vector x is constrained to lie in a region D, called the feasible domain. Constraints to the above problem are included in the specification of the feasible domain. In general, the feasible domain is constrained by J-inequality and/or K-equality constraints as

$$D = \{x : g_j(x) \le 0, \ h_k(x) = 0, \ j = 1, \ldots, J, \ k = 1, \ldots, K\} \tag{13.2}$$

An optimization problem in which the objective and constraint functions are linear functions of their variables is referred to as a linear programming problem. On the other hand, if at least one of the objective or constraint functions is nonlinear, then it is referred to as a nonlinear programming problem.

The classes of optimization problems, the MATLAB solution functions, and the examples appearing in this chapter are summarized in Table 13.1.

13.1.2 Graphical Solution

Solutions to optimization problems with two variables can be visualized with MATLAB's plotting capabilities. This is demonstrated with the following example.

Example 13.1 Two-spring system

Consider a two-spring system[1] shown in Figure 13.1. The system in Figure 13.1(a) shows an unloaded and undeformed spring system. After the loads are applied at joint A, the system is deformed until it is in equilibrium. This is shown by the loaded and deformed system in Figure 13.1(b). We are interested in finding the equilibrium state of the loaded system—that is, the location (x_1, x_2) of joint A in Figure 13.1(b).

The equilibrium state of the system is obtained by deriving the potential energy (PE) for the system and then minimizing it with respect to the design variables x_1 and x_2 to obtain the location of joint A. The potential energy is computed from the difference between the strain energies of the springs, which is given by the first two terms in the Eq. (13.3), and the work done by external forces, which is given by the last two terms in Eq. (13.3). The quantities k_1, k_2, L_1, L_2, P_1, and P_2 are constants whose values are shown in Figure 13.1. Hence, the objective function of the unconstrained optimization problem is

---

[1] G. Vanderplaats, *Numerical Optimization Techniques for Engineering Design*, McGraw-Hill, New York, 1984, pp. 72–73.

TABLE 13.1
Classification of Optimization Problems, MATLAB Functions, and Examples Given in Chapter 13

Problem Class	MATLAB Function	Example
Linear Programming	`linprog`	13.2 Production planning
Nonlinear Programming:		
Single-objective unconstrained:		
multivariable	`fminunc`	13.1 & 13.3 Two-spring system
	`fminsearch`	
curve fitting	`lsqcurvefit`	13.4 Stress-strain relationship
least-squares	`lsqnonlin`	13.5 Stress-strain relationship
		13.6 Semi-empirical P-v-T relationship
Single-objective constrained:		
single-variable	`fminbnd`	13.7 Piping cost in a plant
multivariable	`fmincon`	13.8 Two-bar truss
		13.9 Helical compression spring
		13.10 Gear reducer
quadratic	`quadprog`	13.11 Production planning
semi-infinite	`fseminf`	13.12 Planar two-link manipulator
Multiobjective:	`fminimax`	13.13 Vibrating platform
	`fgoalattain`	13.14 Production planning

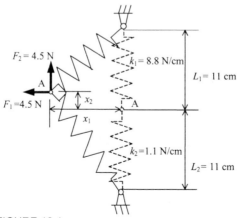

FIGURE 13.1
Two-spring system.

$$\underset{x_1, x_2}{\text{minimize}}\ PE(x_1, x_2) = 0.5k_1 \left(\sqrt{x_1^2 + (L_1 - x_2)^2} - L_1 \right)^2 +$$

$$0.5k_2 \left(\sqrt{x_1^2 + (L_2 + x_2)^2} - L_2 \right)^2 - F_1 x_1 - F_2 x_2 \qquad (13.3)$$

There are two variables, x_1 and x_2, in the objective function, and, hence, their approximate values can be estimated graphically. The script is

```
k1 = 8.8; k2 = 1.1; L1 = 11; L2 = 11; F1 = 4.5; F2 = 4.5;
[x1,x2] = meshgrid(linspace(-5,15,15),linspace(-5,15,15));
PE1 = 1/2*k1*(sqrt(x1.^2+(L1-x2).^2)-L1).^2;
PE2 = 1/2*k2*(sqrt(x1.^2+(L2+x2).^2)-L2).^2;
PE = PE1+PE2-F1*x1-F2*x2;
subplot(1,2,1);
h = contour(x1,x2,PE,[-40:20:20 70:70:490],'k');
clabel(h);
axis([-5 15 -5 15])
subplot(1,2,2);
surfc(x1,x2,PE);
axis([-10 15 -10 15 -100 500])
```

The execution of the script produces the results shown in Figure 13.2, wherein Figure 13.2(a) shows a contour plot of *PE*. The contours are labeled with their numerical values so that the location of the minimum/maximum point can be visually located. Figure 13.2(b) shows the surface plot of *PE* with the contours shown below the surface. It also shows the approximate location of the minimum/maximum point, the point where the *PE* function reaches its minimum/maximum value. The exact location of the minimum/maximum point for this example is obtained in Section 13.3.1 using an unconstrained minimization technique in fminunc.

13.2 Linear Programming

Linear programming (LP) refers to an optimization method applicable to the solution of problems in which the objective and constraint functions are linear functions of the design variables. An LP problem can be stated as follows:

$$\text{minimize}\ f'x$$
$$\text{subject to}:\ \ Ax \le b$$
$$A_{eq} x = b_{eq} \qquad (13.4)$$
$$L_{bound} \le x \le U_{bound}$$

where f', b, and b_{eq} are vectors and A and A_{eq} are matrices. The quantity x is a vector of design variables, and the apostrophe indicates the transpose. The matrix A and the vector b

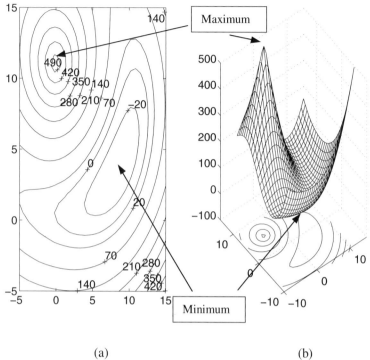

(a)   (b)

FIGURE 13.2
(a) Contour and (b) surface plots of the PE function for the two-spring system shown in Figure 13.1.

are the coefficients of the linear inequality constraints, and A_{eq} and b_{eq} are the coefficients of the equality constraints. The MATLAB linear programming solver is linprog, which is used to solve the problem given by Eq. (13.4). The basic command is

[xopt,fopt] = linprog (f,A,b,Aeq,beq,LBnd,UBnd,x0,options)

which returns a vector x_{opt} of the design variables and the scalar $f(x_{opt})$. The quantities *LBnd* and *UBnd* are vectors representing the lower and upper bounds L_{bound} and U_{bound}, respectively. The quantity $x0$ sets the starting points to x, and *options* sets the parameters described in optimset.

We now demonstrate the use of linprog in the following example.

Example 13.2 Production planning

Consider two liquid products, A and B, that require production time in two departments. Product A requires 1 hour in the first department and 1.25 hours in the second department. Product B requires 1 hour in the first department and 0.75 hours in the second department. The available hours in each department are 200 hours monthly. Furthermore, there is a maximum market potential of 150 units for product B. Assume that the profits are \$4 and \$5 per unit of product A and B, respectively. We shall determine the number of units of products A and B that should be produced so that the producer's profit is maximized.

We first assume that x_1 represents the number of units of product A to be produced, and x_2 the number of units of product B. Then the objective function and the constraints are[2]

$$\text{minimize } f(x_1, x_2) = -4x_1 - 5x_2$$

subject to :

$$g_1 : \quad x_1 + x_2 \le 200$$
$$g_2 : \quad 1.25\, x_1 + 0.75\, x_2 \le 200$$
$$g_3 : \quad x_2 \le 150$$
$$(x_1, x_2) \ge 0$$

Thus,

$$f' = [-4\ -5]$$

and the inequality constraints are expressed as

$$\begin{bmatrix} 1 & 1 \\ 1.25 & 0.75 \\ 0 & 1 \end{bmatrix} \begin{bmatrix} x_1 \\ x_2 \end{bmatrix} \le \begin{bmatrix} 200 \\ 200 \\ 150 \end{bmatrix}$$

The script is

```
f = [-4,-5];
A = [1,1; 1.25,0.75; 0,1];
b = [200,200,150];
LBnd = [0 0];
x = linprog(f,A,b,[],[],LBnd,[])
```

which, upon execution, gives the optimum number of units of product A and B, respectively: $x_1 = 50$ and $x_2 = 150$.

13.3 NONLINEAR PROGRAMMING

Nonlinear programming (NLP) refers to an optimization method in which the objective or constraint function (or both) is a nonlinear function of the design variables. NLP problems and the corresponding methods are divided into two classes: the unconstrained methods and the constrained methods.

---

[2] A. Osyczka, *Multicriterion Optimization in Engineering with Fortran Programs*, Ellis Horwood Limited, West Sussex, England, p. 4, 1984.

13.3.1 Unconstrained Methods

Unconstrained NLP methods find the minimum of an unconstrained multivariable function formulated as

$$\underset{x}{\text{minimize}} \quad f(x) \qquad (13.5)$$

where x is a vector of design variables and f is a scalar objective function. There are two functions that can be used to solve the problem of the type given by Eq. (13.5):

    fminunc

and

    fminsearch

which are, respectively, based on derivative- and nonderivative-based optimization solution techniques. The command to invoke fminunc is

    [xopt,fopt] = fminunc(UserFunction,x0,options,p1,p2,...)

where *UserFunction* is the name of the function file that computes the objective function f and is in *single quotes*, but without the suffix ".m". When *UserFunction* is created by inline, the variable name is written *without any quotes*. The quantity $x0$ is the vector of starting values for x, and *options* set the parameters described in optimset. An empty matrix [] is used for *options* to indicate that the default quantities are to be used. The quantities $p1$, $p2$, ... are parameters that are passed to *UserFunction*.

The command to invoke fminsearch is

    x = fminsearch(UserFunction,x0,options,p1,p2,...)

where the definitions of its arguments are the same as for fminunc.

We now illustrate the use of fminunc.

Example 13.3 Two-spring system revisited

The two-spring system of Example 13.1 is now solved numerically as an unconstrained optimization problem. First, the following unconstrained objective function is created with the design variables x_1 and x_2:

```
function PE = SpringEquilibrium(x,k1,k2,L1,L2,F1,F2)
PE1 = 1/2*k1*(sqrt(x(1)^2+(L1−x(2))^2)−L1)^2;
PE2 = 1/2*k2*(sqrt(x(1)^2+(L2+x(2))^2)−L2)^2;
PE = PE1+PE2−F1*x(1)−F2*x(2);
```

Then the script is

```
x0 = [0.5,5];
k1 = 8.8; k2 = 1.1; L1 = 11; L2 = 11; F1 = 4.5; F2 = 4.5;
options = optimset('MaxIter',600);
[x,f] = fminunc('SpringEquilibrium',x0,options,k1,k2,L1,L2,F1,F2)
```

which gives x = [8.4251 3.6331] and f = PE = –35.0507. This solution agrees with the approximate location of solution shown in Figure 13.2. To obtain the maximum value of the PE function, one can either minimize the inverse (1/PE) or the negative (–PE) of the potential energy function. Thus, *SpringEquilibrium* is changed to

```
function PE = SpringEquilibriumMax(x,k1,k2,L1,L2,F1,F2)
PE1 = 1/2*k1*(sqrt(x(1)^2+(L1–x(2))^2)–L1)^2;
PE2 = 1/2*k2*(sqrt(x(1)^2+(L2+x(2))^2)–L2)^2;
PE = –(PE1+PE2–F1*x(1)–F2*x(2));
```

When this is done, we find that x = [0 11] and PE = 549.45. We see that the coordinates agree with the approximate location of the maximum shown in Figure 13.2 but, because of the course grid used to plot these results, the magnitude does not. This solution is sensitive to both the starting guess and to the maximum number of iterations. To obtain these results, the maximum number of iterations was increased to 600.

13.3.2 Fitting Curves to Data

Nonlinear curve-fitting problems can be solved in a least-squares sense with `lsqcurvefit`. Given a set of input values x_i and a corresponding set of output values y_i, this function finds the coefficients x_c for the "best-fit" of the equation $f(x_c, x_i)$—that is,

$$\text{minimize} \; \underset{x_c}{} \; \frac{1}{2} \sum_i \left[f(x_c, x_i) - y_i \right]^2 \tag{13.6}$$

MATLAB uses two optimization methods for solving the problem of the type shown in Eq. (13.6). The default method is based on a combination of the gradient and Newton methods. The other method is based on the Gauss-Newton method. The basic command is

```
[xopt,res] = lsqcurvefit (UserFunction,x0,xdata,ydata,
                          LBnd,UBnd,options,p1,p2,...)
```

where $xopt = x_{opt}$ is the optimum value of x_c, $res = f(x_{opt}, x_i)$ and *UserFunction* is the name of the function file that computes the objective function and is in *single quotes*, but without the suffix ".m". When *UserFunction* is created by `inline` the variable name is written *without any quotes*. The quantity $x0$ is the vector of starting values, *xdata* and *ydata* are, respectively, vectors of the input and output dat; x_i and y_i, and *options* set the parameters

TABLE 13.2
Stress-Strain Data for a Plastic Material

σ	ε
925	0.11
1125	0.16
1620	0.35
2125	0.48
2625	0.61
3125	0.71
3625	0.85

described in optimset. The quantities *LBnd* and *UBnd*, respectively, are vectors representing the lower and upper bounds on *x*—that is,

$$L_{bound} \le x \le U_{bound}$$

An empty matrix [] is used for *LBnd* and *UBnd* when they are not used and for *options* to indicate that the default quantities are to be used. The quantities *p1, p2, ...* are parameters that are passed to *UserFunction*.

The lsqcurvefit function is now demonstrated.

Example 13.4 Stress-strain relationship

Stress-strain data are given for a plastic material in Table 13.2, where σ is the stress in ksi and ε is the strain. Assume that the relationship between the stress and strain is of the form

$$\varepsilon = a + b \ln \sigma \tag{13.7}$$

The objective is to find the design variables *a* and *b* that produce the best-fit function based on the data values given in Table 13.2. The function required by lsqcurvefit is given by the inline function *SigmaEpsilonFit*. The script is

```
sigma = [925,1125,1625,2125,2625,3125,3625];
epsilon = [0.11,0.16,0.35,0.48,0.61,0.71,0.85];
x0 = [0.1,0.1];
SigmaEpsilonFit = inline('x(1)+x(2)*log(sigma)','x','sigma');
[x,resid] = lsqcurvefit(SigmaEpsilonFit,x0,sigma,epsilon)
```

which, upon execution, gives $x(1) = a = -3.581$ and $x(2) = b = 0.5344$ with a residual of *resid* = 0.0064. Thus, the best-fit function is

$$\varepsilon = -3.581 + 0.5344 \ln \sigma \tag{13.8}$$

13.3.3 Least Squares

Nonlinear least-squares problems are solved with lsqnonlin. This function can also be used for curve fitting, as shown in Example 13.5. However, lsqnonlin is mainly used for problems with multiple sets of input data and single set of observed output data, as shown in Example 13.6. The lsqnonlin function finds x such that

$$\underset{x}{\text{minimize}} \quad \sum_i [f_i(x)]^2 \tag{13.9}$$

The lsqnonlin function is

[xopt,residual] = lsqnonlin(UserFunction,x0,LowBnd,UpBnd,options,,p1,p2,...)

where

$$\text{residual} = \sum_i f_i(x_{opt})^2$$

UserFunction is the name of the function file that computes the objective function and is in *single quotes*, but without the suffix ".m". When *UserFunction* is created by inline, the variable name is written *without any quotes*. *UserFunction* creates the objective functions $f_i(x)$ *not* $f_i^2(x)$. The quantitiy $x0$ is the vector of starting values, *LowBnd* and *UpBnd* are the lower and upper bounds on x, *options* sets the parameters described in optimset, and $p1$, $p2$, ... are parameters passed to *UserFunction*. Empty matrices [] may be used when *LowBnd* and *UpBnd* are not specified and for *options* to indicate that the default values are used.

The lsqnonlin function is now demonstrated.

Example 13.5 Stress-strain relationship revisited

The stress-strain relationship of Example 13.4 is now solved with lsqnonlin. The design variables a and b are determined by minimizing

$$\underset{a,b}{\text{minimize}} \quad \sum_{i=1}^{7} [\varepsilon_i - (a + b \ln \sigma_i)]^2 \tag{13.10}$$

where ε_i and σ_i correspond to the experimentally obtained values in Table 13.2.
The script is

```
sigma = [925,1125,1625,2125,2625,3125,3625];
epsilon = [0.11,0.16,0.35,0.48,0.61,0.71,0.85];
x0 = [0.1,0.1];
SigmaEpsilonLeastSq = inline('epsilon-(x(1)+x(2)*log(sigma))','x','sigma',
            'epsilon');
[x,residual] = lsqnonlin(SigmaEpsilonLeastSq,x0,[],[],[],sigma,epsilon)
```

TABLE 13.3
P-v-T Data for a gas

Run i	P (atm)	v, (cm³/g.mol)	T (K)
1	32.7	480	283
2	42.6	480	313
3	44.5	576	375
4	25.7	672	283
5	36.6	576	313
6	38.6	672	375
7	37.6	384	283
8	63.0	384	375

which, upon execution, gives $x(1) = a = -3.581$, $x(2) = b = 0.5344$, and $residual = 0.0064$. These results are the same as those obtained in Example 13.4.

Example 13.6 Semi-empirical P-v-T relationship

It is well known that the P-v-T relationship of real gases deviates from that estimated by the ideal gas

$$Pv = RT \tag{13.11}$$

where P is the pressure in atm, v is the molar volume in cm³/g mol, T is the temperature in K, and R is a gas constant equal to 82.06 atm cm³/g mol K. A semi-empirical relationship used to correct the departure from the ideal gas is[3]

$$P = \frac{RT}{v-b} - \frac{a}{v(v+b)\sqrt{T}} \tag{13.12}$$

where the values of a and b are obtained from experimental data. Listed in Table 13.3 are the P-v-T experimental measurements obtained for the gas. The design variables a and b are determined by minimizing the following least-squares objective function:

$$\underset{a,b}{\text{minimize}} \sum_{i=1}^{8} \left[P_i - \frac{RT_i}{v_i - b} + \frac{a}{v_i(v_i + b)\sqrt{T_i}} \right]^2 \tag{13.13}$$

where P_i, v_i, and T_i correspond to the values at the ith experimentally obtained conditions shown in Table 13.3. If the semi-empirical relationship given by Eq. (13.12) is to exactly match the experimental data, then at the optimum the objective function of Eq. (13.13) would be equal to zero. However, because of the experimental error and the simplicity of

---

[3] G.V. Reklaitis, et al., *Engineering Optimization*, John Wiley & Sons, New York, pp. 20–22, 1983.

the semi-empirical relationship to model the gas nonlinearities, the objective function of Eq. (13.13) will not be equal to zero at the optimum.

The script is

```
x0 = [8000,40]; R = 82.06;
T = [283,313,375,283,313,375,283,375];
v = [480,480,576,672,576,672,384,384];
P = [32.7,42.7,47.5,25.7,36.6,38.6,37.6,63.0];
pvt = inline('P–R*T./(v–x(2))+x(1)./(sqrt(T).*v.*(v+x(2)))','x','R','T','v','P');
format long e;
options = optimset('MaxFunEvals','600');
[x,residual] = lsqnonlin(pvt,x0,[],[],options,R,T,v,P)
format short
```

which, upon execution, gives $a = x(1) = 5.424 \times 10^7$ and $b = x(2) = 3.32$, with *residual* = 23.4. Thus, the best-fit function is

$$P = \frac{RT}{v} - \frac{5.425 \times 10^7}{v(v + 3.32)\sqrt{T}}$$

(13.14)

13.4 SINGLE-OBJECTIVE CONSTRAINED METHODS

Constrained nonlinear optimization methods find the minimum of a constrained function as formulated by Eqs. (13.1) and (13.2) for the case of a single objective function—that is, $m = 1$.

13.4.1 Constrained Single-Variable Method

The constrained single-variable method finds the minimum of a function of one variable on a fixed interval

$$\text{minimize } f(x) \quad \text{subject to} \quad a_1 \leq x \leq a_2$$
$$x$$

(13.15)

The MATLAB command is

```
[xopt,fxopt] = fminbnd(UserFunction,a1,a2,options,p1,p2,...)
```

where $xopt = x_{opt}$ is the optimum value of x, $fxopt = f(x_{opt})$, and *UserFunction* is the name of the function file that computes the objective function and is in *single quotes*, but without the suffix ".m". When *UserFunction* is created by inline, the variable name is written *without any quotes*. The quantities $a1$ and $a2$ define the interval over which *UserFunction* is minimized with respect to x, *options* sets parameters described in optimset, and $p1, p2,...$ are additional parameters passed to *UserFunction*. The fminbnd function is now demonstrated.

Example 13.7 Piping cost in a plant

Piping costs, including the fittings and pumping costs, are important considerations in the design of a chemical plant. Consider the design of a pipeline that is L feet long and is to carry fluid at the rate of Q gpm. The objective is to determine the pipe diameter D (in inches) that minimizes the annual pumping cost. For a standard carbon steel pump, the annual pumping cost can be estimated from[4]

$$f(D) = 0.45L + 0.245LD^{1.5} + 325(hp)^{0.5} + 61.6(hp)^{0.925} + 102 \qquad (13.16)$$

where

$$hp = 4.4 \times 10^{-8} \frac{LQ^3}{D^5} + 1.92 \times 10^{-9} \frac{LQ^{2.68}}{D^{4.68}} \qquad (13.17)$$

We shall now obtain the pipe diameter D for a minimum cost of a pipe with the length of 1,000 ft and a flow rate of 20 gpm. First we create the following function.

```
function f = PipeLineCost(D,L,Q)
hp = 4.4*10^(-8)*L*Q^3/D^5+(1.92*10^(-9)*L*Q^2.68)/(D^4.68);
f = 0.45*L+0.245*L*D^1.5+325*hp^0.5+61.6*hp^0.925+102;
```

The pipe diameter for the minimum piping cost is determined from the following script.

```
L = 1000; Q = 20;
[D,fD] = fminbnd('PipeLineCost',0.25,6,[],L,Q)
```

which, upon execution, gives $D = 1.117$ inches and $fD = f(D) = 1{,}003$ \$/yr.

13.4.2 Constrained Multivariable Method

The constrained multivariable method is invoked by `fmincon`, which finds the minimum of a nonlinear multivariable constrained optimization problem. Both equality and inequality constraints can be considered. Also, both the objective and/or the constraint functions can be nonlinear. A nonlinear multivariable constrained optimization problem is stated as

$$\begin{aligned}
\underset{x}{\text{minimize}} \ \ & f(x) \\
\text{subject to}: \ \ & Ax \le b && \text{(linear inequality constraints)} \\
& A_{eq}x = b_{eq} && \text{(linear equality constraints)} \\
& C(x) \le 0 && \text{(nonlinear inequality constraints)} \\
& C_{eq}(x) = 0 && \text{(nonlinear equality constaints)} \\
& L_{bound} \le x \le U_{bound}
\end{aligned} \qquad (13.18)$$

---

[4] G.V. Reklaitis, et al., *ibid.*, pp.66–67.

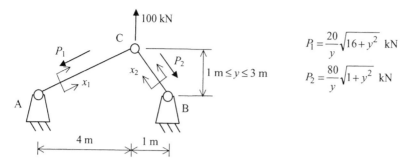

$$P_1 = \frac{20}{y}\sqrt{16+y^2} \text{ kN}$$

$$P_2 = \frac{80}{y}\sqrt{1+y^2} \text{ kN}$$

FIGURE 13.3
Two-bar truss: x_1 and x_2 are cross-sectional areas.

The basic command is

$$[xopt,fxopt] = \texttt{fmincon}(UserFunction,x0,A,b,Aeq,beq,LBnd,UBnd,$$
$$\text{'NonLinConstr',options,p1,p2, ...)}$$

where $xopt = x_{opt}$ is the optimum value of x, fxopt $= f(x_{opt})$, and *UserFunction* is the name of the function file that computes the objective function and is in *single quotes*, but without the suffix ".m". It must create an output in the order specified in the help file for `fmincon`. When *UserFunction* is created by `inline`, the variable name is written *without any quotes*. The quantity $x0$ is the vector of starting values; the matrix A and the vector b are the coefficients of the linear inequality constraints; the matrix *Aeq* and the vector *beq* are the coefficients of the equality constraints; *LBnd* and *UBnd* are the vectors of the lower and upper bounds on x, respectively; *options* sets the parameters described in `optimset`; and $p1, p2, \ldots$ are the additional arguments that are passed to *UserFucntion* and *NonLinConstr*. The quantity *NonLinConstr* is a function that defines the nonlinear constraints in the order prescribed in the help file for `fmincon`. The arguments $p1$, $p2$, ... of *UserFunction* and *NonLinConstr must be identical*, even if only one of the functions uses these values. If *LowBnd*, *Upbnd*, and *options* are not specified, use []; similarly for A, b, *Aeq*, and *beq*.

We now demonstrate the use of `fmincon`.

Example 13.8 Two-bar truss

Consider the two-bar truss shown in Figure 13.3. The objective is to minimize the volume of the two bars AC and BC. There are three variables in the problem. They are x_1 and x_2, the cross-sectional areas of the two bars AC and BC, respectively, and y, which is the vertical position of joint C. There are also several constraints. The tensile stresses on the two bars are limited by a permissible stress $\sigma = 10^5$ kPa. The variable y is to remain between 1 and 3 m. Finally, x_1 and x_2 are non-negative. The optimization problem is formulated as[5]

---

[5] U. Kirsch, *Optimal Structural Design*, McGraw-Hill, New York, 1981.

$$\text{minimize } f_{volume} = x_1\sqrt{16 + y^2} + x_2\sqrt{1 + y^2}$$

subject to :

$$g_1 : \frac{20\sqrt{16 + y^2}}{yx_1} - \sigma \le 0$$

$$g_2 : \frac{80\sqrt{1 + y^2}}{yx_2} - \sigma \le 0$$ (13.19)

$$1 \le y \le 3$$

$$(x_1, x_2) \ge 0$$

Therefore, $A = b = A_{eq} = b_{eq} = C_{eq} = 0$, $L_{bound} = [1, 0, 0]$, and $U_{bound} = [3, \infty, \infty]$.
The functions are

```
function f = TrussNonLinF(x,sigma)
y = x(1); x1 = x(2); x2 = x(3);
f = x1*sqrt(16+y^2)+x2*sqrt(1+y^2);
```

and

```
function [C,Ceq] = TrussNonLinCon(x,sigma)
y = x(1); x1 = x(2); x2 = x(3);
C(1) = 20*sqrt(16+y^2)–sigma*y*x1;
C(2) = 80*sqrt(1+y^2)–sigma*y*x2;
Ceq = [];
```

The script is

```
x0 = [1,1,1]; sigma = 10^5;
Lbnd = [1 0 0]; Ubnd = [3 inf inf];
[x,f] = fmincon('TrussNonLinF',x0,[],[],[],[],Lbnd,Ubnd,'TrussNonLinCon',[],sigma)
```

which, upon execution, gives $x(1) = y = 1.952$, $x(2) = x_1 = 0.0005$, $x(3) = x_2 = 0.0009$, and $f = 0.004$.

Example 13.9 Helical compression spring

Helical compression springs can be found in numerous mechanical devices. They are used to exert force, to provide flexibility, and to either store or absorb energy. To design a helical compression spring, design criteria such as fatigue, yielding, surging, and buckling may have to be taken into consideration. To obtain a solution that meets the various mechanical requirements, an optimization study is performed. The problem as formulated below has one design objective, two design variables, seven constraints, and upper and lower bounds on the variables.

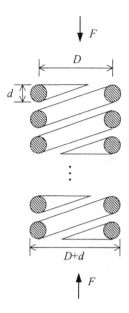

FIGURE 13.4
Helical compression spring.

The design objective is to minimize the inverse of the safety factor, which is equivalent to maximizing the safety factor. Referring to Figure 13.4, the two design variables are c and d, where $c = D/d$ is the spring index, D is the mean coil diameter, and d is the wire diameter. The design objective is to minimize the inverse of the safety factor for fatigue or yielding, whichever is critical. For fatigue, the inverse of the safety factor SF_f is obtained from

$$\frac{1}{SF_f} = \frac{\tau_a}{S_{ns}} + \frac{\tau_m}{S_{us}} \tag{13.20}$$

where τ_a and τ_m are, respectively, the alternating and mean components of the shear stress; S_{ns} is the spring's material fatigue strength; and S_{us} is the ultimate strength. For yielding, the inverse of the safety factor SF_y is obtained from

$$\frac{1}{SF_y} = \frac{\tau_a + \tau_m}{S_{ys}} \tag{13.21}$$

where S_{ys} is the shear yield strength. If the following condition is satisfied

$$\frac{\tau_a}{\tau_m} \geq \frac{S_{ns}(S_{ys} - S_{us})}{S_{us}(S_{ns} - S_{ys})} \tag{13.22}$$

then the inverse of the safety factor for fatigue, Eq. (13.20), will be the objective function; otherwise, the inverse of the safety factor for yielding, Eq. (13.21), will be the objective function. The mean and alternating components of the shear stress are, respectively,

$$\tau_a = \frac{8F_a c K_w}{\pi d^2}$$

$$\tau_m = \frac{8F_m c K_w}{\pi d^2}$$

(13.23)

where

$$K_w = \frac{4c-1}{4c+4} + \frac{0.615}{c}$$

$$F_a = (F_U - F_L)/2$$

$$F_m = (F_U + F_L)/2$$

(13.24)

and F_U and F_L are, respectively, the maximum and minimum applied compressive forces along the spring's axis; F_a and τ_a are, respectively, the alternating force and shear stress; F_m and τ_m are, respectively, the mean force and shear stress; and K_w is the Wahl correction factor for the curvature and direct shear effects on the spring.

The overall design optimization formulation for the helical compression spring is as follows. The design objective is to either

$$\text{minimize} \quad \frac{1}{SF_f} = \frac{\tau_a}{S_{ns}} + \frac{\tau_m}{S_{us}}$$

(13.25)

for fatigue or to

$$\text{minimize} \quad \frac{1}{SF_y} = \frac{\tau_a + \tau_m}{S_{ys}}$$

(13.26)

for yielding, depending on whether or not Eq. (13.22) is satisfied. The objective function is subjected to the following constraints:

g_1: $K_1 d^2 - c \le 0$ Surging

g_2: $K_2 - c^5 \le 0$ Buckling

g_3: $K_3 c^3 - d \le 0$ Minimum number of coils

g_4: $K_4 d^2 c^{-3} + K_8 d - 1 \le 0$ Pocket length   (13.27)

g_5: $K_5(cd + d) - 1 \le 0$ Maximum coil diameter

g_6: $c^{-1} + K_6 d^{-1} c^{-1} - 1 \le 0$ Minimum coil diameter

$g_7: K_7 c^3 - d^2 \leq 0$ Clash allowance

where

$$K_1 = \frac{G f_r \Delta}{112800(F_U - F_L)} \qquad K_2 = \frac{G F_U(1 + A)}{22.3 k^2} \qquad K_3 = \frac{8 k N_{min}}{G}$$

$$K_4 = \frac{G(1 + A)}{8 k L_m} \qquad K_5 = \frac{1}{OD} \qquad K_6 = ID$$

$$K_7 = \frac{0.8(F_U - F_L)}{AG} \qquad K_8 = \frac{Q}{L_m} \qquad k = \frac{F_U - F_L}{\Delta} \qquad (13.28)$$

$$S_{ns} = C_1 d^{A_1} \overline{NC}^{B_1} \qquad S_{us} = C_2 d^{A_1} \qquad S_{ys} = C_3 d^{A_1}$$

The above quantities are identified below along with their assumed values for this problem as follows:

$A = 0.4$	dimensionless clearance constant
$f_r = 500$ Hz	minimum allowable natural frequency
$G = 11.5 \times 10^6$ psi	shear modulus for steel
$ID = 0.75$ in	minimum allowable inside diameter of the spring
$OD = 1.5$ in	maximum allowable outside diameter of the spring
$N_{min} = 3$	minimum allowable number of coils
$L_m = 1.25$ in	maximum spring length under maximum load
$Q = 2$	number of inactive coils
$\overline{NC} = 10^6$ cycles	number of cycles to failure
$\Delta = 0.25$ in	spring deflection

The spring material is piano wire for which $A_1 = 0.14$, $B_1 = -0.2137$, $C_1 = 630,500$, $C_2 = 160,000$, and $C_3 = 86,550$. The lower and upper bounds on the spring index c and wire diameter d are

$$4 \leq c \leq 20$$

and

$$0.004 \leq d \leq 0.25$$

respectively.

Thus, we first create the following three functions. The first is *SpringParameters*, which computes the various spring constants required by the subsequent two functions.

```
function [K,Fa,Fm] = SpringParameters(A,FL,FU,G,fr,ID,OD,Lm,Nmin,Q,Delta)
Fa = (FU–FL)/2;
Fm = (FU+FL)/2;
```

```
k = (FU–FL)/Delta;
K(1) = G*fr*Delta/(112800*(FU–FL));
K(2) = G*FU*(1+A)/(22.3*k^2);
K(3) = 8*k*Nmin/G;
K(4) = G*(1+A)/(8*k*Lm);
K(5) = 1/OD;
K(6) = ID;
K(7) = 0.8*(FU–FL)/(A*G);
K(8) = Q/Lm;
```

The second is *SpringNLConstr*, which computes the nonlinear constraints.

```
function [C,Ceq] = SpringNLConstr(x,K,Fa,Fm,NC,A1,B1,C1,C2,C3)
c = x(1); d = x(2);
C(1) = K(1)*d^2–c;
C(2) = K(2)–c^5;
C(3) = K(3)*c^3–d;
C(4) = K(4)*d^2/c^3+K(8)*d–1;
C(5) = K(5)*(c*d+d)–1;
C(6) = 1/c+K(6)/c/d–1;
C(7) = K(7)*c^3–d^2;
Ceq = [];
```

The third is *SpringObjFunct*, which computes the objective function.

```
function f = SpringObjFunct(x,K,Fa,Fm,NC,A1,B1,C1,C2,C3)
c = x(1); d = x(2);
Sns = C1*d^A1*NC^B1;
Sus = C2*d^A1;
Sys = C3*d^A1;
Kw = (4*c–1)/(4*c+4)+0.615/c;
Temp = 8*c*Kw/(pi*d^2);
TauA = Fa*Temp;
TauM = Fm*Temp;
Ratio = TauA/TauM;
SS = Sns*(Sys –Sus)/(Sus*(Sns–Sys));
if (Ratio–SS)>=0
  f = TauA/Sns+TauM/Sus;
else
  f = (TauA+TauM)/Sys;
end
```

The script is

```
A = 0.4; FL = 15; FU = 30; G = 11.5e6;
```

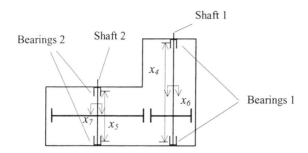

FIGURE 13.5
Reduction gear.

```
fr = 500; ID = 0.75; OD = 1.5; Lm = 1.25;
NC = 10^6; Nmin = 3; Q = 2; Delta = 0.25;
A1 = -0.14; B1 = -0.2137;
C1 = 630500; C2 = 160000; C3 = 86550;
[K,Fa,Fm] = SpringParameters(A,FL,FU,G,fr,ID,OD,Lm,Nmin,Q,Delta);
x0 = [10,10];
LBnd = [4 0.004]; UBnd = [20 0.25];
[x,f] = fmincon('SpringObjFunct',x0,[],[],[],[],LBnd,UBnd,'SpringNLConstr',[],...
                K,Fa,Fm,NC,A1,B1,C1,C2,C3)
SafetyFactor = 1/f
```

which, upon execution, gives $x(1) = c = 8.499$, $x(2) = d = 0.100$, and safety factor $= 1.84$.

Example 13.10 Gear reducer

Consider the design of a gear train with two gears, a gear and a pinion, shown in Figure 13.5. We shall minimize the volume of these two gears and their corresponding shafts. There are seven design variables as follows:

x_1 = gear face width

x_2 = module

x_3 = number of teeth of the pinion

x_4 = distance between bearing set 1

x_5 = distance between bearing set 2

x_6 = diameter of shaft 1

x_7 = diameter of shaft 2

The application is such that the lower and upper limits on these variables are

$$2.6 \le x_1 \le 3.6$$
$$0.7 \le x_2 \le 0.8$$

$$17 \leq x_3 \leq 28$$
$$7.3 \leq x_4 \leq 8.3 \tag{13.29}$$
$$7.3 \leq x_5 \leq 8.3$$
$$2.9 \leq x_6 \leq 3.9$$
$$5.0 \leq x_7 \leq 5.5$$

The design objective is to minimize the overall volume of the shafts, which is given by

$$\text{minimize} \quad f = 0.7854 x_1 x_2^2 \left(3.3333 x_3^2 + 14.933 x_3 - 43.0934\right) - 1.508 x_1 \left(x_6^2 + x_7^2\right) +$$
$$7.477 \left(x_6^3 + x_7^3\right) + 0.7854 \left(x_4 x_6^2 + x_5 x_7^2\right) \tag{13.30}$$

where all the dimensions are in centimeters. The gears are subject to the following constraints:[6]

$g_1: \quad \dfrac{1}{(x_1 x_2^2 x_3)} - \dfrac{1}{27} \leq 0$ Bending stress of gear tooth

$g_2: \quad \dfrac{1}{(x_1 x_2^2 x_3^2)} - \dfrac{1}{397.5} \leq 0$ Contact stress of gear tooth

$g_3: \quad \dfrac{x_4^3}{(x_2 x_3 x_6^4)} - \dfrac{1}{1.93} \leq 0$ Shaft 1 deflection

$g_4: \quad \dfrac{x_5^3}{(x_2 x_3 x_7^4)} - \dfrac{1}{1.93} \leq 0$ Shaft 2 deflection

$g_5: \quad \dfrac{1}{0.1 x_6^3} \sqrt{\left(\dfrac{745 x_4}{x_2 x_3}\right)^2 + 16.9 \times 10^6} - 1100 \leq 0$ Shaft 1 stress

$g_6: \quad \dfrac{1}{0.1 x_7^3} \sqrt{\left(\dfrac{745 x_5}{x_2 x_3}\right)^2 + 157.5 \times 10^6} - 850 \leq 0$ Shaft 2 stress

$g_7: \quad x_2 x_3 - 40 \leq 0$ Space restriction

$g_8: \quad 5 x_2 - x_1 \leq 0$ Space restriction

$g_9: \quad x_1 - 12 x_2 \leq 0$ Space restriction

$g_{10}: \quad 1.9 - x_4 + 1.5 x_6 \leq 0$ Shaft requirement

---

[6] J. Golinski, "Optimum Synthesis Problems Solved by Means of Nonlinear Programming and Random Methods," *Journal of Mechanisms*, 5 (1970), pp. 287–309.

$g_{11}:\quad 1.9 - x_5 + 1.1 x_7 \le 0$ Shaft requirement

Thus, g_1 to g_7 form the nonlinear inequality constraints, and g_8 to g_{11} form the linear inequality constraints. From the linear inequality constraints we see that

$$A = \begin{bmatrix} -1 & 5 & 0 & 0 & 0 & 0 & 0 \\ 1 & -12 & 0 & 0 & 0 & 0 & 0 \\ 0 & 0 & 0 & -1 & 0 & 1.5 & 0 \\ 0 & 0 & 0 & 0 & -1 & 0 & 1.1 \end{bmatrix}$$

$$b = \begin{bmatrix} 0 & 0 & -1.9 & -1.9 \end{bmatrix}'$$

and $A_{eq} = b_{eq} = C_{eq} = 0$. From Eq. (13.29) we find that $L_{bound} = [2.6, 0.7, 17, 7.3, 7.3, 2.9, 5]$ and $L_{bound} = [3.6, 0.8, 28, 8.3, 8.3, 3.9, 5.5]$.

The two functions required by `fmincon` are

```
function f = GearObjFunct(x)
f =  0.7854*x(1)*x(2)^2*(3.3333*x(3)^2+14.9334*x(3)–43.0934)...
          –1.508*x(1)*(x(6)^2+x(7)^2)+7.477*(x(6)^3+x(7)^3)...
          +0.7854*(x(4)*x(6)^2+x(5)*x(7)^2);
```

and

```
function [C,Ceq] = GearNonLinConstr(x)
C(1) = 1/(x(1)*x(2)^2*x(3))–1/27;
C(2) = 1/(x(1)*x(2)^2*x(3)^2)–1/397.5;
C(3) = x(4)^3/(x(2)*x(3)*x(6)^4)–1/1.93;
C(4) = x(5)^3/(x(2)*x(3)*x(7)^4)–1/1.93;
C(5) = sqrt((745*x(4)/(x(2)*x(3)))^2+16.9*10^6)/(0.1*x(6)^3)–1100;
C(6) = sqrt((745*x(5)/(x(2)*x(3)))^2+157.5*10^6)/(0.1*x(7)^3)–850;
C(7) = x(2)*x(3)–40;
Ceq = [];
```

The script is

```
x0 = [2.6, 0.7, 17, 7.3, 7.3, 2.9, 5];
LBnd = [2.6, 0.7, 17, 7.3, 7.3, 2.9, 5];
UBnd = [3.6, 0.8, 28, 8.3, 8.3, 3.9, 5.5];
A = zeros(4,7);
A(1,1) = –1; A(1,2) = 5;
A(2,1) = 1; A(2,2) = –12;
A(3,4) = –1; A(3,6) = 1.5;
A(4,5) = –1; A(4,7) = 1.1;
b = [0 0 –1.9 –1.9 ]';
```

[x,f] = fmincon('GearObjFunct',x0,A,b,[],[],LBnd,UBnd,'GearNonLinConstr')

which, upon execution, gives: $[x_1, x_2, x_3, x_4, x_5, x_6, x_7]$ = [3.500, 0.700, 17.000, 7.300, 7.715, 3.350, 5.287] and f = 2994.3.

13.4.3 Quadratic Programming

Quadratic programming refers to a special class of constrained optimization problems in which the objective function is quadratic and the constraints are linear—that is,

$$\text{minimize}_{x} \quad f = 0.5x'Hx + c'x$$
$$\text{subject to}: \quad Ax \leq b$$
$$A_{eq}x = b_{eq}$$
$$L_{bound} \leq x \leq U_{bound}$$

(13.31)

where H, A, and A_{eq} are matrices and b, b_{eq}, c, x, L_{bound}, and U_{bound} are column vectors. The MATLAB function used to obtain a solution to this class of problems is

[xopt,fopt] = quadprog(H,f,A,b,Aeq,beq,LBnd,Ubnd,x0,options)

where $xopt = x_{opt}$ is the optimum value of x, $fopt = f(x_{opt})$, the symmetric matrix H and the vector c are the set of coefficients of the quadratic objective function f, the matrix A and the vector b are the coefficients of the linear inequality constraints, the matrix Aeq and the vector beq are the coefficients of the linear equality constraints, the vectors $LBnd$ and $Ubnd$ specify the lower and upper bounds on the design variables x, the vector $x0$ sets the starting point, and *options* sets the parameters described in optimset.

We now demonstrate the use of quadprog.

Example 13.11 Production planning revisited

The production-planning scenario discussed in Example 13.2 is slightly revised. It is now assumed that the profits of product A and B are functions of the number of units of each product. For product A, the dollar profit per unit varies according to

$$4+2x_1 +3x_2$$

and that for product B according to

$$5+5x_1 +4x_2$$

The remaining aspects of the problem are the same as those given in Example 13.2. Accordingly, the objective function to be minimized is

$$f = -(4+2x_1 +3x_2)x_1 -(5+5x_1 +4x_2)x_2$$
$$= -(4+2x_1)x_1 -(5+4x_2)x_2 -8x_1x_2$$

or

$$f = \frac{1}{2}[x_1 \quad x_2]\begin{bmatrix} -4 & -8 \\ -8 & -8 \end{bmatrix}\begin{bmatrix} x_1 \\ x_2 \end{bmatrix} + [-4 \quad -5]\begin{bmatrix} x_1 \\ x_2 \end{bmatrix} \tag{13.32}$$

The script is

```
H = [-4, -8; -8, -8];
c = [-4; -5];
A = [1, 1; 1.25, 0.75; 0, 1];
b = [200; 200; 150];
LBnd = [0, 0]; UBnd = [inf, inf];
[xopt,fopt] = quadprog(H,c,A,b,[],[],LBnd,UBnd)
```

which, upon execution, gives $xopt(1) = x_1 = 50$, $xopt(2) = x_2 = 150$, and $-fopt = -f(x_{opt}) = 155,950$.

13.4.4 Semi-Infinitely Constrained Method

The semi-infinitely constrained method finds the solution of optimization problems formulated as

$$\begin{aligned}
&\underset{x}{\text{minimize}} \quad f(x) \\
&\text{subject to}: \ Ax \leq b \\
&\qquad\qquad A_{eq}x = b_{eq} \\
&\qquad\qquad C(x) \leq 0 \\
&\qquad\qquad C_{eq}(x) = 0 \\
&\qquad\qquad K_1(x,\omega_1) \leq 0 \\
&\qquad\qquad K_2(x,\omega_2) \leq 0 \\
&\qquad\qquad \vdots \\
&\qquad\qquad K_n(x,\omega_n) \leq 0 \\
&\qquad\qquad \forall(\omega_1, ..., \omega_n)
\end{aligned} \tag{13.33}$$

where x is the design variable vector, f is the scalar objective function, A is the vector representing the linear inequality constraints, b is the vector of linear inequality constraints, A_{eq} is the vector representing the linear equality constraints, b_{eq} is the vector of linear equality constraints, C is the vector representing the nonlinear inequality constraints, and C_{eq} is the vector of nonlinear equality constraints. The quantity $K_n(x,\omega_n)$ is the vector (or the matrix) of semi-infinite functions, a function of vectors x and ω_n, with the free variable ω_n representing a range of values over which the solution for the design variable x is sought, and $\forall(\omega_1, ..., \omega_n)$, with $\forall =$ "for all," indicating that the problem is considered for all values of the free variables $\omega_1, ..., \omega_n$ within their corresponding ranges. For example, ω_n may represent a temperature range in a heat-transfer problem or a frequency range in a vibration problem over which the K_n-constraint has to be satisfied for all temperature or frequency values in the range. The vector ω_n has, at most, length two.

The MATLAB function is

$$[\text{xopt,fxopt}] = \texttt{fseminf}(\text{UserFunction,x0,n,'SemiConstr'},$$
$$\text{A,b,Aeq,Beq,LBnd,UBnd,options,p1,p2,...})$$

where $xopt = x_{opt}$ is the optimum value of x, $fopt = f(x_{opt})$, and *UserFunction* is the name of the function file that computes the scalar function f and is in *single quotes*, but without the suffix ".m". When *UserFunction* is created by `inline`, the variable name is written *without any quotes*. The quantity $x0$ sets the starting point, n is the number of semi-infinite constraints in Eq. (13.40); the matrix A and the vector b are the coefficients of the linear inequality constraints; the matrix *Aeq* and the vector *beq* are the coefficients of the linear equality constraints; *LBnd* and *Ubnd* specify the lower and upper bounds, respectively, on the design variables x; *options* sets the parameters described in `optimset`; and $p1$, $p2$, ... are the additional arguments that are passed to *UserFucntion* and *SemiConstr*. The arguments $p1$, $p2$, ... of *UserFunction* and *SemiConstr* must be identical, even if only one of the functions uses these values. If *LowBnd*, *Upbnd*, and *options* are not specified use []; similarly for A, b, *Aeq*, and *beq*. The quantity *SemiConstr* is a function that defines the nonlinear constraints as follows:

$$[\text{C,Ceq,K1,K2, ..., Kn,s}] = \text{SemiConstr}(\text{x,s,p1,p2,...})$$

where $K1$, $K2$, ..., Kn, are the semi-infinite constraints evaluated for a range of sampled values of the free variables ω_1, ..., ω_n, respectively. The rows of the two-column matrix s have the sampling interval for the corresponding values of ω_1, ..., ω_n, which are used to calculate $K1$, $K2$, ..., Kn—that is, the ith row of s contains the sampling interval for evaluating K_i. In the first iteration, s is set to NaN so that the initial sampling interval is specified. If C and/or *Ceq* do not exist, then set them to [].

We now demonstrate the use of `fseminf`.

Example 13.12 Planar two-link manipulator

Consider a planar two-link manipulator shown in Figure 13.6. This manipulator is capable of positioning to a point in its plane. The design objective is to maximize the workspace area covered by the manipulator. There are two design variables, a and b, which represent the lengths of the two links. The constraints are the lower (C_1) and upper (C_2) bounds on the ratio a/b, the upper bound (K_1) on a measure of dexterity, and the lower and upper bounds on the two design variables a and b. The dexterity refers to the ease with which the manipulator can either move or exert force or torque in arbitrary directions within its workspace. The condition number κ of the Jacobian matrix for the manipulator is used as a metric for

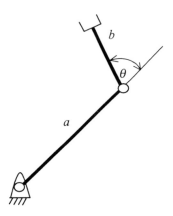

FIGURE 13.6
Planar two-link manipulator.

dexterity[7]. It is desired that this condition number to be as close to unity as possible. The problem formulation is

$$\text{minimize } f(a,b) = -\pi[(a+b)^2 - (a-b)^2]$$

subject to :

$$G_1: \quad a/b \geq 1.1$$
$$G_2: \quad a/b \leq 2$$
$$K_1: \quad \kappa \leq 1.26 \tag{13.34}$$
$$0.1 \leq a \leq 2$$
$$0.1 \leq b \leq 2$$
$$\forall \theta \in [100°, 150°]$$

where the condition number κ is given by

$$\kappa = (a^2 + 2b^2 + 2ab\cos\theta)/2ab\cos\theta \tag{13.35}$$

and the semi-infinite constraints are to be satisfied for the entire range of $\theta \in [100°, 150°]$ with a sampling interval of 5°. We first create the following function:

```
function [C,Ceq,K1,s] = TwoLinkConstr(x,s)
a = x(1); b = x(2);
if isnan(s(1,1))
  s = [5 0];
end
```

---

[7] C. Gosselin and J. Angeles, "A Global Performance Index for the Kinetic Optimization of Robotic Manipulators," *ASME Journal of Mechanical Design*, 113, (Sept. 1991), p. 222.

```
theta = (100:s(1,1):150)*pi/180;
K1 = (a^2+2*b^2+2*(a*b)*cos(theta))./(2*(a*b)*sin(theta))-1.26;
C(1) = -a/b+1.1;
C(2) = a/b-2;
Ceq = [];
plot(theta*180/pi,K1+1.26,'k')
hold on
```

The function that evaluates the scalar *f* is

```
function f = TwoLinkObjFunct(x)
a = x(1); b = x(2);
f = -pi*((a+b)^2-(a-b)^2);
```

The script is

```
x0 = [1,1];
LBnd = [.1,.1]; UBnd = [2,2];
[x,fopt] = fseminf('TwoLinkObjFunct',x0,1,'TwoLinkConstr',[],[],[],[],LBnd,UBnd)
text(120,1.17,'Initial')
text(113,1.05,'Optimum')
ylabel('Condition number \kappa')
xlabel('\theta (degrees)')
```

which, upon execution, produces Figure 13.7 and gives $x(1) = a = 2.000$ and $x(2) = b = 1.443$, with the corresponding workspace area of $-f = 36.2$. In Figure 13.7, we have plotted the condition number κ as a function of θ for each iteration to show the improvement in the condition number from its initial range to its optimum range. In this optimum range of the condition number, when $\theta = 136°$, we see that the condition number is almost unity. This angle is the most desired configuration for the manipulator in terms of its dexterity.

13.5 MULTIOBJECTIVE OPTIMIZATION

Multiobjective optimization refers to the solution of problems in which there is more than one design objective. The objectives in such problems are often in conflict with each other. The conflict arises because of the inherent properties of the problem. For example, consider a structural member in tension with the two design objectives of minimizing weight and stress. These two objectives conflict with each other—that is, as the weight of the member is reduced, the stress is increased and vice versa. During the optimization process for such a problem then, one reaches a point where it may not be possible to simultaneously improve all such objectives. Hence, the term "optimize" in a multiobjective problem generally refers to a solution point for which there is no way of further improving any objective without worsening at least one other objective. Such a solution point is referred to as a Pareto point or noninferior point. Many such Pareto solutions may exist in a multiobjective optimization

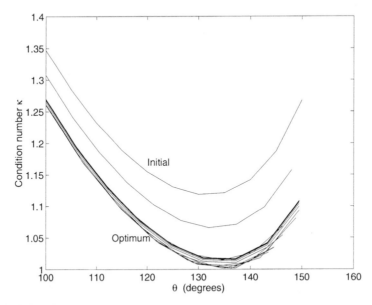

FIGURE 13.7
The condition number of the planar two-link manipulator as a function of θ as the `fseminf` constraint K_1 progresses from the initial values of a and b to their optimum values.

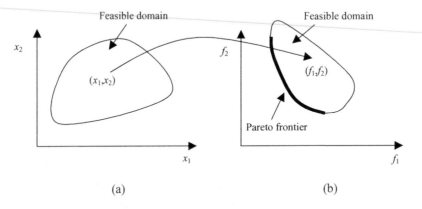

FIGURE 13.8
Feasible domains in (*a*) the variable space and (*b*) the objective space with its Pareto frontier.

problem, and these solutions collectively form a "Pareto frontier." Figure 13.8 shows for a two-variable two-objective problem the feasible domains in the variable space and the objective space and the Pareto frontier when both f_1 and f_2 are minimized. As shown in the figure, the feasible domain in the objective space is obtained as a result of a mapping from the variable space, and the Pareto frontier solution set corresponds to the "best" that can be achieved. Tradeoffs exist between the solutions in the Pareto set—that is, as one objective is improved in the set the other is worsened.

The final preferred solution to a multiobjective problem is selected from the Pareto set according to the decisionmaker's preference. MATLAB has two functions to solve multiobjective problems: fminimax and fgoalattain. The fminimax method solves the problem

$$\min_{x} \ \max_{f} \ \{f_1, f_2, \ldots, f_m\}$$

$$\text{subject to}: \quad Ax \le b \qquad \text{(Linear inequality constraints)}$$

$$A_{eq}x = b_{eq} \qquad \text{(Linear equality constraints)}$$

$$C(x) \le 0 \qquad \text{(Nonlinear inequality constraints)} \qquad (13.36)$$

$$C_{eq}(x) = 0 \qquad \text{(Nonlinear equality constraints)}$$

$$L_{bound} \le x \le U_{bound}$$

where x is the design variable vector; $f_1, f_2, \ldots, f_m$, are the objective functions; the matrix A and the vector b are the coefficients of the linear inequality constraints; the matrix A_{eq} and the vector b_{eq} are the coefficients of the linear equality constraints; C contains the nonlinear inequality constraints; C_{eq} contains the nonlinear equality constraints; and L_{bound} and U_{bound} specify the lower and upper bounds, respectively, on the design variables x. The fminimax method iteratively minimizes the worst-case value (or maximum) of the objective functions subject to the constraints.

The MATLAB function is

[xopt,fxopt] = fminimax(UserFunction,x0,A,b,Aeq,beq,LBnd,UBnd,
                        'NonLinConstr',options,p1,p2, ...)

where $xopt = x_{opt}$ is the optimum value of x, $fxopt = f_i(x_{opt})$, *UserFunction* is the name of the function file that computes the objective function and is in *single quotes*, but without the suffix ".m". This function must create an output in a specified order. When *UserFunction* is created by inline, the variable name is written *without any quotes*. The quantity $x0$ is the vector of starting values; the matrix A and the vector b are the coefficients of the linear inequality constraints; the matrix Aeq and the vector beq are the coefficients of the equality constraints; *LBnd* and *UBnd* are the vectors of the lower and upper bounds on x, respectively; *options* sets the parameters described in optimset; and $p1$, $p2$, ... are the additional arguments that are passed to *UserFucntion* and *NonLinConstr*. The quantity *NonLinConstr* is a function that defines the nonlinear constraints in a prescribed order as follows:

[C,Ceq] = NonLinConstr(x,p1,p2,...)

The arguments $p1, p2, \ldots$ of *UserFunction* and *NonLinConstr must be identical,* even if only one of the functions uses these values or one of the functions uses only some of the quantities. If *LowBnd, Upbnd,* and *options* are not specified, use []; similarly for *A, b, Aeq,* and *beq.*

The function `fgoalattain` solves the following multiobjective problem:

$$
\begin{aligned}
\text{maximize} \quad & \gamma \\
\text{subject to:} \quad & f_i(x) - \omega_i \gamma \le (\text{goal})_i \qquad i = 1, \ldots, m \\
& Ax \le b \qquad \qquad \text{(Linear inequality constraints)} \\
& A_{eq}x = b_{eq} \qquad \text{(Linear equality constraints)} \\
& C(x) \le 0 \qquad \qquad \text{(Nonlinear inequality constraints)} \\
& C_{eq}(x) = 0 \qquad \text{(Nonlinear equality constraints)} \\
& L_{bound} \le x \le U_{bound}
\end{aligned}
\tag{13.37}
$$

where γ is a scalar variable unrestricted in sign, f_i is the ith objective function, and ω_i and $(\text{goal})_i$ are, respectively, the weighting coefficient and target for the ith objective function. The weighting coefficient controls the relative degree of under- or over-attainment of the goal. The term $\omega_i \gamma$ provides an element of slackness in the formulation. For instance, setting all of the weighting coefficients equal to the initial goals indicates that the same percentage of the under- or over-attainment of the goals is desired.

The MATLAB function is

x = fgoalattain(UserFunction,x0,Goal,Weight,A,b,Aeq,beq,LBnd,UBnd,
                'NonLinConstr',options,p1,p2, ...)

where the vector *Weight* contain the elements ω_i, the vector *Goal* contains the elements $(\text{goal})_i$, and the remaining quantities are as defined for `fminimax`.

We now demonstrate the use of `fminimax` and `fgoalattain`.

Example 13.13 Vibrating platform

Consider the system shown in Figure 13.9. The motor is mounted on a beam-type platform composed of three layers of materials. It is assumed that the beam is simply supported at both ends. A vibratory disturbance is imparted from the motor to the beam. The design objectives are to minimize:

1. The negative of the fundamental natural frequency of the beam, denoted f_1

2. The cost of the material comprising the beam, denoted f_2

The constraints include an upper bound on the mass of the beam g_1, upper bounds on the thickness of layer two g_2 and layer three g_3, and upper and lower bounds on the design variables. The five design variables are the beam's length L, its width b, the distance d_1 to the central axis of the interface of layers one and two, the distance d_2 to the interface of the layers, and the distance to the top of the beam, d_3. The mass density ρ, Young's modulus E,

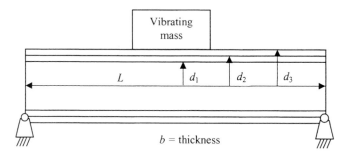

FIGURE 13.9
Vibrating multilayered simply supported platform.

TABLE 13.4
Material Properties and Cost for the Vibrating Platform

Layer i	ρ_i (Kg/m³)	E_i (N/m²)	c_i ($/volume)
1	100	1.6×10^9	500
2	2,770	70×10^9	1,500
3	7,780	200×10^9	800

and cost per unit volume c for the material of each of the three layers are given in Table 13.4. The problem formulation is

$$\text{minimize} \quad f_1(d_1, d_2, d_3, b, L) = -(\pi / 2L^2)\sqrt{EI/\mu}$$
$$\text{minimize} \quad f_2(d_1, d_2, d_3, b) = 2b(c_1 d_1 + c_2(d_2 - d_1) + c_3(d_3 - d_2))$$

where

$$EI = (2b/3)\left(E_1 d_1^3 + E_2(d_2^3 - d_1^3) + E_3(d_3^3 - d_2^3)\right)$$
$$\mu = 2b\left(\rho_1 d_1 + \rho_2(d_2 - d_1) + \rho_3(d_3 - d_2)\right)$$

subject to:

$$g_1 : \mu L - 2800 \le 0 \qquad \text{beam mass}$$
$$g_2 : d_2 - d_1 - 0.15 \le 0 \qquad \text{layer thickness}$$
$$g_3 : d_3 - d_2 - 0.01 \le 0 \qquad \text{layer thickness}$$
$$0.05 \le d_1 \le 0.5$$

$$0.2 \leq d_2 \leq 0.5$$
$$0.2 \leq d_3 \leq 0.6$$
$$0.35 \leq b \leq 0.5$$
$$3 \leq L \leq 6$$

We see that g_1 is a nonlinear inequality constraint and g_2 and g_3 are linear inequality constraints. Thus,

$$A = \begin{bmatrix} -1 & 1 & 0 & 0 & 0 \\ 0 & -1 & 1 & 0 & 0 \end{bmatrix}$$

$$b = \begin{bmatrix} 0.15 & 0.01 \end{bmatrix}'$$

and, since there are no linear and nonlinear equality constraints, $C_{eq} = A_{eq} = b_{eq} = 0$.

In order to have the same order of magnitude of the computed functions, the design objectives are scaled according to

$$scaled\_value = \frac{raw - good}{bad - good} \tag{13.38}$$

where the quantity *raw* refers to the actual value (before scaling) of the function, *good* refers to the target (or desired) value of the function, and *bad* refers to the undesirable value of the function. We see from Eq. (13.38) that when *raw* is equal to *good*, *scaled_value* = 0, and when *raw* is equal to *bad*, *scaled_value* = 1.

We now create the following three functions, the first being used by the other two. The first function computes *EI* and μ.

```
function [EI,mu] = BeamProperties(x,E,Rho,c)
EI = (2*x(4)/3)*(E(1)*x(1)^3+E(2)*(x(2)^3-x(1)^3)+E(3)*(x(3)^3-x(2)^3));
mu = 2*x(4)*(Rho(1)*x(1)+Rho(2)*(x(2)-x(1))+Rho(3)*(x(3)-x(2)));
```

where $[x_1, x_2, x_3, x_4, x_5] = [d_1, d_2, d_3, b, L]$. The second function computes the nonlinear inequality constraint.

```
function [C,Ceq] = VibPlatNLConstr(x,E,Rho,c,good,bad)
[EI,mu] = BeamProperties(x,E,Rho,c);
C(1) = mu*x(5)-2800;
Ceq = [];
```

The third function computes the objective functions.

```
function f = VibPlatformObj(x,E,Rho,c,good,bad)
[EI,mu] = BeamProperties(x,E,Rho,c);
f1 = pi/(2*x(5)^2)*sqrt(EI/mu);
f(1) = (f1-good(1))/(bad(1)-good(1));
```

f2 = 2*x(4)*(c(1)*x(1)+c(2)*(x(2)–x(1))+c(3)*(x(3)–x(2)));
f(2) = (f2–good(2))/(bad(2)–good(2));

The script is

```
x0 = [0.3, 0.35, 0.4, 5,0.4];
LBnd = [0.05, 0.2, 0.2, 0.35, 3];
UBnd = [0.5, 0.5, 0.6, 0.5, 6];
E = [1.6, 70, 200]*10^9;
Rho = [100, 2770, 7780];
c = [500, 1500, 800];
good = [500, 100];
A = [–1 1 0 0 0; 0 –1 1 0 0];
b = [0.15 0.01]';
for k = 1:5
  bad = [100+k*10 500–k*50]
  [xopt,fxopt] = fminimax('VibPlatformObj',x0,A,b,[],[],LBnd,UBnd,...
                  'VibPlatNLConstr',[],E,Rho,c,good,bad);
  for m = 1:2
    ff(m) = fxopt(m)*(bad(m)–good(m))+good(m);
  end
  f1(k) = ff(1);
  f2(k) = ff(2);
end
[f2sort indxf2] = sort(f2);
f1sort = f1(indxf2);
plot(–f1sort,f2sort,'ko-');
xlabel('Negative frequency (Hz)');
ylabel('Cost ($)');
title('Trade-off (Pareto) solutions');
```

which, upon execution, gives the Pareto frontier shown in Figure 13.10.

Example 13.14 Production planning revisited

Consider the production-planning problem given in Example 13.2. We now introduce a second design objective, which is to maximize (or minimize the negative of) the production units of product A. Then the objective function and the constraints are

$$\text{minimize } f(x_1, x_2) = -4x_1 - 5x_2$$
$$f(x_1) = -x_1$$

subject to :

$$g_1 : \quad x_1 + x_2 \leq 200$$

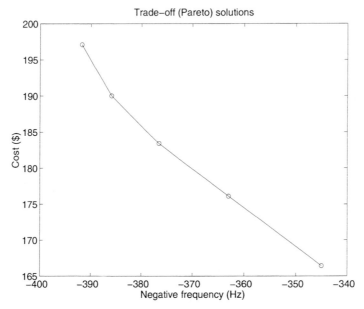

FIGURE 13.10
Pareto frontier of the vibrating platform.

$$g_2: \quad 1.25\, x_1 + 0.75\, x_2 \le 200$$
$$g_3: \quad x_2 \le 150$$
$$(x_1, x_2) \ge 0$$

Thus

$$A = \begin{bmatrix} 1 & 1 \\ 1.25 & 0.75 \\ 0 & 1 \end{bmatrix}$$

$$b = \begin{bmatrix} 200 & 200 & 150 \end{bmatrix}'$$

and L_{bound} = [0 0] and U_{bound} = [∞ ∞]. Since there are no equality constraints and no nonlinear constraints, $C_{eq} = A_{eq} = b_{eq} = C = 0$.

The script is

```
A = [1 1; 1.25 0.75; 0 1];
b = [200 200 150]';
goal = [−950 −50]; x0 = [50 50];
LBnd = [0 0]; UBnd = [inf inf];
Weight = abs(goal);
```

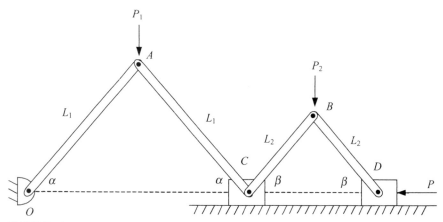

FIGURE 13.11
Two-pair bar mechanism of Exercise 13.1.

```
options = optimset('GoalsExactAchieve','2');
ProdPlanObj = inline('[−4*x(1)−5*x(2), −x(1)]','x');
[x,fevall] = fgoalattain(ProdPlanObj,x0,goal,Weight,A,b,[],[],...
                     LBnd,UBnd,[],options)
```

where we have set the option *GoalsExactAchieve* to 2 (the number of independent variables), which tells the algorithm to try to satisfy the goals exactly, not over- or underachieve it. If the default value is used, then the solution is a function of x0. The execution of the script gives a Pareto solution $[x_1, x_2] = [50, 150]$ with *fevall* = [−950 −50].

EXERCISES

13.1 Consider a two-pair bar mechanism, shown in Figure 13.11, in which links *OA* and *AC* have the same length $L_1 = 0.5$ m, and links *CB* and *BD* have the same length $L_2 = 0.3$ m. Joint *O* is a fixed joint, and joints *C* and *D* are pin connections on two slides that can move without friction along a horizontal line. The mechanism is subjected to three external forces. They are the vertical forces $P_1 = 3$ kN and $P_2 = 1$ kN at joints *A* and *B*, respectively, and a horizontal force $P = 3$ kN at joint *D*. We assume that before the loads are applied, the bars are lined up (stretched out) along the horizontal line. We also assume that the weight of the mechanism is negligible. The equilibrium of the mechanism under the applied loads is obtained by minimizing its potential energy (*PE*) function

$$\text{minimize} \quad PE = -P_1 L_1 \sin\alpha - P_2 L_2 \sin\beta + P\left[L_1(1-\cos\alpha) + L_2(1-\cos\beta)\right]$$

(a) Graphically obtain the contour and surface plots for *PE* and from these plots obtain approximate values of the optimum angles for α and β in radians.

(b) Use fminunc to validate the graphical solution. [Answer: $\alpha = 0.785$ rad, $\beta = 0.322$ rad.]

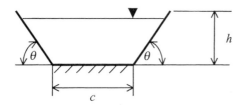

FIGURE 13.12
Water canal of Exercise 13.2.

13.2 Consider the water canal[8] shown in Figure 13.12. A water canal with a fixed cross-sectional area is to be designed so that its discharge flow rate is maximized. The design variables are the height h, the width of base c, and the side angle θ. It can be shown that the flow rate is proportional to the inverse of the wetted perimeter p, which is given by

$$p = c + (2h/\sin\theta)$$

The cross-sectional area A is given by

$$A = ch + h^2\cot\theta$$

If $A = 100$ ft^2, then

(a) Formulate the problem in an unconstrained form to maximize the flow rate as a function of the design variables h and θ.

(b) Create Figure 13.13.

(c) Use `fminunc` to validate the graphical solution with an initial point $(h,\theta) = (1,1)$. [Answer: $[h, \theta] = [7.59, 1.01\ \text{rad}]$.]

13.3 The average total production time per work piece for a machining operation is given by[9]:

$$T = t_m + \frac{t_m t_c}{T_l} + t_{aux}$$

where t_m is the cutting time, T_l is the tool life, t_c is the time it takes to change the tool, and t_{aux} is the auxiliary time. Here, $t_c = 7$ and $t_{aux} = 3$ are assumed to be empirical constants. For a turning operation, the cutting time is obtained by

$$t_m = \frac{\pi DL}{1000Vf}$$

where the diameter of the machined surface is $D = 100$ mm, and the length of the work piece to be machined is $L = 500$ mm. Also, V and f are the cutting surface speed and feed rate of the cutting tool, respectively. The influence of the cutting speed, the feed rate, and the depth of cut d on the tool life are estimated from the extended Taylor equation

$$VT_l^n f^a d^b = K_t$$

---

[8] P. Y. Papalambros and D. J. Wilde, *Principles of Optimal Design: Modeling and Computation*, Cambridge University Press, New York, 1988, p. 151.

[9] D. A. Stephenson and J. S. Agapiou, *Metal Cutting Theory and Practice*, Marcel Dekker, New York, 1997.

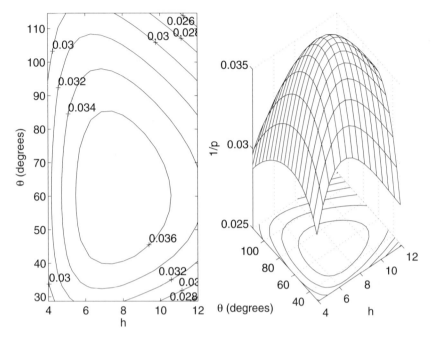

FIGURE 13.13
Contour and surface plots of Exercise 13.2.

where $n = 0.17$, $a = 0.77$, $b = 0.37$, and $K_t = 200$ are empirical constants. If V and f are the design variables, then the optimization problem is

$$\text{minimize } T(V,f) \text{ subject to: } f \le 2$$

If $d = 0.3$, then

(a) Create the contour plot of solution to the problem.

(b) Use `fmincon` to numerically obtain the optimum solutions. [Answers: $T = 3.94$, $V = 100$, $f = 2$.]

13.4 Figure 13.14 shows two frictionless rigid carts, A and B, connected by three linear elastic springs having spring constants $k_1 = 5$ N/m, $k_2 = 10$ N/m, and $k_3 = 8$ N/m.[10] The springs are at their natural positions when the applied force P is zero. Use the following potential energy function to obtain a contour and surface plot and an estimate of the displacements x_1 and x_2 when $P = 100$ N.

$$\text{minimize } PE = 0.5k_2x_1^2 + 0.5k_3(x_2 - x_1)^2 + 0.5k_1x_2^2 - Px_2$$

[Answers: $PE = 530$, $x_1 = 4.5$, $x_2 = 13.5$.]

13.5 Three carts, interconnected by springs and initially at an unstressed equilibrium state, are subjected to the loads P_1, P_2, and P_3 as shown in Figure 13.15.[11] The displacements of the carts from

---

[10] S. S. Rao, *Engineering Optimization, Theory and Practice*, 3rd ed., John Wiley and Sons, New York, 1996.
[11] S. S. Rao, *ibid.*, p. 420.

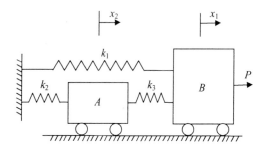

FIGURE 13.14
Spring-mass system of Exercise 13.4.

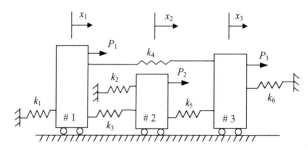

FIGURE 13.15
Spring-mass system of Exercise 13.5.

their original equilibrium position ($x_i = 0$; for all i) are sought by minimizing the potential energy of the system (PE)

$$PE = 0.5X'KX - X'P$$

where

$$K = \begin{bmatrix} k_1 + k_3 + k_4 & -k_3 & -k_4 \\ -k_3 & k_2 + k_3 + k_5 & -k_5 \\ -k_4 & -k_5 & k_4 + k_5 + k_6 \end{bmatrix}$$

$$P = \begin{bmatrix} P_1 & P_2 & P_3 \end{bmatrix}'$$

$$X = \begin{bmatrix} x_1 & x_2 & x_3 \end{bmatrix}'$$

The input data are

$k_1 = 4500$ N/m	$k_4 = 2250$ N/m	$P_1 = 1100$ N
$k_2 = 1650$ N/m	$k_5 = 550$ N/m	$P_2 = 1800$ N
$k_3 = 1100$ N/m	$k_6 = 9300$ N/m	$P_3 = 3300$ N

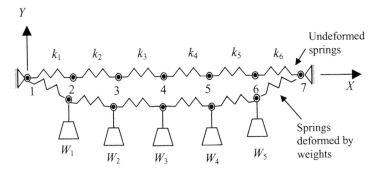

FIGURE 13.16
Spring-weight system of Exercise 13.6: (*a*) undeformed position, (*b*) deformed position.

Find the equilibrium position of the carts using fminunc. [Answer: $[x_1, x_2, x_3]$ = [0.322, 0.714, 0.365]]

13.6 Figure 13.16 shows a spring-weight system in its undeformed position with no supporting weights, and in its deformed position with supporting weights at the joints between the springs.[12] The stiffness of the spring i is k_i, and is defined by

$$k_i = 450 + 225(N/3 - i)^2 \quad \text{N/m} \quad i = 1,...,6$$

where $N = 5$ is the number of weights. Weight W_j is defined by

$$W_j = 60j \quad \text{N} \quad j = 1,...5$$

The length of each spring before the weights are applied is $L_i = 7.5$ m. The coordinates of the spring joints (points 2 to 6) are represented by 10 design variables: (X_i, Y_i), $i = 2,..., 6$. To solve for the equilibrium, the following *PE* function is minimized:

$$PE = 0.5 \sum_{i=1}^{6} K_i \Delta L_i^2 + \sum_{j=1}^{5} W_j Y_j$$

where

$$\Delta L_i = \sqrt{(X_{i+1} - X_i)^2 + (Y_{i+1} - Y_i)^2} - L_i$$

Determine the equilibrium positions using fminunc, that is, the joint positions for the deformed system shown in Figure 13.16. [Answer: $X_2 = 7.92$, $X_3 = 16.25$, $X_4 = 24.36$, $X_5 = 32.22$, $X_6 = 39.30$, $Y_2 = -3.86$, $Y_3 = -7.15$, $Y_4 = -8.84$, $Y_5 = -8.29$, $Y_6 = -5.16$.]

13.7 The buckling load P for a tubular column shown in Figure 13.17 is known to follow the following equation with unknown constants a and b:

$$P = \frac{\pi^a E R^b t}{4l^2}$$

---

[12] G. N. Vanderplaats, *ibid.*, p. 94.

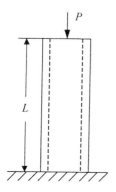
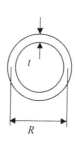

FIGURE 13.17
Column geometry for Exercise 13.7.

TABLE 13.5
Radius R and Load P Data of Exercise 13.7.

Experiments	R (in)	P (lb.)
1	1.1	86.6
2	1.7	120.5
3	2.1	520.88
4	2.9	1758
5	3.9	4098

where E is the modulus of elasticity, R is the mean radius, t is the thickness, and l is the length of the column. It is assumed that the exact relation for the buckling is unknown, and the constants will be determined through curve fitting of experimental data. To do this, an experiment is conducted wherein columns of different sizes, with $E = 250$ ksi, $l = 5$ in, $t = 1$ in, are loaded until they buckle. The loads at which the buckling occurs for different values of R are recorded in Table 13.5. Determine a and b using lsqcurvefit, and recreate Figure 13.18 wherein experimental and curve fitted data are shown. [Answer: $a = -3.3181$ and $b = 3.1599$.]

13.8 Suppose that one of the ingredients in a pharmaceutical drug is to be kept at 0.5 percent of the drug volume and that this ingredient decreases over time. In the eight weeks before the drug reaches the market, a decline to a level 0.51 may occur. Since many other uncontrolled factors may also arise, theoretical calculations are not reliable for making an extended prediction of the decrease of this ingredient at later times. To assist the management in making such decisions as to whether or not the stored drug in a warehouse for an extended period of time should be scrapped or replaced, it is recommended that cartons of the drug be analyzed over a period of time to measure its ingredient content. The results of one such measurement is shown in Table 13.6. It is postulated that a nonlinear model of the form

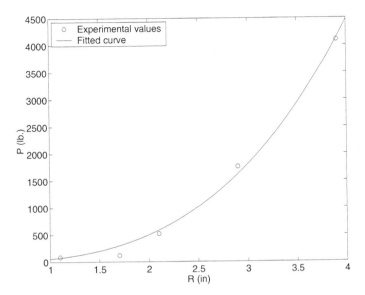

FIGURE 13.18
Tubular column results of Exercise 13.7.

TABLE 13.6
Data for Exercise 13.8

Length of time since production (weeks), t	Amount of ingredient, Y	Length of time since production (weeks), t	Amount of ingredient, Y
7	0.488	25	0.405
9	0.473	27	0.403
11	0.448	29	0.391
13	0.435	31	0.403
15	0.431	33	0.398
17	0.453	35	0.393
19	0.421	37	0.398
21	0.405	39	0.388
23	0.405	41	0.388

$$Y = a + (0.51 - a)e^{-b(t-8)}$$

accounts for the variation observed in the data. Estimate the parameters a and b of the nonlinear model using lsqcurvefit. [Answer: $[a, b] = [0.392\ 0.139]$.]

TABLE 13.7
Position and Time for the Vehicle of Exercise 13.9

Position (ft)	Time (s)
0	0
9	2.05
20	3.1
60	4.8
90	5.6
120	6.8

13.9 Suppose that you are observing a vehicle at a stop sign. The vehicle stops, and then it rapidly accelerates past five houses whose distances from the stop sign are known. As the vehicle starts from rest, you time the vehicle with your stopwatch as it passes each house. The data collected are shown in Table 13.7. The acceleration as a function of time is of the form

$$a(t) = Ct^2 + Dt + a_0$$

where t is travel time (s), a_0 is initial acceleration (ft/s^2), and C and D are constants. Hence, the position of the vehicle as a function of time is given by

$$x(t) = At^4 + Bt^3 + 2t^2$$

Estimate the equation for the car's velocity $v(t)$ as a function of time using the `lsqnonlin`. Assume that the initial position, velocity, and acceleration of the vehicle are, respectively, $x_0 = 0$ ft, $v_0 = 0$ ft/s, and $a_0 = 2$ ft/s^2. Calculate the error of the least square estimation. If this error is high, explain a way to reduce it. [Answer: $v(t) = -0.1084t^3 + 0.8307t^2 + 4t$.]

13.10 The optimal design of a three-bar truss shown in Figure 13.19 is considered. The vertical deflection of its loaded joint gives the objective function[13]

$$\text{minimize } f = \frac{Ph}{E} \frac{1}{x_1 + \sqrt{2}x_2}$$

where the cross-sectional areas of its members are $A_1 = x_1$ and $A_2 = x_2$; hence x_1 and x_2 are the design variables. Load P is applied in the direction shown in Figure 13.19. The constraints are the applicable stresses on the three members and lower and upper bounds on the design variables, as follows:

$$P\frac{x_2 + \sqrt{2}x_1}{\sqrt{2}x_1^2 + 2x_1x_2} - \sigma^{(u)} \le 0$$

$$P\frac{1}{x_1 + \sqrt{2}x_2} - \sigma^{(u)} \le 0$$

$$P\frac{x_2}{\sqrt{2}x_1^2 + 2x_1x_2} + \sigma^{(l)} \le 0$$

---

[13] S.S. Rao, *ibid.*, p. 530.

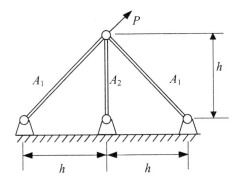

FIGURE 13.19
Three-bar truss of Exercise 13.10.

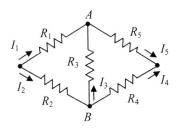

FIGURE 13.20
Bridge network of Exercise 13.11.

$$x_i^{(l)} \leq x_i \leq x_i^{(u)}, \quad i = 1, 2$$

where $\sigma^{(u)}$ is the maximum permissible stress in tension, $\sigma^{(l)}$ is the maximum permissible stress in compression, $x_i^{(l)}$ is the lower bound on x_i, and $x_i^{(u)}$ is the upper bound on x_i. The values for the parameters are $\sigma^{(u)} = 17.5$, $\sigma^{(l)} = -12$, $x_i^{(l)} = 0.2$, $x_i^{(u)} = 6.0$ ($i = 1,2$), $P = 25$, $E = 2$, and $h = 2$. Use fmincon to obtain the optimized values for the cross-sectional areas and the vertical deflection. Assume an initial value of $(x_1, x_2) = (0,0)$. [Answer: $[x_1, x_2] = [0.938, 6.00]$ and $f = 2.653$.]

13.11 Consider the bridge network shown in Figure 13.20 consisting of five resistors R_i, each carrying a current I_i, $i = 1, \ldots, 5$. The voltage drop across each resistor is $V_i = R_i I_i$. Suppose that the voltage drop must be constant for each resistor R_i—that is, $V_i = V_o$ volts, $i = 1, \ldots, 5$. Also assume that the current I_i varies between a lower limit of one amp and an upper limit of two amps for all resistors. (a) Formulate this problem in a constrained optimization form to find R_i for a minimum total power dissipation in the network; (b) use fmincon to obtain the optimum values for each resistor and total power dissipation. Power dissipation in the resistor R_i is equal to $I_i^2 R_i$. Also, Kirchhoff's first law states that in any branching network of wires, the algebraic sum of the currents in all the wires that meet at a point (point A or B of Figure 13.20) is zero. [Answer: $[R_1, R_2, R_3, R_4, R_5] = [1, 1, 1.5, 4, 5]$ and total power dissipation = 20 W.]

13.12 A Company has m manufacturing facilities to produce a product. The product is shipped to n warehouses. The warehouse at the jth location requires at least b_j units of the product to satisfy its demand. The manufacturing facility at the ith location has a capacity to produce a_i units of the product. The cost of shipping x_{ij} units of the product from manufacturing facility i to warehouse j is represented by $c_{ij}x_{ij} + d_{ij}x_{ij}^2$ where c_{ij} and d_{ij} are constants. Thus, the problem can be formulated in a quadratic programming form as

$$\text{minimize} \quad \sum_{i=1}^{m}\sum_{j=1}^{n}(c_{ij}x_{ij} + d_{ij}x_{ij}^2)$$

$$\text{subject to:} \quad \sum_{i=1}^{m}x_{ij} \geq b_j \quad j = 1,...,n$$

$$\sum_{j=1}^{n}x_{ij} \leq a_i \quad i = 1,...,m$$

$$x_{ij} \geq 0 \quad \text{for all } i, j$$

Assume $m = 6$, $n = 4$, $a = [8,24,20,24,16,12]'$, $b = [29,41,13,21]'$,

$$c = \begin{bmatrix} 300 & 270 & 460 & 800 \\ 740 & 600 & 540 & 380 \\ 300 & 490 & 380 & 760 \\ 430 & 250 & 390 & 600 \\ 210 & 830 & 470 & 680 \\ 360 & 290 & 400 & 310 \end{bmatrix}$$

$$d = (-1)\begin{bmatrix} 7 & 4 & 6 & 8 \\ 12 & 9 & 14 & 7 \\ 13 & 12 & 8 & 4 \\ 7 & 9 & 16 & 8 \\ 4 & 10 & 21 & 13 \\ 17 & 9 & 8 & 4 \end{bmatrix}$$

Solve this problem using `quadprog` to obtain the optimum number of units that should be produced at manufacturing facility i and shipped to warehouse j, x_{ij}. [Answer: $[x_{11}, x_{21}, x_{31}, x_{41}, x_{51}, x_{61}; x_{12}, x_{22}, x_{23},$ $x_{24}, x_{25}, x_{26}; x_{31}, x_{32}, x_{33}, x_{34}, x_{35}, x_{36}; x_{41}, x_{42}, x_{43}, x_{44}, x_{45}, x_{46}]' = [2.44, 4.44, 0, 1.11, 6.51, 8.51; 3.80,$ $5.17, 5.51, 7.51, 2.80, 4.17; 6.51, 8.51, 3.80, 5.17, 4.51, 6.51; 1.80, 3.17, 3.51, 5.51, 0.80, 2.17]'$.]

13.13 The two-bar truss shown in Figure 13.21 is symmetric about the y-axis. The nondimensional position of links 1 and 2, x/h, and the nondimensional cross-sectional area of the links A/A_{ref}, are treated as the design variables x_1 and x_2, respectively, where A_{ref} is the reference value of the area A, and h is the height of the truss. The direction of the applied load P is subject to change within the range $-90° \leq \theta \leq 90°$. The weight of the truss w is to be minimized. Thus,

$$w = 2\rho h x_2 A_{ref}\sqrt{1+x_1^2}$$

where ρ is the weight density. The constraints corresponding to the stresses induced in links 1 and 2 are given by

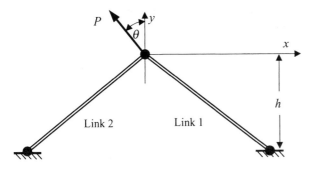

FIGURE 13.21
Two-bar truss of Exercise 13.13.

TABLE 13.8
Input Parameters for Exercise 13.14

ρ (lb/in^3)	P (lb)	σ_0 (psi)	h (in)	A_{ref} (in^2)	x_1^{min}	x_2^{min}	x_1^{max}	x_2^{max}
0.283	8,000	18,500	85	1	0.15	0.15	3.0	3.5

$$-\sigma_0 \leq \frac{P\sqrt{1+x_1^2}\,(x_1\cos\theta+\sin\theta)}{2x_1x_2A_{ref}} \leq \sigma_0$$

$$-\sigma_0 \leq \frac{P\sqrt{1+x_1^2}\,(x_1\cos\theta-\sin\theta)}{2x_1x_2A_{ref}} \leq \sigma_0$$

where P is the applied load. In addition, the following upper and lower bounds are imposed on the design variables x_1 and x_2

$$x_i^{min} \leq x_i \leq x_i^{max} \quad i=1,2$$

where the values of the parameters are listed in Table 13.8. Use `fseminf` to obtain the optimum design variables and create the plot of stresses as a function of θ sampled in 5° intervals as the optimum is approached. The result should look like that shown in Figure 13.22 when an initial design

$$\left(x_1^0, x_2^0\right) = (0.1, 0.1)$$

is assumed. [Answer: $[x_1, x_2] = [0.80, 0.45]$ and $w = 27.87$.]

BIBLIOGRAPHY

J. S. Arora, *Introduction to Optimum Design*, McGraw-Hill, New York, 1989.

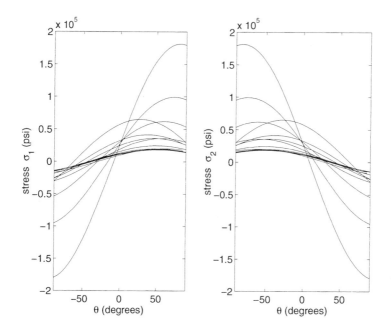

FIGURE 13.22
Stresses in links 1 and 2 in Figure 13.21 as the optimum is approached.

M. Austin and D. Chancogne, *Engineering Programming in C, MATLAB and JAVA*, John Wiley & Sons, New York, 1998.

M. Branch and A. Grace, *MATLAB Optimization Toolbox User's Guide*, The Math Works, Natick, MA, 1996.

V. Changkong and Y. Y. Haimes, *Multiobjective Decision Making: Theory and Methodology*, Elsevier Science Publishing Co., New York, 1983.

N. Draper and H. Smith, *Applied Regression Analysis*, John Wiley & Sons, New York, 1966.

Eschenauer, H., J. Koski and A. Osyczka, Eds., *Multicriteria Design Optimization*, Springer-Verlag, New York, 1990.

J. Golinski, "Optimum Synthesis Problems Solved by Means of Nonlinear Programming and Random Methods," *Journal of Mechanisms*, 5, 1970, pp. 287–309.

C. Gosselin and J. Angeles, "A Global Performance Index for the Kinetic Optimization of Robotic Manipulators," *ASME Journal of Mechanical Design*, 113, September 1991, p. 222.

U. Kirsch, *Optimal Structural Design*, McGraw-Hill, New York, 1981.

A. Messac, "Physical Programming: Effective Optimization for Computational Design," *AIAA Journal 34*, 1996, pp. 149–158.

A. Osyczka, *Multicriterion Optimization in Engineering with Fortran Programs*, Ellis Horwood Limited, West Sussex, England, 1984.

P. Y. Papalambros and D. J. Wilde, *Principles of Optimal Design*, Cambridge University Press, Cambridge, England, 1988.

S. S. Rao, *Engineering Optimization, Theory and Practice*, 3rd ed., John Wiley & Sons, New York, 1996.

G. N. Reklaitis, A. Ravindran, and K. M. Ragsdell, *Engineering Optimization*, John Wiley & Sons, New York, 1983.

J. Shigley and C. Mischke, *Mechanical Engineering Design*, McGraw-Hill, New York, 1989.

D. A. Stephenson and J. S. Agapiou, *Metal Cutting Theory and Practice*, Marcel Dekker, New York, 1997.

G. N. Vanderplaats, *Numerical Optimization Techniques for Engineering Design*, McGraw-Hill, New York, 1984.

D. J. Wilde, *Globally Optimal Design*, John Wiley & Sons, New York, 1978.

CHAPTER 14

ENGINEERING STATISTICS

Edward B. Magrab

The solutions to a wide range of engineering statistics applications are illustrated using the Statistics Toolbox.

14.1 DESCRIPTIVE STATISTICAL QUANTITIES

Consider a collection of measured values x_j, $j = 1, 2, \ldots , n$. The sample mean of these values is

$$\bar{x} = \frac{1}{n} \sum_{j=1}^{n} x_j \tag{14.1}$$

and sample variance

$$s^2 = \frac{1}{n-1}\left[\sum_{j=1}^{n} x_j^2 - n\bar{x}^2\right]$$

(14.2)

where s is the standard deviation. These quantities are the estimates of the true mean μ and the true standard deviation σ. The mean value is determined from

MeanValue = mean(x)

and the standard deviation from

StandardDeviation = std(x)

where x is either a vector or matrix of measured values.

We now create N equal segments over the region that the measured values fall, called bins, and place each x_j into that bin whose lower limit is less than or equal to x_j and whose upper limit is greater than x_j. We denote the center of each bin b_k, $k = 1,2, \dots , N$. After all the x_j have been assigned to a bin, the number of x_j falling into each bin is counted. We denote this value n_k, which is the number of data values that fell in the bin whose center is b_k. When the number of values n_k is plotted as a function of the value of the center of each bin, and each bin is represented by a bar whose width is equal to its upper and lower limits, then the resulting figure is called a histogram. The number of values in each bin can be determined from

[nk,b] = hist(x,N)

where nk is the vector of n_k, b is the vector of bin centers computed by hist, x are the n data samples, and N is the number of bins desired. When N is omitted MATLAB, uses $N = 10$. This same function without the left-hand side plots the histogram—that is,

hist(x)

One can also use

bar(b,nk)

where hist is frequently used to determine n_k.

If we define $f_k = n_k/n$, then we have the fraction of the n samples that fall in the bin centered at b_k. If we let

$$c_k = \sum_{j=1}^{k} f_j \qquad k = 1,2,\dots, N$$

then c_k is called the cumulative distribution function and is obtained from ck = cumsum(f)

where $f = [f_1 \ f_2 \ ... \ f_k] = [n_1/n \ n_2/n \ ... \ n_k/n]$. We can also plot c_k versus b_k, which is an approximation to the probability that a measurement has a value less than or equal to x_k.

Now let us sort the x_j from its lowest value to its highest value. The lowest value can be obtained using $\min(x)$, and the highest value from $\max(x)$. The range of the values is the difference between the highest and lowest values of the samples and can be determined from either

rangex = range(x)

or

rangex = max(x)–min(x)

The center of the sorted values is called the median value. If the number of samples n is odd, then the median value is $x_{(n+1)/2}$; if it is even, then the median value is $(x_{n/2} + x_{n/2+1})/2$. The median value is determined from

MedianValue = median(x)

Another statistical metric that is sometimes useful is the geometric mean, which is defined as the nth root of the product of the measurements of n samples—that is

$$\bar{x}_g = \sqrt[n]{\prod_{j=1}^{n} x_j}$$

This quantity can be determined from either

GeometricMean = geomean(x)

or from the expression

GeometricMean = prod(x)^(1/length(x))

We now apply these functions to the data given in Table 14.1 to produce Figure 14.1. The data are placed in a function *DataSet141*. Thus,

```
function d = DataSet141
d = [105 97 245 163 207 134 218 199 ...
    160 196 221 154 228 131 180 178 ...
    157 151 175 201 183 153 174 154 ...
    190 76 101 142 149 200 186 174 ...
    199 115 193 167 171 163 87 176 ...
    121 120 181 160 194 184 165 145 ...
```

← Histogram   Cumulative distribution →

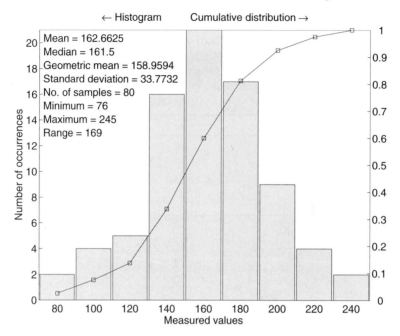

FIGURE 14.1
Histogram and cumulative distribution function of *DataSet141*.

TABLE 14.1
Data Comprising *DataSet141*

105	97	245	163	207	134	218	199
160	196	221	154	228	131	180	178
157	151	175	201	183	153	174	154
190	76	101	142	149	200	186	174
199	115	193	167	171	163	87	176
121	120	181	160	194	184	165	145
160	150	181	168	158	208	133	135
172	171	237	170	180	167	176	158
156	229	158	148	150	118	143	141
110	133	123	146	169	158	135	149

```
160 150 181 168 158 208 133 135 …
172 171 237 170 180 167 176 158 …
156 229 158 148 150 118 143 141 …
110 133 123 146 169 158 135 149];
```

The script is

```
data = DataSet141;
ldat = length(data);
b = 80:20:240;
nn = hist(data,b);
maxn = max(nn);
cs = cumsum(nn*maxn/ldat);
bar(b,nn,.95,'y')
axis([70 250 0 maxn])
box off
hold on
plot(b,cs,'k-s')
title('\leftarrow Histogram        Cumulative distribution \rightarrow')
ylabel('Number of occurrences')
xlabel('Measured values')
text(72,.97*maxn, ['Mean = ' num2str(mean(data))])
text(72,.92*maxn, ['Median = ' num2str(median(data))])
text(72,.87*maxn, ['Geometric mean = ' num2str(geomean(data))])
text(72,.82*maxn, ['Standard deviation = ' num2str(std(data))])
text(72,.77*maxn, ['No. of samples = ' num2str(ldat)])
text(72,.67*maxn, ['Maximum = ' num2str(max(data))])
text(72,.72*maxn, ['Minimum = ' num2str(min(data))])
text(72,.62*maxn, ['Range = ' num2str(range(data))])
plot([70 250],[maxn maxn],'k',[250 250],[0 maxn],'k')
j = 0:.1:1;
lenj = length(j);
text(repmat(251,lenj,1),maxn*j',num2str(j',2))
plot([repmat(248.5,1,lenj);repmat(250,1,lenj)],[maxn*j;maxn*j],'k')
```

Although the centers of the bins are computed by `hist`, we have chosen to specify them. This permits us to more easily control the presentation of the data. We had to turn off the `box` function because this function repeats the tic marks from the horizontal and vertical axes to the top and right-hand vertical axis, respectively. Also, `plotyy` cannot be used because two different types of graphs are being plotted. Therefore, we have to consider the labels independently from the tic marks, and we have to draw the top and right-hand figure boundaries separately. Thus, the tic marks appear at $21j$, where, in this problem, 21 is the maximum value of the y-axis. The maximum value is determined with the `axis` function.

If the bin centers had not been specified, then the resulting histogram would look slightly different because the centers of the bins would be different. This difference may change n_k. Thus, the execution of the statements

```
[nn,b] = hist(DataSet141,9);
bar(b,nn,.95,'y');
axis([70 250 0 max(nn)])
```

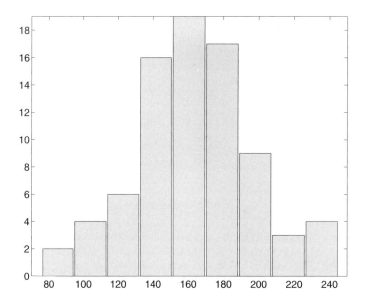

FIGURE 14.2
Resulting histogram for *DataSet141* when `hist` computes the bin centers.

results in Figure 14.2.

The differences between the histograms in Figures 14.1 and 14.2 are due to the differences in the bin centers. In the first case the bin centers were defined as

b = [80 100 120 140 160 180 200 220 240]

whereas in the new script the bin centers were computed by `hist` and found to be

b = [85.38 104.16 122.94 141.72 160.50 179.27 198.05 216.83 235.61]

We see that the number of x_j in several of the bins differs.

Another way of presenting these data is to use a box plot. A box plot of *DataSet141* is shown in Figure 14.3, which is obtained from the statement

`boxplot(DataSet141,1)`

whereby setting the second argument to 1 produced the notched box. The notch indicates the median of the data. The region within the top and bottom limits of the box represents 50% of the data, with the bottom of the box indicating the end of the first quartile q_1 and its top the end of the third quartile q_3. Note that, in general, the box is not symmetrical about the median value. The lines (whiskers) extending from the bottom and top of the box represent the extreme values defined by the regions $q_1 - 1.5(q_3 - q_1)$ and $q_3 + 1.5(q_3 - q_1)$, respectively.

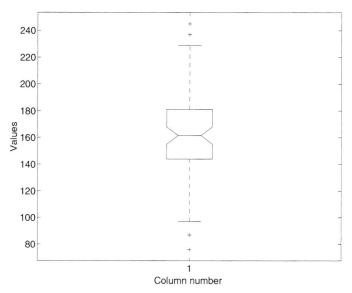

FIGURE 14.3
Box plot of *DataSet141*.

Any data points that lie outside these whiskers are called outliers and are denoted in this figure by plus signs. The more general usage of a box plot is to compare several sets of data in this manner. See, for example, Figure 14.14b.

To obtain the values of q_1 and q_3 we use, respectively,

q1 = prctile(DataSet141,25)
q3 = prctile(DataSet141,75)

which gives $q_1 = 144$ and $q_3 = 181$. The second argument in prctile specifies the percentile of interest. When the percentile equals 25%, this is referred to as the first quartile.

To determine whether or not the data are symmetrically distributed about the mean we use

s = skewness(DataSet141)

which returns $s = -0.0246$. This negative magnitude means that the distribution is slightly skewed to the left.

14.2 PROBABILITY DISTRIBUTIONS

14.2.1 Discrete Distributions

The probability $P(X)$ that a discrete random variable $X = x$, where x is from the set of all possible values of X, is defined as

$$f(x) = P(X = x) \tag{14.3}$$

where $f(x) \geq 0$ for all x and

$$\sum_{\text{all } x_i} f(x_i) = 1 \tag{14.4}$$

The quantity $f(x)$ is called the probability mass function for a discrete random variable.

If we are interested in the probability that $X \leq x$—that is, $P(X \leq x)$—then

$$P(X \leq x) = \sum_{x_k \leq x} f(x_k) = 1 - \sum_{x_k > x} f(x_k) \tag{14.5}$$

which is called the cumulative distribution function. Conversely, if we are interested in the probability that $X \geq x$ — that is $P(X \geq x)$—then

$$P(X \geq x) = \sum_{x_k \geq x} f(x_k) \tag{14.6}$$

Binomial Distribution. If we conduct n repeated trials such that (1) the trials are independent, (2) each trial results in only two possible outcomes, "success" or "failure," and (3) the probability p of a success on each trial remains constant, then the probability mass function is called the binomial distribution given by

$$f_b(x) = P(X = x) = \frac{n!}{x!(n-x)!} p^x (1-p)^{n-x} \quad x = 0, 1, \ldots, n \tag{14.7}$$

where x is the number of trials that meets with success.

The mean of this distribution is

$$\bar{x} = np \tag{14.8a}$$

and its standard deviation

$$s = \sqrt{np(1-p)} \tag{14.8b}$$

The function that computes the probability mass function of the binomial distribution is

```
binopdf(x,n,p)
```

and that which computes its mean and variance (s^2) is

[Bmean, Bvariance] = `binostat(n,p)`

where $x = 0, 1, 2, \ldots, n$.

Consider a die. The probability of getting any one of its sides to be the top surface is $p = 1/6$. Let the side with three dots be of interest. Then the probability that with one toss of the die, the side with three dots will appear is

$$P(X = \text{side with three dots}) = \frac{1!}{1!(0!)}(1/6)^1(1 - 1/6)^{1-1} = \frac{1}{6}$$

which can be determined from the expression

    h = `binopdf(1,1,1/6)`

However, the probability that we can get the side with three dots to show up exactly once in two tries is

    h = `binopdf(1,2,1/6)`

which gives $h = 0.2778 < 1/3$.

Now, consider a coin toss; thus, $p = 0.5$. The probability of getting exactly 4 "heads" ($x = 4$) in ten tosses ($n = 10$) is determined from

    h = `binopdf(4,10,0.5)`

which yields $h = 0.2051$.

Example 14.1 Probability of getting airplanes airborne[1]

An air force squadron of 16 airplanes should always be ready to become airborne immediately. There is, however, a 20% percent chance that an aircraft will not start, at which time several minutes must elapse before another start procedure can be attempted. Thus, the probability of an aircraft starting immediately is 0.80. The probability that exactly 12 airplanes can successfully become airborne is

    h = `binopdf(12,16,.80)`

which yields $h = 0.2001$.

On the other hand, the probability that at least 14 aircraft can become airborne immediately is determined from (recall Eqs. (14.5) and (14.6))

    h = `1−binocdf(13,16,.80)`   % or h = `sum(binopdf(14:16,16,0.80))`

which gives $h = 0.3518$.

---

[1] A. J. Hayter, *Probability and Statistics for Engineers and Scientists*, PWS Publishing Co., Boston, 1996, p. 167.

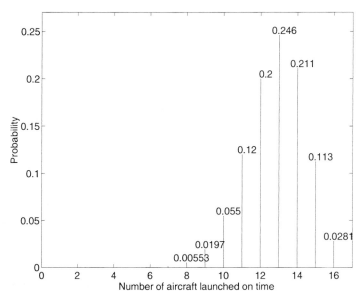

FIGURE 14.4
Probability mass function of launching 0 to 16 aircraft on time.

A graphical representation of this distribution can be obtained from the following script, which results in Figure 14.4.

```
n = 1:16;
h = binopdf(n,16,.80);
plot([n;n],[zeros(1,16);h],'k')
text(8-.7:16-.7, h(8:16)+.005,num2str(h(8:16)',3))
axis([0 17 0 0.27])
xlabel('Number of aircraft launched on time')
ylabel('Probability')
```

Poisson Distribution. Assume that an event occurs randomly throughout an interval and that this interval can be partitioned into smaller subintervals such that (1) the probability of more than one event in the subinterval is zero, (2) the probability of the event is the same for all subintervals and proportional to the length of the subinterval, and (3) the number of events in each subinterval is independent of the other subintervals. Such a series of events is called a Poisson process. If the mean of the number of events in the interval is $\lambda > 0$, then the probability mass distribution

$$f_p(x) = \frac{e^{-\lambda}\lambda^x}{x!} \quad x = 0,1,2,... \tag{14.9}$$

is a Poisson distribution for x events occurring in the interval.

The mean value of the Poisson distribution is

$$\bar{x} = \lambda \qquad (14.10a)$$

and its standard deviation

$$s = \sqrt{\lambda} \qquad (14.10b)$$

The probability mass function of the Poisson distribution is obtained from

h = poisspdf(x,lambda)

and that which computes its mean and variance (s^2) is

[Pmean, Pvariance] = poisstat(lambda)

Example 14.2 Adequacy of hospital resources

A hospital emergency room receives an average of 46 heart attack cases per week (46/7 per day). The hospital currently is able to handle nine such cases per day. The hospital staff is interested in knowing the probability that their current resources are adequate. Consequently, they want to know the value of $P(X \leq 9)$. Thus,

h = poisscdf(9,46/7)

which gives $h = 0.8712$. Thus, on 13% of the days additional resources will be required.

14.2.2 Continuous Distributions

The probability $P(X)$ that a continuous random variable X lies in the range $x_1 \leq X \leq x_2$, where x_1 and x_2 are from the set of all possible values of X, is defined as

$$P(x_1 \leq X \leq x_2) = \int_{x_1}^{x_2} f(u)\,du \qquad (14.11a)$$

where $f(x) \geq 0$ for all x, and

$$\int_{-\infty}^{\infty} f(x)\,dx = 1 \qquad (14.11b)$$

The quantity $f(x)$ is called the probability density function (pdf) for a continuous random variable.

The cumulative distribution function (cdf) $F(x)$ is

$$F(x) = P(X \le x) = \int_{-\infty}^{x} f(u)du = 1 - \int_{x}^{\infty} f(u)du \qquad (14.12)$$

and, therefore,

$$P(X \ge x) = 1 - F(x) \qquad (14.13)$$

MATLAB has a large family of probability density functions. We examine two of them: the normal distribution and the Weibull distribution. The others are used in a similar manner.

Normal Distribution. The normal probability distribution function is

$$f_n(x) = \frac{1}{\sigma\sqrt{2\pi}} e^{-\frac{(x-\mu)^2}{2\sigma^2}} \qquad -\infty < x < \infty \qquad (14.14)$$

where $-\infty < \mu < \infty$ and $\sigma > 0$ are independent parameters. It can be shown that μ is the mean of the distribution and σ^2 its variance (σ is the standard deviation). If we have a set of data $x_j, j = 1, 2, \ldots, n$, then the normal pdf is obtained from

    mu = mean(x);
    sigma = std(x);
    h = normpdf(x0,mu,sigma)

where $x0$ is the value (or values if $x0$ is a vector) of interest, $mu = \mu$, $sigma = \sigma$, the size of h is equal to the size of $x0$. Estimates for the values of μ and σ can also be obtained from

    [meanx, stddev] = normfit(x)

The cumulative distribution function $\Phi(x)$ is

$$\Phi(x) = P(X \le x) = \frac{1}{\sigma\sqrt{2\pi}} \int_{-\infty}^{x} e^{-(u-\mu)^2/2\sigma^2} du = \frac{1}{\sqrt{2\pi}} \int_{-\infty}^{(x-\mu)/\sigma} e^{-u^2/2} du \qquad -\infty < x < \infty \qquad (14.15)$$

or

$$\Phi(z) = P(Z \le z) = \frac{1}{\sqrt{2\pi}} \int_{-\infty}^{z} e^{-u^2/2} du \qquad -\infty < z < \infty \qquad (14.16)$$

where

$$z = (x-\mu)/\sigma \qquad (14.17)$$

is called the standard normal random variable, for which $\mu_z = 0$ and $\sigma_z = 1$. Thus,

$$P(Z \geq z) = 1 - \Phi(z)$$
$$P(Z \leq -z) = \Phi(-z)$$
$$P(-z \leq Z \leq z) = \Phi(z) - \Phi(-z) \qquad (14.18)$$
$$P(z_L \leq Z \leq z_H) = \Phi(z_H) - \Phi(z_L)$$

Equations (14.18) are also valid when z is replaced by x. The regions given by Eq. (14.18) are shown in Figure 14.5.

The normal cdf is obtained from

```
mu = mean(x);
sigma = std(x);
h = normcdf(x0,mu,sigma)
```

where $x0$ is the value (or values, if $x0$ is a vector) of interest, $mu = \mu$, $sigma = \sigma$, and the size of h is equal to the size of $x0$. If the x are converted to z, then $mu = 0$ and $sigma = 1$. These are the default values and, therefore, when $x \rightarrow z$ these arguments can be omitted.

Referring to Figure 14.5(c) and Eq. (14.18), we see that if we are interested in $P(x_L \leq X \leq x_H)$, then

```
h = diff(normcdf([xL xH],mean(x),std(x)))
```

For example, the probability of finding a measured value in *DataSet141* between 120 and 200 is obtained from

```
h = diff(normcdf([120 200],mean(DataSet141),std(DataSet141)))
```

which yields $h = 0.7623$. The value compares well with the estimated value obtained from Figure 14.1.

In some instances, one would like to determine the inverse of $\Phi(x)$—that is,

$$x = \Phi^{-1}[P(X \leq x)] \qquad (14.19)$$

This is accomplished with the function

```
x = norminv(p,mean(x),std(x))
```

where p is the cumulative probability—that is, the shaded area in Figure 14.5a.

In order to determine whether or not a set of data can be modeled with the normal pdf, one usually plots the data on a normal probability graph in which the ordinate (y-axis) is scaled using the cumulative normal distribution function. This is analogous to plotting data on which the ordinate has been scaled by the logarithm. On a graph in which the ordinate has been scaled logarithmically, an exponential function will appear as a straight line. Similarly, on a graph in which the ordinate has been scaled with the normal cumulative probability function, a process that has its ordered values distributed normally will appear as a straight line. In other words, for a normal distribution, the cumulative probability values

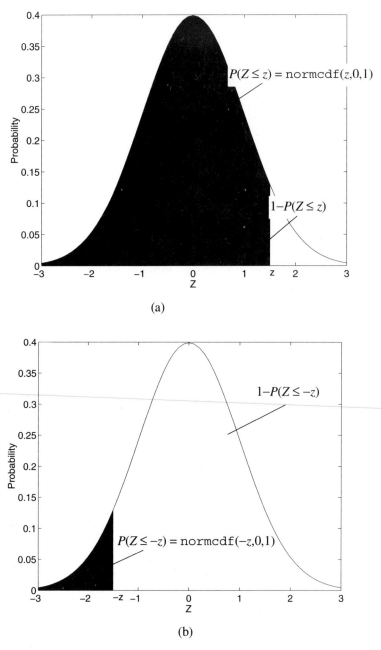

FIGURE 14.5
Relationship of the cdf to `normcdf`: (a) $Z \le z$; (b) $Z \le -z$;

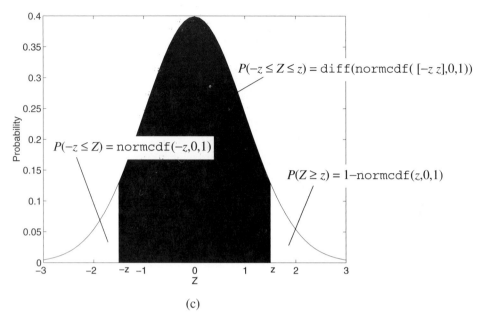

(c)

FIGURE 14.5 (CONTINUED)
Relationship of cdf to `normcdf`: (c) $-z \le Z \le z$.

that are one standard deviation σ on either side of the mean μ are $P(X \le \mu + \sigma) = 0.84$ and $P(X \le \mu - \sigma) = 0.16$, respectively, while that of the mean is $P(X \le \mu) = 0.5$. Thus, on a probability-transformed graph, the three sets of coordinates $(\mu - \sigma, 0.16)$, $(\mu, 0.5)$ and $(\mu + \sigma, 0.84)$ specify three points that lie on a straight line. The values of μ and σ are estimated by Eqs. (14.1) and (14.2), respectively, and computed using `mean` and `std`, respectively.

The procedure for plotting data on a probability graph is as follows. Consider a set of m data values y_i, $i = 1, 2, ..., m$. Order the data from the smallest (most negative) to the largest (most positive) value and assign the lowest value the number 1, and the next-lowest value the number 2, and so on, with the highest value having the number m. Call these ordered data values w_j, $j = 1, 2, ..., m$. Corresponding to each w_j we assign a cumulative probability of $(j-0.5)/m$, $j = 1, 2, ..., m$—that is, $P(w \le w_j)$. The coordinates of each data value that is to be plotted on the probability distribution graph are $(w_j, (j-0.5)/m)$. When only a linear graph is available, one plots instead (w_j, z_j), where $z_j = $ `norminv((j-0.5)/m)`. The function that performs these computations and does the plotting is

```
normplot(y)
```

where $y = [y_1\ y_2\ ...\ y_m]$. The straight line appearing in this plot is determined from the coordinate pairs of the first and third quartiles of y_j and z_j. Recall the determination of $q1$ and $q3$ in Section 14.1 and the interpretation of Figure 14.3.

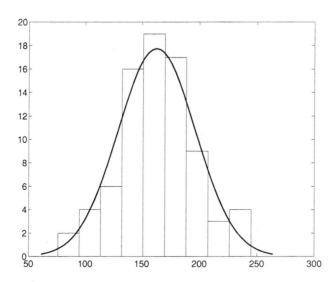

FIGURE 14.6
Histogram with a superimposed normal pdf.

Example 14.3 Verification of the normality of data

Let us revisit *DataSet141*. First, we re-plot its histogram and superimpose on this bar graph the corresponding normal pdf. This is accomplished with the expressions

```
histfit(DataSet141,9)
colormap([1 1 1])
```

which results in Figure 14.6. Next we see whether or not the data are normally distributed. We use

```
normplot(DataSet141)
whitebg('white')
```

and obtain Figure 14.7. It is seen that a fairly large portion of the data are close to the straight line, leading one to conclude that the normal distribution is a reasonable approximation to these data.

If we accept the normal distribution as an adequate representation of these data, then we can determine the values at which, say, 90% of the data lie. Then, referring to Figures 14.5a and 14.5c and Eq. (1.19) we use `norminv` as follows:

```
zh = norminv(.95,mean(DataSet141),std(DataSet141))
zl = norminv(.05,mean(DataSet141),std(DataSet141))
```

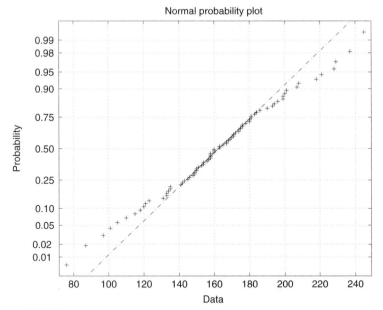

FIGURE 14.7
Normal cumulative probability plot of *DataSet141*.

and obtain $z_h = 218.2145$ and $z_l = 107.1105$. As a check, we find the difference between the probabilities of these two limits, which are determined from the following script:

```
ph = normcdf(218.2145,mean(DataSet141),std(DataSet141))
pl = normcdf(107.1105,mean(DataSet141),std(DataSet141))
```

The execution of this script gives $p_h - p_l = 0.9500 - 0.0500 = 0.90$.

The normal distribution is a good approximation to the binomial distribution when $np > 5$ and $n(1-p) > 5$, and is also a good approximation to the Poisson distribution to obtain $P(X \le x)$ when $\lambda > 5$. For the case of the binomial distribution, the normal standard random variable is (recall Eq. (14.8))

$$Z_b = \frac{X - np}{\sqrt{np(1-p)}}$$

and that for the Poisson distribution (recall Eq. (14.10))

$$Z_p = \frac{X - \lambda}{\sqrt{\lambda}}$$

To illustrate the normal approximation to the Poisson distribution, we return to Example 14.2, where we determined the probability that a hospital will treat nine or fewer

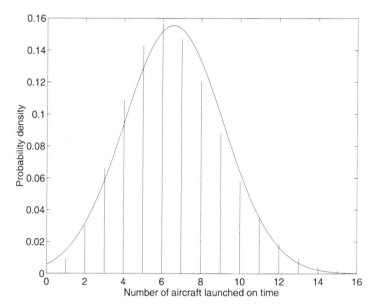

FIGURE 14.8
Poisson distribution of Example 14.1 and its normal approximation.

heart attacks a day was 0.8712. We now solve this problem using the normal distribution. Since $\mu = 46/7$ and $\sigma = \sqrt{46/7}$ we have

```
h = normcdf((9–46/7)/sqrt(46/7),0,1)
```

which gives $h = 0.8283$, a result that is within 4.9% of the exact value. In order to visualize this approximation, we create the following script, which draws the Poisson distribution from Example 14.2 and its approximation given by the above expression:

```
x = 1:16;
y = 0:.2:16;
yPoisson = poisspdf(x,46/7);
NormApprox = normpdf(y,46/7,sqrt(46/7));
plot([x;x],[zeros(1,16);yPoisson],'k',y ,NormApprox,'k')
xlabel('Number of aircraft launched on time')
ylabel('Probability density')
```

The results from the execution of this script are shown on Figure 14.8.

Weibull Distribution. The Weibull probability distribution function is

$$f_w(x) = \alpha\beta x^{\beta-1}e^{-\alpha x^\beta} \qquad x > 0 \tag{14.20}$$

where $\alpha > 0$ is a scale parameter and $\beta > 0$ is a shape parameter. (Another notation that is commonly used is obtained with the transformation $\alpha = \delta^{-\beta}$.) When $\beta = 1$, Eq. (14.20) reduces to the exponential distribution, and when $\beta = 2$, to the Rayleigh distribution. The mean value of this pdf is

$$\mu = \alpha^{-1/\beta}\Gamma\left(1 + \frac{1}{\beta}\right)$$

and its variance

$$\sigma^2 = \alpha^{-2/\beta}\Gamma\left(1 + \frac{2}{\beta}\right) - \alpha^{-2/\beta}\left[\Gamma\left(1 + \frac{1}{\beta}\right)\right]^2$$

where $\Gamma(x)$ is the gamma function. The Weibull pdf is obtained from

h = weibpdf(x,alpha,beta)

where alpha = α, beta = β, and the size of h is equal to the size of x. The mean and variance are obtained from

[Wmean,Wvariance] = weibstat(alpha,beta)

The cumulative distribution function $F_w(x)$ is

$$F_w(x) = P(X \le x) = 1 - e^{-\alpha x^\beta} \qquad x > 0 \tag{14.21}$$

and is obtained from

h = weibcdf(x,alpha,beta)

where the size of h is equal to the size of x.

In some instances, one would like to determine the inverse of $F(x)$—that is, when

$$x = F_w^{-1}[P(X \le x)] \tag{14.22}$$

This is accomplished with the function

x = weibinv(p,alpha,beta)

where p is the value of the cumulative probability distribution.

TABLE 14.2
Sorted Component Life Data

Component life	$F(t) = (j{-}0.5)/14$	j
72	0.0357	1
82	0.1071	2
97	0.1786	3
103	0.2500	4
113	0.3214	5
117	0.3929	6
126	0.4643	7
127	0.5357	8
127	0.6071	9
139	0.6786	10
154	0.7500	11
159	0.8214	12
199	0.8929	13
207	0.9643	14

Example 14.4 Verification that data can be represented by a Weibull distribution

Consider the sorted data on the longevity of a component given in Table 14.2. We create a function *DataSet142* for these data as follows:

```
function d = DataSet142
d = [72 82 97 103 113 117 126 127 127 139 154 159 199 207]';
```

We now plot these data to determine whether or not a Weibull distribution can be used to model it. Thus, we use the `weibplot` function as shown below to obtain Figure 14.9.

```
weibplot(DataSet142)
whitebg('white')
```

It is seen that these data are fairly well represented by the Weibull distribution and, therefore, we shall adopt it as a model for these data.

First, we must determine the values of α and β. We do this by first rearranging Eq. (14.21) and take the natural logarithm twice to obtain

$$y = \beta x + b \tag{14.23}$$

where

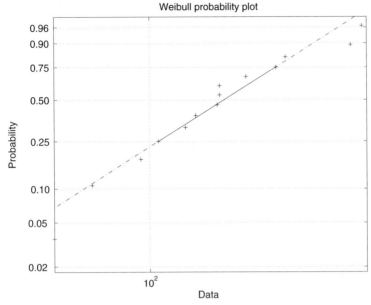

FIGURE 14.9
Weibull cumulative probability plot of *DataSet142*.

$$y = \ln\{\ln(1/[1 - F(t)])\}$$
$$x = \ln(t) \qquad b = \ln(\alpha) \tag{14.24}$$

and, therefore,

$$\alpha = e^b \tag{14.25}$$

Equation (14.23) is the equation of a straight line. Its slope β and intercept b can be determined using `polyfit`. Once they are known, α can be obtained from Eq. (14.25). The values of $F(t)$ are determined in the manner discussed in Example 14.3, and their values are shown in the second column of Table 14.2.

The script is

```
x = log(DataSet142)';
y = log(log(1./(1−((1:14)−.5)/14)));
c = polyfit(x,y,1);
[Wmean,Wvariance] = weibstat(exp(c(2)),c(1));
disp(['beta = ' num2str(c(1)) ' alpha = ' num2str(exp(c(2)))])
disp(['Mean = ' num2str(Wmean) ' Std dev = ' num2str(sqrt(Wvariance))])
```

which, upon execution, displays in the MATLAB command window

    beta = 3.9862   alpha = 2.5234e-009

Mean = 130.0703   Std dev = 36.6047

If a normal distribution had been assumed, then

Nmean = mean(DataSet142)
Stddev = std(DataSet142)

gives $\mu_{norm} = 130.1429$ and $\sigma_{norm} = 39.3854$.

We now plot the Weibull probability density function and, for comparison, the normal probability density function. The script is

```
x = log(DataSet142)';
y = log(log(1./(1–((1:14)–.5)/14)));
c = polyfit(x,y,1);
xx = 50:2.5:200;
yW = weibpdf(xx,exp(c(2)),c(1));
yN = normpdf(xx, mean(DataSet142), std(DataSet142));
plot(xx,yW,'k-',xx,yN,'k--')legend('Weibull','normal')
xlabel('x')
ylabel('Probability density function')
```

The execution of this script results in Figure 14.10.

We now determine the probability that a component's life is less than 100 hours. The script is

```
x = log(DataSet142)';
y = log(log(1./(1–((1:14)–.5)/14)));
c = polyfit(x,y,1);
p = weibcdf(100,exp(c(2)),c(1))
```

which yields $p = 0.2109$, or 21%.

The techniques of transforming the cumulative distribution function into an equation of a straight line are also used with data that can be represented by the exponential and the lognormal distribution. For these cases MATLAB does not explicitly provide the equivalent of normplot and weibplot. However, they are special cases of the weibplot and normplot, respectively. (For the lognormal distribution, see Exercise 14.11.)

14.3 CONFIDENCE INTERVALS

Let θ be a numerical value of a statistic (e.g., the mean, variance, difference in means, etc.) of a collection of n samples. What we are interested in determining is the values of l and u such that the following is true

$$P(l \le \theta \le u) = 1 - \alpha$$

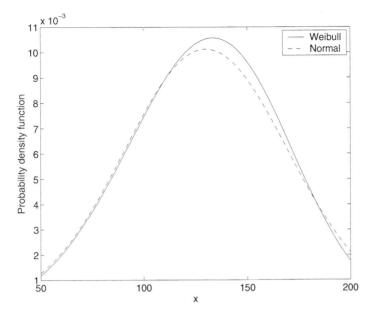

FIGURE 14.10
Comparison of the Weibull and normal probability density functions for *DataSet142*.

where $0 < \alpha < 1$. This means that we will have a probability of $1-\alpha$ of selecting a collection of n samples that will produce an interval that contains the true value of θ. The interval

$$l \leq \theta \leq u$$

is called the $100(1-\alpha)\%$ two-sided confidence interval for θ. The quantities l and u are called the upper and lower confidence limits, respectively. Similarly, the $100(1-\alpha)\%$ one-sided lower confidence interval is

$$l \leq \theta$$

and that for the $100(1-\alpha)\%$ one-sided upper confidence interval is

$$\theta \leq u$$

The confidence limits depend on the distribution of the samples and on whether or not the standard deviation of the population is known. Several commonly used relationships to determine these confidence limits are summarized in Table 14.3. In this table the following definitions are used:

μ and σ are the true mean and standard deviation, respectively

$\bar{x}$ and s^2 are determined from Eqs. (14.1) and (14.2), respectively

$t_{\alpha,n-1}$ is the value of the t distribution with $n-1$ degrees of freedom obtained from
  `tinv`

TABLE 14.3
Summary of Several Confidence Interval Procedures

Problem type	Statistic $\hat{\theta}$	θ	100(1−α)% confidence interval $\hat{\theta}-q \le \theta \le \hat{\theta}+q$ q	Case
mean with σ^2 known	$\bar{x}$	μ	$z_{\alpha/2}\sigma/\sqrt{n}$	1
difference in means with σ_1^2, σ_2^2 known	$\bar{x}_1-\bar{x}_2$	$\mu_1-\mu_2$	$z_{\alpha/2}\sqrt{\dfrac{\sigma_1^2}{n_1}+\dfrac{\sigma_2^2}{n_2}}$	2
mean with σ^2 unknown	$\bar{x}$	μ	$t_{\alpha/2,n-1}s/\sqrt{n}$	3
difference in means with $\sigma_1^2 = \sigma_2^2$ unknown	$\bar{x}_1-\bar{x}_2$	$\mu_1-\mu_2$	$t_{\alpha/2,n_1+n_2-2}S_p\sqrt{\dfrac{1}{n_1}+\dfrac{1}{n_2}}$	4
difference in means with $\sigma_1^2 \ne \sigma_2^2$ unknown	$\bar{x}_1-\bar{x}_2$	$\mu_1-\mu_2$	$t_{\alpha/2,v}\sqrt{\dfrac{s_1^2}{n_1}+\dfrac{s_2^2}{n_2}}$	5

	Statistic $\hat{\theta}$	θ	100(1−α)% confidence interval $q_1\hat{\theta} \le \theta \le q_2\hat{\theta}$ q_1	q_2	
variance	s^2	σ^2	$\dfrac{n-1}{\chi_{\alpha/2,n-1}^2}$	$\dfrac{n-1}{\chi_{1-\alpha/2,n-1}^2}$	6
ratio of variances	$\dfrac{s_1^2}{s_2^2}$	$\dfrac{\sigma_1^2}{\sigma_2^2}$	$\dfrac{1}{f_{\alpha/2,n_1-1,n_2-1}}$	$f_{\alpha/2,n_2-1,n_1-1}$	7

$z_{\alpha/2}$ is the value of the normal distribution obtained from `norminv`

$\chi^2_{\alpha/2,n-1}$ is the chi square distribution with $n-1$ degrees of freedom obtained from `chi2inv`

$f_{\alpha/2,n-1,m-1}$ is f distribution with $n-1$ and $m-1$ degrees of freedom obtained from `finv`

Furthermore, for Case 4

$$s_p = \sqrt{\frac{(n_1-1)s_1^2 + (n_2-1)s_2^2}{n_1+n_2-2}}$$

and for Case 5

$$v = \left(\frac{s_1^2}{n_1} + \frac{s_2^2}{n_2}\right)^2 \left[\frac{\left(s_1^2/n_1\right)^2}{n_1+1} + \frac{\left(s_2^2/n_2\right)^2}{n_2+1}\right]^{-1} - 2$$

We now illustrate the determination of the two-sided confidence limits for Cases 3 and 7 of Table 14.3. For Case 3, the two-sided confidence limits are

$$\bar{x} - t_{\alpha/2,n-1}\, s/\sqrt{n} \le \mu \le \bar{x} + t_{\alpha/2,n-1}\, s/\sqrt{n}$$

and those for Case 7 are

$$\frac{s_1^2}{s_2^2} \frac{1}{f_{\alpha/2,n_1-1,n_2-1}} \le \frac{\sigma_1^2}{\sigma_2^2} \le \frac{s_1^2}{s_2^2} f_{\alpha/2,n_2-1,n_1-1}$$

Notice that the degrees of freedom in the subscripts of f are reversed.

<u>Case 3</u>

For Case 3, we again consider the data in Table 14.1, which resides in function *DataSet141*. If we set the confidence level to 95%, then the script to determine the confidence interval is

```
meen = mean(DataSet141);
L = length(DataSet141);
q = std(DataSet141)*tinv(0.975,L-1)/sqrt(L);
disp(['Sample mean = ' num2str(meen)])
disp('Confidence interval for sample mean at 95% confidence level -')
disp(['   ' num2str(meen-q) ' <= Sample mean <= ' num2str(meen+q)])
```

which, upon execution, displays to the MATLAB command window

```
Sample mean = 162.6625
Confidence interval for sample mean at 95% confidence level -
     155.1466 <= Sample mean <= 170.1784
```

Another way to obtain this confidence interval is with `ttest`, which is illustrated in Section 14.4.

<u>Case 7</u>

For Case 7, we consider the two columns of data in Table 14.4, which are placed in function *DataFci* shown below.

```
function [set1,set2] = DataFci
set1 = [41.60 41.48 42.34 41.95 41.86 42.18 41.72 42.26 41.81 42.04];
set2 = [39.72 42.59 41.88 42.00 40.22 41.07 41.90 44.29];
```

TABLE 14.4
Data for Case 7

Set 1	Set 2
41.60	39.72
41.48	42.59
42.34	41.88
41.95	42.00
41.86	40.22
42.18	41.07
41.72	41.90
42.26	44.29
41.81	
42.04	

The script is

```
[data1,data2] = DataFci;
r = var(data1)/var(data2);
L1 = length(data1);
L2 = length(data2);
q2 = r*finv(.975,L2 −1,L1−1);
q1 = r/finv(.975,L1−1,L2−1);
disp(['Ratio of sample variances = ' num2str(r)])
disp('Confidence interval for ratio of sample variances at 95% confidence level -')
disp(['   ' num2str(q1) ' <= Ratio of sample variances <= ' num2str(q2)])
```

which, upon execution, displays to the MATLAB command window

```
Ratio of sample variances = 0.039874
Confidence interval for ratio of sample variances at 95% confidence level -
   0.0082672 <= Ratio of sample variances <= 0.16736
```

14.4 HYPOTHESIS TESTING

In engineering, there are many situations where one has to either accept or reject a statement (hypothesis) about some parameter. A statistical hypothesis can be thought of as a statement about the parameters of one or more populations. A population is the totality of the observations with which we are concerned. A sample is a subset of a population. Since we use probability distributions to represent populations, a statistical hypothesis can be thought of as a statement about the statistical distribution of the population.

Suppose that we have a parameter θ that has been obtained from n samples of a population, and we are interested in determining whether or not this parameter is equal to θ_o. The hypothesis testing procedure requires one to

1. Postulate a hypothesis, called the null hypothesis, H_0
2. Form the appropriate test statistic, q_0
3. Select a confidence level (recall that $100(1-\alpha)\%$ is the confidence level for θ)
4. Compare the test statistic to a value that corresponds to the magnitude of the test statistic that one can expect to occur naturally, q

Based on the respective magnitudes of q_0 and q, the null hypothesis is either accepted or rejected. If the null hypothesis is rejected, then we accept an alternative one, which is denoted H_1.

There are three cases to consider:

$$H_0: \theta = \theta_0 \qquad\qquad H_0: \theta = \theta_0 \qquad\qquad H_0: \theta = \theta_0$$
$$H_1: \theta \neq \theta_0 \qquad\qquad H_1: \theta > \theta_0 \qquad\qquad H_1: \theta < \theta_0$$

For each case, there are the corresponding test statistics $q_0(n,\alpha)$ and $q(n,\alpha)$. Several hypothesis-testing procedures are summarized in Table 14.5, which parallel the confidence-interval procedures in Table 14.3. The terms appearing in Table 14.5 have been defined in Section 14.3.

There are two types of errors that can be made in hypothesis testing:

Type I: Rejecting the null hypothesis H_0 when it is true

Type II: Accepting the null hypothesis H_0 when it is false—that is, when really $\theta = \theta_1$

The probability of making a Type I error is α and that for the Type II is denoted β.

It is becoming more common to replace the confidence parameter α with a quantity called the *p*-value, which is the smallest level of significance that would lead to the rejection of the null hypothesis. That is, the smaller the *p*-value, the less plausible is the null hypothesis.

We now illustrate these concepts with three examples from Table 14.5: Cases 2, 4, and 7.

Case 2

For Case 2 we again consider again *DataSet141*, which appears in Table 14.1. We want to know whether there is any statistically significant difference between the sample mean and a mean value of 168 ($\mu_0 = 168$) at a 95% confidence level. Thus, the hypothesis is

$$H_0: \mu = 168$$
$$H_1: \mu \neq 168$$

We use `ttest` to determine the validity of this hypothesis. The `ttest` function is

TABLE 14.5
Several Hypothesis Testing Procedures

Null Hypothesis H_0	Alternative Hypotheses H_1	Criteria for Rejection of H_0	Test Statistic	MATLAB Function	Case
$\mu = \mu_0$ (σ known)	$\mu \neq \mu_0$	$\|z_0\| > z_{\alpha/2}$	$z_0 = \dfrac{\bar{x} - \mu_0}{\sigma/\sqrt{n}}$	ztest	1
	$\mu > \mu_0$	$z_0 > z_\alpha$			
	$\mu < \mu_0$	$z_0 < -z_\alpha$			
$\mu = \mu_0$ (σ unknown)	$\mu \neq \mu_0$	$\|t_0\| > t_{\alpha/2,\, n-1}$	$t_0 = \dfrac{\bar{x} - \mu_0}{s/\sqrt{n}}$	ttest	2
	$\mu > \mu_0$	$t_0 > t_{\alpha,\, n-1}$			
	$\mu < \mu_0$	$t_0 < -t_{\alpha,\, n-1}$			
$\mu_1 = \mu_2$ (σ_1 and σ_2 known)	$\mu_1 \neq \mu_2$	$\|z_0\| > z_{\alpha/2}$	$z_0 = \dfrac{\bar{x}_1 - \bar{x}_2}{\sqrt{\dfrac{\sigma_1^2}{n_1} + \dfrac{\sigma_2^2}{n_2}}}$		3
	$\mu_1 > \mu_2$	$z_0 > z_\alpha$			
	$\mu_1 < \mu_2$	$z_0 < -z_\alpha$			
$\mu_1 = \mu_2$ ($\sigma_1 = \sigma_2$ unknown)	$\mu_1 \neq \mu_2$	$\|t_0\| > t_{\alpha/2,\, n_1+n_2-2}$	$t_0 = \dfrac{\bar{x}_1 - \bar{x}_2}{s_p\sqrt{\dfrac{1}{n_1} + \dfrac{1}{n_2}}}$	ttest2	4
	$\mu_1 > \mu_2$	$t_0 > t_{\alpha,\, n_1+n_2-2}$			
	$\mu_1 < \mu_2$	$t_0 < t_{\alpha,\, n_1+n_2-2}$			
$\mu_1 = \mu_2$ ($\sigma_1 \neq \sigma_2$ unknown)	$\mu_1 \neq \mu_2$	$\|t_0\| > t_{\alpha/2,\, v}$	$t_0 = \dfrac{\bar{x}_1 - \bar{x}_2}{\sqrt{\dfrac{s_1^2}{n_1} + \dfrac{s_2^2}{n_2}}}$		5
	$\mu_1 > \mu_2$	$t_0 > t_{\alpha,\, v}$			
	$\mu_1 < \mu_2$	$t_0 < -t_{\alpha,\, v}$			
$\sigma^2 = \sigma_0^2$	$\sigma^2 \neq \sigma_0^2$	$\chi_0^2 > \chi_{\alpha/2,\, n-1}^2$	$\chi_0^2 = \dfrac{(n-1)s^2}{\sigma_0^2}$		6
	$\sigma^2 > \sigma_0^2$	$\chi_0^2 > \chi_{\alpha,\, n-1}^2$			
	$\sigma^2 < \sigma_0^2$	$\chi_0^2 < \chi_{1-\alpha,\, n-1}^2$			
$\sigma_1^2 = \sigma_2^2$	$\sigma_1^2 \neq \sigma_2^2$	$f_0 > f_{\alpha/2,\, n_1-1,\, n_2-1}$ or $f_0 < f_{1-\alpha/2,\, n_1-1,\, n_2-1}$	$f_0 = \dfrac{s_1^2}{s_2^2}$		7
	$\sigma_1^2 > \sigma_2^2$	$f_0 > f_{\alpha,\, n_1-1,\, n_2-1}$			

$[h,p,ci] = \texttt{ttest}(Data,muzero,alpha)$

where *Data* are the data, *muzero* $= \mu_0$, *alpha* $= \alpha$, $h = 0$ if H_0 and $h = 1$ if H_1, $p = p$-value—that is,

$p = 2*(1-\texttt{tcdf}(\texttt{t0,n-1}));$

for a two-sided confidence interval and $t0 = t_0$ is defined in the fourth column of the second row of Table 14.5, and $ci(1) = l$ and $ci(2) = u$ are the lower and upper confidence limits, respectively. Thus,

[h,p,ci] = ttest(DataSet141,168,0.05)

yields $h = 0$—that is, we cannot reject the null hypothesis, $p = 0.1614$ and $ci(1) = 155.1466$ and $ci(2) = 170.1784$. Recall Case 3 of Section 14.3 where we had determined that $\bar{x} = 162.6625$, and that the confidence interval for this value at the 95% confidence level is $155.1466 \le \bar{x} \le 170.1784$. Since the hypothesized value for the mean, 168, lies within this confidence interval, we should expect that the null hypothesis would not be rejected. In fact, based on its p-value we see that we are only $100(1-0.1614) = 83.9\%$ confident, which is less than our desired confidence level of 95%.

On the other hand, if our null hypothesis is

$$H_0: \mu = 175$$
$$H_1: \mu \ne 175$$

then

[h,p,ci] = ttest(DataSet141,175,0.05)

gives $h = 1$—that is, we reject the null hypothesis and adopt H_1, $p = 0.0016$ and $ci(1) = 155.1466$ and $ci(2) = 170.1784$. In other words, we can be $100(1-0.0016) = 99.84\%$ confident that the mean of *DataSet141* is different from the mean value of 175.

Case 4

For Case 4 we consider again *DataFci*, which appears in Table 14.4. We want to determine whether there is any statistically significant difference between the means of these samples at a 95% confidence level. Thus, the hypothesis is

$$H_0: \mu_1 = \mu_2$$
$$H_1: \mu_1 \ne \mu_2$$

We use ttest2 to determine the validity of this hypothesis. The ttest2 function is

[h,p,ci] = ttest2(x1,x2,alpha)

where $x1$ and $x2$ are the data, $alpha = \alpha$, $h = 0$ if H_0 and $h = 1$ if H_1, $p = p$-value—that is,

p = 2(1−tcdf(t0, n−1))

for a two-sided confidence interval and $t0 = t_0$ is defined in the fourth column of the fourth row of Table 14.5, and $ci(1) = l$ and $ci(2) = u$ are the lower and upper confidence limits, respectively. Thus,

```
[x1,x2] = DataFci;
[h,p,ci] = ttest2(x1,x2,0.05)
```

yields $h = 0$—that is, we cannot reject the null hypothesis, $p = 0.6445$ and $ci(1) = -0.7550$ and $ci(2) = 1.1855$ are the lower and upper confidence limits, respectively, on the *difference* between the means. Based on the p-value, we see that we are only $100(1-0.6445) = 35.55\%$ confident that there is a statistically significant difference between the means, which is substantially less than our desired confidence level of 95%. Therefore, the null hypothesis cannot be rejected.

Case 7

For Case 7 we consider again *DataFci*, which appears in Table 14.4. We want to know whether there is any statistically significant difference between the variances of these samples at a 95% confidence level. Thus, the hypothesis is

$$H_0:\ \sigma_1^2 = \sigma_2^2$$
$$H_1:\ \sigma_1^2 \neq \sigma_2^2$$

The test statistic is

$$f_0 = \frac{s_1^2}{s_2^2}$$

and the criteria for rejection of the null hypothesis is either

$$f_0 > f_{\alpha/2,n_1-1,n_2-1}\quad \text{or}\quad f_0 < f_{1-\alpha/2,n_1-1,n_2-1}$$

Execution of the following script

```
[x1,x2] = DataFci;
L1 = length(x1);
L2 = length(x2);
ratio = var(x1)/var(x2);
if ratio>finv(0.975,L1-1,L2-1)
  disp('Reject null hypothesis')
  disp(['pValue = 'num2str(2*(1-fcdf(ratio,L1-1,L2-1)))])
elseif ratio<finv(0.025,L1-1,L2-1)
  disp('Reject null hypothesis')
  disp(['pValue = 'num2str(2*fcdf(ratio,L1-1,L2-1))])
else
  disp('Null hypothesis cannot be rejected')
end
```

yields

    Reject null hypothesis

pValue = 6.5379e-005

Thus, for these two data sets there is a statistically significant difference in their variances. It is noted that, in general, the p-value for a two-sided F-test is determined from

$$p = 2*(1-\texttt{fcdf}(r, n1, n2))$$

where $r = s_1^2 / s_2^2$ and $n1 = n_1$ and $n2 = n_2$ are the corresponding degrees of freedom.

14.5 LINEAR REGRESSION

14.5.1 Simple Linear Regression

Regression analysis is a statistical technique for modeling and investigating the relationship between two or more variables. A simple linear regression model has only one independent variable. If the input to a process is x and its response y, then a linear model is

$$y = \beta_1 x + \beta_0$$

If there are n values of the independent variable x_i and n corresponding measured responses y_i, $i = 1, 2, \ldots, n$, then estimates of y are obtained from

$$\hat{y} = \hat{y}(x) = \hat{\beta}_1 x + \hat{\beta}_0 \qquad x_{\min} \leq x \leq x_{\max} \tag{14.26}$$

where $x_{\min}$ is the minimum value of x_i, $x_{\max}$ is the maximum value of x_i, and $\hat{\beta}_1$ and $\hat{\beta}_0$, are estimates of β_1 and β_0, respectively, and are given by

$$\hat{\beta}_1 = \frac{S_{xy}}{S_{xx}}$$
$$\hat{\beta}_0 = \bar{y} - \hat{\beta}_1 \bar{x} \tag{14.27}$$

and

$$\bar{x} = \frac{1}{n} \sum_{i=1}^{n} x_i \qquad \bar{y} = \frac{1}{n} \sum_{i=1}^{n} y_i \tag{14.28}$$

$$S_{xx} = \sum_{i=1}^{n} x_i^2 - n\bar{x}^2 \qquad S_{xy} = \sum_{i=1}^{n} x_i y_i - n\bar{x}\bar{y}$$

The values for $\hat{\beta}_1$ and $\hat{\beta}_0$ are obtained from $\texttt{polyfit}$ (recall Section 5.6.1). Thus,

$$[c,s] = \texttt{polyfit}(x,y,1)$$

where $c(1) = \hat{\beta}_1$ and $c(2) = \hat{\beta}_0$, and s is a quantity needed by `polyconf`, which is described below.

The $100(1-\alpha)\%$ confidence limits on the estimate of $y(x)$, for $x_{\min} \le x \le x_{\max}$, are

$$\hat{y}(x) - w(x) \le y(x) \le \hat{y}(x) + w(x) \tag{14.29}$$

where

$$w(x) = t_{\alpha/2,n-2}\hat{\sigma}\sqrt{1 + \frac{1}{n} + \frac{(x-\bar{x})^2}{S_{xx}}}$$

$$\hat{\sigma}^2 = \frac{SS_E}{n-2} \qquad SS_E = S_{yy} - \hat{\beta}_1 S_{xy} \tag{14.30}$$

$$S_{yy} = \sum_{i=1}^{n} y_i^2 - n\bar{y}^2$$

The quantities $w(x)$ and $\hat{y}(x)$ are obtained from `polyconf` as follows:

```
[c,s] = polyfit(x,y,1)
[yhat,w] = polyconf(c,x,s,alpha)
```

where $yhat = \hat{y}(x)$, $w = w(x)$, and alpha $= \alpha$. The vector x determines the values at which $yhat$ and w are evaluated.

One means of determining the adequacy of the model given by Eq. (14.26) is to examine its residuals, which are

$$e_i = y_i - \hat{y}(x_i) \qquad i = 1,2,...,n \tag{14.31}$$

If e_i are approximately normally distributed, then the model has been correctly applied.

Another indicator of the model's representation of the data is the coefficient of determination R^2, which is

$$R^2 = 1 - \frac{SS_E}{S_{yy}} \tag{14.32}$$

The value $100R^2$ is the percentage of the variability of the data that is accounted for by the model. The closer this value is to 100%, the better the model. The quantity R is called the correlation coefficient.

We now illustrate these relationships.

Example 14.5 Regression analysis

Consider the data given in Table 14.6. These data are placed in a function called *DataRegress1*. Notice, however, that these data are not ordered. Since this is inconvenient when it comes time to plotting them with connected with straight lines, we sort them in ascending order. Neither `polyfit` nor `polyconf` requires the sorting. Thus,

TABLE 14.6
Data for Simple Linear Regression—*DataRegress1*

x	y	x	y
2.38	51.11	2.78	52.87
2.44	50.63	2.70	52.36
2.70	51.82	2.36	51.38
2.98	52.97	2.42	50.87
3.32	54.47	2.62	51.02
3.12	53.33	2.80	51.29
2.14	49.90	2.92	52.73
2.86	51.99	3.04	52.81
3.50	55.81	3.26	53.59
3.20	52.93	2.30	49.77

```
function [x,y] = DataRegress1
xx = [2.38 2.44 2.70 2.98 3.32 3.12 2.14 2.86 3.50 3.20 2.78 2.70 2.36 2.42 ...
      2.62 2.80 2.92 3.04 3.26 2.30];
yy = [51.11 50.63 51.82 52.97 54.47 53.33 49.90 51.99 55.81 52.93 52.87 52.36 ...
      51.38 50.87 51.02 51.29 52.73 52.81 53.59 49.77];
[x,index] = sort(xx);
y = yy(index);
```

where *index* gives the original position of each element of x prior to being sorted. This technique has to be used because the correspondence of the elements in x and y must be preserved. If two sort functions were used, one on x and the other on y, then this correspondence would be lost.

We now present a script that determines $\hat{\beta}_1$ and $\hat{\beta}_0$, plots $\hat{y}(x)$ and its confidence limits at the 95% level, plots the data, and connects their values to $\hat{y}(x)$ and includes the appropriate annotation. In addition, the value for the coefficient of determination will be computed and placed on the graph. The results are shown in Figure 14.11.

```
[x,y] = DataRegress1;
[c,s] = polyfit(x,y,1);
[yhat,w] = polyconf(c,x,s,.05);
syy = sum(y.^2)-length(x)*mean(y)^2;
sse = syy-c(1)*(sum(x.*y)-length(x)*mean(x)*mean(y));
plot(x,yhat,'k-',x,yhat-w,'k--',x,yhat+w,'k--',x,y,'ks',[x;x],[yhat;y],'k-')
legend('Regression line','95% confidence interval of y',4)
axis([2 3.6 48 57])
```

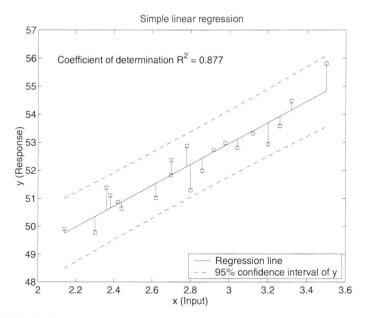

FIGURE 14.11

Linear regression for the data in Table 14.6 and the confidence limits on y.

```
xlabel('x (Input)')
ylabel('y (Response)')
title('Simple linear regression')
text(2.1,56,['Coefficient of determination R^2 = ' num2str(1-sse/syy,3)])
```

We proceed further and investigate the residuals. We first compute the residuals and then plot them using `normplot` (recall Figure 14.7) to determine whether or not they are normally distributed. The script is

```
[x,y] = DataRegress1;
normplot(y-polyval(polyfit(x,y,1),x))
whitebg('white')
```

which, upon execution, results in Figure 14.12. Since the residuals are very close to the line representing the normal distribution, we can say that the residuals are very nearly normally distributed and, therefore, our model is adequate.

14.5.2 Multiple Linear Regression

There are many applications where there is more than one independent factor (variable) that affects the outcome of a process. In this situation, we require a multiple regression model.

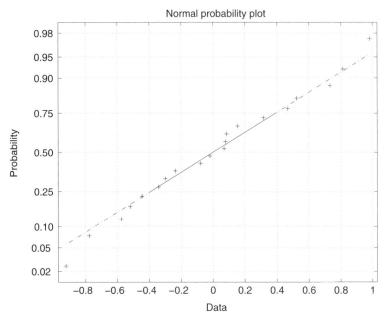

FIGURE 14.12
Normal cumulative distribution plot of the residuals from the fitted line appearing in Figure 14.11.

Consider a process that has one output y and k inputs x_j, $j = 1, 2, ..., k$. This process can be modeled as

$$y = \beta_o + \sum_{j=1}^{k} \beta_j x_j \qquad (14.33)$$

which is called a multiple linear regression model with k independent variables. The parameters β_j, $j = 0, 1, 2, ..., k$ are the regression coefficients. Models that are more complex in appearance may often be analyzed with this multiple linear regression model. For example, suppose that we have a cubic polynomial in *one* independent variable x:

$$y = \beta_o + \beta_1 x + \beta_2 x^2 + \beta_3 x^3$$

If we let $x_1 = x$, $x_2 = x^2$, and $x_3 = x^3$, then we have the linear model shown in Eq. (14.33)—that is,

$$y = \beta_o + \beta_1 x_1 + \beta_2 x_2 + \beta_3 x_3$$

However, this class of models is more easily solved with `polyfit`.
Another example is

$$y = \beta_o + \beta_1 x_1 + \beta_2 x_2 + \beta_3 x_1^2 + \beta_4 x_2^2 + \beta_5 x_1 x_2$$

which is of the form of Eq. (14.33) when we set $x_3 = x_1^2$, $x_4 = x_2^2$, and $x_5 = x_1x_2$.

Thus, we see that any regression model that is linear in the parameters β_j is a linear regression model, regardless of the shape of the surface y that it generates.

In order to estimate the parameters, we run an experiment n times, $n > k + 1$, such that for each set of x_{ij}, $i = 1, 2, \ldots, n$ and $j = 1, 2, \ldots, k$, we obtain a corresponding set of outputs y_i. In tabular form this would appear as

y	x_1	x_2	$\ldots$	x_k
y_1	x_{11}	x_{12}	$\ldots$	x_{1k}
y_2	x_{21}	x_{22}	$\ldots$	x_{2k}
$\vdots$	$\vdots$	$\vdots$		$\vdots$
y_n	x_{n1}	x_{n2}	$\ldots$	x_{nk}

Then Eq. (14.33) becomes

$$y_i = \beta_o + \sum_{j=1}^{k} \beta_j x_{ij} \qquad i = 1,2,\ldots,n \tag{14.34}$$

If these data are arranged in the following matrix form

$$X = \begin{bmatrix} 1 & x_{11} & x_{12} & \cdots & x_{1k} \\ 1 & x_{21} & x_{22} & \cdots & x_{2k} \\ \vdots & \vdots & & & \vdots \\ 1 & x_{n1} & x_{n2} & \cdots & x_{nk} \end{bmatrix} \qquad y = \begin{bmatrix} y_1 \\ y_2 \\ \vdots \\ y_n \end{bmatrix} \qquad \hat{a} = \begin{bmatrix} \hat{\beta}_0 \\ \hat{\beta}_1 \\ \vdots \\ \hat{\beta}_k \end{bmatrix} \tag{14.35}$$

then the solution for the estimates of β_j, denoted $\hat{\beta}_j$, are obtained from the solution of the following matrix equation:

$$\hat{a} = (X'X)^{-1} X'y \tag{14.36}$$

The matrix X is, in general, not square. Then,

$$\hat{y}_i = \hat{\beta}_o + \sum_{j=1}^{k} \hat{\beta}_j x_{ij} \qquad i = 1,2,\ldots,n \tag{14.37}$$

where $\hat{y}_i$ is the estimate of y_i.

Once the regression coefficients have been obtained, one indication of the adequacy of the model is to compute the residuals and see whether they are normally distributed. The residuals are defined as

$$e = y - \hat{y}$$

Thus,

$$e_i = y_i - \hat{y}_i = y_i - \hat{\beta}_o - \sum_{j=1}^{k} \hat{\beta}_j x_{ij} \qquad i = 1, 2, ..., n \tag{14.38}$$

The confidence limits on the regression coefficients β_j are given by

$$\beta_{Lj} \leq \beta_j \leq \beta_{Uj} \qquad j = 0, 1, ..., k \tag{14.39}$$

where

$$\beta_{Lj} = \hat{\beta}_j - t_{\alpha/2, n-k-1} \hat{\sigma} \sqrt{C_{jj}}$$
$$\beta_{Uj} = \hat{\beta}_j + t_{\alpha/2, n-k-1} \hat{\sigma} \sqrt{C_{jj}} \tag{14.40}$$

and

$$\hat{\sigma}^2 = \frac{y'y - \hat{a}'X'y}{n - k - 1}$$

$$C = (X'X)^{-1} = \begin{bmatrix} C_{00} & C_{01} & \cdots & C_{0k} \\ C_{10} & C_{11} & & \\ \vdots & & \ddots & \\ C_{k0} & & & C_{kk} \end{bmatrix} \tag{14.41}$$

In other words

$$\text{var}(\hat{\beta}_j) = \hat{\sigma}^2 C_{jj} \qquad j = 0, 1, ..., k$$

is an estimate of the variance of $\hat{\beta}_j$, and

$$\text{covar}(\hat{\beta}_i, \hat{\beta}_j) = \hat{\sigma}^2 C_{ij} \qquad i, j = 0, 1, ..., k \qquad i \neq j$$

is an estimate of the covariance of $\hat{\beta}_i$ and $\hat{\beta}_j$.

The multiple determination coefficient R^2 is given by

$$R^2 = 1 - \frac{y'y - \hat{a}'X'y}{y'y - n\bar{y}^2} \tag{14.42}$$

where

$$\bar{y} = \frac{1}{n} \sum_{j=1}^{n} y_j$$

The quantity R is the correlation coefficient.

One can also perform a hypothesis test to determine whether or not there exists a linear relationship between at least one regressor variable (x_i, $i = 1, 2, \ldots , k$) and the response y. The hypothesis test is

$$H_0: \beta_1 = \beta_2 = \ldots = \beta_k = 0$$
$$H_1: \beta_j \neq 0 \text{ for at least one } j$$

Rejection of H_0 implies that at least one regressor variable makes a statistically significant contribution. The test statistic is

$$F_0 = \frac{(\hat{a}'X'y - n\bar{y}^2)/k}{(y'y - \hat{a}'X'y)/(n-k-1)} \qquad n > k+1 \tag{14.43}$$

We reject H_0 if

$$F_0 > f_{\alpha,\, k,\, n\text{-}k\text{-}1}$$

The numerical evaluation of these equations can be obtained from either

beta = regress(y,x)

or

[beta,betacl,e,ecl,stats] = regress(y,X,alpha)

where:

$beta = [\hat{\beta}_0\ \hat{\beta}_1\ \ldots\ \hat{\beta}_k]$ as defined by Eq. (14.36)

betacl is a $((k+1)\times 2)$ array of the lower and upper confidence limits β_L and β_U, respectively, as defined by Eq. (14.40) and whose order corresponds to that of *beta*

$e = [e_1\ e_2\ \ldots\ e_n]$ are the residuals given by Eq. (14.38);

ecl are the confidence limits on the residuals

$stats = [R^2\ F_0\ p]$, where

   R^2 is given by Eq. (14.42)

   F_0 is given by Eq. (14.43)

   p is the p-value corresponding to F_0—that is,

   p = 1−fcdf(F0,k,n−k−1)

$y = [y_1\ y_2\ \ldots\ y_n]'$ is the column vector of responses

$X = X$ as defined by Eq. (14.35)

alpha = α

We now illustrate the use of these formulas.

TABLE 14.7
Data Comprising the Function *DataMultiRegress1*

y	x_1	x_2	x_3	y	x_1	x_2	x_3
0.22200	7.3	0.0	0.0	0.10100	7.3	2.5	6.8
0.39500	8.7	0.0	0.3	0.23200	8.5	2.0	6.6
0.42200	8.8	0.7	1.0	0.30600	9.5	2.5	5.0
0.43700	8.1	4.0	0.2	0.09230	7.4	2.8	7.8
0.42800	9.0	0.5	1.0	0.11600	7.8	2.8	7.7
0.46700	8.7	1.5	2.8	0.07640	7.7	3.0	8.0
0.44400	9.3	2.1	1.0	0.43900	10.3	1.7	4.2
0.37800	7.6	5.1	3.4	0.09440	7.8	3.3	8.5
0.49400	10.0	0.0	0.3	0.11700	7.1	3.9	6.6
0.45600	8.4	3.7	4.1	0.07260	7.7	4.3	9.5
0.45200	9.3	3.6	2.0	0.04120	7.4	6.0	10.9
0.11200	7.7	2.8	7.1	0.25100	7.3	2.0	5.2
0.43200	9.8	4.2	2.0	0.00002	7.6	7.8	20.7

Example 14.6 Multiple regression analysis

Consider the data in Table 14.7. We shall fit the following model to these data:

$$y = \beta_0 + \beta_1 x_1 + \beta_2 x_2 + \beta_3 x_3 + \beta_4 x_1 x_2 + \beta_5 x_1 x_3 + \beta_6 x_2 x_3 + \beta_7 x_1^2 + \beta_8 x_2^2 + \beta_9 x_3^2$$

First we create the function *DataMultiRegress1* to generate X according to Eq. (14.35).

```
function [y,X] = DataMultiRegress1
y = [0.22200 0.39500 0.42200 0.43700 0.42800 0.46700 0.44400 0.37800 0.49400 ...
    0.45600 0.45200 0.11200 0.43200 0.10100 0.23200 0.30600 0.09230 0.11600 ...
0.07640 0.43900 0.09440 0.11700 0.07260 0.04120 0.25100 0.00002]';
x1 = [7.3 8.7 8.8 8.1 9.0 8.7 9.3 7.6 10.0 8.4 9.3 7.7 9.8 7.3 8.5 9.5 7.4 7.8 7.7 10.3 ...
    7.8 7.1 7.7 7.4 7.3 7.6]';
x2 = [0.0 0.0 0.7 4.0 0.5 1.5 2.1 5.1 0.0 3.7 3.6 2.8 4.2 2.5 2.0 2.5 2.8 2.8 3.0 1.7 ...
    3.3 3.9 4.3 6.0 2.0 7.8]';
x3 = [0.0 0.3 1.0 0.2 1.0 2.8 1.0 3.4 0.3 4.1 2.0 7.1 2.0 6.8 6.6 5.0 7.8 7.7 8.0 ...
    4.2 8.5 6.6 9.5 10.9 5.2 20.7]';
X = [ones(length(y),1) x1 x2 x3 x1.*x2 x1.*x3 x2.*x3 x1.^2 x2.^2 x3.^2];
```

Next, we determine the estimates of the coefficients $\hat{\beta}_j$ and their confidence limits at the 95% confidence level, display the values of R^2, F_0 and its *p*-value, and plot the residuals to determine whether or not they are normally distributed. The script is

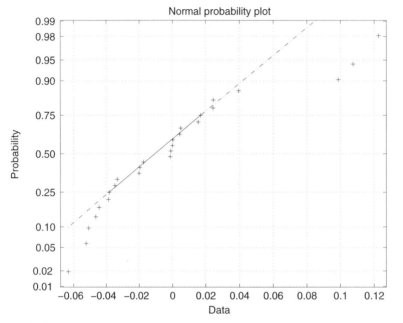

FIGURE 14.13
Normal cumulative distribution plot of the residuals from the surface modeling the data in Table 14.7.

```
[y,X] = DataMultiRegress1;
[b,bcl,e,ecl,stat] = regress(y,X,0.05);
lenb = length(b);
disp('Regression coefficients and their confidence limits')
disp([num2str(bcl(:,1)) repmat(' <= beta(',lenb,1) num2str((0:lenb−1)') ...
    repmat(') = ',lenb,1) num2str(b) repmat(' <= ',lenb,1) num2str(bcl(:,2))])
disp(['Coefficient of determination R^2 = ' num2str(stat(1))])
disp(['Test statistic F0 = ' num2str(stat(2)) ' and corresponding p-value = ' ...
        num2str(stat(3))])
normplot(e)
whitebg('white')
```

Execution of this script displays the following information to the MATLAB command window, which has been manually aligned for readability, and plots the results shown in Figure 14.13. It is seen in this figure that all but five residuals fall close to the line representing the normal distribution. Therefore, the model is adequate.

```
Regression coefficients and their confidence limits
-4.4976    <= beta(0) = -1.7694    <= 0.9589
-0.20282   <= beta(1) = 0.4208     <= 1.0444
-0.054708 <= beta(2) = 0.22245     <= 0.49961
```

TABLE 14.8
Tabulations of the Results of a Single-Factor Experiment with $n > 1$ Replicates

Level	Observations				Average	Variance	Residuals
A_1	x_{11}	x_{12}	$\cdots$	x_{1n}	$\mu_1 = \dfrac{1}{n}\sum_{j=1}^{n} x_{1j}$	$s_1^2 = \dfrac{1}{n-1}\sum_{j=1}^{n}(x_{1j}-\mu_1)^2$	$\varepsilon_{1j} = x_{1j} - \mu_1$
A_2	x_{21}	x_{22}		x_{2n}	$\mu_2 = \dfrac{1}{n}\sum_{j=1}^{n} x_{2j}$	$s_2^2 = \dfrac{1}{n-1}\sum_{j=1}^{n}(x_{2j}-\mu_2)^2$	$\varepsilon_{2j} = x_{2j} - \mu_2$
$\cdots$			$\cdots$	$\cdots$		$\cdots$	
A_a	x_{a1}	x_{a2}	$\cdots$	x_{an}	$\mu_a = \dfrac{1}{n}\sum_{j=1}^{n} x_{aj}$	$s_a^2 = \dfrac{1}{n-1}\sum_{j=1}^{n}(x_{aj}-\mu_a)^2$	$\varepsilon_{aj} = x_{aj} - \mu_a$

```
-0.27691    <= beta(3) = -0.128       <= 0.020918
-0.045395   <= beta(4) = -0.019876    <= 0.0056419
-0.0070049  <= beta(5) = 0.0091515    <= 0.025308
-0.012346   <= beta(6) = 0.0025762    <= 0.017499
-0.054932   <= beta(7) = -0.019325    <= 0.016283
-0.032989   <= beta(8) = -0.0074485   <= 0.018092
-0.002231   <= beta(9) = 0.00082397   <= 0.003879
```
Coefficient of determination $R^2 = 0.91695$
Test statistic $F0 = 19.628$ and corresponding p-value = 5.0513e-007

14.6 DESIGN OF EXPERIMENTS

14.6.1 Single-Factor Experiments: Analysis of Variance

Consider a single-factor experiment with the factor denoted A. We run an experiment varying A at a different levels, $A_j, j = 1, 2, \ldots, a$, and we repeat the experiment n times—that is, we obtain n replicates. The results are given in Table 14.8. The results in the first column of the observations, x_{j1} in Table 14.8, would be obtained by randomly ordering the levels $A_j, j = 1, 2\ldots a$, and then running the experiment in this randomly selected order. Then the results in the second column of the observations, $x_{j2}, j = 1, 2\ldots a$, would be obtained by generating a new random order for the levels A_j and running the experiment in this new random order. This procedure is repeated until the n replicates have been obtained. Running the experiment in this manner ensures that the values obtained for the x_{jk} have each been independently obtained. Thus, we can define two independent variances using the quantities μ_i and s_i^2 defined in Table 14.8 as follows. The variance of the mean of factor A is

$$ s_A^2 = \frac{n}{a-1}\left(\sum_{i=1}^{a}\mu_i^2 - a\bar{x}^2\right) = \frac{SS_A}{a-1} $$

which has $a-1$ degrees of freedom, and $\bar{x}$ is the grand mean given by

$$\bar{x} = \frac{1}{an} \sum_{i=1}^{a} \sum_{j=1}^{n} x_{ij}$$

The variance of the error is

$$s_{error}^2 = \frac{1}{a} \sum_{i=1}^{a} s_i^2 = \frac{1}{a(n-1)} \left(\sum_{i=1}^{a} \sum_{j=1}^{n} x_{ij}^2 - an\bar{x}^2 \right) = \frac{SS_{error}}{a(n-1)}$$

which has $a(n-1)$ degrees of freedom.

These two variances, s_A^2 and s_{error}^2, are related by the following identity, called the sum-of-squares identity, which has $an-1$ degrees of freedom:

$$\sum_{i=1}^{a} \sum_{j=1}^{n} (x_{ij} - \bar{x})^2 = \sum_{i=1}^{a} \sum_{j=1}^{n} [(\mu_i - \bar{x}) + (x_{ij} - \mu_i)]^2$$

$$= n \sum_{i=1}^{a} (\mu_i - \bar{x})^2 + \sum_{i=1}^{a} \sum_{j=1}^{n} (x_{ij} - \mu_i)^2$$

$$SS_{total} = SS_A + SS_{error}$$

$$= (a-1)s_A^2 + a(n-1)s_{error}^2$$

The left-hand side of the equation is called the total sum of squares. Thus, the identity has partitioned the total variance into two independent components: that due to the factor A and that due to the variation in the process as expressed by the residuals ε_{ij}.

In the analysis of variance, the convention is to define a quantity called the mean square, denoted MS, which is the sum of squares divided by the number of degrees of freedom. Thus, for the single factor experiment, we have

$$MS_A = \frac{SS_A}{(a-1)} = s_A^2 \qquad (a>1)$$

$$MS_{error} = \frac{SS_{error}}{a(n-1)} = s_{error}^2 \qquad (n>1)$$

The objective of the experiment is to determine whether or not the various levels of A have any statistically significant effect on the output x_{ij}. We now have the ability to determine this by forming the ratio of the mean square of the factor A with the independent mean square of the random error. This tells us whether or not the variance of A is a statistically significantly large portion of the total variance. Thus, the test statistic is

$$F_0 = \frac{MS_A}{MS_{error}}$$

The hypothesis is

TABLE 14.9
ANOVA Table for a Single-Factor Experiment with $n > 1$ Replicates

Factor	Sum of squares	Degrees of freedom	Mean square	F_0	p-value
A	SS_A	$a-1$	MS_A	MS_A / MS_{error}	
Error	SS_{error}	$a(n-1)$	MS_{error}		
Total	SS_{total}	$an-1$			

TABLE 14.10
Data for Example 14.7

Level	Observations			
1	143	141	150	146
2	152	149	137	143
3	134	133	132	127
4	129	127	132	129
5	147	148	144	142

$$H_0: \mu_1 = \mu_2 = \ldots = \mu_a$$
$$H_1: \mu_j \neq \mu_i \text{ for at least one } j \neq i$$

Thus, when

$$F_0 > f_{\alpha,\, a-1,\, a(n-1)}$$

the null hypothesis is rejected. The results of this analysis are usually presented in the form shown in Table 14.9.

A single-factor analysis of variance is obtained with

```
p = anova1(x)
```

where p is the p-value and x is the *transpose* of data as shown in Table 14.8. There are two additional outputs from this function: one is the ANOVA table shown in Table 14.9, and the other is a box plot of the variations in the medians of each of the a levels.

We now illustrate the analysis of variance of a single-factor experiment.

Example 14.7 Single-factor analysis of variance

Consider the data in Table 14.10. We shall write a script to generate the ANOVA table, display the p-value, compute the residuals, and determine whether or not they are normally distributed. We first create a function to convert the data into a form acceptable to anova1.

```
function d = DataAnoval
d = [143 141 150 146; ...
     152 149 137 143; ...
     134 133 132 127; ...
     129 127 132 129; ...
     147 148 144 142]';
```

The script is

```
vv = DataAnoval;
[r,c] = size(vv);
pp = anoval(vv);
meen = mean(vv);
k = 0;
for n = 1:r
 for m = 1:c
  k = k+1;
  e(k) = vv(n,m)−meen(m);
 end
end
disp(['p-value = ' num2str(pp)])
figure
normplot(e)
whitebg('white')
```

The nested `for` loop is needed to store all the residuals in a single vector. The `figure` function is used to open another figure window, because `anoval` opens two windows of its own. If the `figure` function weren't used, then one of the two figures generated by `anoval` would be overwritten. The following is displayed to the MATLAB command window:

p-value = 2.414e-005

Anoval produces the table in Figure 14.14a and the box plot in Figure 14.14b; Figure 14.14c is produced by `normplot`.

14.6.2 Multiple-Factor Experiments

Factorial Experiments. The results for a single-factor experiment can be extended to experiments with several factors, which are called factorial experiments because the procedure requires that we run all combinations of all the levels of each factor for each replicate of the experiment. We illustrate this for a two-factor experiment, which has the factor A at a levels and the factor B at b levels. The number of replicates is n (>1), and the output is x_{ijk}, where $i = 1, 2, ..., a, j = 1, 2, ..., b$, and $k = 1, 2, ..., n$. The intervals between each level of each factor do not have to be equal. The tabular form of these data is given in Table 14.11.

ANOVA Table

Source	SS	df	MS	F
Columns	1061	4	265.1	16.35
Error	243.3	15	16.22	
Total	1304	19		

(a)

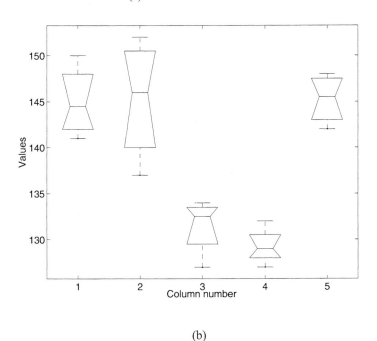

(b)

FIGURE 14.14
Analysis of variance of the data in Table 14.10: (a) ANOVA table; (b) box plot of the five levels;

The starting point is the sum-of-squares identity. Before proceeding with this identity, however, we introduce the following definitions for several different means:

$$\bar{x}_{ijn} = \frac{1}{n} \sum_{k=1}^{n} x_{ijk}$$

$$\bar{x}_{ibn} = \frac{1}{b} \sum_{j=1}^{b} \bar{x}_{ijn} = \frac{1}{bn} \sum_{j=1}^{b} \sum_{k=1}^{n} x_{ijk}$$

$$\bar{x}_{ajn} = \frac{1}{a} \sum_{i=1}^{a} \bar{x}_{ijn} = \frac{1}{an} \sum_{i=1}^{a} \sum_{k=1}^{n} x_{ijk}$$

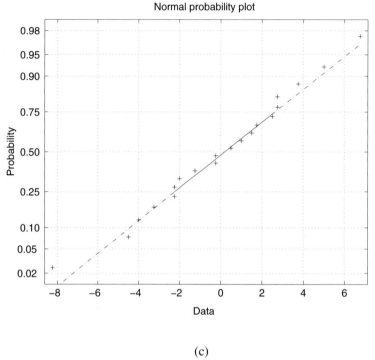

(c)

FIGURE 14.14 (CONTINUED)
Analysis of variance of the data in Table 14.10: (c) normal distribution plot of the residuals.

TABLE 14.11
Data Arrangement for a Two-Factor Factorial Experiment

		Factor B			
		1	2	...	b
Factor A	1	$y_{111}, y_{112}, ..., y_{11n}$	$y_{121}, y_{122}, ..., y_{12n}$		$y_{1b1}, y_{1b2}, ..., y_{1bn}$
	2	$y_{211}, y_{212}, ..., y_{21n}$	$y_{221}, y_{222}, ..., y_{22n}$		$y_{2b1}, y_{2b2}, ..., y_{2bn}$
	⋮				
	a	$y_{a11}, y_{a12}, ..., y_{a1n}$	$y_{a21}, y_{a22}, ..., y_{a2n}$		$y_{ab1}, y_{ab2}, ..., y_{abn}$

and the grand mean

$$\bar{x} = \frac{1}{abn} \sum_{i=1}^{a} \sum_{j=1}^{b} \sum_{k=1}^{n} x_{ijk}$$

TABLE 14.12
ANOVA Table for a Two-Factor Experiment with $n > 1$ Replicates

Factor	Sum of squares	Degrees of freedom	Mean square	F_0	$f_{\alpha, z, ab(n-1)}$	$p-$value
A	SS_A	$a-1$	$MS_A = SS_A/(a-1)$	MS_A/MS_{error}	(f-table, $z = a-1$)	
B	SS_B	$b-1$	$MS_B = SS_B/(b-1)$	MS_B/MS_{error}	(f-table, $z = b-1$)	
AB	SS_{AB}	$(a-1)(b-1)$	$MS_{AB} = SS_{AB}/(a-1)(b-1)$	MS_{AB}/MS_{error}	(f-table, $z = (a-1)(b-1)$)	
Error	SS_{error}	$ab(n-1)$	$MS_{error} = SS_{error}/ab(n-1)$			
Total	SS_{total}	$abn-1$				

The sum-of-squares identity for a two-factor analysis of variance is

$$SS_{total} = \sum_{i=1}^{a}\sum_{j=1}^{b}\sum_{k=1}^{n}(x_{ijk} - \bar{x})^2 = SS_A + SS_B + SS_{AB} + SS_{error}$$

where

$$SS_A = \sum_{i=1}^{a}\sum_{j=1}^{b}\sum_{k=1}^{n}(\bar{x}_{ibn} - \bar{x})^2 = bn\sum_{i=1}^{a}\bar{x}_{ibn}^2 - abn\bar{x}^2$$

$$SS_B = \sum_{i=1}^{a}\sum_{j=1}^{b}\sum_{k=1}^{n}(\bar{x}_{ajn} - \bar{x})^2 = an\sum_{j=1}^{b}\bar{x}_{ajn}^2 - abn\bar{x}^2$$

$$SS_{AB} = n\sum_{i=1}^{a}\sum_{j=1}^{b}(\bar{x}_{ijn} - \bar{x}_{ibn} - \bar{x}_{ajn} + \bar{x})^2$$

and

$$SS_{error} = \sum_{i=1}^{a}\sum_{j=1}^{b}\sum_{k=1}^{n}(x_{ijk} - \bar{x}_{ijn})^2 = \sum_{i=1}^{a}\sum_{j=1}^{b}\sum_{k=1}^{n}x_{ijk}^2 - n\sum_{i=1}^{a}\sum_{j=1}^{b}\bar{x}_{ijn}^2$$

The quantities SS_A, SS_B, SS_{AB}, SS_{error}, and SS_{total} have $(a-1)$, $(b-1)$, $(a-1)(b-1)$, $ab(n-1)$, and $abn-1$ degrees of freedom, respectively. The sum-of-squares term SS_{AB} indicates the interaction of factors A and B. The ANOVA table for a two-factor experiment is given in Table 14.12. The definitions of the mean-square values are also given in this table. It is seen that the analysis of variance isolates the interaction effects of the two factors and provides a means of ascertaining, through the ratio MS_{AB}/MS_{error}, whether or not the interaction of the factors is statistically significant at a stated confidence level.

The solution to a two factor factorial experiment is obtained from

```
p = anova2(y,n)
```

TABLE 14.13
Data for Example 14.8—*DataAnova2*

		Factor B		
		1	2	3
	1	130, 155, 74, 180	34, 40, 80, 75	20, 70, 82, 58
Factor A	2	150, 188, 159, 126	136, 122, 106, 115	25, 70, 58, 45
	3	138, 110, 168, 160	174, 120, 150, 139	96, 104, 82, 60

where n is the number of replicates and p is a three-element vector of p-values corresponding to the two factors and their interaction: $p(1)$ = column factor; $p(2)$ = row factor; and $p(3)$ = interaction of row and column factors. The matrix y follows the form of the data in Table 14.11 as follows:

$$
y = \begin{bmatrix}
y_{111} & y_{121} & \cdots & y_{1b1} \\
y_{112} & y_{122} & & y_{1b2} \\
\vdots & & & \\
y_{11n} & y_{12n} & & y_{1bn} \\
y_{211} & y_{221} & & y_{2b1} \\
y_{212} & y_{222} & & y_{2b2} \\
\vdots & & & \\
y_{21n} & y_{22n} & & y_{2bn} \\
\vdots & & & \\
y_{a11} & y_{a21} & & y_{ab1} \\
y_{a12} & y_{a22} & & y_{ab2} \\
\vdots & & & \\
y_{a1n} & y_{a2n} & & y_{abn}
\end{bmatrix}
$$

We now illustrate these relationships.

Example 14.8 Two-factor analysis of variance

Consider the data shown in Table 14.13. To put these data in the appropriate format we create the following function:

```
function d = DataAnova2
dc1 = [[130 155 74 180]';[150 188 159 126]';[138 110 168 160]'];
dc2 = [[34 40 80 75]';[136 122 106 115]';[174 120 150 139]'];
dc3 = [[20 70 82 58]';[25 70 58 45]';[96 104 82 60]'];
d = [dc1 dc2 dc3];
```

The script is

```
pvalue = anova2(DataAnova2,4);
disp(['p value of column = ' num2str(pvalue(1))])
disp(['p value of row = ' num2str(pvalue(2))])
disp(['p value of column and row = ' num2str(pvalue(3))])
```

which, upon execution, displays in the MATLAB command window

p value of column = 1.9086e-007
p value of row = 0.0019761
p value of column and row = 0.018611

and displays the following table in a figure window:

ANOVA Table

Source	SS	df	MS	F
Columns	3.912e+004	2	1.956e+004	28.97
Rows	1.068e+004	2	5342	7.911
Interaction	9614	4	2403	3.56
Error	1.823e+004	27	675.2	
Total	7.765e+004	35		

Thus, based on the p-values, we see that factors A and B are statistically significant at the greater than 99.8% level and that their interaction is significant at the 98% level.

2^k **Factorial Experiments.** If the factorial experiments described in the previous section contain k factors and each factor is considered at only two levels, then the experiment is called a 2^k factorial design. It implicitly assumes that there is a linear relationship between the two levels of each factor. This assumption leads to certain simplifications in how the tests are conducted and how the results are analyzed.

The convention is to denote the value of the high level of a factor with either "1" or "+," and the value of the low level "0" or "−." Then the 2^k combination of factors that comprise one run, which represents one replicate, is given in Table 14.14 for $k = 2$, 3, and 4. The table is used as follows. For the 2^2 ($k = 2$) factorial experiment, only the columns labeled A and B and the first four rows ($m = 1, ..., 4$) are used. The four combinations of the factors are run in a random order. One such random order is shown in the column labeled 2^2. Thus, the combination in row 2 is run first, with A high (A_{high}) and B low (B_{low}). This yields the output value $y_{2,1}$. Then the combination shown in the fourth row is run, where both A and B are at their high levels (A_{high} and B_{high}, respectively). This gives the output response $y_{4,1}$. After the remaining combinations have been run, one replicate of the experiment has been completed. A newly obtained random order for the run is obtained, one that is most likely different from the one shown in the column labeled 2^2, and the four combinations are run in the new order to get the output response for the second replicate. For $k = 3$, the factors are A, B, and C, and the first 8 rows of the table are used; for $k = 4$, the factors are A, B, C, and D,

TABLE 14.14

The Levels and Run Order of Each Factor for a 2^2, 2^3, and 2^4 Factorial Experiment

m	A	B	C	D	$j = 1$	$j = 2$	...	2^2	2^3	2^4
1	−	−	−	−	$y_{1.1}$	$y_{1.2}$		3	5	6
2	+	−	−	−	$y_{2.1}$	$y_{2.2}$		1	7	11
3	−	+	−	−	$y_{3.1}$	$y_{3.2}$		4	8	14
4	+	+	−	−	$y_{4.1}$	$y_{4.2}$		2	4	5
5	−	−	+	−	$y_{5.1}$	$y_{5.2}$			2	13
6	+	−	+	−	$y_{6.1}$	$y_{6.2}$			1	2
7	−	+	+	−	$y_{7.1}$	$y_{7.2}$			3	16
8	+	+	+	−	$y_{8.1}$	$y_{8.2}$			6	15
9	−	−	−	+	$y_{9.1}$	$y_{9.2}$				9
10	+	−	−	+	$y_{10.1}$	$y_{10.2}$				7
11	−	+	−	+	$y_{11.1}$	$y_{11.2}$				10
12	+	+	−	+	$y_{12.1}$	$y_{12.2}$				3
13	−	−	+	+	$y_{13.1}$	$y_{13.2}$				8
14	+	−	+	+	$y_{14.1}$	$y_{14.2}$				4
15	−	+	+	+	$y_{15.1}$	$y_{15.2}$				1
16	+	+	+	+	$y_{16.1}$	$y_{16.2}$				12

Run no. Factors and their levels — Data $(y_{m.j})$ — Run order number*

* One set of randomly ordered runs for $j = 1$ only. For $j = 2$, a new set of a randomly generated run order is used, and so on.

and all 16 rows of the table are used. One set of a random run order is given for each of these cases in the columns labeled 2^3 and 2^4, respectively.

After the data have been collected, they are analyzed as follows, provided that the number of replicates is greater than one. Consider the tabulations in Table 14.15. (Recall Table 4.2.) The + and − signs in each column represent +1 and −1, respectively. The columns for the primary factors A, B, C, and D are the same as those given in Table 14.14, where, again, the + and − signs stand for +1 and −1, respectively. The columns representing all the interaction terms are obtained by multiplying the corresponding signs in the columns of the primary factors. Thus, the signs in the columns designating the interaction ABC are obtained by multiplying the signs in the columns labeled A, B, and C. For example, in row seven ($m = 7$) $A = -1$, $B = +1$, and $C = +1$; therefore, the sign in the seventh row of the column labeled ABC is −1 [= (−1)(+1)(+1)]. Furthermore, for the 2^2 experiment the first three columns and the rows $m = 1, 2, ..., 4$ are used; for the 2^3 experiment, the first seven columns and the rows $m = 1, 2, ..., 8$ are used; and for the 2^4 experiment all 15 columns and the rows $m = 1, 2, ..., 16$ are used. The method for computing the signs in Table 14.15 was shown in Section 4.3.1.

TABLE 14.15
Definitions of Various Terms That Are Used to Calculate the Sum of Squares and Mean-Square Values for a 2^2, 2^3, and 2^4 Experiment

Factors and their interactions (λ)†															Data‡			
A	B	A B	C	A C	B C	A B C	D	A D	B D	A B D	C D	A C D	B C D	A B C D	$j=1$	... $j=n$	$S_m{}^{\#}$	m
−	−	+	−	+	+	−	−	+	+	−	+	−	−	+	$y_{1,1}$	$y_{1,n}$	S_1	1
+	−	−	−	−	+	+	−	−	+	+	+	+	−	−	$y_{2,1}$	$y_{2,n}$	S_2	2
−	+	−	−	+	−	+	−	+	−	+	+	−	+	−	$y_{3,1}$	$y_{3,n}$	S_3	3
+	+	+	−	−	−	−	−	−	−	−	+	+	+	+	$y_{4,1}$	$y_{4,n}$	S_4	4
−	−	+	+	−	−	+	−	+	+	−	−	+	+	−	$y_{5,1}$	$y_{5,n}$	S_5	5
+	−	−	+	+	−	−	−	−	+	+	−	−	+	+	$y_{6,1}$	$y_{6,n}$	S_6	6
−	+	−	+	−	+	−	−	+	−	+	−	+	−	+	$y_{7,1}$	$y_{7,n}$	S_7	7
+	+	+	+	+	+	+	−	−	−	−	−	−	−	−	$y_{8,1}$	$y_{8,n}$	S_8	8
−	−	+	−	+	+	−	+	−	−	+	−	+	+	−	$y_{9,1}$	$y_{9,n}$	S_9	9
+	−	−	−	−	+	+	+	+	−	−	−	−	+	+	$y_{10,1}$	$y_{10,n}$	S_{10}	10
−	+	−	−	+	−	+	+	−	+	−	−	+	−	+	$y_{11,1}$	$y_{11,n}$	S_{11}	11
+	+	+	−	−	−	−	+	+	+	+	−	−	−	−	$y_{12,1}$	$y_{12,n}$	S_{12}	12
−	−	+	+	−	−	+	+	−	−	+	+	−	−	+	$y_{13,1}$	$y_{13,n}$	S_{13}	13
+	−	−	+	+	−	−	+	+	−	−	+	+	−	−	$y_{14,1}$	$y_{14,n}$	S_{14}	14
−	+	−	+	−	+	−	+	−	+	−	+	−	+	−	$y_{15,1}$	$y_{15,n}$	S_{15}	15
+	+	+	+	+	+	+	+	+	+	+	+	+	+	+	$y_{16,1}$	$y_{16,n}$	S_{16}	16

† The '+' and '−' stand for +1 and −1, respectively, although they also indicate the high and low levels of the factors.
‡ The data are obtained as indicated in Table 14.14.

$$^{\#}\ S_m = \sum_{j=1}^{n} y_{m,j}$$

The sum of squares is obtained for $n > 1$ and for a given value of k as follows:

$$SS_{total} = \sum_{j=1}^{n} \sum_{m=1}^{2^k} y_{m,j}^2 - 2^k n \bar{y}^2$$

$$SS_{error} = SS_{total} - \sum_{\lambda} SS_{\lambda}$$

$$SS_\lambda = \frac{C_\lambda^2}{n2^k} \qquad \lambda = A, B, AB, \dots$$

where

$$C_\lambda = \sum_{m=1}^{2^k} S_m \times (\text{sign in row } m \text{ of column } \lambda) \qquad \lambda = A, B, AB, \dots$$

$$\bar{y} = \frac{1}{n2^k} \sum_{m=1}^{2^k} S_m$$

and S_m is defined in Table 14.15.

The average value of the effect of the primary factors and their interactions is obtained from the relation

$$\text{Effect}_\lambda = \frac{C_\lambda}{n2^{k-1}} \qquad \lambda = A, B, AB, \dots$$

where $Effect_\lambda$ is called the effect of λ. As seen in Table 14.15, for $k = 2$ there are three λ's: A, B, and AB; for $k = 3$ there are seven λ's: A, B, C, AB, AC, BC, and ABC; and for $k = 4$ there are fifteen λ's: A, B, C, D, AB, AC, BC, AD, BD, CD, ABC, ABD, ACD, BCD, and $ABCD$.

The mean-square values for the main effects and their interactions are simply

$$MS_\lambda = SS_\lambda$$

since the number of degrees of freedom for each primary factor and their interactions is one. The mean square for the error is

$$MS_{error} = \frac{SS_{error}}{2^k(n-1)} \qquad n > 1$$

The test statistic for each factor and their interactions is

$$F_\lambda = \frac{MS_\lambda}{MS_{error}} = \frac{MS_\lambda}{SS_{error}/[2^k(n-1)]} \qquad \lambda = A, B, AB, \dots \quad n > 1$$

The ANOVA table for the 2^k factorial analysis is given in Table 14.16.

The results of ANOVA for the 2^k factorial design can be used directly to obtain a multiple-regression model that estimates the output of the process as a function of the statistically significant primary factors and the statistically significant interactions. We first introduce the coded variable x_β

$$x_\beta = \frac{2\beta - \beta_{low} - \beta_{high}}{\beta_{high} - \beta_{low}}$$

TABLE 14.16
ANOVA Table for a 2^k Factorial Experiment with $n > 1$ Replicates

Factor	Sum of squares	Degrees of freedom	Mean square	F_λ	$f_{\alpha,1,(n-1)2^k}$
A	SS_A	1	MS_A	MS_A/MS_{error}	(value from f-table)
B	SS_B	1	MS_B	MS_B/MS_{error}	(value from f-table)
C	SS_C	1	MS_C	MS_C/MS_{error}	(value from f-table)
$\vdots$					
AB	SS_{AB}	1	MS_{AB}	MS_{AB}/MS_{error}	(value from f-table)
AC	SS_{AC}	1	MS_{AC}	MS_{AC}/MS_{error}	(value from f-table)
BC	SS_{BC}	1	MS_{BC}	MS_{BC}/MS_{error}	(value from f-table)
$\vdots$					
ABC	SS_{ABC}	1	MS_{ABC}	MS_{ABC}/MS_{error}	(value from f-table)
$\vdots$					
Error	SS_{error}	$2^k(n-1)$	MS_{error}		
Total	SS_{total}	$n2^k-1$			

where β is a primary variable—that is, $\beta = A, B, C, \ldots$ Thus, if $\beta = A$, then when $\beta = A_{high}$, $x_A = +1$, and when $\beta = A_{low}$, $x_A = -1$. If $A_{low} \le A \le A_{high}$, then $-1 \le x_A \le +1$.

An estimate of the average output y_{avg} is

$$y_{avg} = \bar{y} + 0.5\left[\sum_\lambda \text{Effect}_\lambda x_\lambda + \sum_\lambda \sum_\beta \text{Effect}_{\lambda\beta} x_\lambda x_\beta + \sum_\lambda \sum_\beta \sum_\gamma \text{Effect}_{\lambda\beta\gamma} x_\lambda x_\beta x_\gamma \cdots\right]$$

where $\lambda, \beta, \gamma, \ldots$ have the values of $A, B, C, \ldots$ and correspond only to those combinations of subscripts that indicate statistically significant factors and interactions, and the x_α ($-1 \le x_\alpha \le +1$) are the coded values.

We now illustrate these relationships.

Example 14.9 Analysis of a 2^4 factorial experiment

We generate the ANOVA table for the data in Table 14.17, which were obtained from a two-replicate 2^4 factorial experiment. We shall include in the ANOVA table the effects. The run numbers correspond to those of Table 14.14. First, we create a function *FactorialData* for these data.

```
function dat = FactorialData
dat1 = [159 168 158 166 175 179 173 179 164 187 163 185 168 197 170 194]';
dat2 = [163 175 163 168 178 183 168 182 159 189 159 191 174 199 174 198]';
dat = [dat1 dat2];
```

TABLE 14.17
Data for a Two-Replicate 2^4 Experiment

Run no.*	Data ($y_{m,j}$)	
m	$j = 1$	$j = 2$
1	159	163
2	168	175
3	158	163
4	166	168
5	175	178
6	179	183
7	173	168
8	179	182
9	164	159
10	187	189
11	163	159
12	185	191
13	168	174
14	197	199
15	170	174
16	194	198

* Run number corresponds to level combinations given in Table 14.14.

Next we convert the script from Section 4.3.1 into a function called *FactorialSigns*, which determines the signs in Table 14.15. Thus,

```
function s = FactorialSigns(k)
s = ones(2^k,2^k-1);
for r = 1:2:2^k
  s(r,1) = -1;
end
for c = 2:k
  e = 2^(c-1);
  for r = 1:e
    s(r,e) = -1;
  end
  for r = e+1:2^(k)
    s(r,2^(c-2)) = s(r-e,2^(c-2));
  end
end
for m = 2:k
```

```
  e = 2^(m–1);
  for j = 1:e–1
    s(:,e+j) = s(:,j).*s(:,e);
  end
end
```

The script to create the ANOVA table is

```
tag = str2mat('A','B','AB','C','AC','BC','ABC','D','AD','BD','ABD',...
                     'CD','ACD','BCD','ABCD');
k = 4; n = 2;
fdata = FactorialData;
s = FactorialSigns(k);
Sm = sum(fdata')';
yBar = sum(Sm)/n/2^k;
SStotal = sum(sum(fdata.^2))–yBar^2*n*2^k;
for nn = 1:2^k–1
  Clambda = sum(s(:,nn).*Sm);
  SSlambda(nn) = Clambda^2/2^(k+1);
  EffectLambda(nn) = Clambda./2^k;
end
SSerror = SStotal–sum(SSlambda);
MSerror = SSerror/2^k;
f0 = SSlambda/MSerror;
pValue = 1–fcdf(f0,1,2^k);
disp('Factor      SS         MS         Effect       f-lambda   p-value')
disp([tag repmat('    ',15,1) num2str(SSlambda',6) repmat('    ',15,1)...
     num2str(SSlambda',6) repmat('    ',15,1) num2str(EffectLambda',6)...
     repmat('    ',15,1) num2str(f0',6) repmat('    ',15,1) num2str(pValue',6)])
disp(['SSerror ' num2str(SSerror,6) ' ' num2str(MSerror,6)])
disp(['SStotal ' num2str(SStotal,6)])
disp(['yBar = ' num2str(yBar,6)])
```

The execution of this script results in the following information being displayed to the MATLAB window, which has been manually realigned for clarity.

Factor	SS	MS	Effect	f-lambda	p-value
A	2312	2312	17	241.778	4.45067e-011
B	21.125	21.125	-1.625	2.20915	0.156633
AB	0.125	0.125	-0.125	0.0130719	0.910397
C	946.125	946.125	10.875	98.9412	2.95785e-008
AC	3.125	3.125	-0.625	0.326797	0.575495
BC	0.5	0.5	-0.25	0.0522876	0.822026
ABC	4.5	4.5	0.75	0.470588	0.502537
D	561.125	561.125	8.375	58.6797	9.69219e-007

AD	666.125	666.125	9.125	69.6601	3.18663e-007
BD	12.5	12.5	1.25	1.30719	0.269723
ABD	2	2	-0.5	0.20915	0.653583
CD	12.5	12.5	-1.25	1.30719	0.269723
ACD	0	0	0	0	1
BCD	0.125	0.125	0.125	0.0130719	0.910397
ABCD	21.125	21.125	-1.625	2.20915	0.156633
SSerror	153	9.5625			
SStotal	4716				
yBar =	175.25				

It is seen that at the considerably better than 95% confidence level, factors A, C, and D and interaction AD are statistically significant and, therefore, influence the outcome of the process. In fact, the sum of the sum of squares of these four quantities is 4,485. Thus, the sum-of-squares contribution of the quantities that are not statistically significant is $78 = 4716 - 4485 - 153$, or 1.65% of the total sum of squares.

We now use these results to obtain the following regression equation at the greater than 95% confidence level.

$$y_{\text{avg}} = 175.25 + 8.50x_A + 5.44x_C + 4.10x_D + 4.56x_A x_D$$

The residuals are the differences between the measured values $y_{m,j}$ and y_{avg} at the 2^4 combinations of coded values of x_γ shown in Table 14.14. We now use the following script to determine the residuals and plot them using normplot.

```
fdata = FactorialData;
s = FactorialSigns(4);
yAvg = 175.25+8.5*s(:,1)+5.44*s(:,3)+4.1*s(:,4)+4.56*s(:,1).*s(:,4);
normplot([fdata(:,1)–yAvg; fdata(:,2)–yAvg])
whitebg('white')
```

which, when executed, results in Figure 14.15. We see that the residuals are acceptable.

EXERCISES

14.1 Consider the data shown in Table 14.18. We shall assume two scenarios: (1) all the data in Table 14.18 comprise one set denoted S_0; and (2) the data in each of the five pairs of columns represent five separate sets denoted S_j, $j = 1, 2, ..., 5$.

a) Determine the harmonic mean of data set S_0 and compare it with the mean and the geometric mean. The harmonic mean $\bar{x}_h$ is defined as

$$\frac{1}{\bar{x}_h} = \sum_{i=1}^{n} \frac{1}{x_i}$$

b) What are the mean values and standard deviations of the six data sets S_j, $j = 0, 1, 2, ..., 5$.

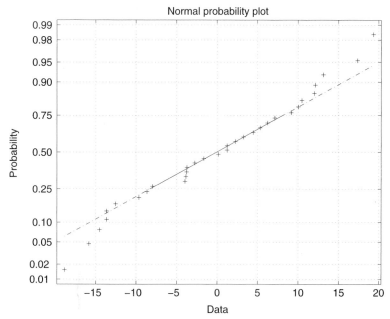

FIGURE 14.15
Residual plot for the data used in Example 14.9.

TABLE 14.18
Data for Exercise 14.1

1		2		3		4		5	
1115	1567	1223	1782	1055	798	1016	2100	910	1501
1310	1883	375	1522	1764	1020	1102	1594	1730	1238
1540	1203	2265	1792	1330	865	1605	2023	1102	990
1502	1270	1910	1000	1608	2130	706	1315	1578	1468
1258	1015	1018	1820	1535	1421	2215	1269	758	1512
1315	845	1452	1940	1781	1109	785	1260	1416	1750
1085	1674	1890	1120	1750	1481	885	1888	1560	1642

c) Display a vertical box plot of data sets $S_j, j = 1, 2, \ldots, 5$.

d) Determine the confidence limits on the differences in the mean values of S_0 and each $S_j, j = 1, 2, \ldots,$ 5, at the 95% confidence level assuming that the standard deviations are unknown but equal (Case 4 in Tables 14.3 and 14.5). What are the p-values for each of the data sets? Are any of the mean values of the data sets S_j statistically significantly different from the mean of S_0? Do these conclusions qualitatively agree with the results displayed in (c) above?

TABLE 14.19
Data for Exercise 14.4

Process #1		Process #2	
88.4	89.0	92.6	93.2
93.2	90.5	93.2	91.7
87.4	90.8	89.2	91.5
94.3	93.1	94.8	92.0
93.0	92.8	93.3	90.7
94.3	91.9	94.0	93.8

14.2 (a) A company's telephone help line receives an average of five calls per minute during its working hours. What is the probability that it could receive: (i) eight calls per minute; (ii) two calls per minute?

(b) The telephone system can handle 10 calls per minute; if there is more than this number, the caller gets a busy signal. What is the probability of getting a busy signal? [Answers: (a) (i) 0.065278; (ii) 0.084224; (b) 0.013695.]

14.3 The probability that a structural member can withstand a load L_o is 0.7. If 15 of these members are to be used, then what is the probability that at least 12 of them can withstand L_o? [Answer: 0.29687.]

14.4 Taguchi defines the average loss factor of a process as being proportional to

$$L_{avg} = s^2 + (\bar{x} - \tau)^2$$

where τ is the target mean. In other words, when comparing two processes the one whose mean is closest to τ and whose variance is the smallest is the process with the lowest loss factor. For the data in Table 14.19, determine which process has the lowest average loss factor when $\tau = 92.0$. [Answer: $L_1 = 5.5904$ and $L_2 = 2.6936$.]

14.5 A manufacturer found that 20% of one of its products were underweight. There are 24 of these items to a case. If we assume that the weight of each item is independent of the weight of another item, then one can apply the binomial distribution.

a) What is the expected number of underweight items in a case and its variance?

b) What is the probability that there are no more than two underweight items in a case?

c) What is the probability that none of the items in the case is underweight?

d) Plot on the same figure the probability mass function and the cumulative distribution function as a function of the number of underweight items in a case.

[Answer: (a) expected value = 4.8 and variance = 3.84; (b) 0.11452; (c) 0.0047224.]

14.6 The chi-square statistic is used to perform goodness-of-fit tests. Let there be k categories (cells) and in each category, the expected value is $\hat{p}_i$, $i = 1, 2, ..., k$. If, in an experiment, the number of observations (occurrences) that fall in each category is x_i, $i = 1, 2, ..., k$, then the chi-square test statistic is

$$X^2 = \sum_{i=1}^{k} (x_i - e_i)^2 / e_i$$

where $e_i = n\ \hat{p}_i$ and

$$n = \sum_{i=1}^{k} x_i = \sum_{i=1}^{k} e_i$$

If, in any category, $e_i < 5$, then the corresponding e_i and x_i must be combined with their respective next adjacent e_i and x_i until $e_i \geq 5$. See Exercise 4.5.

We use this test statistic to test the hypothesis

$$H_0 : p_i = \hat{p}_i \quad i = 1, ..., k$$

where $p_i = x_i / n$. If

$$X^2 \leq \chi^2_{\alpha, k-1}$$

then H_0 is accepted. In practice, α is not given, and instead the p-value is determined. The closer the p-value is to 1, the more confident we are that the observed category occurrences x_i are close to the expected number of occurrences e_i.

(a) Suppose that a piece of equipment is assumed to have a probability of malfunctioning as follows: from a mechanical malfunction, 0.60 ($\hat{p}_1 = 0.6$); from an electrical malfunction, 0.25 ($\hat{p}_2 = 0.25$); and from an operator-caused malfunction, 0.15 ($\hat{p}_3 = 0.15$). From 55 ($n = 55$) recorded equipment breakdowns, 32 are due to mechanical malfunctions ($x_1 = 32$), 14 are due to electrical malfunctions ($x_2 = 14$), and 9 are due to operator-caused malfunctions ($x_3 = 9$). Using the method described above, determine the plausibility that these $\hat{p}_i$ are representative of this piece of equipment's breakdowns. [Answer: p-value = 0.94979; therefore, very plausible.]

(b) The probabilities $\hat{p}_i$ can also be determined from a statistical model. For example, let us assume a Poisson distribution, which is based on a choice (guess) for λ. In this case,

$$e_i = n \frac{e^{-\lambda} \lambda^{i-1}}{(i-1)!} \quad i=1,2,...,k+1$$

For $i > k+1$,

$$e_i = n \left(1 - \sum_{i=1}^{k+1} \frac{e^{-\lambda} \lambda^{i-1}}{(i-1)!} \right) \quad i > k+1$$

If the number of defects found in each product of a sample of 85 products is as shown in Table 14.20, then determine whether it is plausible that the number of defects found in the product has a Poisson distribution with $\lambda = 3$. In this case, $k = 8$. Also, some regrouping of e_i and x_i is required. Use the results of Exercise 4.4. [Answer: $x_i = $ [17 20 25 14 6 3]; $e_i = $ [16.9276 19.0436 19.0436 14.2827 8.5696 7.1330]; p-value = 0.40592 and, therefore, somewhat plausible.]

TABLE 14.20
Data for Exercise 14.6

i	Number of defects $(i-1)$	Number of occurrences, x_i
1	0	3
2	1	14
3	2	20
4	3	25
5	4	14
6	5	6
7	6	2
8	7	0
9	8	1
10	≥ 9	0

TABLE 14.21
Data for Exercise 14.7

Group 1		Group 2	
88	81	76	79
79	83	83	85
84	90	78	76
89	87	80	80
81	78	84	82
83	80	86	78
82	87	77	78
79	85	75	77
82	80	81	81
85	88	78	80

14.7 To determine whether or not one should use Case 4 or Case 5 in Table 14.5, an F-test is first performed on the ratio of the variances as denoted in Case 7 of the table. If the variances are statistically significantly different, then Case 5 is used; otherwise, Case 4 is used. Write a script to determine whether or not there is a difference between the means of the data given in Table 14.21, and then based on the results, determine whether or not the means are different. Also create a box plot to visualize the data and qualitatively support your conclusions. [Answer: From F-test on the ratio of variances $p = 0.47092$; therefore, there is no difference in the variances. From a t-test on differences in means $p = 0.0009342$; therefore, means are different.]

TABLE 14.22
Data for Exercise 14.8

2.5629	2.5630
2.5630	2.5628
2.5628	2.5623
2.5634	2.5631
2.5619	2.5635
2.5613	2.5623

14.8 The process capability ratio (PCR) is a measure of the ability of a process to meet specifications that are given in terms of a lower specification limit LSL and an upper specification limit USL. It is defined as

$$PCR = \frac{USL - LSL}{6\hat{\sigma}}$$

for a centered process and as

$$PCR_k = \min\left[\frac{USL - \bar{x}}{3\hat{\sigma}}, \frac{\bar{x} - LSL}{3\hat{\sigma}}\right]$$

for a noncentered process. The quantity $\hat{\sigma}$ is the estimate of the standard deviation of the process and $\bar{x}$ an estimate of its mean. When $PCR > 1$, very few defective or nonconforming units are produced; when $PCR = 1$, then 0.27% (or 2700 parts per million) non conforming units are produced; and when $PCR < 1$, a large number of nonconforming units are produced. The quantity $100/PCR$ is the percentage of the specification width used by the process. When $PCR = PCR_k$, then the process is centered.

The number of nonconforming parts is Np, where N is the total number of parts produced and

$$p = 1 - \Phi\left(\frac{USL - \bar{x}}{\hat{\sigma}}\right) + \Phi\left(\frac{LSL - \bar{x}}{\hat{\sigma}}\right)$$

where Φ is given by Eq. (14.16). Recall, also, Figure 14.5c and Eq. (14.18).

For the data in Table 14.22 use the MATLAB function `capable` to determine p, PCR, and PCR_k when $LSL = 2.560$ and $USL = 2.565$. Is the process centered? [Answer: $p = 1.5351\text{e}{-}004$, $PCR = 1.3103$ and $PCR_k = 1.2099$.]

14.9 The reliability of a component $R(t)$ is the probability that it operates without failure for a length of time t. If the probability distribution function of the life of the component is $f(t)$, then its cumulative distribution is

$$F(t) = P(T \le t) = \int_{-\infty}^{t} f(u)\,du = \int_{0}^{t} f(u)\,du$$

which is the probability of the time to failure. Thus,

$$R(t) = 1 - F(t)$$

TABLE 14.23
Data for Exercise 14.10

y	x_1	x_2
144	18	52
142	24	40
124	12	40
64	30	48
96	30	32
74	26	56
136	26	24
54	22	64
92	22	16
96	14	64
92	10	56
82	10	24
76	6	48
68	6	32

The hazard rate function $h(t)$ is the chance of a component, which has not yet failed at time t, suddenly failing. It is given as

$$h(t) = \frac{f(t)}{R(t)} = \frac{f(t)}{1 - F(t)}$$

(a) Plot the hazard-rate function and the reliability on the same graph when $f(t)$ is the exponential distribution given by

$$f(t) = \frac{1}{\mu} e^{-t/\mu}$$

Assume $\mu = 1$ and use exppdf and expcdf.

(b) Plot the hazard-rate function and the reliability when $f(t)$ is the Weibull distribution with $\alpha = 1$ and $\beta = 0.5, 1, 2,$ and 4. Use subplot to create a 2×2 array of four figures, each with a pair of curves corresponding to a β.

14.10 (a) For the model below determine β_j for the data in Table 14.23, and show that this model is a good fit to these data.

$$y = \beta_0 + \beta_1 x_1 + \beta_2 x_2 + \beta_3 x_1^2 + \beta_4 x_2^2 + \beta_5 x_1 x_2$$

(b) Using the values found for β_j plot its surface and contour to plot the contours of the projection of this surface onto the (x_1, x_2)-plane.

(c) Determine the coordinates of the maximum value of this fitted surface. [Answer: $x_1 = 18.7635$ and $x_2 = 38.0156$.]

TABLE 14.24
Data for Exercise 14.11

1.55	15.70
3.05	16.35
3.65	17.70
5.20	17.95
7.75	19.45
10.45	19.80
10.85	20.05
10.90	32.75
12.65	35.45
15.25	49.35

14.11 The cumulative distribution function for the lognormal distribution is given by

$$F(t) = \Phi\left(\frac{\ln(t) - \bar{x}_L}{s_L}\right)$$

where

$$\bar{x}_L = \frac{1}{n}\sum_{i=1}^{n}\ln(t_i) \qquad s_L^2 = \frac{1}{n-1}\left[\sum_{i=1}^{n}(\ln(t_i))^2 - n\bar{x}_L^2\right] \qquad \text{(a)}$$

If we take the inverse of this equation we obtain

$$y = \beta_0 + \beta_1 x$$

where

$$y = \Phi^{-1}(F(t)) \qquad x = \ln(t) \qquad \beta_0 = -\frac{\bar{x}_L}{s_L} \qquad \beta_1 = \frac{1}{s_L}$$

and $\Phi^{-1}(\ldots)$ is obtained from `norminv`. The mean and variance of t (not $\ln(t)$, which has a normal distribution) are given, respectively, by

$$\bar{x}_t = \exp\left(\bar{x}_L + s_L^2/2\right) \qquad s_t^2 = \left(\exp\left(s_L^2\right) - 1\right)\exp\left(2\bar{x}_L + s_L^2\right)$$

which can be obtained from `lognstat`.

(a) For the data in Table 14.24, which have already been sorted, determine whether or not they are distributed lognormally using the technique outlined prior to Example 14.3. In other words, plot $F(t)$ as a function of $\ln(t)$ and the fitted line, and also use `normplot` to display the residuals.

(b) Compare the values of x_L and s_L obtained by the graphical method to those obtained from Eq. (a). [Answer: From curve fit: $x_L = 2.5072$ and $s_L = 0.88841$; from Eq. (a): $x_L = 2.5072$ and $s_L = 0.85441$.]

14.12 The correlation coefficient R for a simple linear regression analysis can be obtained from Eq. (14.32). We can test the hypothesis that

TABLE 14.25
Data for Exercise 14.12

x	y	x	y
10.0	4.746	11.6	5.211
12.0	5.466	14.8	6.264
6.8	3.171	7.2	3.411
5.4	1.500	15.7	6.537
20.0	6.708	17.6	6.336
19.4	7.158	14.0	5.400
19.1	6.882	10.9	4.503
6.1	1.674	18.2	6.909
16.3	6.498	20.4	6.930
12.4	5.598	8.2	3.582
5.8	1.959	7.9	3.432
12.7	5.790	4.9	0.369
9.2	4.686		

$$H_0: R = 0$$
$$H_1: R \neq 0$$

by forming the test statistic

$$t_0 = \frac{R\sqrt{n-2}}{\sqrt{1-R^2}}$$

and comparing it with $t_{\alpha/2,n-2}$. If $t_0 > t_{\alpha/2,n-2}$, then we reject H_0. In practice, we examine the p-value corresponding to t_0. The confidence limits on the correlation coefficient r, for $n \geq 25$, can be estimated from

$$\tanh\left(\tanh^{-1}(R) - \frac{z_{\alpha/2}}{\sqrt{n-3}}\right) \leq r \leq \tanh\left(\tanh^{-1}(R) + \frac{z_{\alpha/2}}{\sqrt{n-3}}\right)$$

where $z_{\alpha/2} = \texttt{norminv}(1-\alpha/2)$ [recall Eq. (14.19)].

For the data given in Table 14.25:

(a) Determine the regression coefficients when the model is of the form $y = \beta_0 + \beta_1/x$.

(b) Plot the fitted line and the data points.

(c) Determine whether or not the residuals are normally distributed.

(d) Determine: (i) whether or not the correlation coefficient is different than 0; and (ii) its confidence limits at the 95% confidence level.

[Answer: (a) $\beta_0 = 8.9366$, $\beta_1 = -41.6073$; (d) $0.976998 \leq 0.98996 \leq 0.99564$.]

TABLE 14.26
Data for a 2^4 Factorial Experiment with $n = 1$

Run no.[†]	y_m	Run no.[†]	y_m
1	86	9	90
2	200	10	142
3	90	11	96
4	208	12	130
5	150	13	136
6	172	14	120
7	140	15	160
8	192	16	130

[†] Run number corresponds to level combinations given in Table 14.14.

14.13 In multiple linear regression analysis one of two types of residuals are frequently examined: (a) the standardized residuals, which are defined as

$$d_i = \frac{e_i}{\hat{\sigma}}$$

where $\hat{\sigma}^2$ is given by Eq. (14.41); and (b) the studentized residuals, which are defined as

$$r_i = \frac{e_i}{\hat{\sigma}\sqrt{1 - h_{ii}}}$$

where h_{ii} is the ith diagonal element of

$$\mathbf{H} = \mathbf{X}(\mathbf{X}'\mathbf{X})^{-1}\mathbf{X}'$$

and $\mathbf{X}$ is given by Eq. (14.35).

Using the model in Example 14.6 and the corresponding data in Table 14.7 determine the standardized and studentized residuals. Plot these residuals as a function of the average output $\hat{y}_i (= y_i - e_i, y_i$ are the output values given in Table 14.7) on the same graph using two different symbols to differentiate them. Are any of these residuals outliers—that is, do any if them exceed 3. Label the figure and identify the two different sets of residuals with `legend`.

14.14 The formulas given for the 2^k factorial experiment can be applied when $n = 1$ by modifying the method as follows. The effects $Effects_\lambda$ are computed as described in Section 14.6.2, and then ordered from most positive to most negative. See the column in the tabulated results of Example 14.9 labeled "Effect." During the ordering one must be keep track of the factors and their corresponding interactions. The ordered effects are then plotted using `normplot`. The effects that are negligible (not statistically significant) will be normally distributed and will tend to fall on a straight line on this plot, whereas the effects that are statistically significant will lie considerably off this straight line. Consider the data given in Table 14.26, which were obtained from a 2^4 design with a single replicate, and determine which values are statistically significant. This determination is made visually from the results of `normplot` and the listing of the ordered effects and their corresponding factor or interaction. [Answer: A, C, D, AD and AC, which account for 96.6% of the total sum of squares. The ordered factors and their interactions are, from most positive to most negative: A, C, B, BCD, BC, ABC, ACD, CD, BD, AB, ABCD, ABD, D, AD, AC. $Effect_A = 43.25$, $Effect_C = 19.75$, $Effect_D = -29.25$, $Effect_{AD} = -33.25$, $Effect_{AC} = -36.25$.]

BIBLIOGRAPHY

T. B. Barker, *Quality by Experimental Design*, Marcel Dekker, New York, 1985.

G. E. P. Box, W. G. Hunter, and J. S. Hunter, *Statistics for Experimenters*, John Wiley & Sons, New York, 1978.

F. W. Breyfogle III. *Statistical Methods for Testing, Development and Manufacturing*, John Wiley & Sons, New York, 1992.

N. Draper and H. Smith, *Applied Regression Analysis*, 2nd ed., John Wiley & Sons, New York, 1981.

E. A. Elsayed, *Reliability Engineering*, Addison Wesley Longman, Inc., Reading, MA, 1996.
N. L. Frigon and D. Mathews, *Practical Guide to Experimental Design*, John Wiley & Sons, New York, 1997.

A. J. Hayter, *Probability and Statistics for Engineers and Scientists*, PWS Publishing Co., Boston, 1996.

L. L. Lapin, *Modern Engineering Statistics*, Duxbury Press, Belmont CA, 1997.

E. E. Lewis, *Introduction to Reliability Engineering*, 2nd ed., John Wiley & Sons, New York, 1996.

D. C. Montgomery, *Design and Analysis of Experiments*, 3rd ed., John Wiley & Sons, New York, 1991.

D. C. Montgomery, and G. C. Runger, *Applied Statistics and Probability for Engineers*, John Wiley & Sons, New York, 1994.

R. H. Myers and D. C. Montgomery, *Response Surface Methodology: Process and Product Optimization Using Designed Experiments*, John Wiley & Sons, New York, 1995.

R. E. Walpole, R. H. Myers, and S. L. Myers, *Probability and Statistics for Engineers and Scientists*, 6th ed., Prentice Hall, Upper Saddle River, NJ, 1998.

INDEX

694